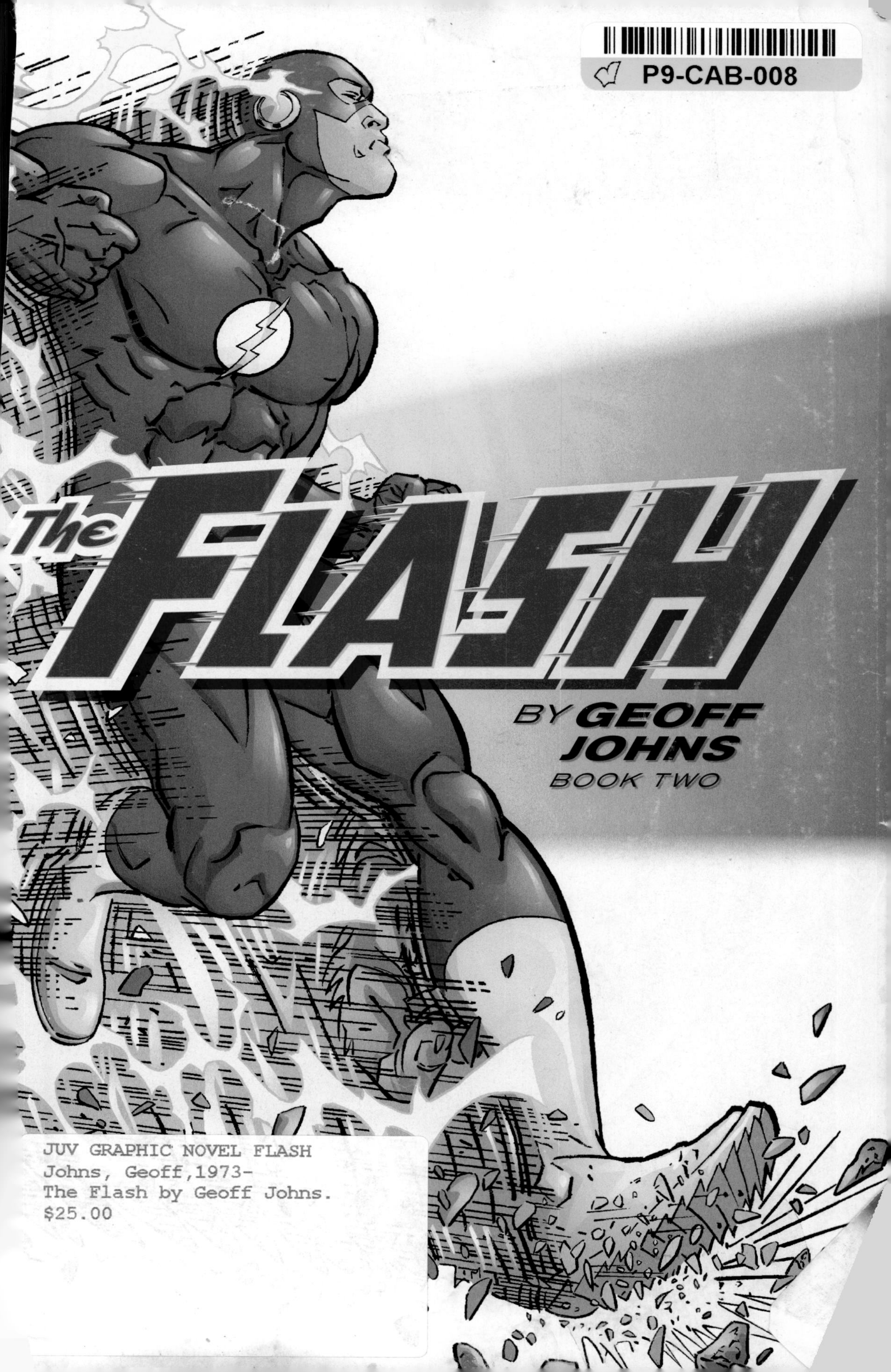
The FLASH
BY GEOFF JOHNS
BOOK TWO

The FLASH

BY GEOFF JOHNS

BOOK TWO

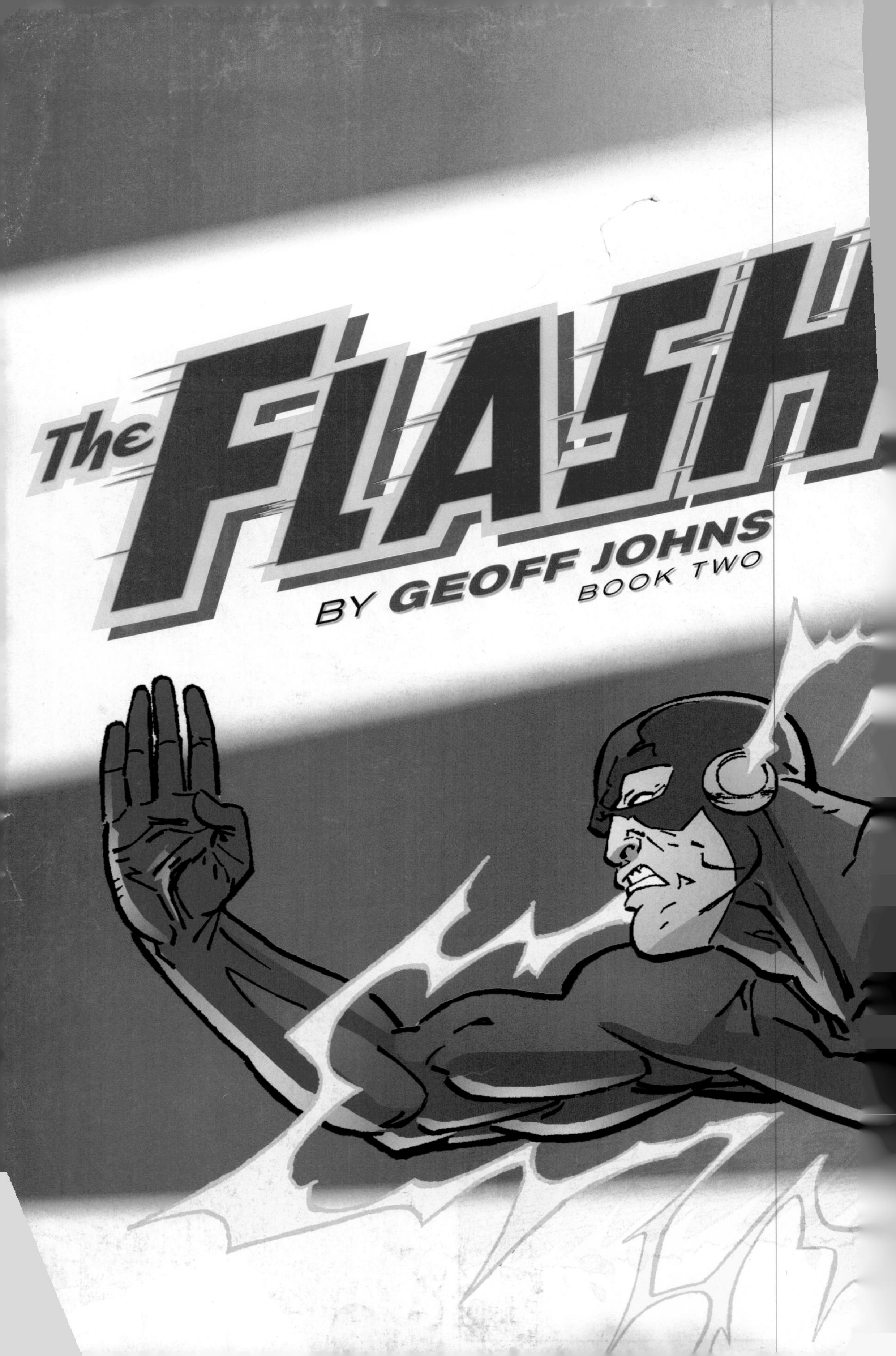

WRITTEN BY **GEOFF JOHNS**

PENCILS BY
SCOTT KOLINS RICK BURCHETT ANGEL UNZUETA

INKS BY
DOUG HAZLEWOOD DAN PANOSIAN
PRENTIS ROLLINS JOSÉ MARZAN JR.

COLORS BY
JAMES SINCLAIR TOM McCRAW

LETTERS BY
GASPAR SALADINO
JOHN COSTANZA KURT HATHAWAY

COLLECTION COVER ART BY **BRIAN BOLLAND**

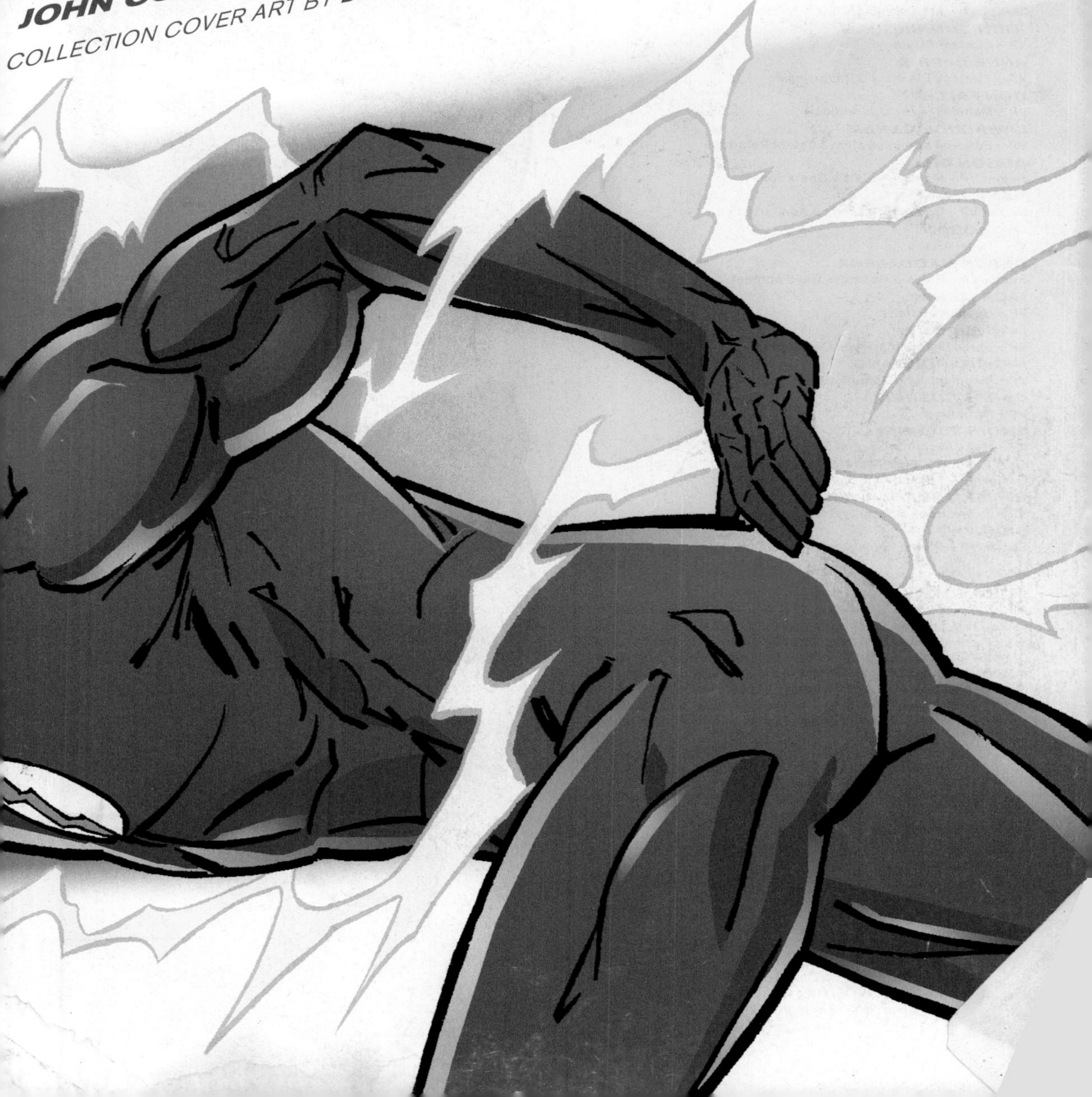

THE FLASH BY GEOFF JOHNS BOOK TWO

Published by DC Comics. Compilation and all new material copyright © 2016 DC Comics. All Rights Reserved. All Rights Reserved. Originally published in single magazine form in FLASH 177-188, FLASH SECRET FILES AND ORIGINS 3, FLASH: OUR WORLDS AT WAR 1, and DC FIRST: THE FLASH/SUPERMAN 1. Copyright © 2001, 2002 DC Comics. All Rights Reserved. All characters, their distinctive likenesses and related elements featured in this publication are trademarks of DC Comics. The stories, characters and incidents featured in this publication are entirely fictional. DC Comics does not read or accept unsolicited submissions of ideas, stories or artwork.

DC Comics, 2900 West Alameda Ave., Burbank, CA 91505
Printed by RR Donnelley, Salem, VA, USA. 4/15/16. First Printing.
ISBN: 978-1-4012-6101-6

Library of Congress Cataloging-in-Publication Data

Names: Johns, Geoff, 1973- author. | Kolins, Scott, illustrator. | Van Sciver, Ethan, illustrator.
Title: The Flash by Geoff Johns. Book two / Geoff Johns, writer ; Scott Kolins, Ethan Van Sciver, artists.
Description: Burbank, CA : DC Comics,]2016] | "Originally published in single magazine form in FLASH 177-188, FLASH SECRET FILES 1, FLASH: OUR WORLDS AT WAR 1, and DC FIRST: THE FLASH/SUPERMAN 1."
Identifiers: LCCN 2016006451 | ISBN 9781401261016
Subjects: LCSH: Graphic novels. | Superhero comic books, strips, etc.
Classification: LCC PN6728.F53 J6333 2016 | DDC 741.5/973—dc23
LC record available at http://lccn.loc.gov/2016006451

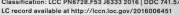

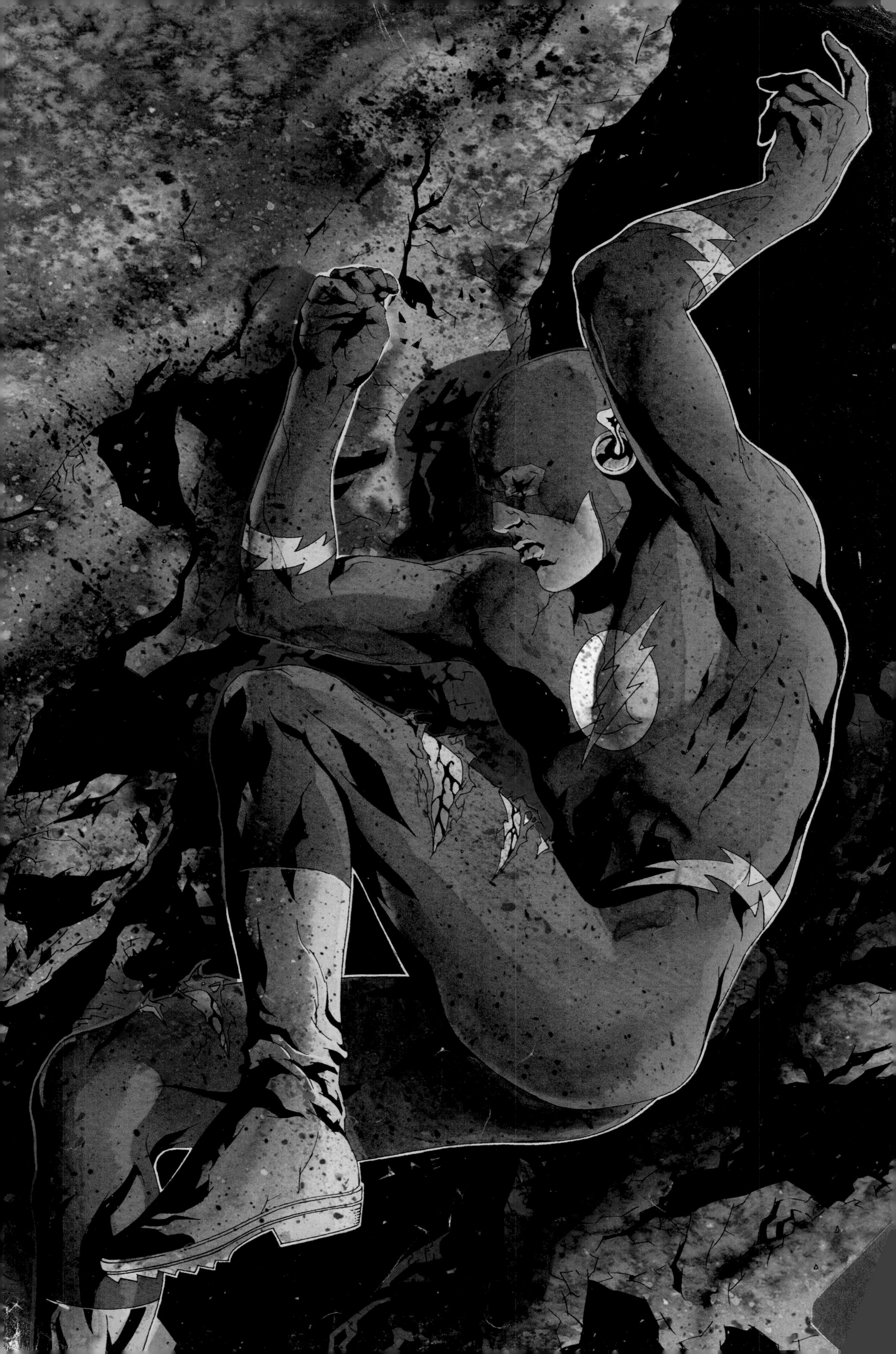

COVER ART BY ***JAE LEE*** *AND* ***JOSE VILLARRUBIA***

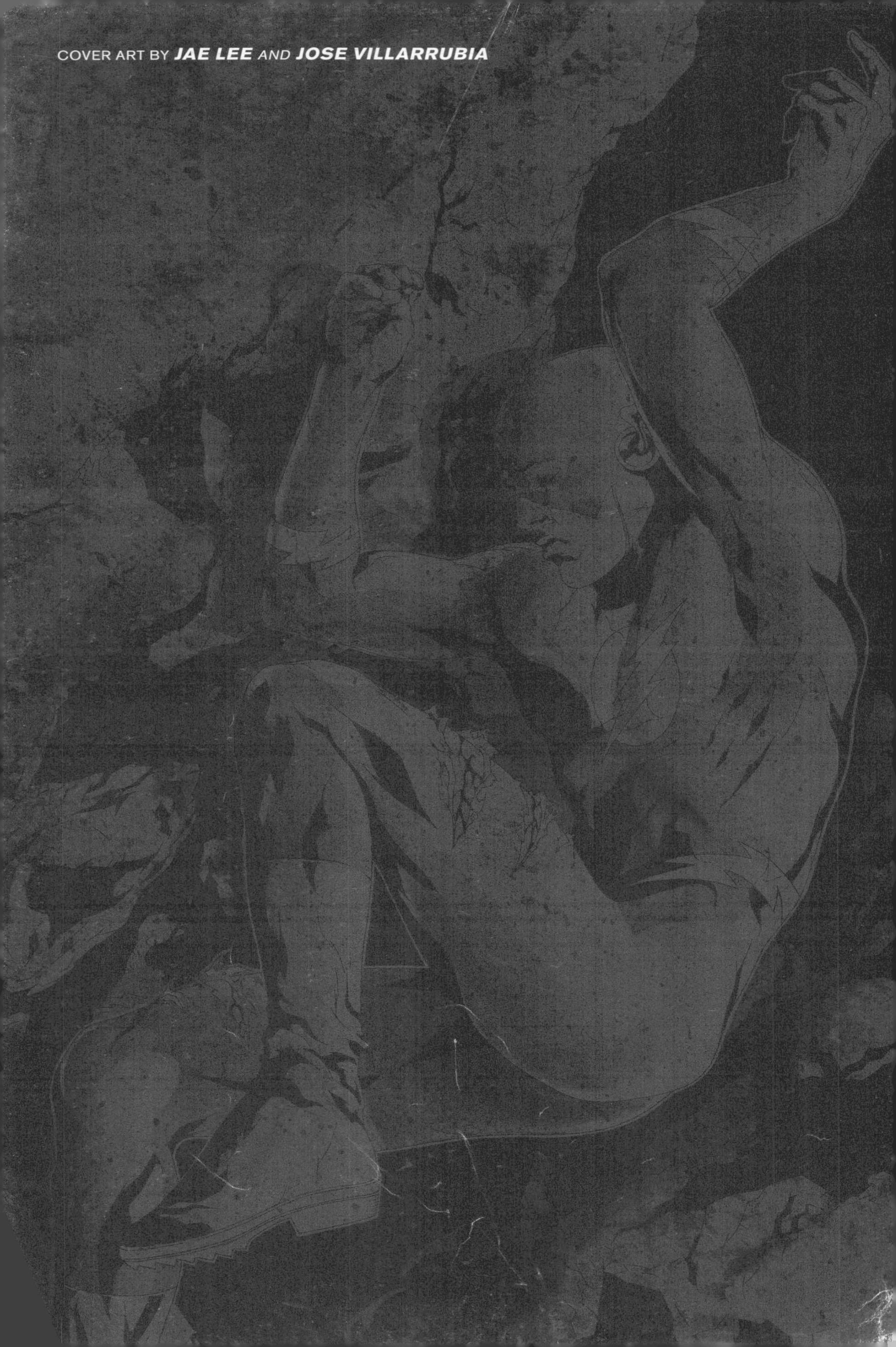

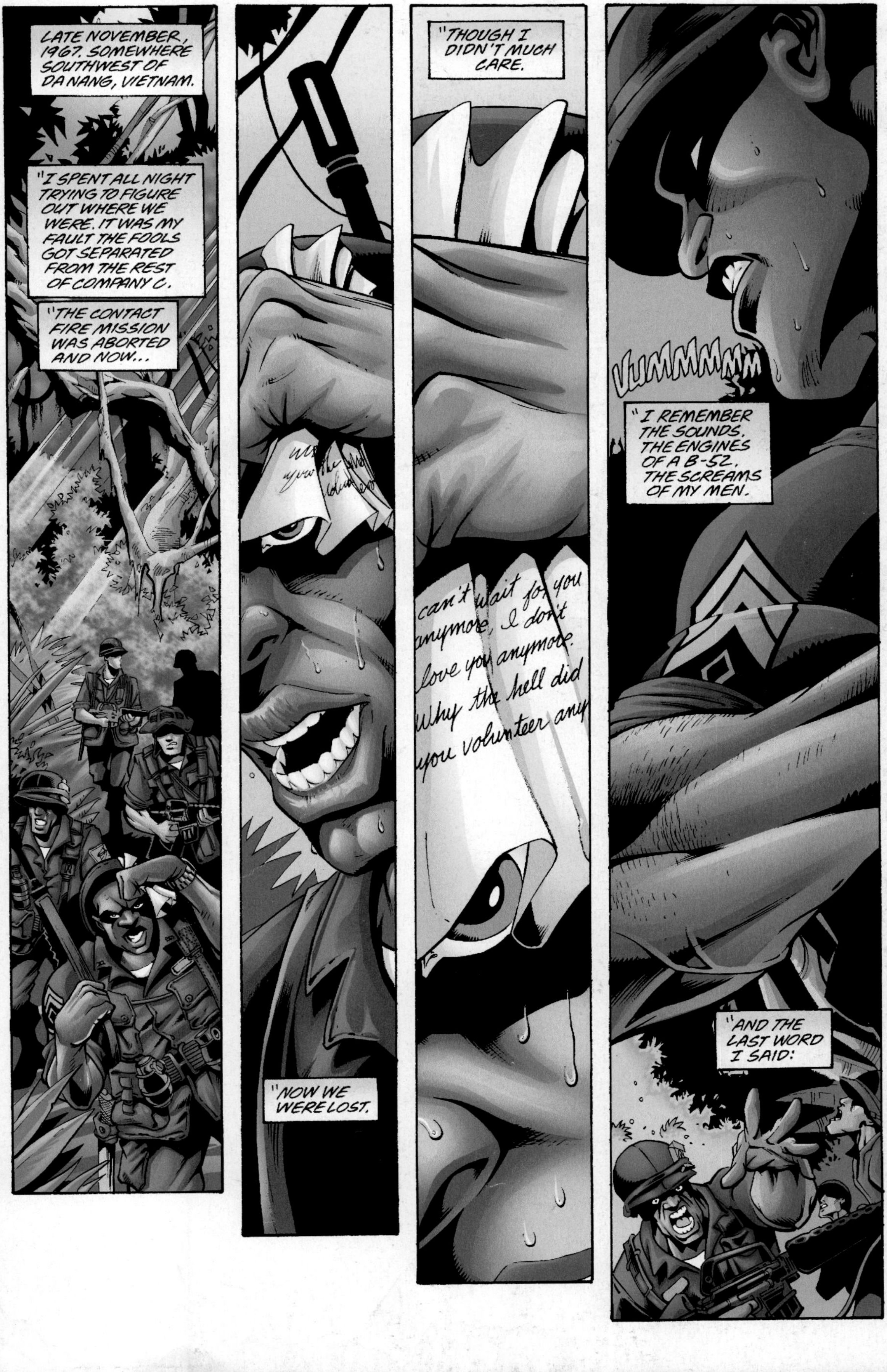
LATE NOVEMBER, 1967. SOMEWHERE SOUTHWEST OF DA NANG, VIETNAM.
"I SPENT ALL NIGHT TRYING TO FIGURE OUT WHERE WE WERE. IT WAS MY FAULT THE FOOLS GOT SEPARATED FROM THE REST OF COMPANY C.
"THE CONTACT FIRE MISSION WAS ABORTED AND NOW...
"NOW WE WERE LOST.
"THOUGH I DIDN'T MUCH CARE.
can't wait for you
anymore, I don't
love you anymore.
Why the hell did
you volunteer any
VUMMMMM
"I REMEMBER THE SOUNDS. THE ENGINES OF A B-52. THE SCREAMS OF MY MEN.
"AND THE LAST WORD I SAID:

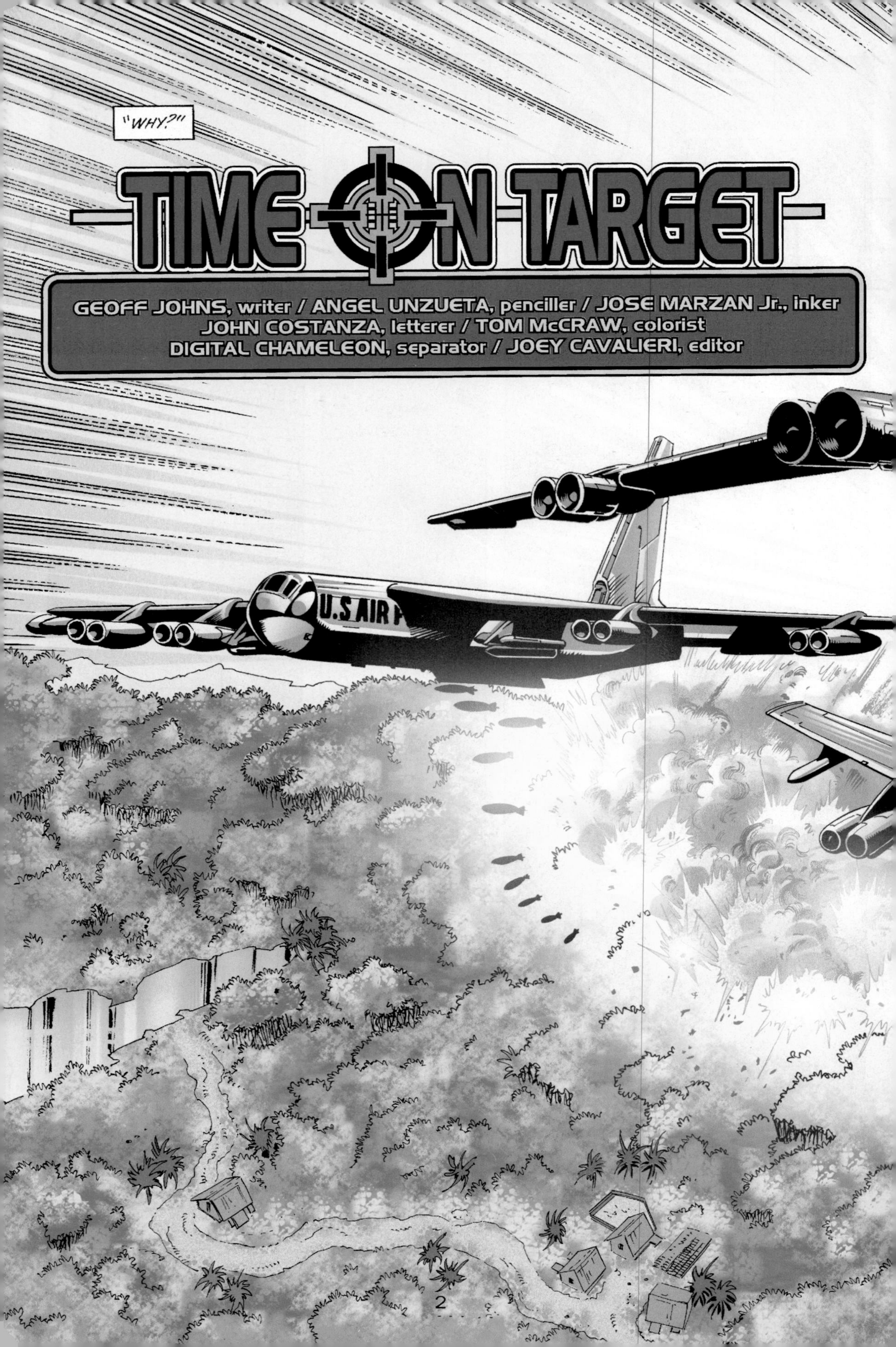

"WHY?"
TIME ON TARGET
GEOFF JOHNS, writer / ANGEL UNZUETA, penciller / JOSE MARZAN Jr., inker
JOHN COSTANZA, letterer / TOM McCRAW, colorist
DIGITAL CHAMELEON, separator / JOEY CAVALIERI, editor
U.S AIR F

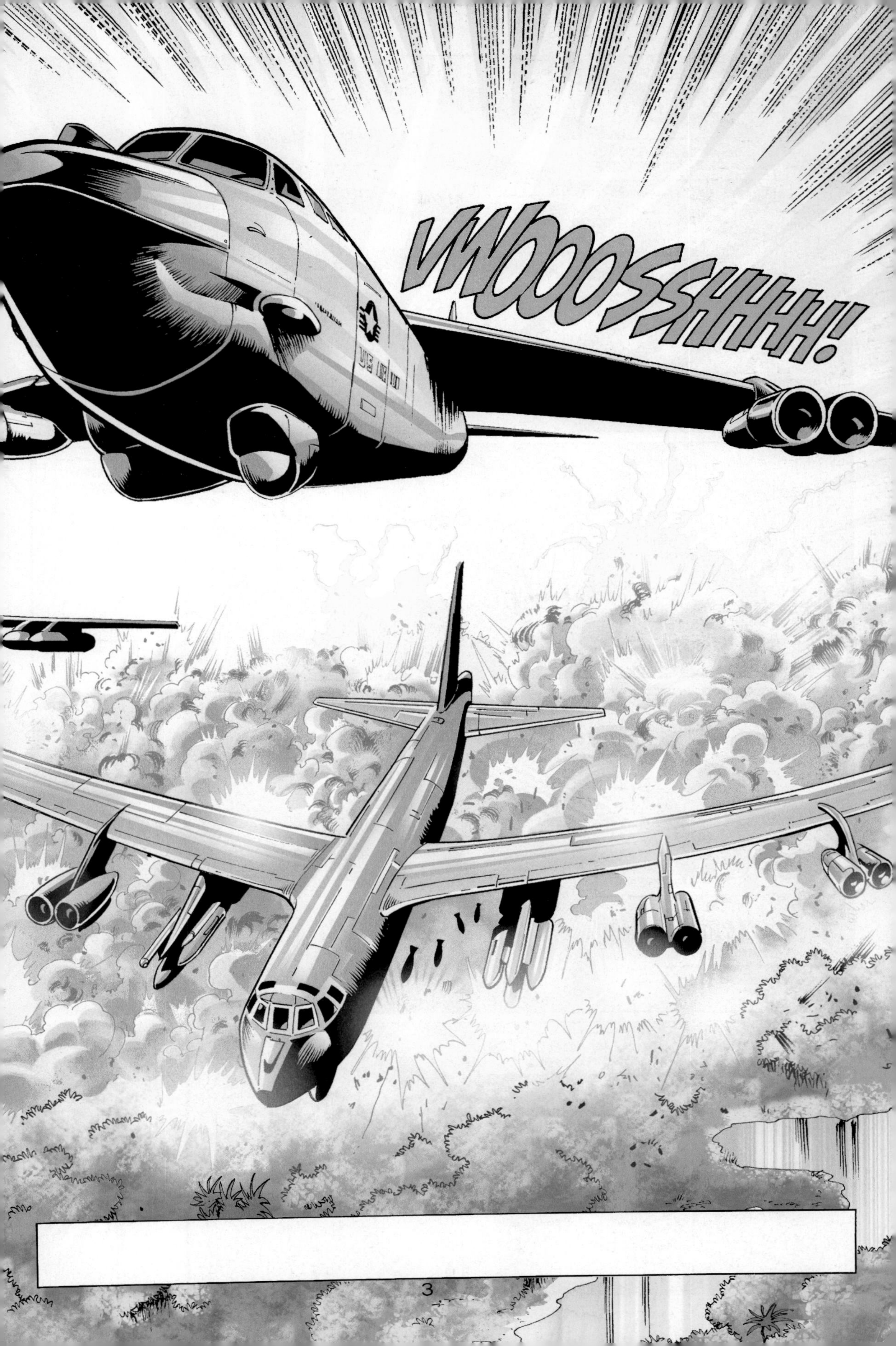
VWOOOSSHHHH!

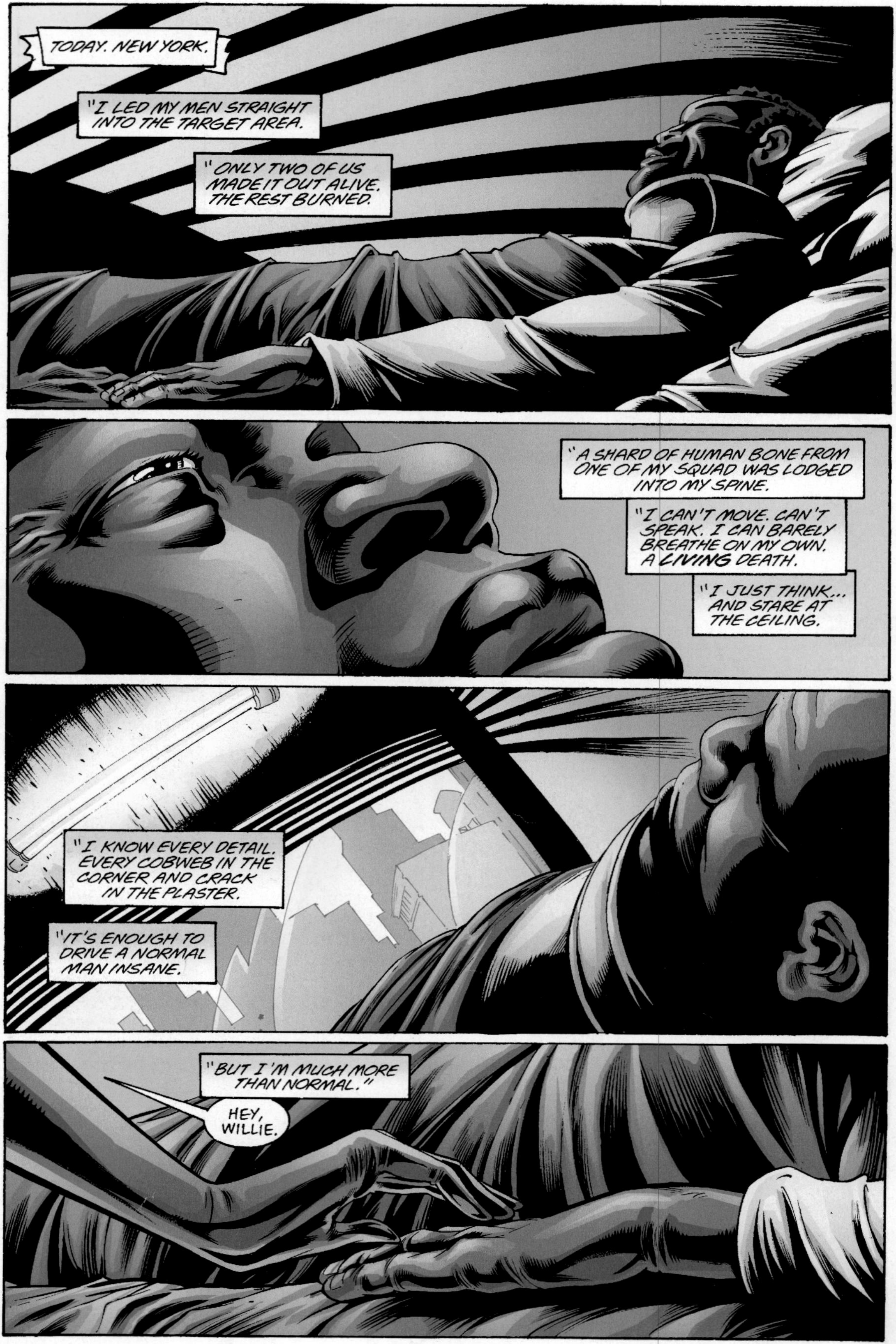
TODAY. NEW YORK.
"I LED MY MEN STRAIGHT INTO THE TARGET AREA.
"ONLY TWO OF US MADE IT OUT ALIVE. THE REST BURNED.
"A SHARD OF HUMAN BONE FROM ONE OF MY SQUAD WAS LODGED INTO MY SPINE.
"I CAN'T MOVE. CAN'T SPEAK. I CAN BARELY BREATHE ON MY OWN. A LIVING DEATH.
"I JUST THINK... AND STARE AT THE CEILING.
"I KNOW EVERY DETAIL. EVERY COBWEB IN THE CORNER AND CRACK IN THE PLASTER.
"IT'S ENOUGH TO DRIVE A NORMAL MAN INSANE.
"BUT I'M MUCH MORE THAN NORMAL."
HEY, WILLIE.

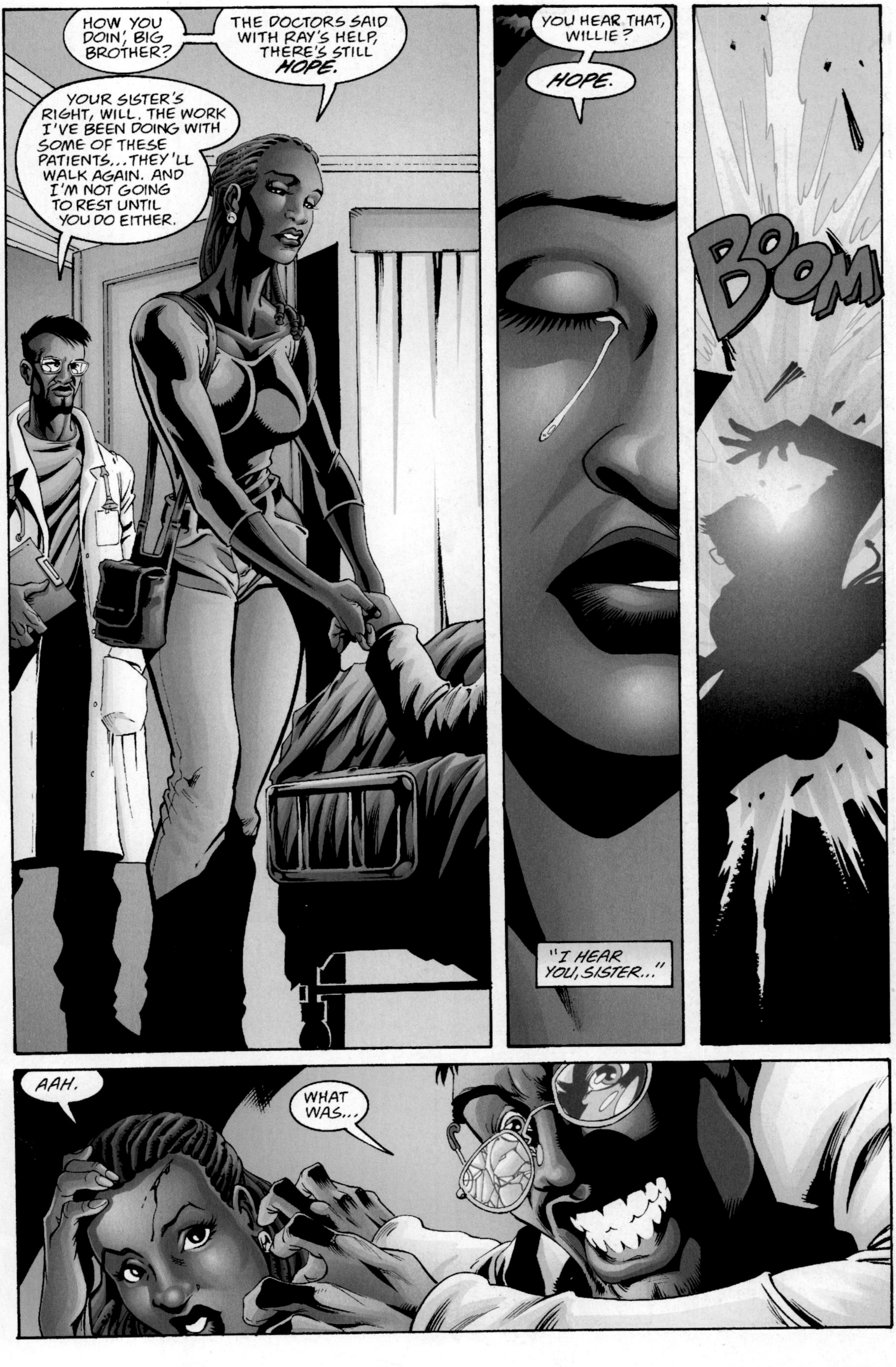

HOW YOU DOIN', BIG BROTHER?
THE DOCTORS SAID WITH RAY'S HELP, THERE'S STILL *HOPE.*
YOUR SISTER'S RIGHT, WILL. THE WORK I'VE BEEN DOING WITH SOME OF THESE PATIENTS... THEY'LL WALK AGAIN. AND I'M NOT GOING TO REST UNTIL YOU DO EITHER.
YOU HEAR THAT, WILLIE?
HOPE.
"I HEAR YOU, SISTER..."
BOOM
AAH.
WHAT WAS...

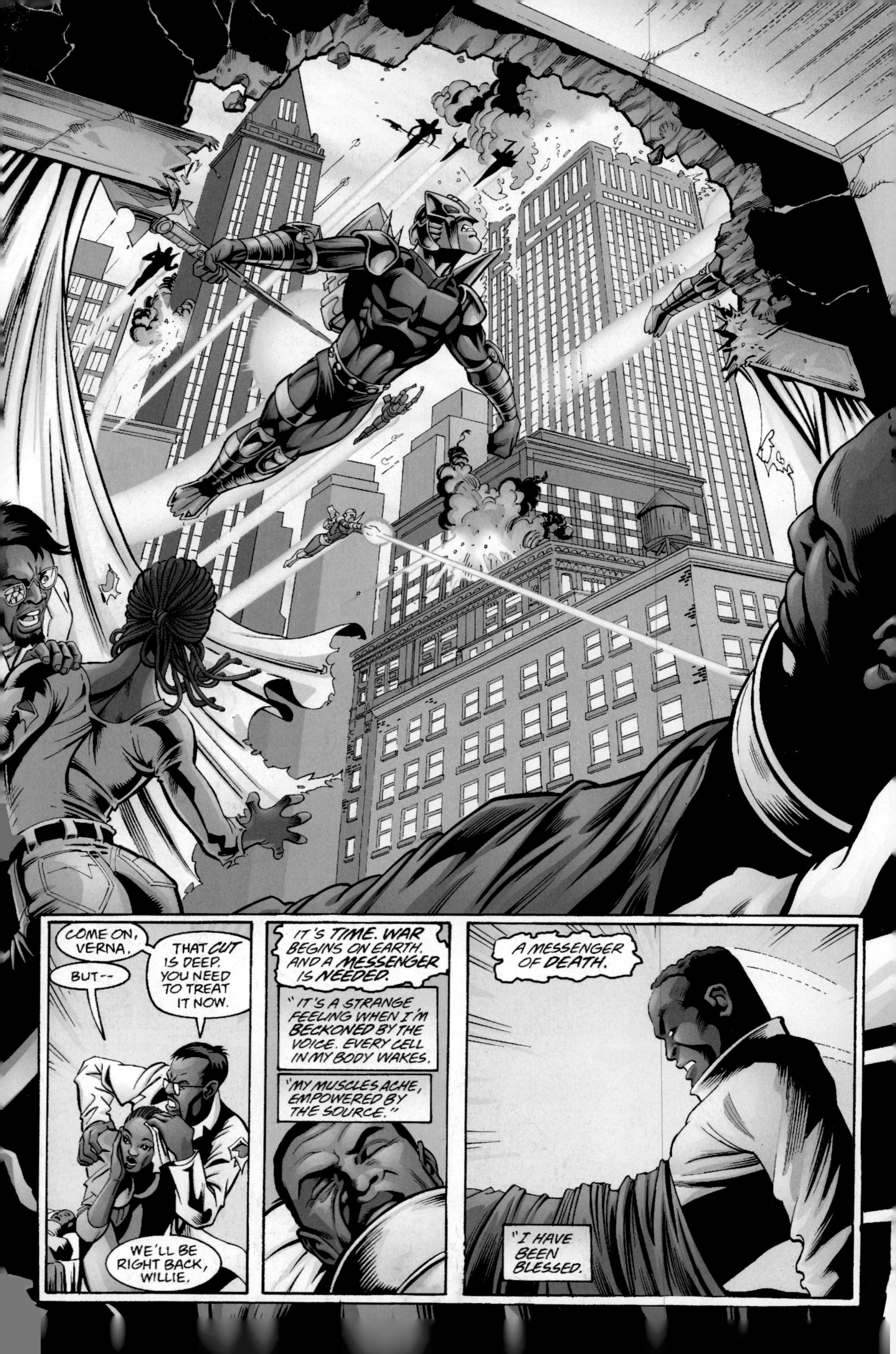
COME ON, VERNA.
THAT CUT IS DEEP. YOU NEED TO TREAT IT NOW.
BUT--
WE'LL BE RIGHT BACK, WILLIE.
IT'S TIME. WAR BEGINS ON EARTH. AND A MESSENGER IS NEEDED.
"IT'S A STRANGE FEELING WHEN I'M BECKONED BY THE VOICE. EVERY CELL IN MY BODY WAKES.
"MY MUSCLES ACHE, EMPOWERED BY THE SOURCE."
A MESSENGER OF DEATH.
"I HAVE BEEN BLESSED.

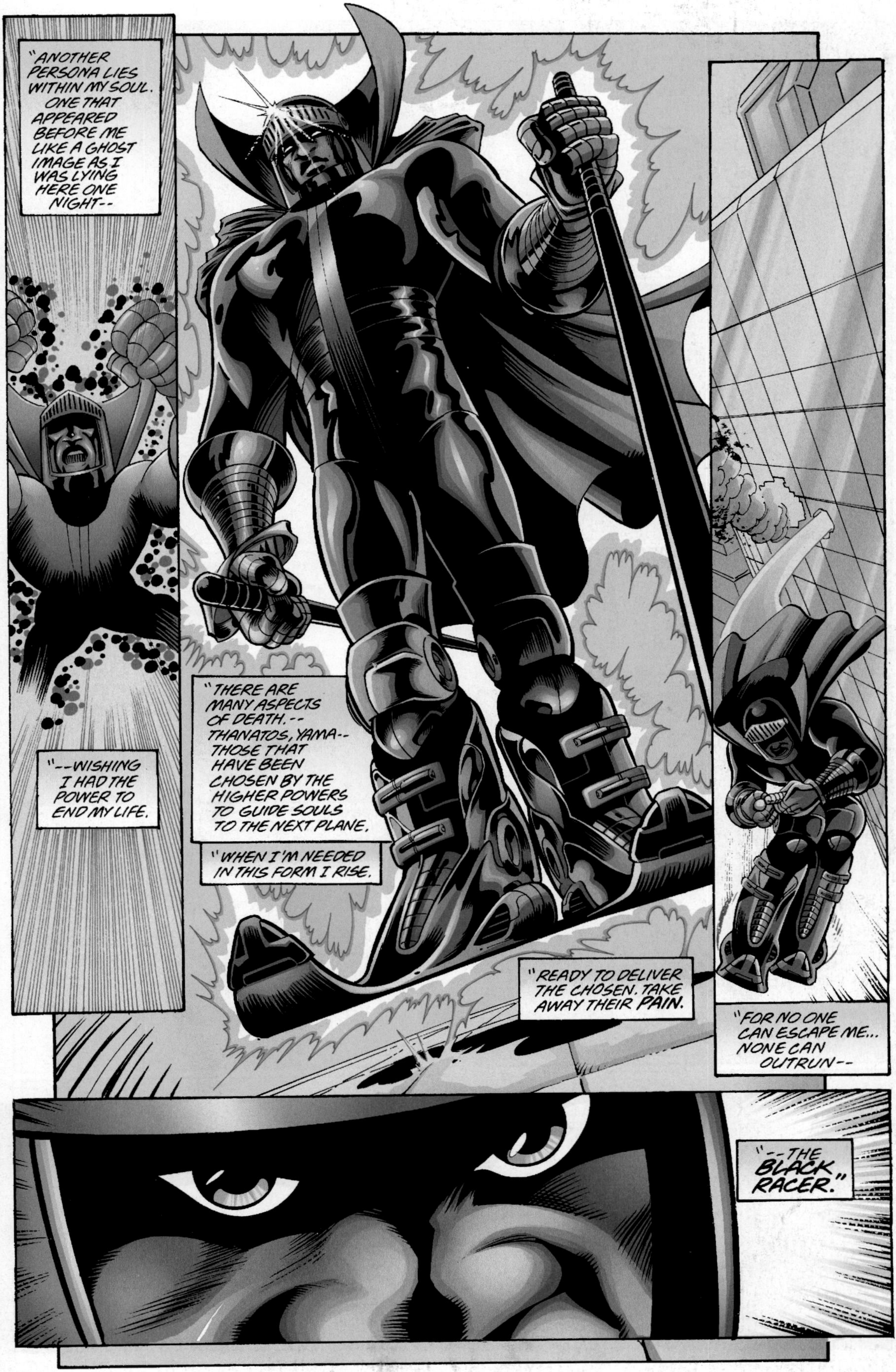
"ANOTHER PERSONA LIES WITHIN MY SOUL. ONE THAT APPEARED BEFORE ME LIKE A GHOST IMAGE AS I WAS LYING HERE ONE NIGHT--
"--WISHING I HAD THE POWER TO END MY LIFE.
"THERE ARE MANY ASPECTS OF DEATH.--THANATOS, YAMA--THOSE THAT HAVE BEEN CHOSEN BY THE HIGHER POWERS TO GUIDE SOULS TO THE NEXT PLANE.
"WHEN I'M NEEDED IN THIS FORM I RISE.
"READY TO DELIVER THE CHOSEN. TAKE AWAY THEIR PAIN.
"FOR NO ONE CAN ESCAPE ME... NONE CAN OUTRUN--
"--THE BLACK RACER."

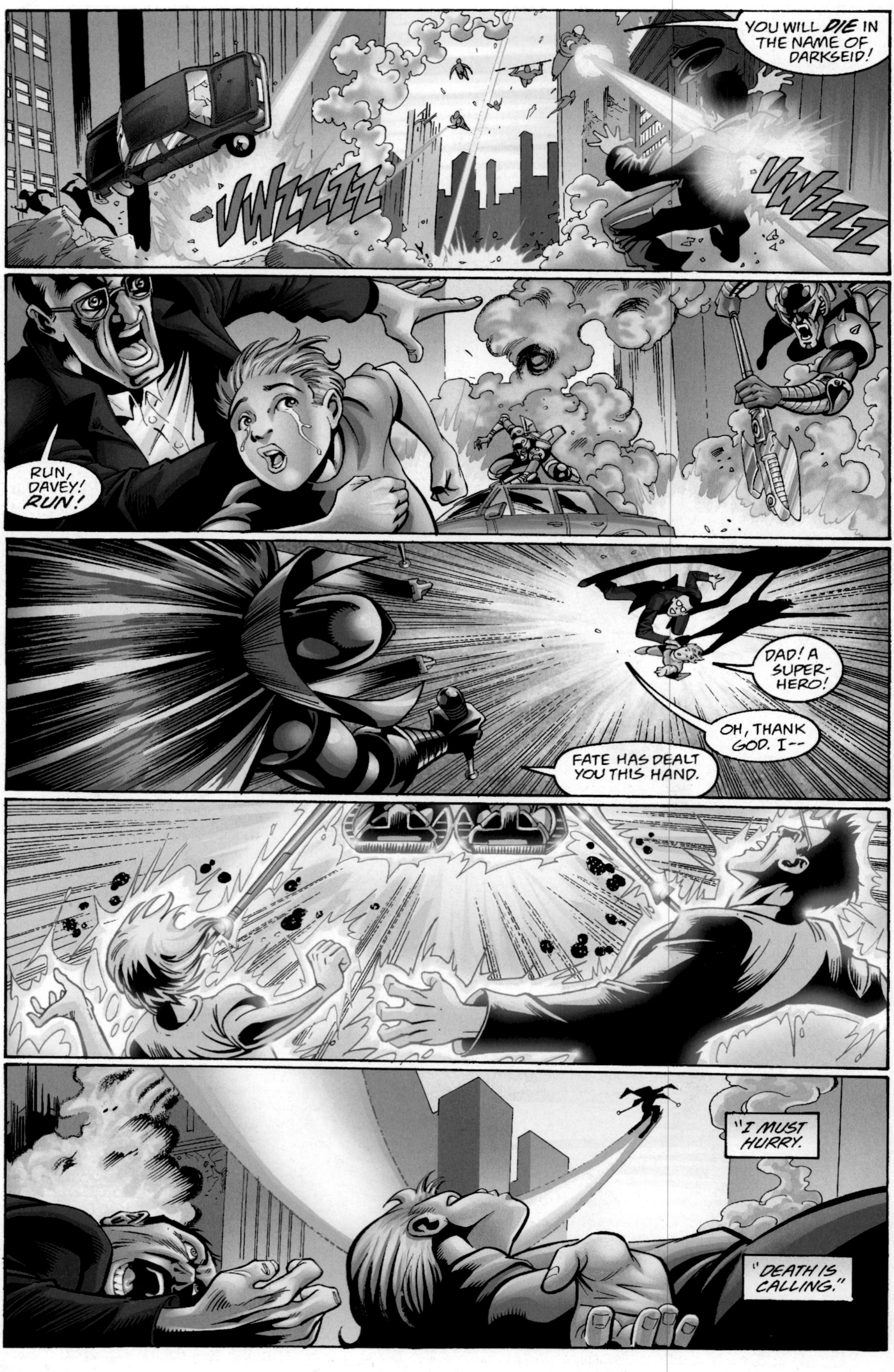

YOU WILL DIE IN THE NAME OF DARKSEID!
VWZZZZ
VWZZZ
RUN, DAVEY! RUN!
DAD! A SUPER-HERO!
OH, THANK GOD. I--
FATE HAS DEALT YOU THIS HAND.
"I MUST HURRY.
"DEATH IS CALLING."

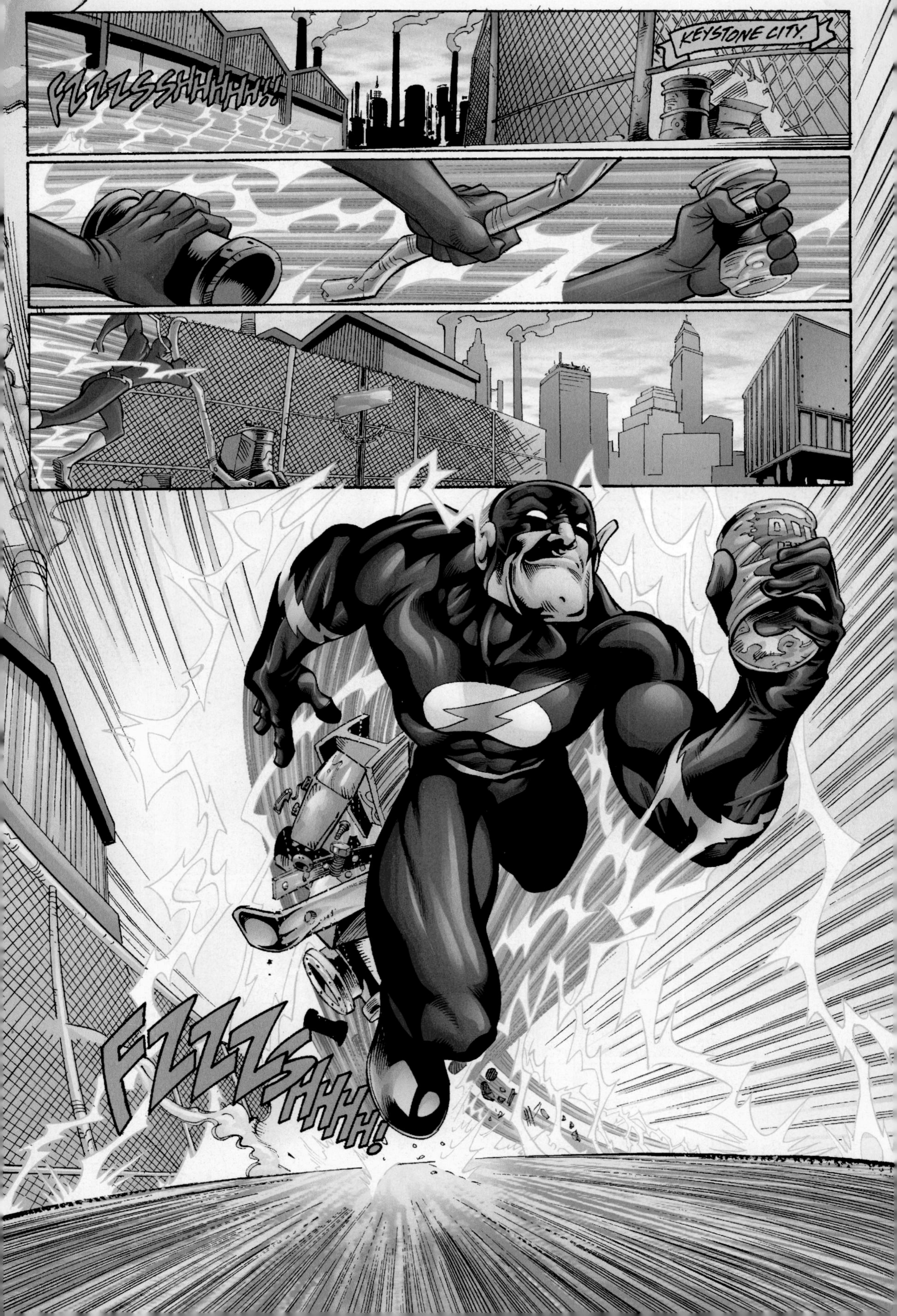
FZZZSSHHHH!!
KEYSTONE CITY.
FZZZSHHHH!

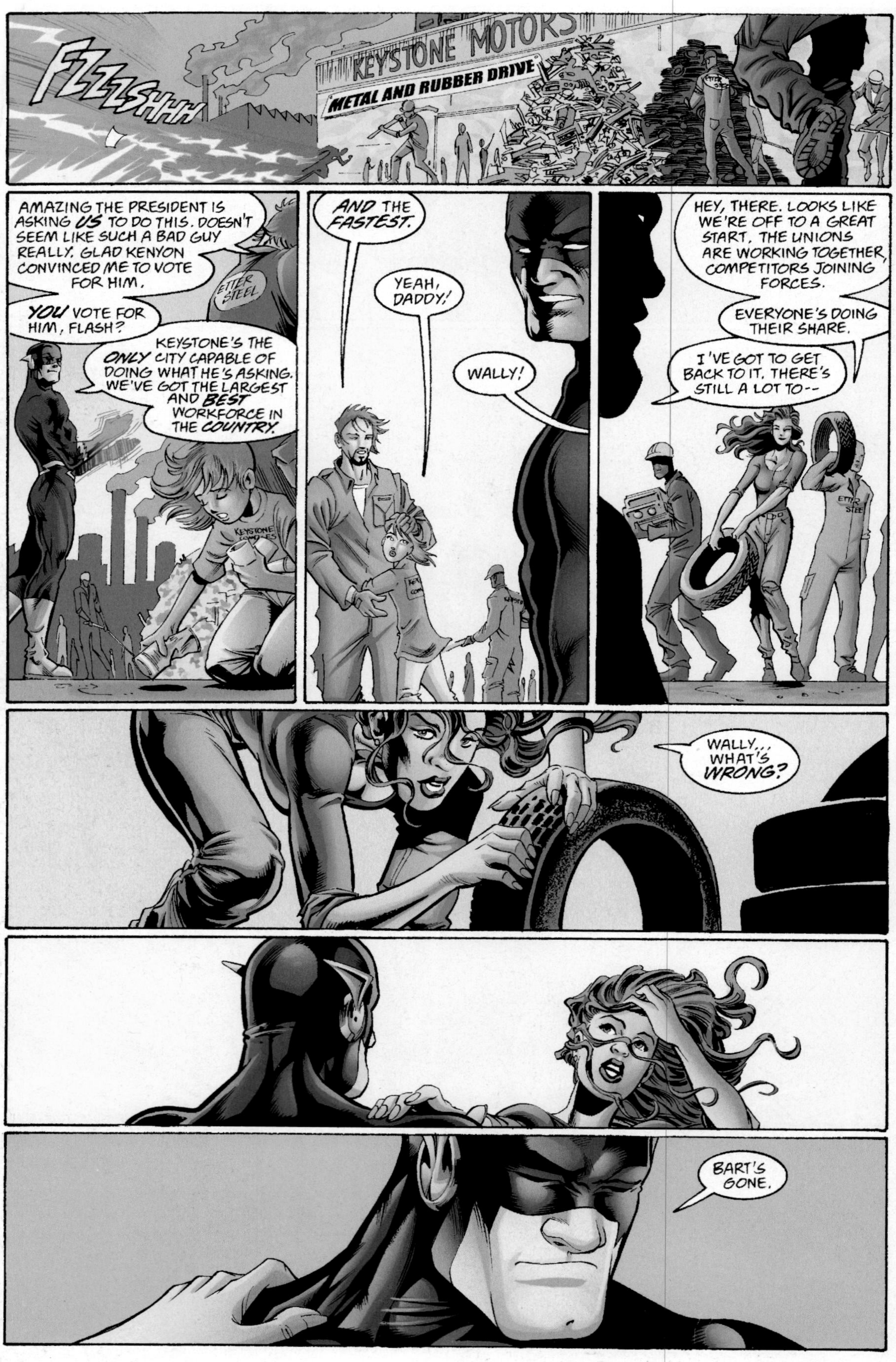

FZZZSHHH
KEYSTONE MOTORS
KEYSTONE METAL AND RUBBER DRIVE
AMAZING THE PRESIDENT IS ASKING US TO DO THIS. DOESN'T SEEM LIKE SUCH A BAD GUY REALLY. GLAD KENYON CONVINCED ME TO VOTE FOR HIM.
YOU VOTE FOR HIM, FLASH?
KEYSTONE'S THE ONLY CITY CAPABLE OF DOING WHAT HE'S ASKING. WE'VE GOT THE LARGEST AND BEST WORKFORCE IN THE COUNTRY.
AND THE FASTEST.
YEAH, DADDY!
WALLY!
HEY, THERE. LOOKS LIKE WE'RE OFF TO A GREAT START. THE UNIONS ARE WORKING TOGETHER, COMPETITORS JOINING FORCES.
EVERYONE'S DOING THEIR SHARE.
I'VE GOT TO GET BACK TO IT. THERE'S STILL A LOT TO--
WALLY... WHAT'S WRONG?
BART'S GONE.

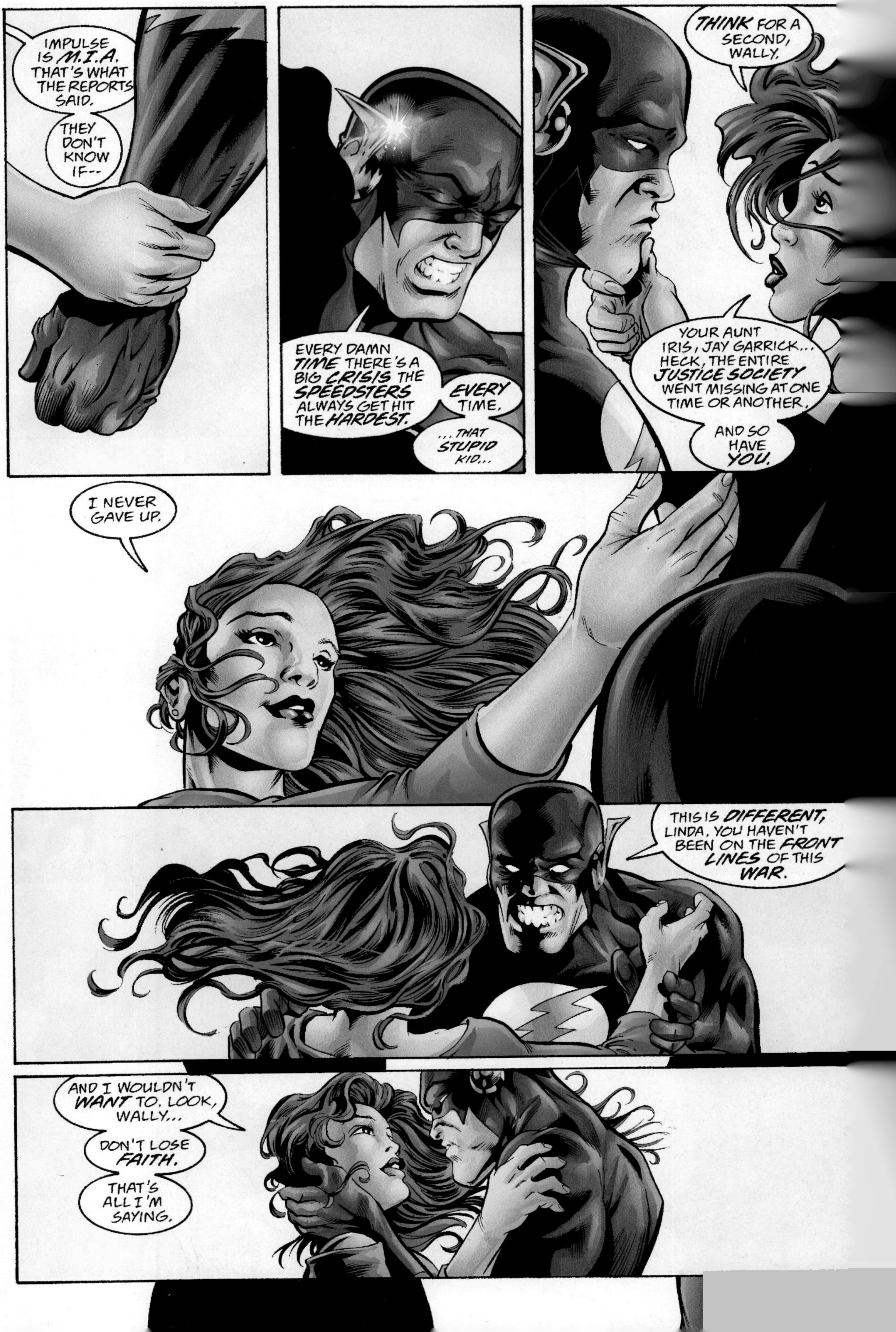

IMPULSE IS M.I.A. THAT'S WHAT THE REPORTS SAID.
THEY DON'T KNOW IF--
EVERY DAMN TIME THERE'S A BIG CRISIS THE SPEEDSTERS ALWAYS GET HIT THE HARDEST.
EVERY TIME.
...THAT STUPID KID...
THINK FOR A SECOND, WALLY.
YOUR AUNT IRIS, JAY GARRICK... HECK, THE ENTIRE JUSTICE SOCIETY WENT MISSING AT ONE TIME OR ANOTHER.
AND SO HAVE YOU.
I NEVER GAVE UP.
THIS IS DIFFERENT, LINDA. YOU HAVEN'T BEEN ON THE FRONT LINES OF THIS WAR.
AND I WOULDN'T WANT TO. LOOK, WALLY...
DON'T LOSE FAITH.
THAT'S ALL I'M SAYING.

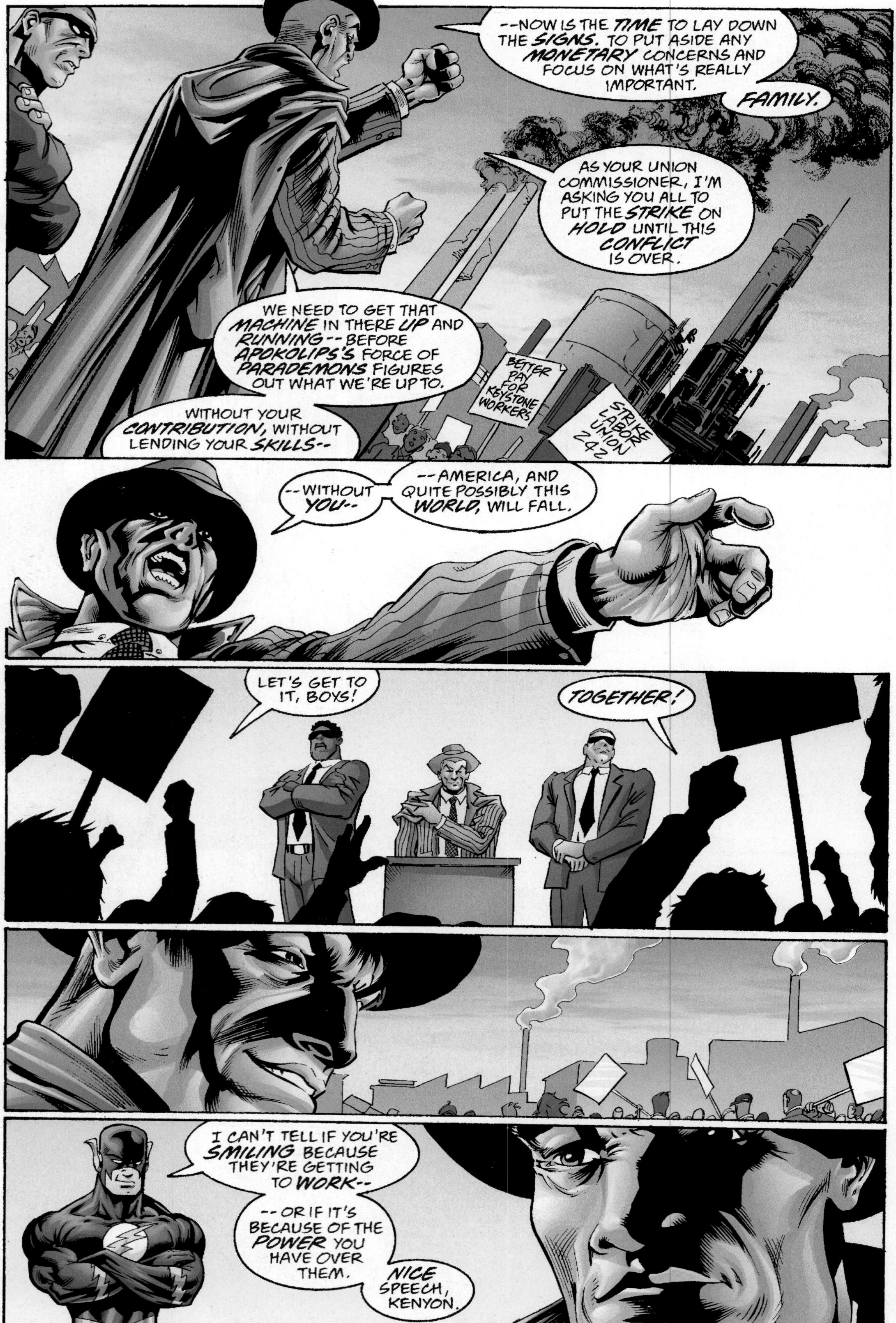
--NOW IS THE TIME TO LAY DOWN THE SIGNS. TO PUT ASIDE ANY MONETARY CONCERNS AND FOCUS ON WHAT'S REALLY IMPORTANT.
FAMILY.
AS YOUR UNION COMMISSIONER, I'M ASKING YOU ALL TO PUT THE STRIKE ON HOLD UNTIL THIS CONFLICT IS OVER.
WE NEED TO GET THAT MACHINE IN THERE UP AND RUNNING--BEFORE APOKOLIPS'S FORCE OF PARADEMONS FIGURES OUT WHAT WE'RE UP TO.
BETTER PAY FOR KEYSTONE WORKERS
STRIKE LABOR UNION 242
WITHOUT YOUR CONTRIBUTION, WITHOUT LENDING YOUR SKILLS--
--WITHOUT YOU--
--AMERICA, AND QUITE POSSIBLY THIS WORLD, WILL FALL.
LET'S GET TO IT, BOYS!
TOGETHER!
I CAN'T TELL IF YOU'RE SMILING BECAUSE THEY'RE GETTING TO WORK--
--OR IF IT'S BECAUSE OF THE POWER YOU HAVE OVER THEM.
NICE SPEECH, KENYON.

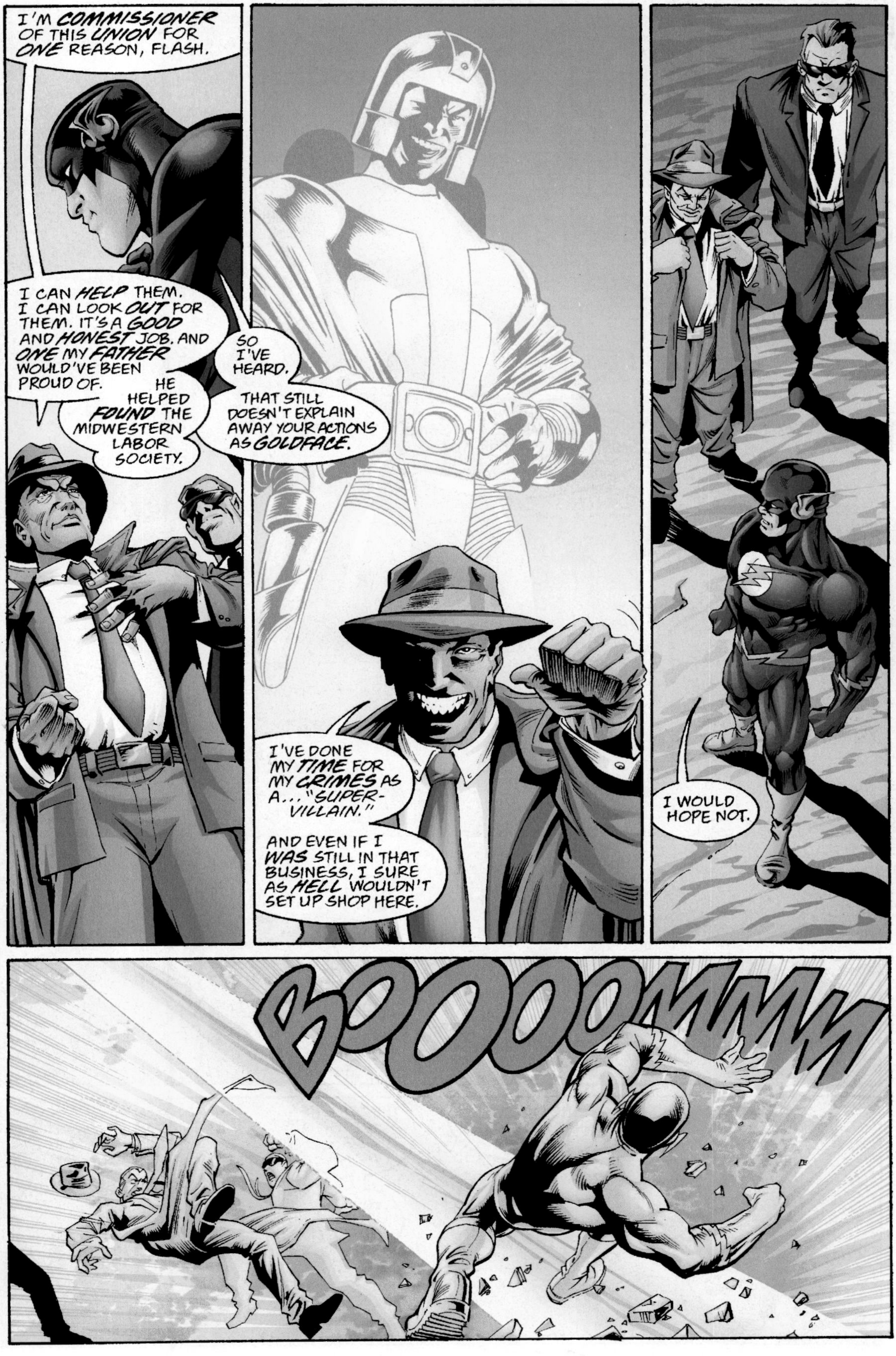

I'M COMMISSIONER OF THIS UNION FOR ONE REASON, FLASH.
I CAN HELP THEM. I CAN LOOK OUT FOR THEM. IT'S A GOOD AND HONEST JOB. AND ONE MY FATHER WOULD'VE BEEN PROUD OF.
HE HELPED FOUND THE MIDWESTERN LABOR SOCIETY.
SO I'VE HEARD.
THAT STILL DOESN'T EXPLAIN AWAY YOUR ACTIONS AS GOLDFACE.
I'VE DONE MY TIME FOR MY CRIMES AS A... "SUPER-VILLAIN."
AND EVEN IF I WAS STILL IN THAT BUSINESS, I SURE AS HELL WOULDN'T SET UP SHOP HERE.
I WOULD HOPE NOT.
BOOOOMMM

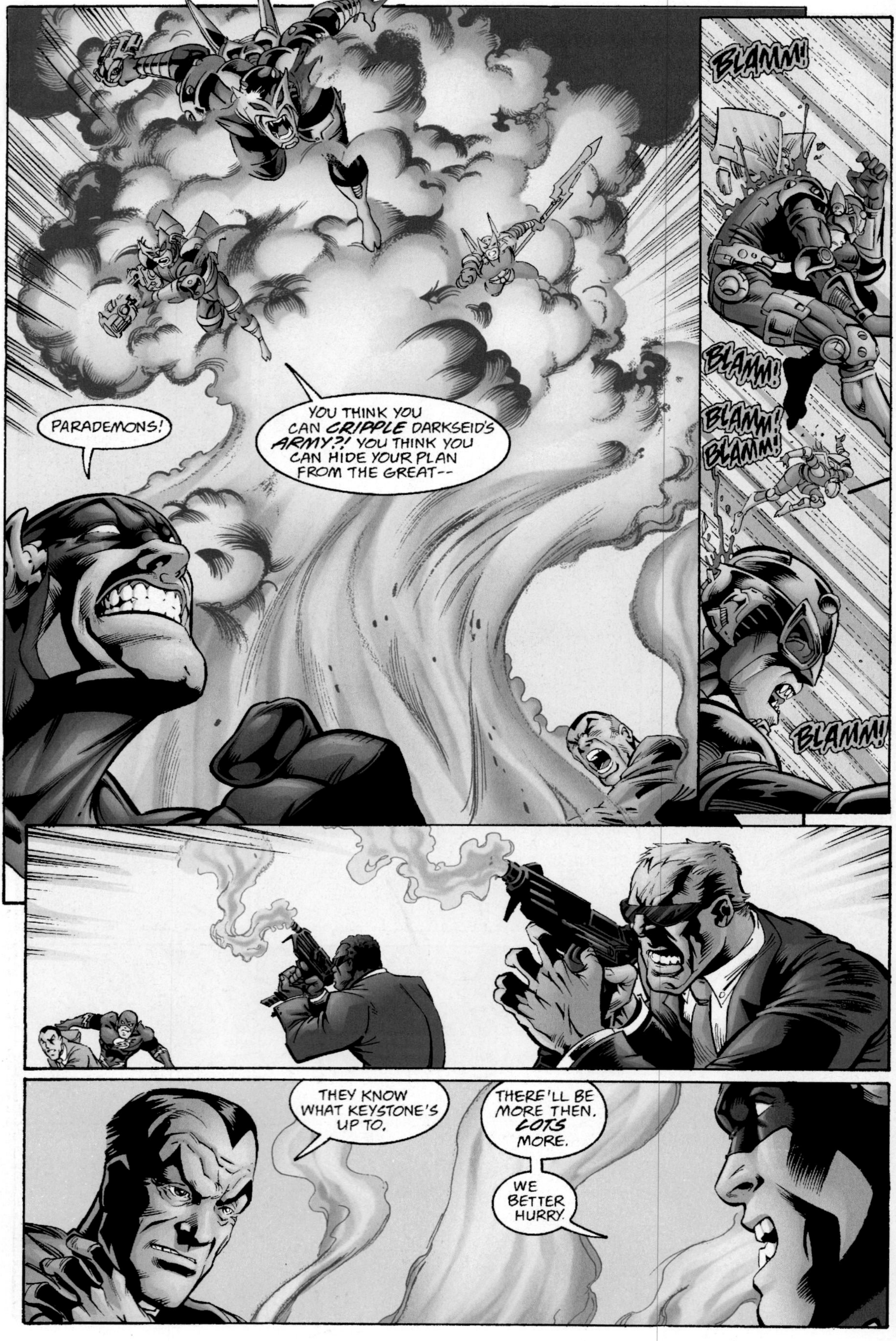
BLAMM!
BLAMM!
BLAMM! BLAMM!
BLAMM!
PARADEMONS!
YOU THINK YOU CAN CRIPPLE DARKSEID'S ARMY?! YOU THINK YOU CAN HIDE YOUR PLAN FROM THE GREAT--
THEY KNOW WHAT KEYSTONE'S UP TO.
THERE'LL BE MORE THEN. LOTS MORE.
WE BETTER HURRY.

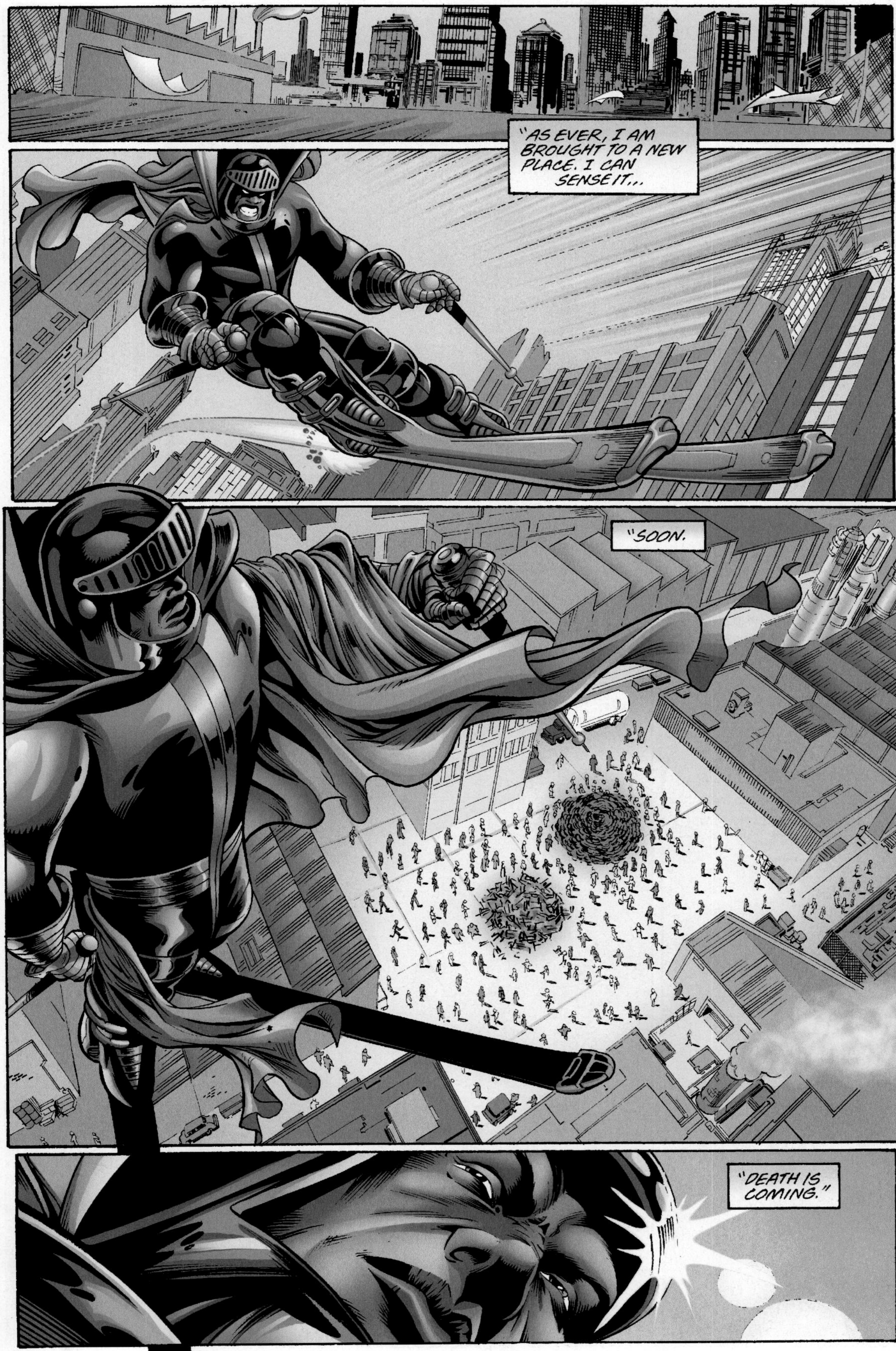

"AS EVER, I AM BROUGHT TO A NEW PLACE. I CAN SENSE IT...
"SOON.
"DEATH IS COMING."

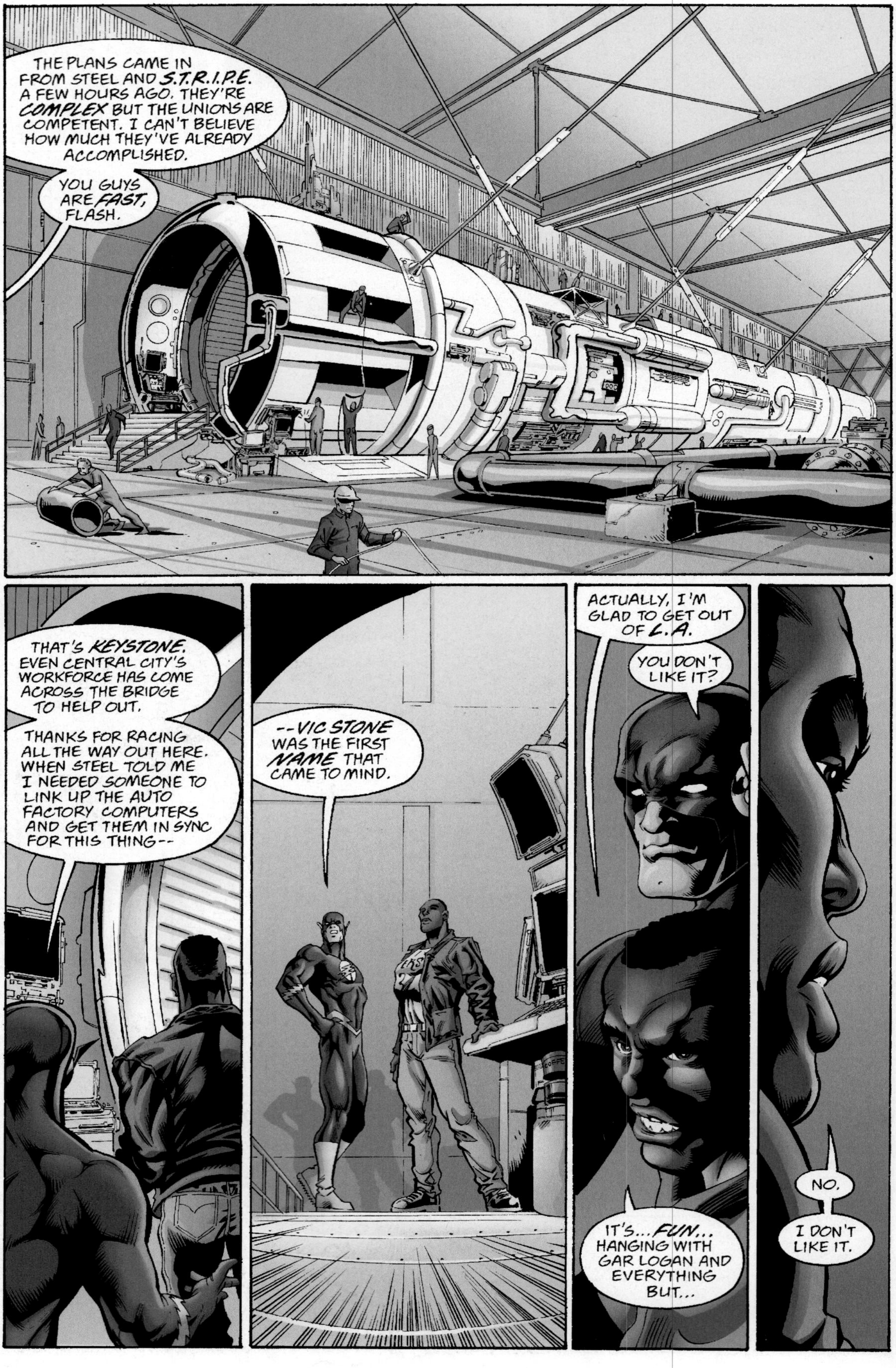
THE PLANS CAME IN FROM STEEL AND S.T.R.I.P.E. A FEW HOURS AGO. THEY'RE COMPLEX BUT THE UNIONS ARE COMPETENT. I CAN'T BELIEVE HOW MUCH THEY'VE ALREADY ACCOMPLISHED.
YOU GUYS ARE FAST, FLASH.
THAT'S KEYSTONE. EVEN CENTRAL CITY'S WORKFORCE HAS COME ACROSS THE BRIDGE TO HELP OUT.
THANKS FOR RACING ALL THE WAY OUT HERE. WHEN STEEL TOLD ME I NEEDED SOMEONE TO LINK UP THE AUTO FACTORY COMPUTERS AND GET THEM IN SYNC FOR THIS THING--
--VIC STONE WAS THE FIRST NAME THAT CAME TO MIND.
ACTUALLY, I'M GLAD TO GET OUT OF L.A.
YOU DON'T LIKE IT?
IT'S...FUN... HANGING WITH GAR LOGAN AND EVERYTHING BUT...
NO.
I DON'T LIKE IT.

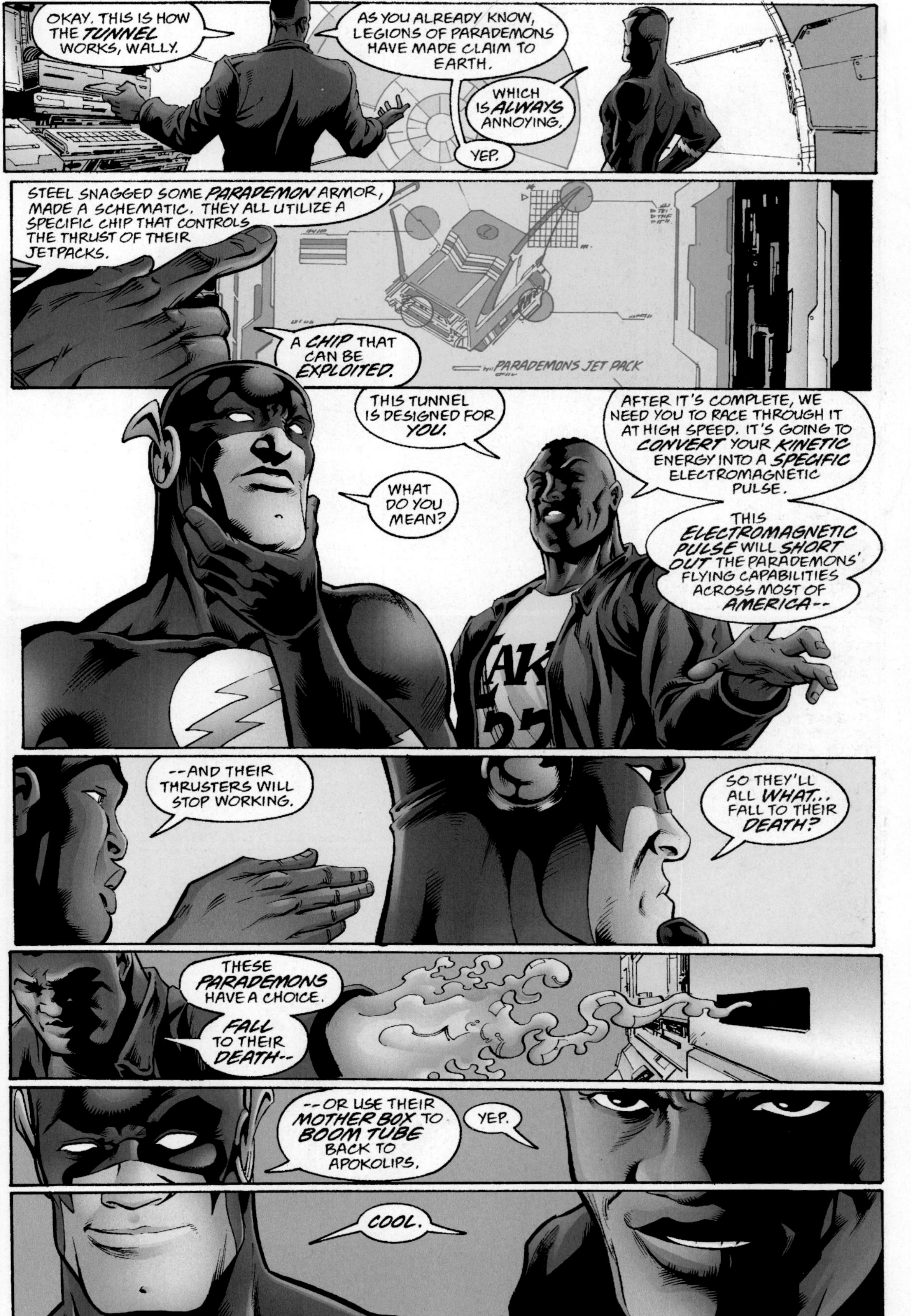
OKAY. THIS IS HOW THE TUNNEL WORKS, WALLY.
AS YOU ALREADY KNOW, LEGIONS OF PARADEMONS HAVE MADE CLAIM TO EARTH.
WHICH IS ALWAYS ANNOYING.
YEP.
STEEL SNAGGED SOME PARADEMON ARMOR, MADE A SCHEMATIC. THEY ALL UTILIZE A SPECIFIC CHIP THAT CONTROLS THE THRUST OF THEIR JETPACKS.
A CHIP THAT CAN BE EXPLOITED.
PARADEMONS JET PACK
THIS TUNNEL IS DESIGNED FOR YOU.
WHAT DO YOU MEAN?
AFTER IT'S COMPLETE, WE NEED YOU TO RACE THROUGH IT AT HIGH SPEED. IT'S GOING TO CONVERT YOUR KINETIC ENERGY INTO A SPECIFIC ELECTROMAGNETIC PULSE.
THIS ELECTROMAGNETIC PULSE WILL SHORT OUT THE PARADEMONS' FLYING CAPABILITIES ACROSS MOST OF AMERICA--
--AND THEIR THRUSTERS WILL STOP WORKING.
SO THEY'LL ALL WHAT... FALL TO THEIR DEATH?
THESE PARADEMONS HAVE A CHOICE.
FALL TO THEIR DEATH--
--OR USE THEIR MOTHER BOX TO BOOM TUBE BACK TO APOKOLIPS.
YEP.
COOL.

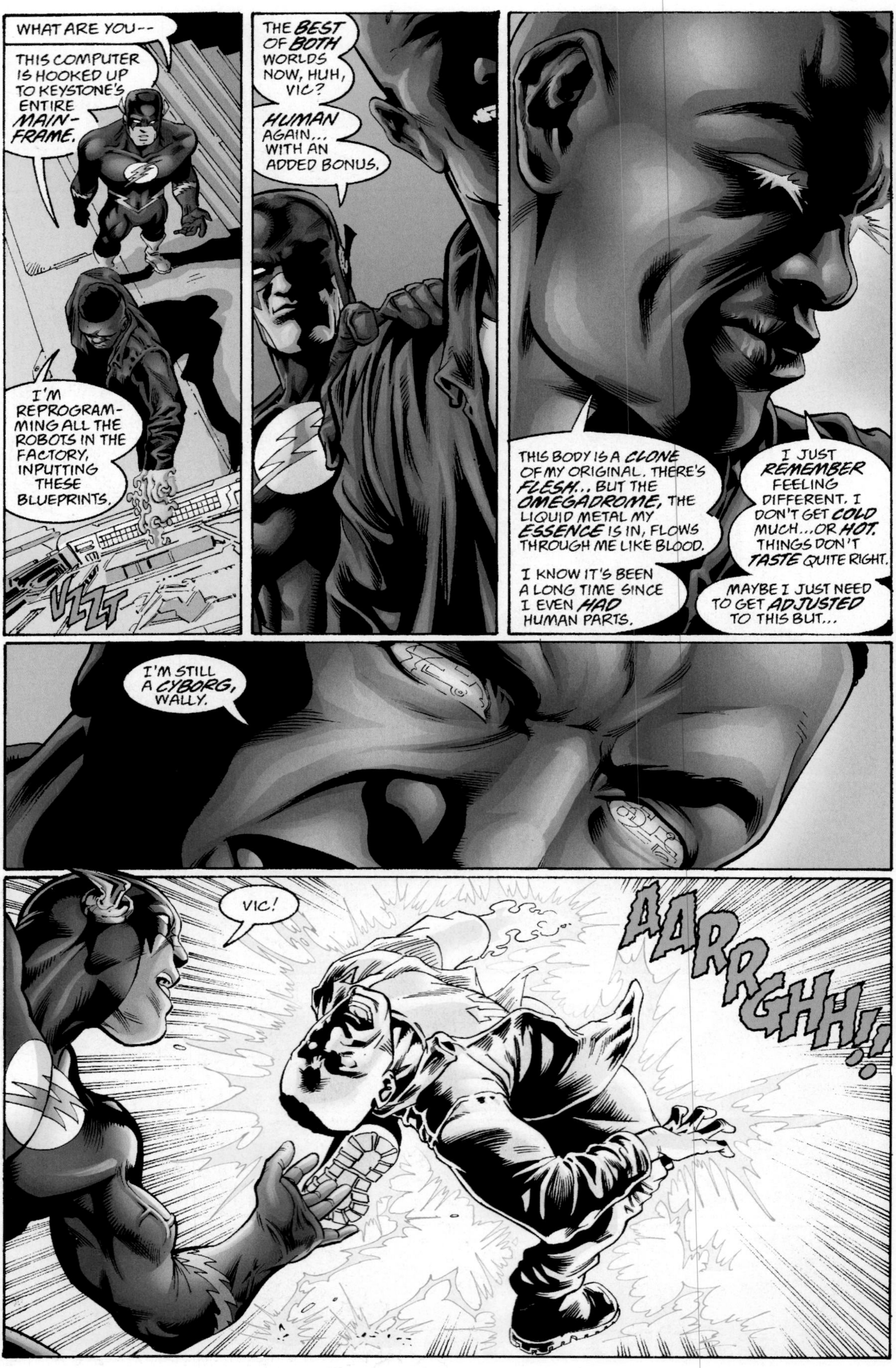
WHAT ARE YOU--
THIS COMPUTER IS HOOKED UP TO KEYSTONE'S ENTIRE MAIN-FRAME.
I'M REPROGRAMMING ALL THE ROBOTS IN THE FACTORY, INPUTTING THESE BLUEPRINTS.
VZZT
THE BEST OF BOTH WORLDS NOW, HUH, VIC?
HUMAN AGAIN... WITH AN ADDED BONUS.
THIS BODY IS A CLONE OF MY ORIGINAL. THERE'S FLESH... BUT THE OMEGADROME, THE LIQUID METAL MY ESSENCE IS IN, FLOWS THROUGH ME LIKE BLOOD.
I KNOW IT'S BEEN A LONG TIME SINCE I EVEN HAD HUMAN PARTS.
I JUST REMEMBER FEELING DIFFERENT. I DON'T GET COLD MUCH...OR HOT. THINGS DON'T TASTE QUITE RIGHT.
MAYBE I JUST NEED TO GET ADJUSTED TO THIS BUT...
I'M STILL A CYBORG, WALLY.
VIC!
AARRGHH!!

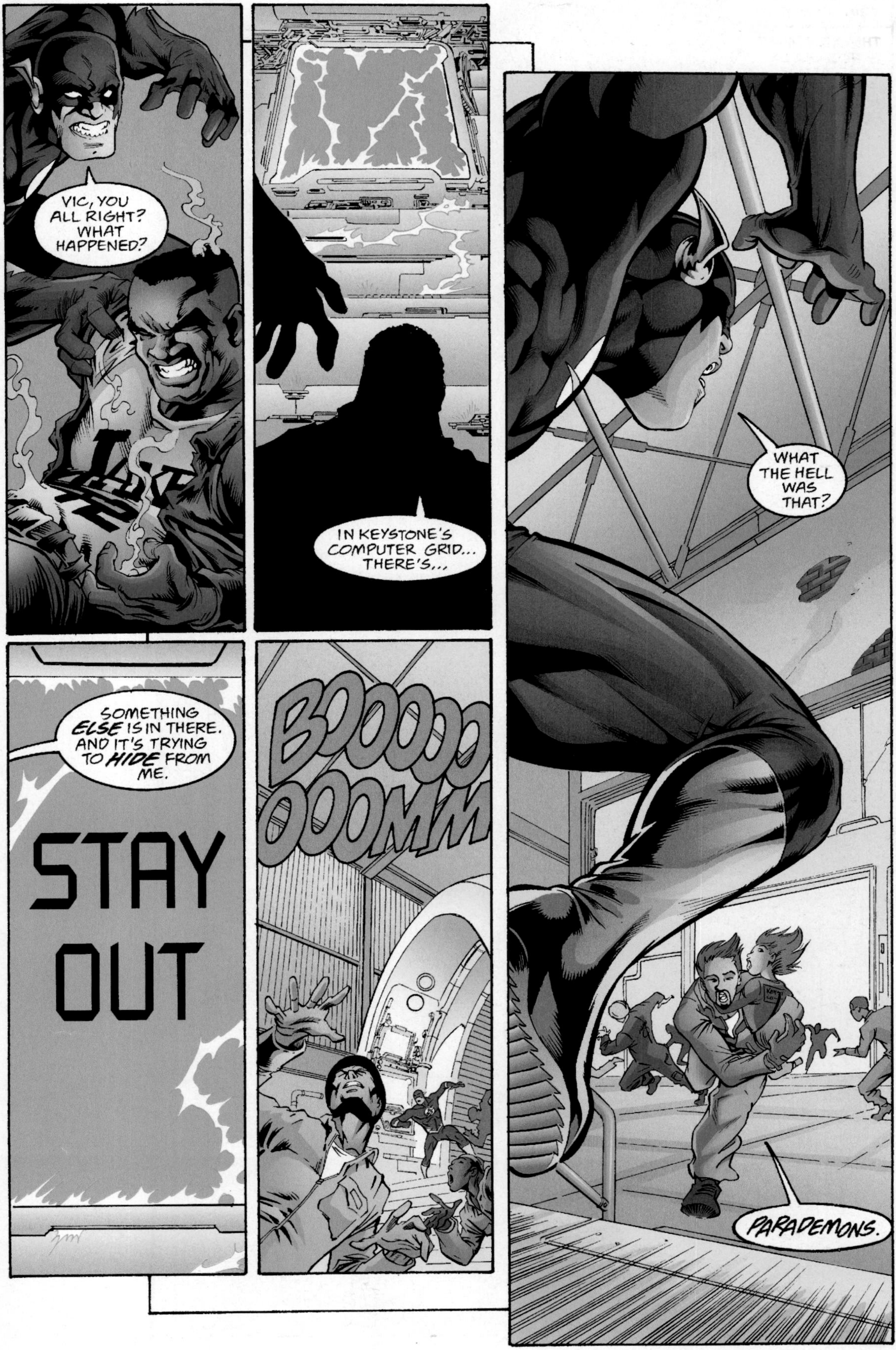
VIC, YOU ALL RIGHT? WHAT HAPPENED?
IN KEYSTONE'S COMPUTER GRID... THERE'S...
WHAT THE HELL WAS THAT?
SOMETHING ELSE IS IN THERE. AND IT'S TRYING TO HIDE FROM ME.
STAY OUT
BOOOOOOOOOMM
PARADEMONS.

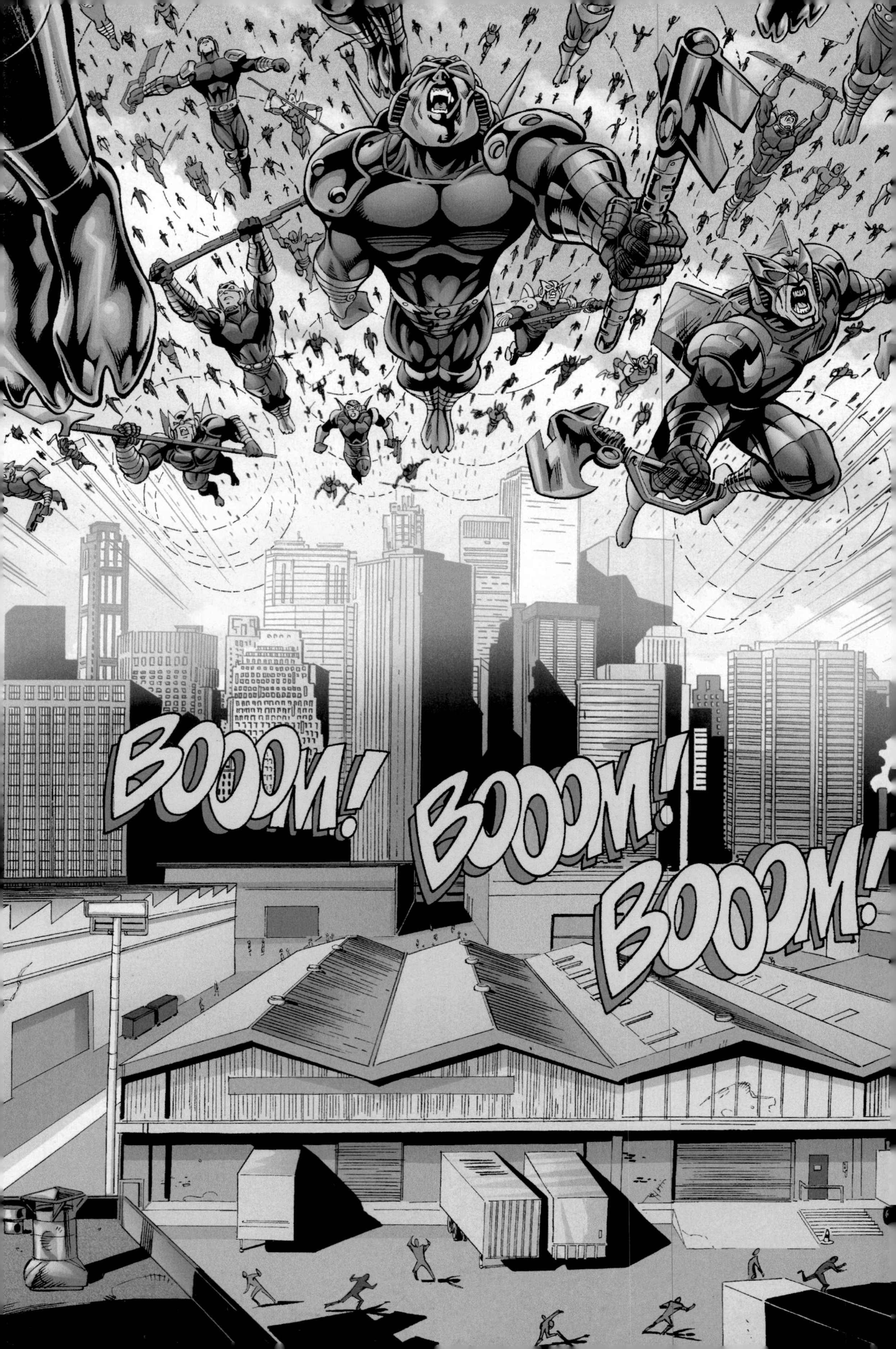
BOOOM!
BOOOM!
BOOOM!

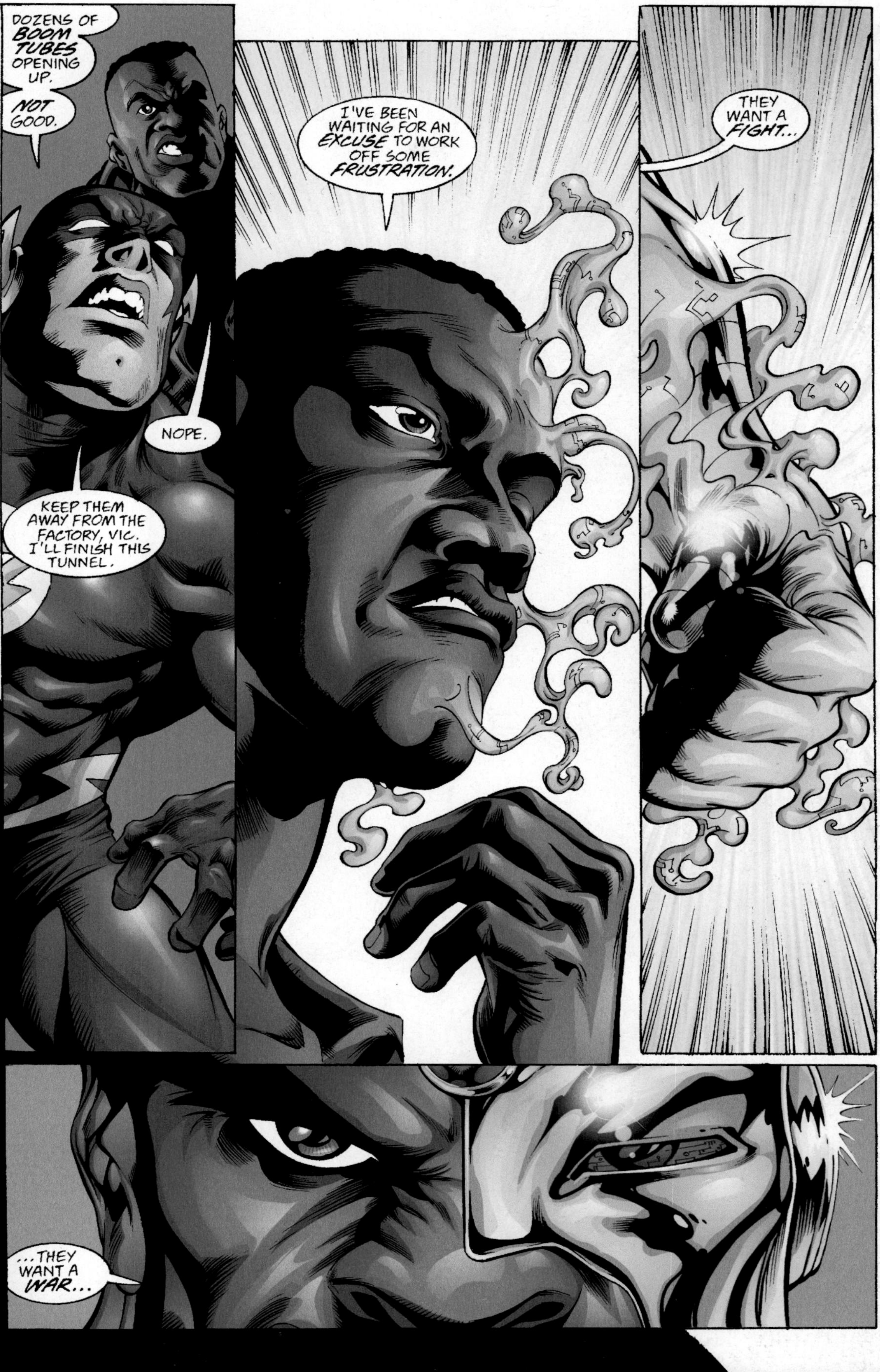
DOZENS OF BOOM TUBES OPENING UP.
NOT GOOD.
NOPE.
KEEP THEM AWAY FROM THE FACTORY, VIC. I'LL FINISH THIS TUNNEL.
I'VE BEEN WAITING FOR AN EXCUSE TO WORK OFF SOME FRUSTRATION.
THEY WANT A FIGHT...
...THEY WANT A WAR...

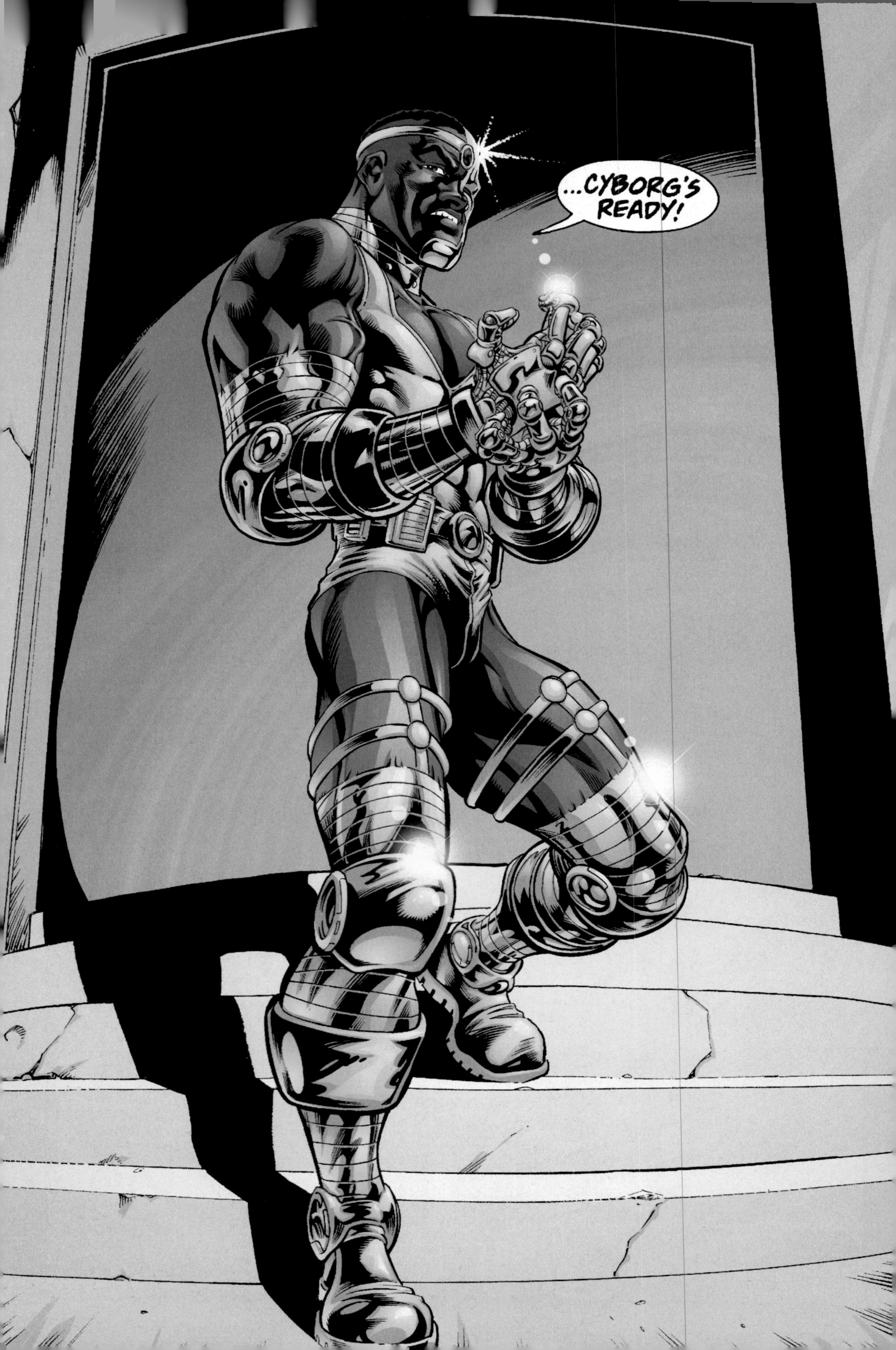
...CYBORG'S READY!

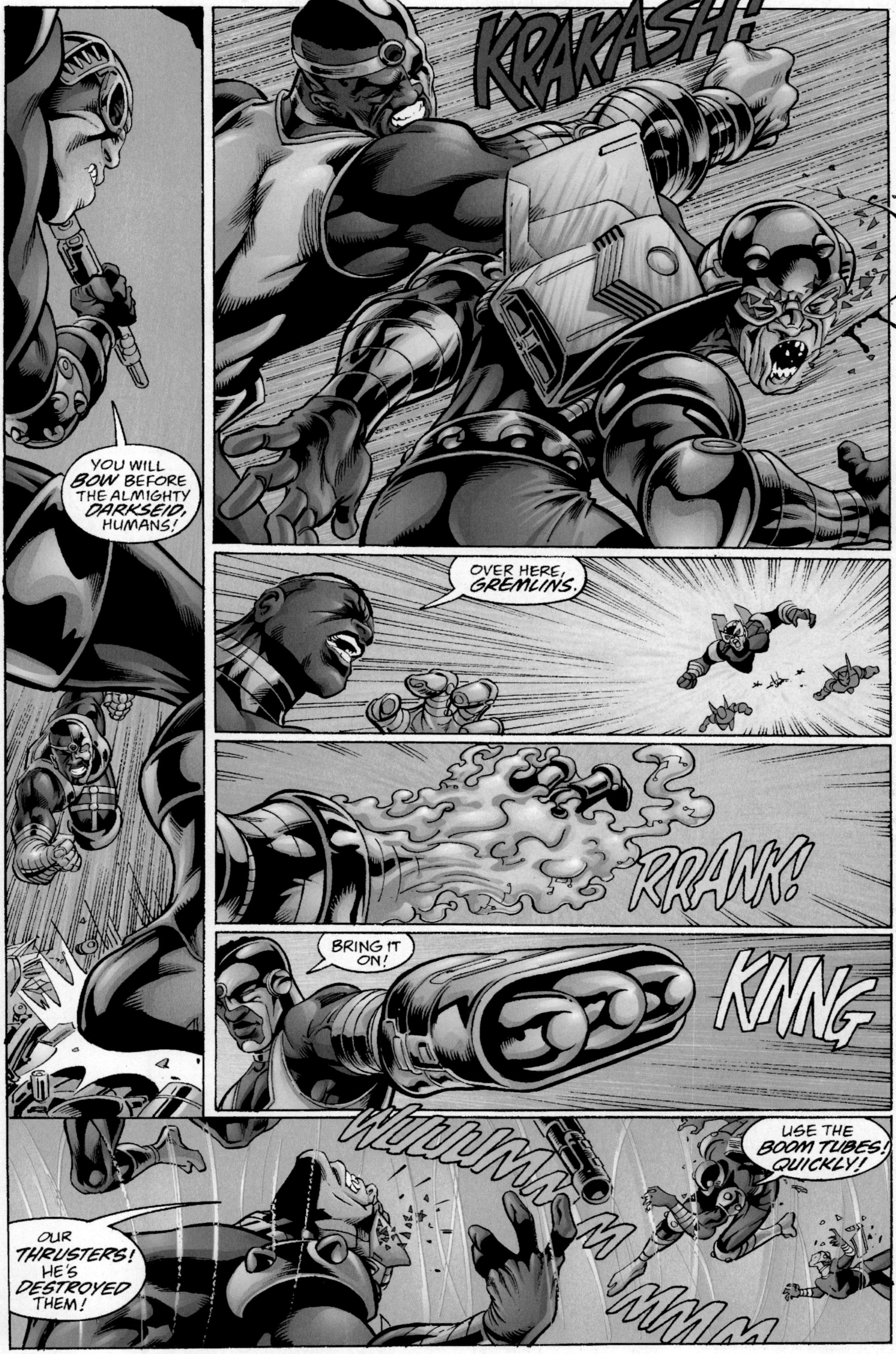
KRAKASH!
YOU WILL BOW BEFORE THE ALMIGHTY DARKSEID, HUMANS!
OVER HERE, GREMLINS.
RRANK!
BRING IT ON!
KINNG
WUUUMMMM
USE THE BOOM TUBES! QUICKLY!
OUR THRUSTERS! HE'S DESTROYED THEM!
MMMMM

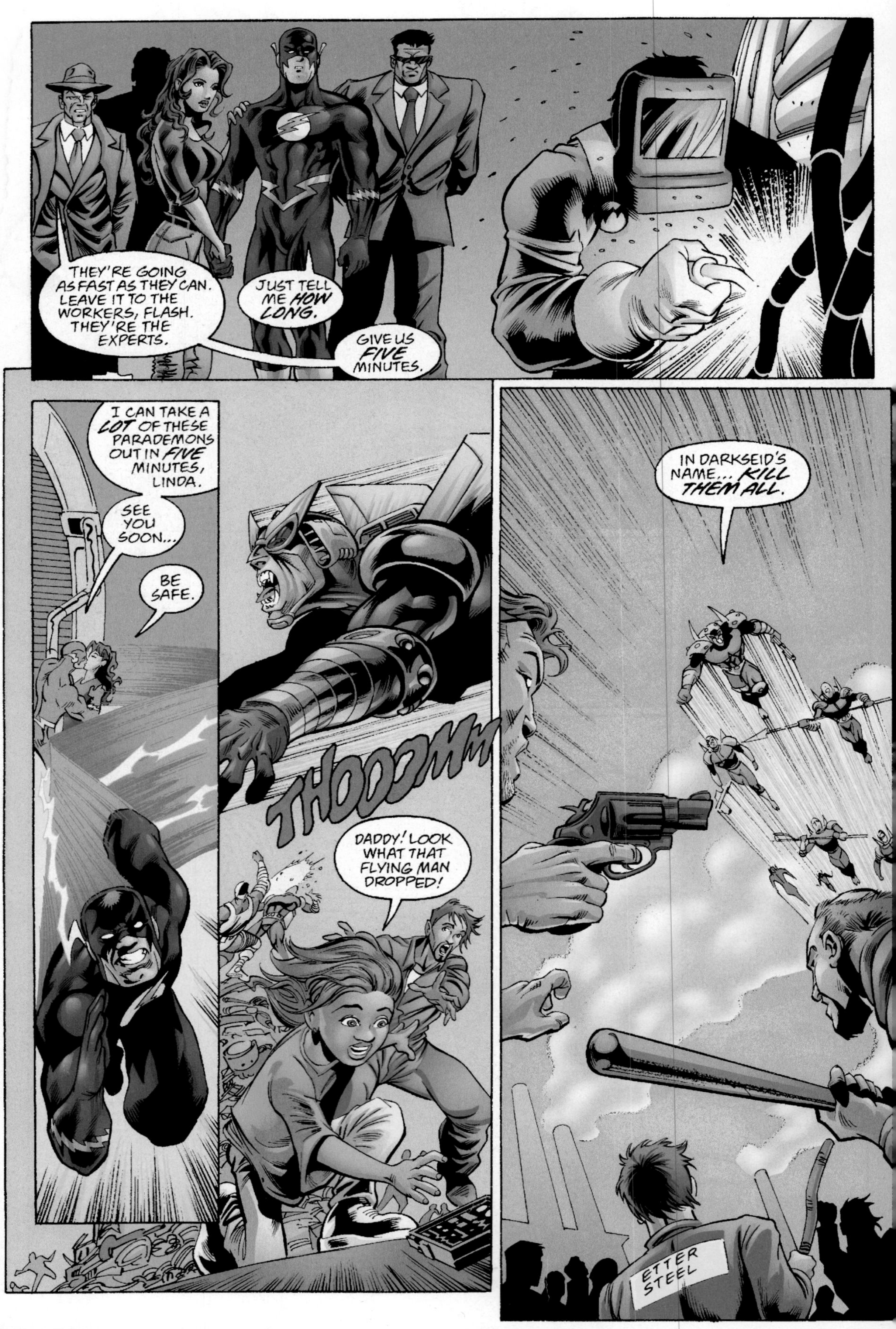

THEY'RE GOING AS FAST AS THEY CAN. LEAVE IT TO THE WORKERS, FLASH. THEY'RE THE EXPERTS.
JUST TELL ME HOW LONG.
GIVE US FIVE MINUTES.
I CAN TAKE A LOT OF THESE PARADEMONS OUT IN FIVE MINUTES, LINDA.
SEE YOU SOON...
BE SAFE.
THOOOMM
DADDY! LOOK WHAT THAT FLYING MAN DROPPED!
IN DARKSEID'S NAME... KILL THEM ALL.
ETTER STEEL

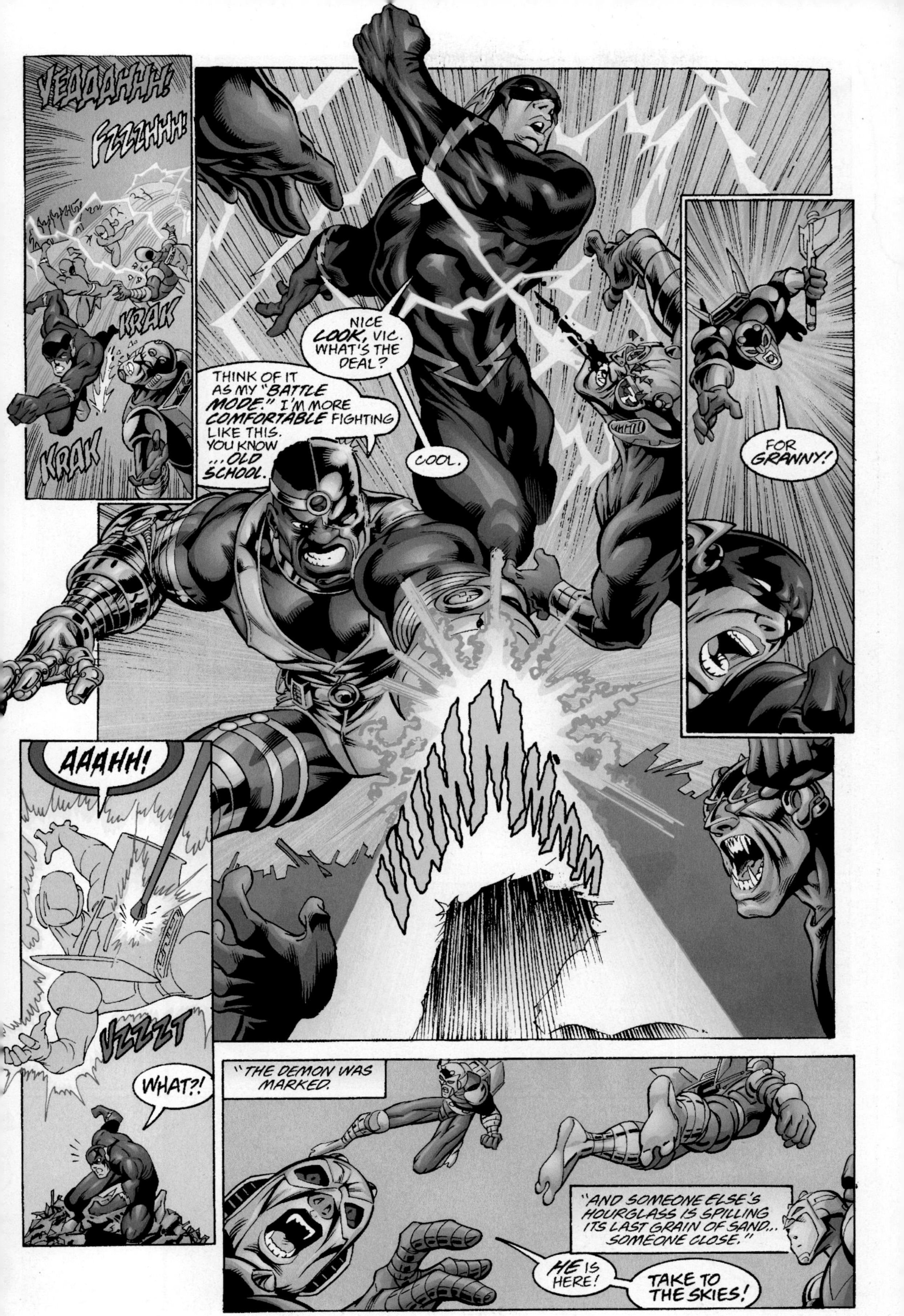

YEAAAHHH!
FZZZHHH!
KRAK
KRAK
NICE LOOK, VIC. WHAT'S THE DEAL?
THINK OF IT AS MY "BATTLE MODE." I'M MORE COMFORTABLE FIGHTING LIKE THIS. YOU KNOW ...OLD SCHOOL.
COOL.
FOR GRANNY!
VUMMMMMM
AAAHH!
VZZZT
WHAT?!
"THE DEMON WAS MARKED.
"AND SOMEONE ELSE'S HOURGLASS IS SPILLING ITS LAST GRAIN OF SAND... SOMEONE CLOSE."
HE IS HERE!
TAKE TO THE SKIES!

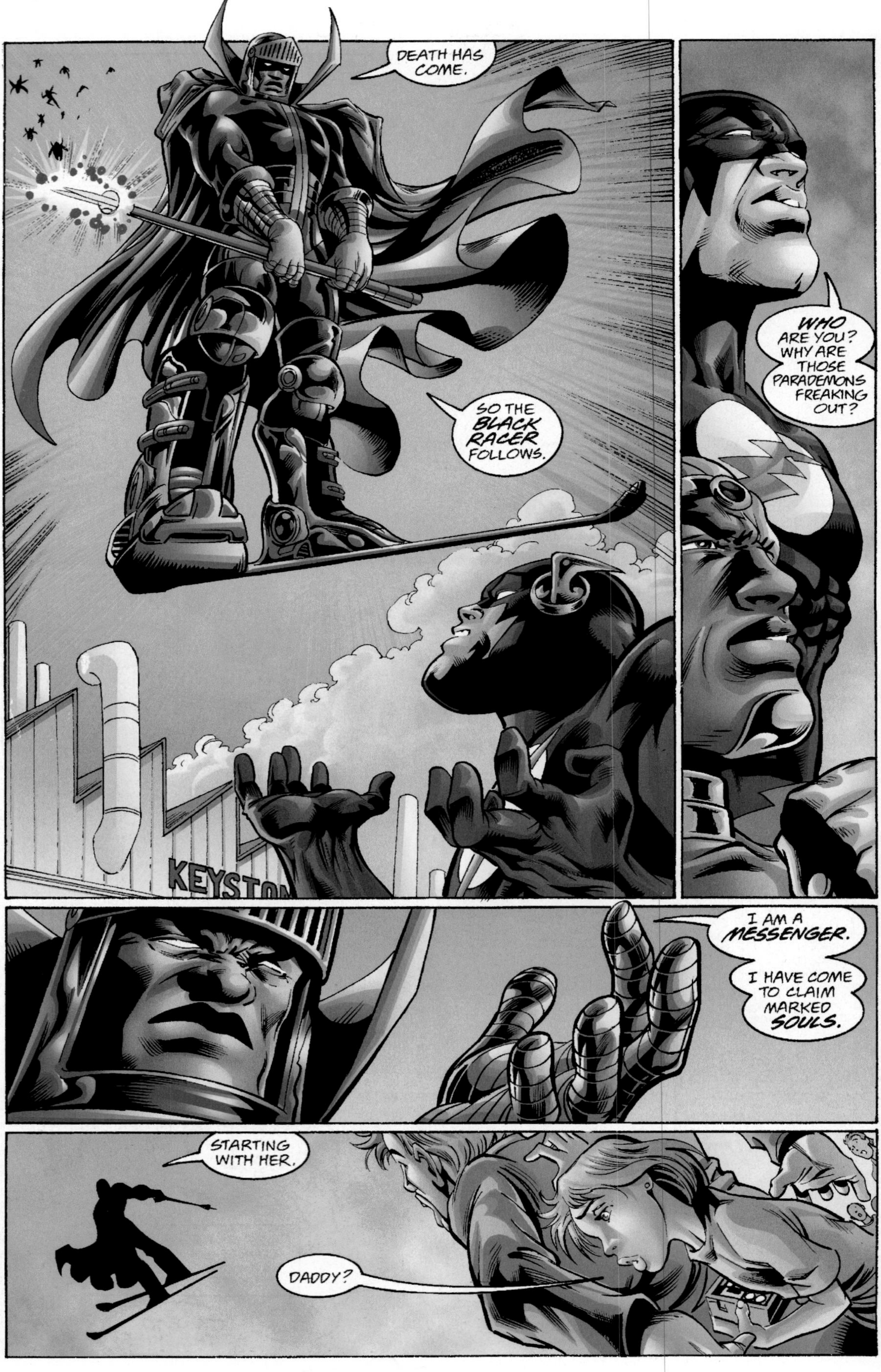
DEATH HAS COME.
SO THE BLACK RACER FOLLOWS.
KEYSTON
WHO ARE YOU? WHY ARE THOSE PARADEMONS FREAKING OUT?
I AM A MESSENGER.
I HAVE COME TO CLAIM MARKED SOULS.
STARTING WITH HER.
DADDY?

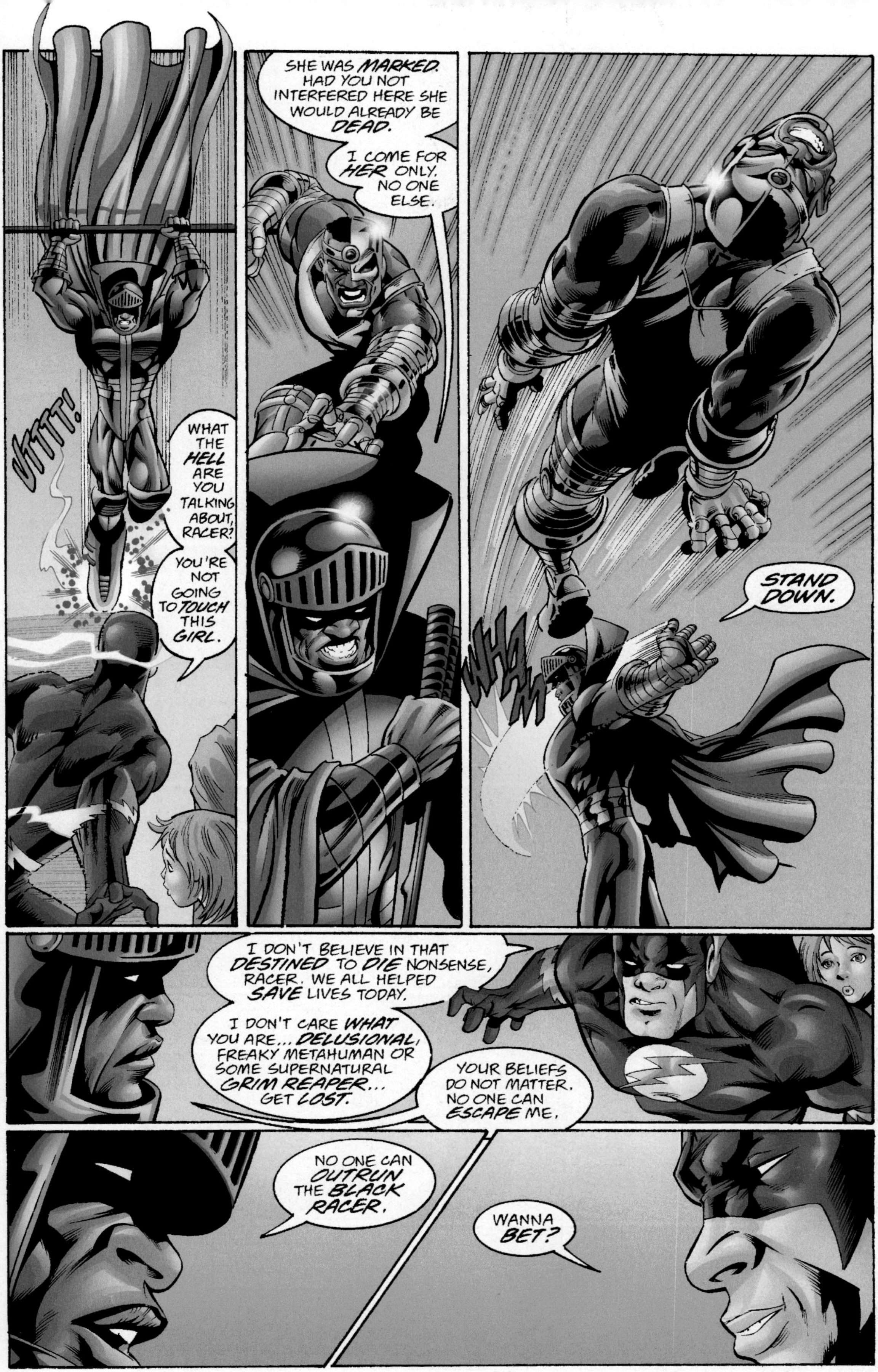

VTTTT!
WHAT THE HELL ARE YOU TALKING ABOUT, RACER?
YOU'RE NOT GOING TO TOUCH THIS GIRL.
SHE WAS MARKED. HAD YOU NOT INTERFERED HERE SHE WOULD ALREADY BE DEAD.
I COME FOR HER ONLY. NO ONE ELSE.
WHAM
STAND DOWN.
I DON'T BELIEVE IN THAT DESTINED TO DIE NONSENSE, RACER. WE ALL HELPED SAVE LIVES TODAY.
I DON'T CARE WHAT YOU ARE... DELUSIONAL, FREAKY METAHUMAN OR SOME SUPERNATURAL GRIM REAPER... GET LOST.
YOUR BELIEFS DO NOT MATTER. NO ONE CAN ESCAPE ME.
NO ONE CAN OUTRUN THE BLACK RACER.
WANNA BET?

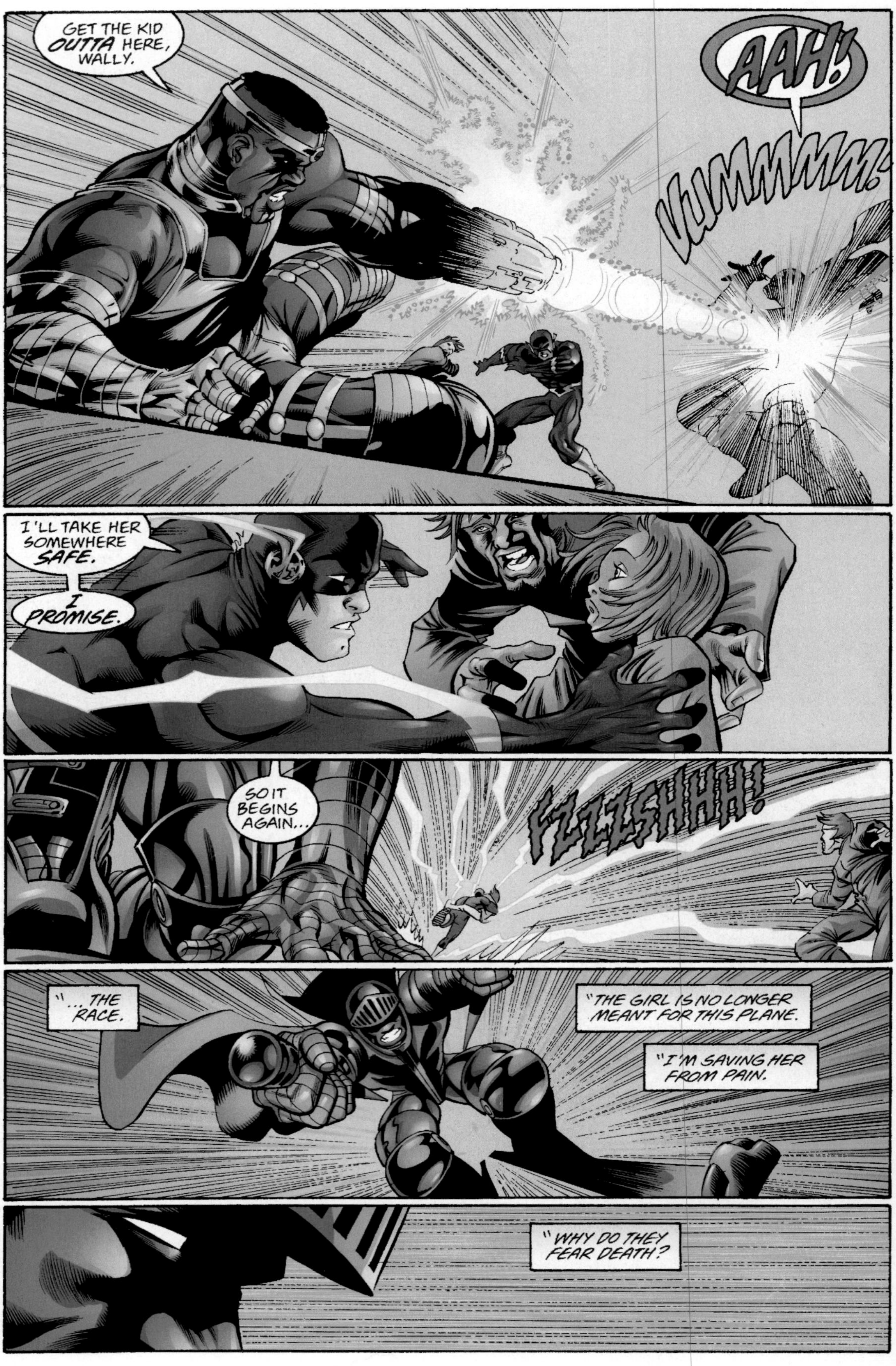
GET THE KID OUTTA HERE, WALLY.
AAH!
VUMMMM!
I'LL TAKE HER SOMEWHERE SAFE.
I PROMISE.
SO IT BEGINS AGAIN...
FZZZSHHH!
"...THE RACE.
"THE GIRL IS NO LONGER MEANT FOR THIS PLANE.
"I'M SAVING HER FROM PAIN.
"WHY DO THEY FEAR DEATH?

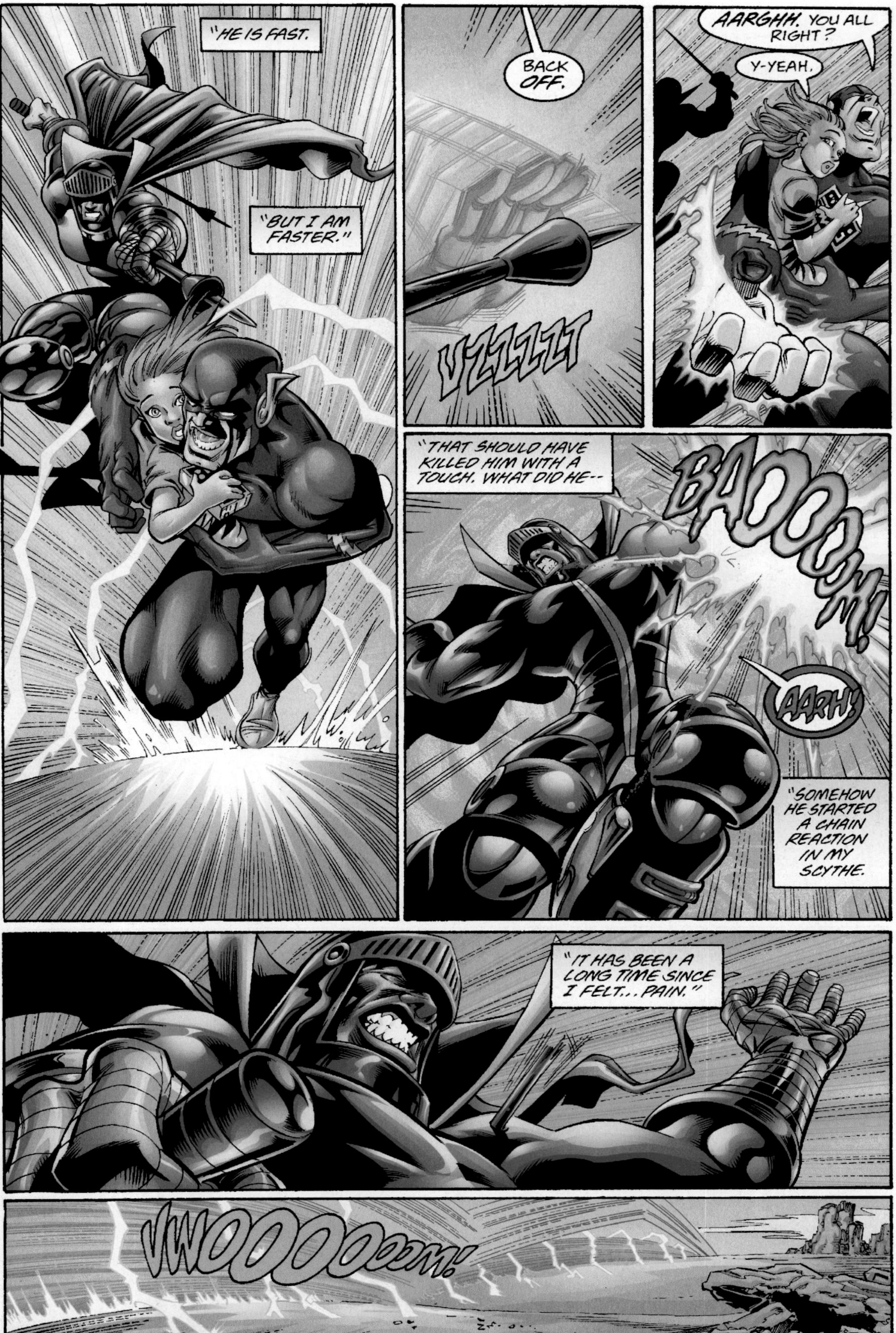
"HE IS FAST.
"BUT I AM FASTER."
BACK OFF.
VZZZZZT
AARGHH. YOU ALL RIGHT?
Y-YEAH.
"THAT SHOULD HAVE KILLED HIM WITH A TOUCH. WHAT DID HE--
BAOOOOM!
AARH!
"SOMEHOW HE STARTED A CHAIN REACTION IN MY SCYTHE.
"IT HAS BEEN A LONG TIME SINCE I FELT... PAIN."
VWOOOOOOM!

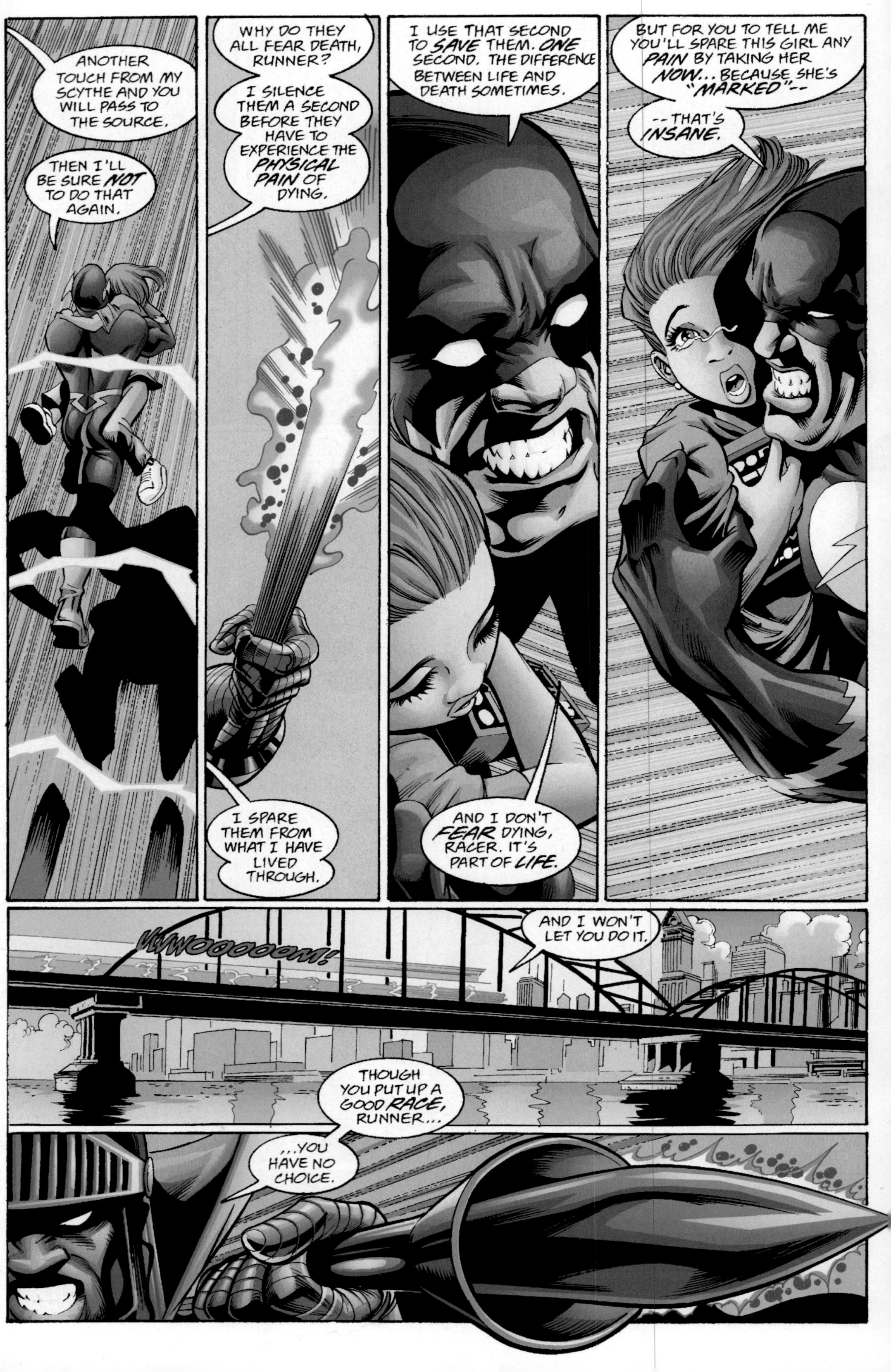
ANOTHER TOUCH FROM MY SCYTHE AND YOU WILL PASS TO THE SOURCE.
THEN I'LL BE SURE NOT TO DO THAT AGAIN.
WHY DO THEY ALL FEAR DEATH, RUNNER?
I SILENCE THEM A SECOND BEFORE THEY HAVE TO EXPERIENCE THE PHYSICAL PAIN OF DYING.
I SPARE THEM FROM WHAT I HAVE LIVED THROUGH.
I USE THAT SECOND TO SAVE THEM. ONE SECOND. THE DIFFERENCE BETWEEN LIFE AND DEATH SOMETIMES.
AND I DON'T FEAR DYING, RACER. IT'S PART OF LIFE.
BUT FOR YOU TO TELL ME YOU'LL SPARE THIS GIRL ANY PAIN BY TAKING HER NOW... BECAUSE SHE'S "MARKED"--
--THAT'S INSANE.
VWWOOOOOOOM!
AND I WON'T LET YOU DO IT.
THOUGH YOU PUT UP A GOOD RACE, RUNNER...
...YOU HAVE NO CHOICE.

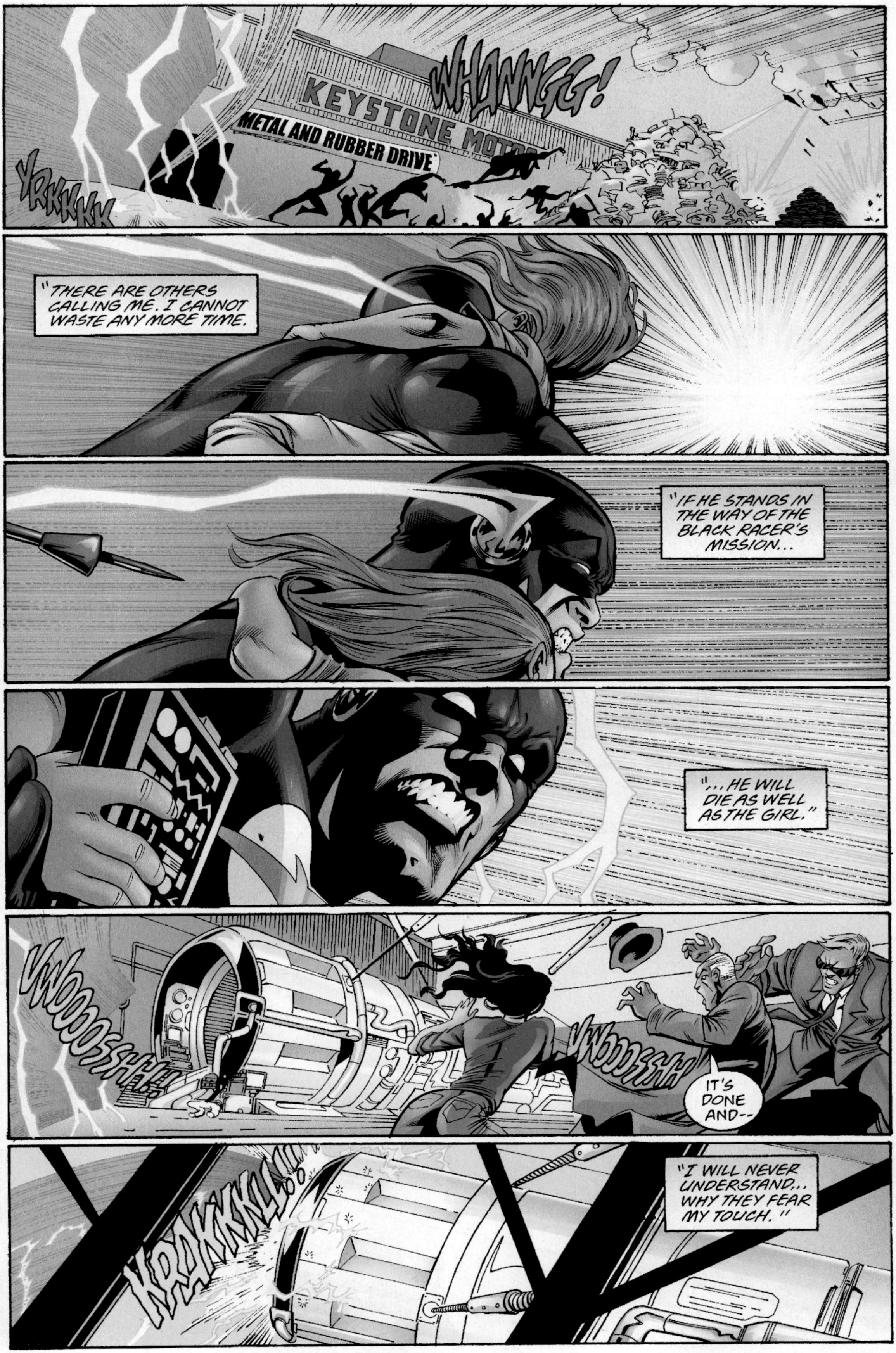
KEYSTONE MOTO
METAL AND RUBBER DRIVE
WHANNGG!
YRKKKKK
"THERE ARE OTHERS CALLING ME. I CANNOT WASTE ANY MORE TIME.
"IF HE STANDS IN THE WAY OF THE BLACK RACER'S MISSION...
"...HE WILL DIE AS WELL AS THE GIRL."
VWOOOSSHH!!
VWOOOSSHH
IT'S DONE AND--
KRAKKKLL!!
"I WILL NEVER UNDERSTAND... WHY THEY FEAR MY TOUCH."

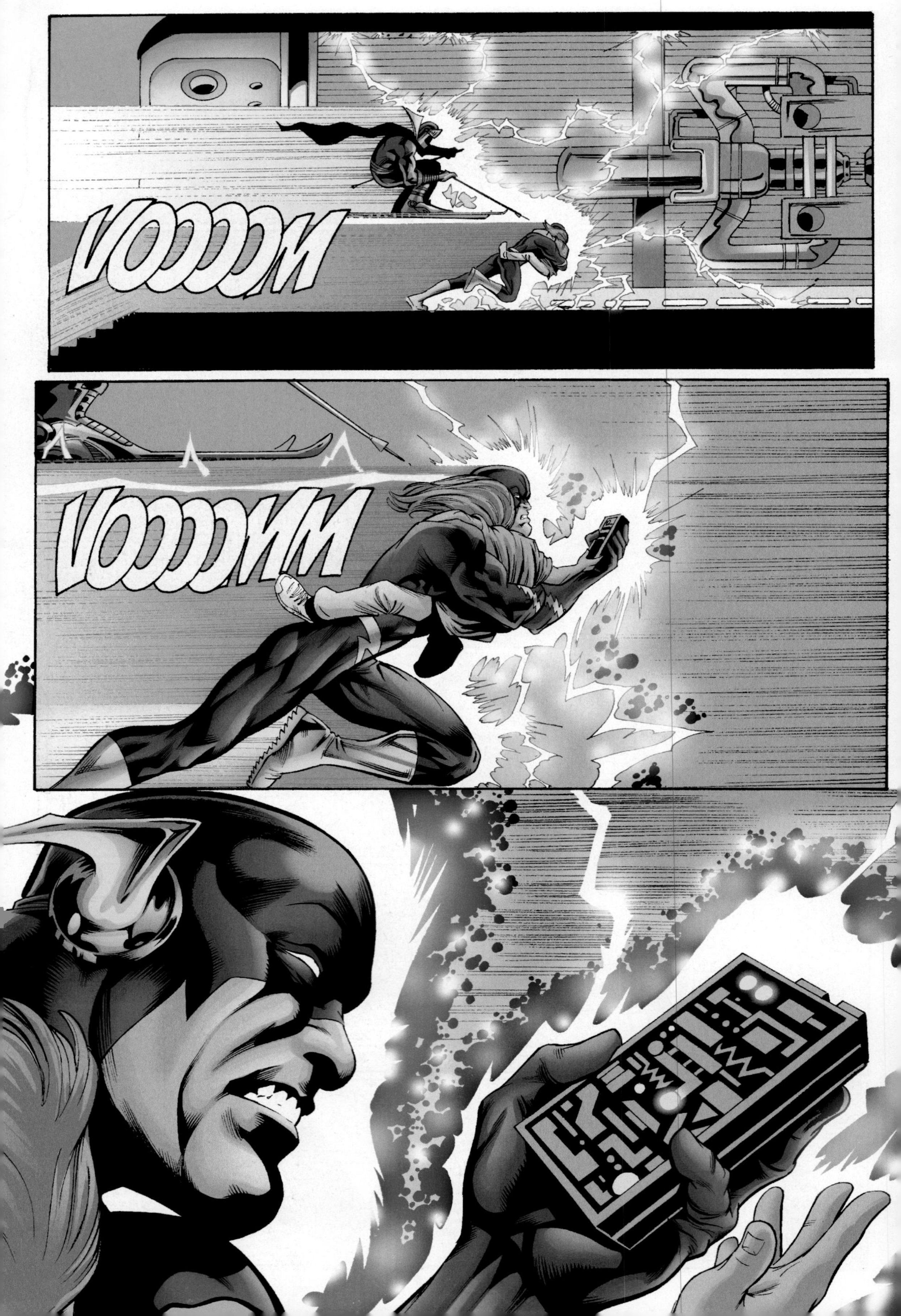
VOOOOM
VOOOOMM

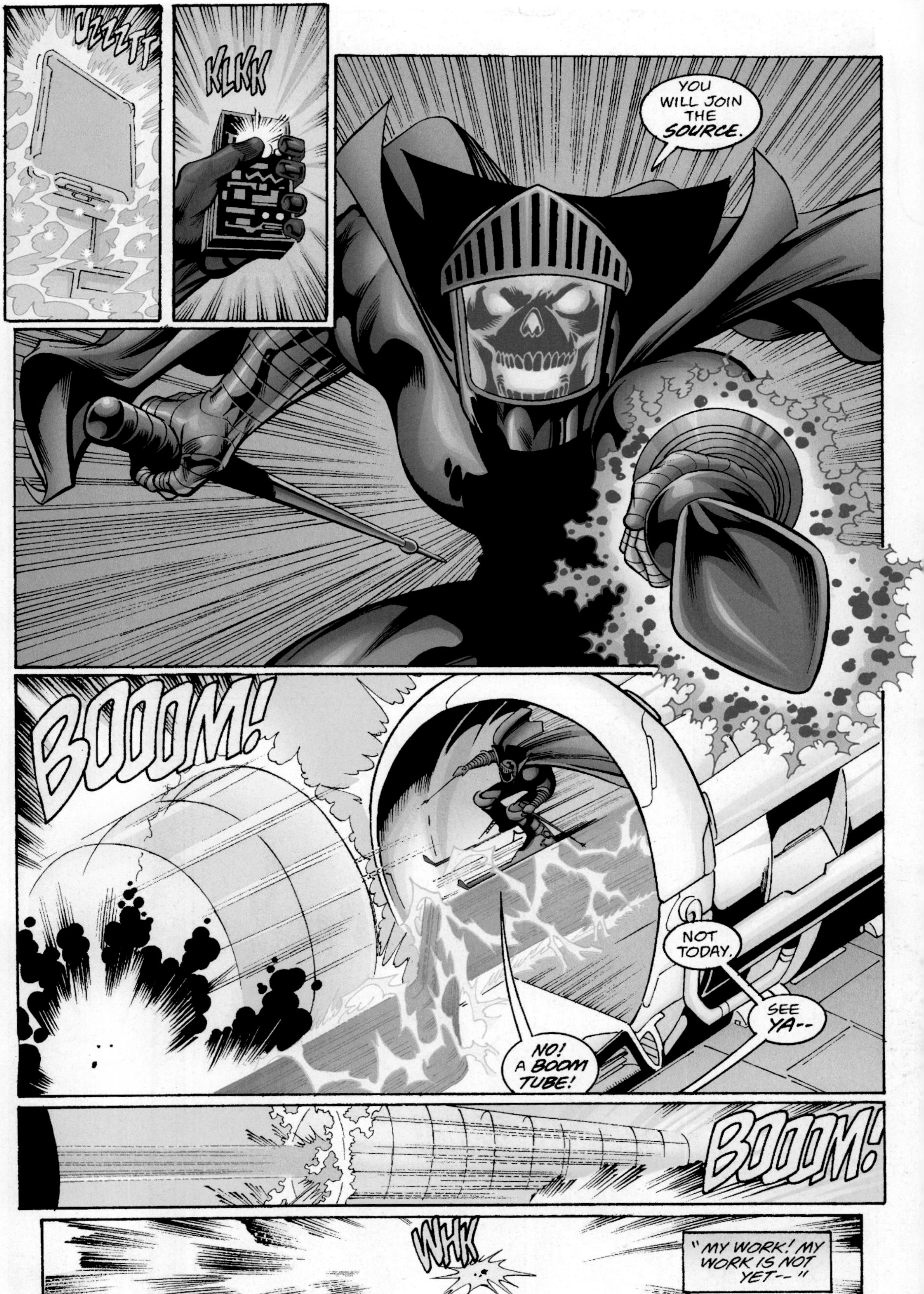

UZZZTT
KLKK
YOU WILL JOIN THE SOURCE.
BOOOM!
NO! A BOOM TUBE!
NOT TODAY.
SEE YA--
BOOOM!
WHK
"MY WORK! MY WORK IS NOT YET--"

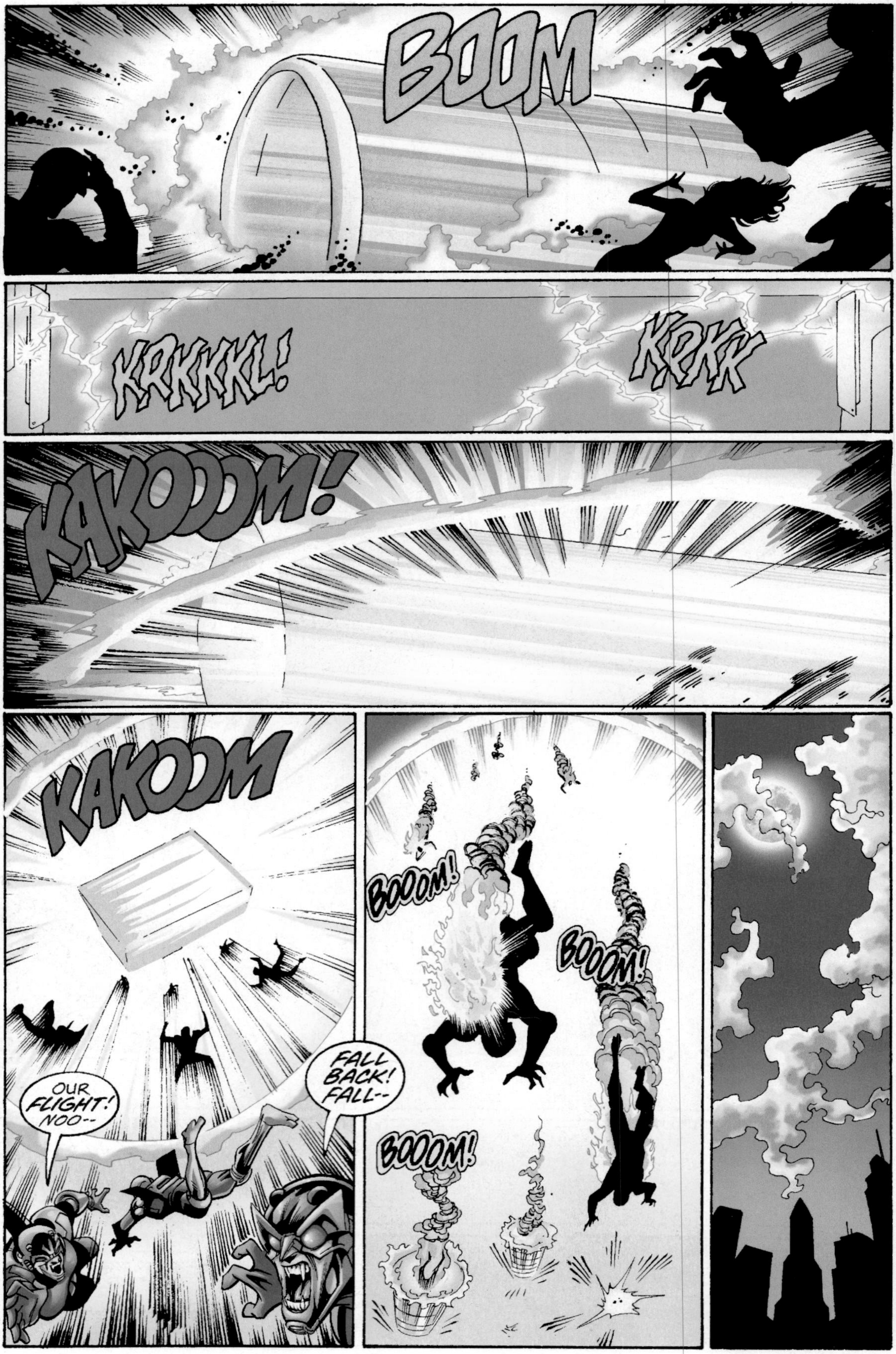
BOOM
KRKKKL!
KRKK
KAKOOOM!
KAKOOM
OUR FLIGHT! NOO--
FALL BACK! FALL--
BOOOM!
BOOOM!
BOOOM!

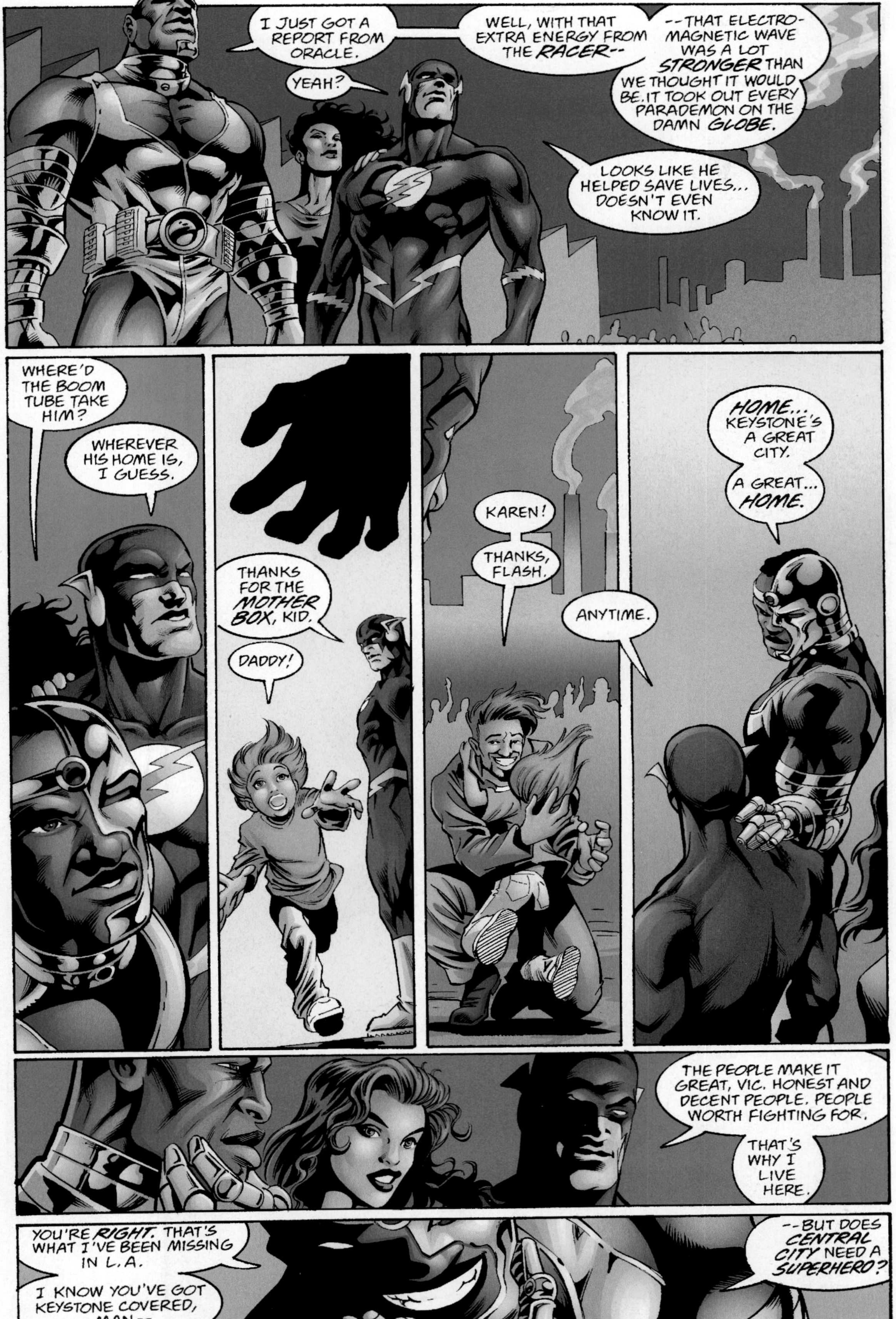
I JUST GOT A REPORT FROM ORACLE.
YEAH?
WELL, WITH THAT EXTRA ENERGY FROM THE RACER--
--THAT ELECTRO-MAGNETIC WAVE WAS A LOT STRONGER THAN WE THOUGHT IT WOULD BE. IT TOOK OUT EVERY PARADEMON ON THE DAMN GLOBE.
LOOKS LIKE HE HELPED SAVE LIVES... DOESN'T EVEN KNOW IT.
WHERE'D THE BOOM TUBE TAKE HIM?
WHEREVER HIS HOME IS, I GUESS.
THANKS FOR THE MOTHER BOX, KID.
DADDY!
KAREN!
THANKS, FLASH.
ANYTIME.
HOME... KEYSTONE'S A GREAT CITY.
A GREAT... HOME.
THE PEOPLE MAKE IT GREAT, VIC. HONEST AND DECENT PEOPLE. PEOPLE WORTH FIGHTING FOR.
THAT'S WHY I LIVE HERE.
YOU'RE RIGHT. THAT'S WHAT I'VE BEEN MISSING IN L.A.
I KNOW YOU'VE GOT KEYSTONE COVERED, MAN--
--BUT DOES CENTRAL CITY NEED A SUPERHERO?

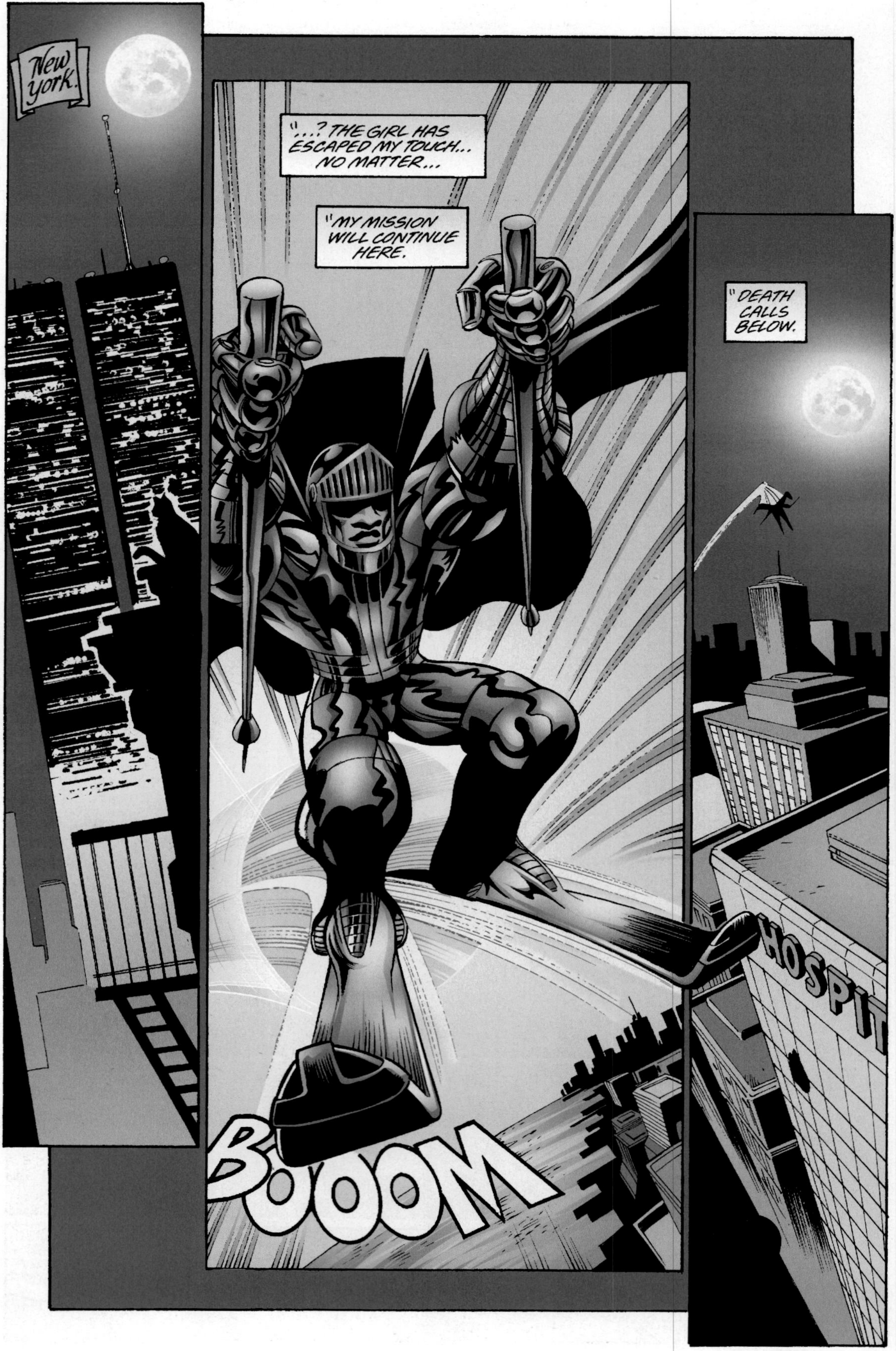
New York.
"...? THE GIRL HAS ESCAPED MY TOUCH... NO MATTER...
"MY MISSION WILL CONTINUE HERE.
"DEATH CALLS BELOW.
BOOOM
HOSPIT

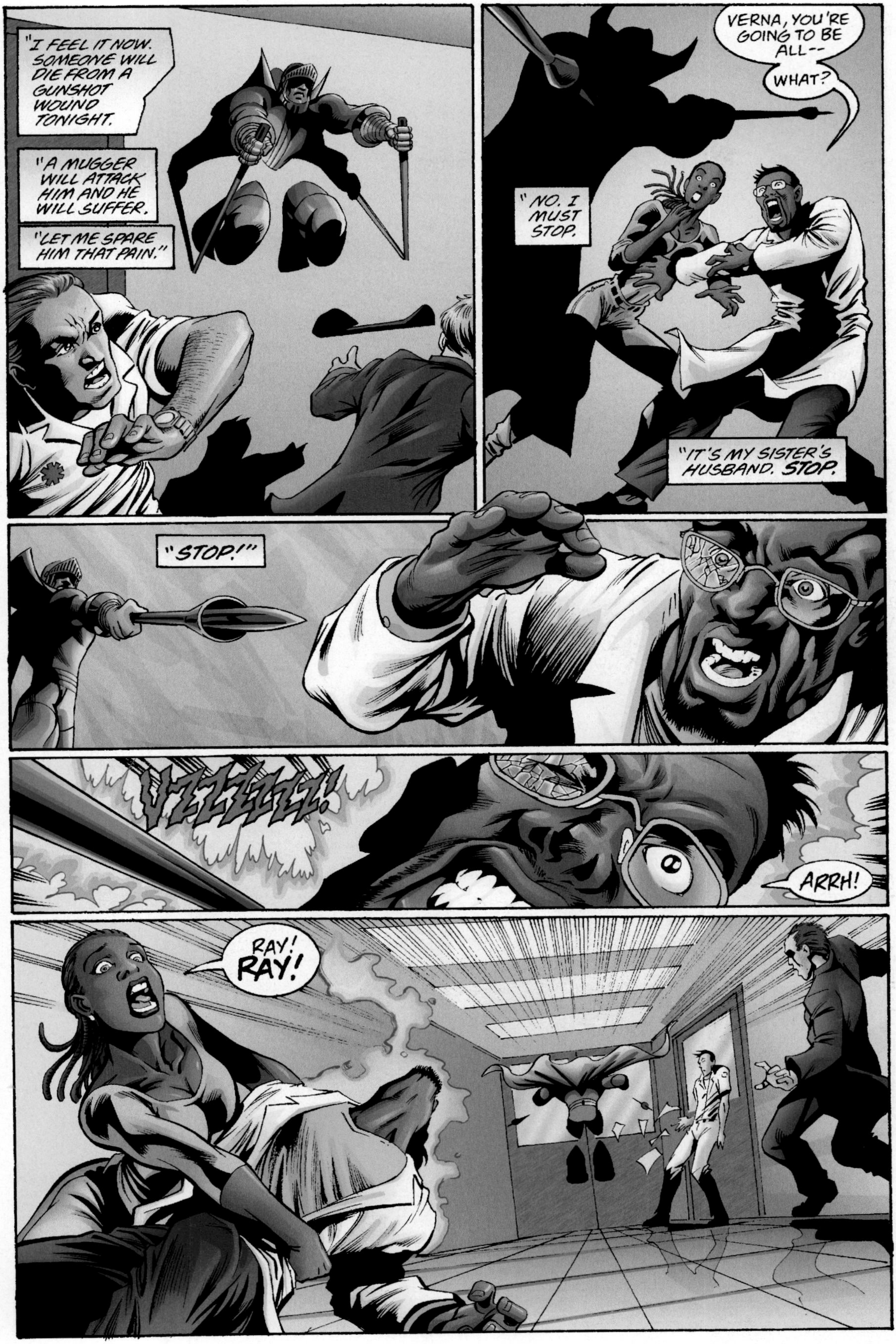
"I FEEL IT NOW. SOMEONE WILL DIE FROM A GUNSHOT WOUND TONIGHT.
"A MUGGER WILL ATTACK HIM AND HE WILL SUFFER.
"LET ME SPARE HIM THAT PAIN."
VERNA, YOU'RE GOING TO BE ALL--
WHAT?
"NO. I MUST STOP.
"IT'S MY SISTER'S HUSBAND. STOP.
"STOP!"
VZZZZZZ!
ARRH!
RAY! RAY!

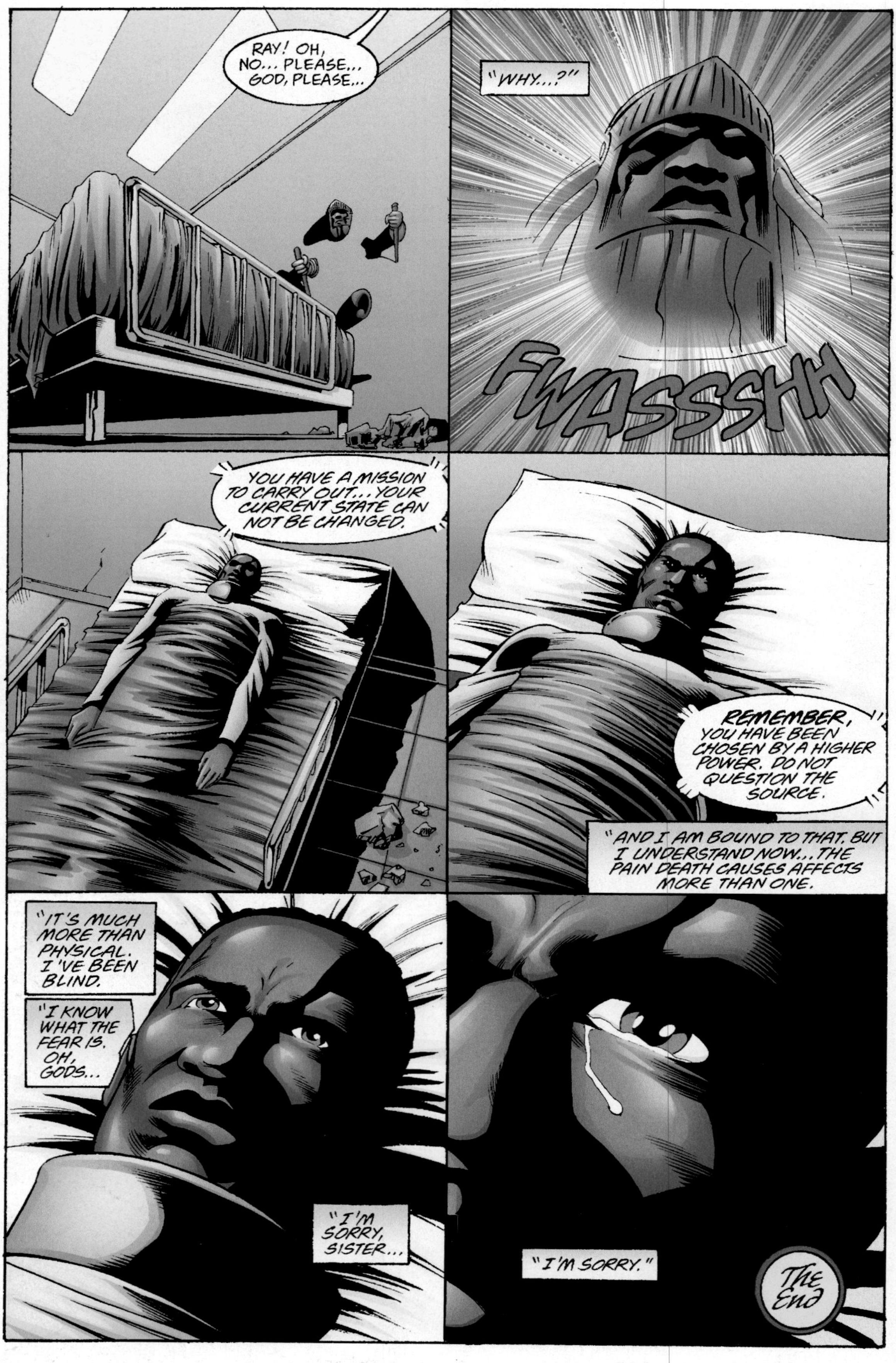
RAY! OH, NO... PLEASE... GOD, PLEASE...
"WHY...?"
FWASSSHH
YOU HAVE A MISSION TO CARRY OUT... YOUR CURRENT STATE CAN NOT BE CHANGED.
REMEMBER, YOU HAVE BEEN CHOSEN BY A HIGHER POWER. DO NOT QUESTION THE SOURCE.
"AND I AM BOUND TO THAT. BUT I UNDERSTAND NOW... THE PAIN DEATH CAUSES AFFECTS MORE THAN ONE.
"IT'S MUCH MORE THAN PHYSICAL. I'VE BEEN BLIND.
"I KNOW WHAT THE FEAR IS. OH, GODS...
"I'M SORRY, SISTER...
"I'M SORRY."
THE END

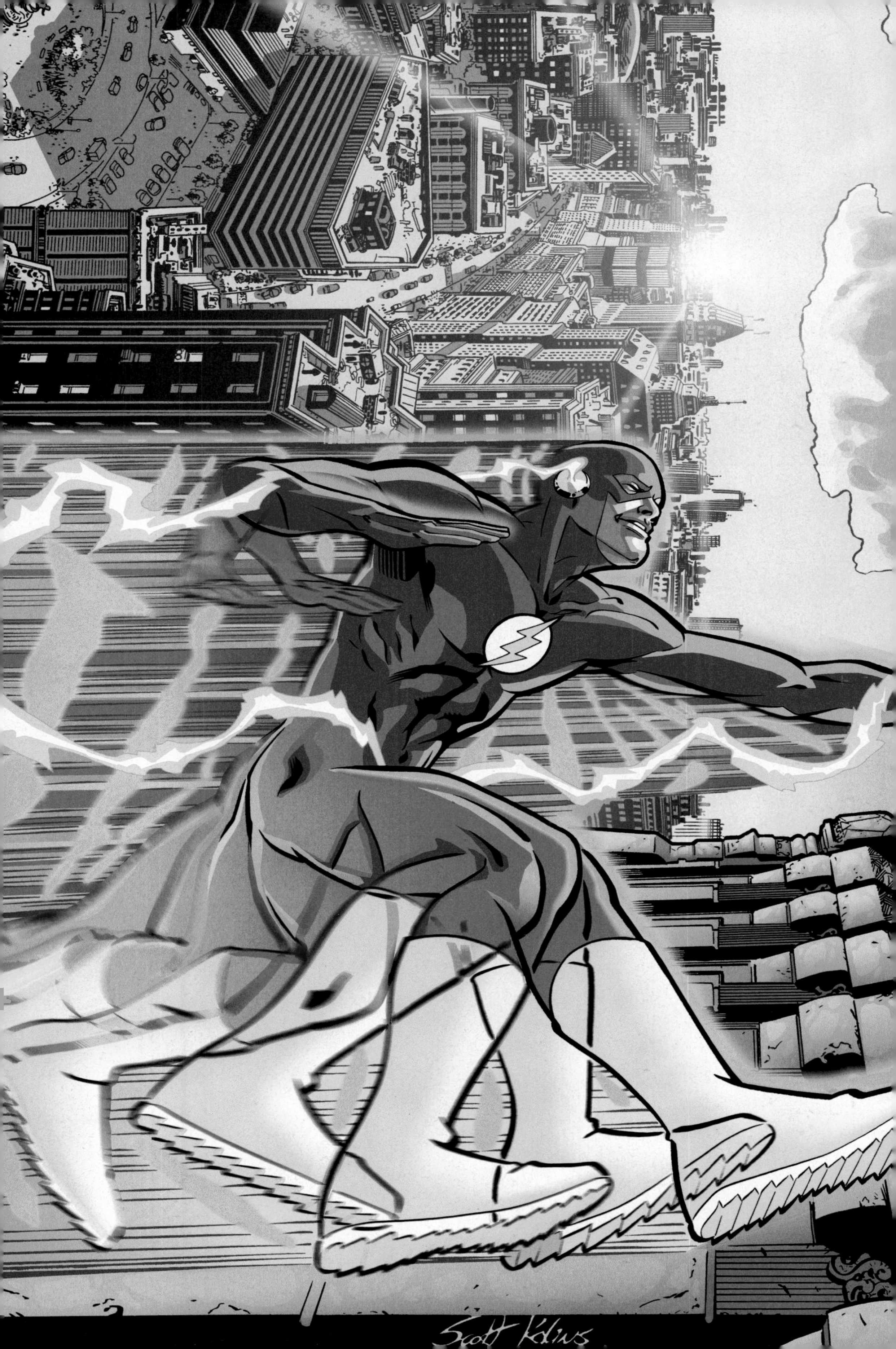
Scott Kolins

COVER ART BY ***SCOTT KOLINS***

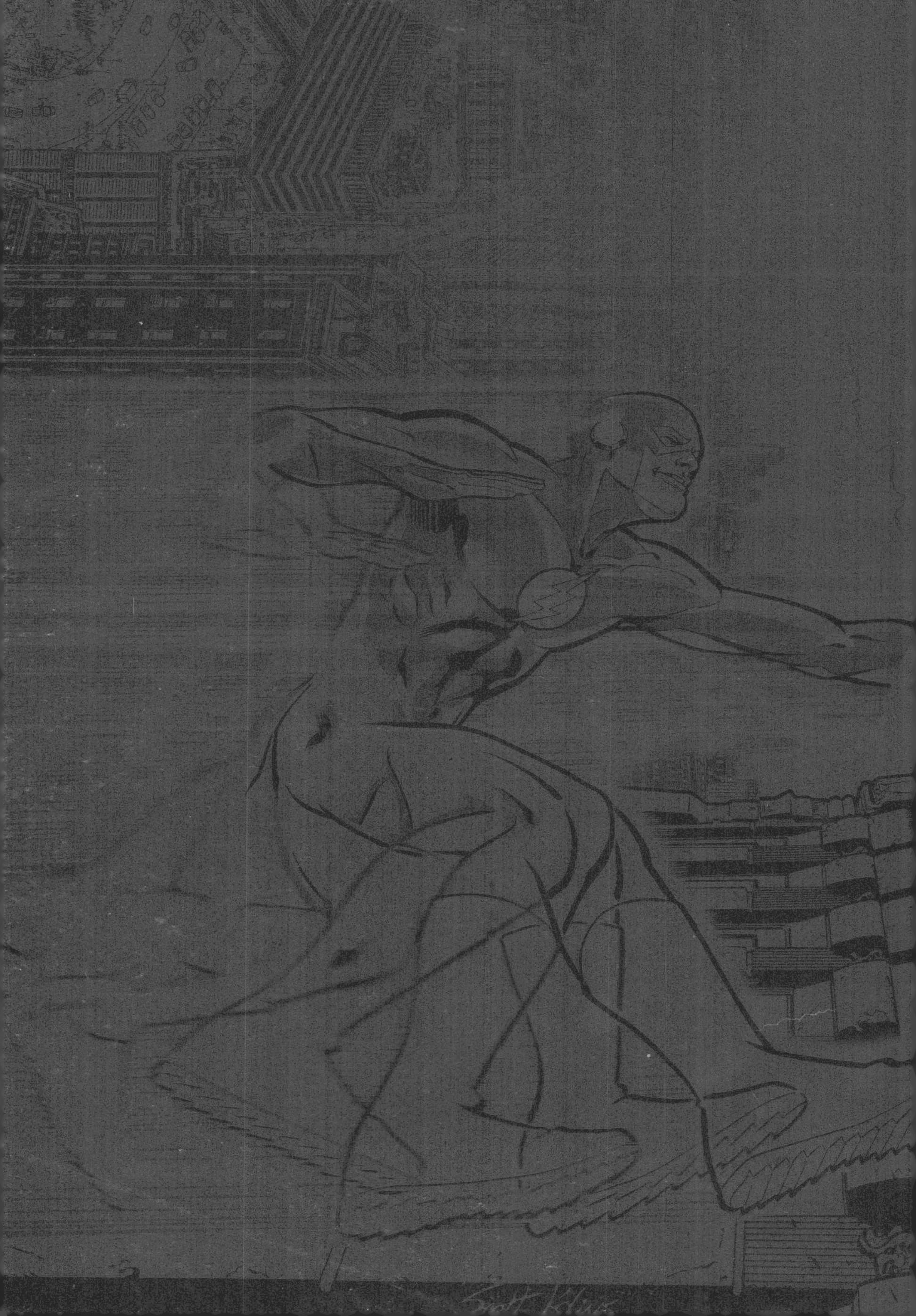

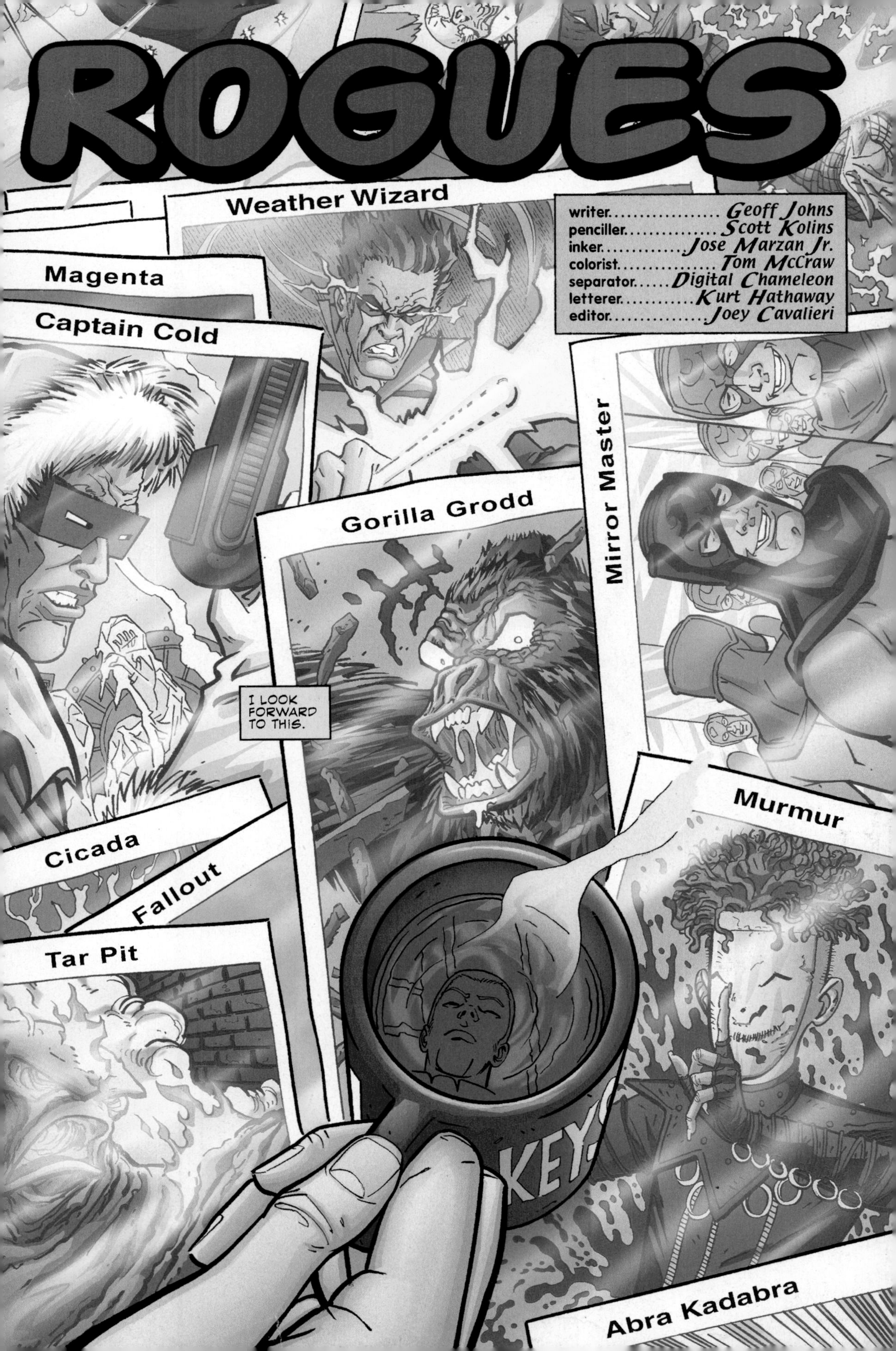
ROGUES
Weather Wizard
writer.................Geoff Johns
penciller..............Scott Kolins
inker............Jose Marzan Jr.
colorist..............Tom McCraw
separator......Digital Chameleon
letterer...........Kurt Hathaway
editor.............Joey Cavalieri
Magenta
Captain Cold
Mirror Master
Gorilla Grodd
I LOOK FORWARD TO THIS.
Murmur
Cicada
Fallout
Tar Pit
Abra Kadabra

GOOD TO GET AWAY-- FORGET ABOUT THE DIVORCE--

I GRADUATED FROM THE F.B.I.'S INVESTIGATIVE SUPPORT UNIT TWO DAYS AGO--AND I'M ALREADY ON MY WAY TO KEYSTONE CITY.

QUITE A CHANGE FROM THE CAMPUS AT QUANTICO. NOT MANY TREES, CLOUDY AIR-- I'VE NEVER BEEN TO KEYSTONE AND NOW I'M CALLING IT HOME.

KEYSTONE'S ONE OF THE MOST IMPORTANT CITIES IN AMERICA, I'M TOLD.

THEY PRACTICALLY INVENTED THE IDEA OF MAKING THINGS MOVE FAST--

--AND YET THE ONLY MODE OF PUBLIC TRANSPORT FROM THE AIRPORT TO DOWNTOWN IS BY TRAIN.

EASY ENOUGH, I SUPPOSE. AND IT IS--FAST. LIKE ITS RESIDENT HERO.

EVERYONE IN AMERICA CONNECTS THIS TOWN WITH THREE THINGS:

TRANSPORTATION.

THE FLASH.

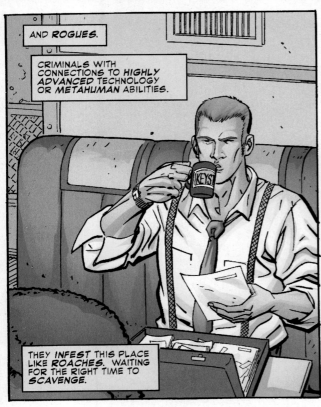

AND ROGUES.

CRIMINALS WITH CONNECTIONS TO HIGHLY ADVANCED TECHNOLOGY OR METAHUMAN ABILITIES.

THEY INFEST THIS PLACE LIKE ROACHES. WAITING FOR THE RIGHT TIME TO SCAVENGE.

THEY'RE OUT THERE--

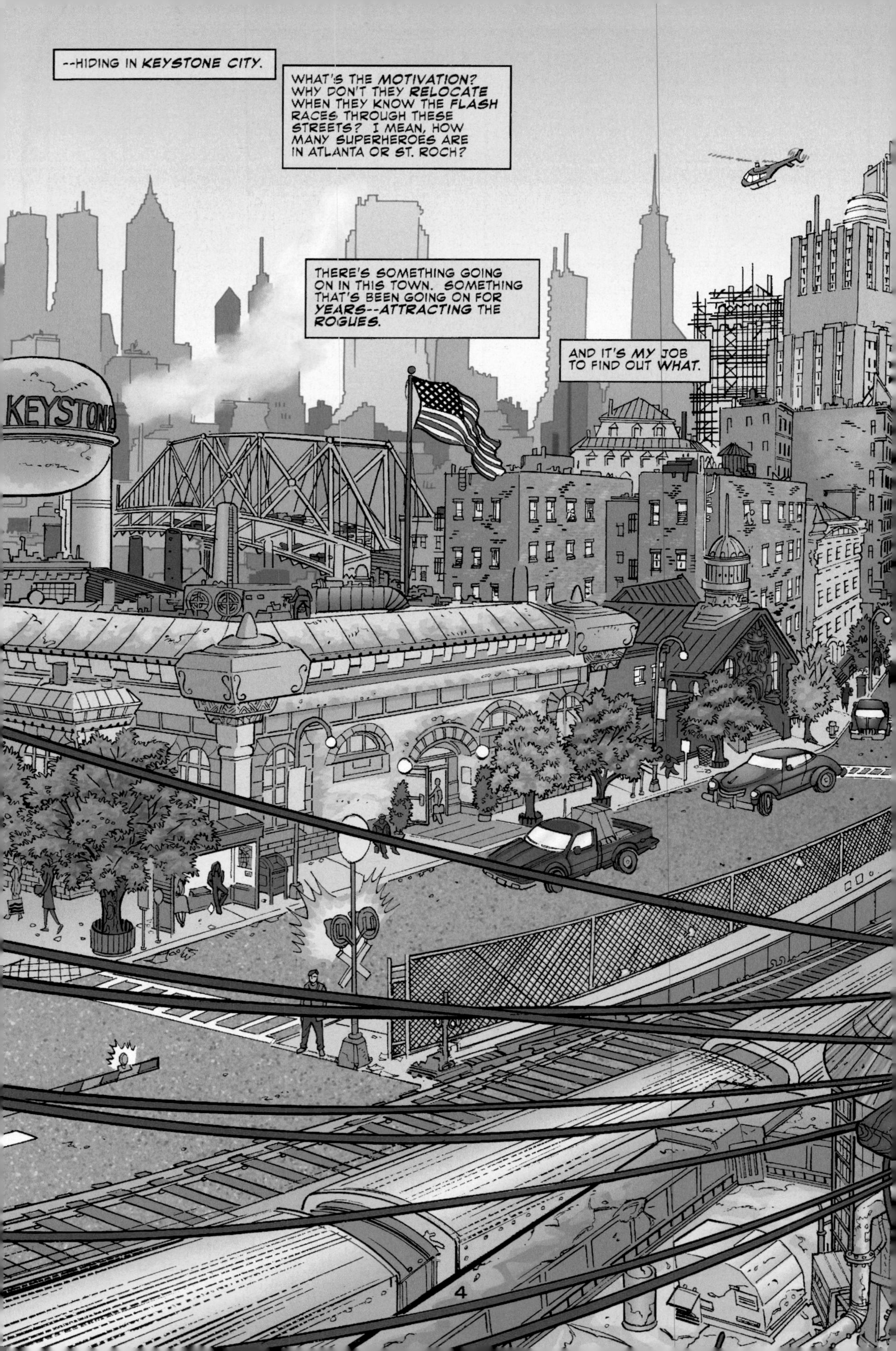
--HIDING IN KEYSTONE CITY.
WHAT'S THE MOTIVATION? WHY DON'T THEY RELOCATE WHEN THEY KNOW THE FLASH RACES THROUGH THESE STREETS? I MEAN, HOW MANY SUPERHEROES ARE IN ATLANTA OR ST. ROCH?
THERE'S SOMETHING GOING ON IN THIS TOWN. SOMETHING THAT'S BEEN GOING ON FOR YEARS--ATTRACTING THE ROGUES.
AND IT'S MY JOB TO FIND OUT WHAT.
KEYSTON

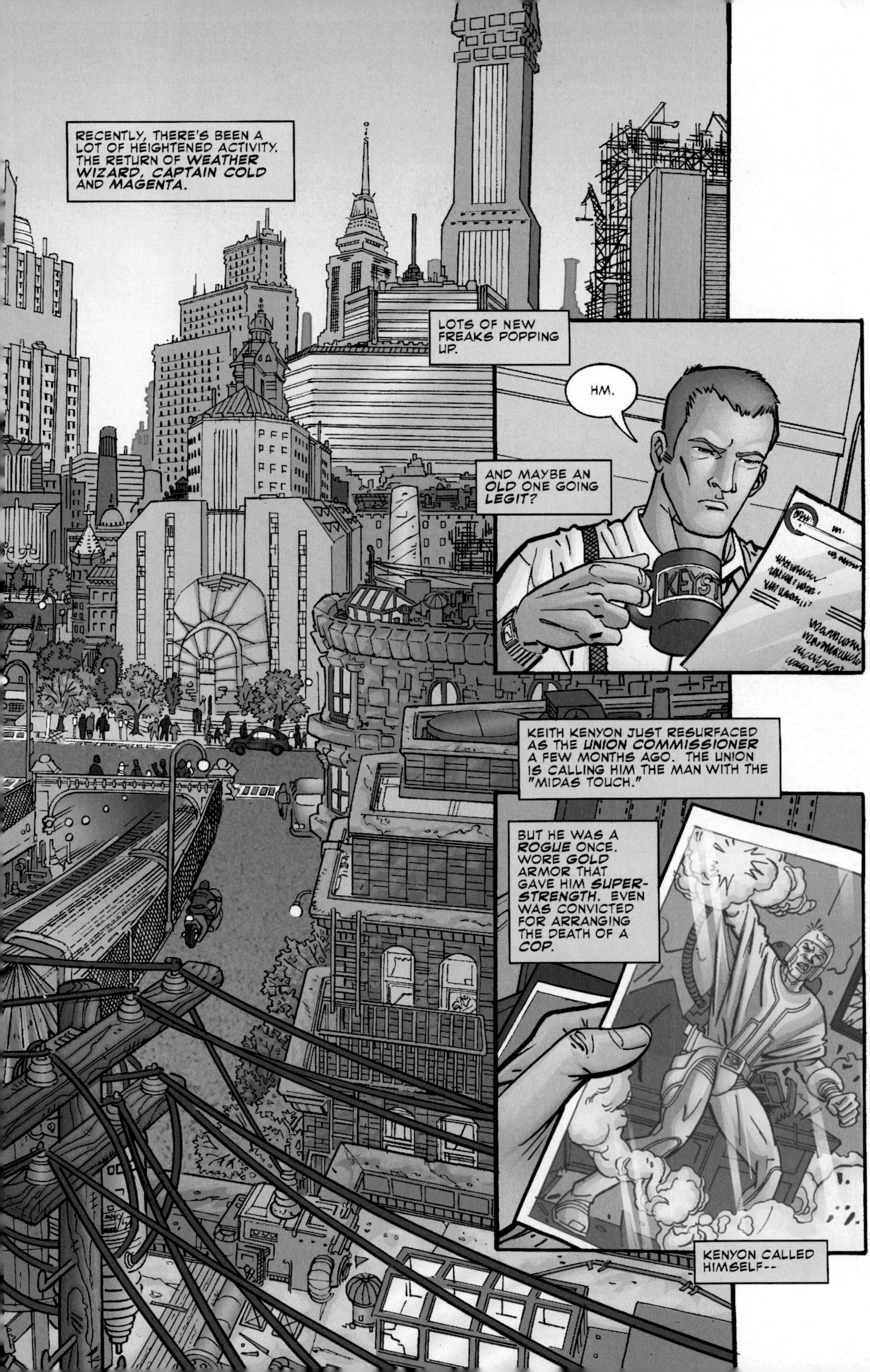

RECENTLY, THERE'S BEEN A LOT OF HEIGHTENED ACTIVITY. THE RETURN OF WEATHER WIZARD, CAPTAIN COLD AND MAGENTA.
LOTS OF NEW FREAKS POPPING UP.
HM.
AND MAYBE AN OLD ONE GOING LEGIT?
KEITH KENYON JUST RESURFACED AS THE UNION COMMISSIONER A FEW MONTHS AGO. THE UNION IS CALLING HIM THE MAN WITH THE "MIDAS TOUCH."
BUT HE WAS A ROGUE ONCE. WORE GOLD ARMOR THAT GAVE HIM SUPER-STRENGTH. EVEN WAS CONVICTED FOR ARRANGING THE DEATH OF A COP.
KENYON CALLED HIMSELF--

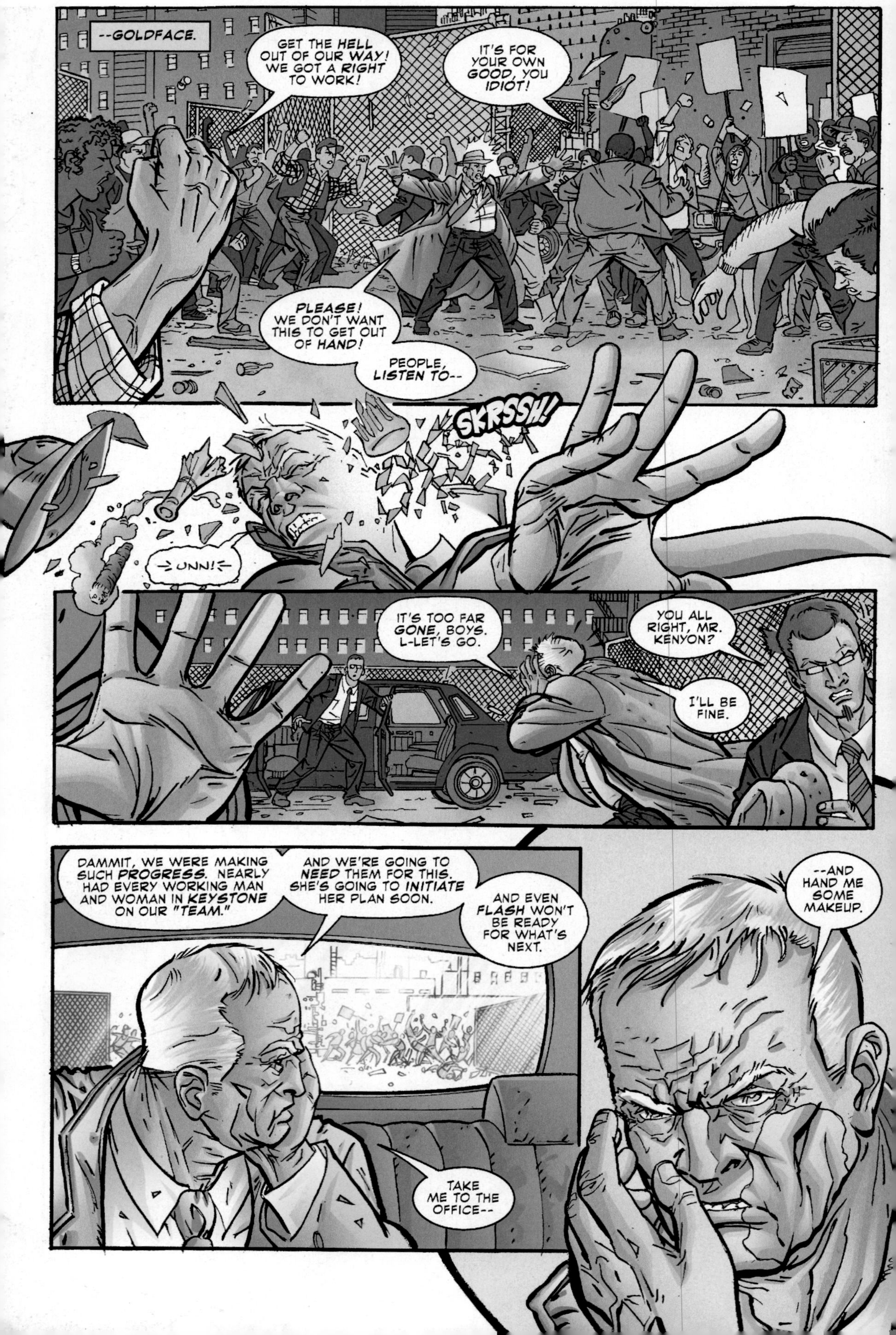
--GOLDFACE.
GET THE HELL OUT OF OUR WAY! WE GOT A RIGHT TO WORK!
IT'S FOR YOUR OWN GOOD, YOU IDIOT!
PLEASE! WE DON'T WANT THIS TO GET OUT OF HAND!
PEOPLE, LISTEN TO--
SKRSSH!
UNN!
IT'S TOO FAR GONE, BOYS. L-LET'S GO.
YOU ALL RIGHT, MR. KENYON?
I'LL BE FINE.
DAMMIT, WE WERE MAKING SUCH PROGRESS. NEARLY HAD EVERY WORKING MAN AND WOMAN IN KEYSTONE ON OUR "TEAM."
AND WE'RE GOING TO NEED THEM FOR THIS. SHE'S GOING TO INITIATE HER PLAN SOON.
AND EVEN FLASH WON'T BE READY FOR WHAT'S NEXT.
TAKE ME TO THE OFFICE--
--AND HAND ME SOME MAKEUP.

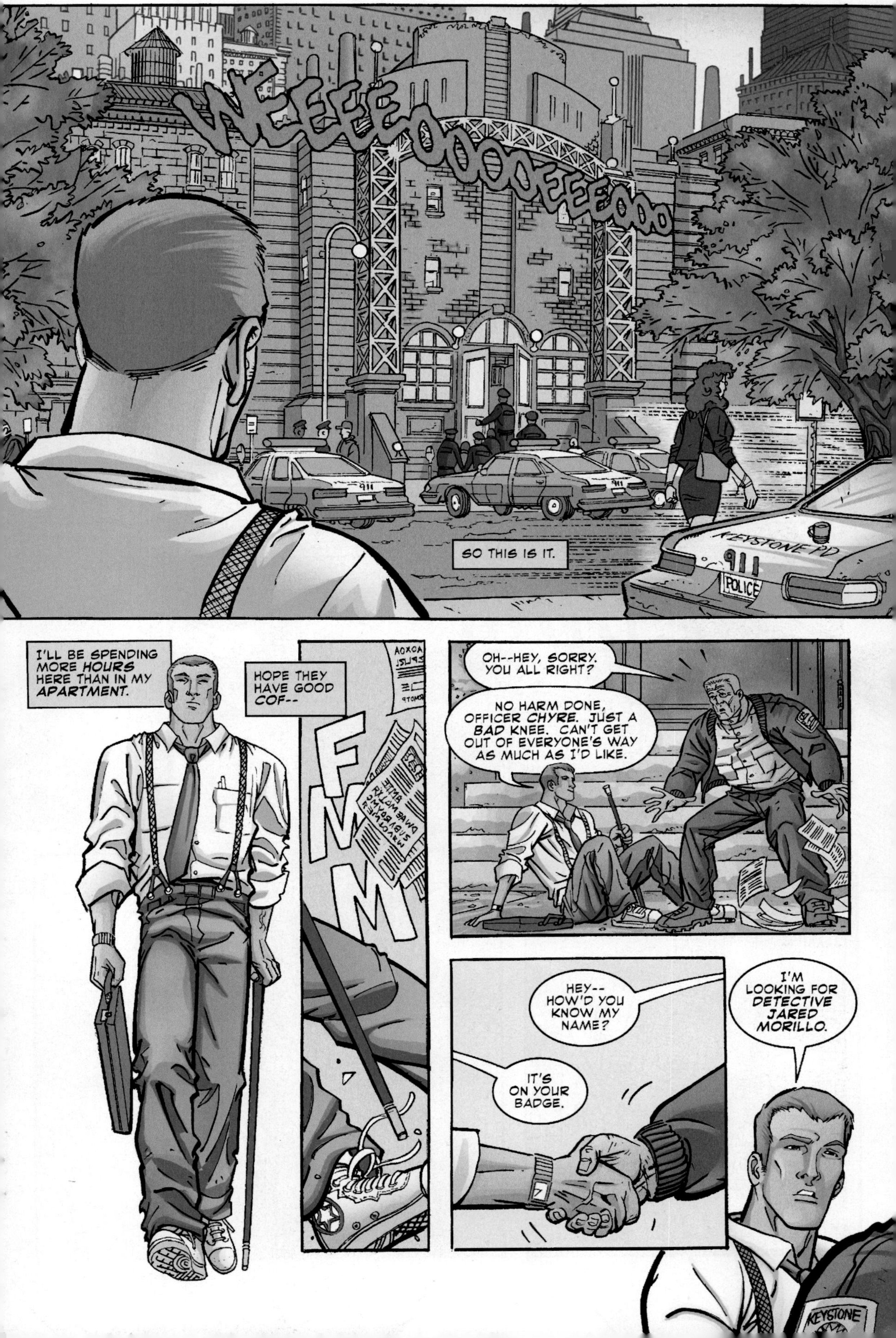

WEEEEOOOOEEEOoo
SO THIS IS IT.
KEYSTONE PD
911
POLICE
I'LL BE SPENDING MORE HOURS HERE THAN IN MY APARTMENT.
HOPE THEY HAVE GOOD COF--
FMM
OH--HEY, SORRY. YOU ALL RIGHT?
NO HARM DONE, OFFICER CHYRE. JUST A BAD KNEE. CAN'T GET OUT OF EVERYONE'S WAY AS MUCH AS I'D LIKE.
HEY-- HOW'D YOU KNOW MY NAME?
IT'S ON YOUR BADGE.
I'M LOOKING FOR DETECTIVE JARED MORILLO.
KEYSTONE

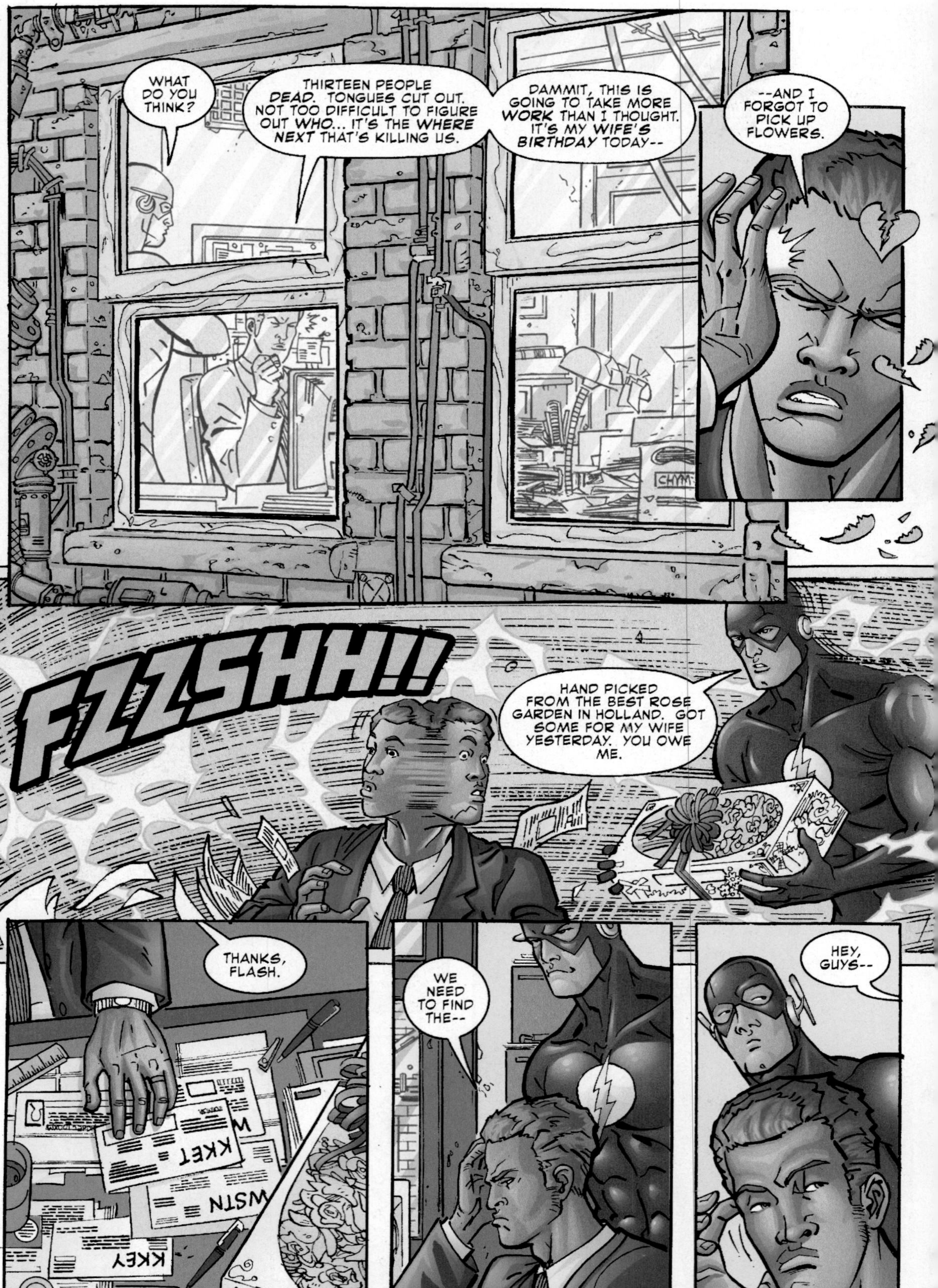
WHAT DO YOU THINK?
THIRTEEN PEOPLE DEAD. TONGUES CUT OUT. NOT TOO DIFFICULT TO FIGURE OUT WHO... IT'S THE WHERE NEXT THAT'S KILLING US.
DAMMIT, THIS IS GOING TO TAKE MORE WORK THAN I THOUGHT. IT'S MY WIFE'S BIRTHDAY TODAY--
--AND I FORGOT TO PICK UP FLOWERS.
CHYM
FZZSHH!!
HAND PICKED FROM THE BEST ROSE GARDEN IN HOLLAND. GOT SOME FOR MY WIFE YESTERDAY. YOU OWE ME.
THANKS, FLASH.
KKET
WSTN
KKEY
WE NEED TO FIND THE--
HEY, GUYS--

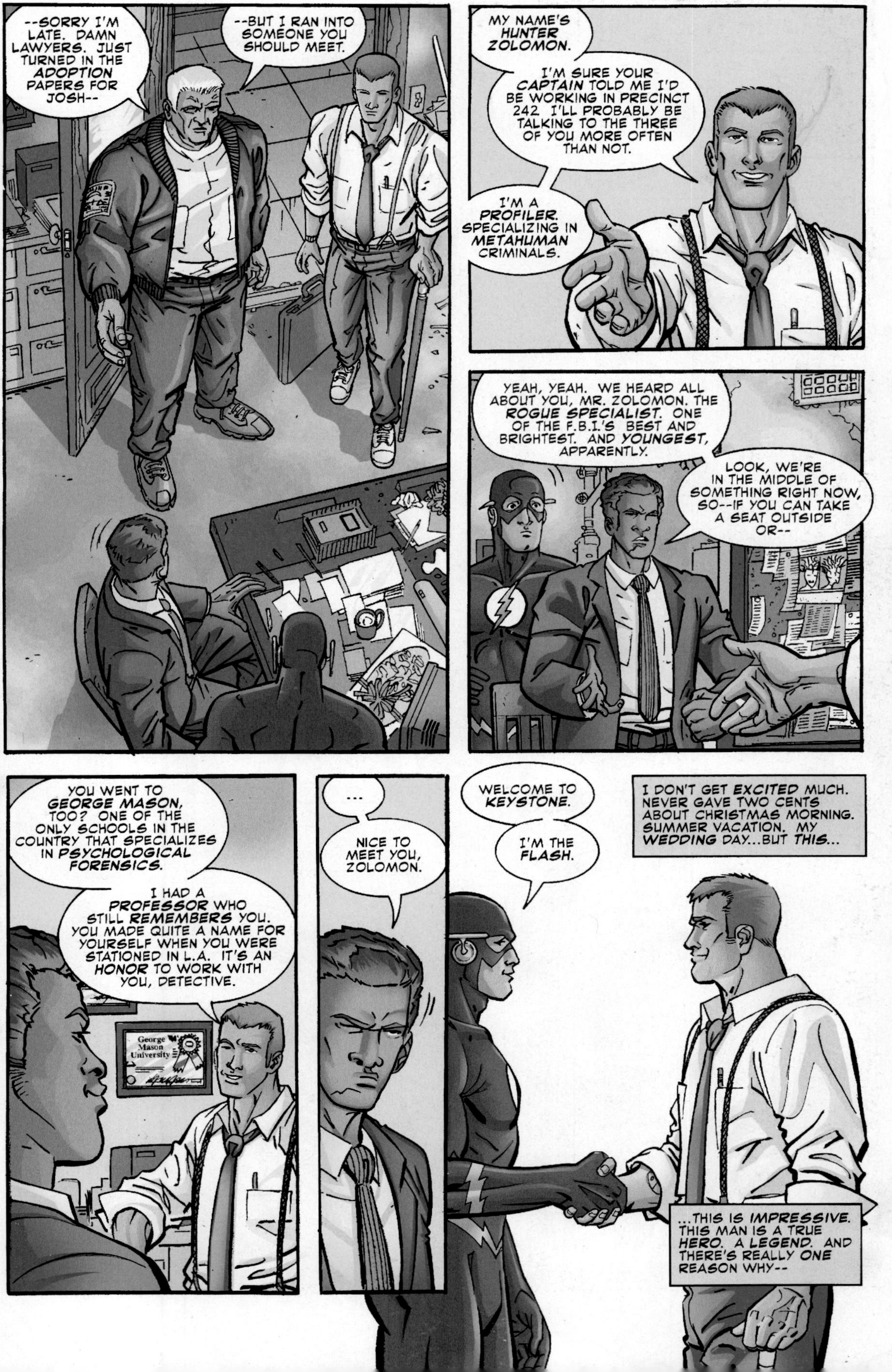
--SORRY I'M LATE. DAMN LAWYERS. JUST TURNED IN THE ADOPTION PAPERS FOR JOSH--
--BUT I RAN INTO SOMEONE YOU SHOULD MEET.
MY NAME'S HUNTER ZOLOMON.
I'M SURE YOUR CAPTAIN TOLD ME I'D BE WORKING IN PRECINCT 242. I'LL PROBABLY BE TALKING TO THE THREE OF YOU MORE OFTEN THAN NOT.
I'M A PROFILER. SPECIALIZING IN METAHUMAN CRIMINALS.
YEAH, YEAH. WE HEARD ALL ABOUT YOU, MR. ZOLOMON. THE ROGUE SPECIALIST. ONE OF THE F.B.I.'S BEST AND BRIGHTEST. AND YOUNGEST, APPARENTLY.
LOOK, WE'RE IN THE MIDDLE OF SOMETHING RIGHT NOW, SO--IF YOU CAN TAKE A SEAT OUTSIDE OR--
YOU WENT TO GEORGE MASON, TOO? ONE OF THE ONLY SCHOOLS IN THE COUNTRY THAT SPECIALIZES IN PSYCHOLOGICAL FORENSICS.
I HAD A PROFESSOR WHO STILL REMEMBERS YOU. YOU MADE QUITE A NAME FOR YOURSELF WHEN YOU WERE STATIONED IN L.A. IT'S AN HONOR TO WORK WITH YOU, DETECTIVE.
George Mason University
...
NICE TO MEET YOU, ZOLOMON.
WELCOME TO KEYSTONE.
I'M THE FLASH.
I DON'T GET EXCITED MUCH. NEVER GAVE TWO CENTS ABOUT CHRISTMAS MORNING. SUMMER VACATION. MY WEDDING DAY...BUT THIS...
...THIS IS IMPRESSIVE. THIS MAN IS A TRUE HERO. A LEGEND. AND THERE'S REALLY ONE REASON WHY--

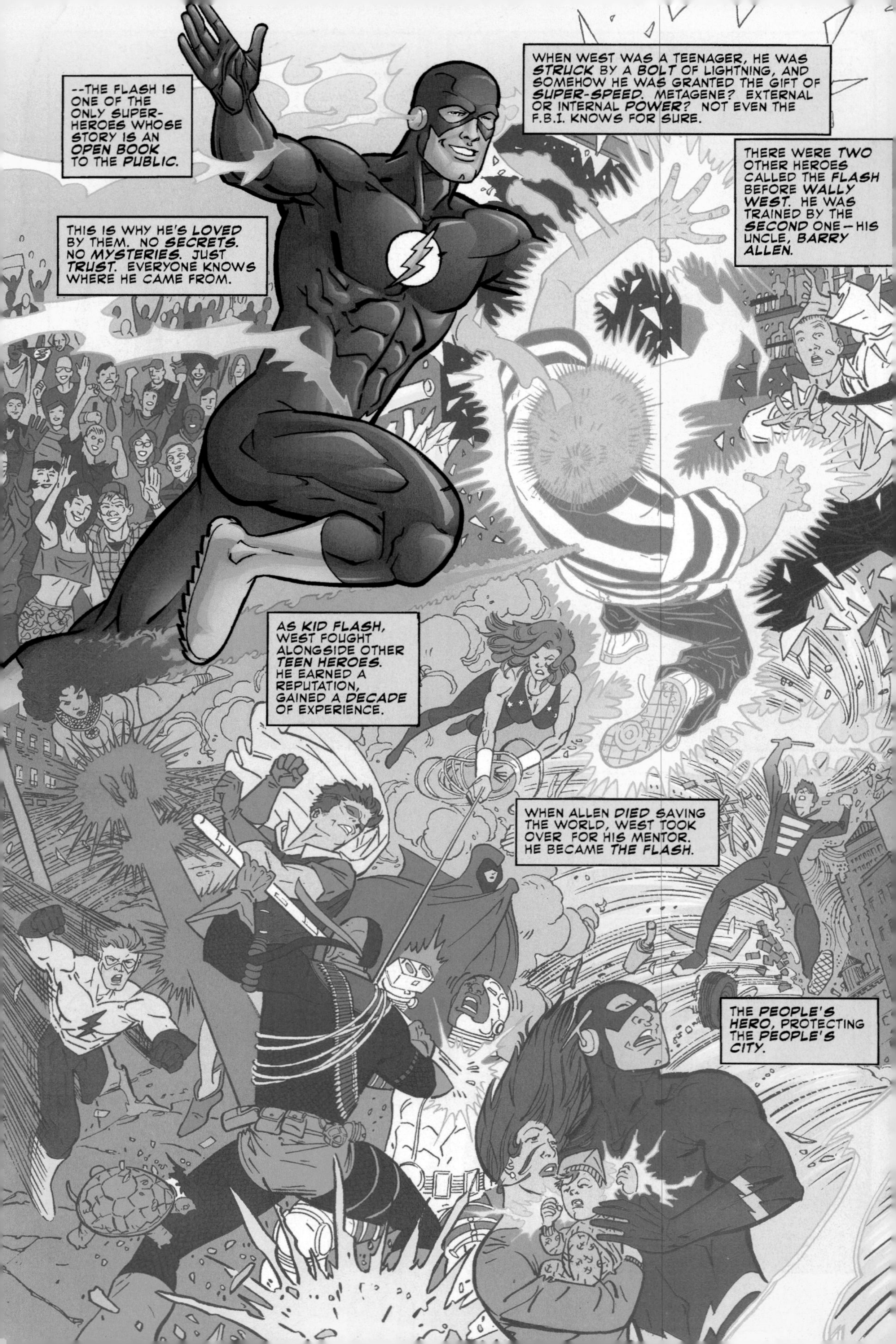
--THE FLASH IS ONE OF THE ONLY SUPER-HEROES WHOSE STORY IS AN OPEN BOOK TO THE PUBLIC.
THIS IS WHY HE'S LOVED BY THEM. NO SECRETS. NO MYSTERIES. JUST TRUST. EVERYONE KNOWS WHERE HE CAME FROM.
WHEN WEST WAS A TEENAGER, HE WAS STRUCK BY A BOLT OF LIGHTNING, AND SOMEHOW HE WAS GRANTED THE GIFT OF SUPER-SPEED. METAGENE? EXTERNAL OR INTERNAL POWER? NOT EVEN THE F.B.I. KNOWS FOR SURE.
THERE WERE TWO OTHER HEROES CALLED THE FLASH BEFORE WALLY WEST. HE WAS TRAINED BY THE SECOND ONE—HIS UNCLE, BARRY ALLEN.
AS KID FLASH, WEST FOUGHT ALONGSIDE OTHER TEEN HEROES. HE EARNED A REPUTATION, GAINED A DECADE OF EXPERIENCE.
WHEN ALLEN DIED SAVING THE WORLD, WEST TOOK OVER FOR HIS MENTOR. HE BECAME THE FLASH.
THE PEOPLE'S HERO, PROTECTING THE PEOPLE'S CITY.

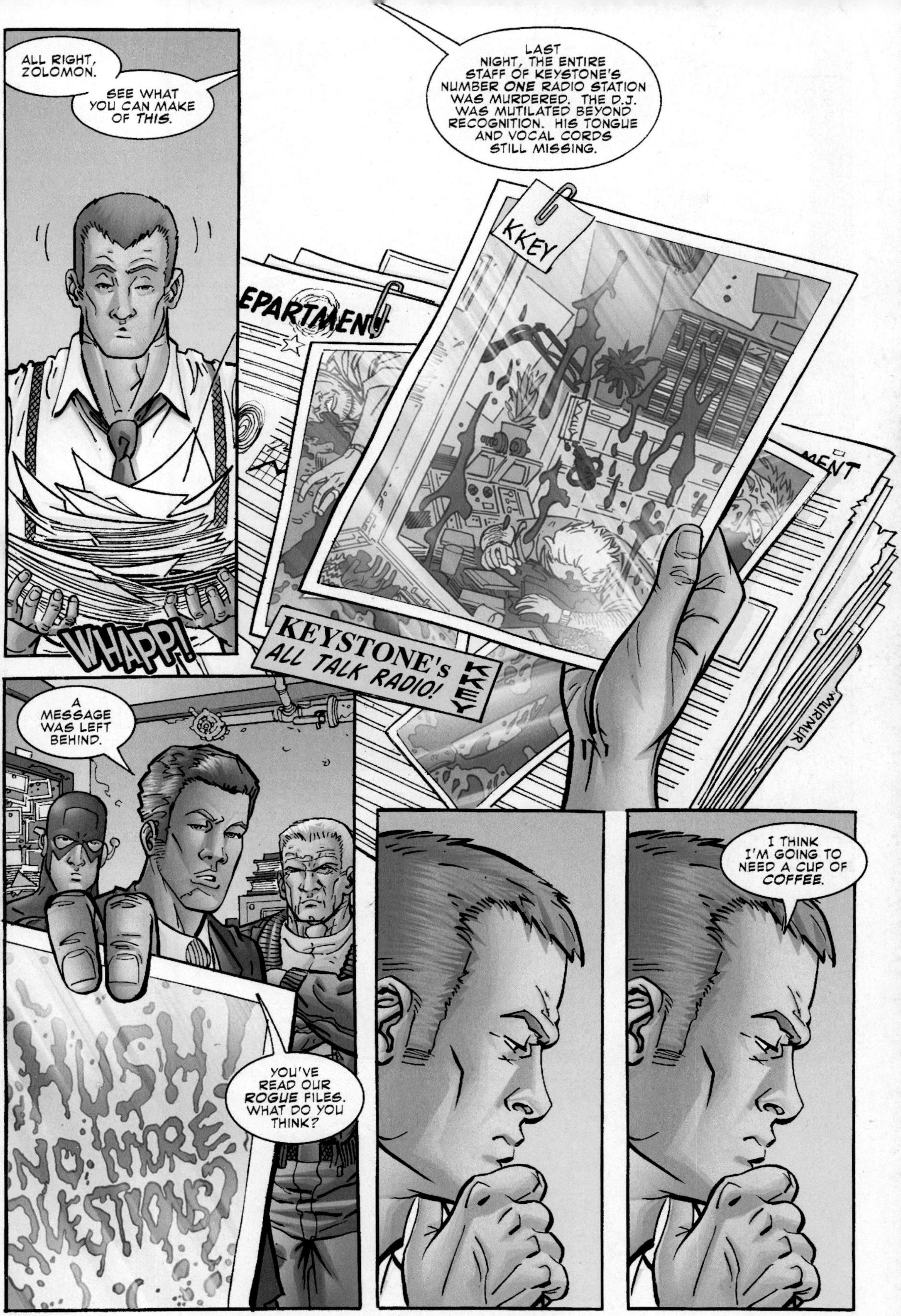

ALL RIGHT, ZOLOMON.
SEE WHAT YOU CAN MAKE OF THIS.
LAST NIGHT, THE ENTIRE STAFF OF KEYSTONE'S NUMBER ONE RADIO STATION WAS MURDERED. THE D.J. WAS MUTILATED BEYOND RECOGNITION. HIS TONGUE AND VOCAL CORDS STILL MISSING.
WHAPP!
KKEY
EPARTMEN
MENT
KEYSTONE's ALL TALK RADIO! KKEY
MURMUR
A MESSAGE WAS LEFT BEHIND.
HUSH! NO MORE QUESTIONS?
YOU'VE READ OUR ROGUE FILES. WHAT DO YOU THINK?
I THINK I'M GOING TO NEED A CUP OF COFFEE.

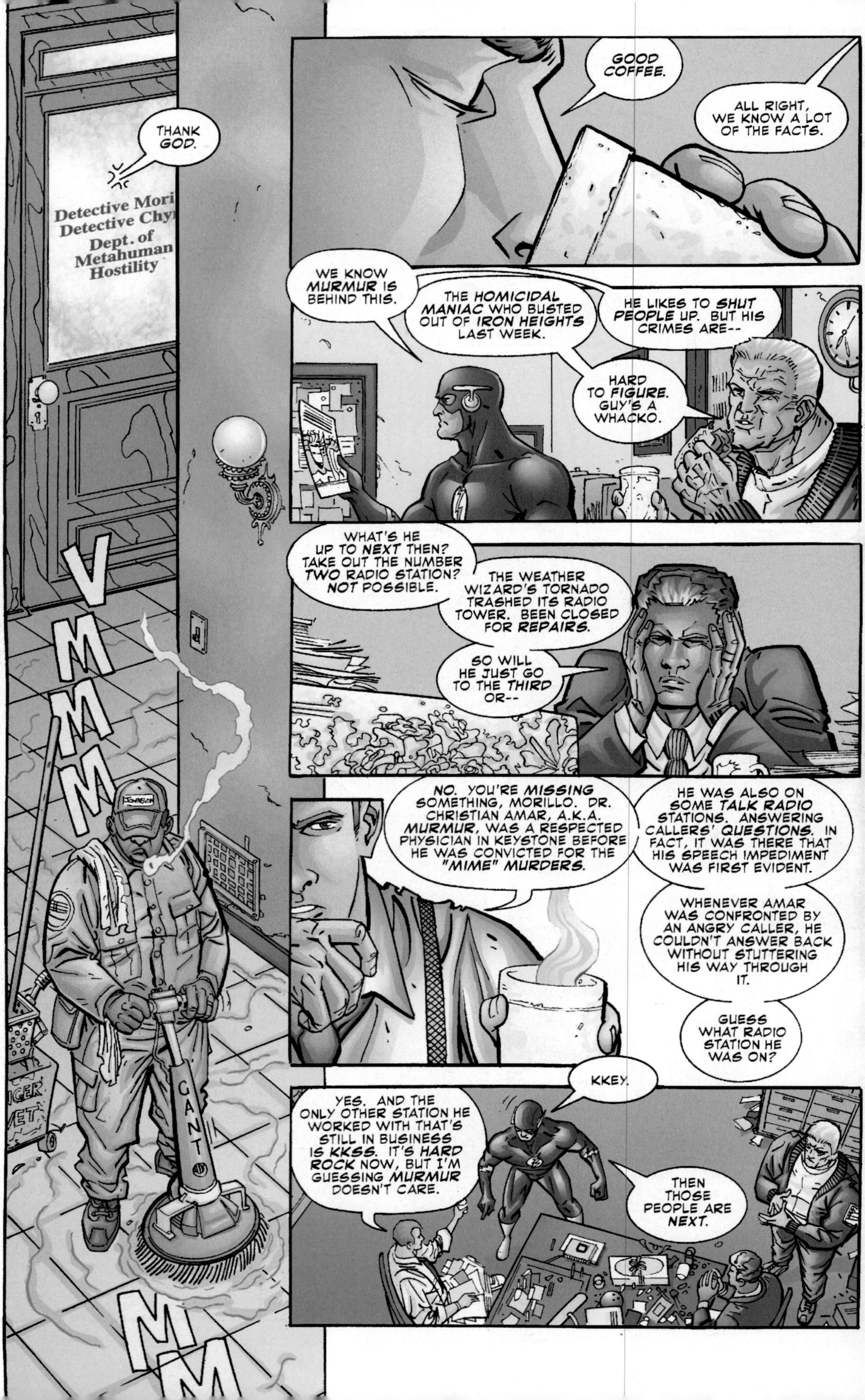
Detective Mori
Detective Chy
Dept. of Metahuman Hostility
THANK GOD.
VMMMM
JOHNSON
GANT
GOOD COFFEE.
ALL RIGHT, WE KNOW A LOT OF THE FACTS.
WE KNOW MURMUR IS BEHIND THIS.
THE HOMICIDAL MANIAC WHO BUSTED OUT OF IRON HEIGHTS LAST WEEK.
HE LIKES TO SHUT PEOPLE UP. BUT HIS CRIMES ARE--
HARD TO FIGURE. GUY'S A WHACKO.
WHAT'S HE UP TO NEXT THEN? TAKE OUT THE NUMBER TWO RADIO STATION? NOT POSSIBLE.
THE WEATHER WIZARD'S TORNADO TRASHED ITS RADIO TOWER. BEEN CLOSED FOR REPAIRS.
SO WILL HE JUST GO TO THE THIRD OR--
NO. YOU'RE MISSING SOMETHING, MORILLO. DR. CHRISTIAN AMAR, A.K.A. MURMUR, WAS A RESPECTED PHYSICIAN IN KEYSTONE BEFORE HE WAS CONVICTED FOR THE "MIME" MURDERS.
HE WAS ALSO ON SOME TALK RADIO STATIONS. ANSWERING CALLERS' QUESTIONS. IN FACT, IT WAS THERE THAT HIS SPEECH IMPEDIMENT WAS FIRST EVIDENT.
WHENEVER AMAR WAS CONFRONTED BY AN ANGRY CALLER, HE COULDN'T ANSWER BACK WITHOUT STUTTERING HIS WAY THROUGH IT.
GUESS WHAT RADIO STATION HE WAS ON?
KKEY.
YES. AND THE ONLY OTHER STATION HE WORKED WITH THAT'S STILL IN BUSINESS IS KKSS. IT'S HARD ROCK NOW, BUT I'M GUESSING MURMUR DOESN'T CARE.
THEN THOSE PEOPLE ARE NEXT.
MMM

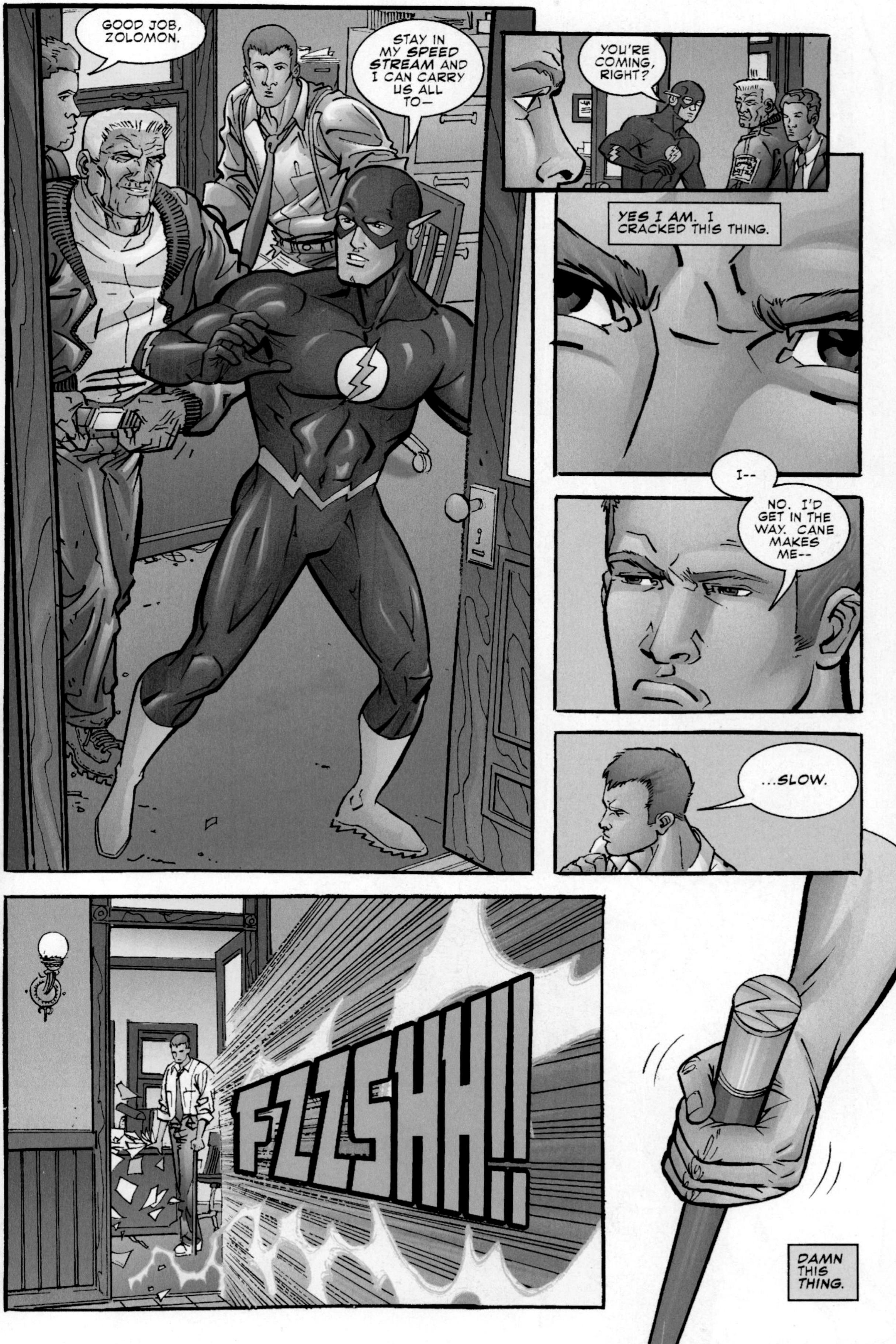
GOOD JOB, ZOLOMON.
STAY IN MY SPEED STREAM AND I CAN CARRY US ALL TO—
YOU'RE COMING, RIGHT?
YES I AM. I CRACKED THIS THING.
I--
NO. I'D GET IN THE WAY. CANE MAKES ME--
...SLOW.
FZZSHH!!
DAMN THIS THING.

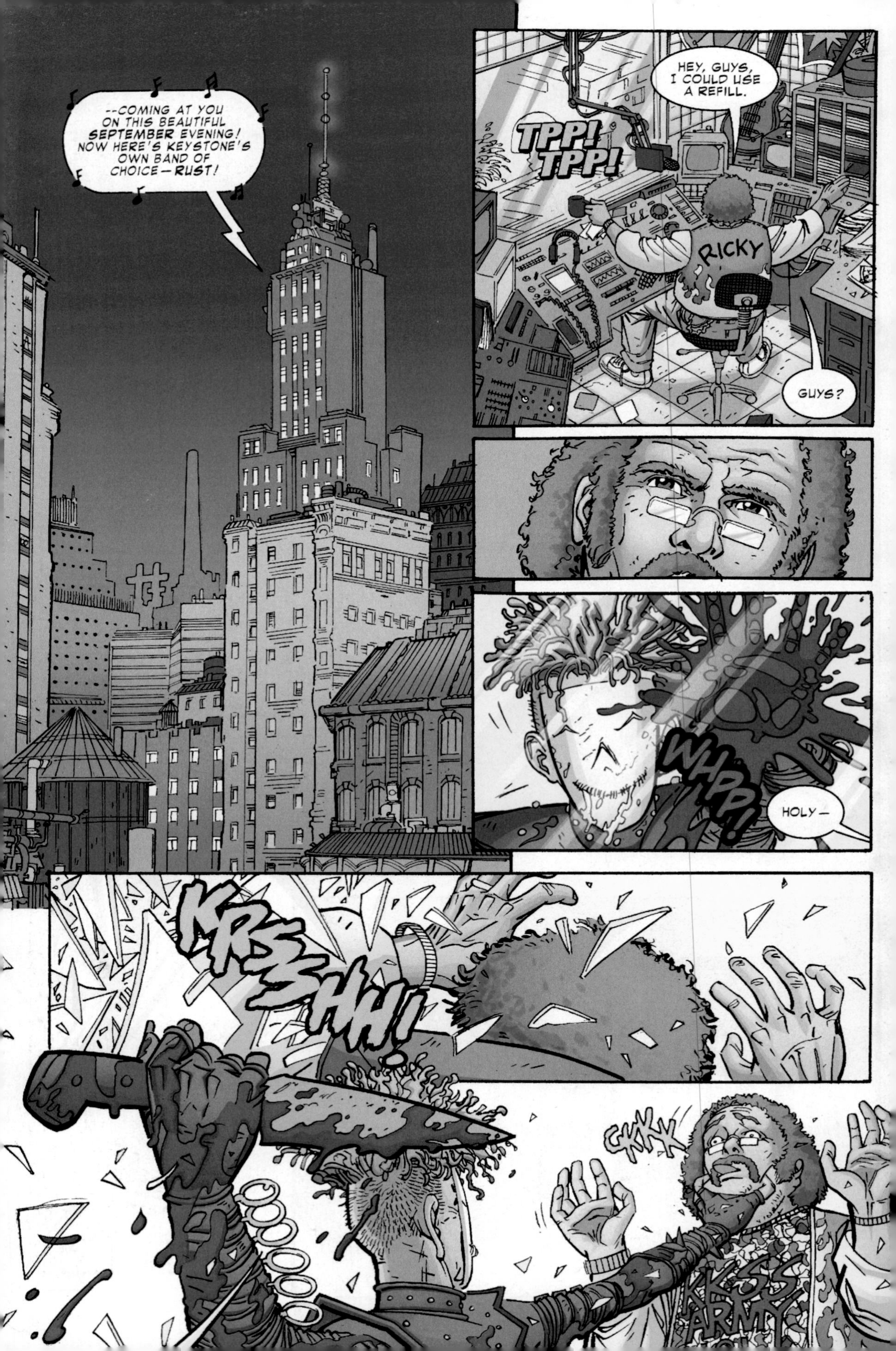
--COMING AT YOU ON THIS BEAUTIFUL SEPTEMBER EVENING! NOW HERE'S KEYSTONE'S OWN BAND OF CHOICE—RUST!
HEY, GUYS, I COULD USE A REFILL.
TPP! TPP!
RICKY
GUYS?
WHPP!
HOLY—
KRSSHH!
GKKK
KISS ARMY

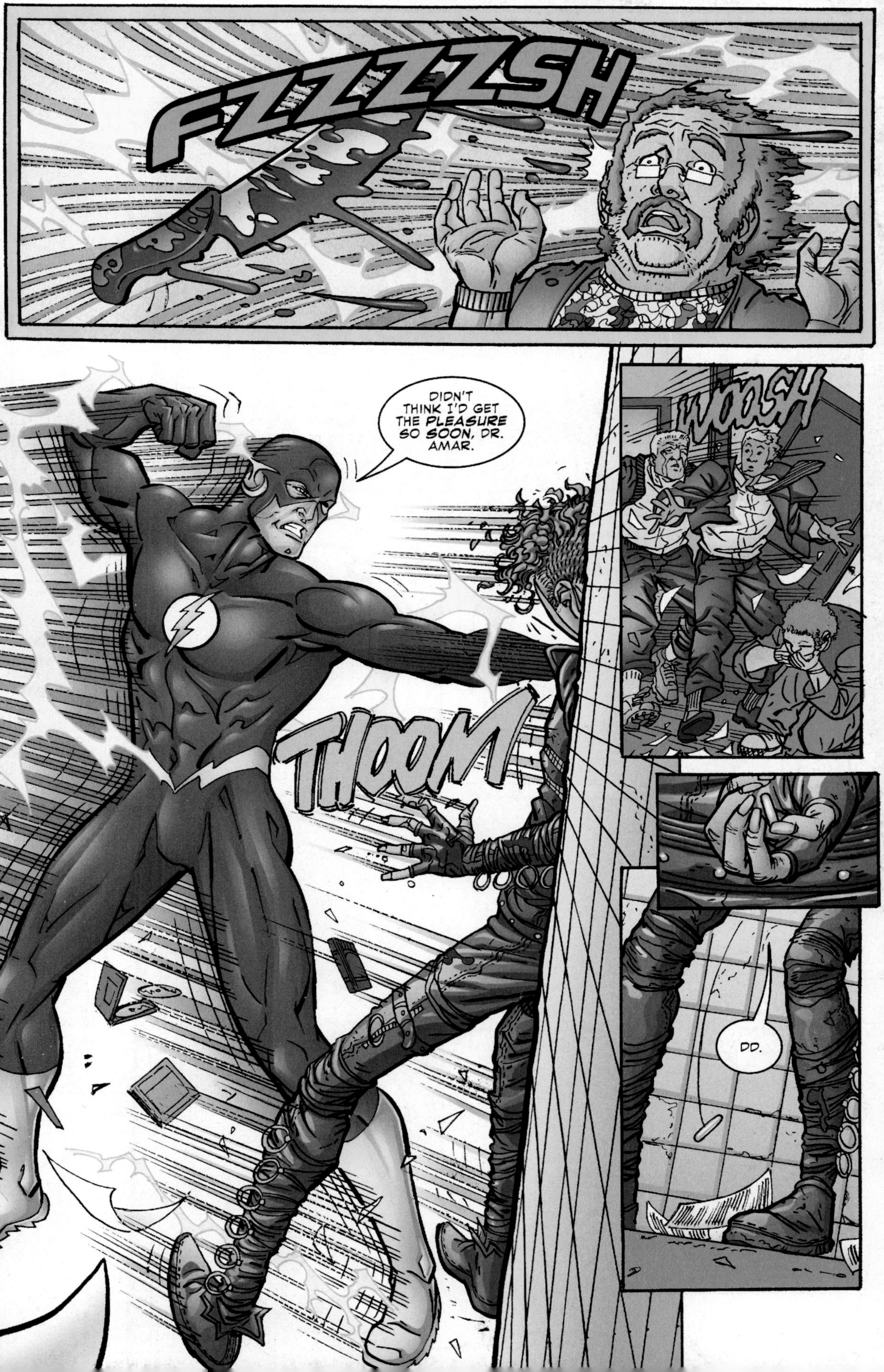
FZZZZSH
DIDN'T THINK I'D GET THE PLEASURE SO SOON, DR. AMAR.
WOOSH
THOOM
DD.

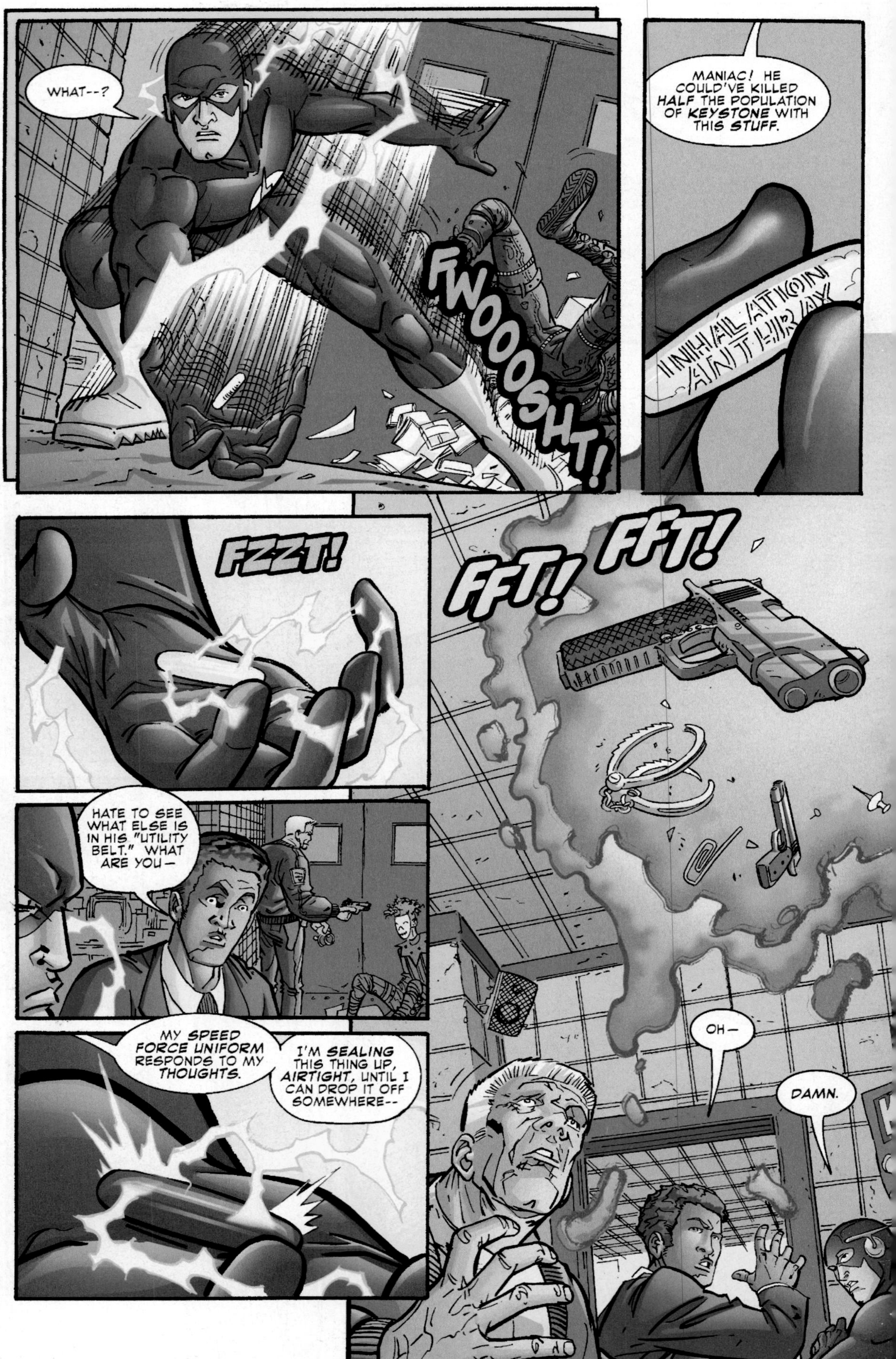
WHAT--?
FWOOOSHT!
MANIAC! HE COULD'VE KILLED HALF THE POPULATION OF KEYSTONE WITH THIS STUFF.
INHALATION ANTHRAX
FZZT!
HATE TO SEE WHAT ELSE IS IN HIS "UTILITY BELT." WHAT ARE YOU—
MY SPEED FORCE UNIFORM RESPONDS TO MY THOUGHTS.
I'M SEALING THIS THING UP, AIRTIGHT, UNTIL I CAN DROP IT OFF SOMEWHERE--
FFT! FFT!
OH—
DAMN.

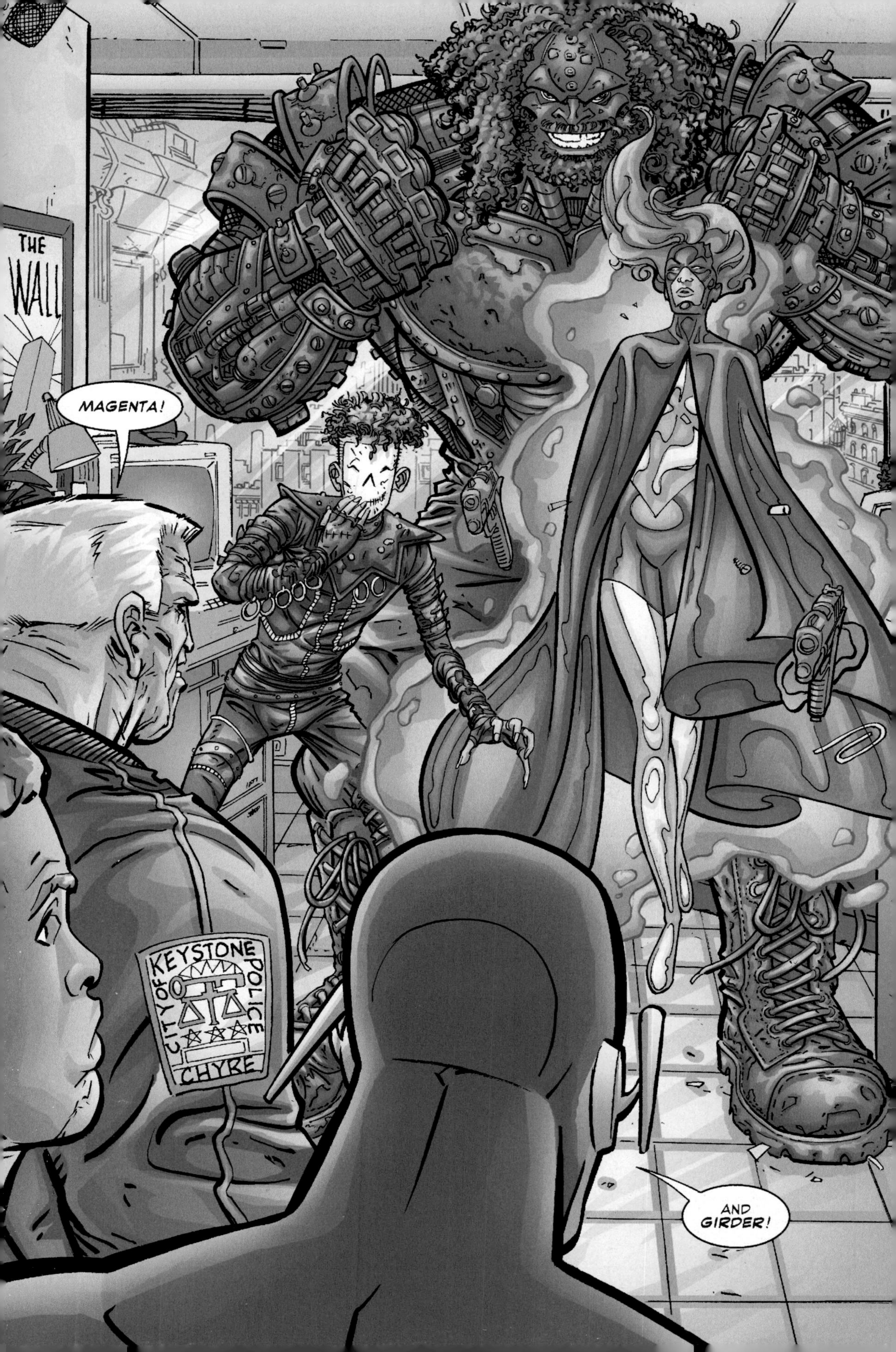
THE WALL
MAGENTA!
KEYSTONE CITY OF POLICE
CHYRE
AND GIRDER!

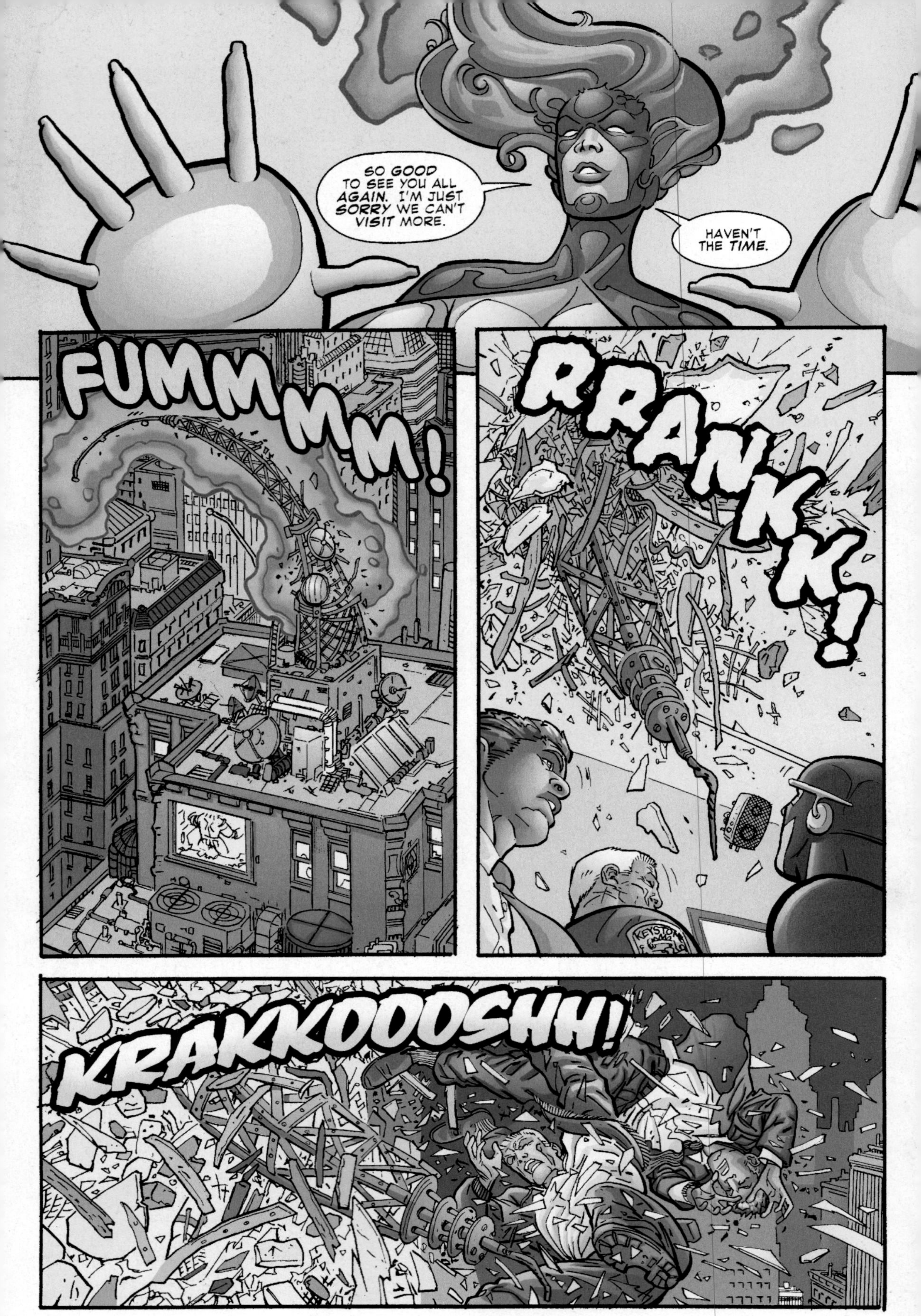
SO GOOD TO SEE YOU ALL AGAIN. I'M JUST SORRY WE CAN'T VISIT MORE.
HAVEN'T THE TIME.
FUMMMMM!
RRANKK!
KRAKKOOOSHH!

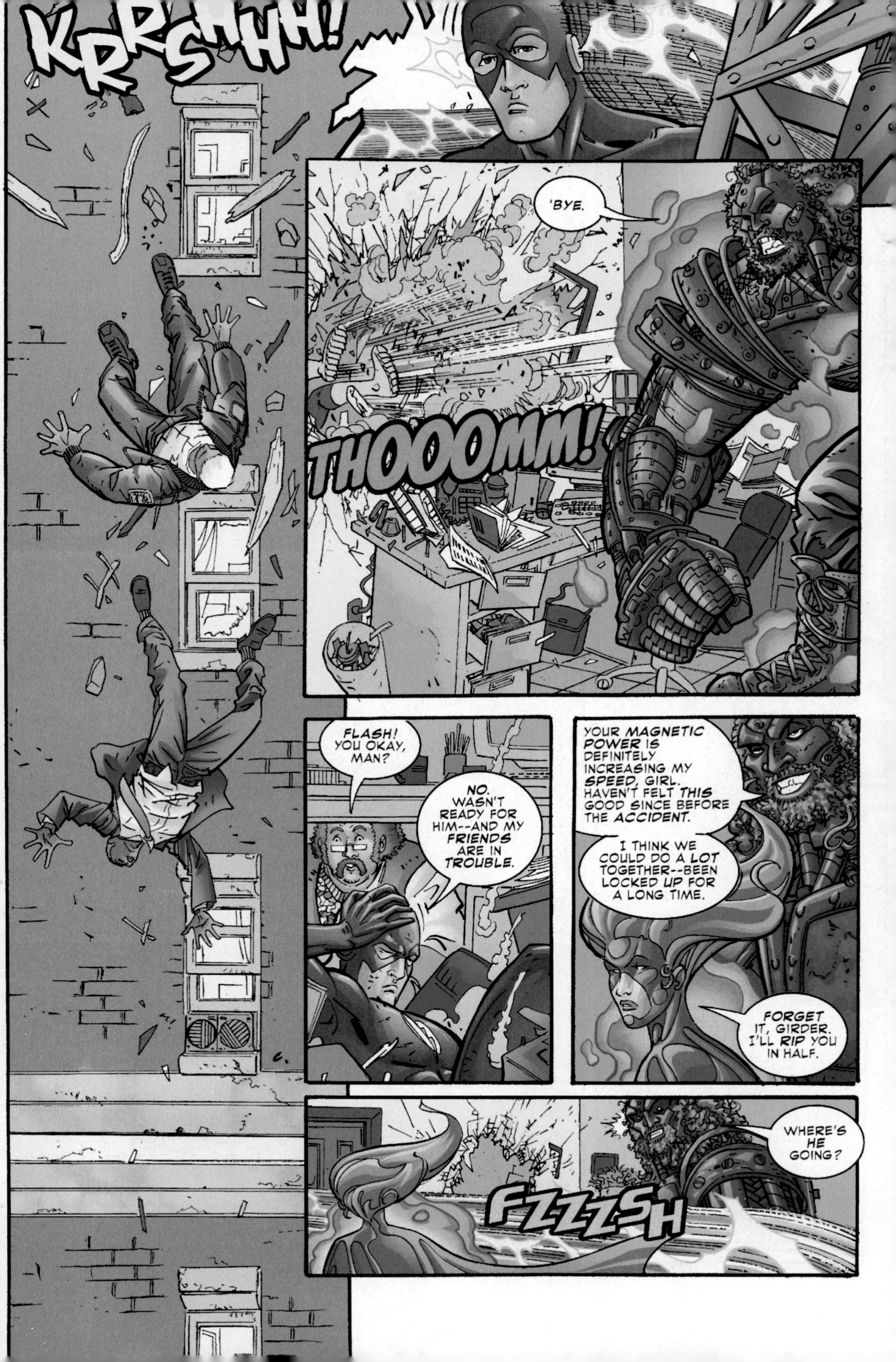
KRRSHHH!
'BYE.
THOOOMM!
FLASH! YOU OKAY, MAN?
NO. WASN'T READY FOR HIM--AND MY FRIENDS ARE IN TROUBLE.
YOUR MAGNETIC POWER IS DEFINITELY INCREASING MY SPEED, GIRL. HAVEN'T FELT THIS GOOD SINCE BEFORE THE ACCIDENT.
I THINK WE COULD DO A LOT TOGETHER--BEEN LOCKED UP FOR A LONG TIME.
FORGET IT, GIRDER. I'LL RIP YOU IN HALF.
WHERE'S HE GOING?
FZZZSH

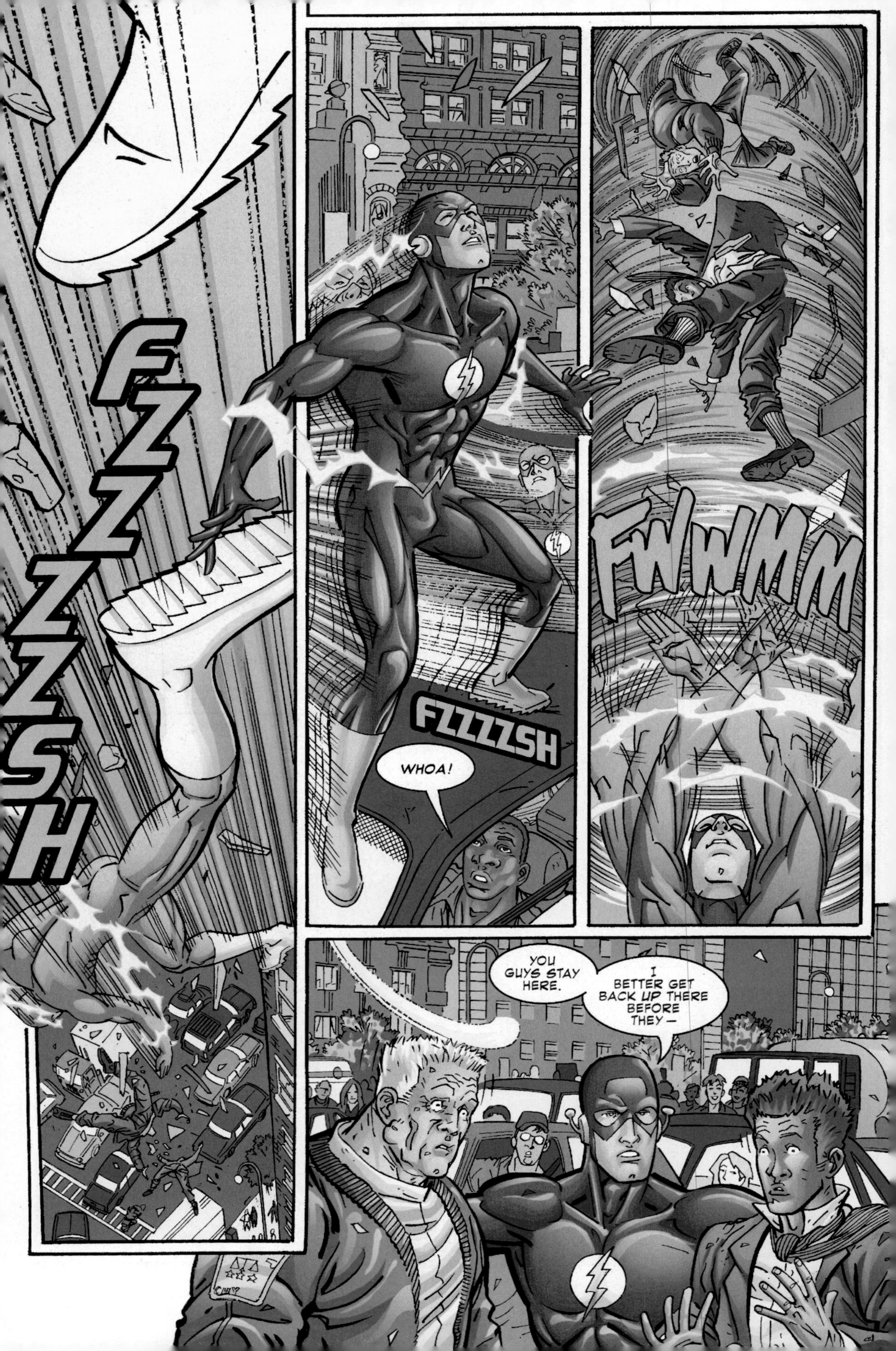
FZZZZSH
FZZZZSH
WHOA!
FWWMM
YOU GUYS STAY HERE.
I BETTER GET BACK UP THERE BEFORE THEY—

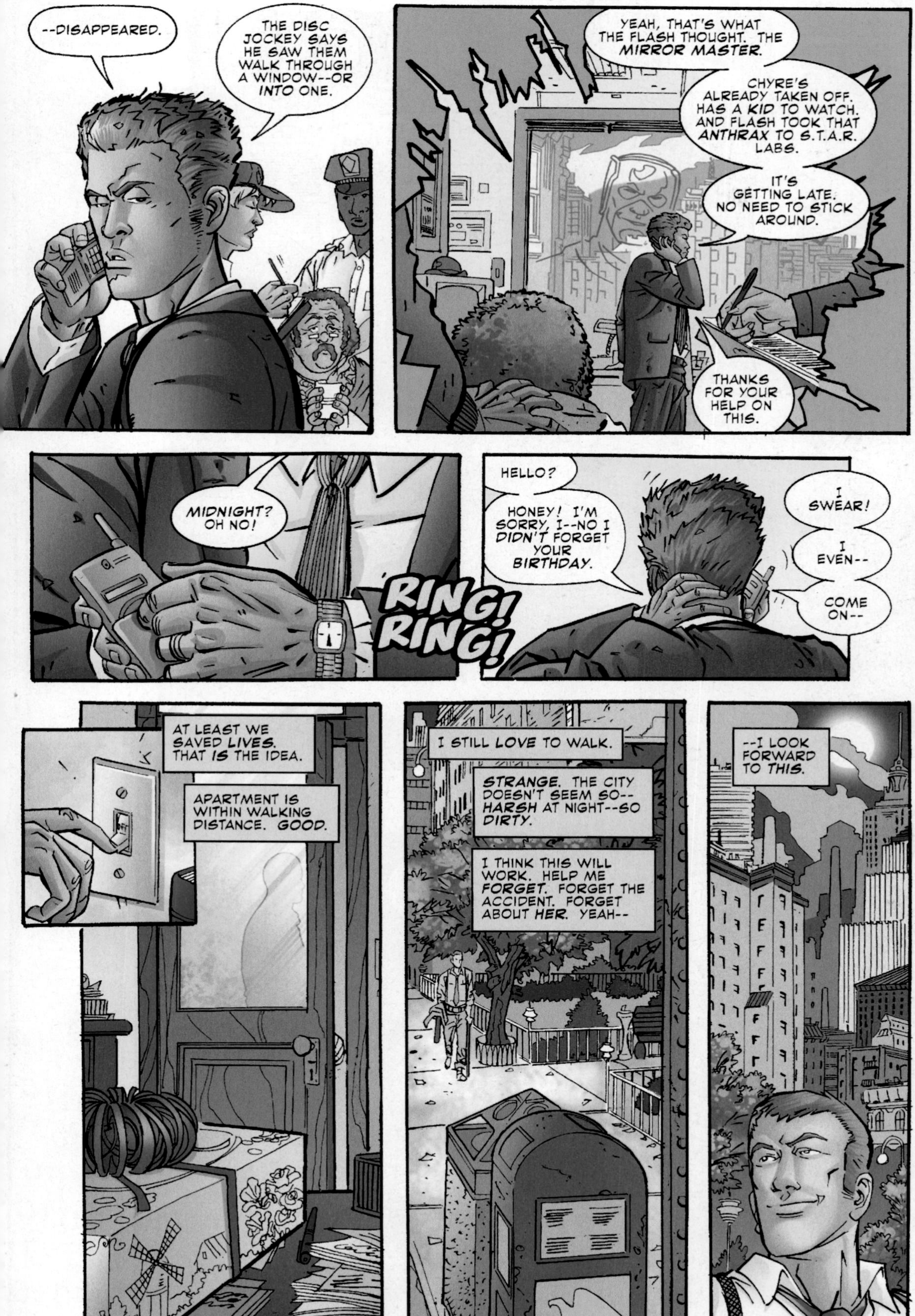
--DISAPPEARED.
THE DISC JOCKEY SAYS HE SAW THEM WALK THROUGH A WINDOW--OR INTO ONE.
YEAH, THAT'S WHAT THE FLASH THOUGHT. THE MIRROR MASTER.
CHYRE'S ALREADY TAKEN OFF. HAS A KID TO WATCH. AND FLASH TOOK THAT ANTHRAX TO S.T.A.R. LABS.
IT'S GETTING LATE. NO NEED TO STICK AROUND.
THANKS FOR YOUR HELP ON THIS.
MIDNIGHT? OH NO!
RING! RING!
HELLO?
HONEY! I'M SORRY, I--NO I DIDN'T FORGET YOUR BIRTHDAY.
I SWEAR!
I EVEN--
COME ON--
AT LEAST WE SAVED LIVES. THAT IS THE IDEA.
APARTMENT IS WITHIN WALKING DISTANCE. GOOD.
I STILL LOVE TO WALK.
STRANGE. THE CITY DOESN'T SEEM SO--HARSH AT NIGHT--SO DIRTY.
I THINK THIS WILL WORK. HELP ME FORGET. FORGET THE ACCIDENT. FORGET ABOUT HER. YEAH--
--I LOOK FORWARD TO THIS.

EPILOGUE

YOU DID WELL.

MURMUR'S-- VICES ARE A PERFECT COVER FOR OUR SETUP.

AS SOON AS THEY PUT THE ANTENNAS BACK UP, THEY'LL BE READY TO BROADCAST. AND THEY DON'T EVEN KNOW IT.

THEN IT'S TIME TO FINISH REMOVING HIS ALLIES.

WE'LL OWN THESE TWIN CITIES, ROGUES.

AND THE FLASH WILL BE TAKEN OUT ONCE AND FOR ALL.

KZZZZ

HUMANS.

THEY WILL SOON UNDERSTAND THE FLASH AND HIS CITY DO NOT BELONG TO THEM--

100 10100 00110 1110 010010 101001 00110 011101 010010

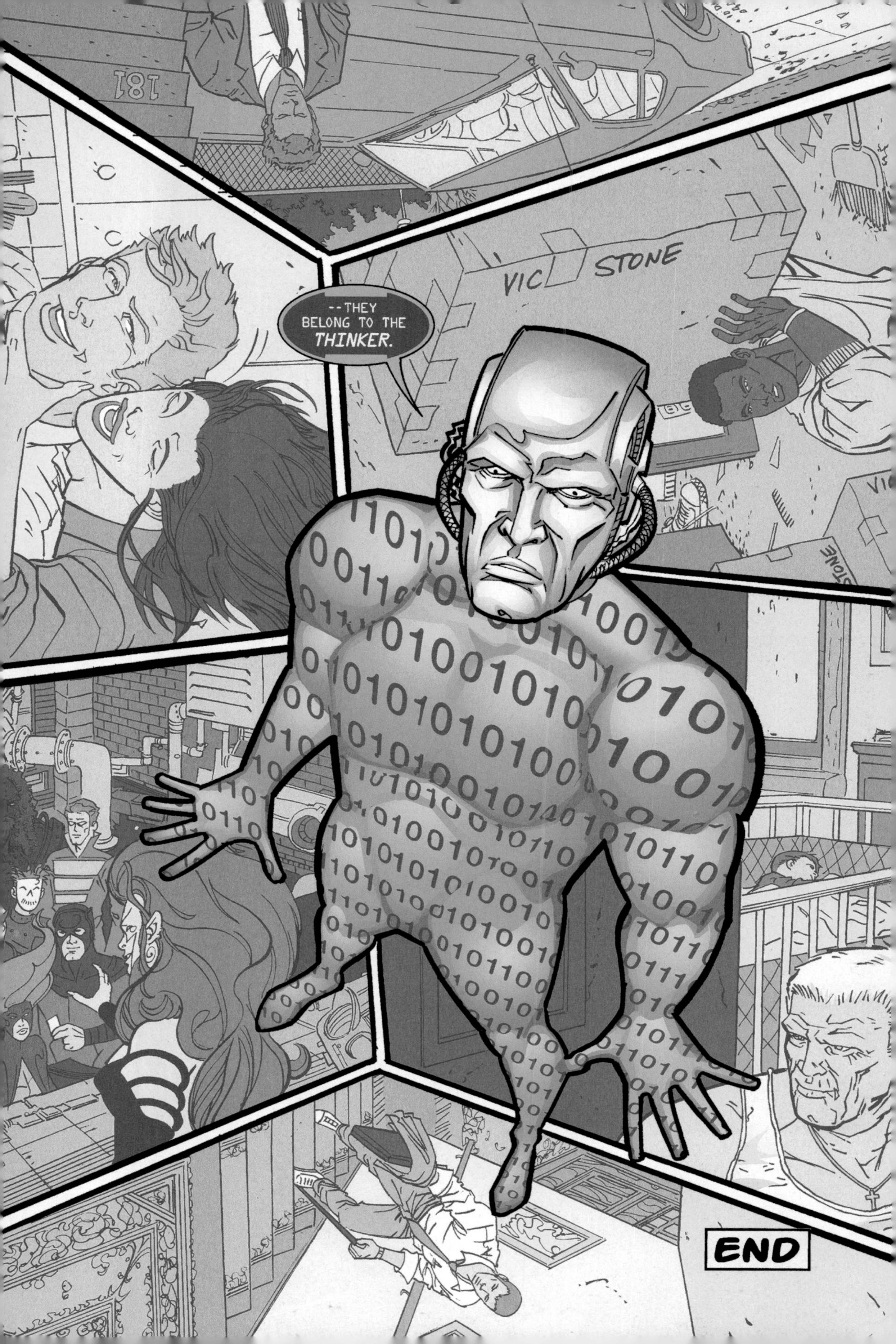
--THEY BELONG TO THE THINKER.
VIC STONE
END

Historical first appearance: THE FLASH (1st series) #130 (July, 1962)
Current team's first appearance: THE FLASH: IRON HEIGHTS (October, 2001)

The Rogues are a group of super-criminals that have plagued both Barry Allen and Wally West. Their motivation remains a mystery.

The current membership includes:

WEATHER WIZARD

Mark Mardon was a small-time crook who either got lucky or was a murderer. A prison escapee, Mardon headed to his older brother's observatory for shelter, where he either found his brother dead (from a heart attack) or killed him. What is indisputable is that he took possession of his brother's invention, a "weather wand" capable of controlling the weather. Using the wand, Mardon became the thief known as Weather Wizard.

Recently, Mardon discovered he has a child—the son of deceased police officer Julie Jackam—who has somehow inherited the powers of the weather wand. Mardon now wants nothing less than to dissect the boy and unlock the secrets of his abilities.

GIRDER

After steelworker Tony Woodward assaulted a young female at work, a riot ensued and he was thrown into a vat of molten steel by his angry co-workers. No ordinary metal, it was, in fact, scrap from S.T.A.R. Labs that had undergone several mysterious experiments. Woodward rose up from the pit in the metallic form of Girder. Endowed with incredible strength, Girder's greatest enemy is rust, which painfully eats away more of his body each day.

MAGENTA

Frances Kane's metahuman magnetic abilities manifested themselves at the worst time conceivable. While in the car with her father and brother, Kane's powers kicked in, causing a terrible accident that left both men dead. From then on,

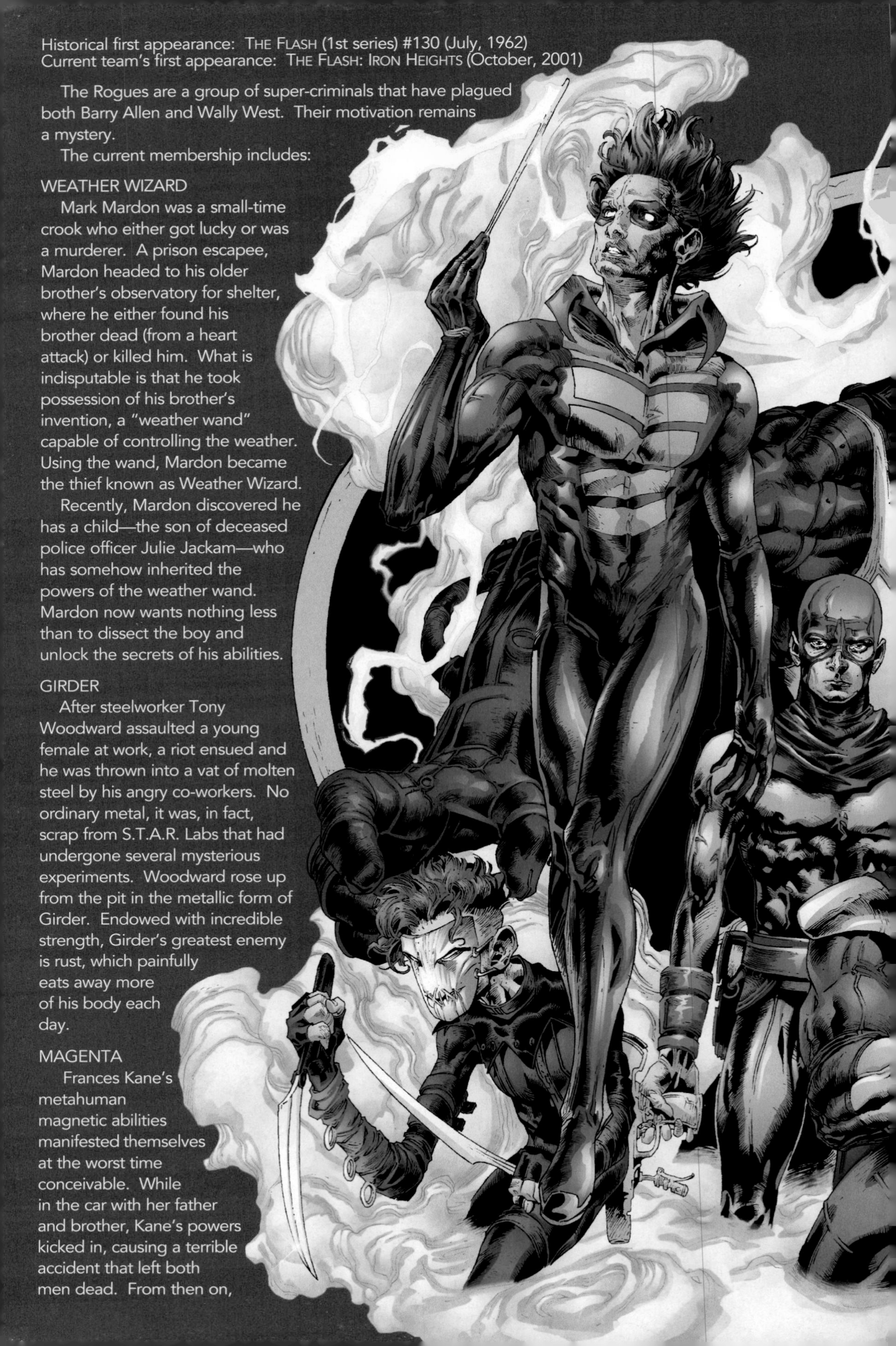

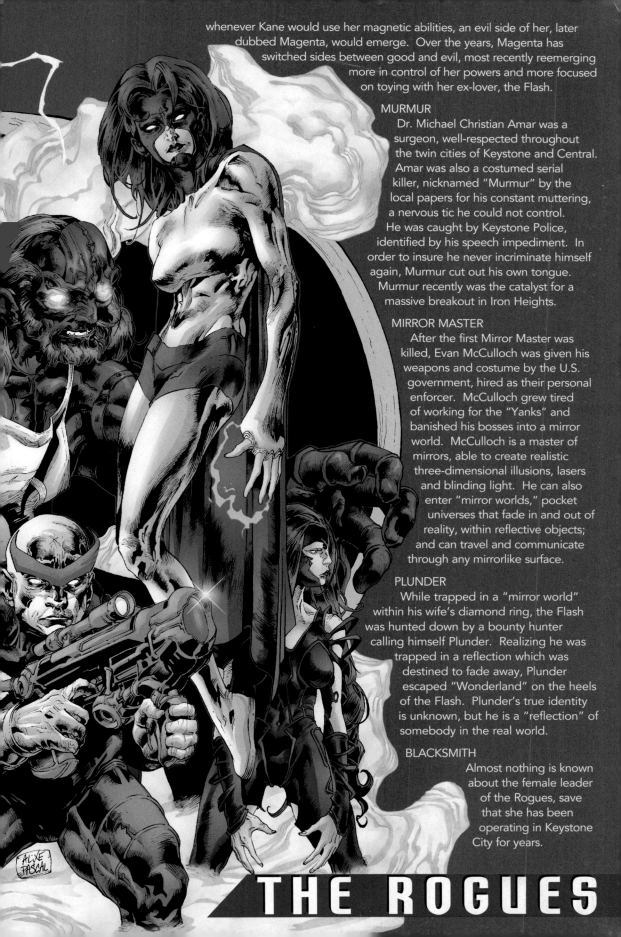

whenever Kane would use her magnetic abilities, an evil side of her, later dubbed Magenta, would emerge. Over the years, Magenta has switched sides between good and evil, most recently reemerging more in control of her powers and more focused on toying with her ex-lover, the Flash.

MURMUR

Dr. Michael Christian Amar was a surgeon, well-respected throughout the twin cities of Keystone and Central. Amar was also a costumed serial killer, nicknamed "Murmur" by the local papers for his constant muttering, a nervous tic he could not control. He was caught by Keystone Police, identified by his speech impediment. In order to insure he never incriminate himself again, Murmur cut out his own tongue. Murmur recently was the catalyst for a massive breakout in Iron Heights.

MIRROR MASTER

After the first Mirror Master was killed, Evan McCulloch was given his weapons and costume by the U.S. government, hired as their personal enforcer. McCulloch grew tired of working for the "Yanks" and banished his bosses into a mirror world. McCulloch is a master of mirrors, able to create realistic three-dimensional illusions, lasers and blinding light. He can also enter "mirror worlds," pocket universes that fade in and out of reality, within reflective objects; and can travel and communicate through any mirrorlike surface.

PLUNDER

While trapped in a "mirror world" within his wife's diamond ring, the Flash was hunted down by a bounty hunter calling himself Plunder. Realizing he was trapped in a reflection which was destined to fade away, Plunder escaped "Wonderland" on the heels of the Flash. Plunder's true identity is unknown, but he is a "reflection" of somebody in the real world.

BLACKSMITH

Almost nothing is known about the female leader of the Rogues, save that she has been operating in Keystone City for years.

THE ROGUES

CHYRE & MORILLO

Names: Fred Chyre/ Jared Morillo
Occupation: Keystone City Police, Department of Metahuman Hostility
Marital Status: Single/Married
Ht: 6′ 1″ / 5′ 10″
Wt: 220 lbs./185 lbs.
Eyes: Blue/Brown
Hair: Gray/Black
First Appearance: THE FLASH (2nd series) #164 (September, 2000)/#171 (April, 2001)

Often driven by his short temper, Officer Fred Chyre has been suspended for excessive force several times. Most of his anger stems from the death of Chyre's first partner, Joe Jackam. Recently, Joe's granddaughter, Julie Jackam, who transferred from the NYPD to the KCPD at Chyre's request, was murdered, leaving behind a two-year-old son, Josh. Chyre hopes to adopt him.

Jared Morillo was the chief homicide detective in Los Angeles, California for several years. He had hoped to join the F.B.I., but his wife persuaded him to give up his dream. She wanted a child, and there was no way in hell she was going to raise one in L.A. Morillo and his wife moved to Keystone City. Unimpressed with Keystone City's police department, and unhappy about giving up his chance to join the F.B.I., Detective Morillo treated his fellow officers with little respect and no courtesy. He quickly became one of the most disliked law officers on the force… second only to Fred Chyre.

During a case in which Morillo was cut by a dagger wielded by the cult leader Cicada, Chyre and Morillo were partnered up at the request of their captain. The two are now the sole members of KCPD's new Department of Metahuman Hostility. Unfortunately, this means they have to share an office.

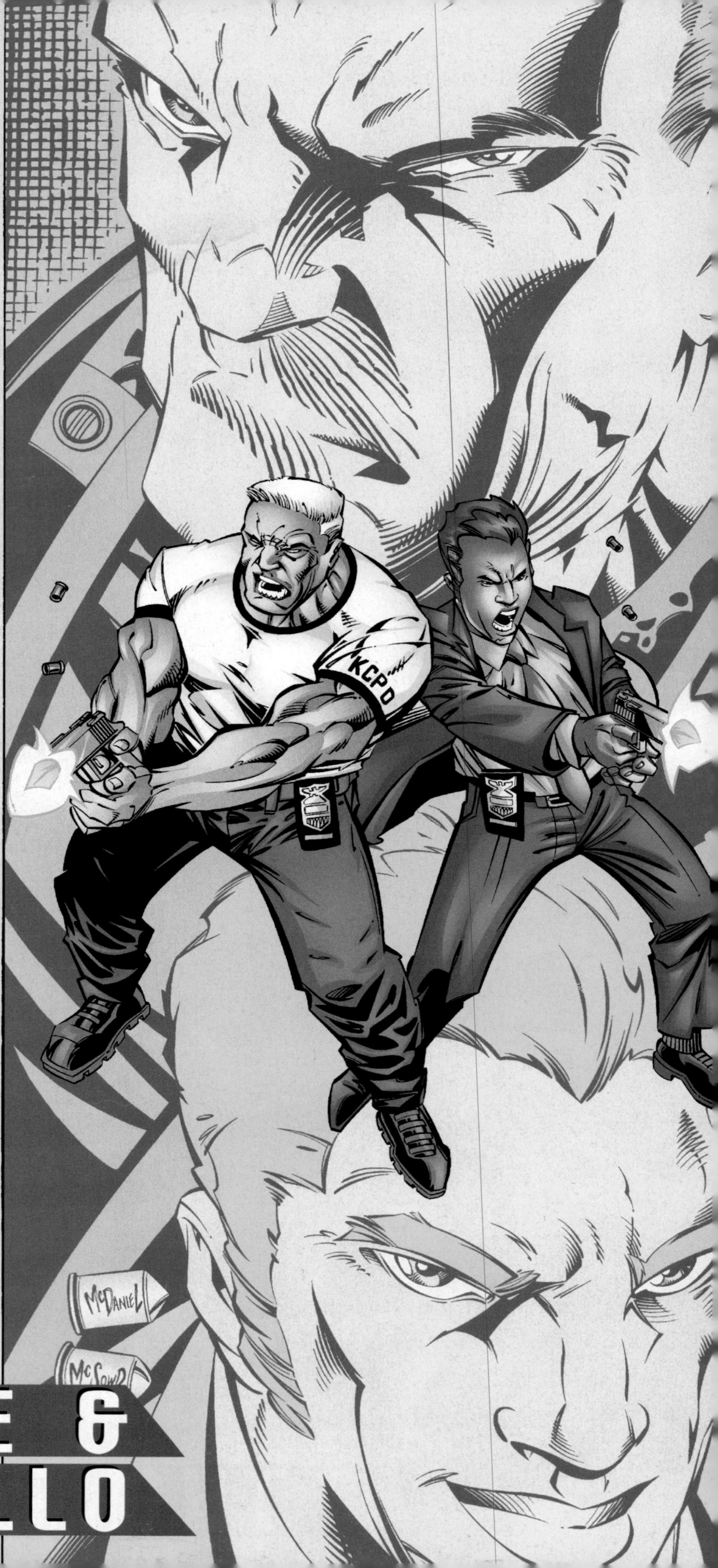
KCPD

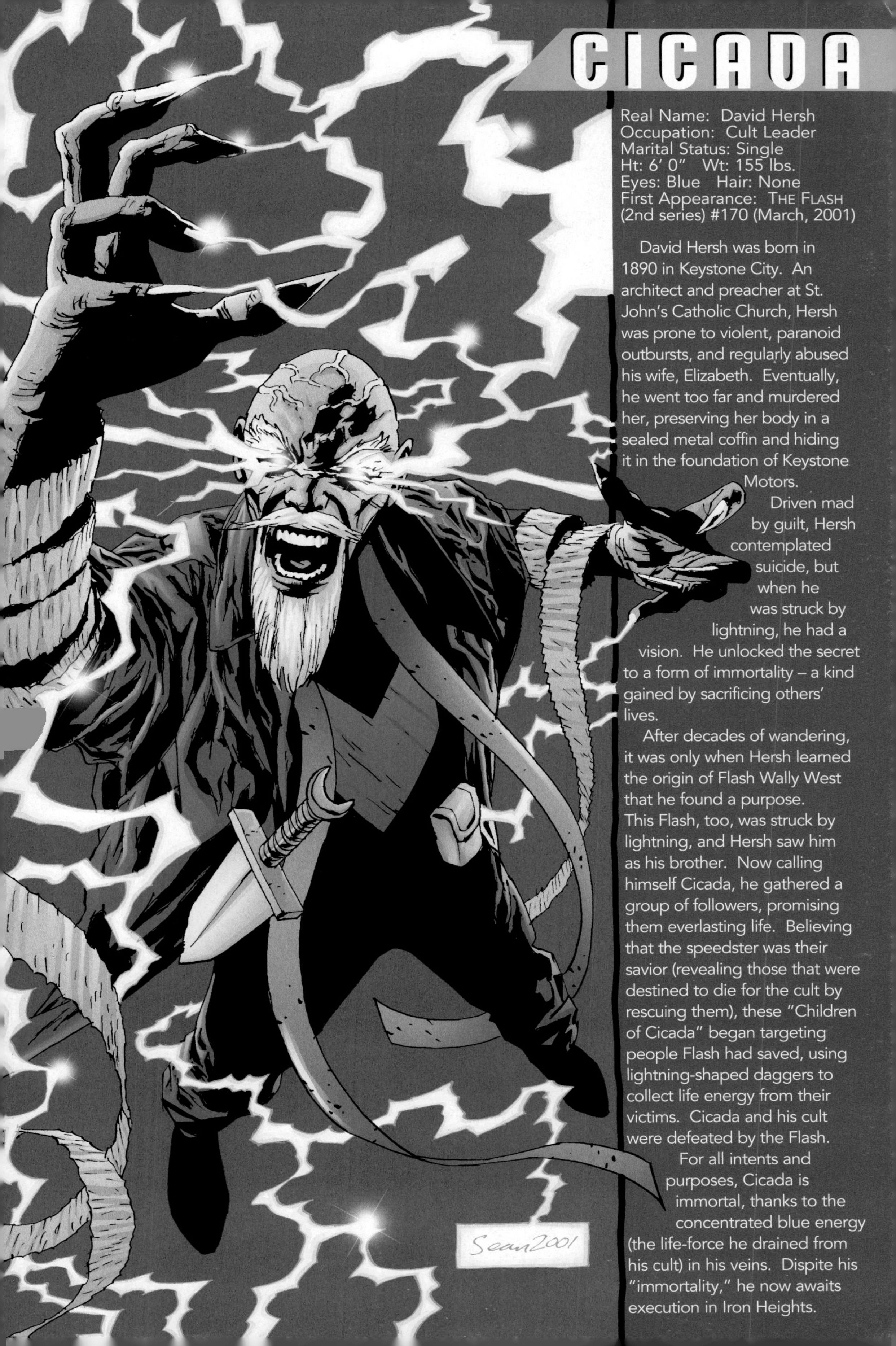
Sean2001

CICADA

Real Name: David Hersh
Occupation: Cult Leader
Marital Status: Single
Ht: 6′ 0″ Wt: 155 lbs.
Eyes: Blue Hair: None
First Appearance: THE FLASH (2nd series) #170 (March, 2001)

David Hersh was born in 1890 in Keystone City. An architect and preacher at St. John's Catholic Church, Hersh was prone to violent, paranoid outbursts, and regularly abused his wife, Elizabeth. Eventually, he went too far and murdered her, preserving her body in a sealed metal coffin and hiding it in the foundation of Keystone Motors.

Driven mad by guilt, Hersh contemplated suicide, but when he was struck by lightning, he had a vision. He unlocked the secret to a form of immortality – a kind gained by sacrificing others' lives.

After decades of wandering, it was only when Hersh learned the origin of Flash Wally West that he found a purpose. This Flash, too, was struck by lightning, and Hersh saw him as his brother. Now calling himself Cicada, he gathered a group of followers, promising them everlasting life. Believing that the speedster was their savior (revealing those that were destined to die for the cult by rescuing them), these "Children of Cicada" began targeting people Flash had saved, using lightning-shaped daggers to collect life energy from their victims. Cicada and his cult were defeated by the Flash.

For all intents and purposes, Cicada is immortal, thanks to the concentrated blue energy (the life-force he drained from his cult) in his veins. Dispite his "immortality," he now awaits execution in Iron Heights.

First Appearance:
THE FLASH: IRON HEIGHTS
(October, 2001)

"The only way out of Iron Heights is in a body bag." Up until the recent breakout, this was the motto among Iron Heights' prisoners…and its staff.

Keystone City Penitentiary was a fairly standard institution until Gregory Wolfe took over as warden. Spending a budget of nearly forty million dollars, Wolfe entirely reinvented the prison, transforming it into Iron Heights.

The main structure of the prison houses the worst criminals the surrounding states have to offer, as well as the infirmary – and the Warden's office. Riots are increasingly infrequent, and no guards had ever lost their lives until the recent breakout.

Over forty feet underground, the lower level of Iron Heights is called the Pipeline. Originally just a utility basement, it has since been converted to house metahuman and costumed inmates. The prisoners in the Pipeline are rarely let out of their cells.

Next to the Pipeline is the Power Room. Once, large generators powered the prison. Now, at Warden Wolfe's request, a radioactive rogue named Fallout serves as the power source. The prison saves hundreds of thousands of dollars thanks to his energies.

Currently over one thousand men and women are held within the walls of Iron Heights.

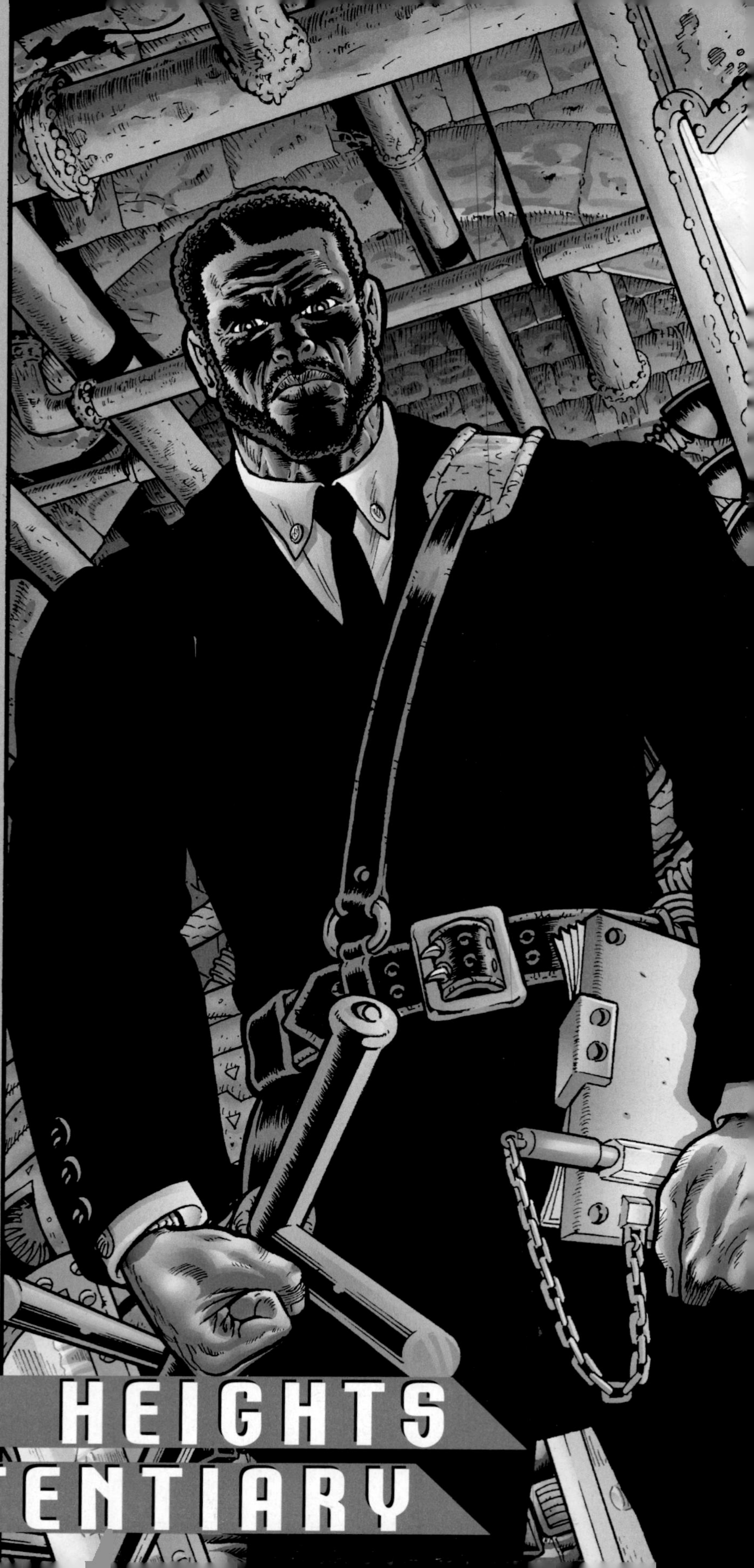

IRON HEIGHTS PENITENTIARY

GREGORY WOLFE

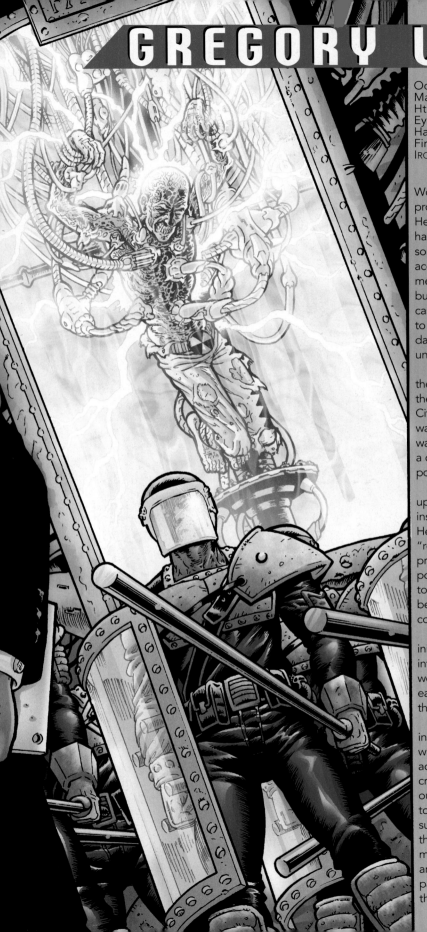

Occupation: Warden
Marital Status: Married
Ht: 6' 2"   Wt: 195 lbs.
Eyes: Brown
Hair: Black
First Appearance: THE FLASH
IRON HEIGHTS (October, 2001)

Prior to his role as warden, Wolfe was an infamous prosecutor for the city of St. Louis. He earned a reputation of being hard on criminals and seeking somewhat shady help in accumulating evidence. His methods were controversial, but Wolfe almost never lost a case. The only man Wolfe failed to convict was murdered two days after the trial, a case as yet unsolved.

Because of his friendship with the Governor, Wolfe was offered the job of Warden of Keystone City Prison after the previous warden suffered a heart attack and was forced to retire. Looking for a challenge, Wolfe accepted the position.

Wolfe was instrumental in updating and remodeling the institution, renaming it Iron Heights. His frustration with the "revolving door" nature of many prisons with large metahuman populations has driven Wolfe to ensure his building has been outfitted with the latest in containment technology.

Wolfe takes great care in initiating costumed "super-villains" into the prison. He forces them to wear their costumes, so they'll be easily spotted when mingling with the general population.

Although Wolfe held the Flash in high regard, his first encounter with him left him cold. The Flash accused the Warden of excessive cruelty towards prisoners, outraging Wolfe. Unbeknownst to the Flash – as well as to his superiors – Gregory Wolfe has the metahuman ability to control muscular impulses in living beings and, at a thought, can trigger painful spasms within any part of the human body.

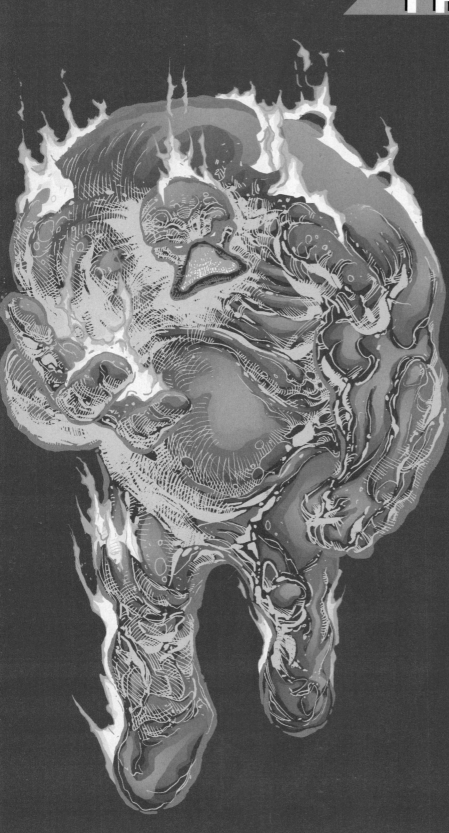

TAR PIT

Real Name: Joey Monteleone
Occupation: Professional Criminal
Marital Status: Single
Ht: 7' 9"
Wt: 325 lbs.
Eyes: Yellow
Hair: None
First Appearance: THE FLASH (2nd series) #174 (July, 2001)

Joey Monteleone is the kid brother of Keystone City's drug czar, Jack Monteleone – a.k.a. "the Candyman." The Candyman struggled to train his younger sibling in drug trading and enforcing, but Joey's mind wandered. Even Jack couldn't keep him out of prison.

Joey was thrown into Iron Heights with a mandatory sentence of seven years. For most people this would've been a wake-up call, but Joey believed his brother would spring him. So he waited. And waited.

After serving six months, Joey realized that he wasn't leaving. Turning to meditation, he soon discovered he had a metahuman ability to make his astral soul depart his body and inhabit inanimate objects. He began to go "joyriding" at night, out for vandalism and fun. During the day, his spirit returned to his body.

Recently, Joey sent his astral self into a vat of tar and crashed the hockey playoffs in a tarry form which his astral self has been unable to escape. Like everything else, his latest predicament is another game to Joey Monteleone.

Currently, Joey's comatose human body resides in one cell in the upper containment units of Iron Heights, his Tar Pit form down in the Pipeline.

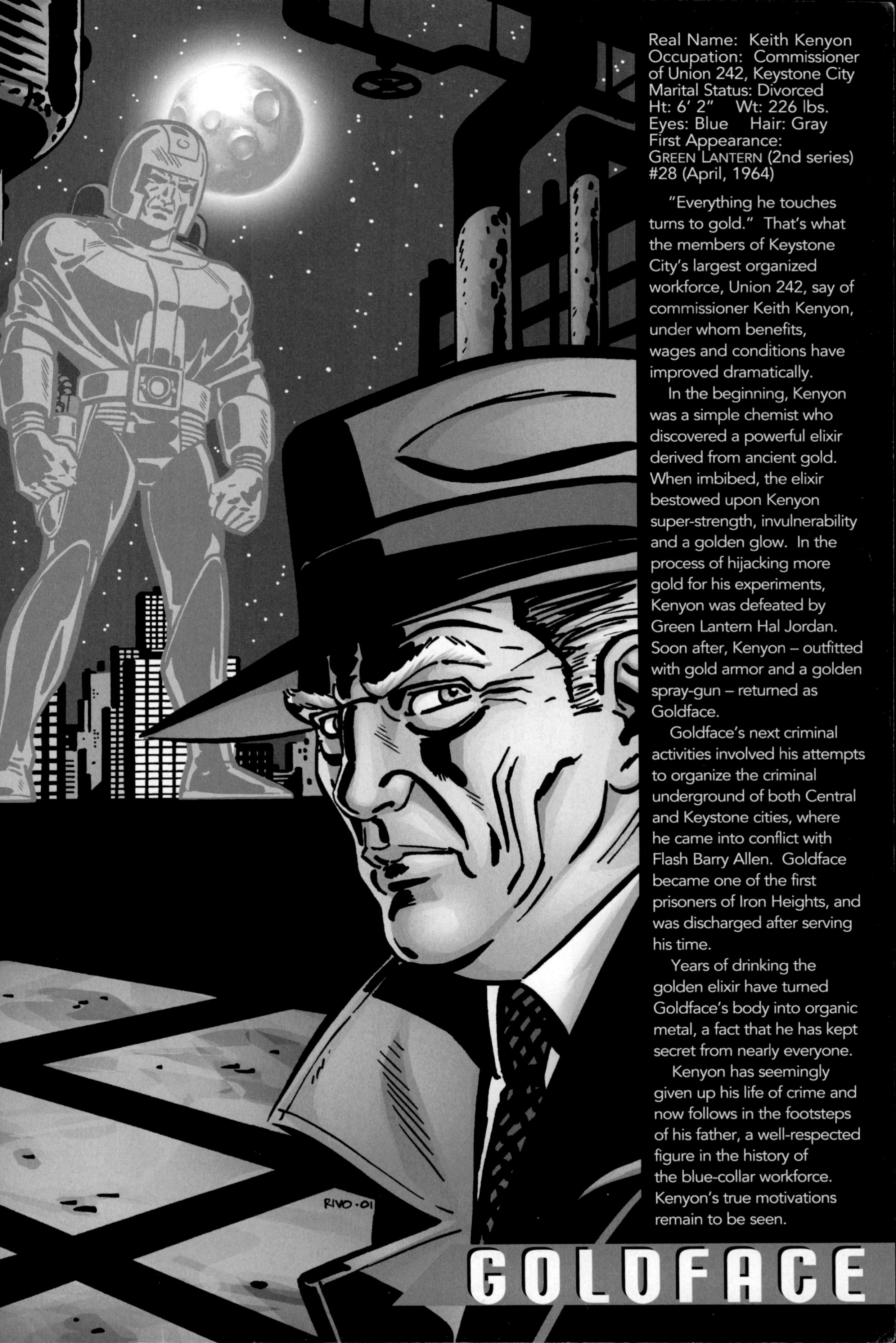
RIVO·01

Real Name: Keith Kenyon
Occupation: Commissioner of Union 242, Keystone City
Marital Status: Divorced
Ht: 6′ 2″ Wt: 226 lbs.
Eyes: Blue Hair: Gray
First Appearance: GREEN LANTERN (2nd series) #28 (April, 1964)

"Everything he touches turns to gold." That's what the members of Keystone City's largest organized workforce, Union 242, say of commissioner Keith Kenyon, under whom benefits, wages and conditions have improved dramatically.

In the beginning, Kenyon was a simple chemist who discovered a powerful elixir derived from ancient gold. When imbibed, the elixir bestowed upon Kenyon super-strength, invulnerability and a golden glow. In the process of hijacking more gold for his experiments, Kenyon was defeated by Green Lantern Hal Jordan. Soon after, Kenyon – outfitted with gold armor and a golden spray-gun – returned as Goldface.

Goldface's next criminal activities involved his attempts to organize the criminal underground of both Central and Keystone cities, where he came into conflict with Flash Barry Allen. Goldface became one of the first prisoners of Iron Heights, and was discharged after serving his time.

Years of drinking the golden elixir have turned Goldface's body into organic metal, a fact that he has kept secret from nearly everyone.

Kenyon has seemingly given up his life of crime and now follows in the footsteps of his father, a well-respected figure in the history of the blue-collar workforce. Kenyon's true motivations remain to be seen.

GOLDFACE

CAPTAIN COLD

Real Name: Leonard Snart
Occupation: Professional Criminal
Marital Status: Single
Ht: 6' 2" Wt: 196 lbs.
Eyes: Brown Hair: Brown
First Appearance: SHOWCASE #8 (May-June, 1957)

Leonard Snart grew up in a trailer park outside of Central City with an alcoholic father and a verbally abusive mother. His only fond memories are of his younger sister, Lisa. The two would shoplift together, beat up the neighbor kids and steal from their own parents. When Snart turned eighteen, he moved out, becoming a small-time thief, and began drinking excessively and experimenting with drugs.

After graduating to armed robbery, Snart was caught by Barry Allen (the second Flash) in Central City and imprisoned. During his jail time, he studied thermal motion, hoping to find a way to slow Flash down. When he was released, Snart broke into a lab and used an unknown radiation to charge a special gun of his own design.

Snart's cold-gun has the unique ability to halt movement at the atomic level, thereby achieving Absolute Zero. It can also create a "cold field" which Snart – renamed Captain Cold – used to slow Flash down so that he could be seen.

After Barry Allen died, Cold briefly teamed with his sister, now a super-villain called the Golden Glider, and the two eventually formed a quasi-legitimate business as bounty hunters. But "good" was not in their blood and it quickly fell apart. Soon after, the Golden Glider was murdered, thrusting Cold back into a life of crime.

Cold often goes on binges with his illicit earnings, spending his money on booze and professional escorts. He has recently returned to Keystone City for reasons yet to be revealed.

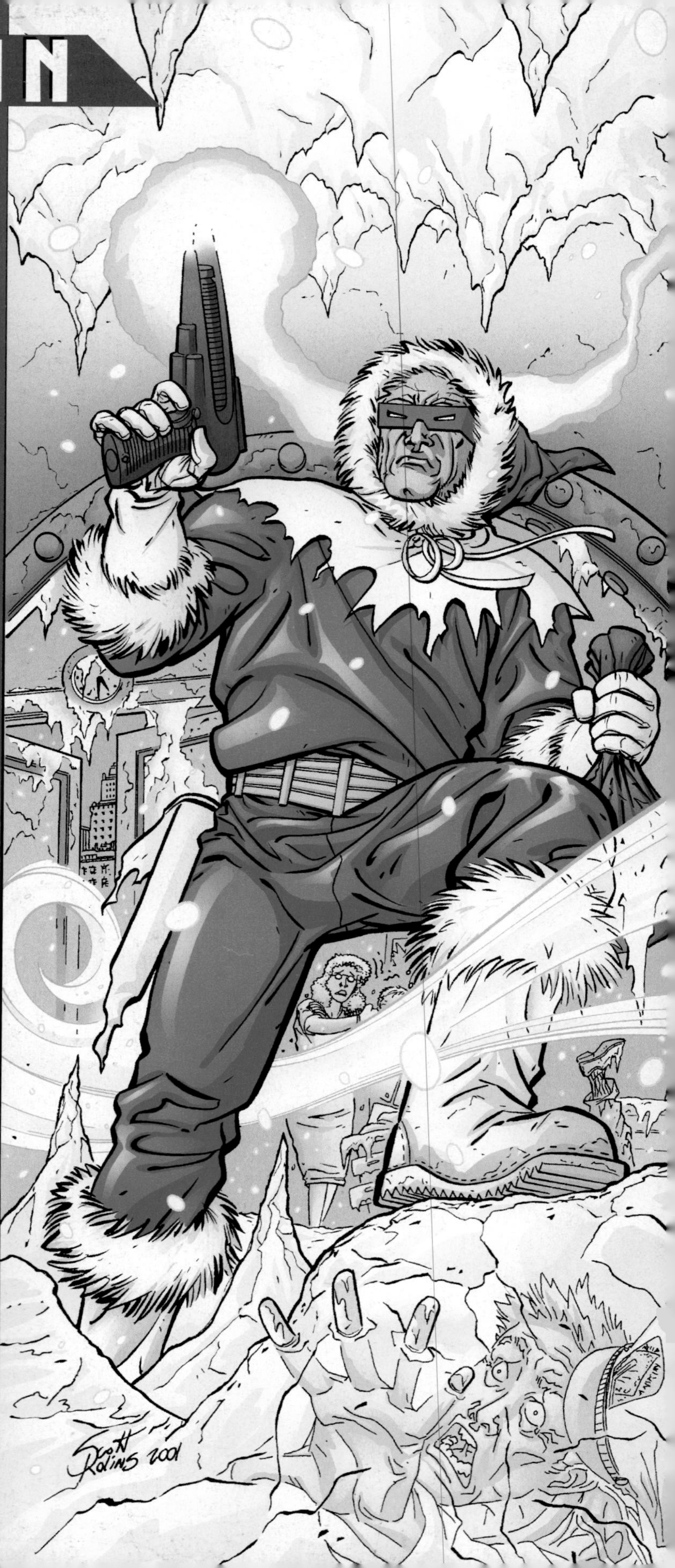

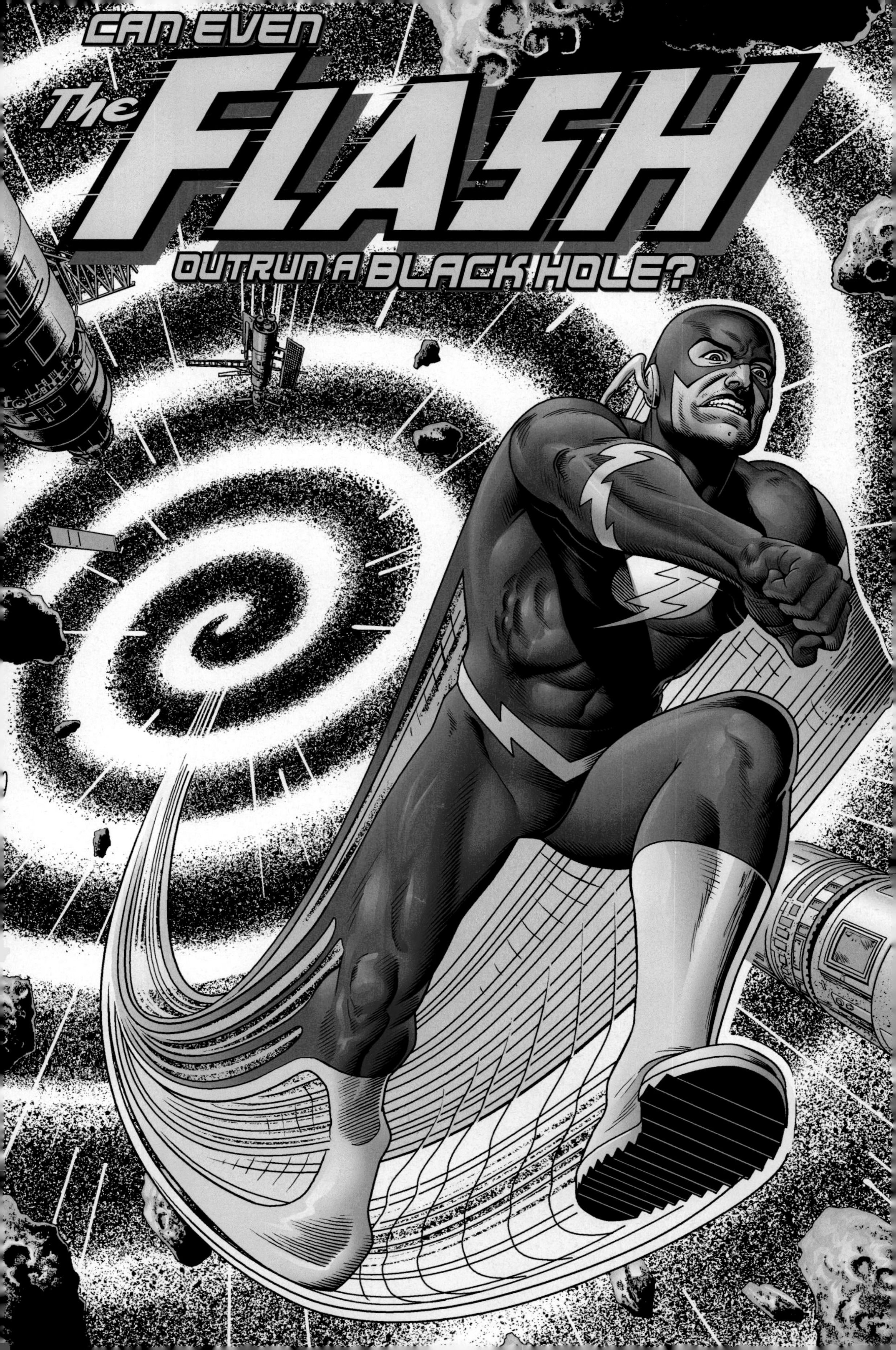
CAN EVEN
The FLASH
OUTRUN A BLACK HOLE?

COVER ART BY **BRIAN BOLLAND**

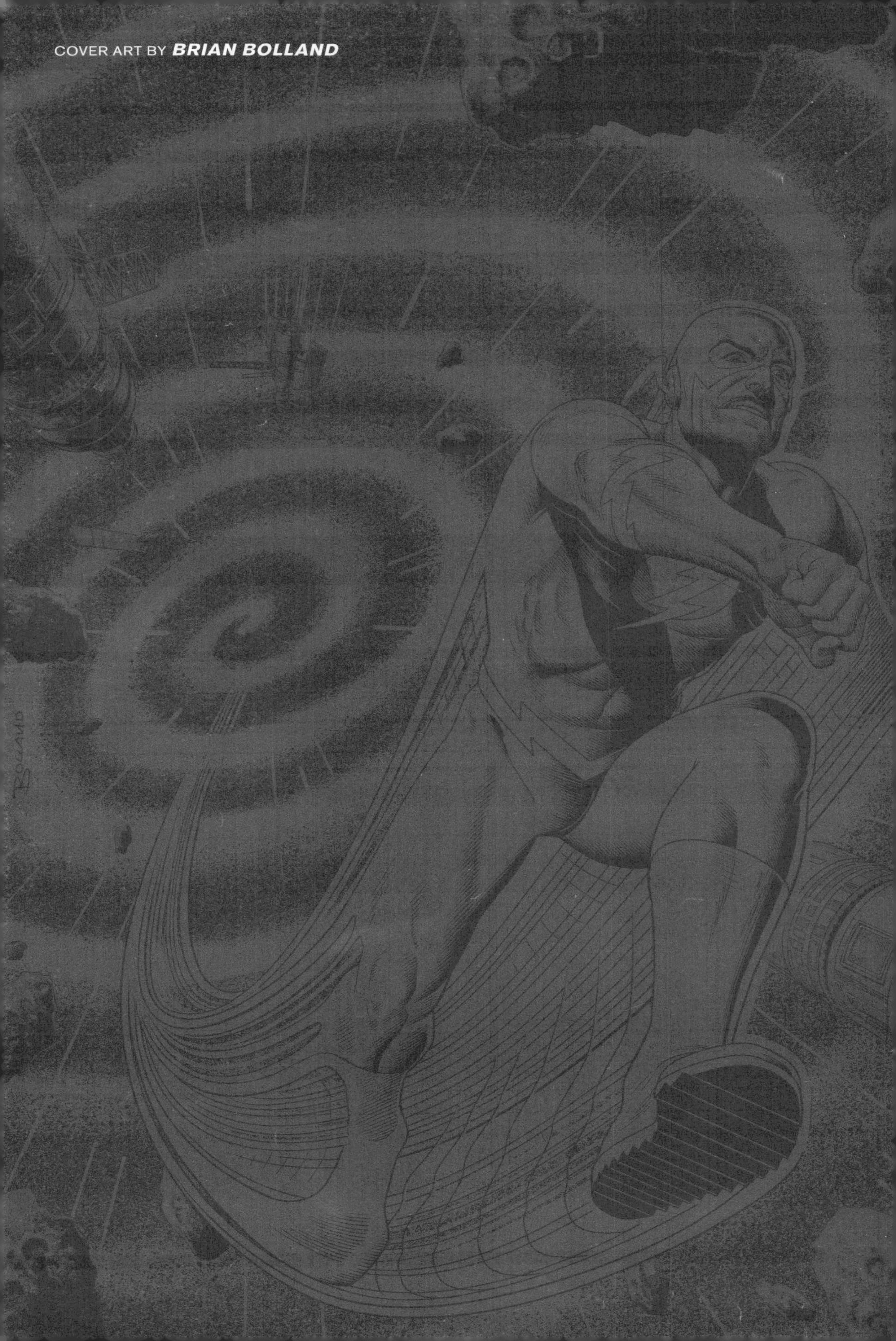
BOLLAND

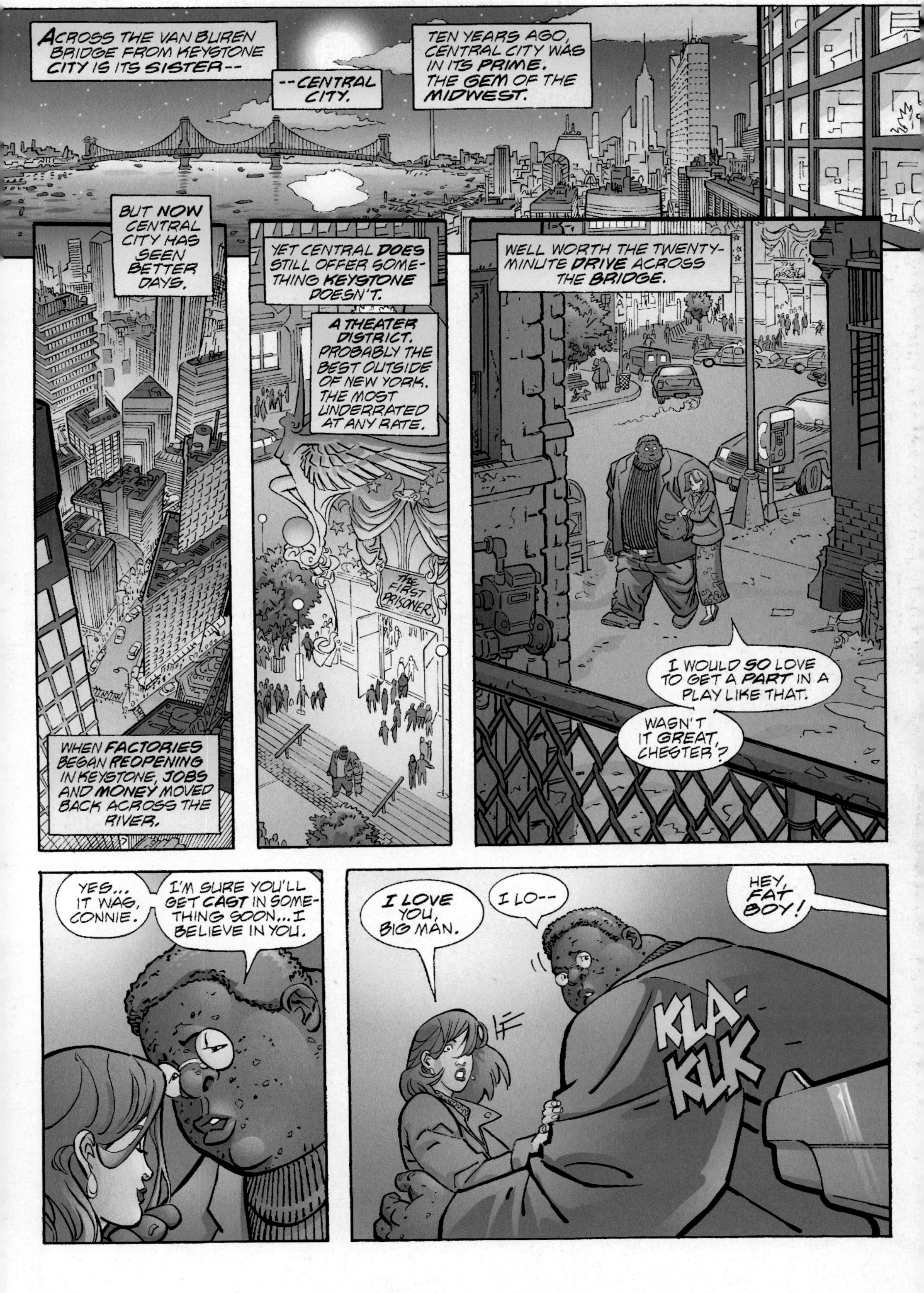
ACROSS THE VAN BUREN BRIDGE FROM KEYSTONE CITY IS ITS SISTER--
--CENTRAL CITY.
TEN YEARS AGO, CENTRAL CITY WAS IN ITS PRIME. THE GEM OF THE MIDWEST.
BUT NOW CENTRAL CITY HAS SEEN BETTER DAYS.
WHEN FACTORIES BEGAN REOPENING IN KEYSTONE, JOBS AND MONEY MOVED BACK ACROSS THE RIVER.
YET CENTRAL DOES STILL OFFER SOMETHING KEYSTONE DOESN'T.
A THEATER DISTRICT. PROBABLY THE BEST OUTSIDE OF NEW YORK. THE MOST UNDERRATED AT ANY RATE.
THE FIRST PRISONER
WELL WORTH THE TWENTY-MINUTE DRIVE ACROSS THE BRIDGE.
I WOULD SO LOVE TO GET A PART IN A PLAY LIKE THAT.
WASN'T IT GREAT, CHESTER?
YES... IT WAS, CONNIE.
I'M SURE YOU'LL GET CAST IN SOMETHING SOON... I BELIEVE IN YOU.
I LOVE YOU, BIG MAN.
I LO--
HEY, FAT BOY!
KLA-KLK

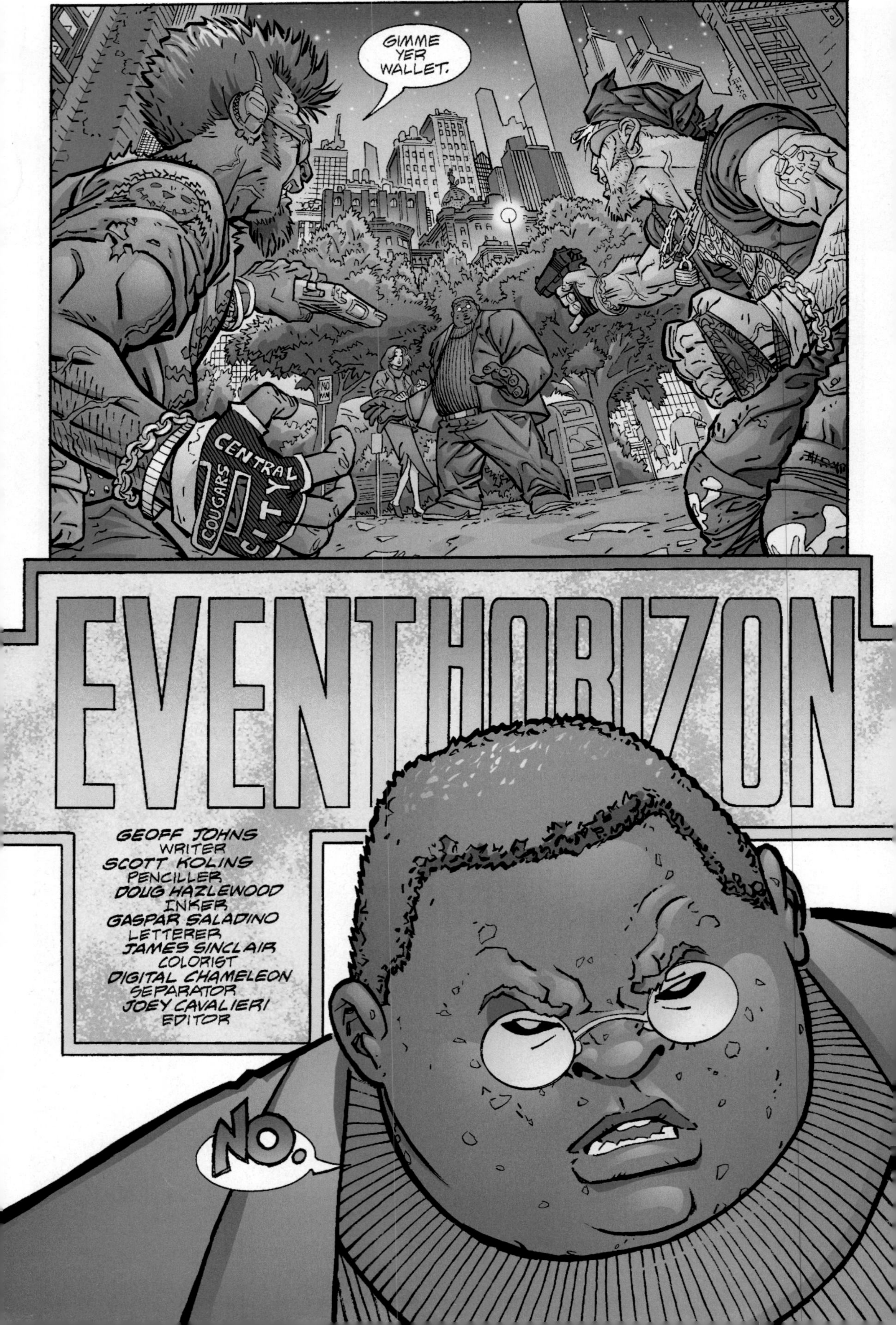
GIMME YER WALLET.
CENTRAL CITY COUGARS
EVENT HORIZON
GEOFF JOHNS WRITER
SCOTT KOLINS PENCILLER
DOUG HAZLEWOOD INKER
GASPAR SALADINO LETTERER
JAMES SINCLAIR COLORIST
DIGITAL CHAMELEON SEPARATOR
JOEY CAVALIERI EDITOR
NO.

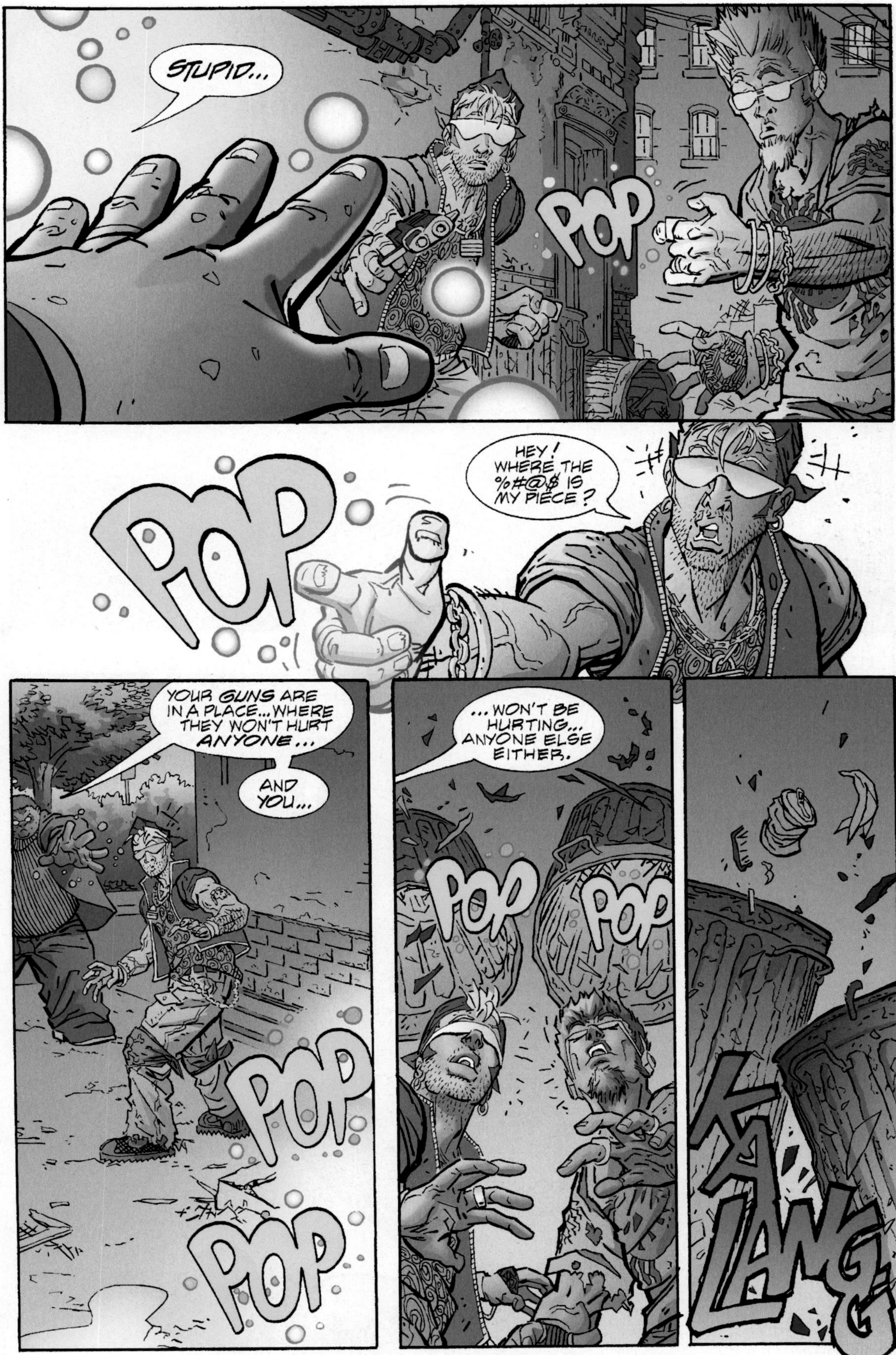
STUPID...
POP
HEY! WHERE THE %#@$ IS MY PIECE?
POP
YOUR GUNS ARE IN A PLACE... WHERE THEY WON'T HURT ANYONE...
AND YOU...
POP
POP
...WON'T BE HURTING... ANYONE ELSE EITHER.
POP
POP
KA LANG

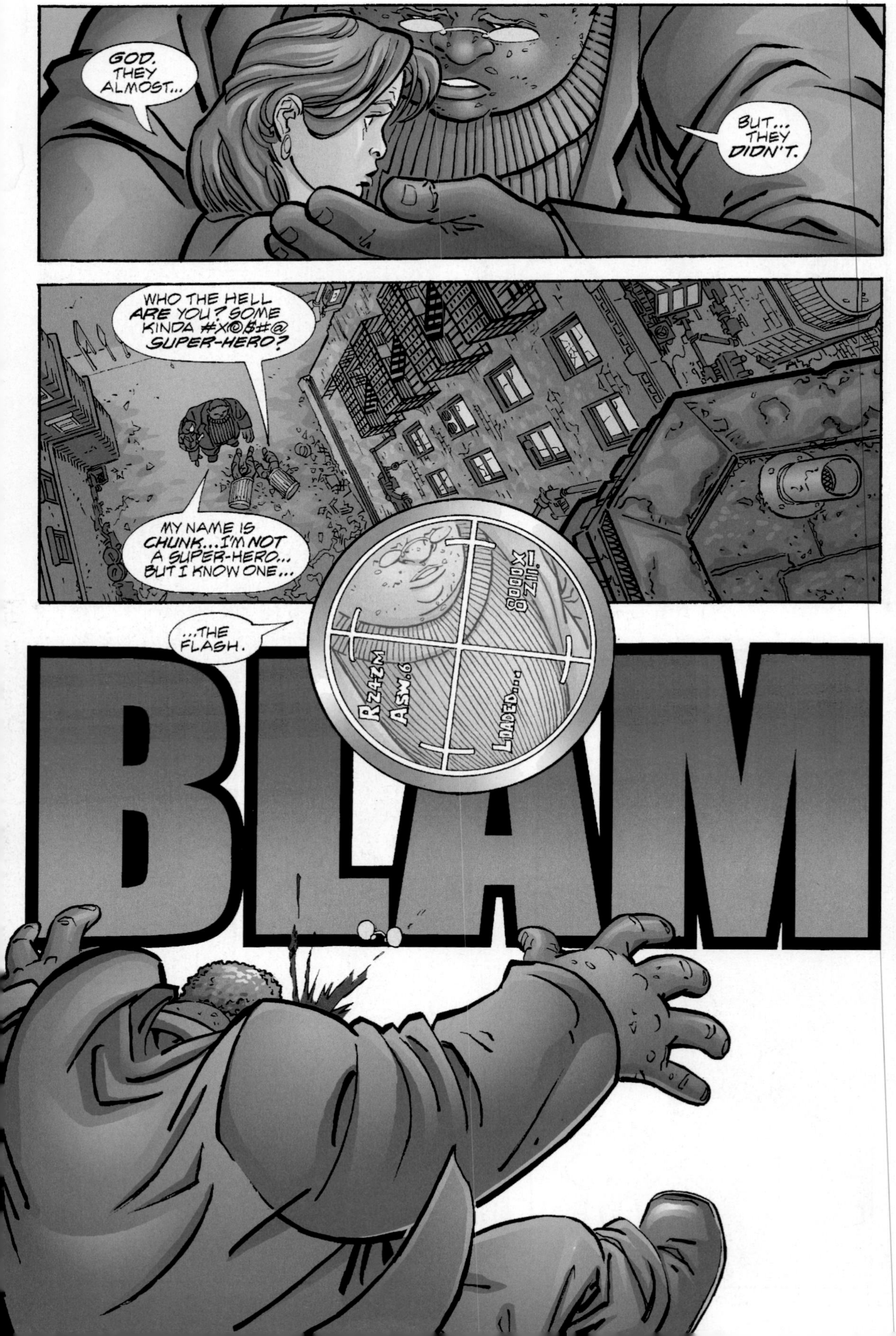
GOD. THEY ALMOST...
BUT... THEY DIDN'T.
WHO THE HELL ARE YOU? SOME KINDA #X©$#@ SUPER-HERO?
MY NAME IS CHUNK...I'M NOT A SUPER-HERO... BUT I KNOW ONE...
...THE FLASH.
R242M
ASW.6
LOADED...
BLAM

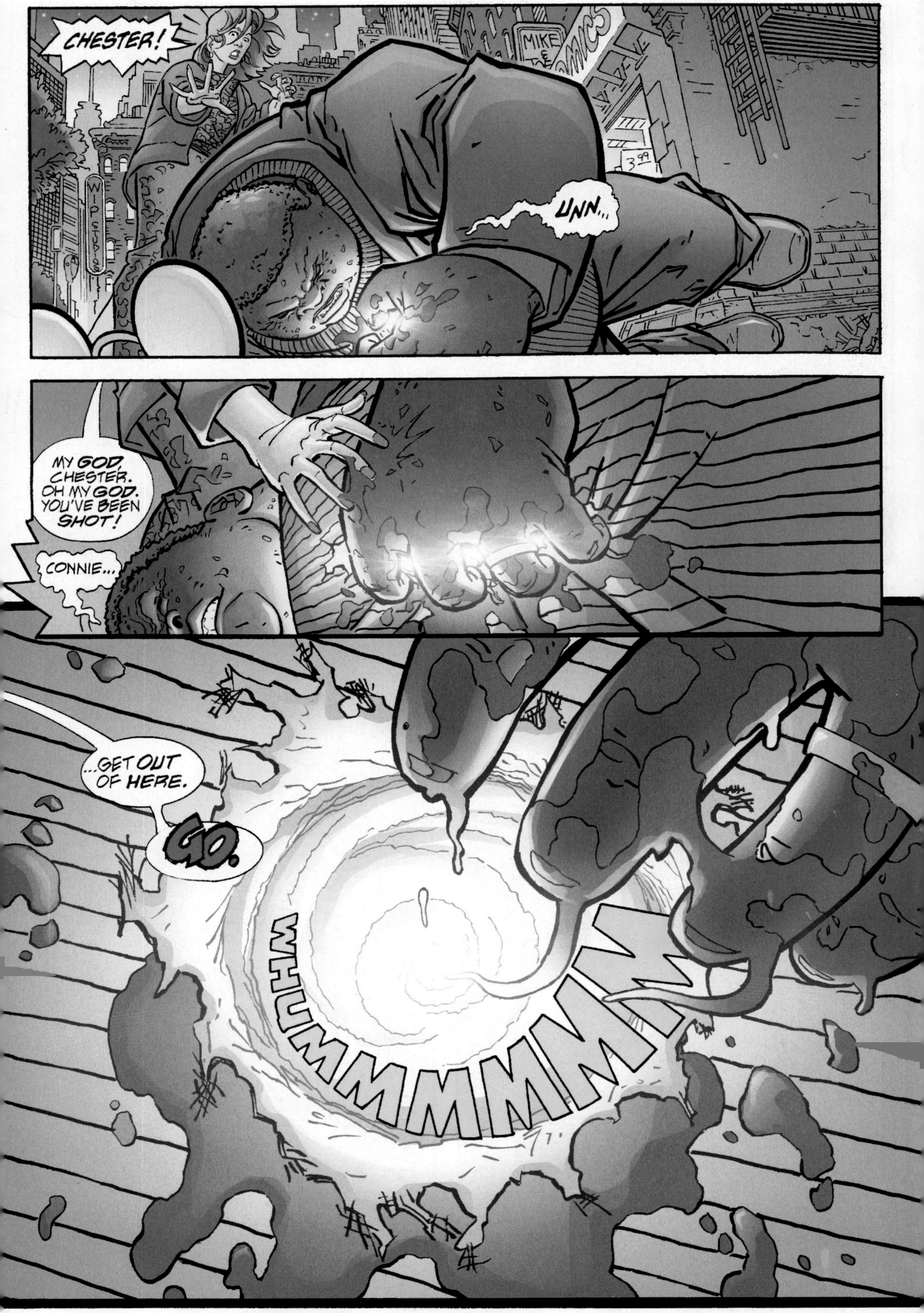
CHESTER!
MIKE
COMICS
3.99
W.I.P STUDIOS
UNN...
MY GOD, CHESTER. OH MY GOD. YOU'VE BEEN SHOT!
CONNIE...
...GET OUT OF HERE.
GO.
WHUMMMMMMM

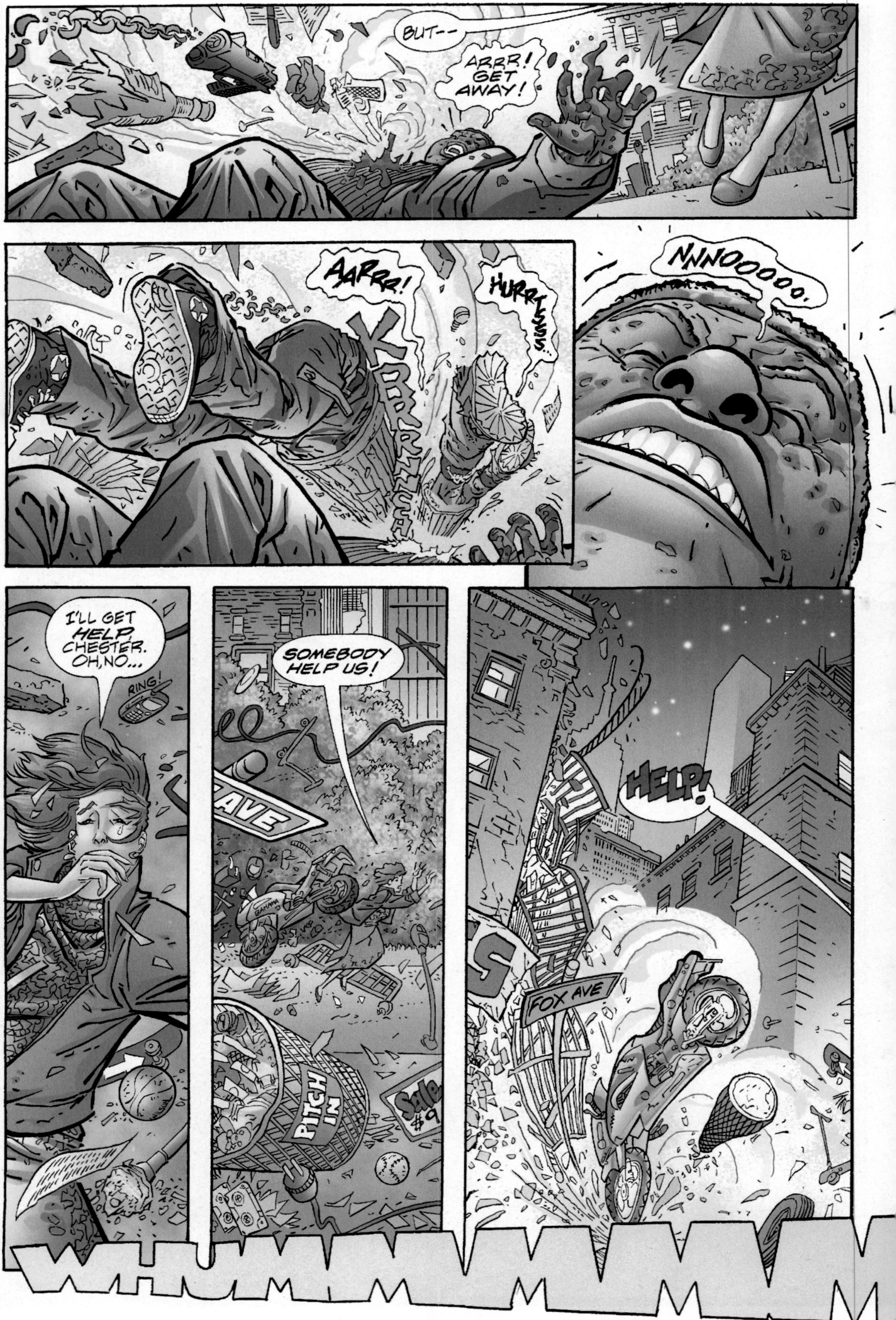
BUT--
ARRR! GET AWAY!
AARRR!
KRRRTTCH
HURRISSSS...
NNNOOOOOO.
I'LL GET HELP, CHESTER. OH, NO...
RING!
AVE
SOMEBODY HELP US!
PITCH IN
HELP!
FOX AVE
WHUMMMMMM

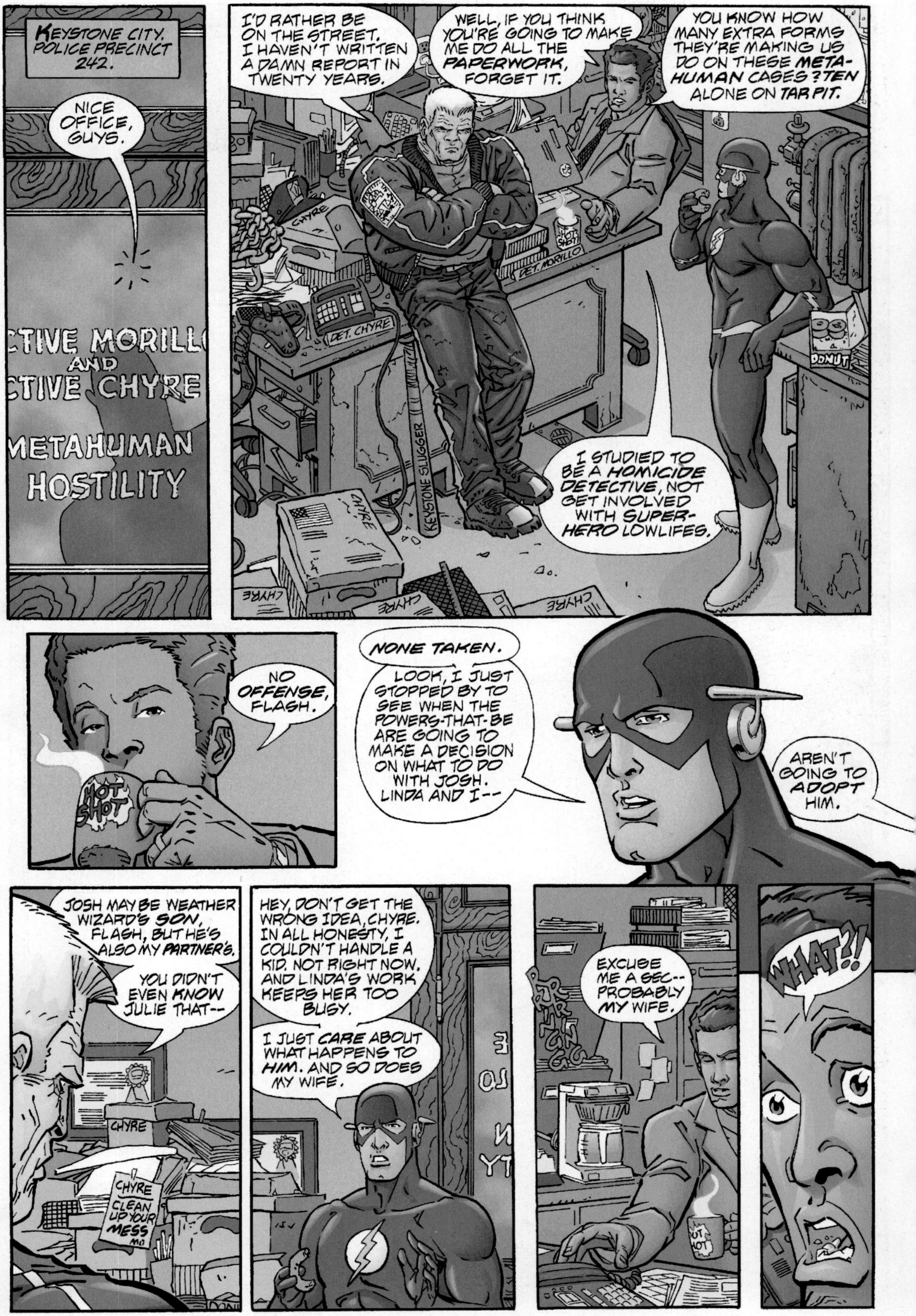
KEYSTONE CITY. POLICE PRECINCT 242.
NICE OFFICE, GUYS.
CTIVE MORILL AND CTIVE CHYRE METAHUMAN HOSTILITY
I'D RATHER BE ON THE STREET. I HAVEN'T WRITTEN A DAMN REPORT IN TWENTY YEARS.
WELL, IF YOU THINK YOU'RE GOING TO MAKE ME DO ALL THE PAPERWORK, FORGET IT.
YOU KNOW HOW MANY EXTRA FORMS THEY'RE MAKING US DO ON THESE META-HUMAN CASES? TEN ALONE ON TAR PIT.
I STUDIED TO BE A HOMICIDE DETECTIVE, NOT GET INVOLVED WITH SUPER-HERO LOWLIFES.
DET. CHYRE
DET. MORILLO
KEYSTONE SLUGGER
DONUT
CHYRE
NO OFFENSE, FLASH.
HOT SHOT
NONE TAKEN.
LOOK, I JUST STOPPED BY TO SEE WHEN THE POWERS-THAT-BE ARE GOING TO MAKE A DECISION ON WHAT TO DO WITH JOSH. LINDA AND I--
AREN'T GOING TO ADOPT HIM.
JOSH MAY BE WEATHER WIZARD'S SON, FLASH, BUT HE'S ALSO MY PARTNER'S.
YOU DIDN'T EVEN KNOW JULIE THAT--
CHYRE
CHYRE CLEAN UP YOUR MESS MO
HEY, DON'T GET THE WRONG IDEA, CHYRE. IN ALL HONESTY, I COULDN'T HANDLE A KID. NOT RIGHT NOW. AND LINDA'S WORK KEEPS HER TOO BUSY.
I JUST CARE ABOUT WHAT HAPPENS TO HIM. AND SO DOES MY WIFE.
BRRRING
EXCUSE ME A SEC-- PROBABLY MY WIFE.
WHAT?!!

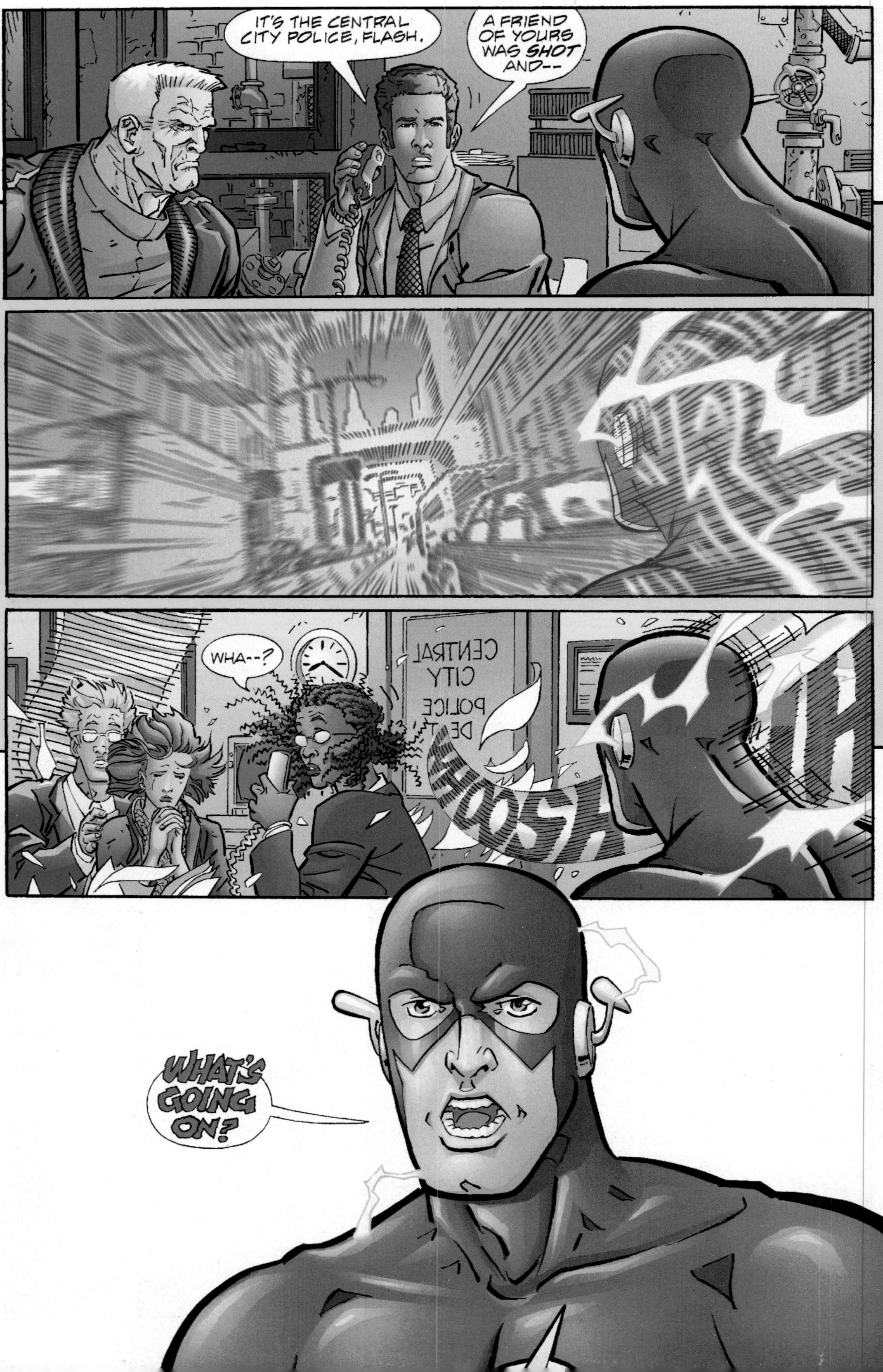
IT'S THE CENTRAL CITY POLICE, FLASH.
A FRIEND OF YOURS WAS SHOT AND--
WHA--?
WHAT'S GOING ON?

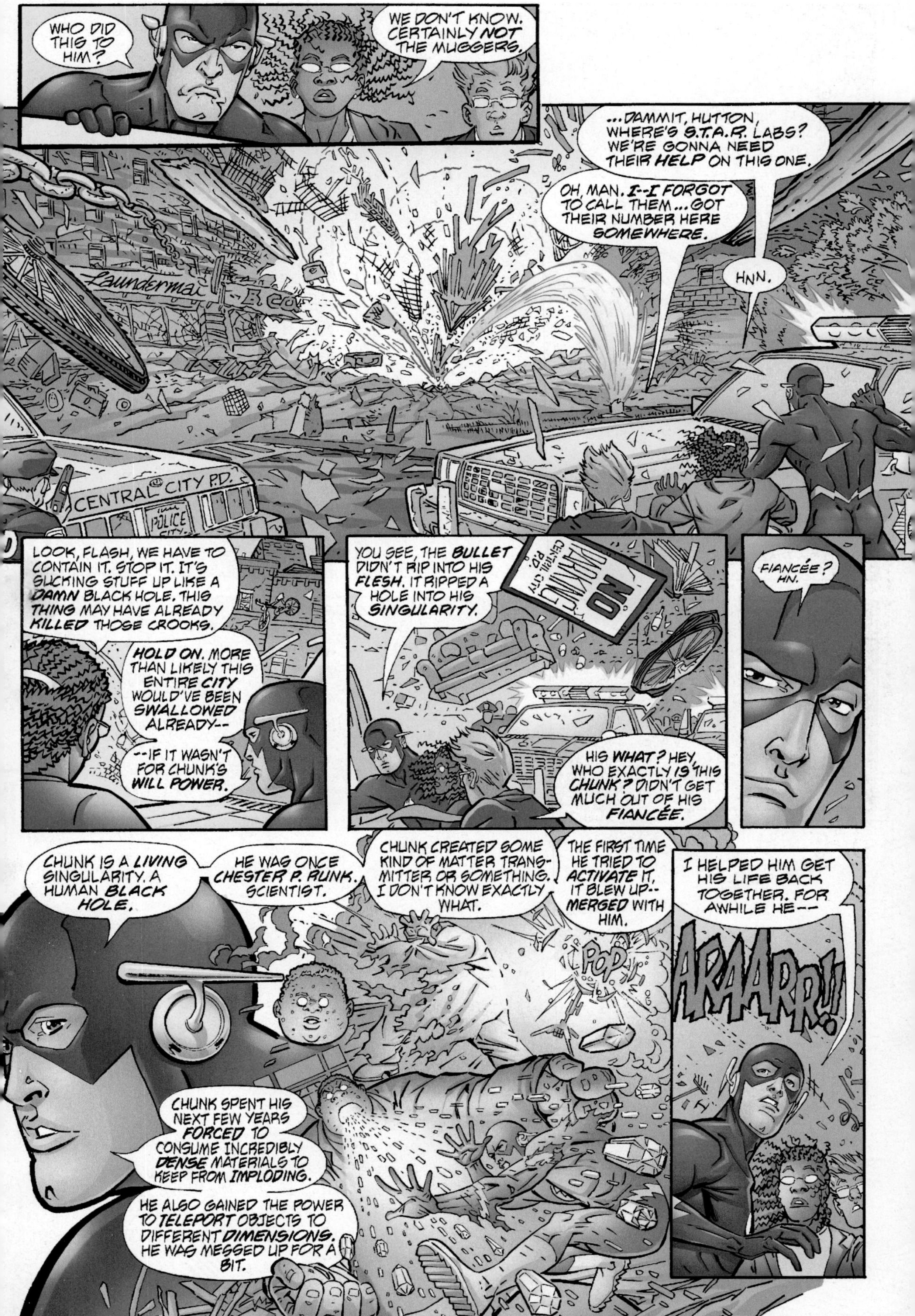
WHO DID THIS TO HIM?
WE DON'T KNOW. CERTAINLY NOT THE MUGGERS.
...DAMMIT, HUTTON, WHERE'S S.T.A.R. LABS? WE'RE GONNA NEED THEIR HELP ON THIS ONE.
OH, MAN. I--I FORGOT TO CALL THEM... GOT THEIR NUMBER HERE SOMEWHERE.
HNN.
CENTRAL CITY P.D.
POLICE
LOOK, FLASH, WE HAVE TO CONTAIN IT. STOP IT. IT'S SUCKING STUFF UP LIKE A DAMN BLACK HOLE. THIS THING MAY HAVE ALREADY KILLED THOSE CROOKS.
HOLD ON. MORE THAN LIKELY THIS ENTIRE CITY WOULD'VE BEEN SWALLOWED ALREADY--
--IF IT WASN'T FOR CHUNK'S WILL POWER.
YOU SEE, THE BULLET DIDN'T RIP INTO HIS FLESH. IT RIPPED A HOLE INTO HIS SINGULARITY.
NO PARKING
HIS WHAT? HEY, WHO EXACTLY IS THIS CHUNK? DIDN'T GET MUCH OUT OF HIS FIANCÉE.
FIANCÉE? HN.
CHUNK IS A LIVING SINGULARITY. A HUMAN BLACK HOLE.
HE WAS ONCE CHESTER P. RUNK. SCIENTIST.
CHUNK CREATED SOME KIND OF MATTER TRANSMITTER OR SOMETHING. I DON'T KNOW EXACTLY WHAT.
THE FIRST TIME HE TRIED TO ACTIVATE IT, IT BLEW UP-- MERGED WITH HIM.
POP
CHUNK SPENT HIS NEXT FEW YEARS FORCED TO CONSUME INCREDIBLY DENSE MATERIALS TO KEEP FROM IMPLODING.
HE ALSO GAINED THE POWER TO TELEPORT OBJECTS TO DIFFERENT DIMENSIONS. HE WAS MESSED UP FOR A BIT.
I HELPED HIM GET HIS LIFE BACK TOGETHER. FOR AWHILE HE--
ARAARR!!

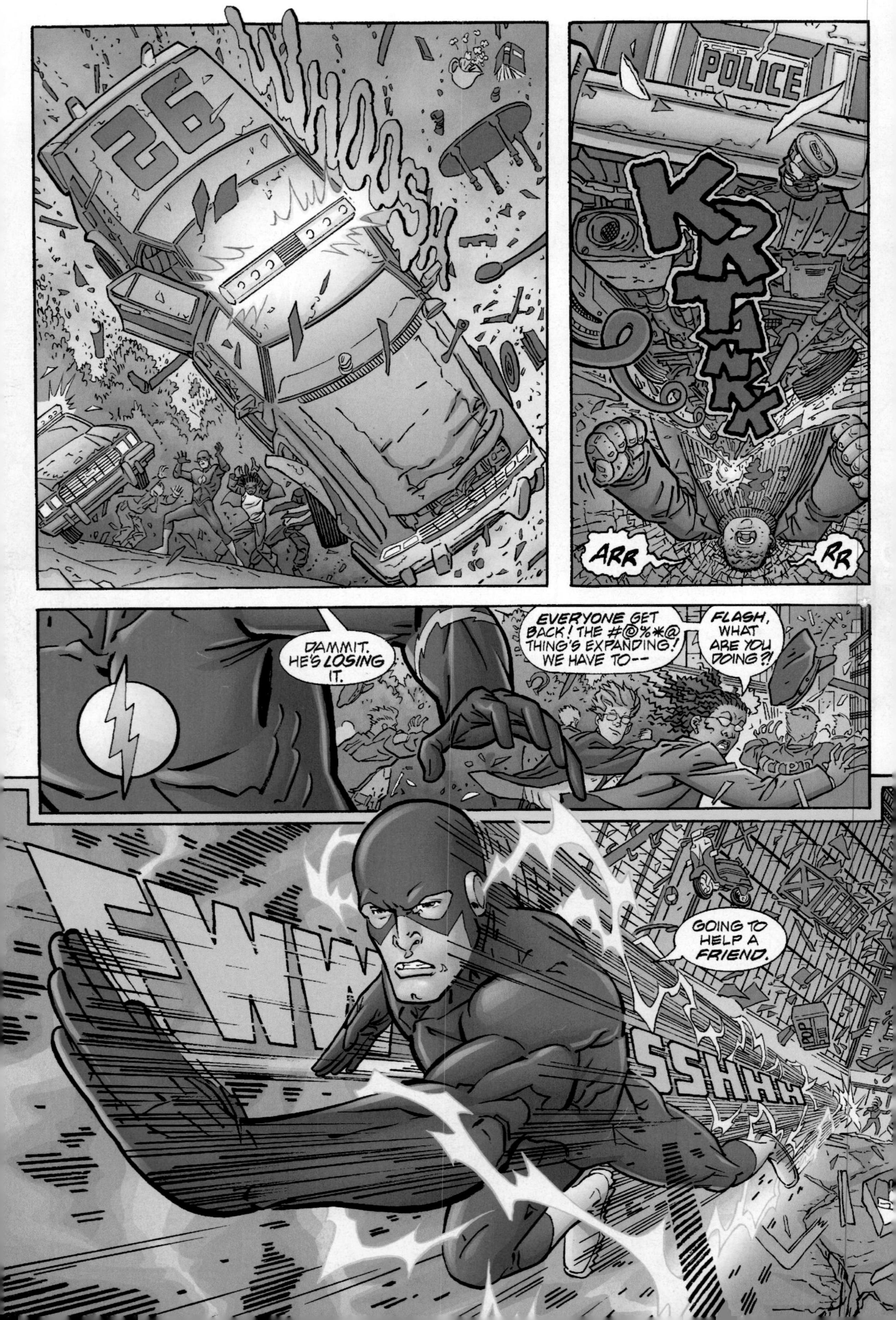
WHOOSH
POLICE
KRTANKK
ARR
RR
DAMMIT. HE'S LOSING IT.
EVERYONE GET BACK! THE #@%*@ THING'S EXPANDING! WE HAVE TO--
FLASH, WHAT ARE YOU DOING?!
GOING TO HELP A FRIEND.
SSHHH

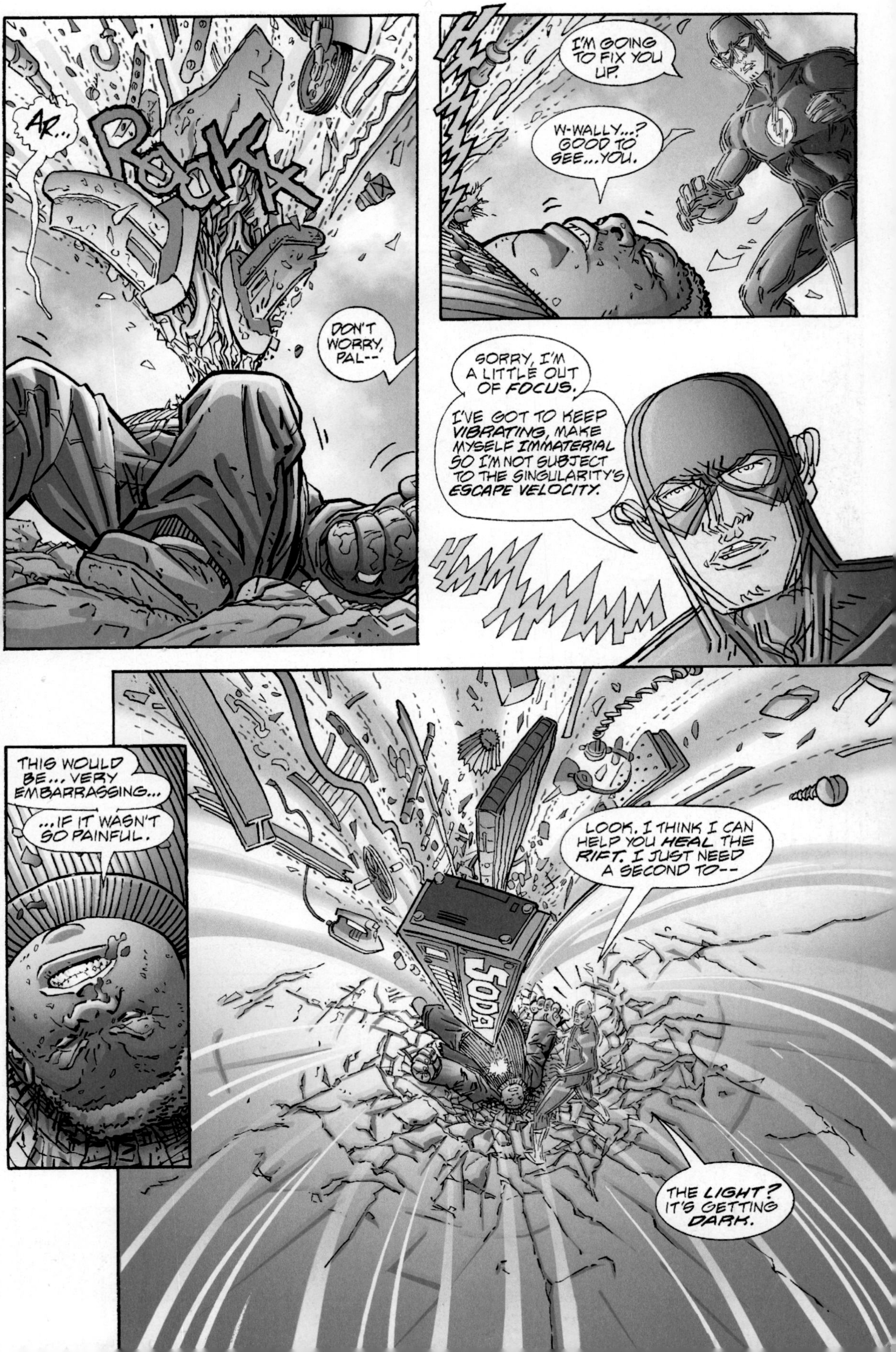
AR...
RAKK
DON'T WORRY, PAL--
HMMM
I'M GOING TO FIX YOU UP.
W-WALLY...? GOOD TO SEE...YOU.
SORRY, I'M A LITTLE OUT OF FOCUS.
I'VE GOT TO KEEP VIBRATING, MAKE MYSELF IMMATERIAL SO I'M NOT SUBJECT TO THE SINGULARITY'S ESCAPE VELOCITY.
HMMMMMMMM
THIS WOULD BE... VERY EMBARRASSING...
...IF IT WASN'T SO PAINFUL.
LOOK. I THINK I CAN HELP YOU HEAL THE RIFT. I JUST NEED A SECOND TO--
SODA
THE LIGHT? IT'S GETTING DARK.

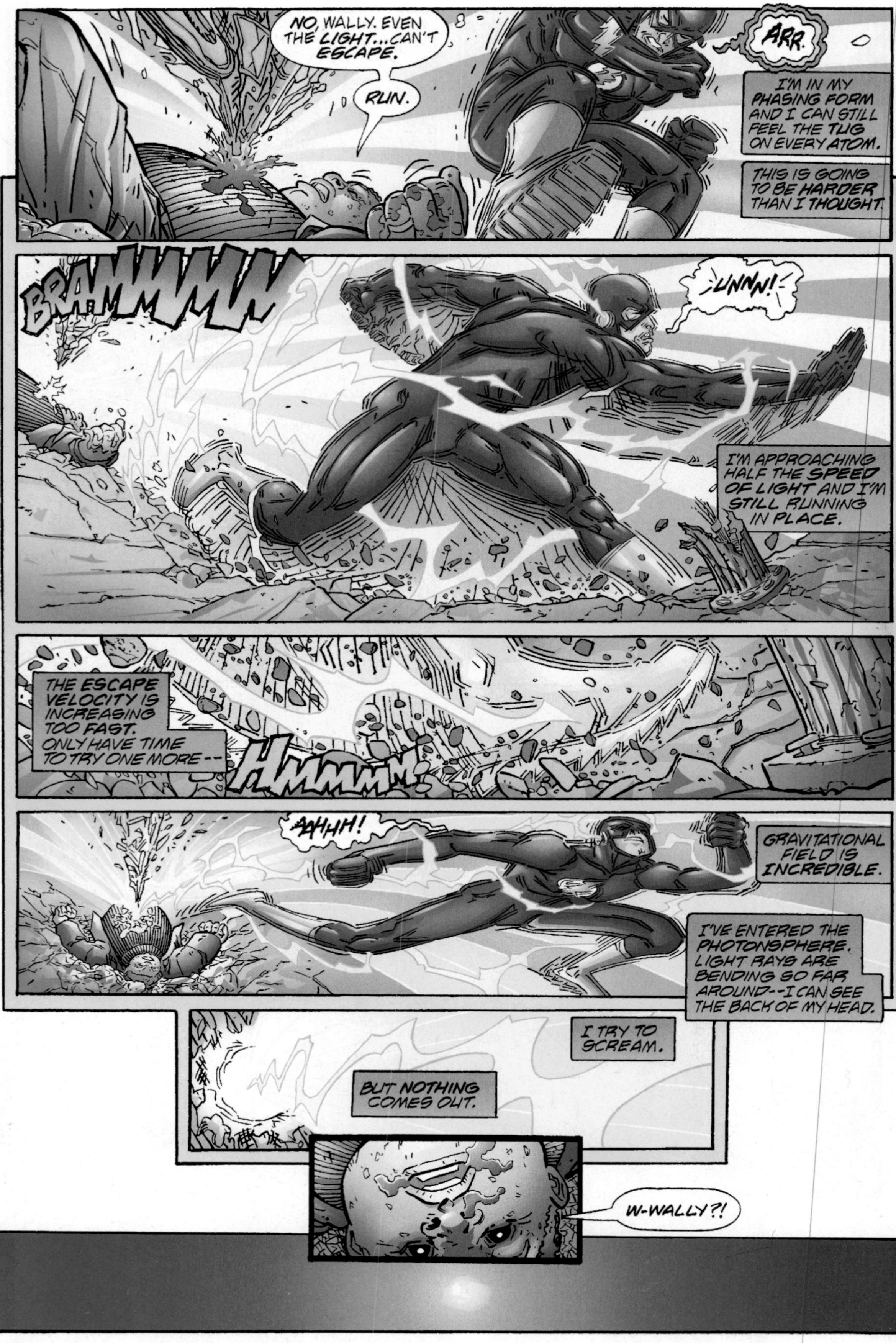
NO, WALLY. EVEN THE LIGHT... CAN'T ESCAPE.
RUN.
ARR.
I'M IN MY PHASING FORM AND I CAN STILL FEEL THE TUG ON EVERY ATOM.
THIS IS GOING TO BE HARDER THAN I THOUGHT.
BRAMMMM
UNNN!
I'M APPROACHING HALF THE SPEED OF LIGHT AND I'M STILL RUNNING IN PLACE.
THE ESCAPE VELOCITY IS INCREASING TOO FAST.
ONLY HAVE TIME TO TRY ONE MORE--
HMMMMM
AAHHH!
GRAVITATIONAL FIELD IS INCREDIBLE.
I'VE ENTERED THE PHOTONSPHERE. LIGHT RAYS ARE BENDING SO FAR AROUND--I CAN SEE THE BACK OF MY HEAD.
I TRY TO SCREAM.
BUT NOTHING COMES OUT.
W-WALLY?!

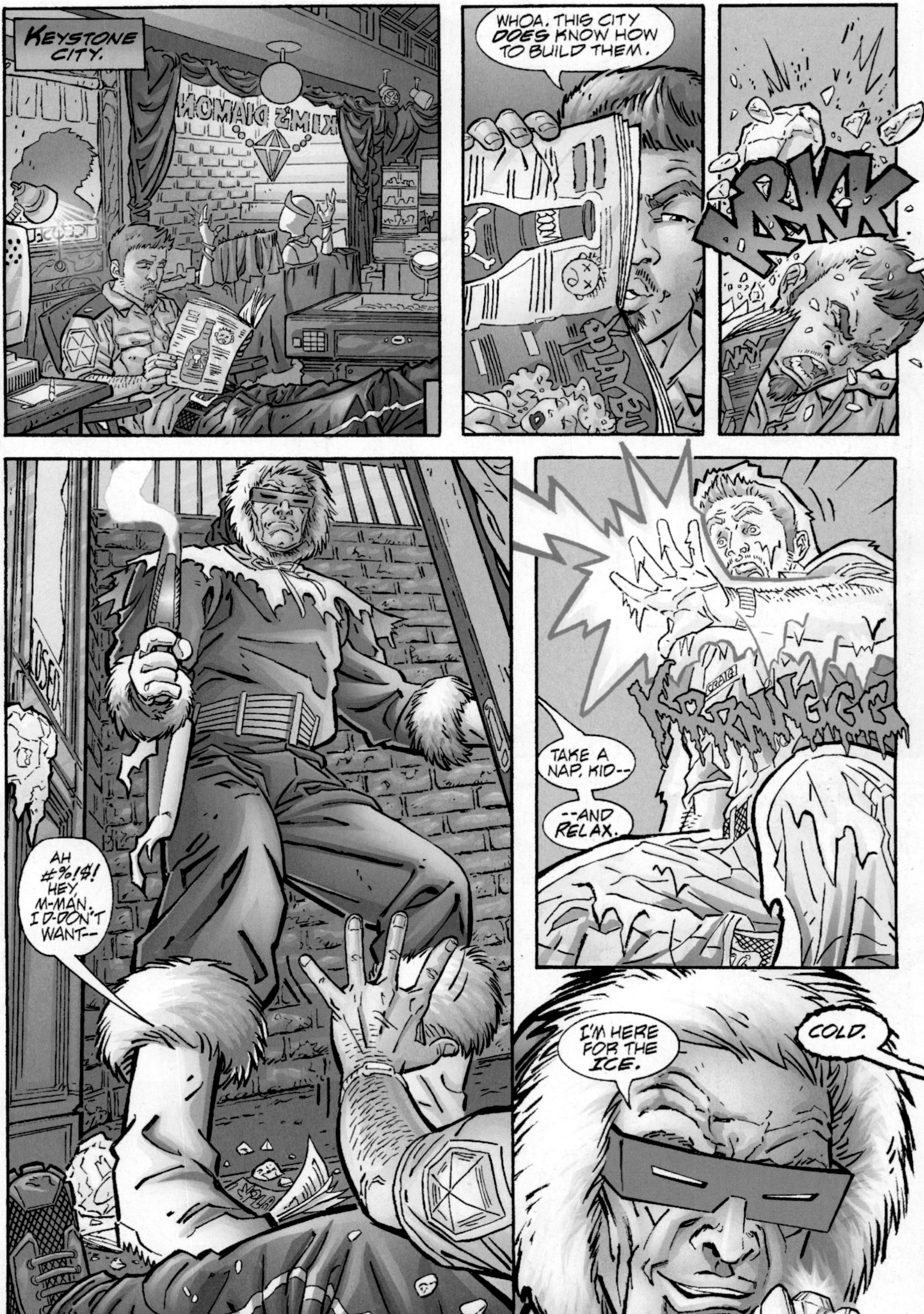
KEYSTONE CITY.
KIM'S DIAMON
WHOA. THIS CITY DOES KNOW HOW TO BUILD THEM.
KRKK
AH #%!$! HEY, M-MAN. I D-DON'T WANT--
KRANGGE
TAKE A NAP, KID--
--AND RELAX.
I'M HERE FOR THE ICE.
COLD.

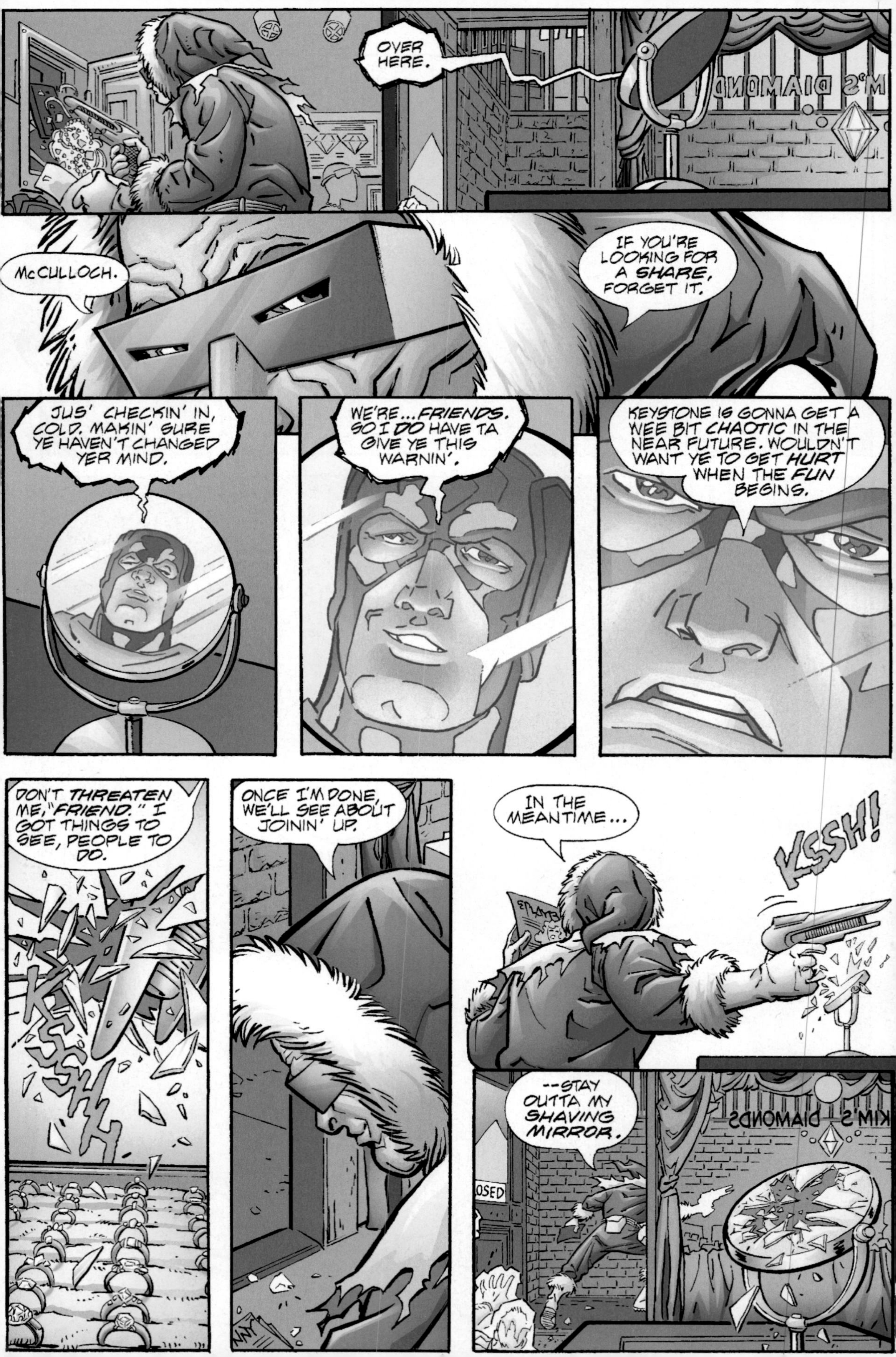
OVER HERE.
M'S DIAMOND
McCULLOCH.
IF YOU'RE LOOKING FOR A SHARE, FORGET IT.
JUS' CHECKIN' IN, COLD. MAKIN' SURE YE HAVEN'T CHANGED YER MIND.
WE'RE...FRIENDS. SO I DO HAVE TA GIVE YE THIS WARNIN'.
KEYSTONE IS GONNA GET A WEE BIT CHAOTIC IN THE NEAR FUTURE. WOULDN'T WANT YE TO GET HURT WHEN THE FUN BEGINS.
DON'T THREATEN ME, "FRIEND." I GOT THINGS TO SEE, PEOPLE TO DO.
KSSH
ONCE I'M DONE, WE'LL SEE ABOUT JOININ' UP.
IN THE MEANTIME...
KSSH!
--STAY OUTTA MY SHAVING MIRROR.
KIM'S DIAMONDS
OSED

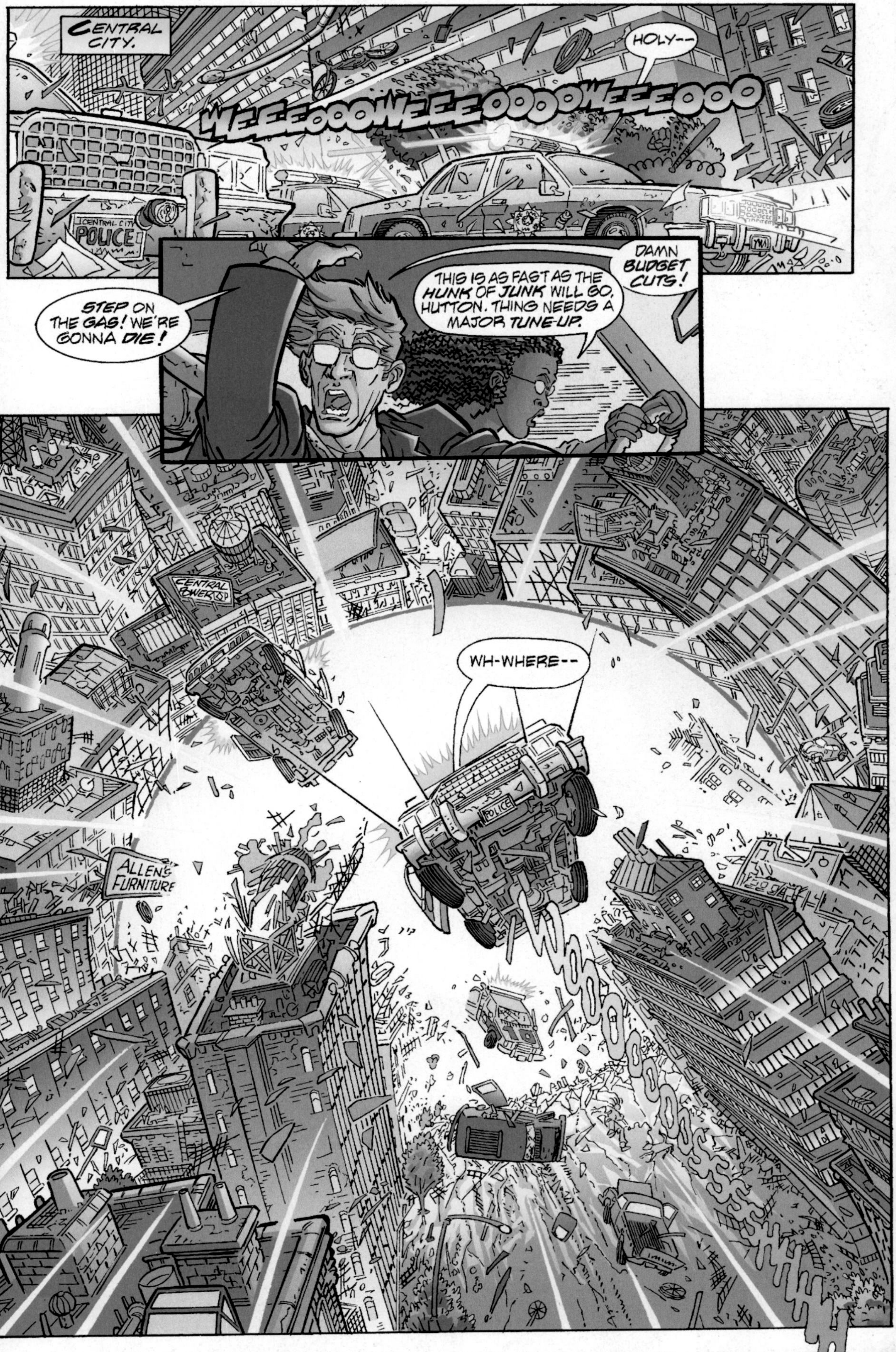
CENTRAL CITY.
HOLY--
WEEEOOOWEEEOOOOWEEEOOO
CENTRAL CITY
POLICE
STEP ON THE GAS! WE'RE GONNA DIE!
THIS IS AS FAST AS THE HUNK OF JUNK WILL GO, HUTTON. THING NEEDS A MAJOR TUNE-UP.
DAMN BUDGET CUTS!
CENTRAL POWER
WH-WHERE--
POLICE
ALLEN'S FURNITURE

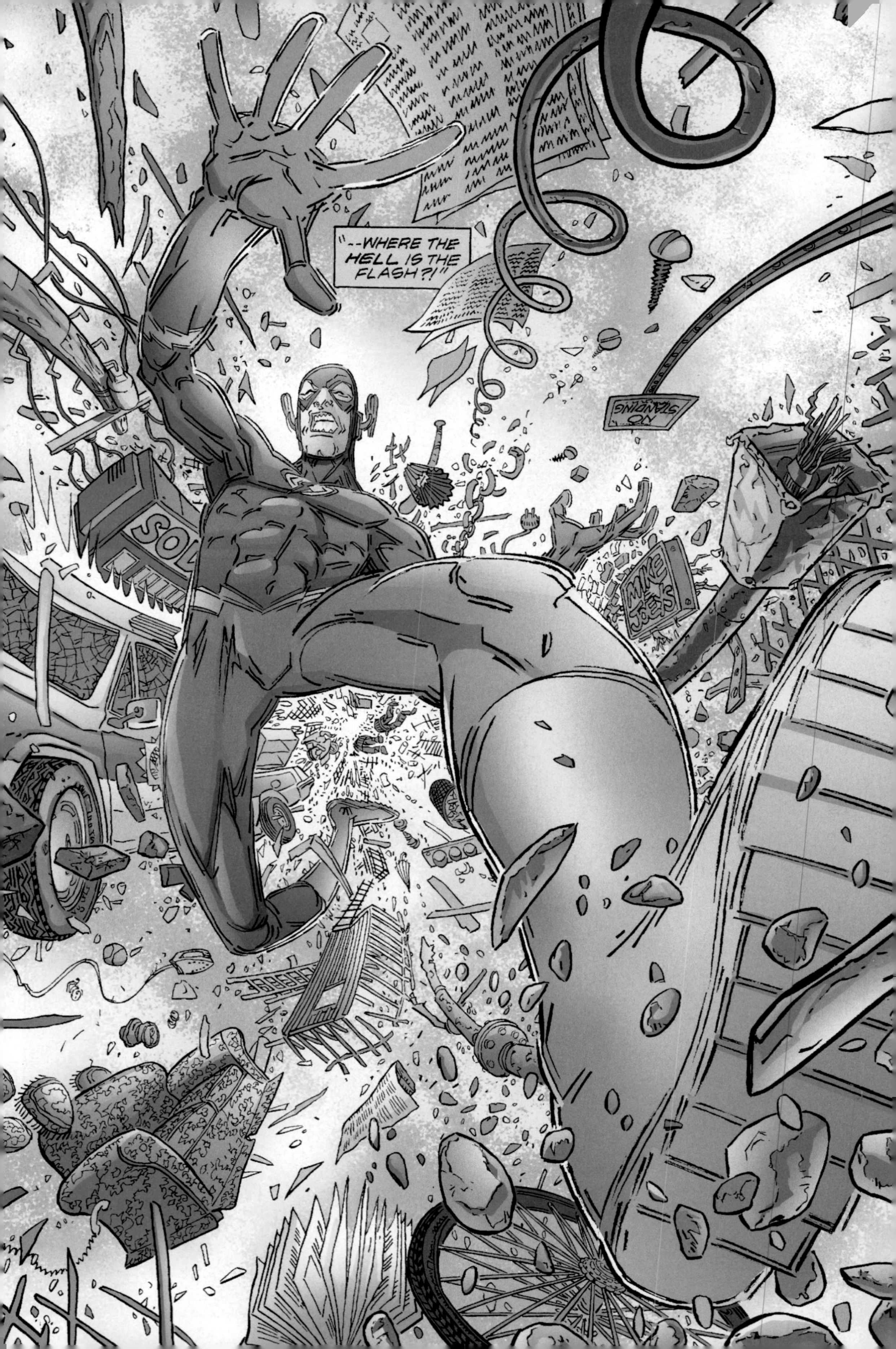
"--WHERE THE HELL IS THE FLASH?!"
NO STANDING
MIKE JOE'S

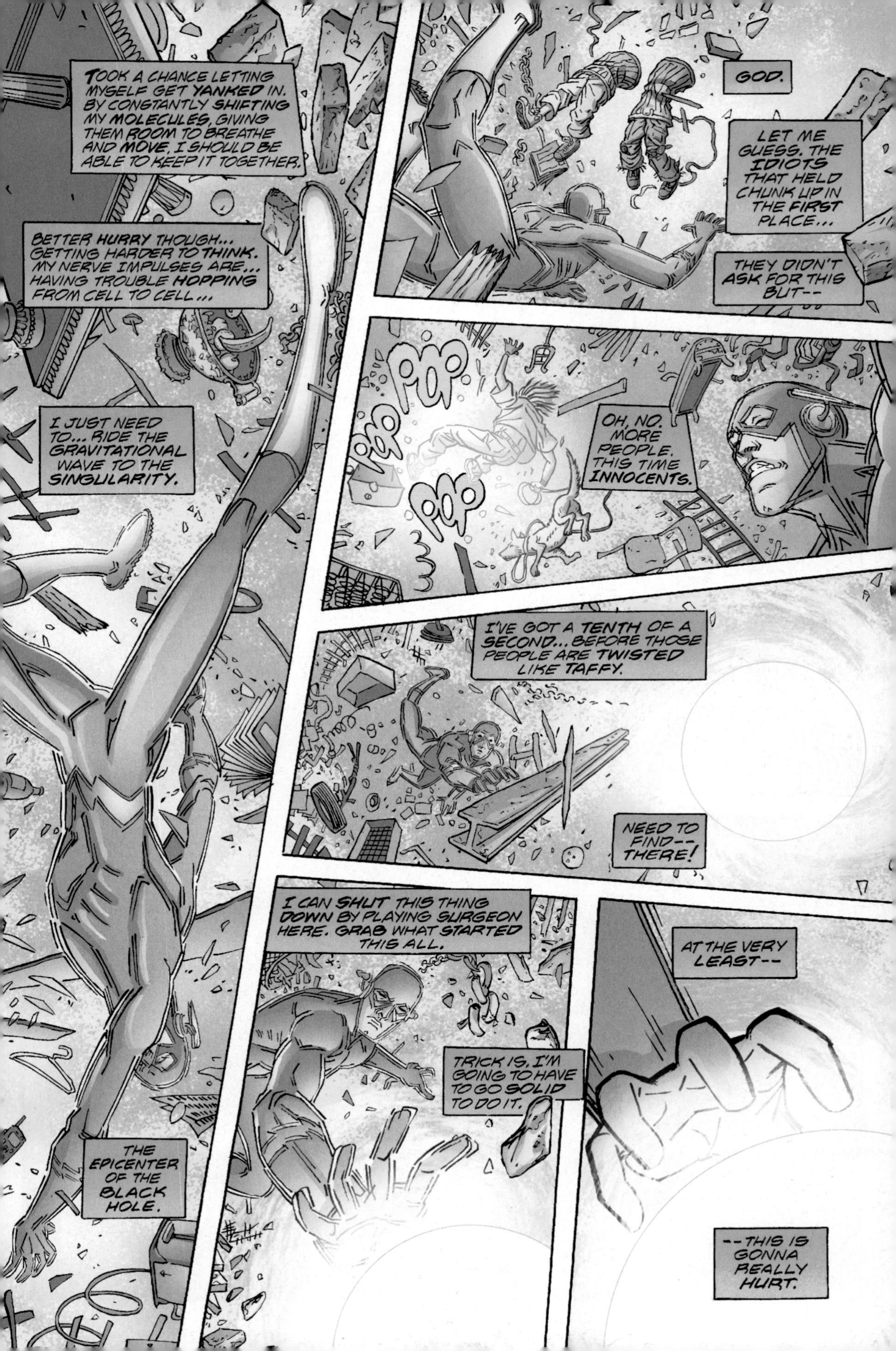
TOOK A CHANCE LETTING MYSELF GET YANKED IN. BY CONSTANTLY SHIFTING MY MOLECULES, GIVING THEM ROOM TO BREATHE AND MOVE, I SHOULD BE ABLE TO KEEP IT TOGETHER.
BETTER HURRY THOUGH... GETTING HARDER TO THINK. MY NERVE IMPULSES ARE... HAVING TROUBLE HOPPING FROM CELL TO CELL...
I JUST NEED TO... RIDE THE GRAVITATIONAL WAVE TO THE SINGULARITY.
THE EPICENTER OF THE BLACK HOLE.
GOD.
LET ME GUESS. THE IDIOTS THAT HELD CHUNK UP IN THE FIRST PLACE...
THEY DIDN'T ASK FOR THIS BUT--
POP POP
POP
POP
OH, NO. MORE PEOPLE. THIS TIME INNOCENTS.
I'VE GOT A TENTH OF A SECOND... BEFORE THOSE PEOPLE ARE TWISTED LIKE TAFFY.
NEED TO FIND-- THERE!
I CAN SHUT THIS THING DOWN BY PLAYING SURGEON HERE. GRAB WHAT STARTED THIS ALL.
TRICK IS, I'M GOING TO HAVE TO GO SOLID TO DO IT.
AT THE VERY LEAST--
--THIS IS GONNA REALLY HURT.

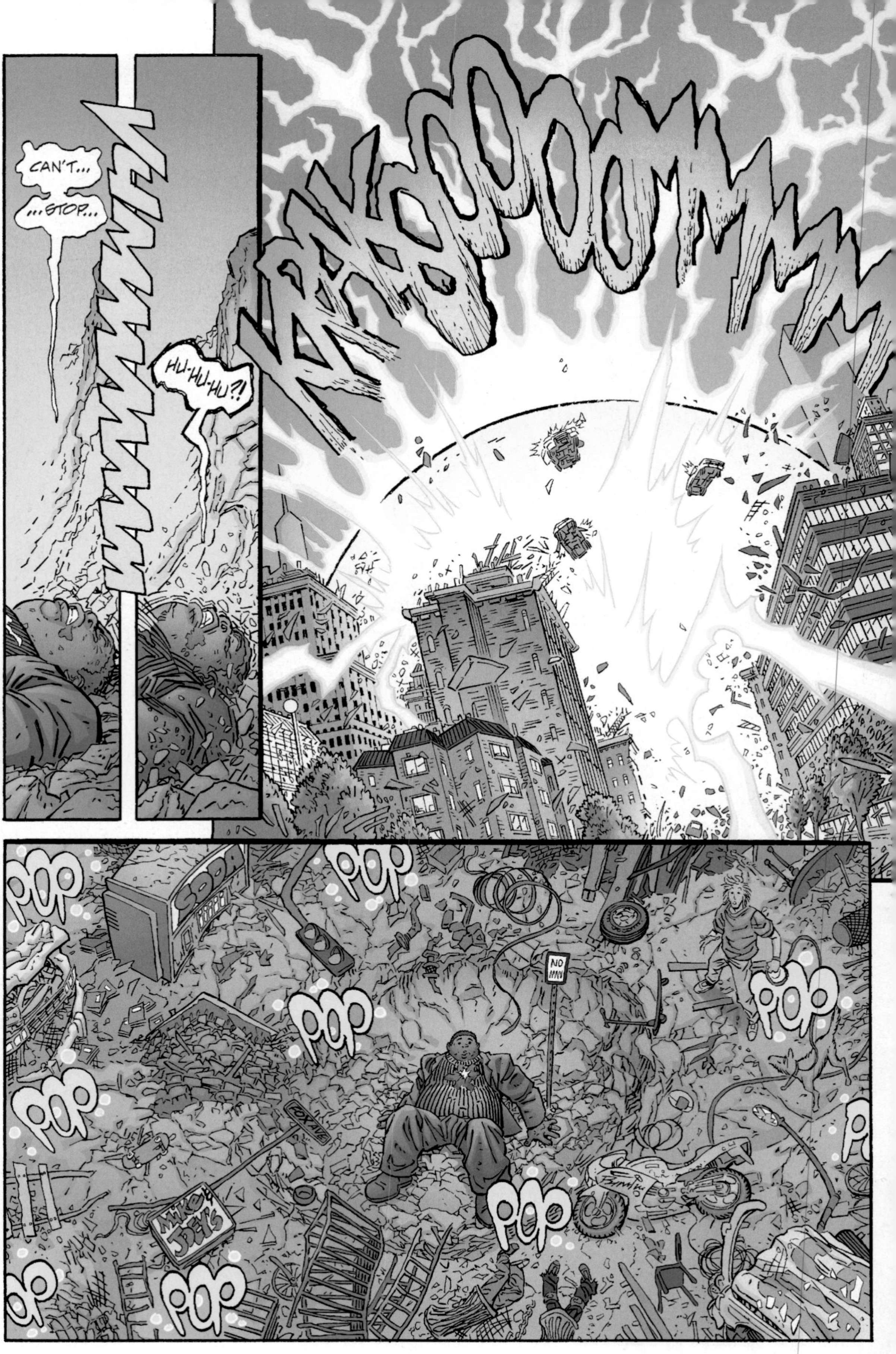
CAN'T...
...STOP...
HU-HU-HU?!
POP
SODA
POP
POP
POP
FOX AVE
MIKE & JOEY'S
POP
POP
POP
POP

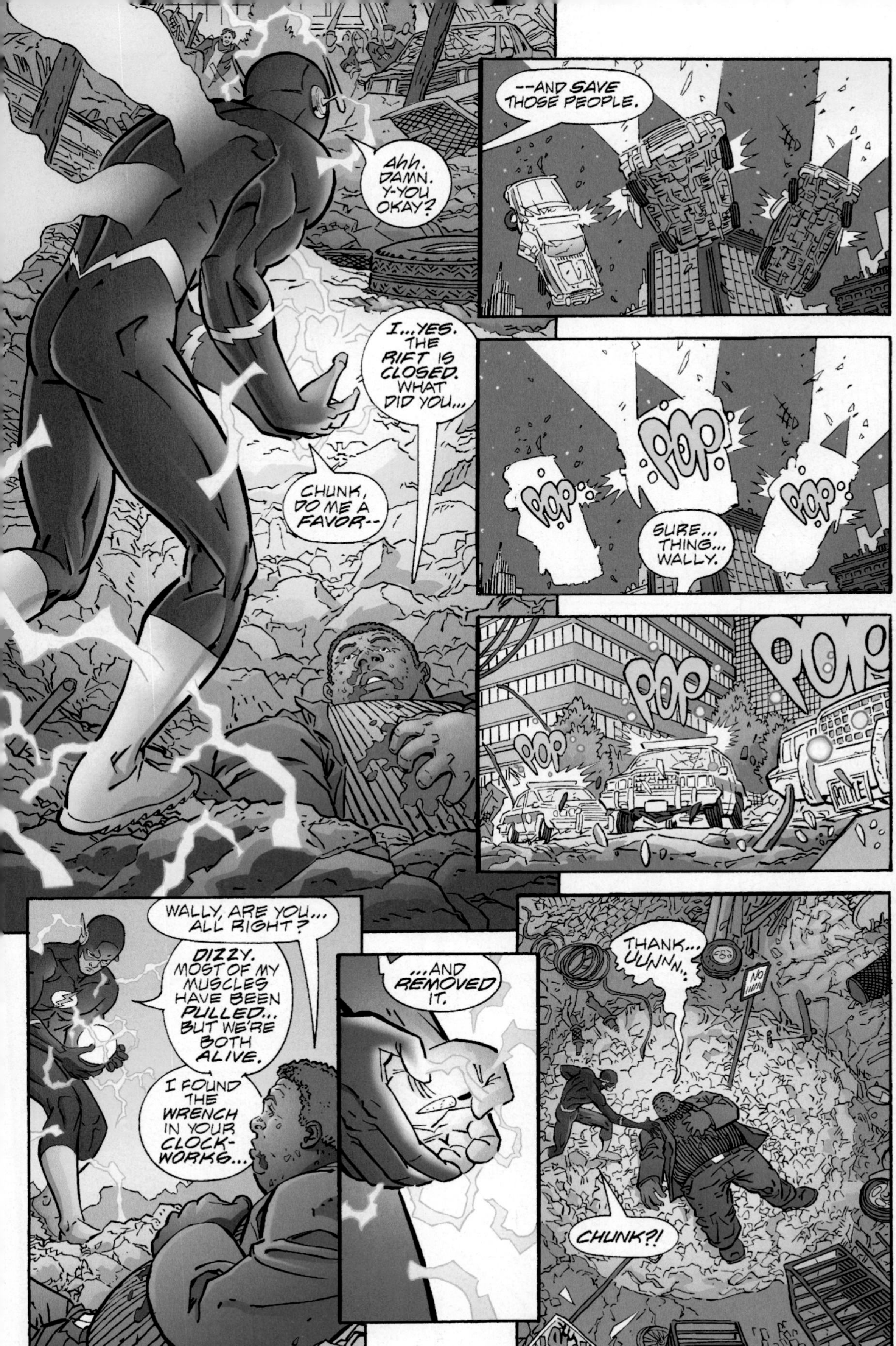
Ahh. DAMN. Y-YOU OKAY?
I...YES. THE RIFT IS CLOSED. WHAT DID YOU...
CHUNK, DO ME A FAVOR--
--AND SAVE THOSE PEOPLE.
POP
POP
POP
SURE... THING... WALLY.
POP
POP
POP
POLICE
WALLY, ARE YOU... ALL RIGHT?
DIZZY. MOST OF MY MUSCLES HAVE BEEN PULLED... BUT WE'RE BOTH ALIVE.
I FOUND THE WRENCH IN YOUR CLOCK-WORKS...
...AND REMOVED IT.
THANK... UUNNN...
NO
CHUNK?!

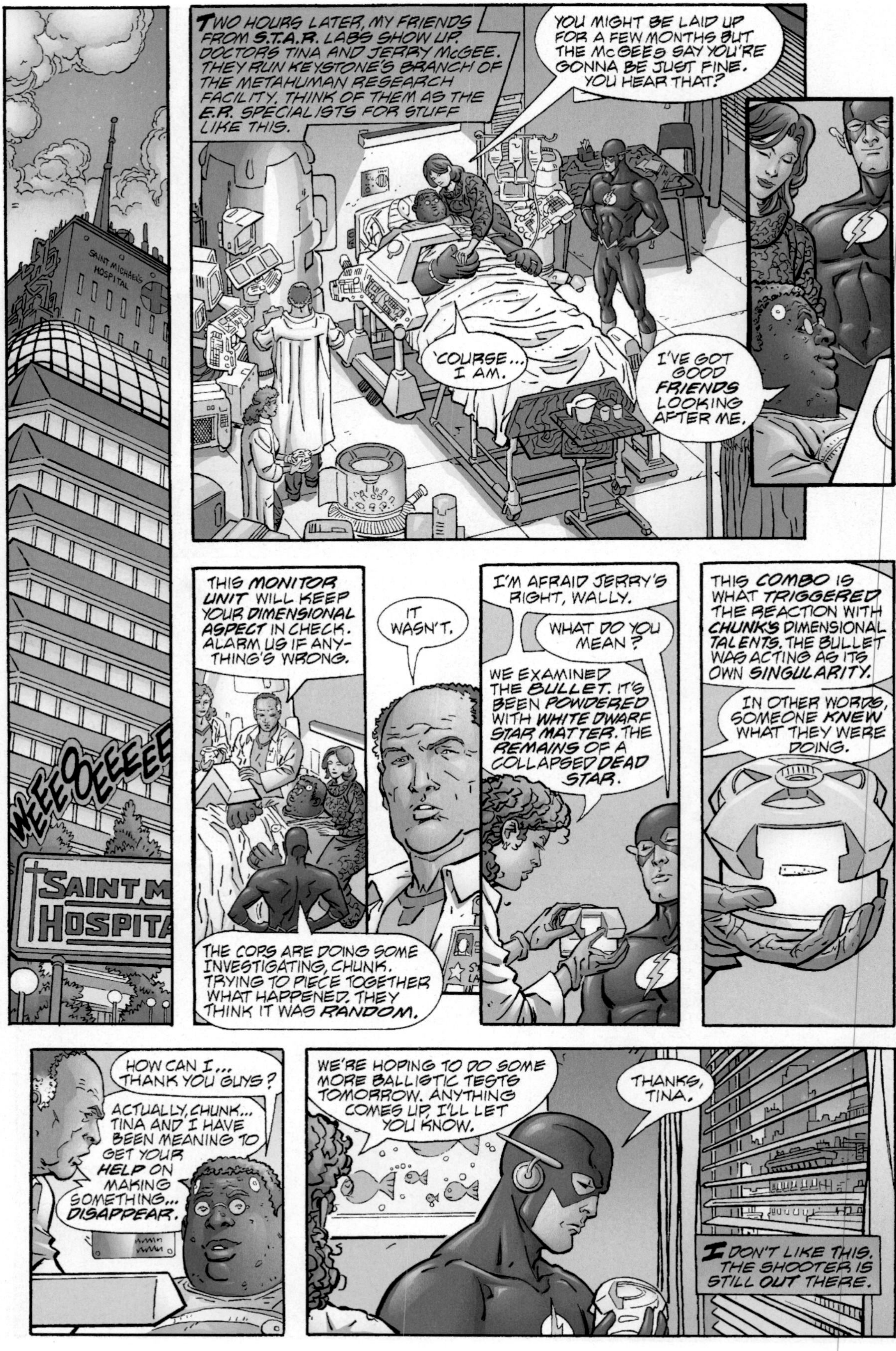

SAINT MICHAEL'S HOSPITAL
WEEEOOEEEEE
SAINT M
HOSPITA
TWO HOURS LATER, MY FRIENDS FROM S.T.A.R. LABS SHOW UP. DOCTORS TINA AND JERRY McGEE. THEY RUN KEYSTONE'S BRANCH OF THE METAHUMAN RESEARCH FACILITY. THINK OF THEM AS THE E.R. SPECIALISTS FOR STUFF LIKE THIS.
YOU MIGHT BE LAID UP FOR A FEW MONTHS BUT THE McGEES SAY YOU'RE GONNA BE JUST FINE. YOU HEAR THAT?
'COURSE... I AM.
I'VE GOT GOOD FRIENDS LOOKING AFTER ME.
THIS MONITOR UNIT WILL KEEP YOUR DIMENSIONAL ASPECT IN CHECK. ALARM US IF ANYTHING'S WRONG.
THE COPS ARE DOING SOME INVESTIGATING, CHUNK. TRYING TO PIECE TOGETHER WHAT HAPPENED. THEY THINK IT WAS RANDOM.
IT WASN'T.
I'M AFRAID JERRY'S RIGHT, WALLY.
WHAT DO YOU MEAN?
WE EXAMINED THE BULLET. IT'S BEEN POWDERED WITH WHITE DWARF STAR MATTER. THE REMAINS OF A COLLAPSED DEAD STAR.
THIS COMBO IS WHAT TRIGGERED THE REACTION WITH CHUNK'S DIMENSIONAL TALENTS. THE BULLET WAS ACTING AS ITS OWN SINGULARITY.
IN OTHER WORDS, SOMEONE KNEW WHAT THEY WERE DOING.
HOW CAN I... THANK YOU GUYS?
ACTUALLY, CHUNK... TINA AND I HAVE BEEN MEANING TO GET YOUR HELP ON MAKING SOMETHING... DISAPPEAR.
WE'RE HOPING TO DO SOME MORE BALLISTIC TESTS TOMORROW. ANYTHING COMES UP, I'LL LET YOU KNOW.
THANKS, TINA.
I DON'T LIKE THIS. THE SHOOTER IS STILL OUT THERE.

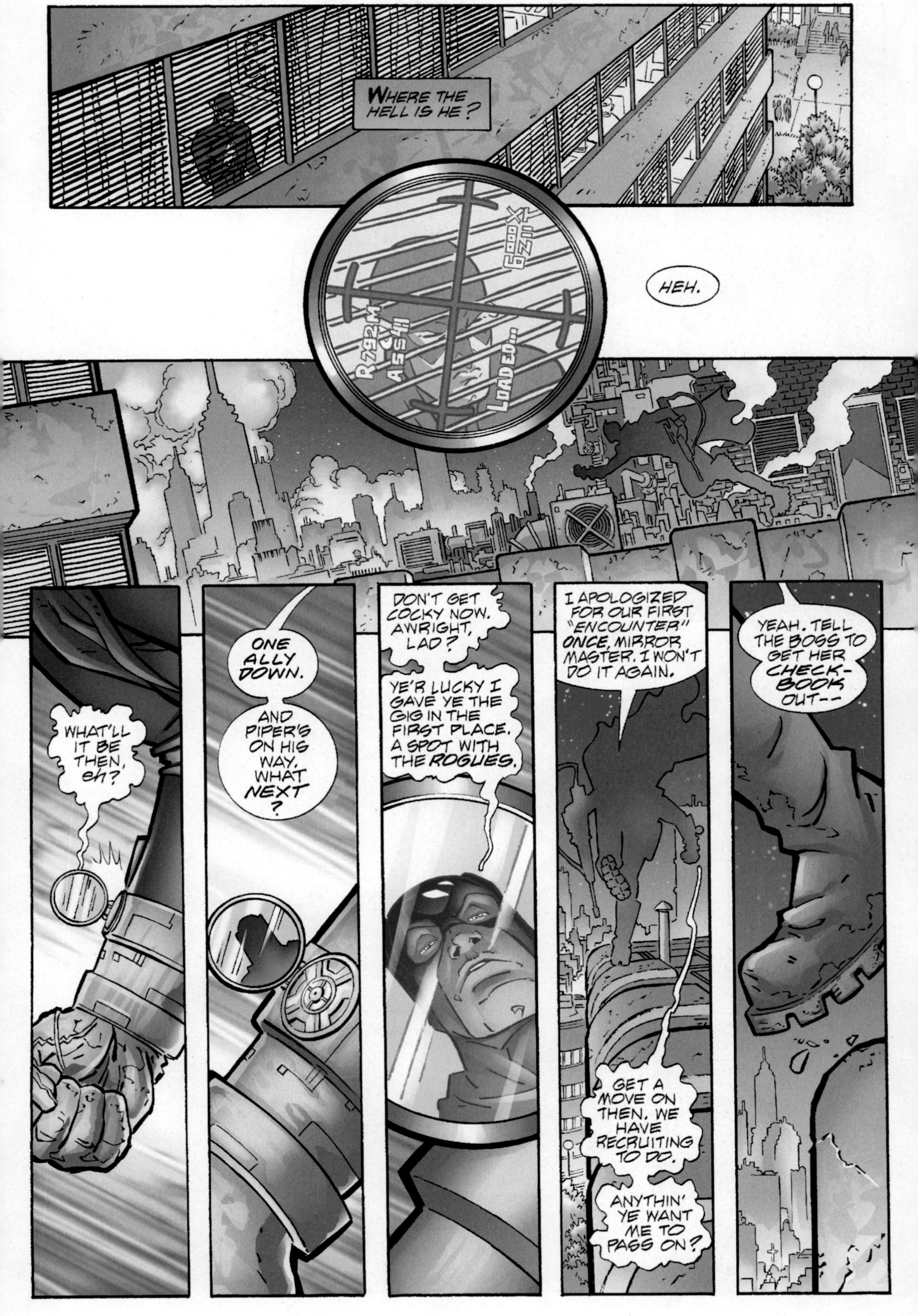
WHERE THE HELL IS HE?
R792M
AS541
LOADED...
6000X
HEH.
WHAT'LL IT BE THEN, eh?
ONE ALLY DOWN.
AND PIPER'S ON HIS WAY. WHAT NEXT?
DON'T GET COCKY NOW. AWRIGHT, LAD?
YE'R LUCKY I GAVE YE THE GIG IN THE FIRST PLACE. A SPOT WITH THE ROGUES.
I APOLOGIZED FOR OUR FIRST "ENCOUNTER" ONCE, MIRROR MASTER. I WON'T DO IT AGAIN.
GET A MOVE ON THEN. WE HAVE RECRUITING TO DO.
ANYTHIN' YE WANT ME TO PASS ON?
YEAH. TELL THE BOSS TO GET HER CHECK-BOOK OUT--

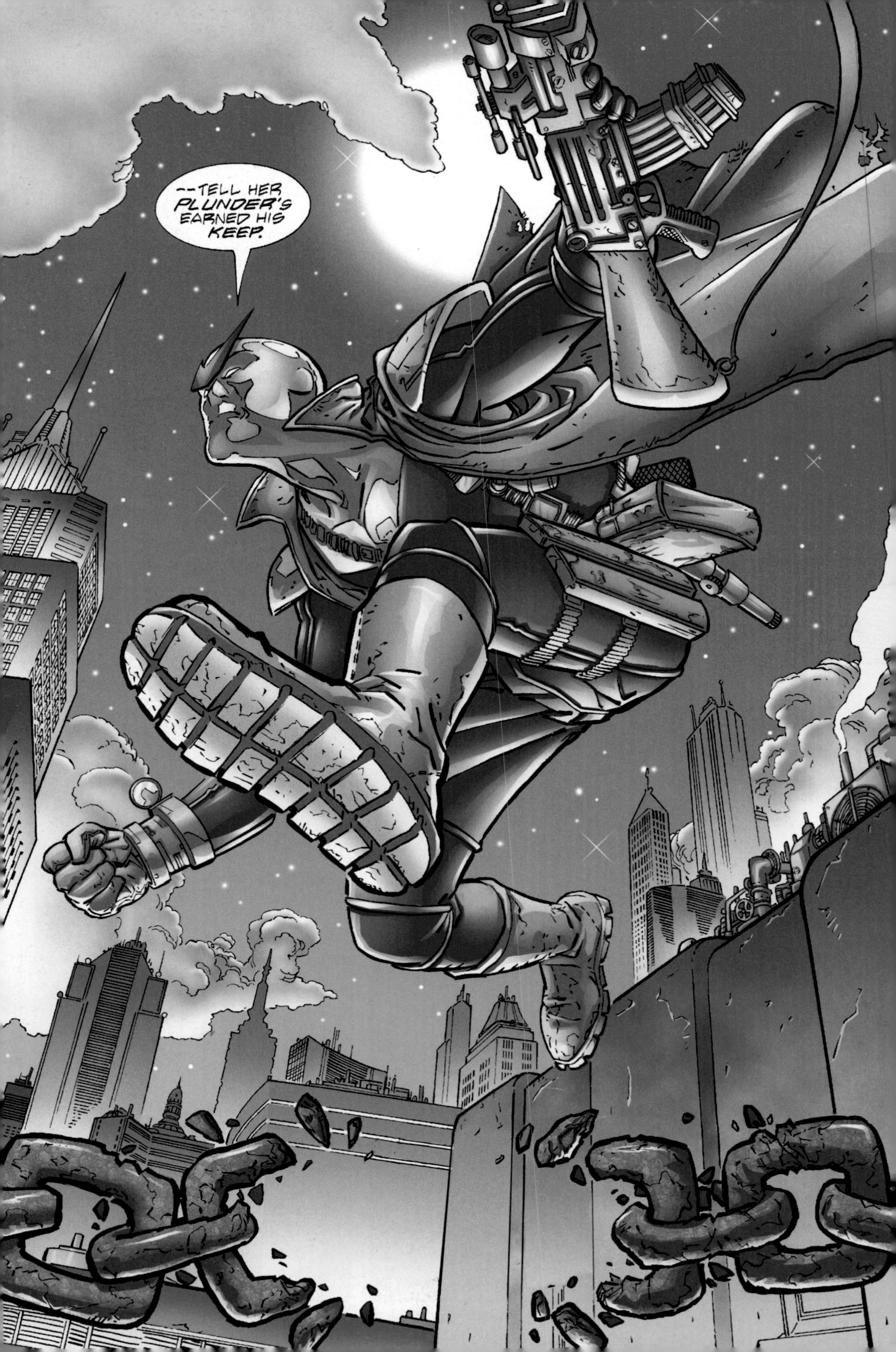
--TELL HER PLUNDER'S EARNED HIS KEEP.

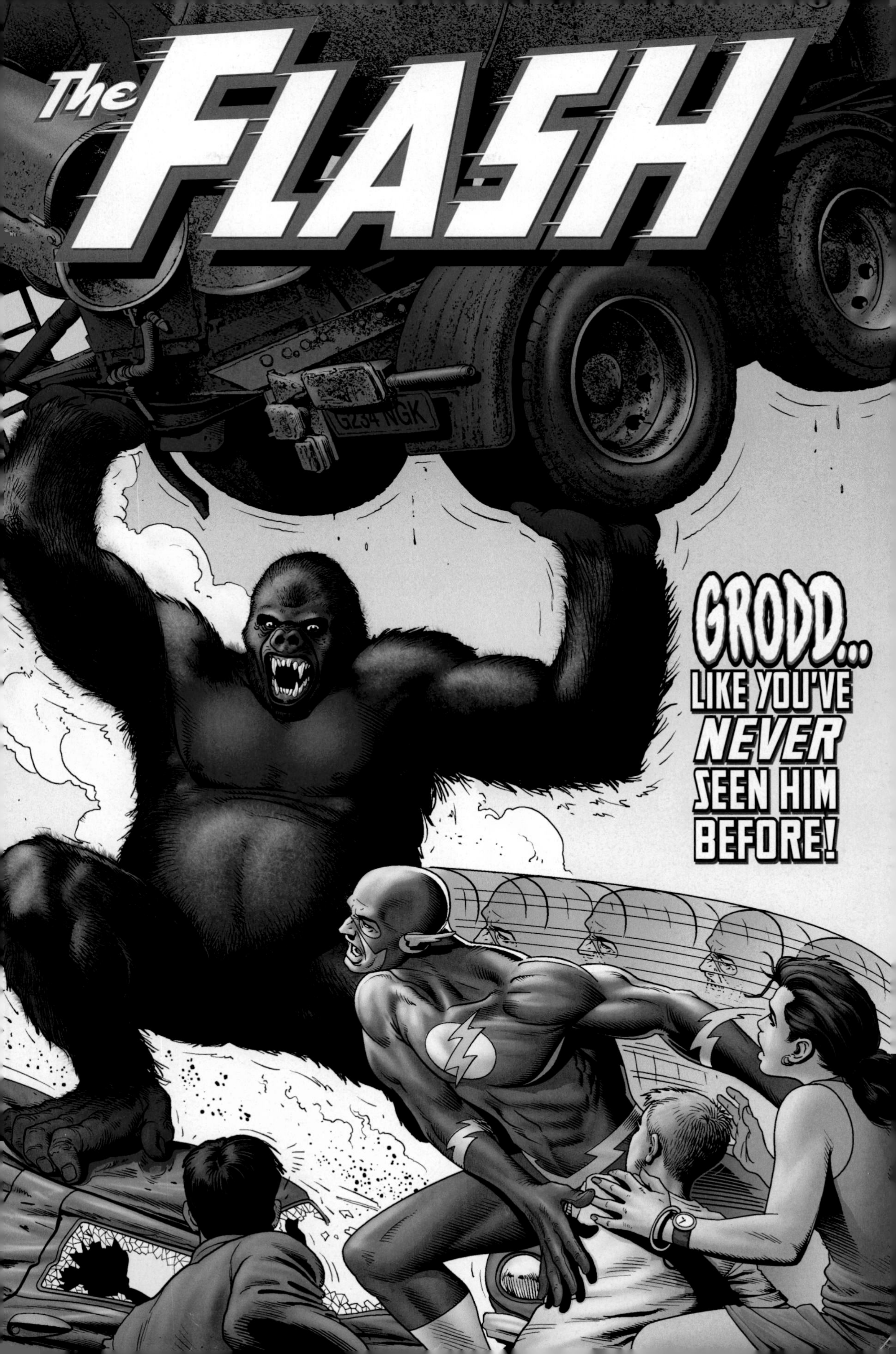
The FLASH
G234 NGK
GRODD... LIKE YOU'VE NEVER SEEN HIM BEFORE!

COVER ART BY ***BRIAN BOLLAND***

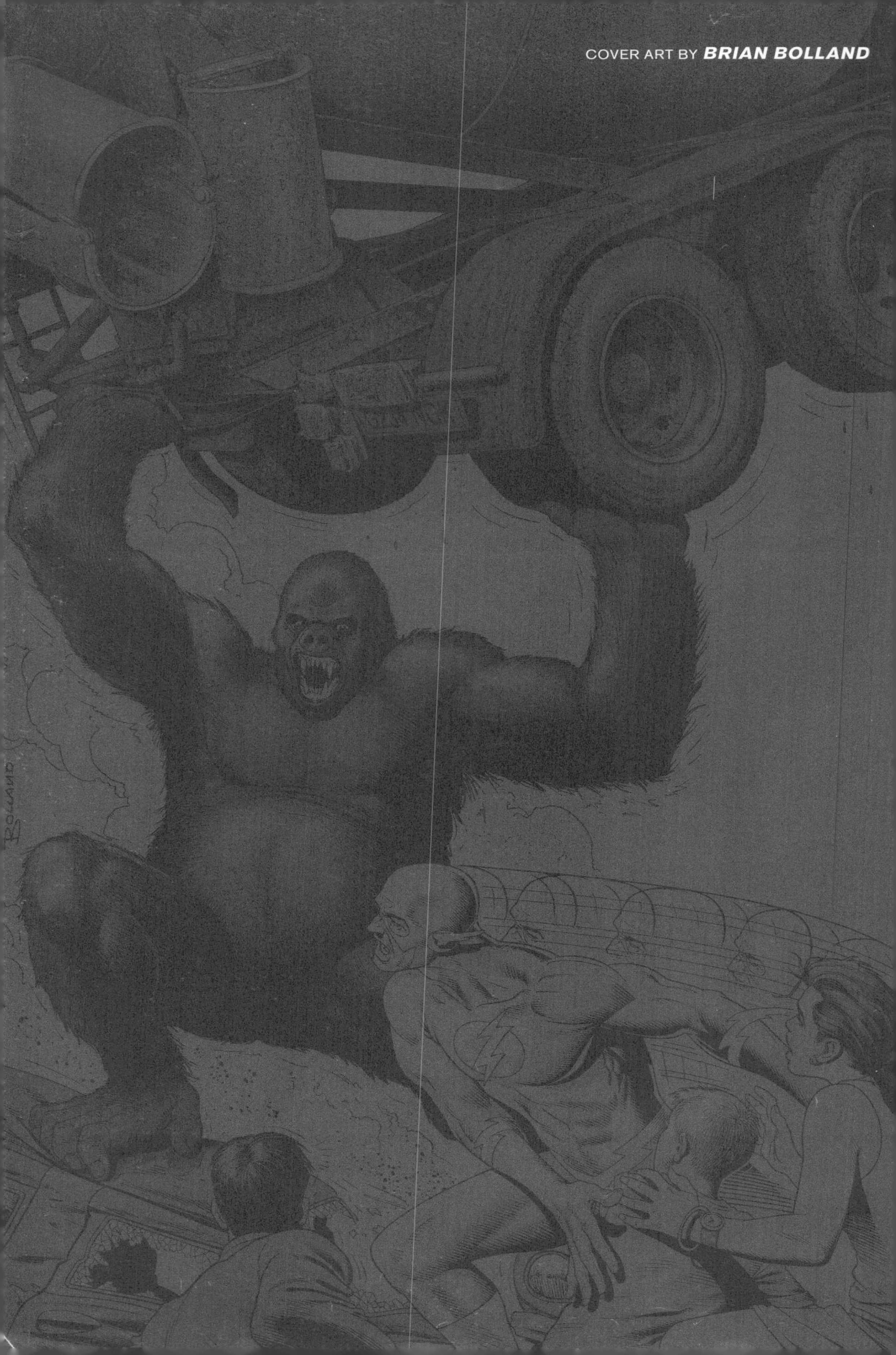
BOLLAND

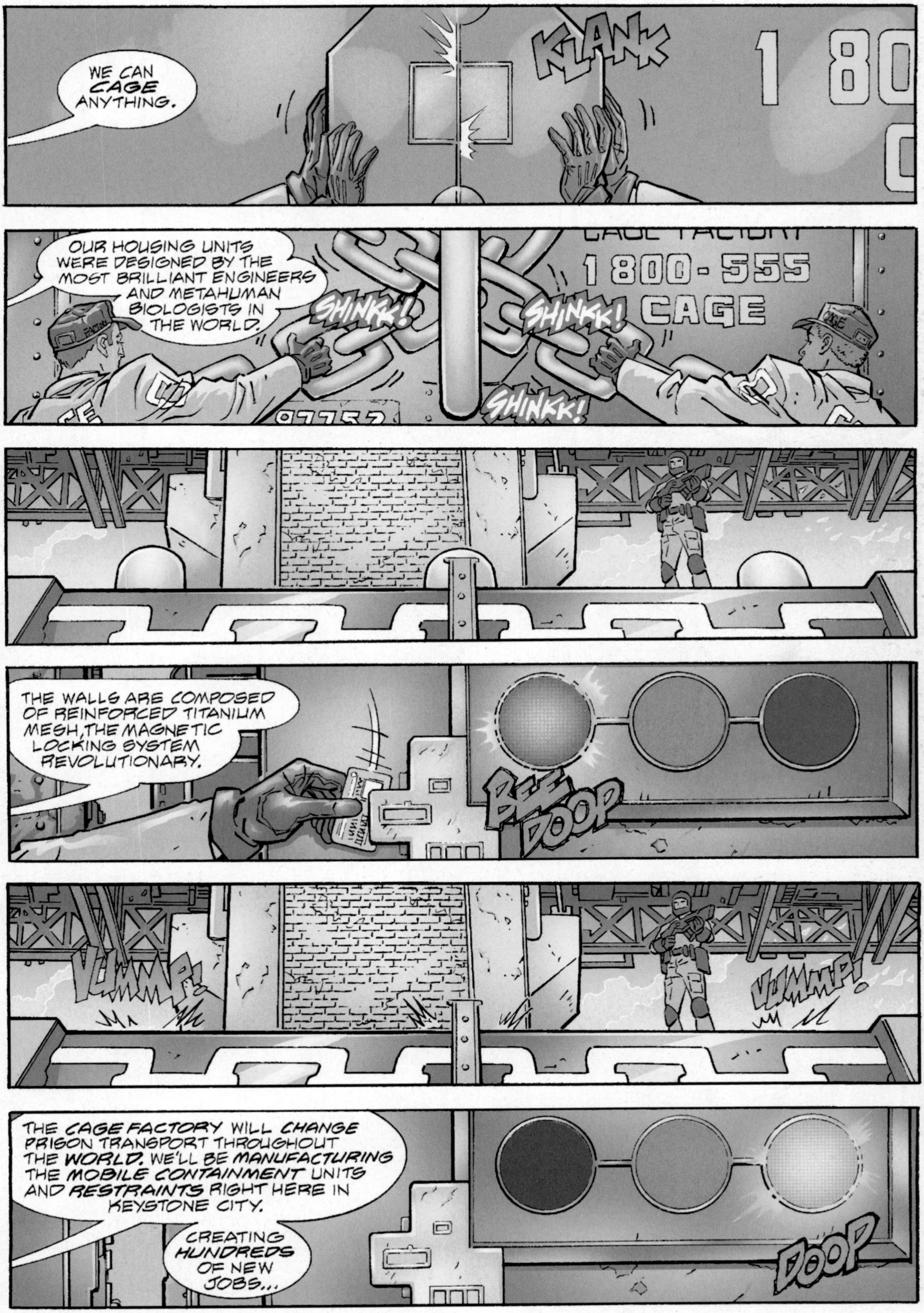
WE CAN CAGE ANYTHING.
KLANK
1 80
OUR HOUSING UNITS WERE DESIGNED BY THE MOST BRILLIANT ENGINEERS AND METAHUMAN BIOLOGISTS IN THE WORLD.
CAGE FACTORY
1 800-555 CAGE
SHINKK!
SHINKK!
SHINKK!
THE WALLS ARE COMPOSED OF REINFORCED TITANIUM MESH, THE MAGNETIC LOCKING SYSTEM REVOLUTIONARY.
BEE DOOP
VUMMP!
VUMMP!
THE CAGE FACTORY WILL CHANGE PRISON TRANSPORT THROUGHOUT THE WORLD. WE'LL BE MANUFACTURING THE MOBILE CONTAINMENT UNITS AND RESTRAINTS RIGHT HERE IN KEYSTONE CITY.
CREATING HUNDREDS OF NEW JOBS...
DOOP

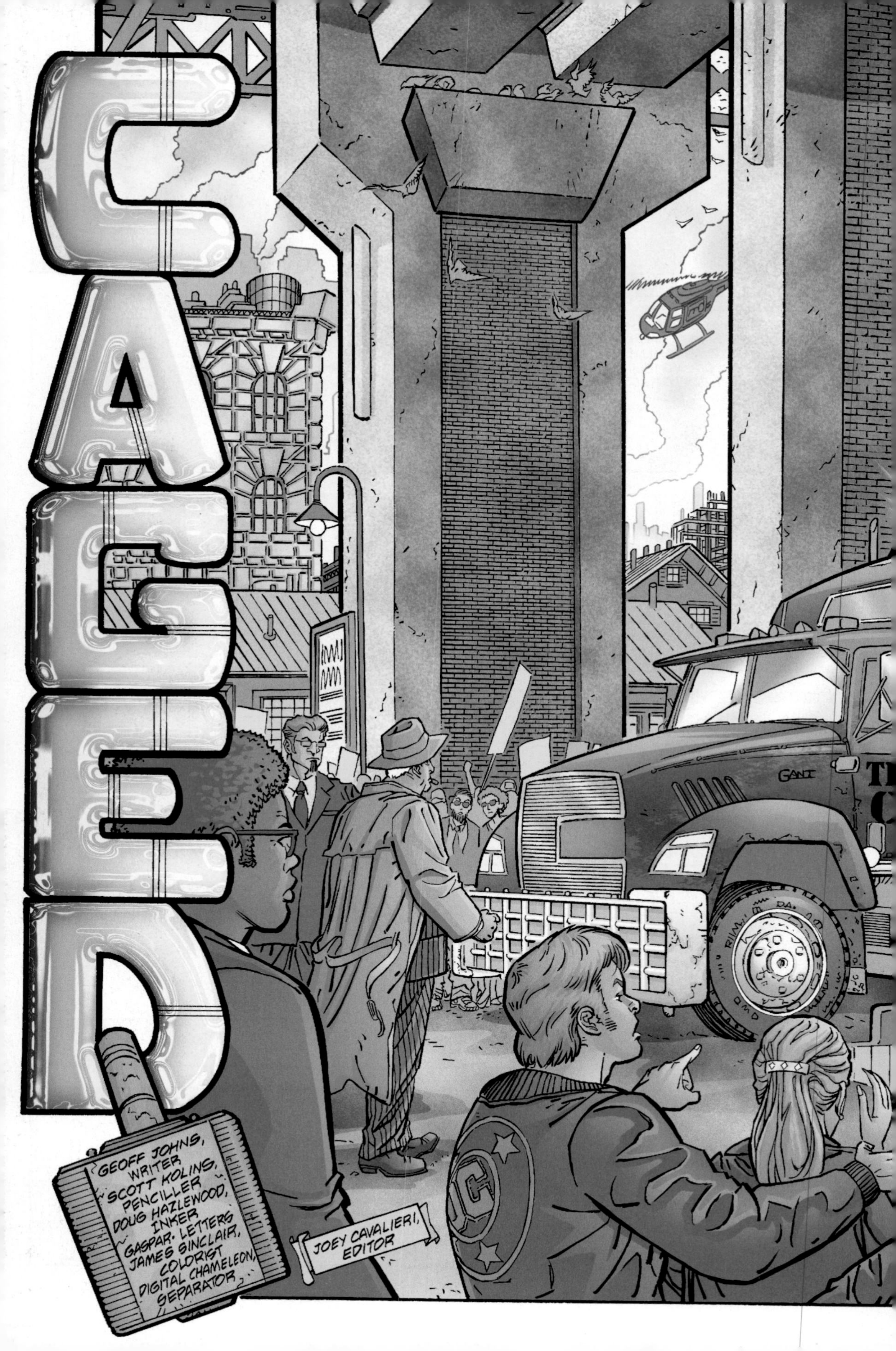
CAGED
GEOFF JOHNS, WRITER
SCOTT KOLINS, PENCILLER
DOUG HAZLEWOOD, INKER
GASPAR. LETTERS
JAMES SINCLAIR, COLORIST
DIGITAL CHAMELEON, SEPARATOR
JOEY CAVALIERI, EDITOR
GANT

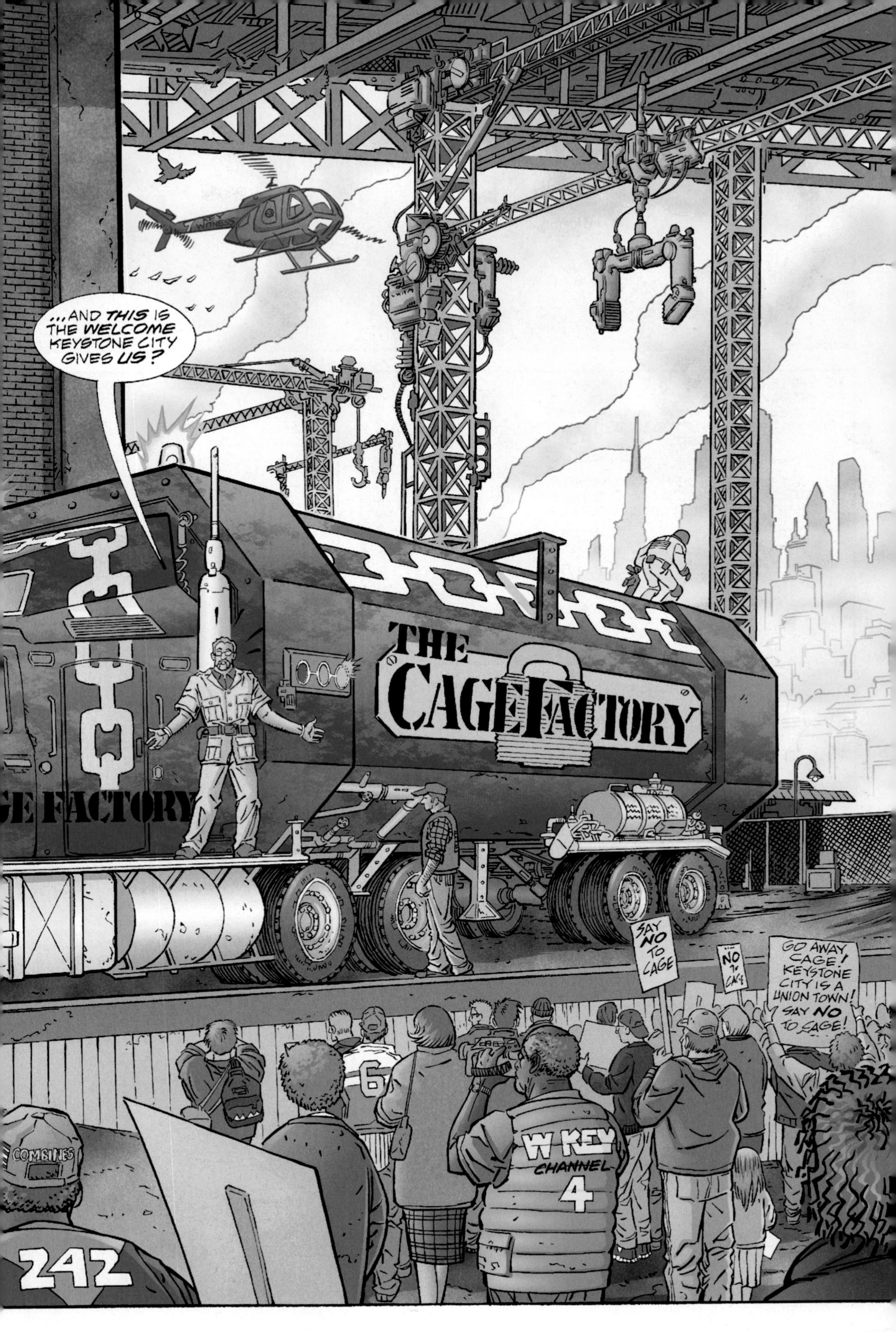

...AND THIS IS THE WELCOME KEYSTONE CITY GIVES US?
KEY WITNESS
THE CAGE FACTORY
GE FACTORY
SAY NO TO CAGE
NO TO CAGE
GO AWAY, CAGE! KEYSTONE CITY IS A UNION TOWN! SAY NO TO CAGE!
COMBINES
W KEY CHANNEL 4

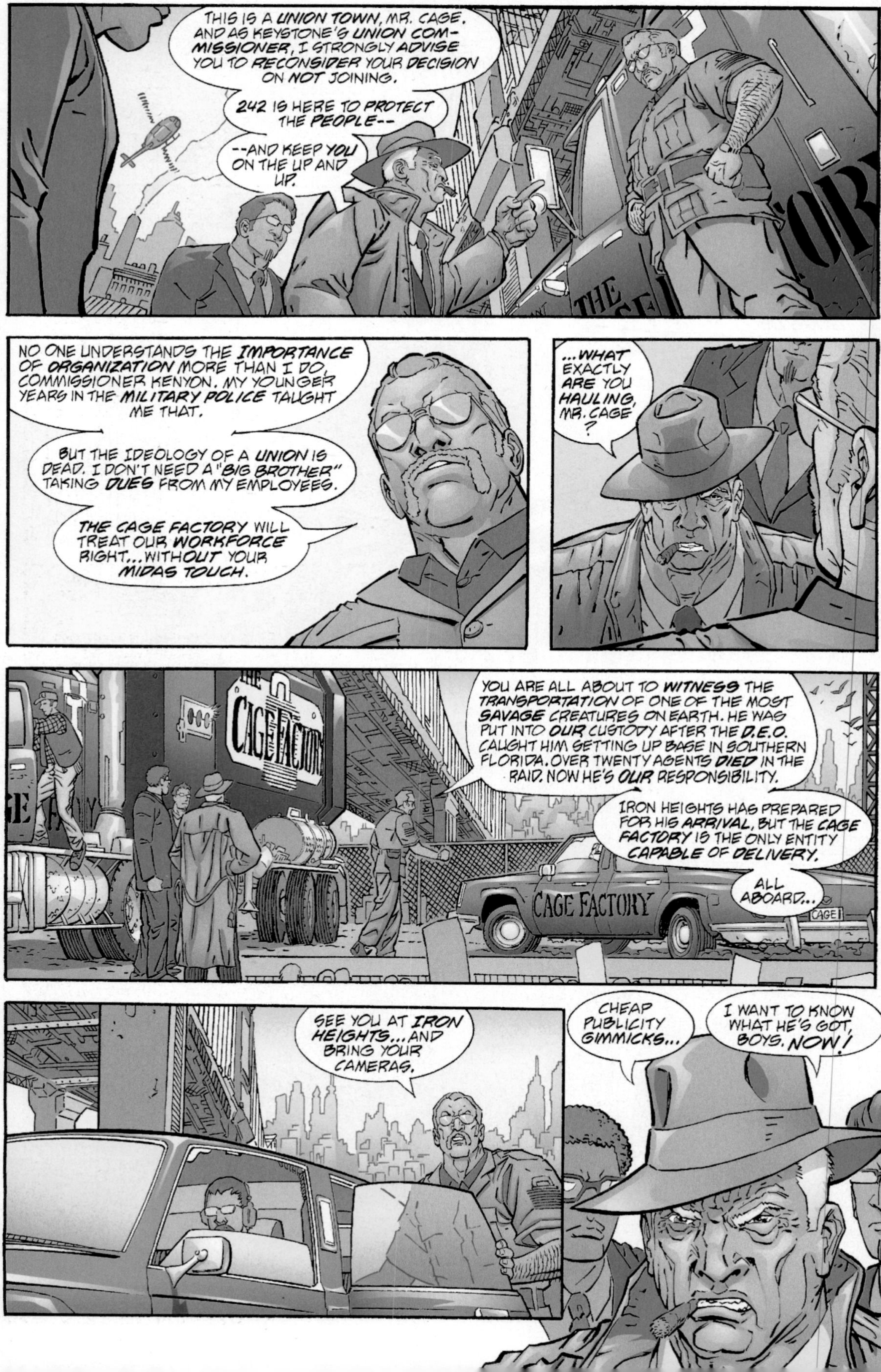
THIS IS A UNION TOWN, MR. CAGE. AND AS KEYSTONE'S UNION COMMISSIONER, I STRONGLY ADVISE YOU TO RECONSIDER YOUR DECISION ON NOT JOINING.
242 IS HERE TO PROTECT THE PEOPLE--
--AND KEEP YOU ON THE UP AND UP.
THE CAGE FACTORY
NO ONE UNDERSTANDS THE IMPORTANCE OF ORGANIZATION MORE THAN I DO, COMMISSIONER KENYON. MY YOUNGER YEARS IN THE MILITARY POLICE TAUGHT ME THAT.
BUT THE IDEOLOGY OF A UNION IS DEAD. I DON'T NEED A "BIG BROTHER" TAKING DUES FROM MY EMPLOYEES.
THE CAGE FACTORY WILL TREAT OUR WORKFORCE RIGHT... WITHOUT YOUR MIDAS TOUCH.
...WHAT EXACTLY ARE YOU HAULING, MR. CAGE?
YOU ARE ALL ABOUT TO WITNESS THE TRANSPORTATION OF ONE OF THE MOST SAVAGE CREATURES ON EARTH. HE WAS PUT INTO OUR CUSTODY AFTER THE D.E.O. CAUGHT HIM SETTING UP BASE IN SOUTHERN FLORIDA. OVER TWENTY AGENTS DIED IN THE RAID. NOW HE'S OUR RESPONSIBILITY.
IRON HEIGHTS HAS PREPARED FOR HIS ARRIVAL, BUT THE CAGE FACTORY IS THE ONLY ENTITY CAPABLE OF DELIVERY.
ALL ABOARD...
THE CAGE FACTORY
CAGE FACTORY
CAGE
SEE YOU AT IRON HEIGHTS... AND BRING YOUR CAMERAS.
CHEAP PUBLICITY GIMMICKS...
I WANT TO KNOW WHAT HE'S GOT, BOYS. NOW!

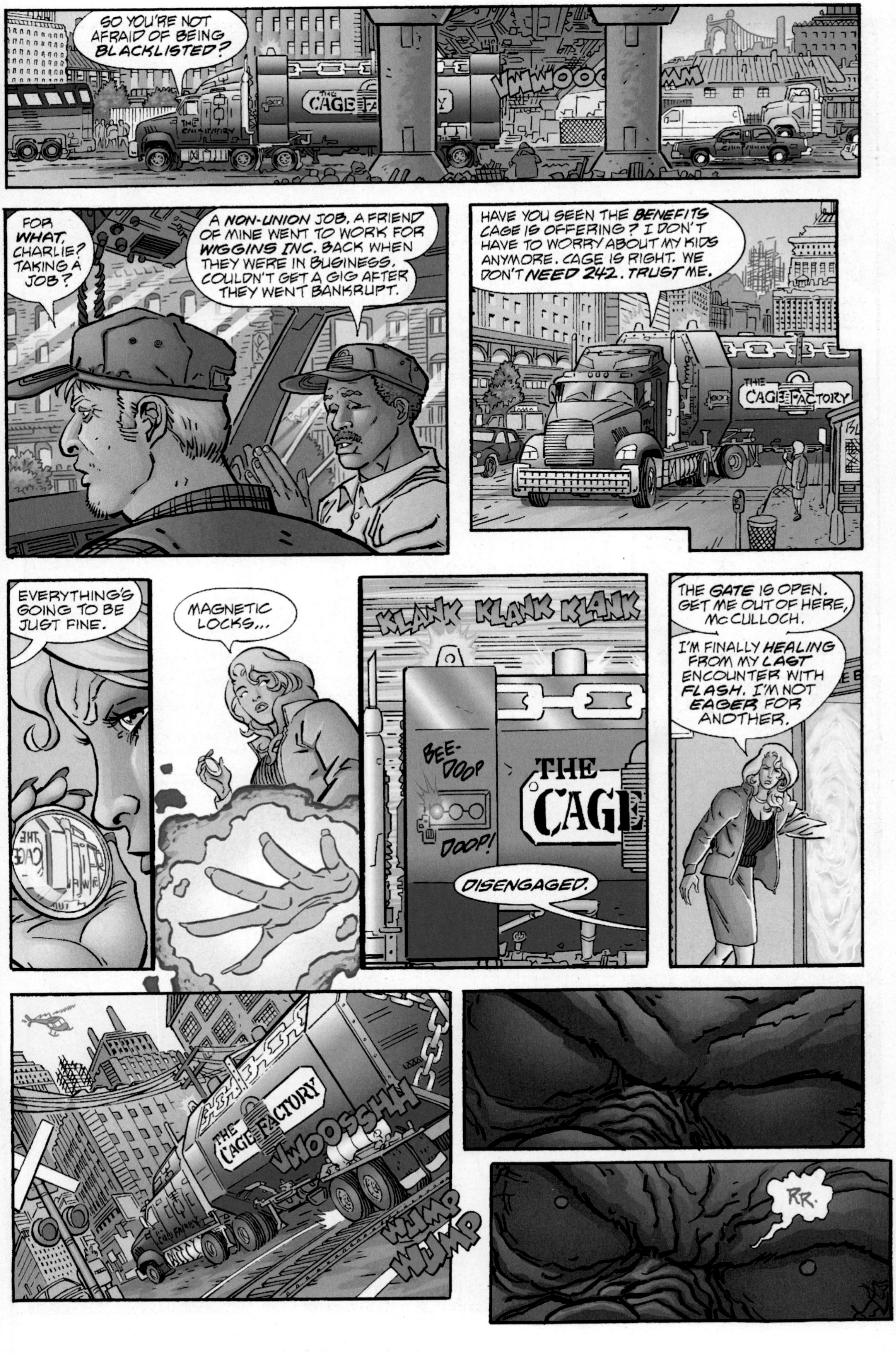
SO YOU'RE NOT AFRAID OF BEING BLACKLISTED?
THE CAGE FACTORY
VWWOOOMM
FOR WHAT, CHARLIE? TAKING A JOB?
A NON-UNION JOB. A FRIEND OF MINE WENT TO WORK FOR WIGGINS INC. BACK WHEN THEY WERE IN BUSINESS. COULDN'T GET A GIG AFTER THEY WENT BANKRUPT.
HAVE YOU SEEN THE BENEFITS CAGE IS OFFERING? I DON'T HAVE TO WORRY ABOUT MY KIDS ANYMORE. CAGE IS RIGHT. WE DON'T NEED 242. TRUST ME.
THE CAGE FACTORY
EVERYTHING'S GOING TO BE JUST FINE.
MAGNETIC LOCKS...
KLANK KLANK KLANK
BEE-DOOP
DOOP!
THE CAGE
DISENGAGED.
THE GATE IS OPEN. GET ME OUT OF HERE, McCULLOCH.
I'M FINALLY HEALING FROM MY LAST ENCOUNTER WITH FLASH. I'M NOT EAGER FOR ANOTHER.
THE CAGE FACTORY
WOOSSHH
WUMP WUMP
RR.

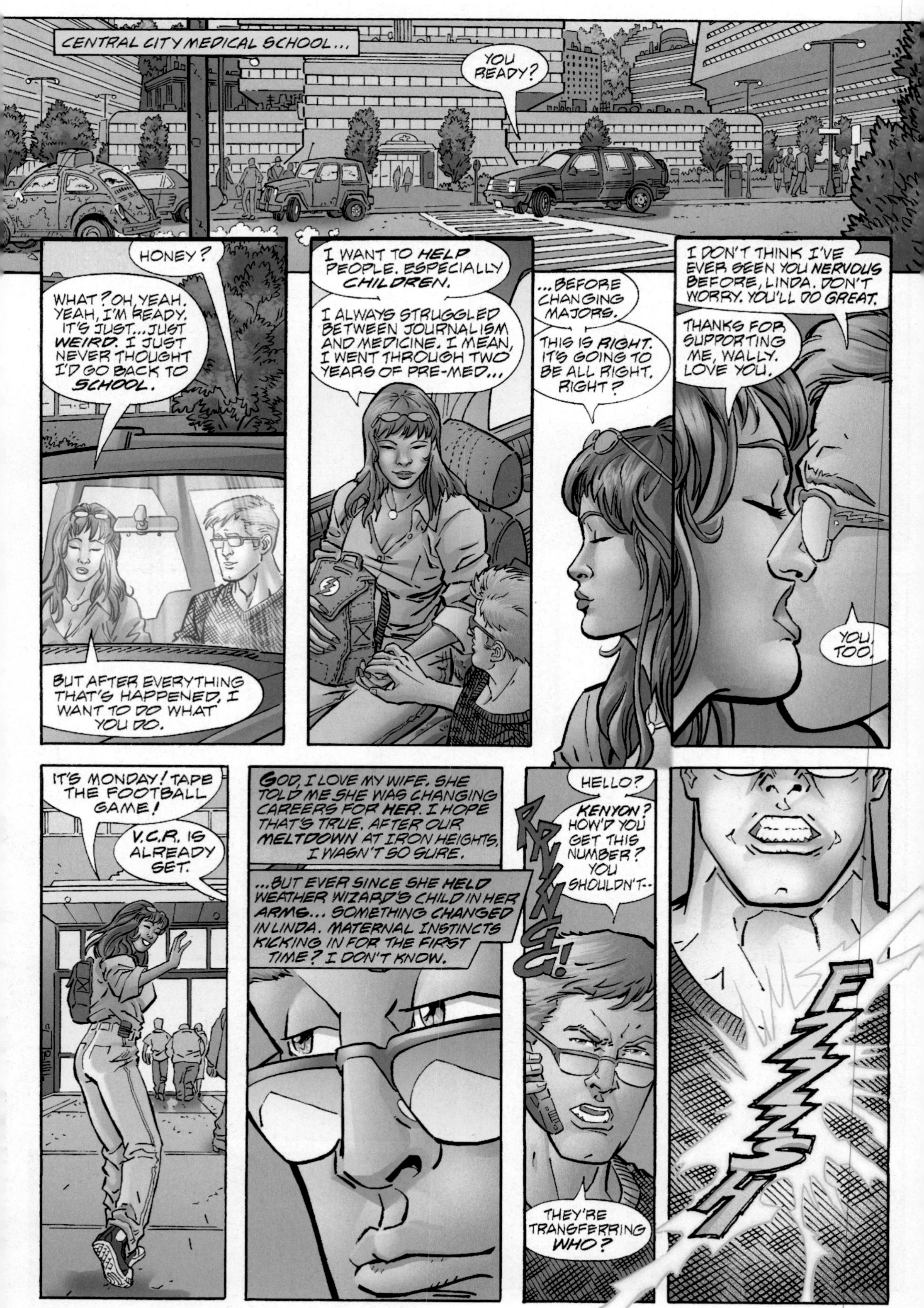

CENTRAL CITY MEDICAL SCHOOL...
YOU READY?
HONEY?
WHAT? OH, YEAH. YEAH, I'M READY. IT'S JUST... JUST WEIRD. I JUST NEVER THOUGHT I'D GO BACK TO SCHOOL.
BUT AFTER EVERYTHING THAT'S HAPPENED, I WANT TO DO WHAT YOU DO.
I WANT TO HELP PEOPLE. ESPECIALLY CHILDREN.
I ALWAYS STRUGGLED BETWEEN JOURNALISM AND MEDICINE. I MEAN, I WENT THROUGH TWO YEARS OF PRE-MED...
...BEFORE CHANGING MAJORS.
THIS IS RIGHT. IT'S GOING TO BE ALL RIGHT. RIGHT?
I DON'T THINK I'VE EVER SEEN YOU NERVOUS BEFORE, LINDA. DON'T WORRY. YOU'LL DO GREAT.
THANKS FOR SUPPORTING ME, WALLY. LOVE YOU.
YOU, TOO.
IT'S MONDAY! TAPE THE FOOTBALL GAME!
V.C.R. IS ALREADY SET.
GOD, I LOVE MY WIFE. SHE TOLD ME SHE WAS CHANGING CAREERS FOR HER. I HOPE THAT'S TRUE. AFTER OUR MELTDOWN AT IRON HEIGHTS, I WASN'T SO SURE.
...BUT EVER SINCE SHE HELD WEATHER WIZARD'S CHILD IN HER ARMS... SOMETHING CHANGED IN LINDA. MATERNAL INSTINCTS KICKING IN FOR THE FIRST TIME? I DON'T KNOW.
RRRING!
HELLO?
KENYON? HOW'D YOU GET THIS NUMBER? YOU SHOULDN'T--
THEY'RE TRANSFERRING WHO?
FZZMMSH

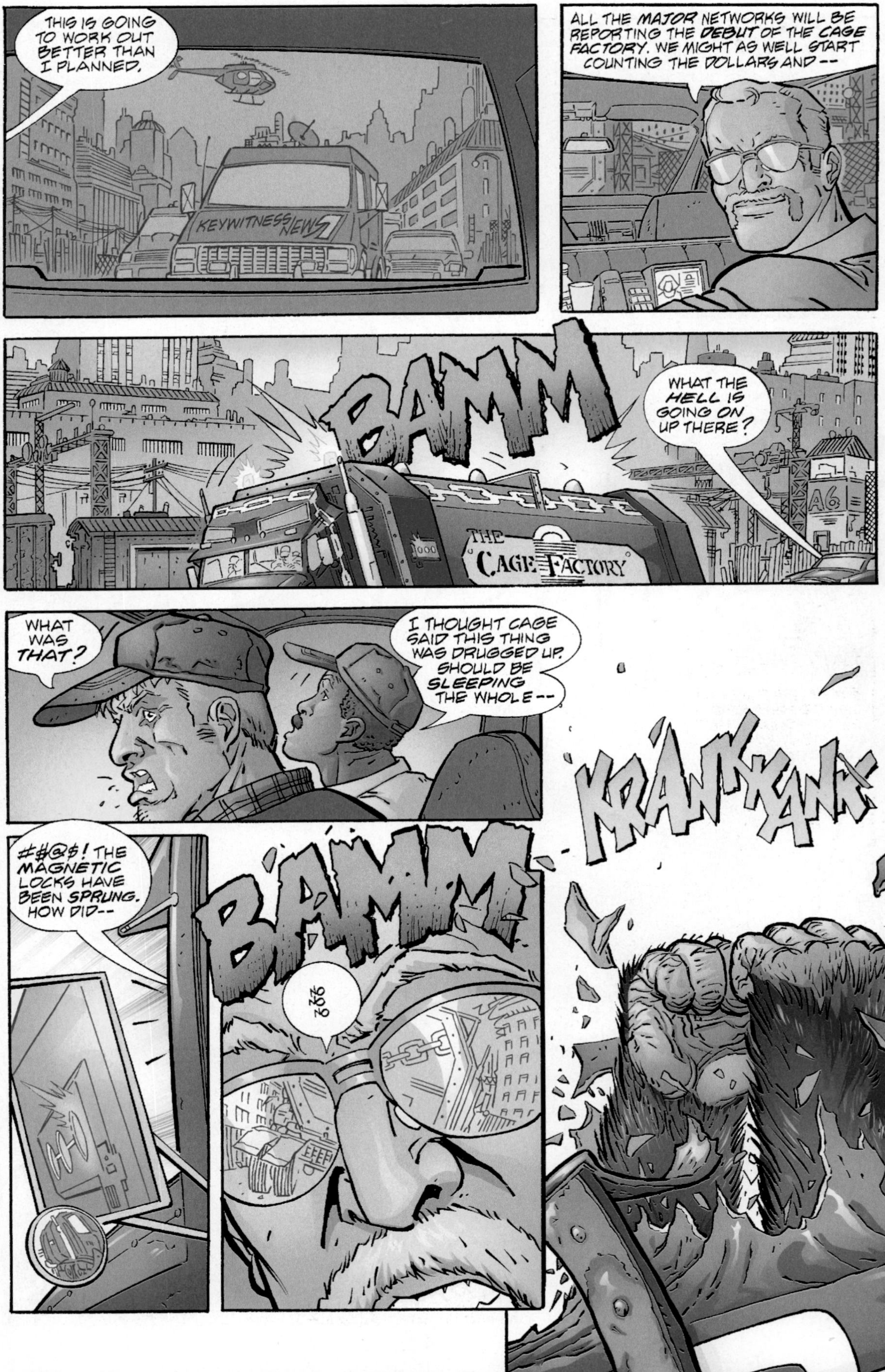
THIS IS GOING TO WORK OUT BETTER THAN I PLANNED.
KEYWITNESS NEWS 7
ALL THE MAJOR NETWORKS WILL BE REPORTING THE DEBUT OF THE CAGE FACTORY. WE MIGHT AS WELL START COUNTING THE DOLLARS AND --
BAMM
WHAT THE HELL IS GOING ON UP THERE?
THE CAGE FACTORY
A6
WHAT WAS THAT?
I THOUGHT CAGE SAID THIS THING WAS DRUGGED UP. SHOULD BE SLEEPING THE WHOLE --
KRANKKANK
#$@$! THE MAGNETIC LOCKS HAVE BEEN SPRUNG. HOW DID--
BAMM
NO NO NO

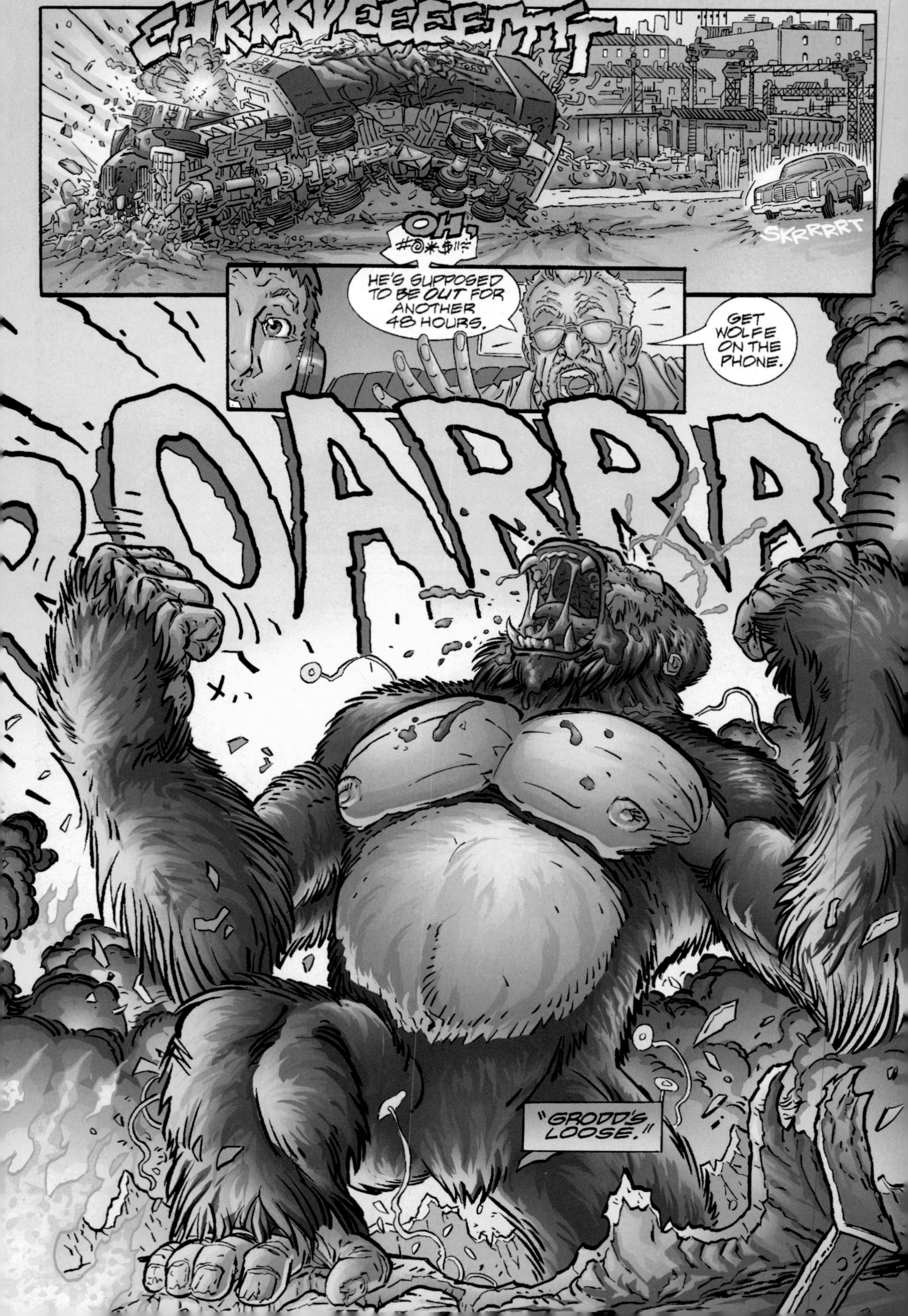
CHKKKVEEEEMMT
OH, #@*$!!
SKRRRRT
HE'S SUPPOSED TO BE OUT FOR ANOTHER 48 HOURS.
GET WOLFE ON THE PHONE.
OARR
"GRODD'S LOOSE."

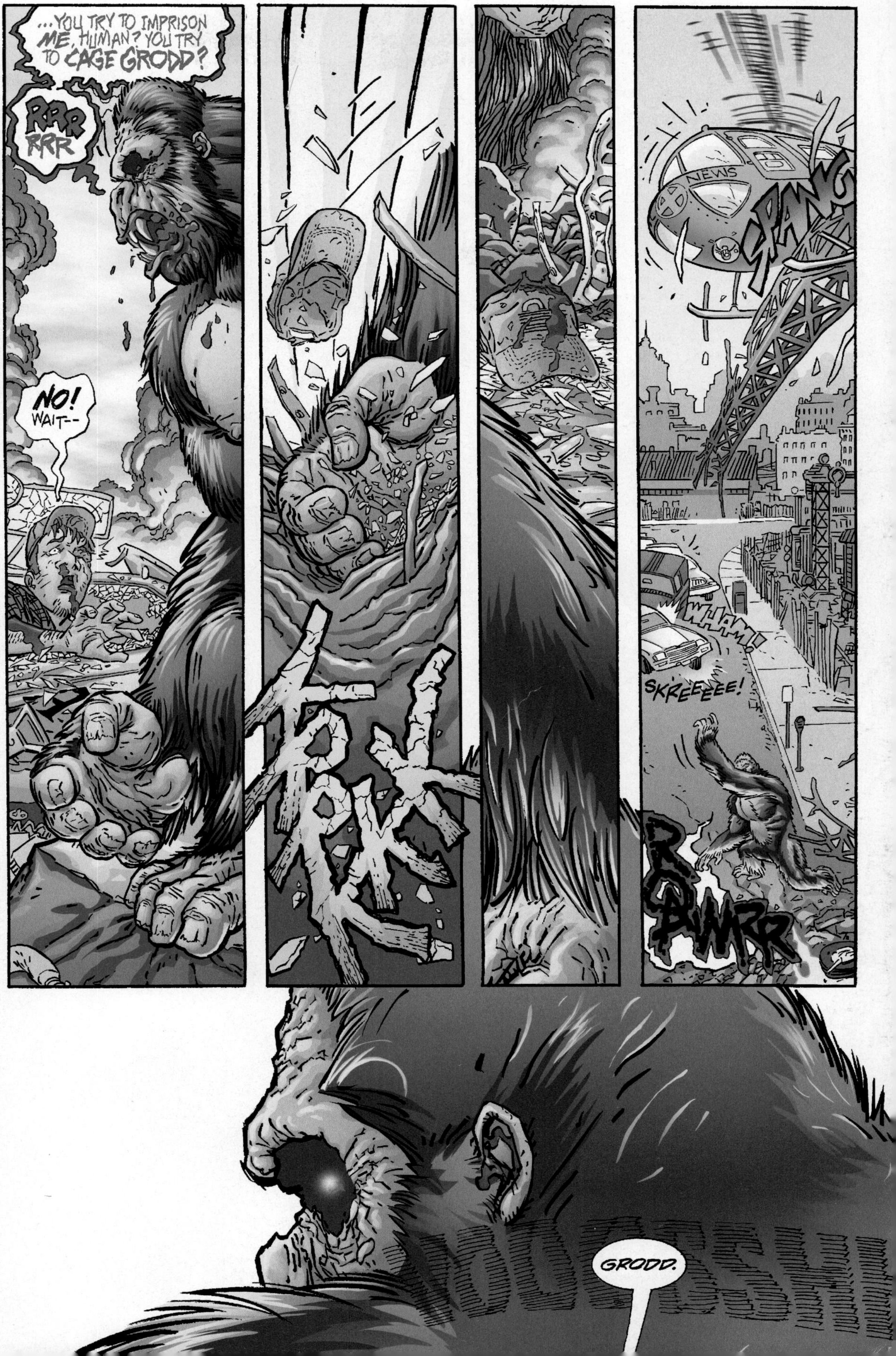
...YOU TRY TO IMPRISON ME, HUMAN? YOU TRY TO CAGE GRODD?
RRR RRR
NO! WAIT--
NEWS
SPANG
WHAM!
SKREEEEEE!
GROOSH
GRODD.

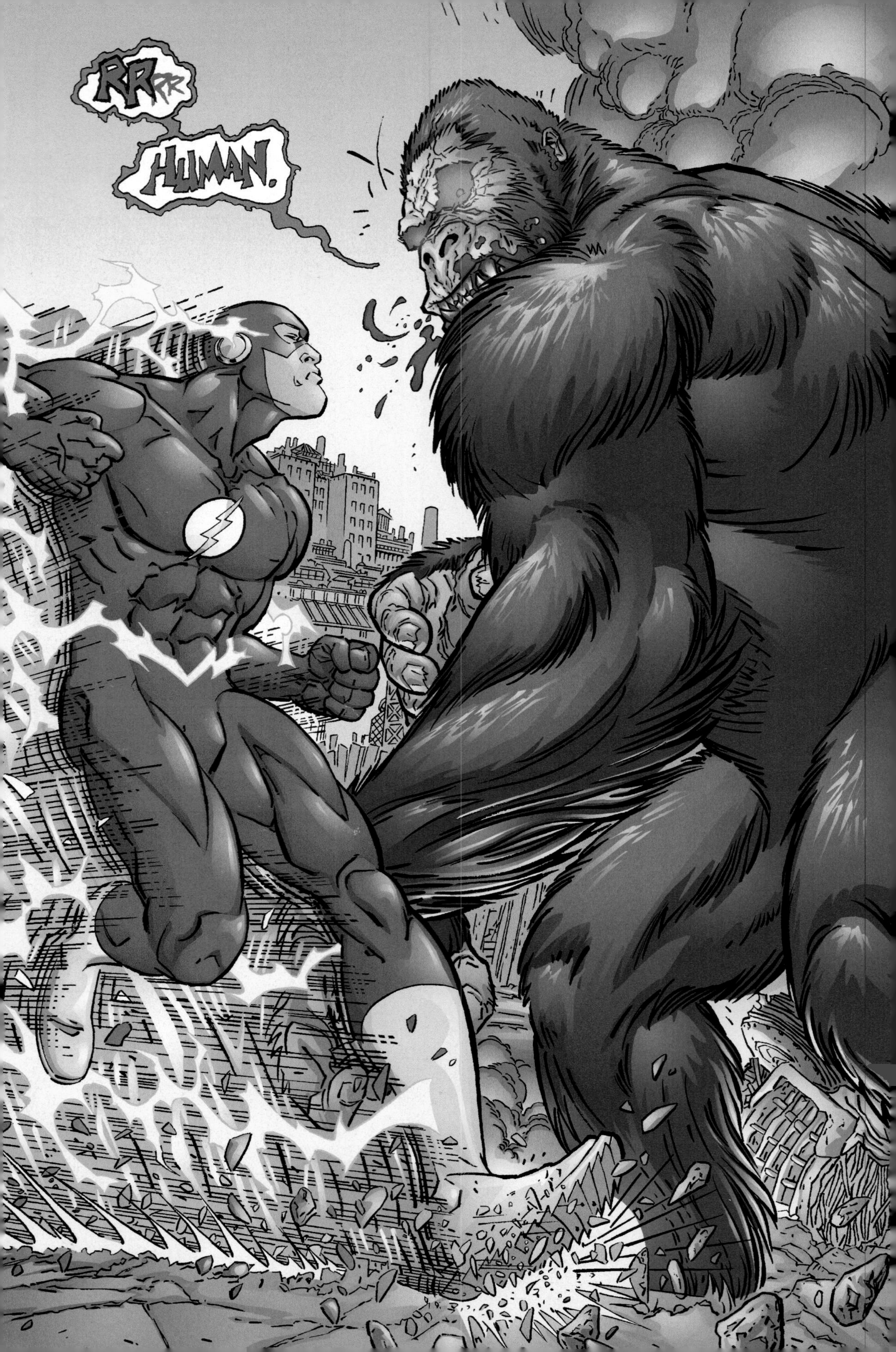
RRrrr
HUMAN.

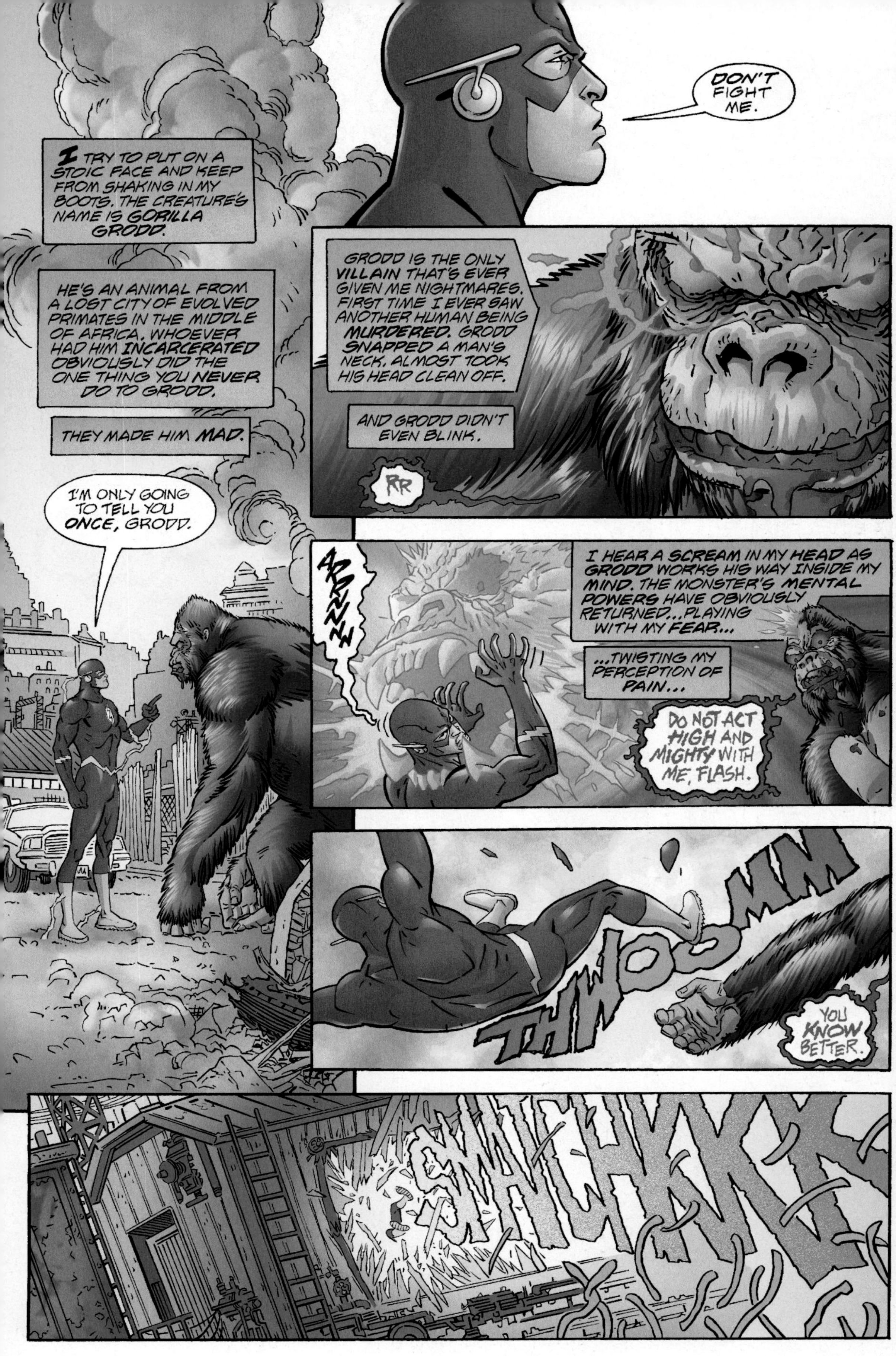
DON'T FIGHT ME.
I TRY TO PUT ON A STOIC FACE AND KEEP FROM SHAKING IN MY BOOTS. THE CREATURE'S NAME IS GORILLA GRODD.
HE'S AN ANIMAL FROM A LOST CITY OF EVOLVED PRIMATES IN THE MIDDLE OF AFRICA. WHOEVER HAD HIM INCARCERATED OBVIOUSLY DID THE ONE THING YOU NEVER DO TO GRODD.
THEY MADE HIM MAD.
GRODD IS THE ONLY VILLAIN THAT'S EVER GIVEN ME NIGHTMARES. FIRST TIME I EVER SAW ANOTHER HUMAN BEING MURDERED. GRODD SNAPPED A MAN'S NECK. ALMOST TOOK HIS HEAD CLEAN OFF.
AND GRODD DIDN'T EVEN BLINK.
RR
I'M ONLY GOING TO TELL YOU ONCE, GRODD.
ARNNNN
I HEAR A SCREAM IN MY HEAD AS GRODD WORKS HIS WAY INSIDE MY MIND. THE MONSTER'S MENTAL POWERS HAVE OBVIOUSLY RETURNED...PLAYING WITH MY FEAR...
...TWISTING MY PERCEPTION OF PAIN...
DO NOT ACT HIGH AND MIGHTY WITH ME, FLASH.
THWOOOMM
YOU KNOW BETTER.
SMATCHKKK

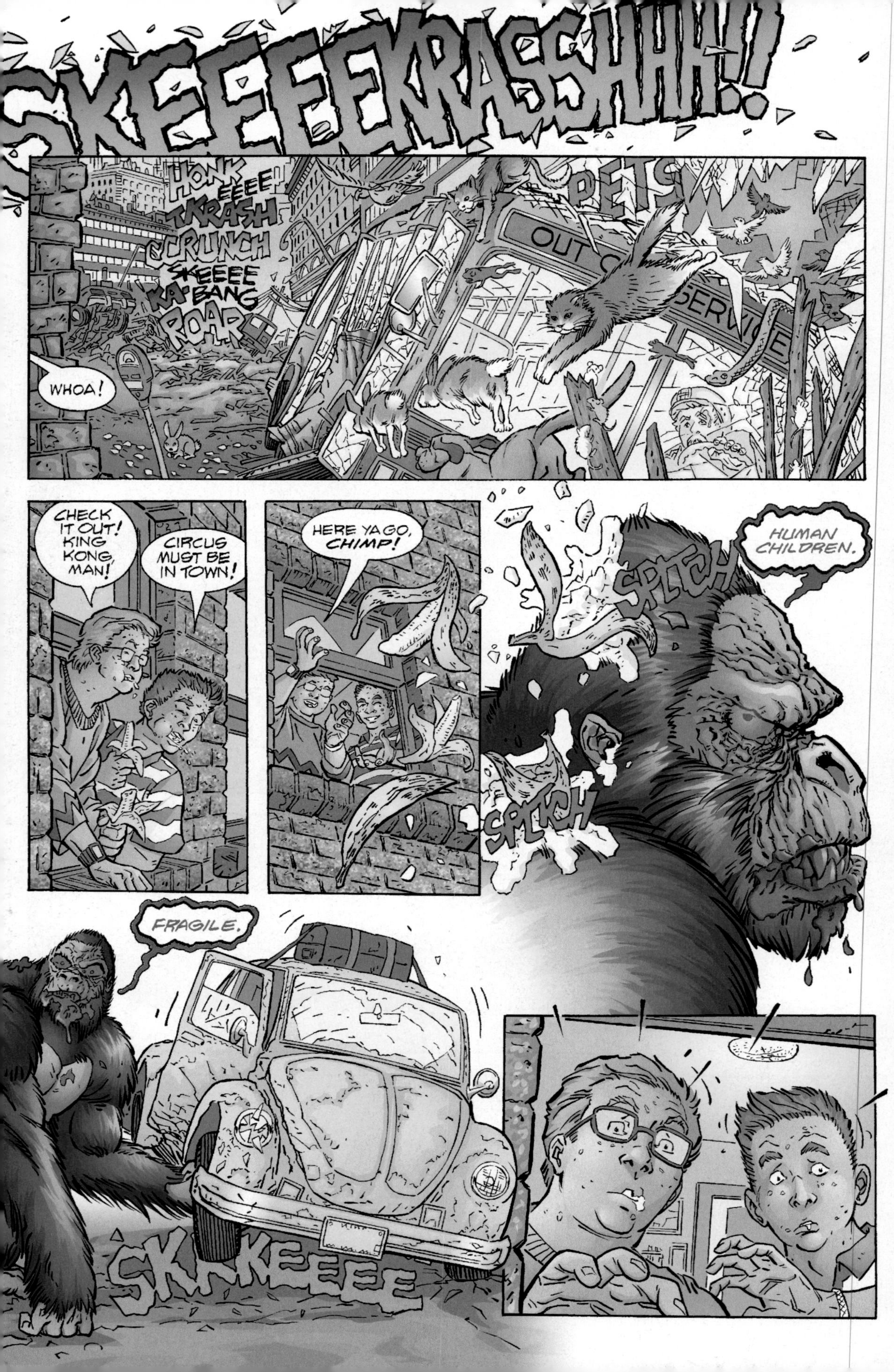

SKEEEEKRASSHHH!!
HONK
EEEE
KRASH
CRUNCH
SKEEEE
KA-BANG
ROAR
PETS
OUT OF
SERVICE
WHOA!
CHECK IT OUT! KING KONG MAN!
CIRCUS MUST BE IN TOWN!
HERE YA GO, CHIMP!
SPLTCH
HUMAN CHILDREN.
SPLTCH
FRAGILE.
SKRKEEEE

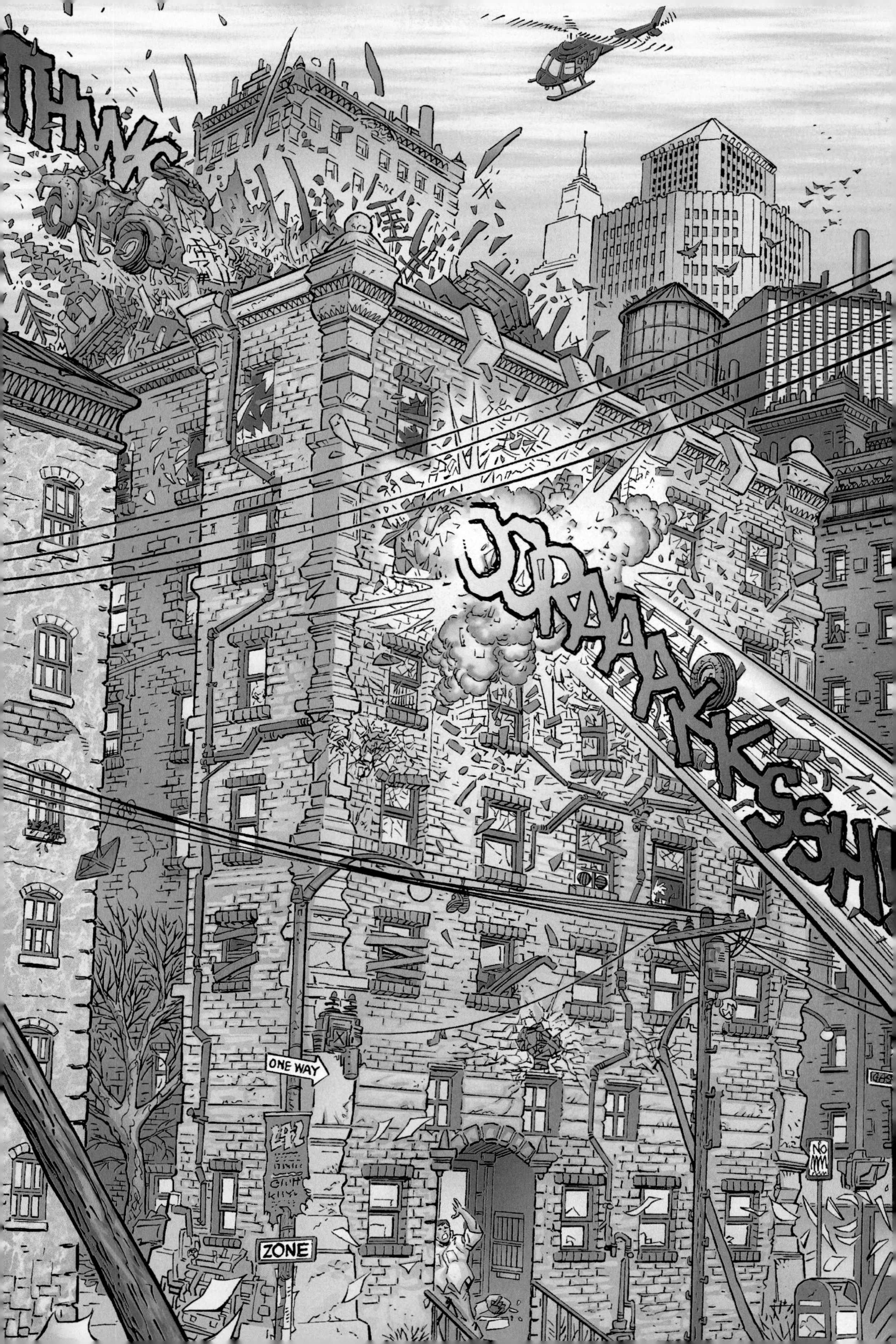
THWK
CRAAAKKSSH
ONE WAY
ZONE
NO

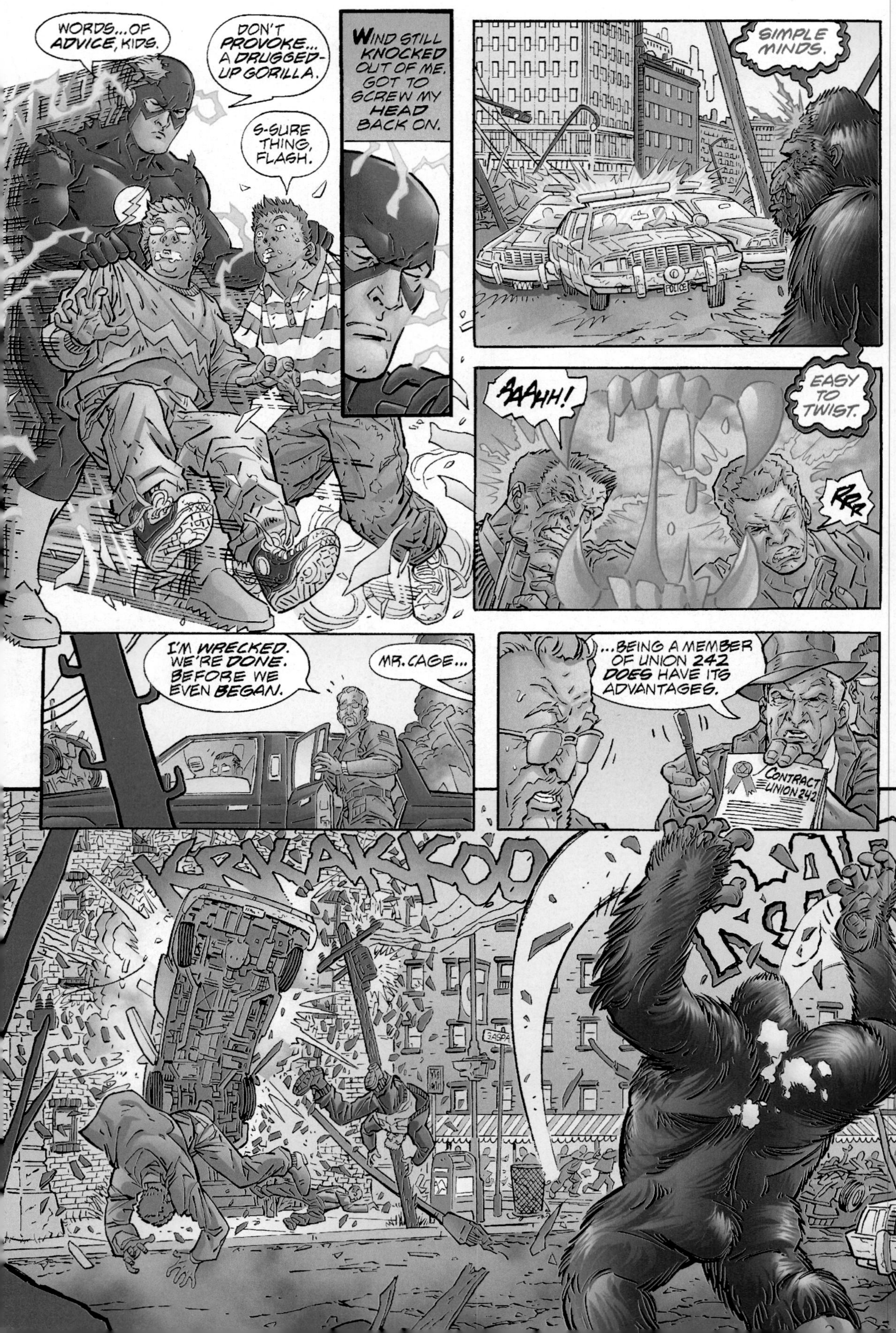
WORDS...OF ADVICE, KIDS.
DON'T PROVOKE... A DRUGGED-UP GORILLA.
S-SURE THING, FLASH.
WIND STILL KNOCKED OUT OF ME. GOT TO SCREW MY HEAD BACK ON.
SIMPLE MINDS.
POLICE
AAAHH!
EASY TO TWIST.
RRR
I'M WRECKED. WE'RE DONE. BEFORE WE EVEN BEGAN.
MR. CAGE...
...BEING A MEMBER OF UNION 242 DOES HAVE ITS ADVANTAGES.
CONTRACT UNION 242

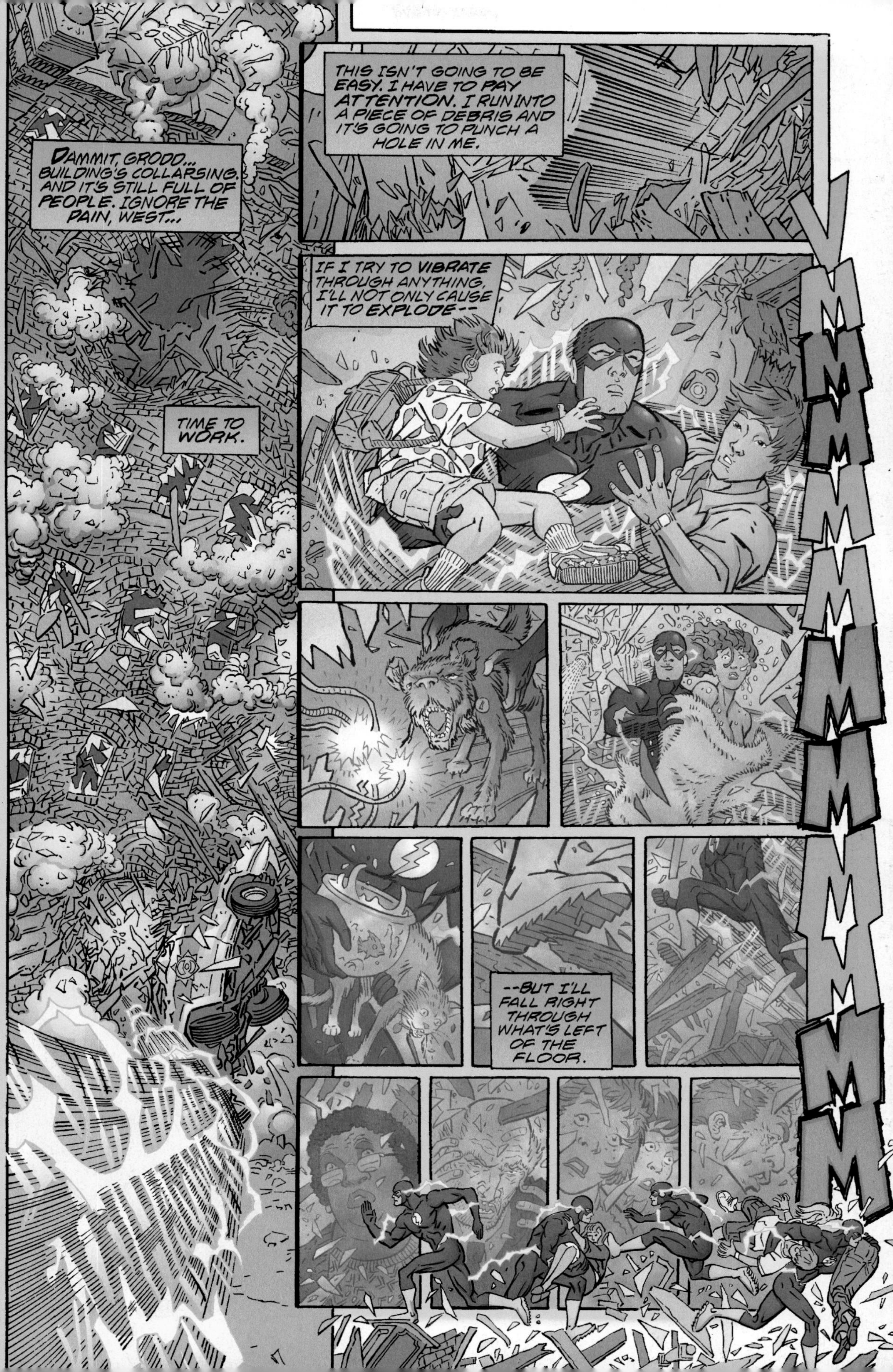
DAMMIT, GRODD... BUILDING'S COLLAPSING. AND IT'S STILL FULL OF PEOPLE. IGNORE THE PAIN, WEST...
TIME TO WORK.
THIS ISN'T GOING TO BE EASY. I HAVE TO PAY ATTENTION. I RUN INTO A PIECE OF DEBRIS AND IT'S GOING TO PUNCH A HOLE IN ME.
IF I TRY TO VIBRATE THROUGH ANYTHING, I'LL NOT ONLY CAUSE IT TO EXPLODE--
--BUT I'LL FALL RIGHT THROUGH WHAT'S LEFT OF THE FLOOR.
VMMMMMMMMMMMMMMM

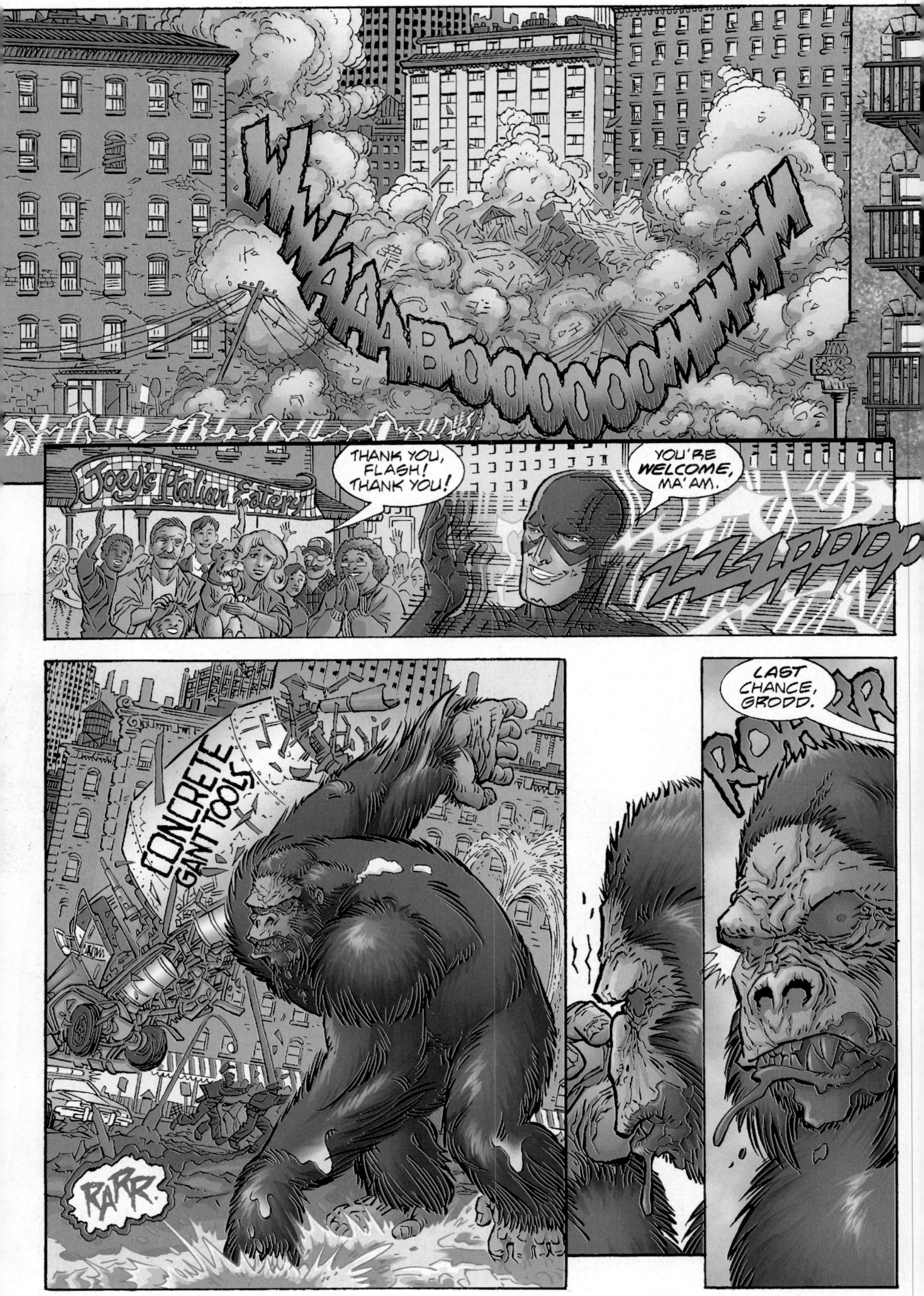
WHAAABOOOOOOMMM
Joey's Italian Eatery
THANK YOU, FLASH! THANK YOU!
YOU'RE WELCOME, MA'AM.
ZZZAPPP
CONCRETE
GANT TOOLS
RARR.
LAST CHANCE, GRODD.

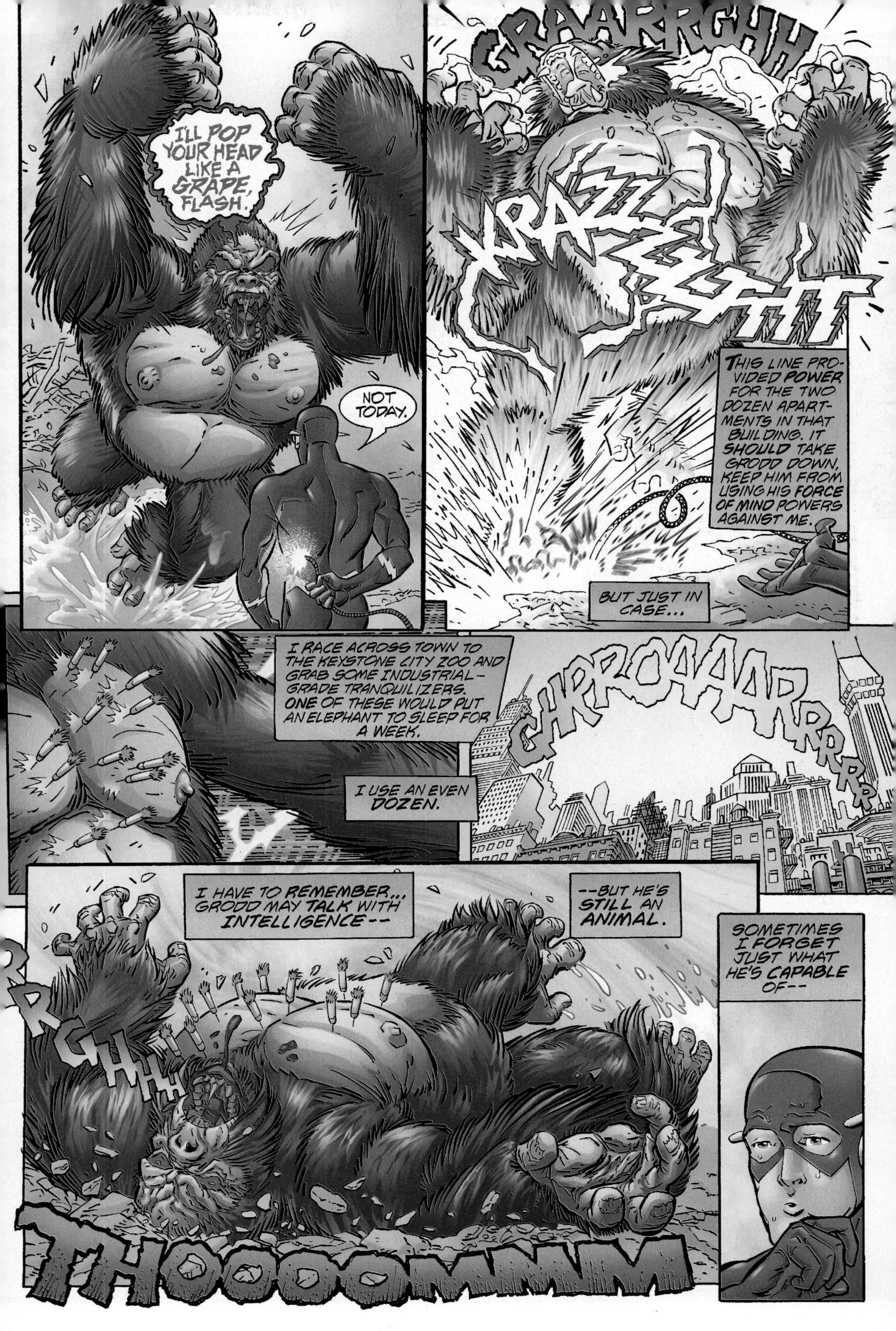
I'LL POP YOUR HEAD LIKE A GRAPE, FLASH.
NOT TODAY.
GRAARRGHH
KRAZZZZAAKKZZTTT
THIS LINE PROVIDED POWER FOR THE TWO DOZEN APARTMENTS IN THAT BUILDING. IT SHOULD TAKE GRODD DOWN, KEEP HIM FROM USING HIS FORCE OF MIND POWERS AGAINST ME.
BUT JUST IN CASE...
I RACE ACROSS TOWN TO THE KEYSTONE CITY ZOO AND GRAB SOME INDUSTRIAL-GRADE TRANQUILIZERS. ONE OF THESE WOULD PUT AN ELEPHANT TO SLEEP FOR A WEEK.
I USE AN EVEN DOZEN.
GHRROAAARRRRR
I HAVE TO REMEMBER... GRODD MAY TALK WITH INTELLIGENCE--
--BUT HE'S STILL AN ANIMAL.
RRGHHH
THOOOOMMM
SOMETIMES I FORGET JUST WHAT HE'S CAPABLE OF--

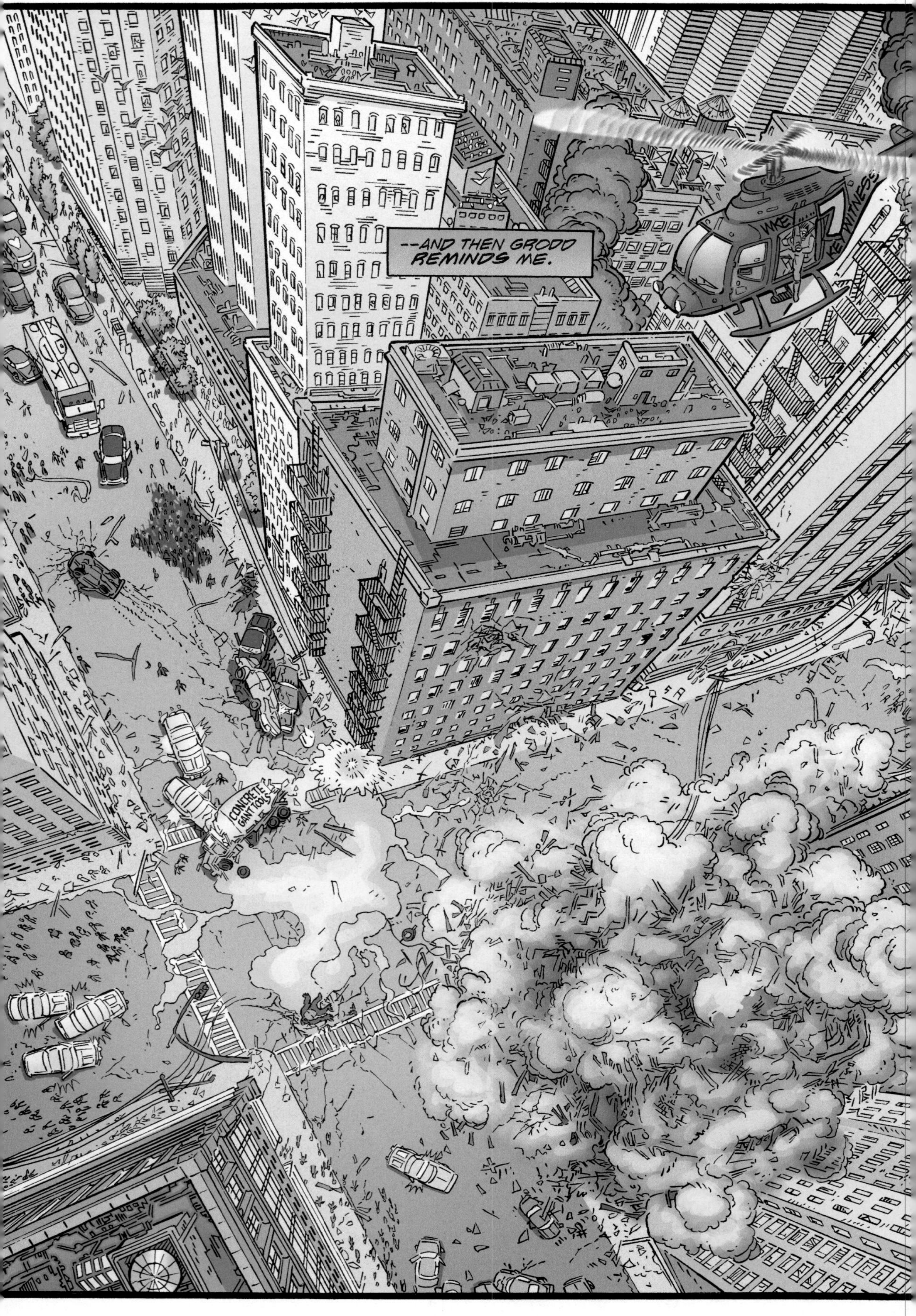
--AND THEN GRODD REMINDS ME.
WKEY 7
KE WITNESS
CONCRETE
GANT TOOLS

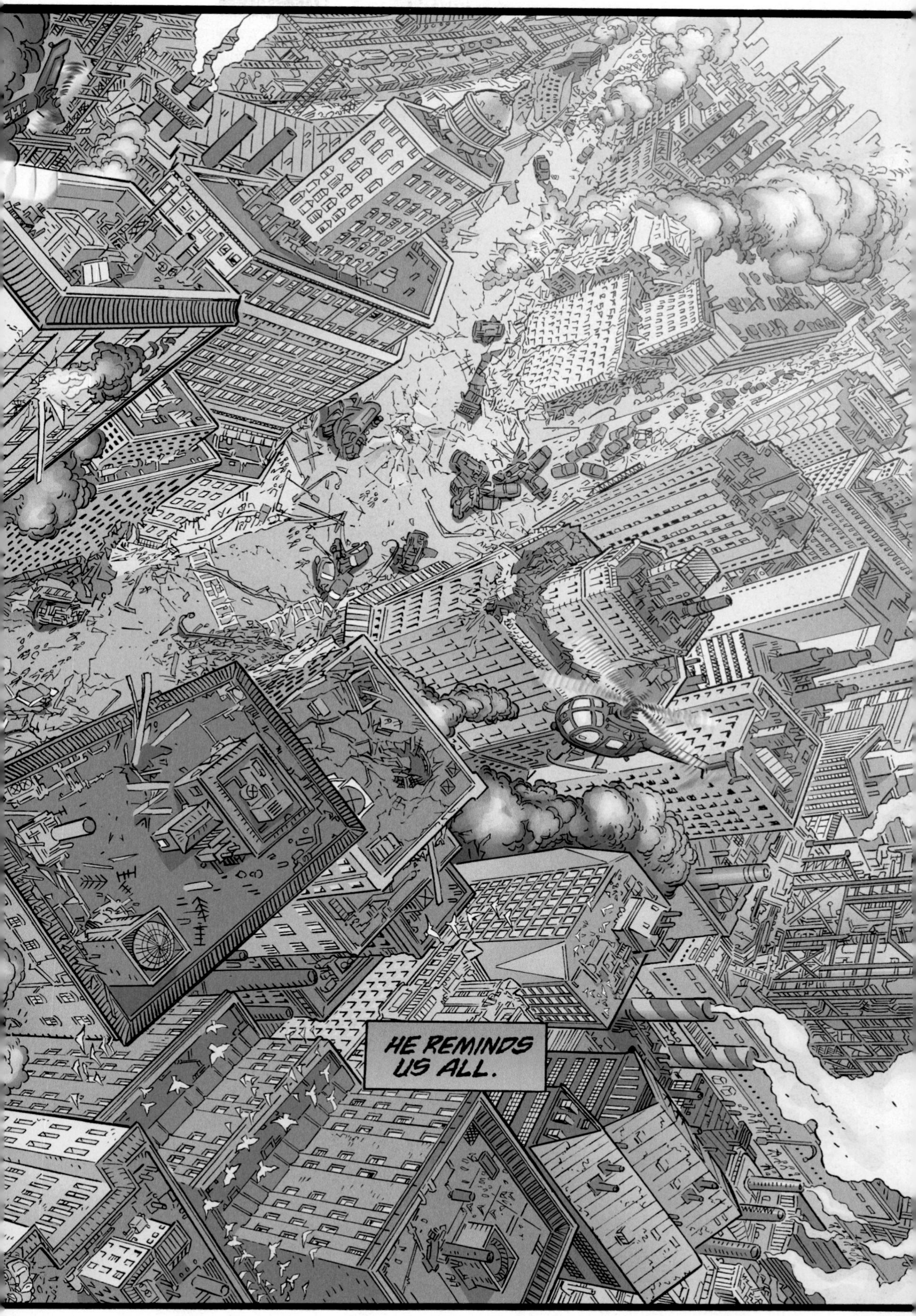
HE REMINDS US ALL.

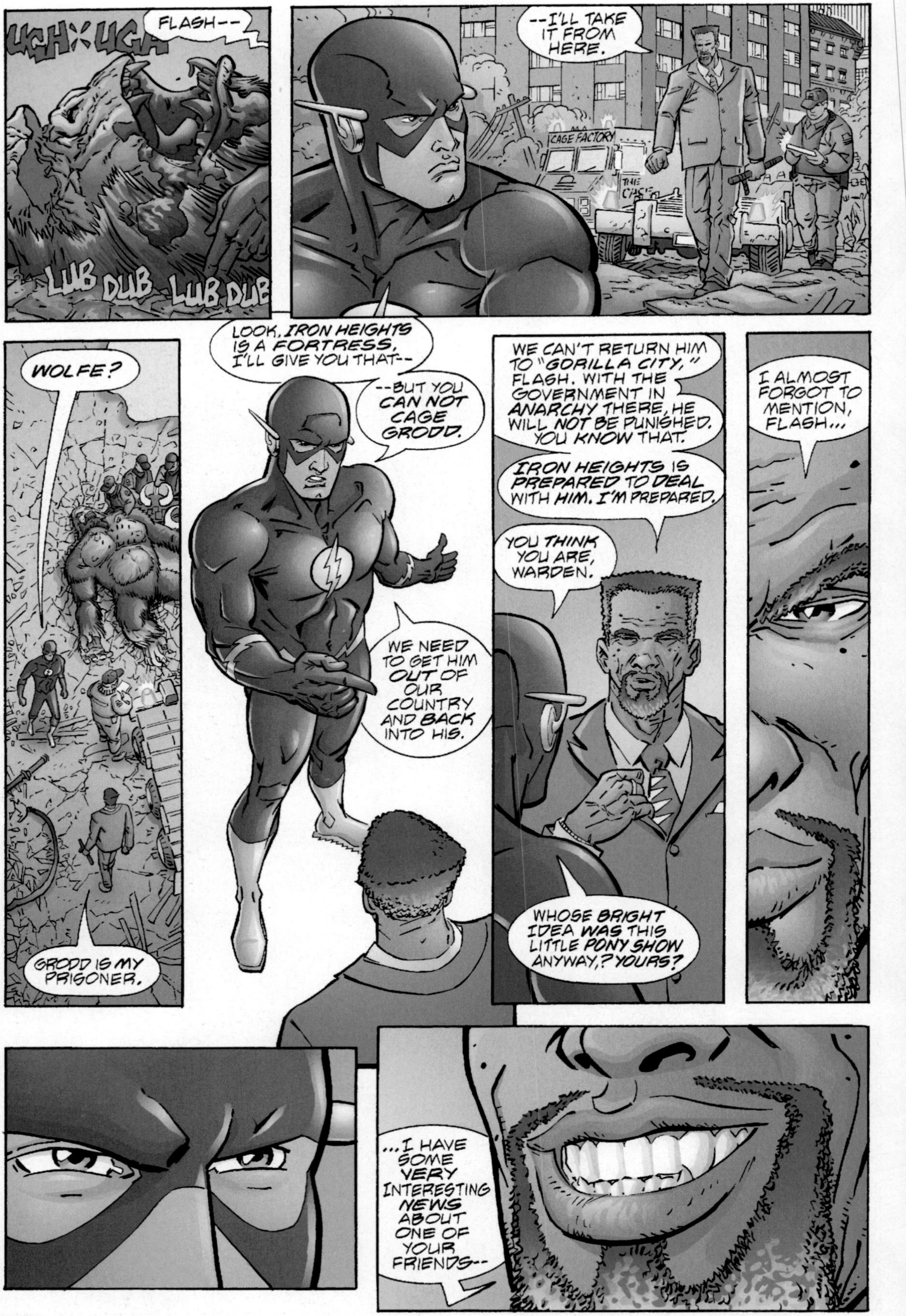
UGH UGH
FLASH--
LUB DUB LUB DUB
--I'LL TAKE IT FROM HERE.
CAGE FACTORY
WOLFE?
GRODD IS MY PRISONER.
LOOK, IRON HEIGHTS IS A FORTRESS, I'LL GIVE YOU THAT--
--BUT YOU CAN NOT CAGE GRODD.
WE NEED TO GET HIM OUT OF OUR COUNTRY AND BACK INTO HIS.
WE CAN'T RETURN HIM TO "GORILLA CITY," FLASH. WITH THE GOVERNMENT IN ANARCHY THERE, HE WILL NOT BE PUNISHED. YOU KNOW THAT.
IRON HEIGHTS IS PREPARED TO DEAL WITH HIM. I'M PREPARED.
YOU THINK YOU ARE, WARDEN.
WHOSE BRIGHT IDEA WAS THIS LITTLE PONY SHOW ANYWAY,? YOURS?
I ALMOST FORGOT TO MENTION, FLASH...
...I HAVE SOME VERY INTERESTING NEWS ABOUT ONE OF YOUR FRIENDS--

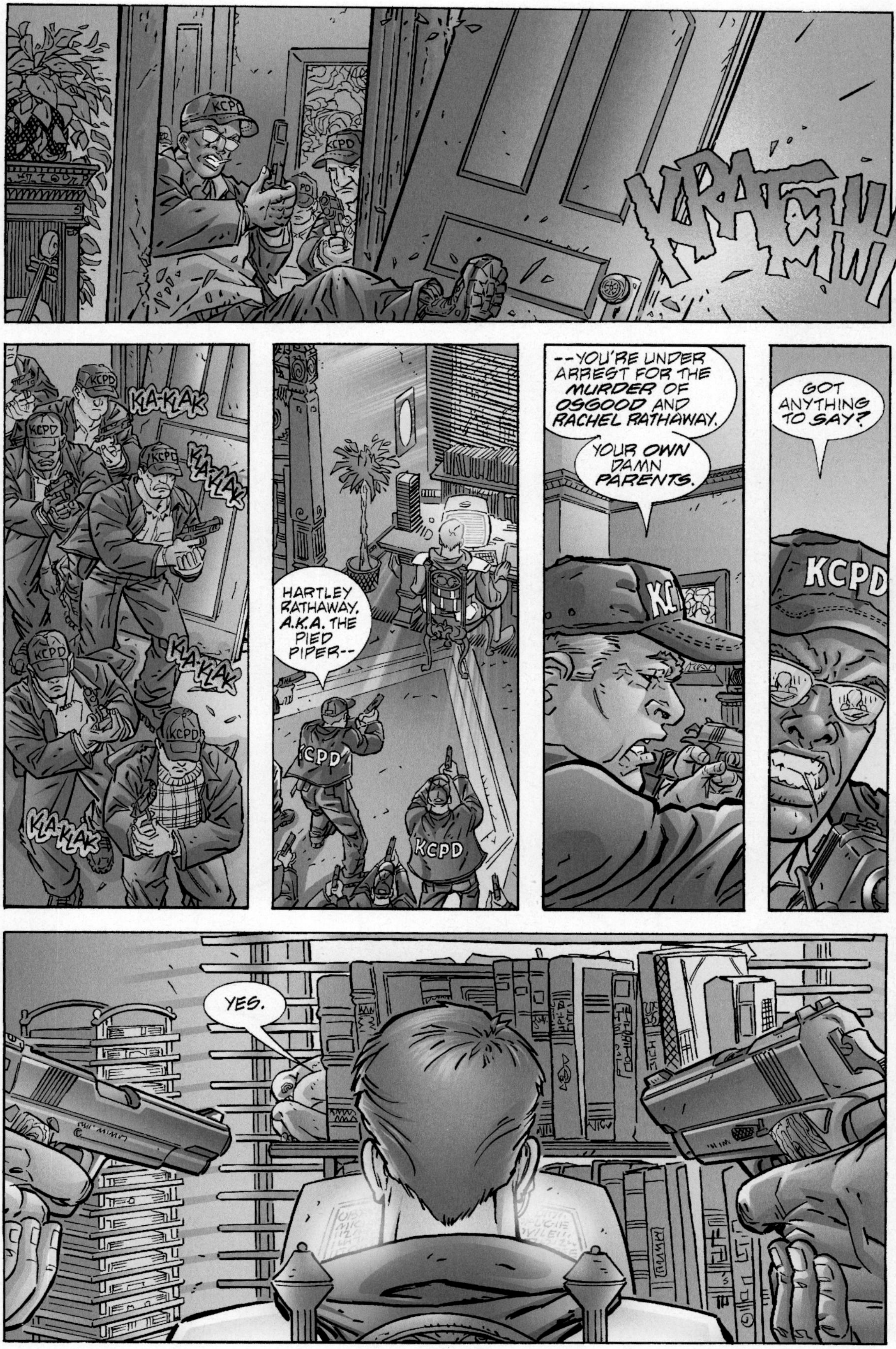
KRATCHH
KLA-KLAK
KLA-KLAK
KLA-KLAK
KLA-KLAK
HARTLEY RATHAWAY. A.K.A. THE PIED PIPER--
--YOU'RE UNDER ARREST FOR THE MURDER OF OSGOOD AND RACHEL RATHAWAY.
YOUR OWN DAMN PARENTS.
GOT ANYTHING TO SAY?
YES.

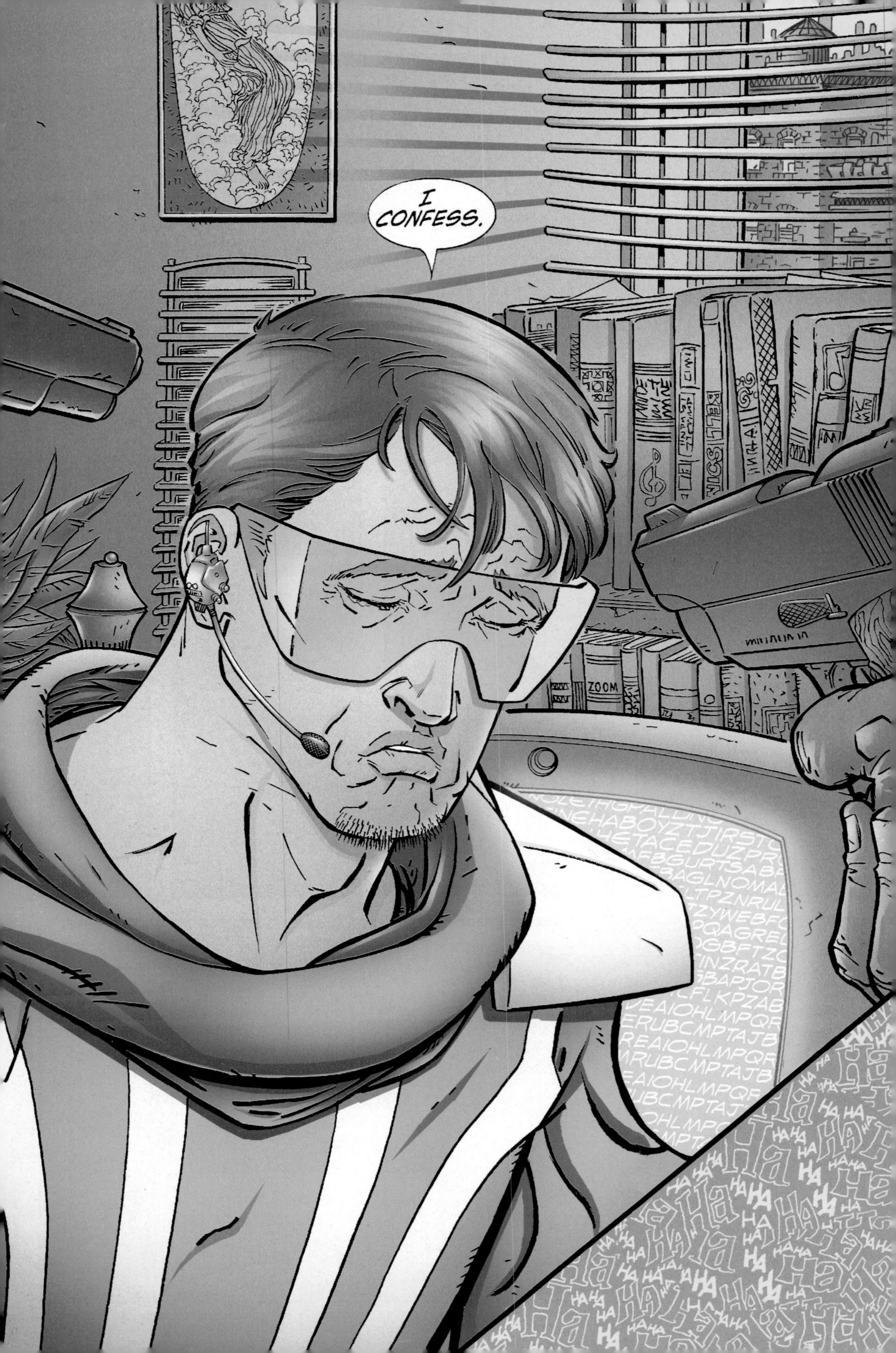
I CONFESS.

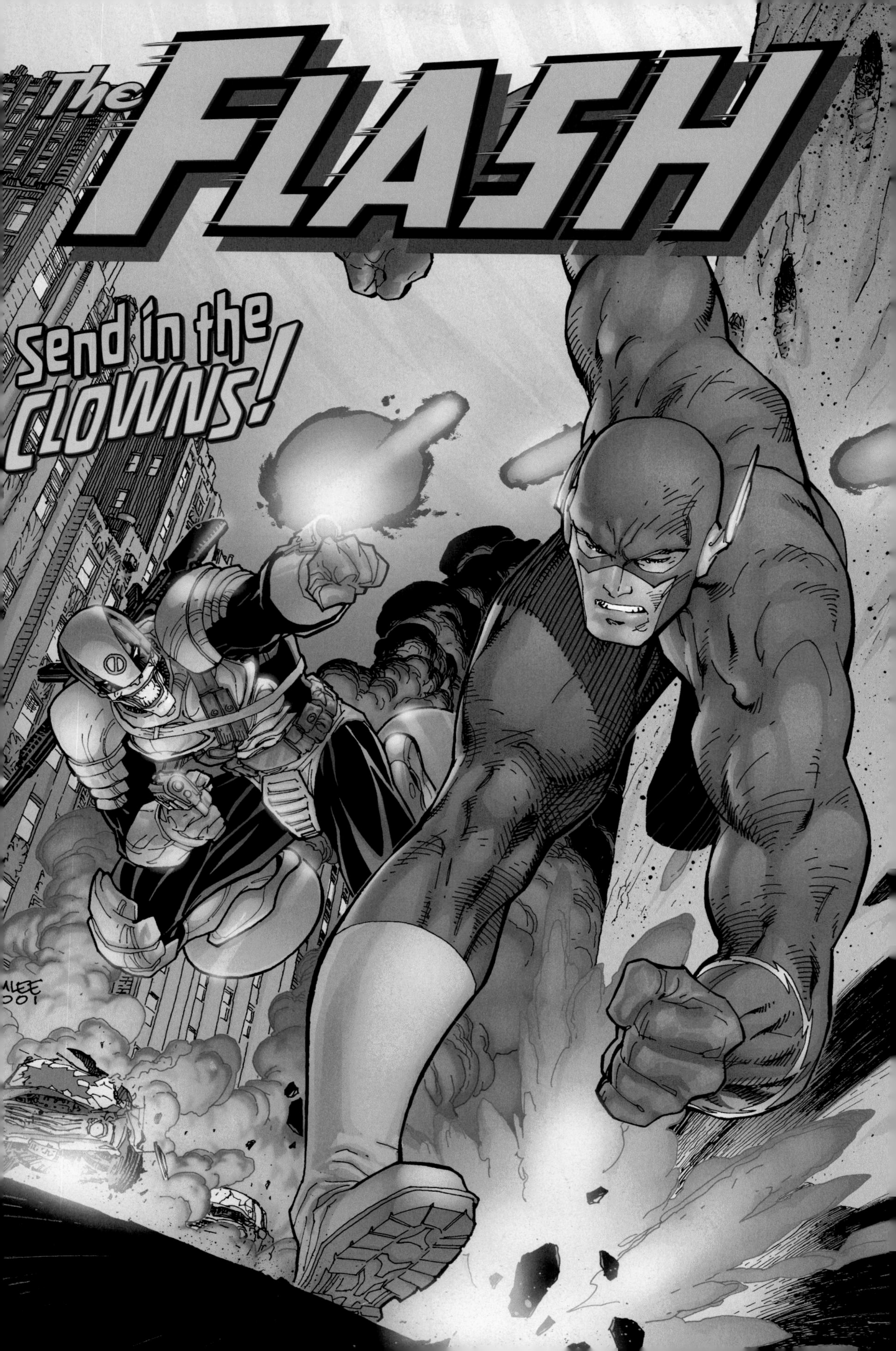
The FLASH
Send in the CLOWNS!
LEE 2001

COVER ART BY ***JIM LEE***

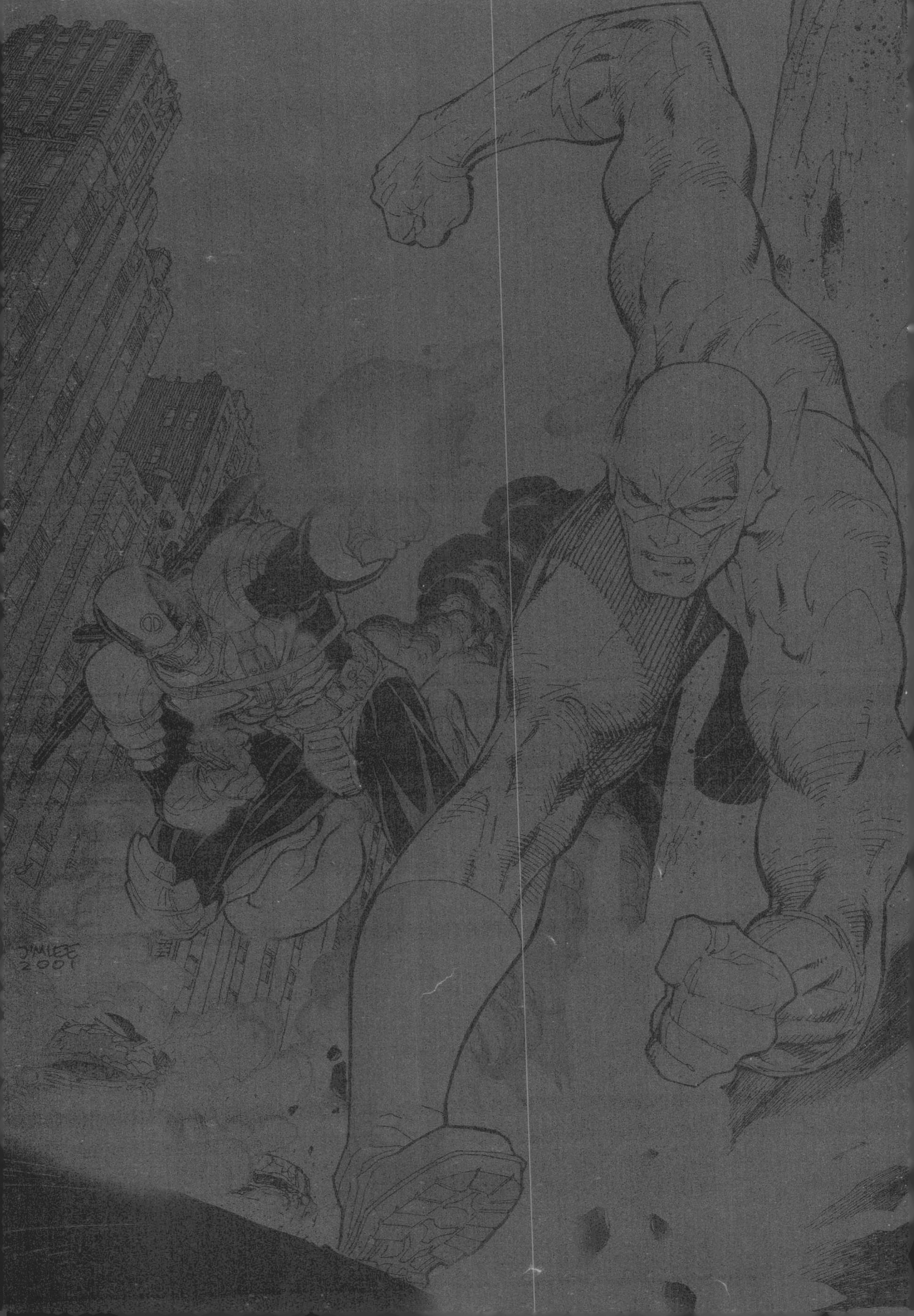
JIM LEE
2001

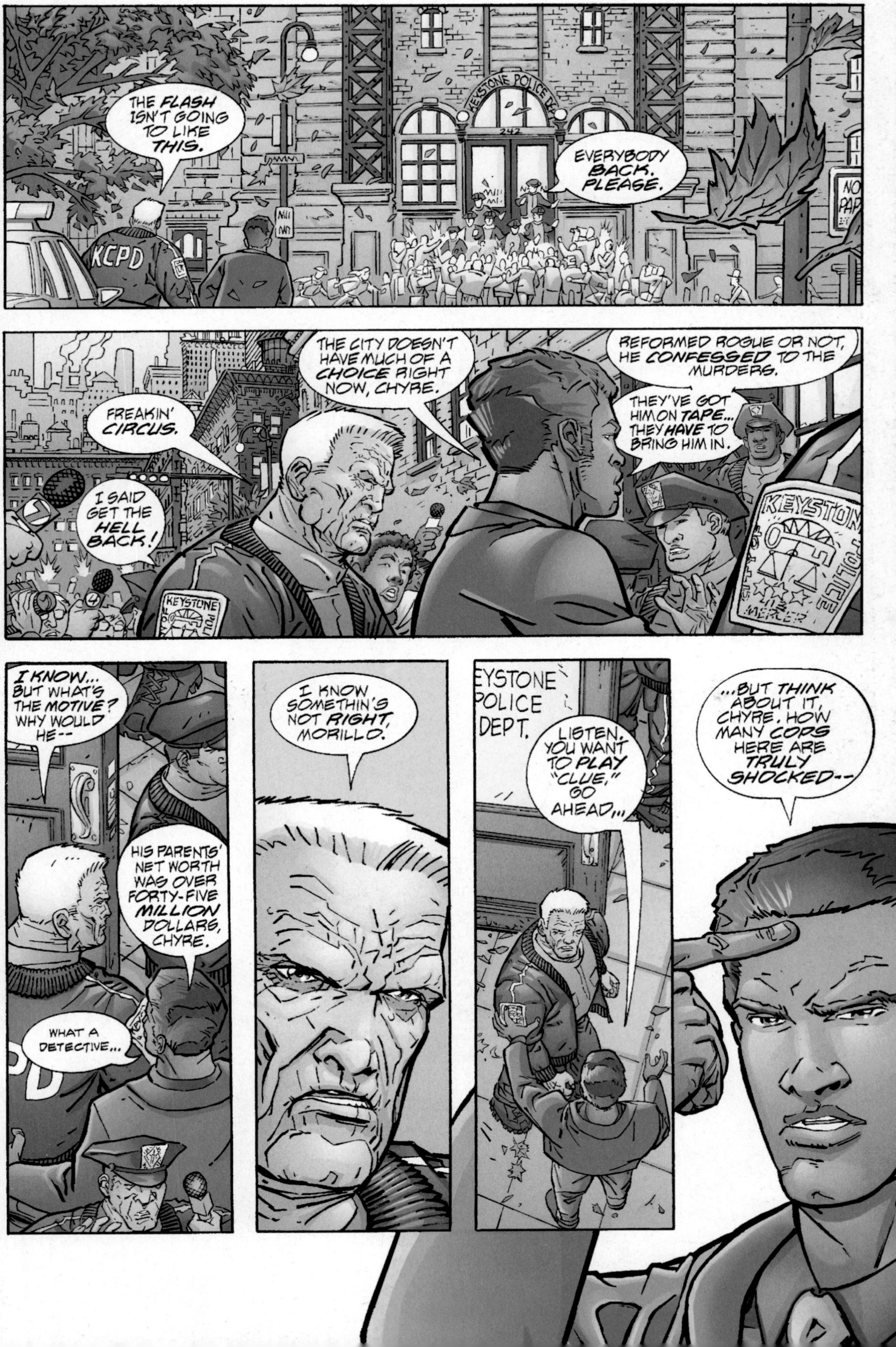
THE FLASH ISN'T GOING TO LIKE THIS.
KEYSTONE POLICE DEPT.
242
EVERYBODY BACK. PLEASE.
KCPD
THE CITY DOESN'T HAVE MUCH OF A CHOICE RIGHT NOW, CHYRE.
REFORMED ROGUE OR NOT, HE CONFESSED TO THE MURDERS.
FREAKIN' CIRCUS.
THEY'VE GOT HIM ON TAPE... THEY HAVE TO BRING HIM IN.
I SAID GET THE HELL BACK!
KEYSTONE
I KNOW... BUT WHAT'S THE MOTIVE? WHY WOULD HE--
HIS PARENTS' NET WORTH WAS OVER FORTY-FIVE MILLION DOLLARS, CHYRE.
WHAT A DETECTIVE...
I KNOW SOMETHIN'S NOT RIGHT, MORILLO.
KEYSTONE POLICE DEPT.
LISTEN. YOU WANT TO PLAY "CLUE," GO AHEAD...
...BUT THINK ABOUT IT, CHYRE. HOW MANY COPS HERE ARE TRULY SHOCKED--

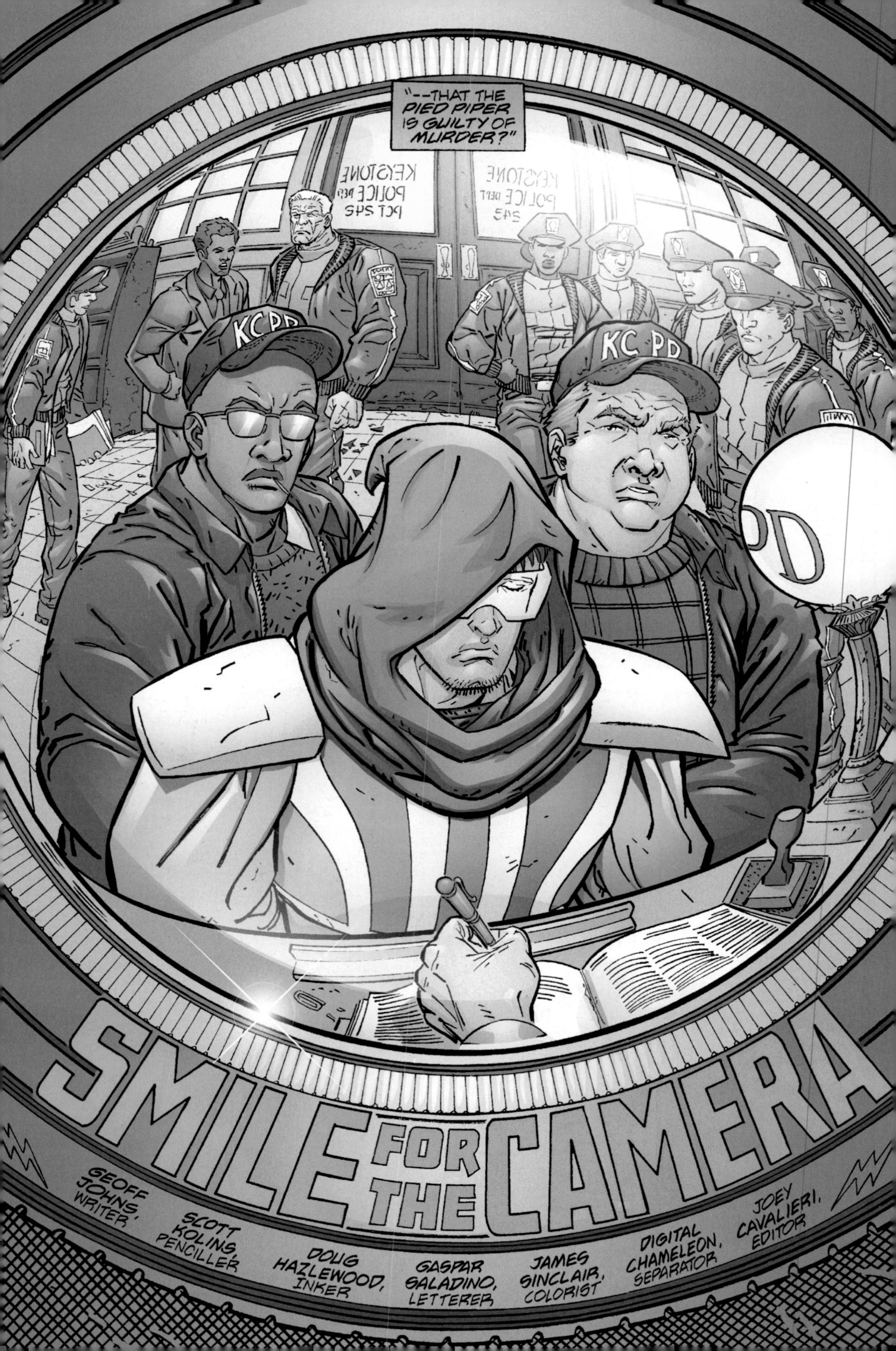
"--THAT THE PIED PIPER IS GUILTY OF MURDER?"
KEYSTONE POLICE DEPT PCT 242
KEYSTONE POLICE DEPT 242
KCPD
KC PD
PD
SMILE FOR THE CAMERA
GEOFF JOHNS, WRITER
SCOTT KOLINS, PENCILLER
DOUG HAZLEWOOD, INKER
GASPAR SALADINO, LETTERER
JAMES SINCLAIR, COLORIST
DIGITAL CHAMELEON, SEPARATOR
JOEY CAVALIERI, EDITOR

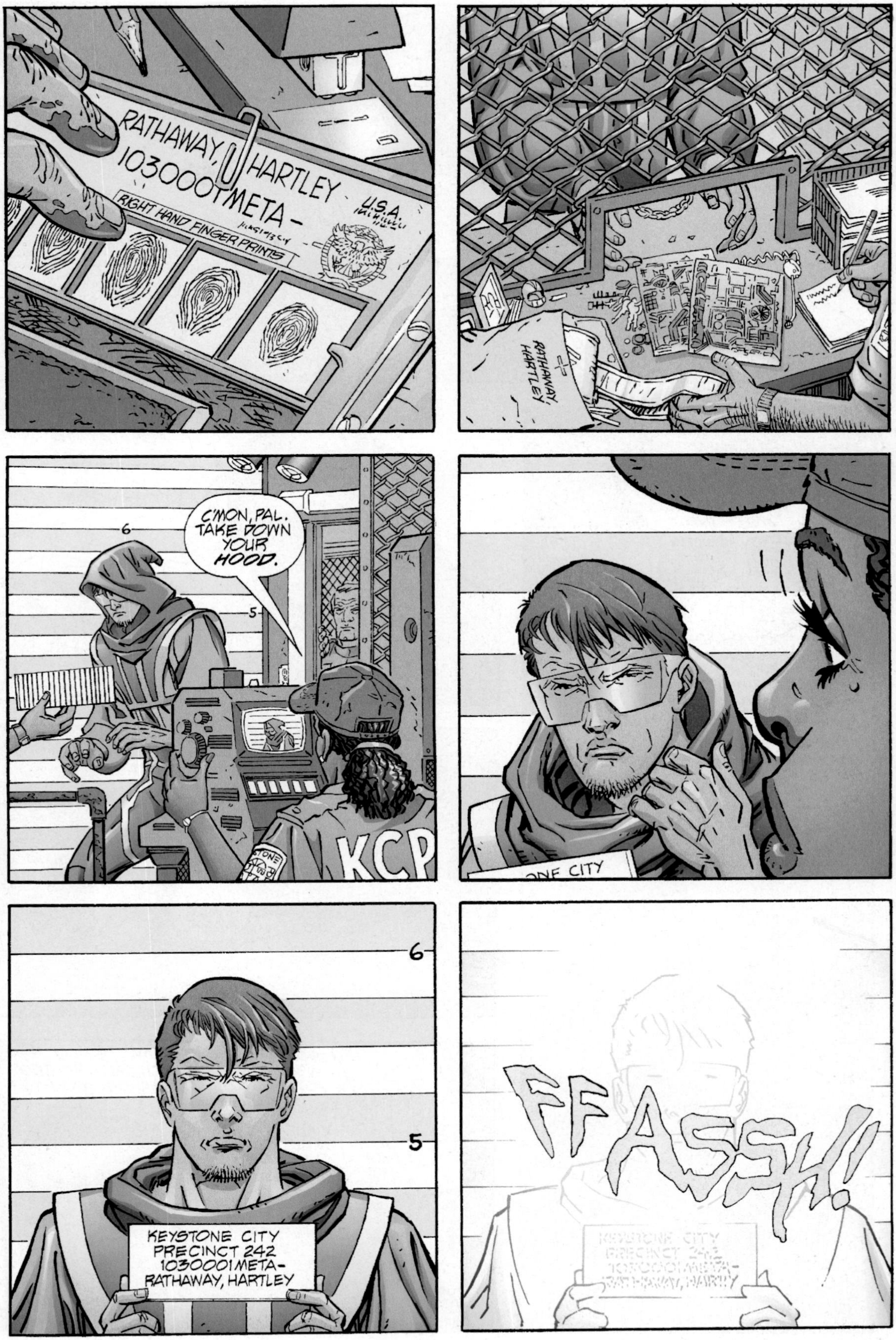
RATHAWAY, HARTLEY
1030001 META-
U.S.A.
RIGHT HAND FINGER PRINTS
RATHAWAY, HARTLEY
6
5
C'MON, PAL. TAKE DOWN YOUR HOOD.
KCP
6
5
KEYSTONE CITY
PRECINCT 242
1030001 META-
RATHAWAY, HARTLEY
FFASSH!

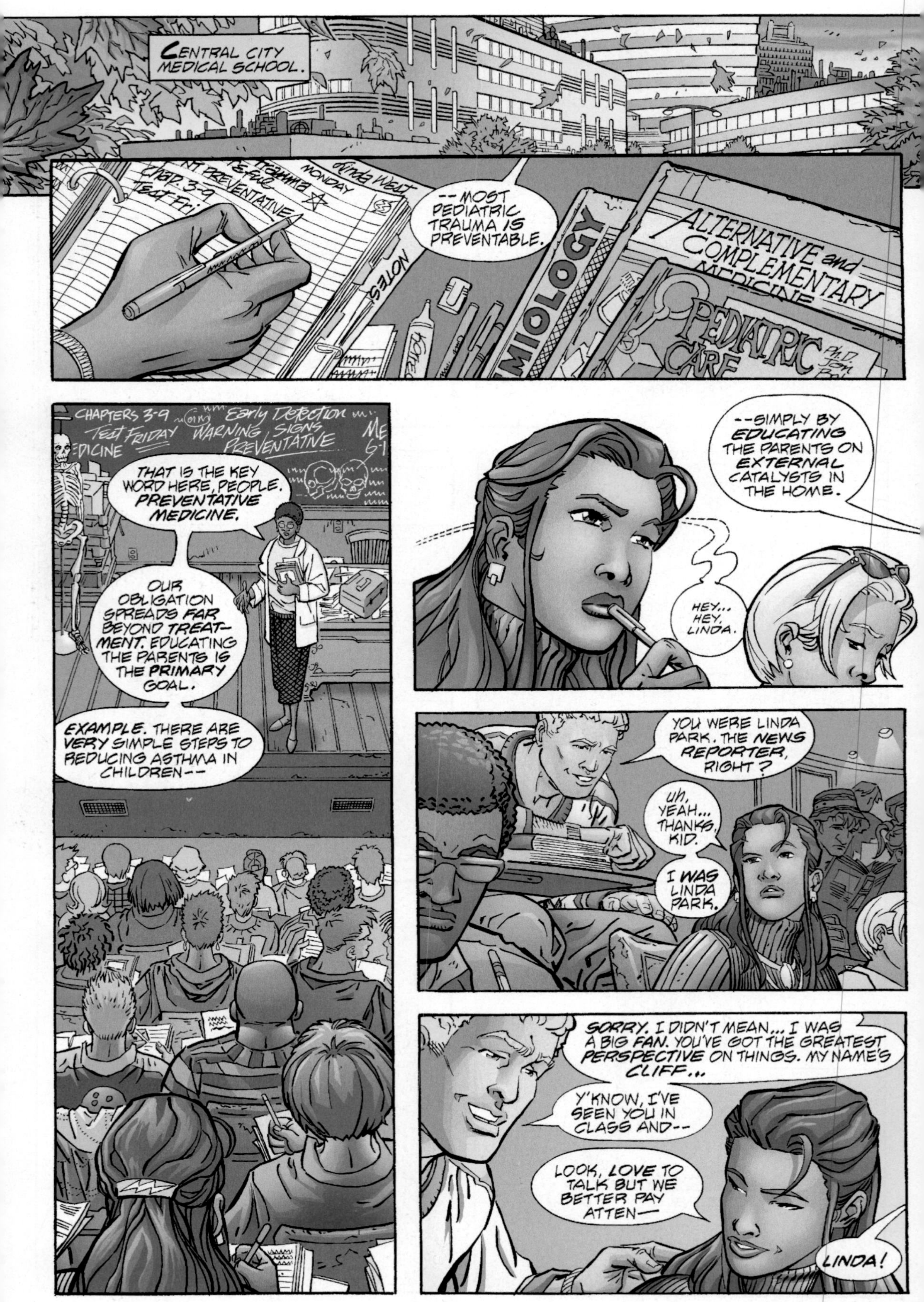
CENTRAL CITY MEDICAL SCHOOL.
--MOST PEDIATRIC TRAUMA IS PREVENTABLE.
ALTERNATIVE and COMPLEMENTARY MEDICINE
PEDIATRIC CARE
CHAPTERS 3-9
TEST FRIDAY
Early Detection
WARNING SIGNS
PREVENTATIVE
THAT IS THE KEY WORD HERE, PEOPLE. PREVENTATIVE MEDICINE.
OUR OBLIGATION SPREADS FAR BEYOND TREATMENT. EDUCATING THE PARENTS IS THE PRIMARY GOAL.
EXAMPLE. THERE ARE VERY SIMPLE STEPS TO REDUCING ASTHMA IN CHILDREN--
--SIMPLY BY EDUCATING THE PARENTS ON EXTERNAL CATALYSTS IN THE HOME.
HEY... HEY, LINDA.
YOU WERE LINDA PARK. THE NEWS REPORTER, RIGHT?
uh, YEAH... THANKS, KID.
I WAS LINDA PARK.
SORRY. I DIDN'T MEAN... I WAS A BIG FAN. YOU'VE GOT THE GREATEST PERSPECTIVE ON THINGS. MY NAME'S CLIFF...
Y'KNOW, I'VE SEEN YOU IN CLASS AND--
LOOK, LOVE TO TALK BUT WE BETTER PAY ATTEN—
LINDA!

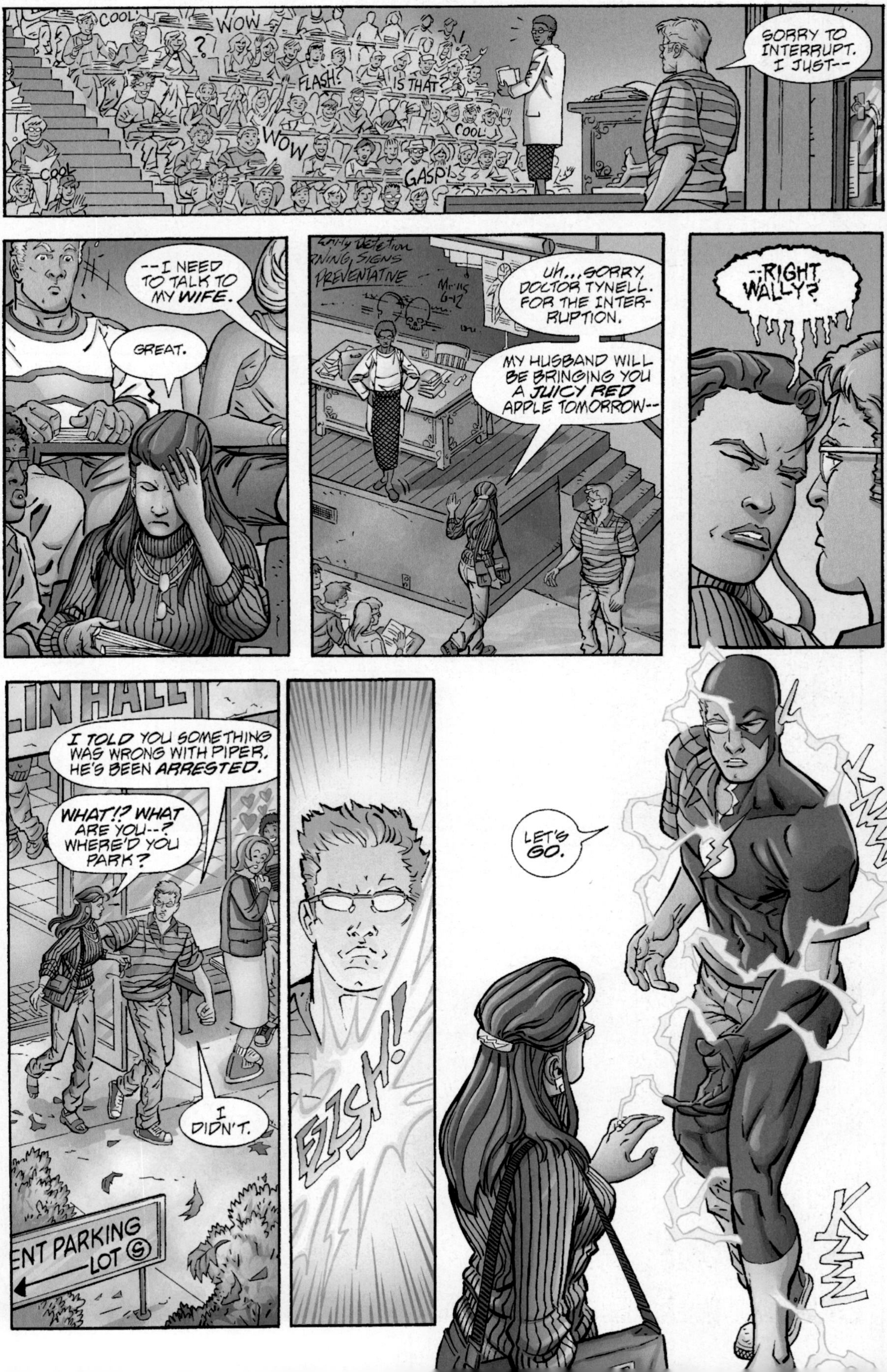
COOL
WOW
?
FLASH?
IS THAT?
COOL
WOW
GASP!
COOL
SORRY TO INTERRUPT. I JUST--
--I NEED TO TALK TO MY *WIFE*.
GREAT.
UH... SORRY, DOCTOR TYNELL. FOR THE INTERRUPTION.
MY HUSBAND WILL BE BRINGING YOU A *JUICY RED* APPLE TOMORROW--
--RIGHT, WALLY?
LIN HALL
I TOLD YOU SOMETHING WAS WRONG WITH PIPER. HE'S BEEN *ARRESTED*.
WHAT!? WHAT ARE YOU--? WHERE'D YOU PARK?
I DIDN'T.
ENT PARKING LOT S
FZZSH!
LET'S *GO*.

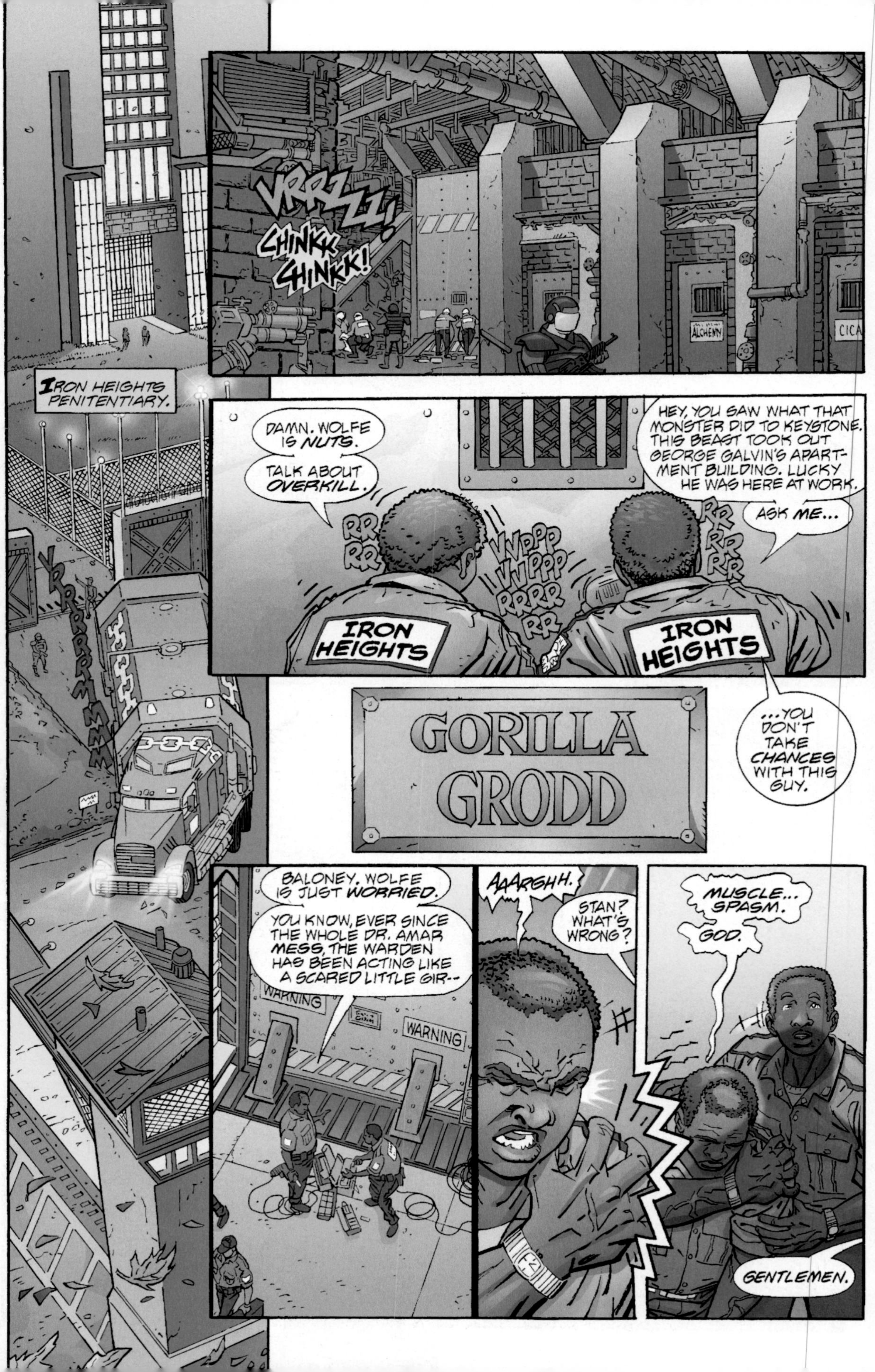
IRON HEIGHTS PENITENTIARY.
VRRRRRMMMM
VRRZZZ!
CHINKK CHINKK!
ALCHEMY
DAMN. WOLFE IS NUTS.
TALK ABOUT OVERKILL.
RR RR
VVPPP VVPPP RRRR RR
RR RR RR
HEY, YOU SAW WHAT THAT MONSTER DID TO KEYSTONE. THIS BEAST TOOK OUT GEORGE GALVIN'S APARTMENT BUILDING. LUCKY HE WAS HERE AT WORK.
ASK ME...
IRON HEIGHTS
IRON HEIGHTS
GORILLA GRODD
...YOU DON'T TAKE CHANCES WITH THIS GUY.
BALONEY. WOLFE IS JUST WORRIED.
YOU KNOW, EVER SINCE THE WHOLE DR. AMAR MESS, THE WARDEN HAS BEEN ACTING LIKE A SCARED LITTLE GIR--
WARNING
WARNING
AAARGHH.
STAN? WHAT'S WRONG?
MUSCLE... SPASM.
GOD.
GENTLEMEN.

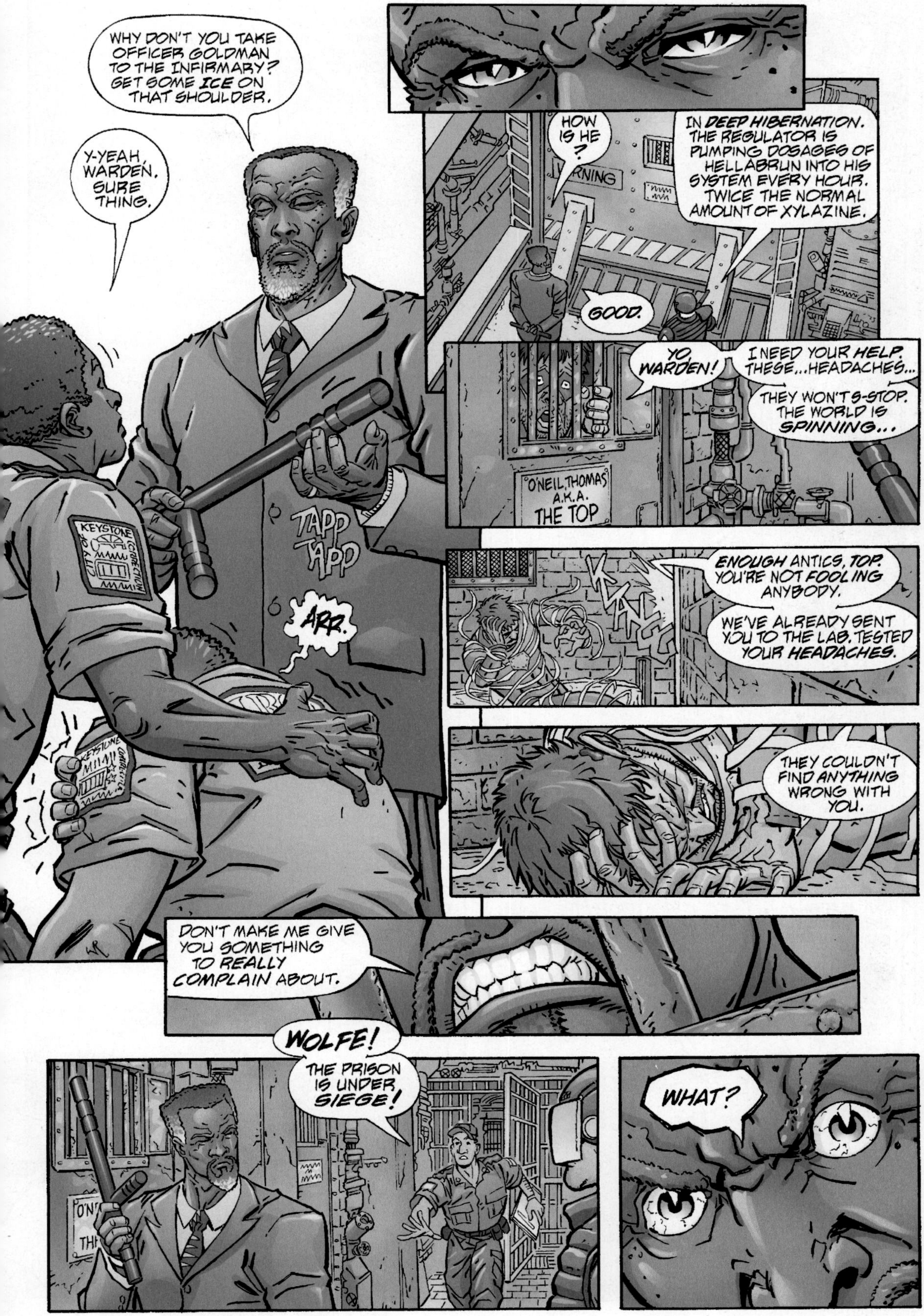
WHY DON'T YOU TAKE OFFICER GOLDMAN TO THE INFIRMARY? GET SOME ICE ON THAT SHOULDER.
Y-YEAH, WARDEN. SURE THING.
TAPP TAPP
ARR.
HOW IS HE?
IN DEEP HIBERNATION. THE REGULATOR IS PUMPING DOSAGES OF HELLABRUN INTO HIS SYSTEM EVERY HOUR. TWICE THE NORMAL AMOUNT OF XYLAZINE.
GOOD.
YO, WARDEN!
I NEED YOUR HELP. THESE...HEADACHES...
THEY WON'T S-STOP. THE WORLD IS SPINNING...
O'NEIL THOMAS A.K.A. THE TOP
ENOUGH ANTICS, TOP. YOU'RE NOT FOOLING ANYBODY.
WE'VE ALREADY SENT YOU TO THE LAB. TESTED YOUR HEADACHES.
THEY COULDN'T FIND ANYTHING WRONG WITH YOU.
DON'T MAKE ME GIVE YOU SOMETHING TO REALLY COMPLAIN ABOUT.
WOLFE!
THE PRISON IS UNDER SIEGE!
WHAT?

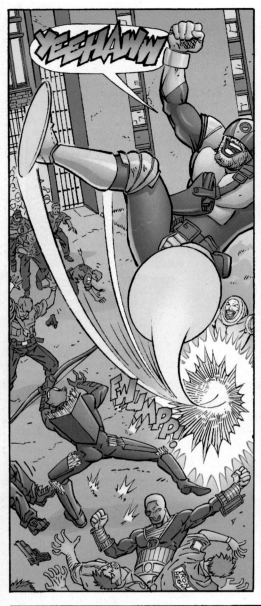

YEEHAWW

FWTMPP!

SHOULD WE JOKERIZE THESE BORING OLD FOLK? PUT A LITTLE RED IN THOSE CHEEKS, DEADSHOT? LIKE THE JOKER SAID, "GO TEACH THEM HOW TO SMILE!"

HEH. YOU WANT TO SPREAD THE LOVE, GO AHEAD, MERLYN.

ME?

I SHOOT TO KILL.

KRAKOW!
KRAKOW!

--A MASSIVE BREAKOUT. JOKER GOT LOOSE, CONTAMINATED CLOSE TO A HUNDRED METAHUMANS WITH HIS JOKER JUICE.

#%~~$@* IDIOTS! THE SLAB IS A JOKE, A REVOLVING DOOR, AND WHOEVER AUTHORIZED THE JOKER'S "RELEASE" SHOULD BE HANGED.

I WANT ALL PERSONNEL TO--

QUIET, WARDEN. THIS IS OUR PRISON NOW.

BOO.

KACHAK

WASN'T HE A **MAJOR PLAYER?** I MEAN--

WINNETKA COLIN, KEYSTONE CITY

AMBULANCE

KEYSTNE EMS

NE CITY JAIL

MAJOR PLAYER? NO WAY. I'VE SEEN THE PICTURES BEFORE HE ACCIDENTALLY BLEW HIMSELF UP WITH HIS OWN **EXPLODING BOOMERANG.**

TRUST ME. THESE BANDAGES ARE A **HUGE IMPROVEMENT.** CHECK HIS COSTUME OUT...

HARKNESS, DIGGER

A.K.A. CAPTAIN BOOMERANG

BLOODY... AAH...

S.T.A.R. LABS SAYS HE'LL NEVER WALK AGAIN.

BUT THEY SAY HE'S WELL ENOUGH TO BE TRANSFERRED TO **IRON HEIGHTS.** JUST NEED TO LOAD UP **PIPER** AND WE'RE ON OUR WAY.

BLOODY... HALF-WITS...

SAVE YOUR **BREATH,** BOOMERANG. WE CAN'T UNDERSTAND A **DAMN** THING YOU'RE SAYING ANYWAY--

"--ALRIGHTY, MATE?"

KLANK

YOU GOT **FIVE MINUTES,** BATHAWAY.

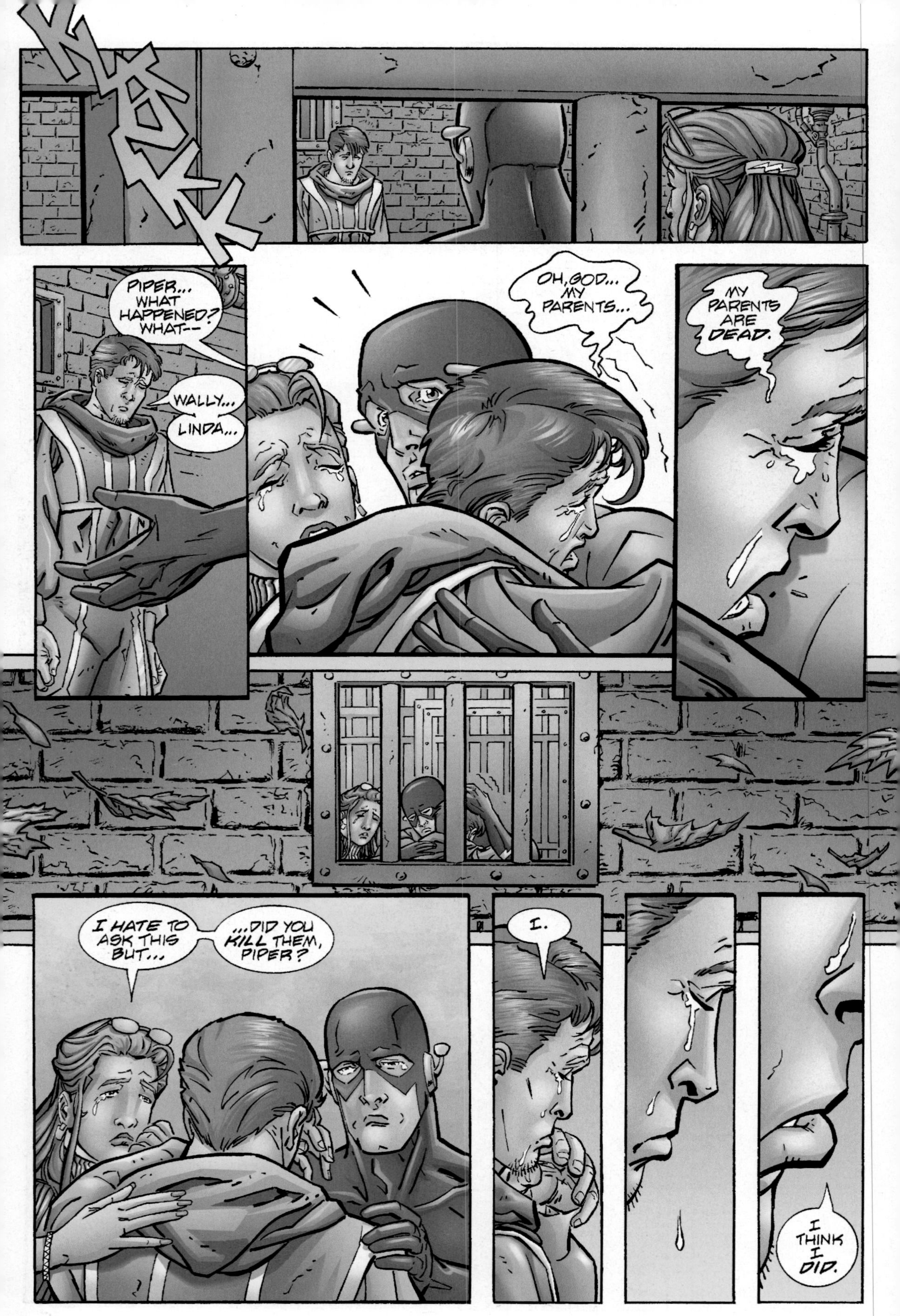
PIPER... WHAT HAPPENED? WHAT--
WALLY...
LINDA...
OH, GOD... MY PARENTS...
MY PARENTS ARE DEAD.
I HATE TO ASK THIS BUT...
...DID YOU KILL THEM, PIPER?
I.
I THINK I DID.

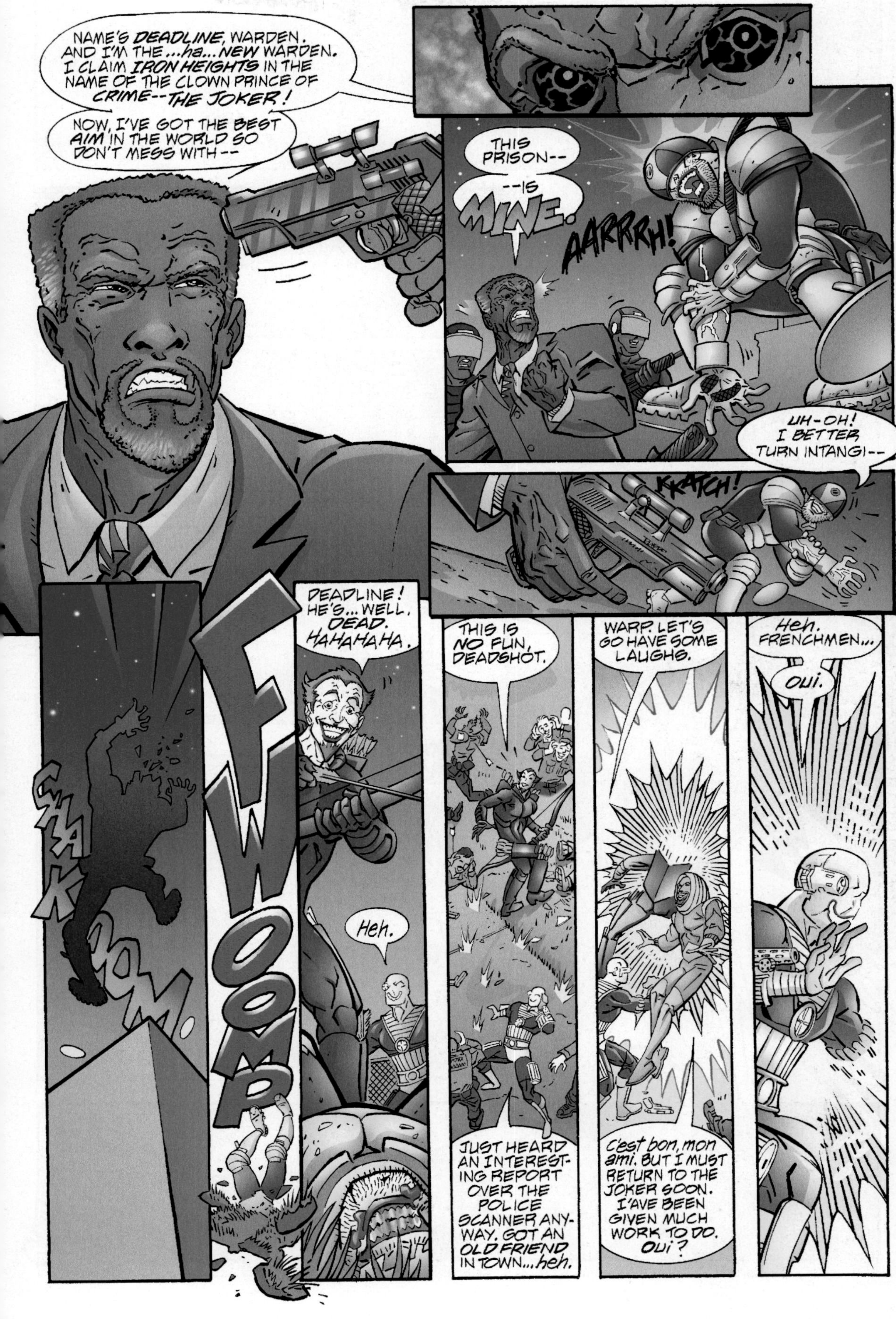
NAME'S DEADLINE, WARDEN. AND I'M THE ...ha... NEW WARDEN. I CLAIM IRON HEIGHTS IN THE NAME OF THE CLOWN PRINCE OF CRIME--THE JOKER!
NOW, I'VE GOT THE BEST AIM IN THE WORLD SO DON'T MESS WITH --
THIS PRISON--
--IS MINE.
AARRRH!
UH-OH! I BETTER TURN INTANGI--
KKATCH!
CHAKOOOM.
FWOOOMP
DEADLINE! HE'S... WELL, DEAD. HAHAHAHA.
Heh.
THIS IS NO FUN, DEADSHOT.
JUST HEARD AN INTERESTING REPORT OVER THE POLICE SCANNER ANYWAY. GOT AN OLD FRIEND IN TOWN... heh.
WARP. LET'S GO HAVE SOME LAUGHS.
C'est bon, mon ami. BUT I MUST RETURN TO THE JOKER SOON. I'AVE BEEN GIVEN MUCH WORK TO DO. Oui?
Heh. FRENCHMEN...
Oui.

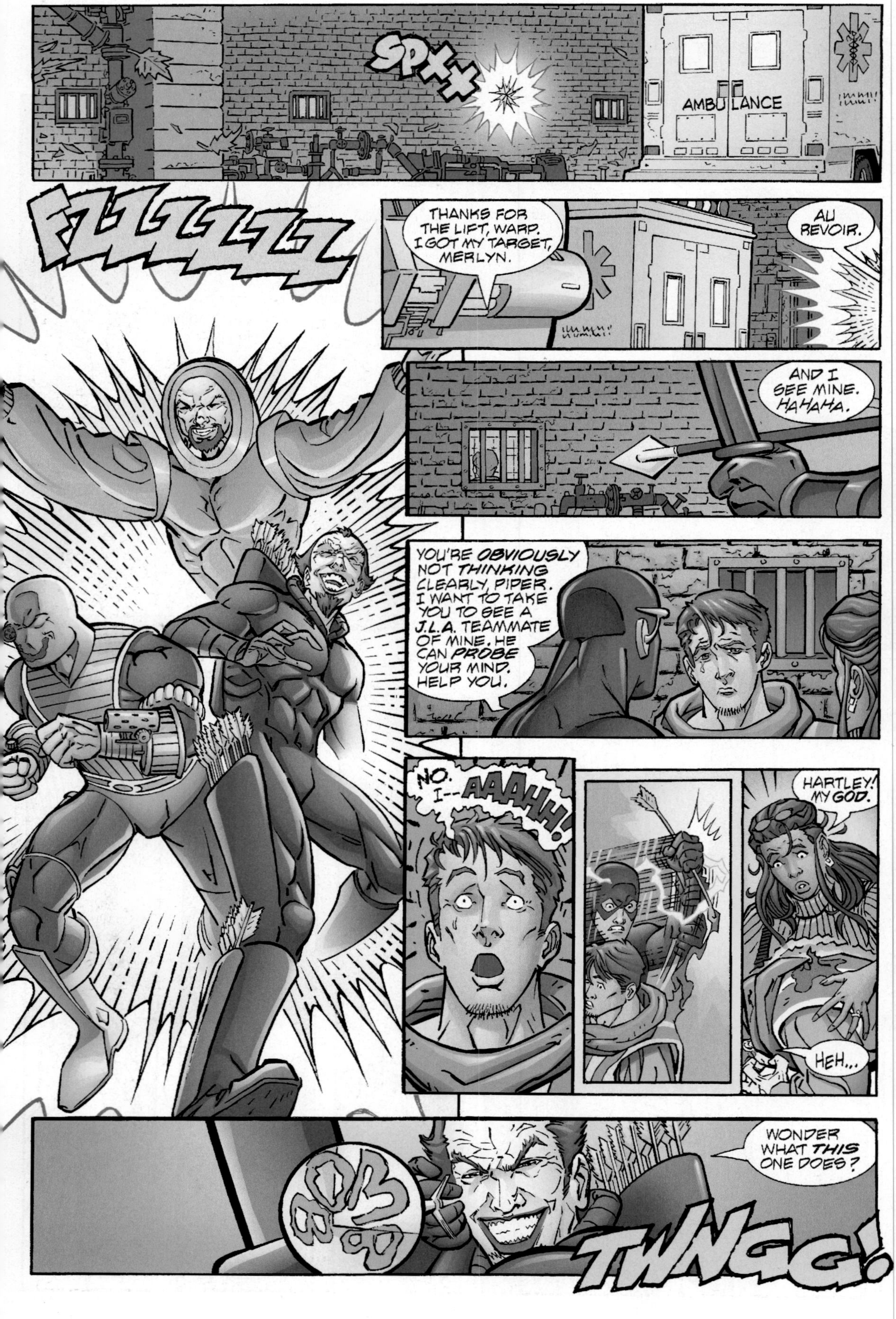
SPXX
AMBULANCE
FZZZZZZ
THANKS FOR THE LIFT, WARP. I GOT MY TARGET, MERLYN.
AU REVOIR.
AND I SEE MINE. HAHAHA.
YOU'RE OBVIOUSLY NOT THINKING CLEARLY, PIPER. I WANT TO TAKE YOU TO SEE A J.L.A. TEAMMATE OF MINE. HE CAN PROBE YOUR MIND. HELP YOU.
NO. I--AAAHH!
HARTLEY! MY GOD.
HEH...
WONDER WHAT THIS ONE DOES?
TWNGG!

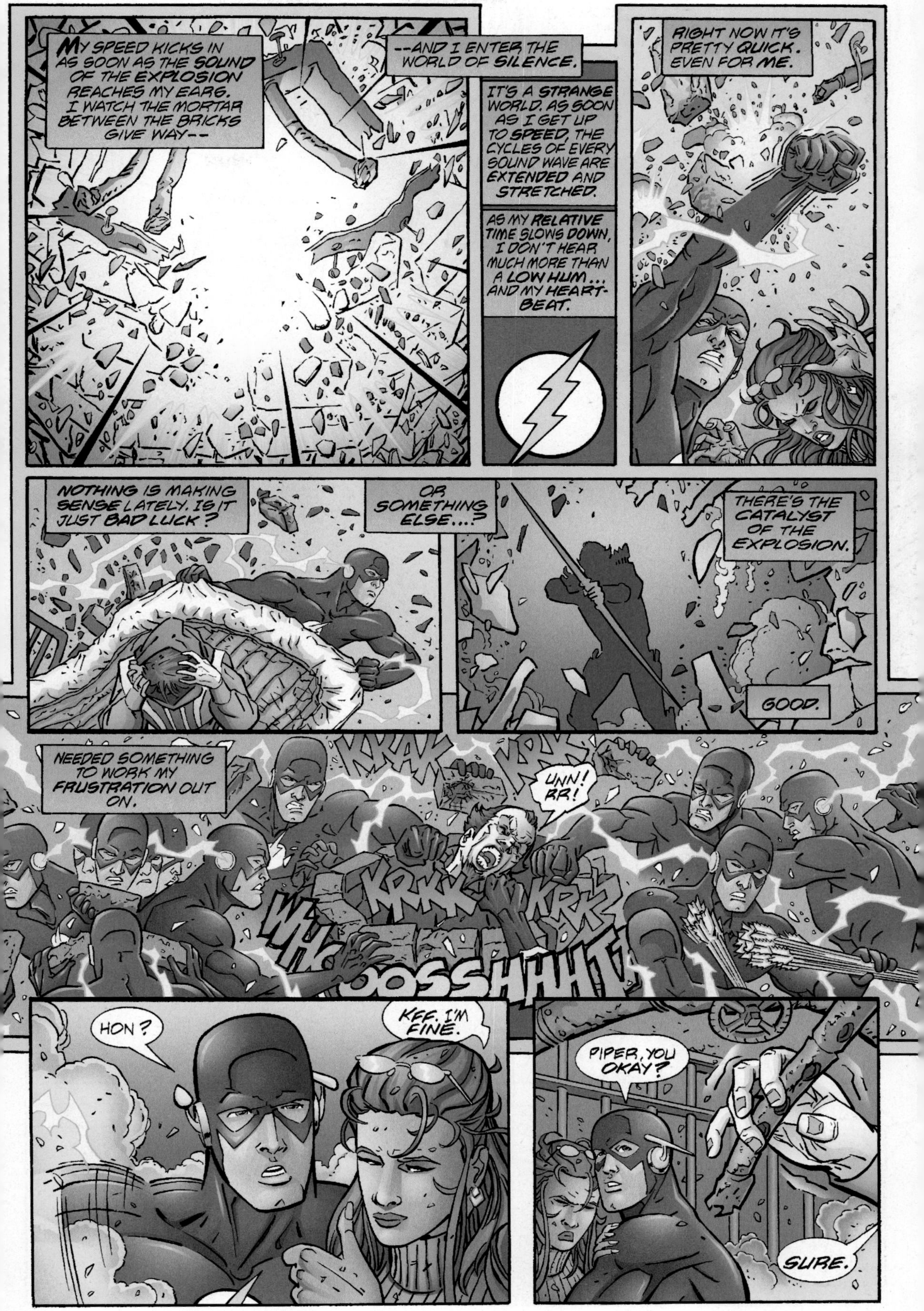
MY SPEED KICKS IN AS SOON AS THE SOUND OF THE EXPLOSION REACHES MY EARS. I WATCH THE MORTAR BETWEEN THE BRICKS GIVE WAY--
--AND I ENTER THE WORLD OF SILENCE.
IT'S A STRANGE WORLD. AS SOON AS I GET UP TO SPEED, THE CYCLES OF EVERY SOUND WAVE ARE EXTENDED AND STRETCHED.
AS MY RELATIVE TIME SLOWS DOWN, I DON'T HEAR MUCH MORE THAN A LOW HUM... AND MY HEART-BEAT.
RIGHT NOW IT'S PRETTY QUICK. EVEN FOR ME.
NOTHING IS MAKING SENSE LATELY. IS IT JUST BAD LUCK?
OR SOMETHING ELSE...?
THERE'S THE CATALYST OF THE EXPLOSION.
GOOD.
NEEDED SOMETHING TO WORK MY FRUSTRATION OUT ON.
UNN! RR!
KRKK
KRKK
WHOOOSSHHHT!
HON?
KFF. I'M FINE.
PIPER, YOU OKAY?
SURE.

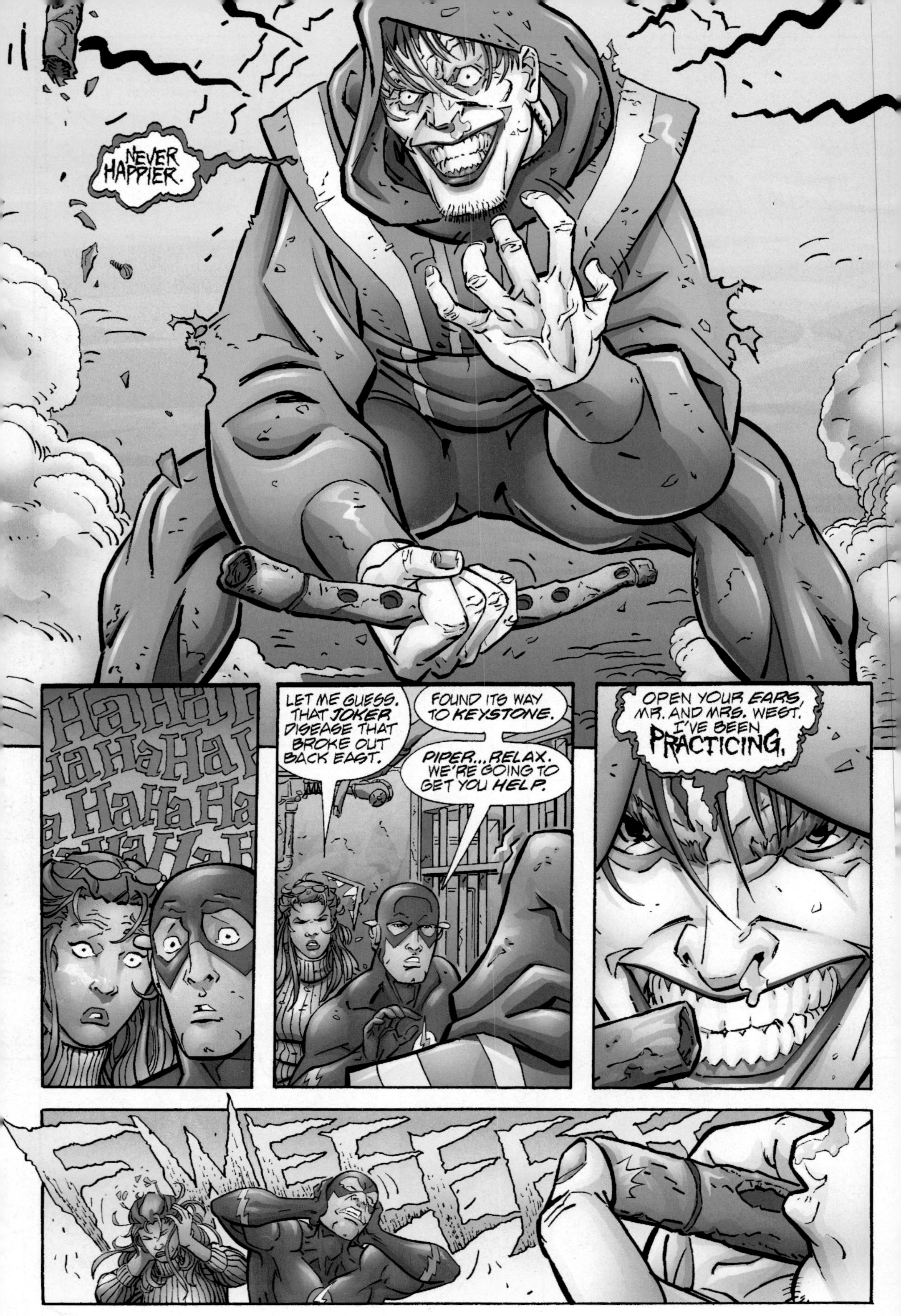
NEVER HAPPIER.
HaHaHa HaHaHa HaHaHa HaHaHa
LET ME GUESS. THAT JOKER DISEASE THAT BROKE OUT BACK EAST.
FOUND ITS WAY TO KEYSTONE.
PIPER...RELAX. WE'RE GOING TO GET YOU HELP.
OPEN YOUR EARS, MR. AND MRS. WEST. I'VE BEEN PRACTICING.
EWEEEEP

WHAT THE HELL IS GOING ON OUT--

WRUNNCH

KRAKOW! KRAKOW!

D-DEADSHOT? APPRECIATE YA SHUTTIN' THEM... EARBASHERS UP BUT... *ksff*...

...WH-WHAT ARE YA... DOIN' HERE, COBBER?

COME TO FINISH OL'... *ksff*... DIGGER OFF?

NAW. JUST COME TO SHOW MY *BUDDY* A GOOD TIME--

SHMM

SHWWMP

AAAAHH--

AAAA!

--AND HELP HIM GET BACK ON HIS FEET. *Heh Heh.*

BAWHAHAHAHA

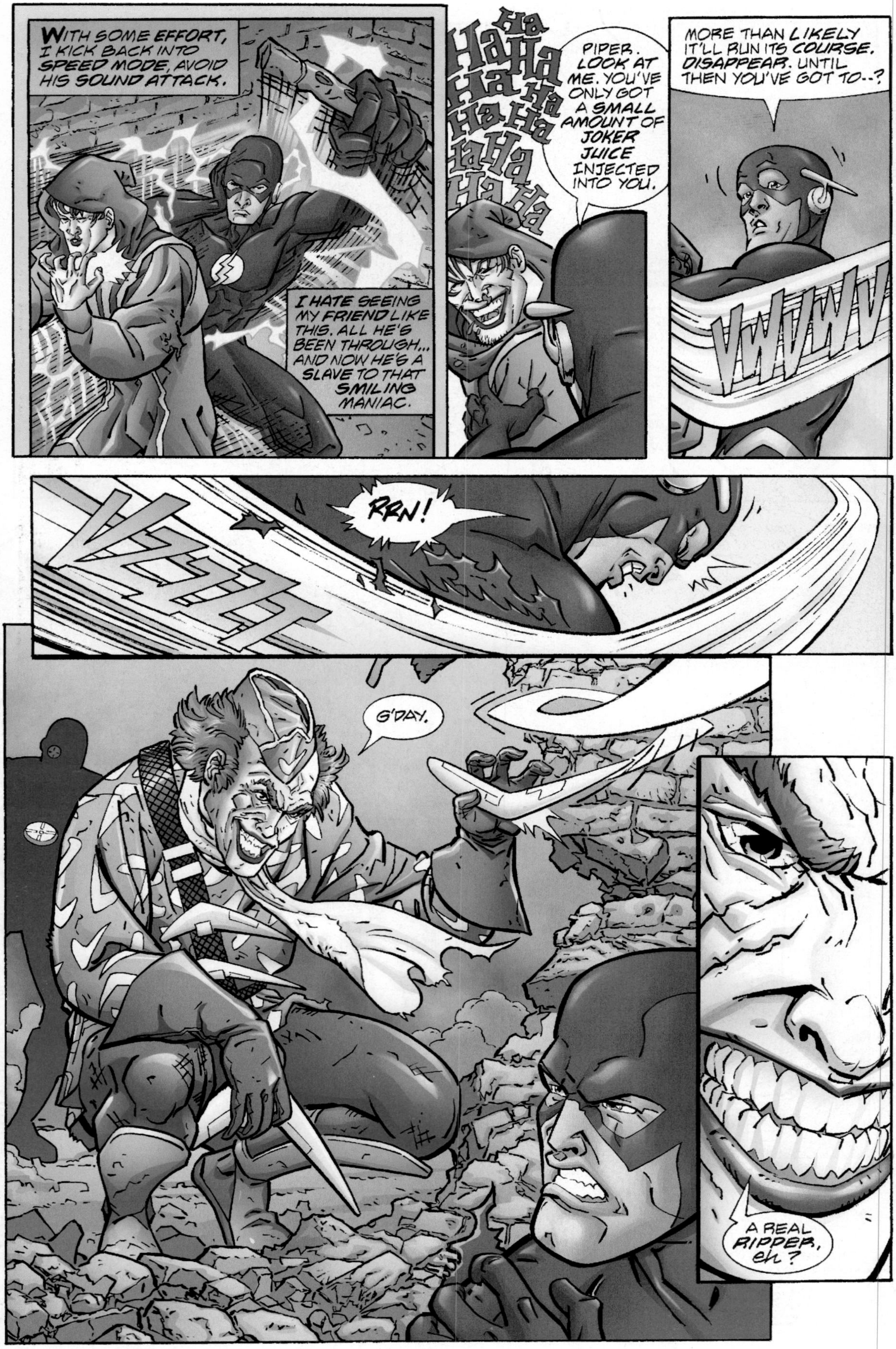

WITH SOME EFFORT, I KICK BACK INTO SPEED MODE, AVOID HIS SOUND ATTACK.
I HATE SEEING MY FRIEND LIKE THIS. ALL HE'S BEEN THROUGH... AND NOW HE'S A SLAVE TO THAT SMILING MANIAC.
HA HA HA HA HA HA HA HA HA HA HA HA HA
PIPER. LOOK AT ME. YOU'VE ONLY GOT A SMALL AMOUNT OF JOKER JUICE INJECTED INTO YOU.
MORE THAN LIKELY IT'LL RUN ITS COURSE. DISAPPEAR. UNTIL THEN YOU'VE GOT TO..?
VWVWV
RRN!
G'DAY.
A REAL RIPPER, eh?

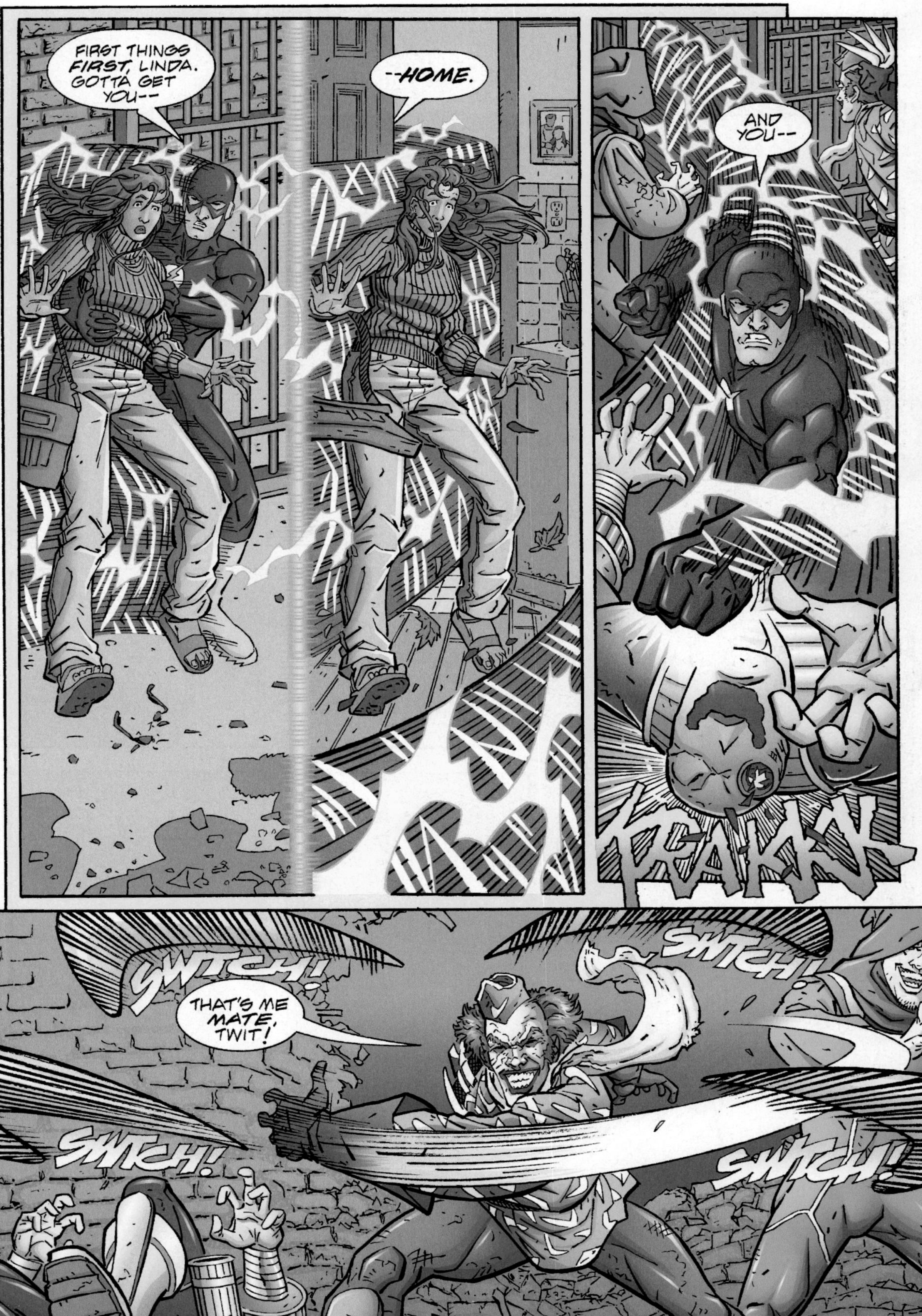
FIRST THINGS FIRST, LINDA. GOTTA GET YOU--
--HOME.
AND YOU--
KRAKKK
SWITCH!
THAT'S ME MATE, TWIT!
SWITCH!
SWITCH!
SWITCH!

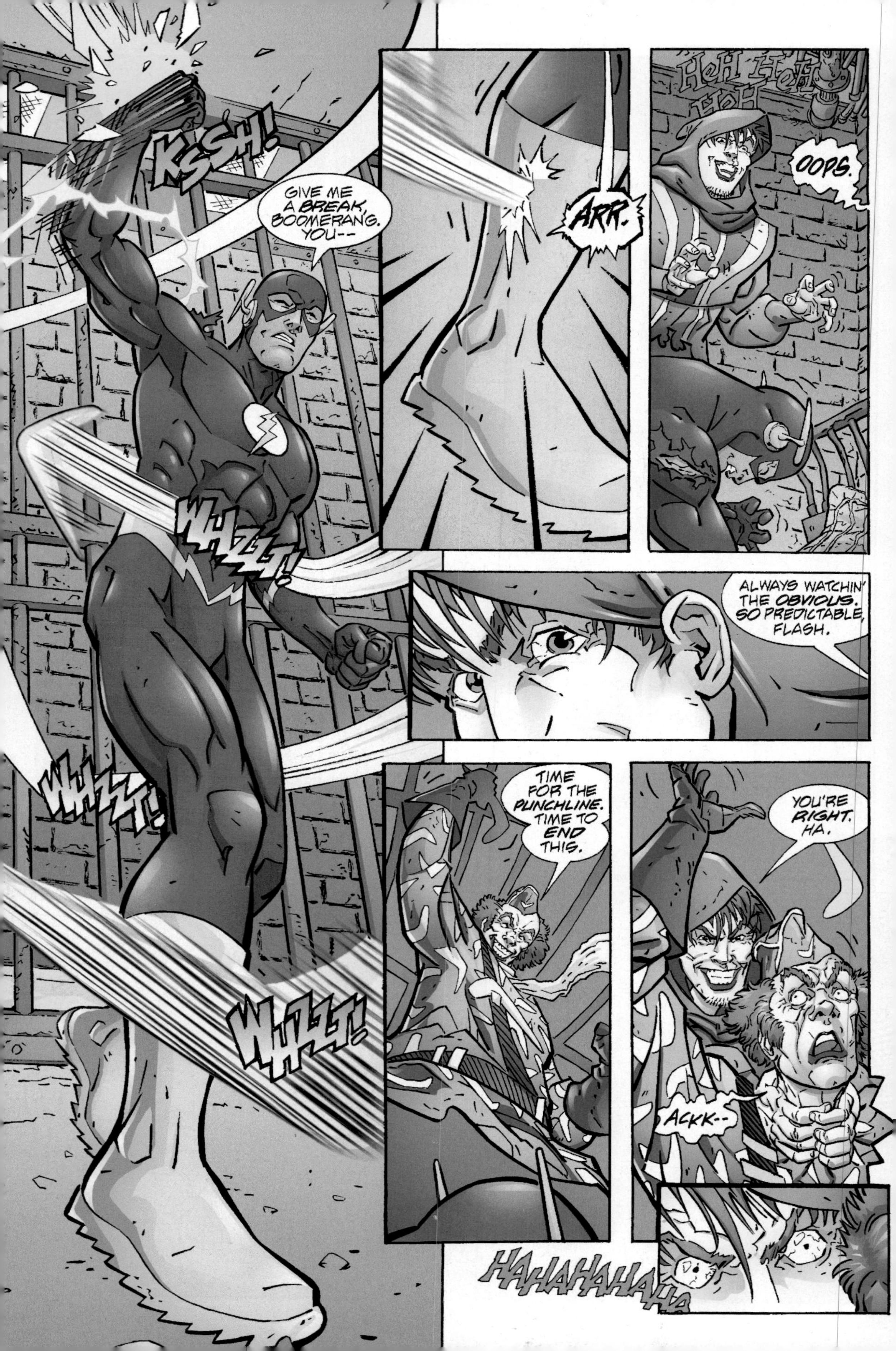
K'SSH!
GIVE ME A BREAK, BOOMERANG. YOU--
WHZZT!
WHZZT!
WHZZT!
ARR.
HEH HEH HEH HEH
OOPS.
ALWAYS WATCHIN' THE OBVIOUS. SO PREDICTABLE, FLASH.
TIME FOR THE PUNCHLINE. TIME TO END THIS.
YOU'RE RIGHT. HA.
ACKK--
HAHAHAHAHA

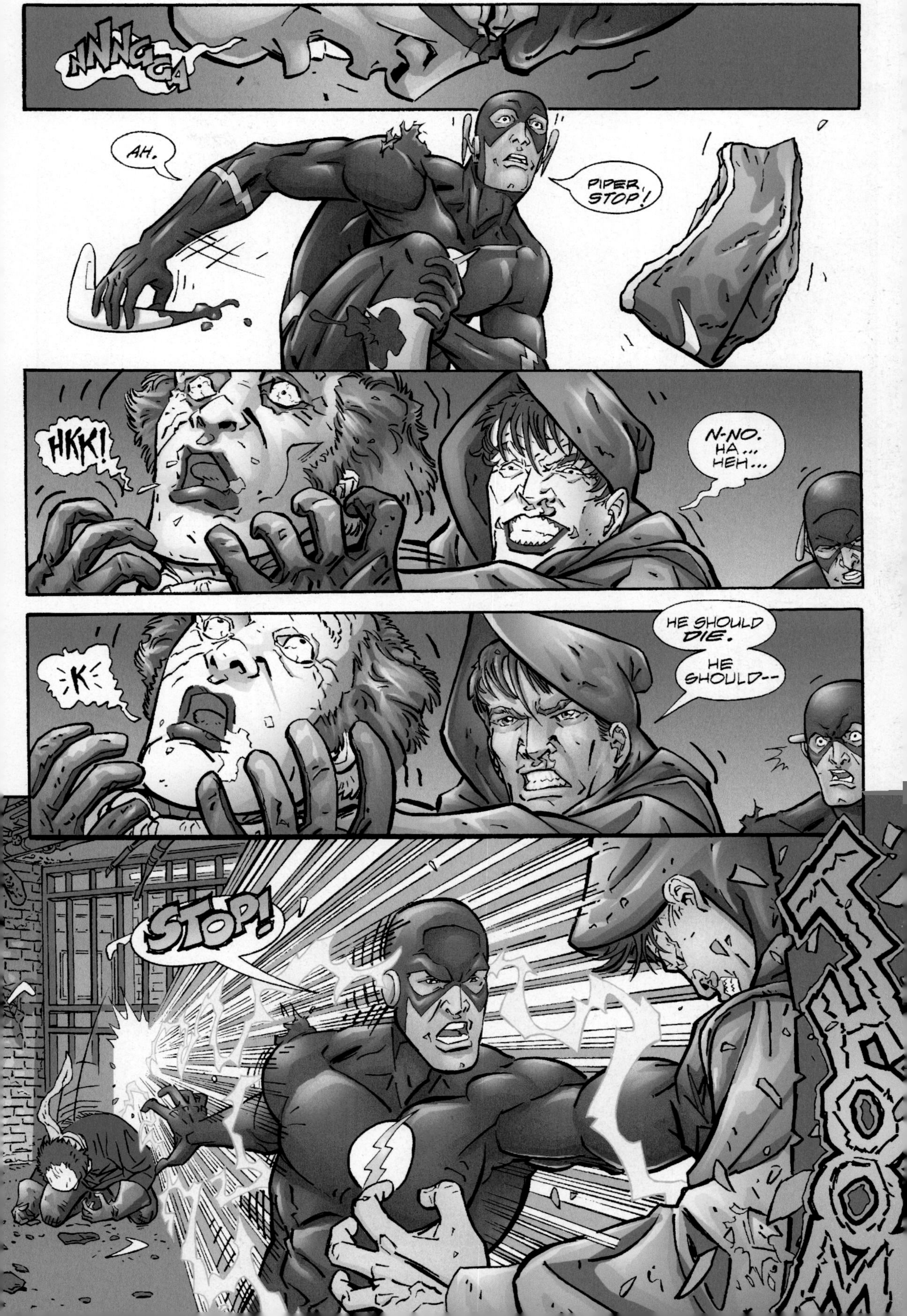
NNNGGA
AH.
PIPER. STOP!
HKK!
N-NO. HA... HEH...
K
HE SHOULD DIE.
HE SHOULD--
STOP!
THOOM

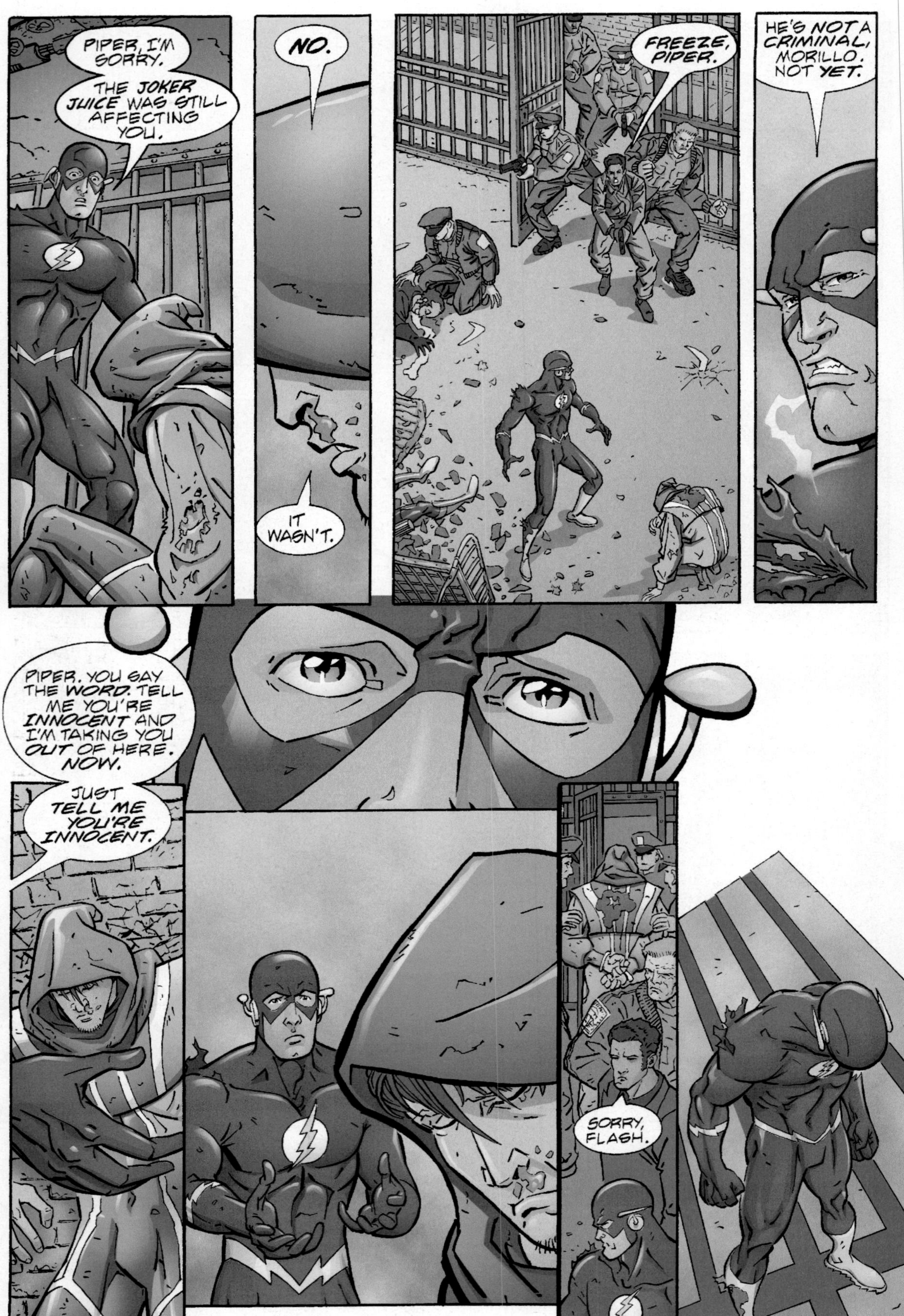

PIPER, I'M SORRY.
THE JOKER JUICE WAS STILL AFFECTING YOU.
NO.
IT WASN'T.
FREEZE, PIPER.
HE'S NOT A CRIMINAL, MORILLO. NOT YET.
PIPER. YOU SAY THE WORD. TELL ME YOU'RE INNOCENT AND I'M TAKING YOU OUT OF HERE. NOW.
JUST TELL ME YOU'RE INNOCENT.
SORRY, FLASH.

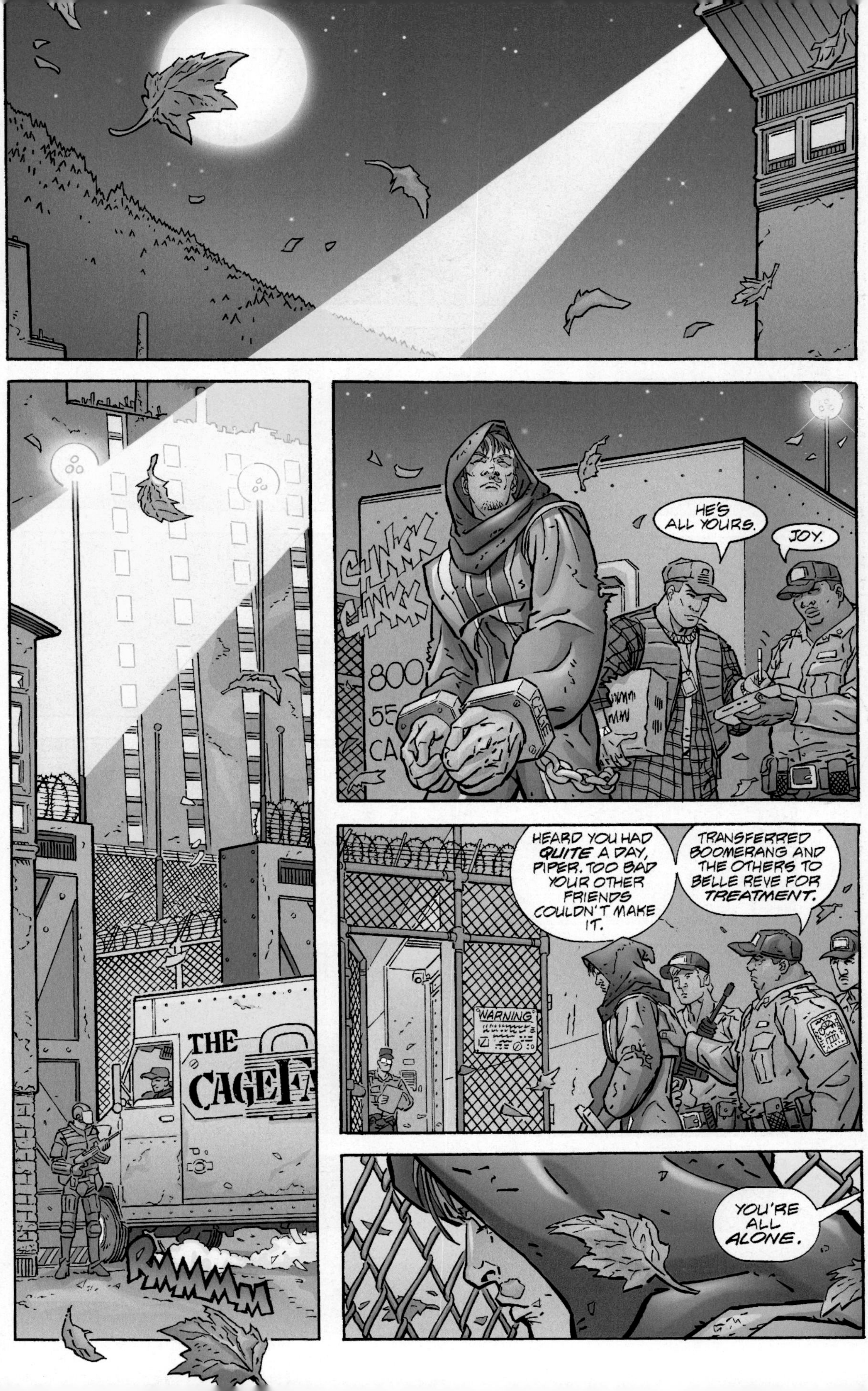
THE CAGE
HE'S ALL YOURS.
JOY.
WARNING
HEARD YOU HAD QUITE A DAY, PIPER. TOO BAD YOUR OTHER FRIENDS COULDN'T MAKE IT.
TRANSFERRED BOOMERANG AND THE OTHERS TO BELLE REVE FOR TREATMENT.
YOU'RE ALL ALONE.

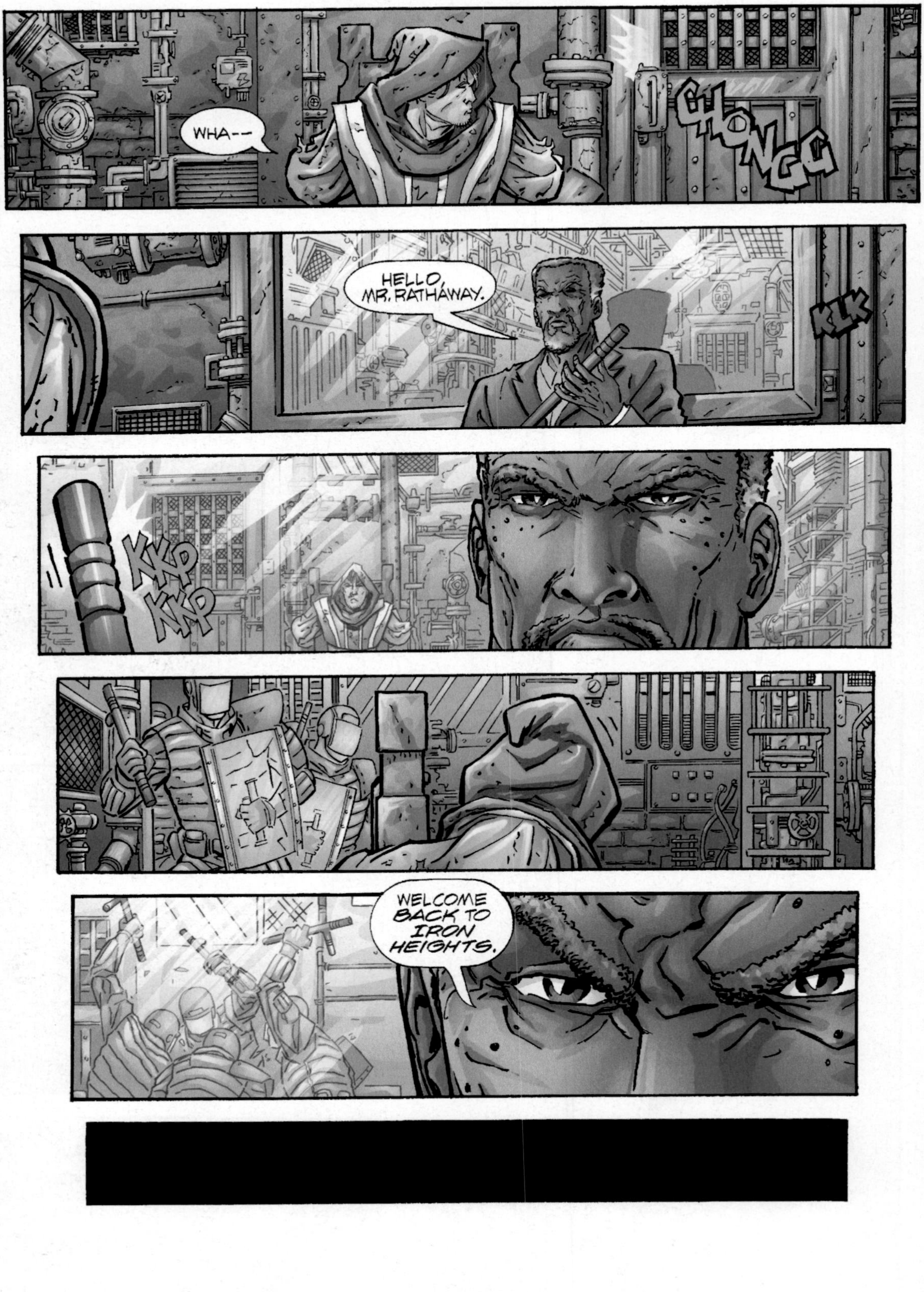
WHA--
CHONGG
HELLO, MR. RATHAWAY.
KLK
KKP KKP
WELCOME BACK TO IRON HEIGHTS.

[redacted]

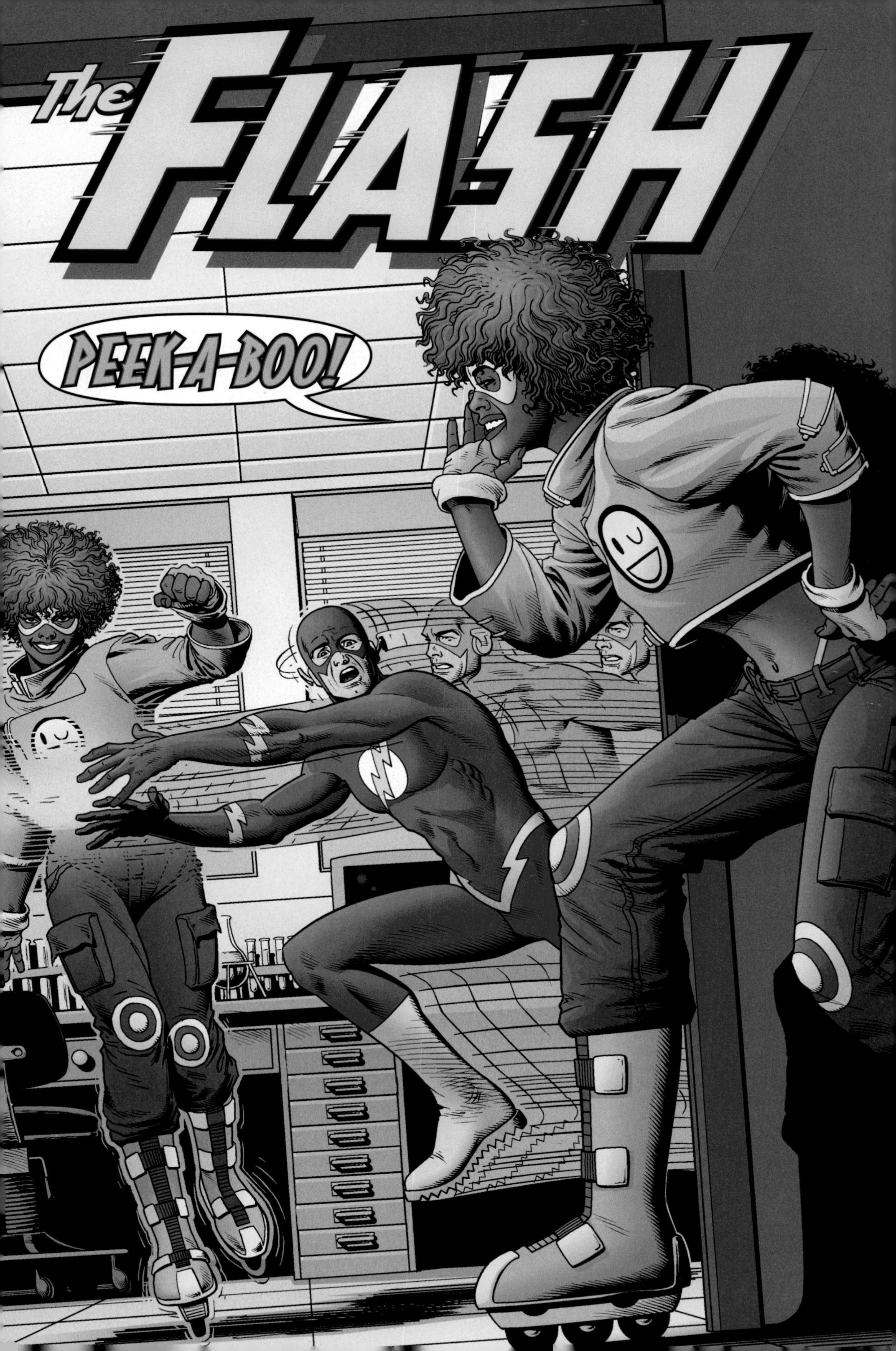
The FLASH
PEEK-A-BOO!

COVER ART BY **BRIAN BOLLAND**

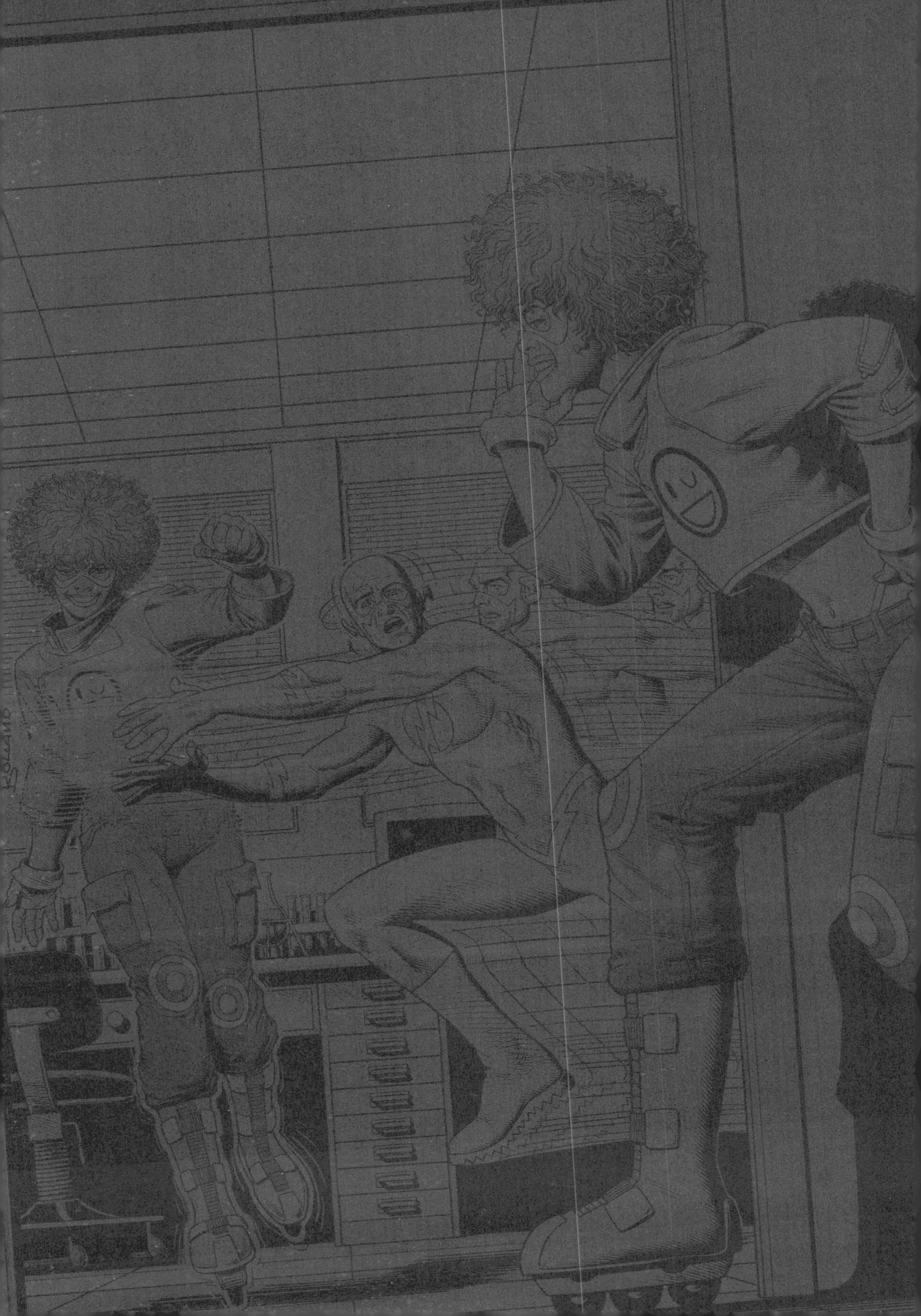
BOLLAND

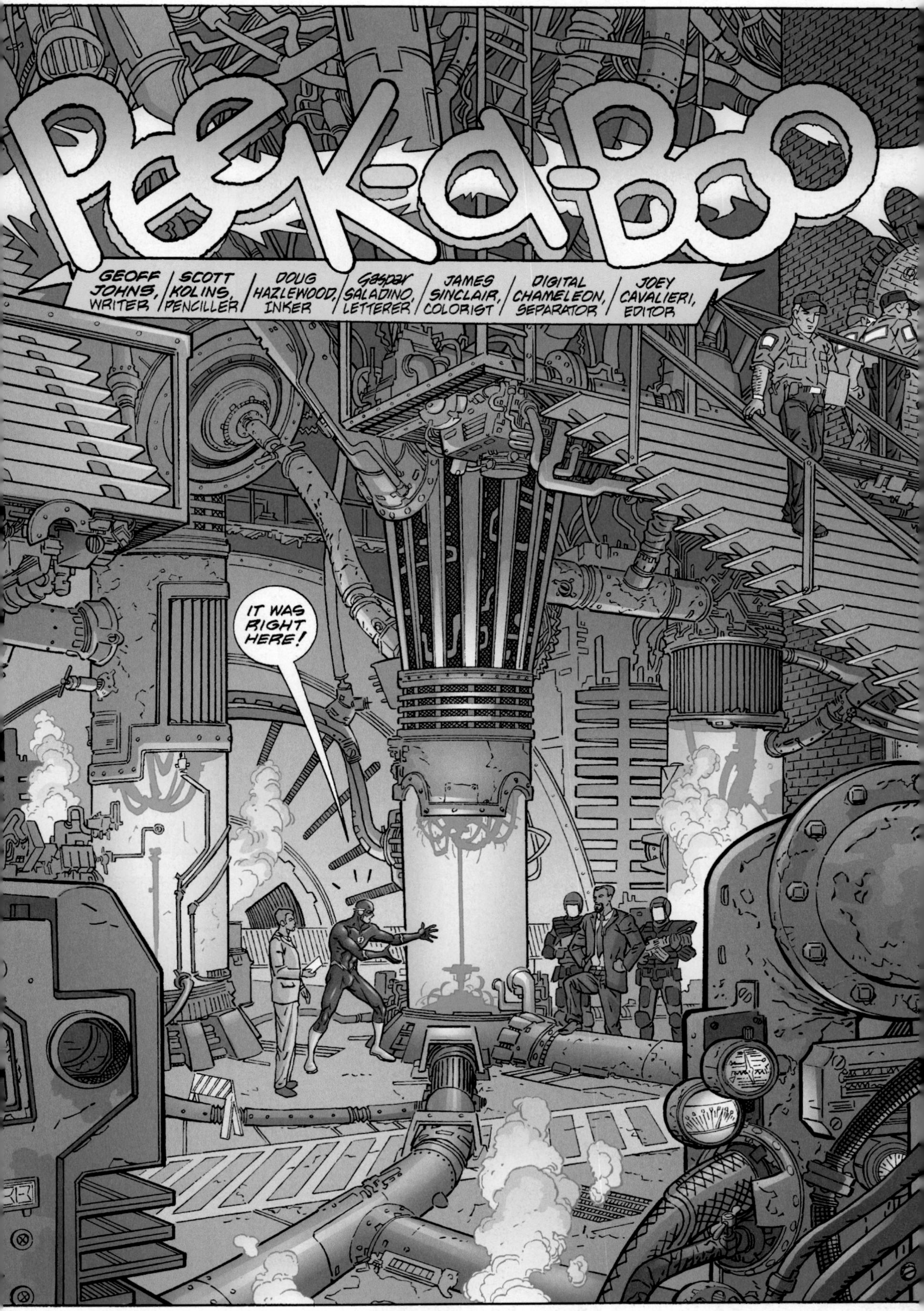
PEEK-A-BOO
GEOFF JOHNS, WRITER
SCOTT KOLINS, PENCILLER
DOUG HAZLEWOOD, INKER
Gaspar SALADINO, LETTERER
JAMES SINCLAIR, COLORIST
DIGITAL CHAMELEON, SEPARATOR
JOEY CAVALIERI, EDITOR
IT WAS RIGHT HERE!

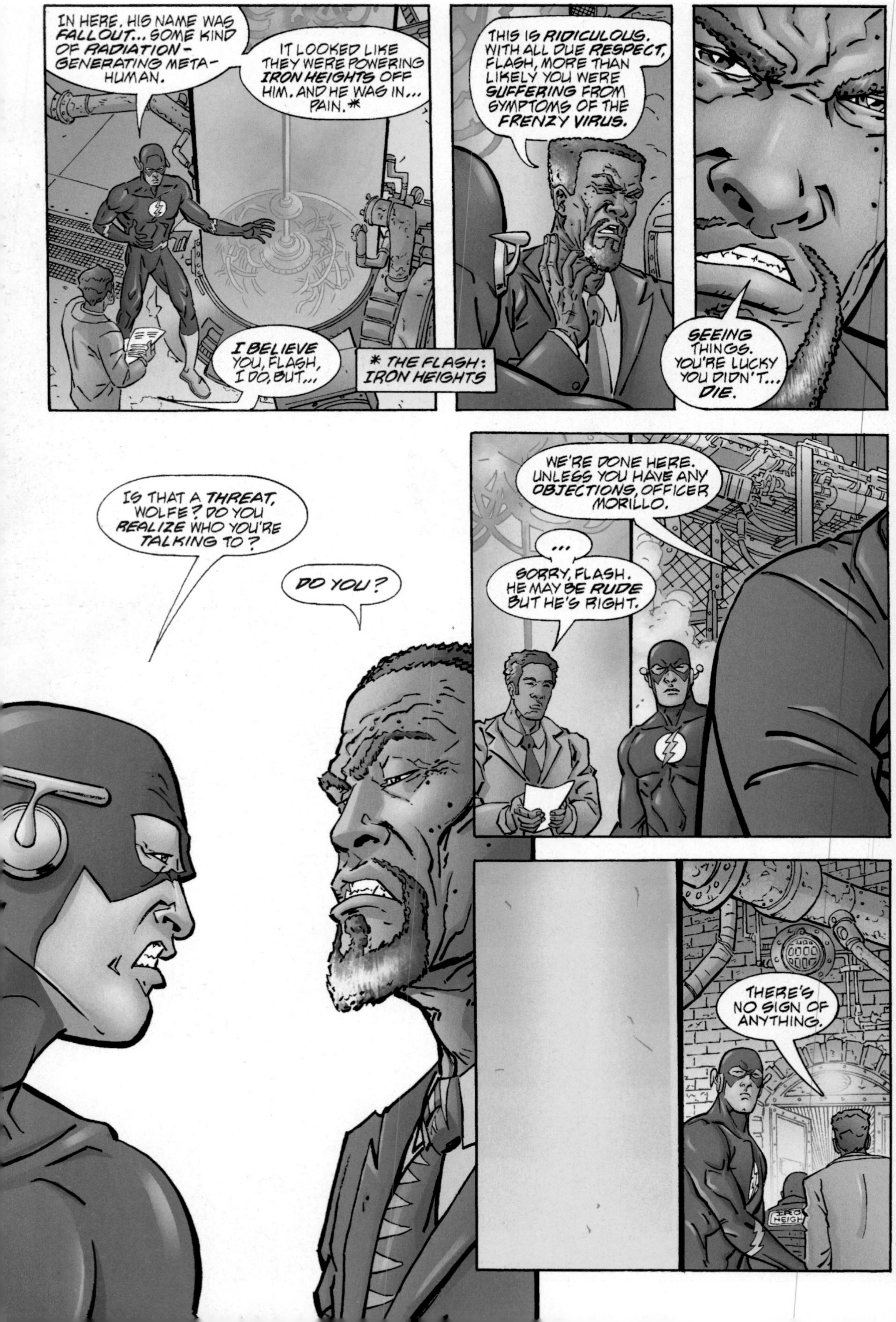
IN HERE. HIS NAME WAS FALLOUT... SOME KIND OF RADIATION-GENERATING META-HUMAN.
IT LOOKED LIKE THEY WERE POWERING IRON HEIGHTS OFF HIM. AND HE WAS IN... PAIN.*
I BELIEVE YOU, FLASH, I DO, BUT...
* THE FLASH: IRON HEIGHTS
THIS IS RIDICULOUS. WITH ALL DUE RESPECT, FLASH, MORE THAN LIKELY YOU WERE SUFFERING FROM SYMPTOMS OF THE FRENZY VIRUS.
SEEING THINGS. YOU'RE LUCKY YOU DIDN'T... DIE.
IS THAT A THREAT, WOLFE? DO YOU REALIZE WHO YOU'RE TALKING TO?
DO YOU?
WE'RE DONE HERE. UNLESS YOU HAVE ANY OBJECTIONS, OFFICER MORILLO.
...
SORRY, FLASH. HE MAY BE RUDE BUT HE'S RIGHT.
THERE'S NO SIGN OF ANYTHING.

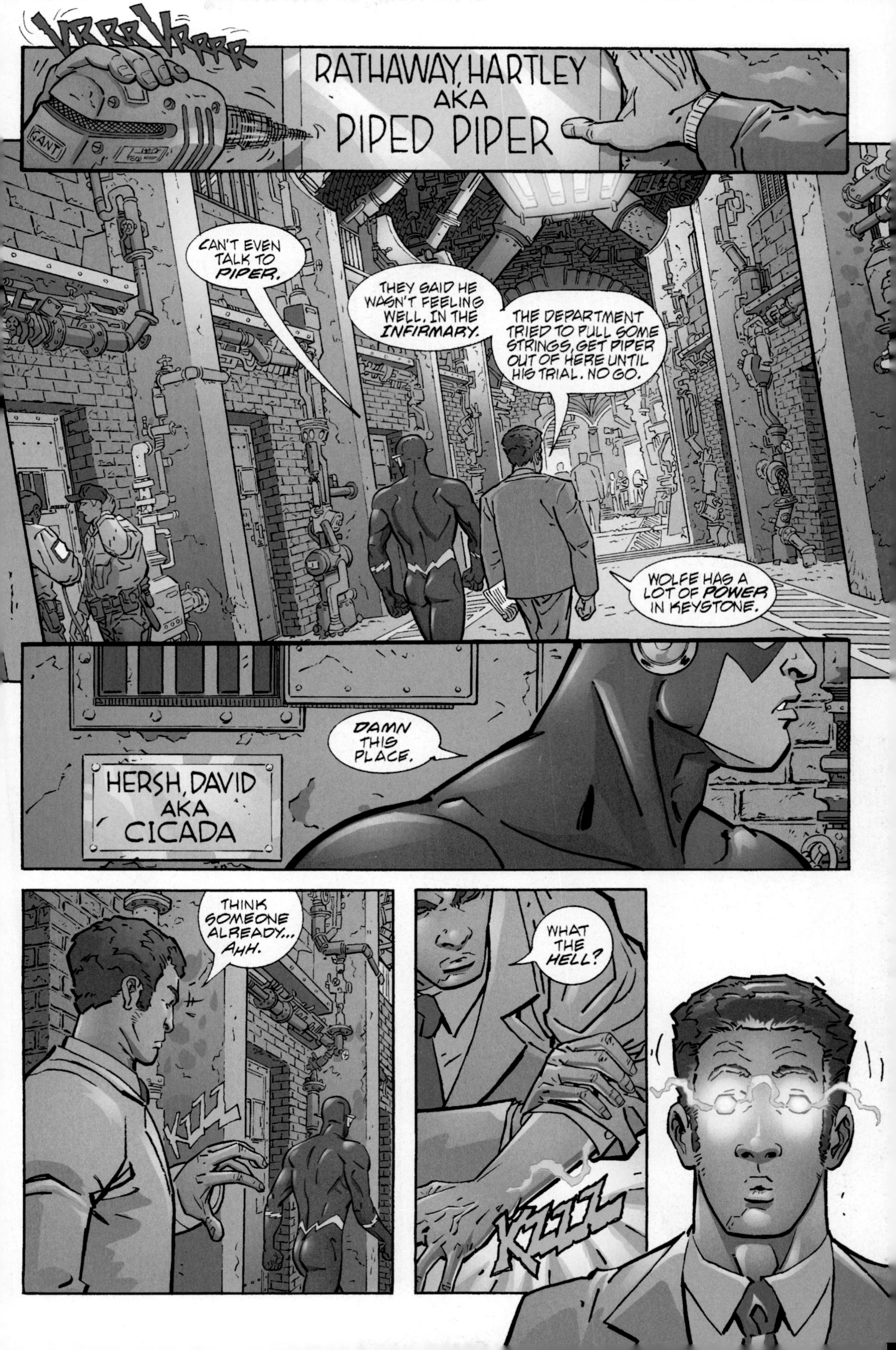
VRRRVRRRR
RATHAWAY, HARTLEY AKA PIPED PIPER
CAN'T EVEN TALK TO PIPER.
THEY SAID HE WASN'T FEELING WELL. IN THE INFIRMARY.
THE DEPARTMENT TRIED TO PULL SOME STRINGS, GET PIPER OUT OF HERE UNTIL HIS TRIAL. NO GO.
WOLFE HAS A LOT OF POWER IN KEYSTONE.
HERSH, DAVID AKA CICADA
DAMN THIS PLACE.
THINK SOMEONE ALREADY... AHH.
KZZZ
WHAT THE HELL?
KZZZ

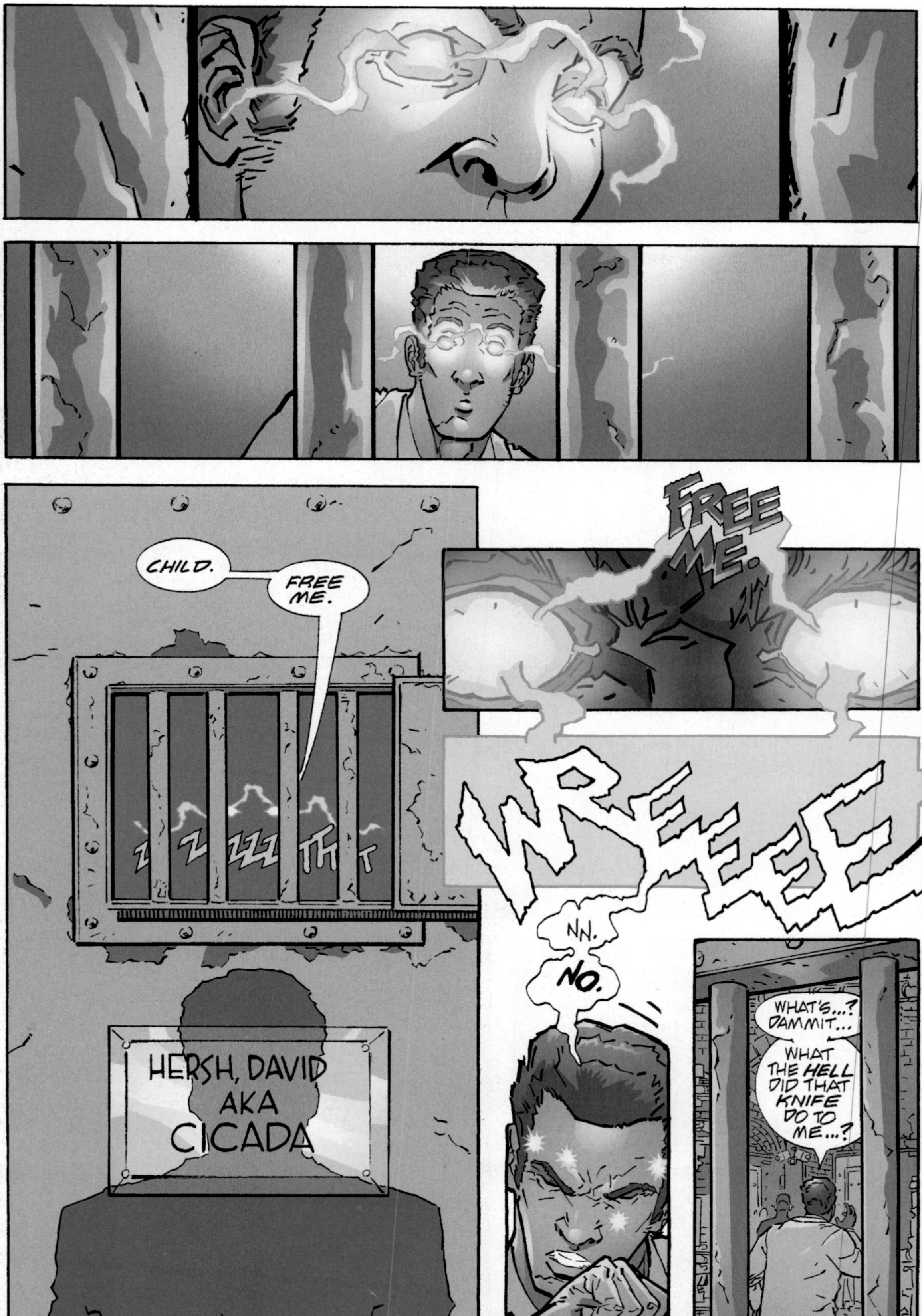
CHILD.
FREE ME.
HERSH, DAVID AKA CICADA
ZZZZZTHT
FREE ME.
WREEEEE
NN.
NO.
WHAT'S...? DAMMIT...
WHAT THE HELL DID THAT KNIFE DO TO ME...?

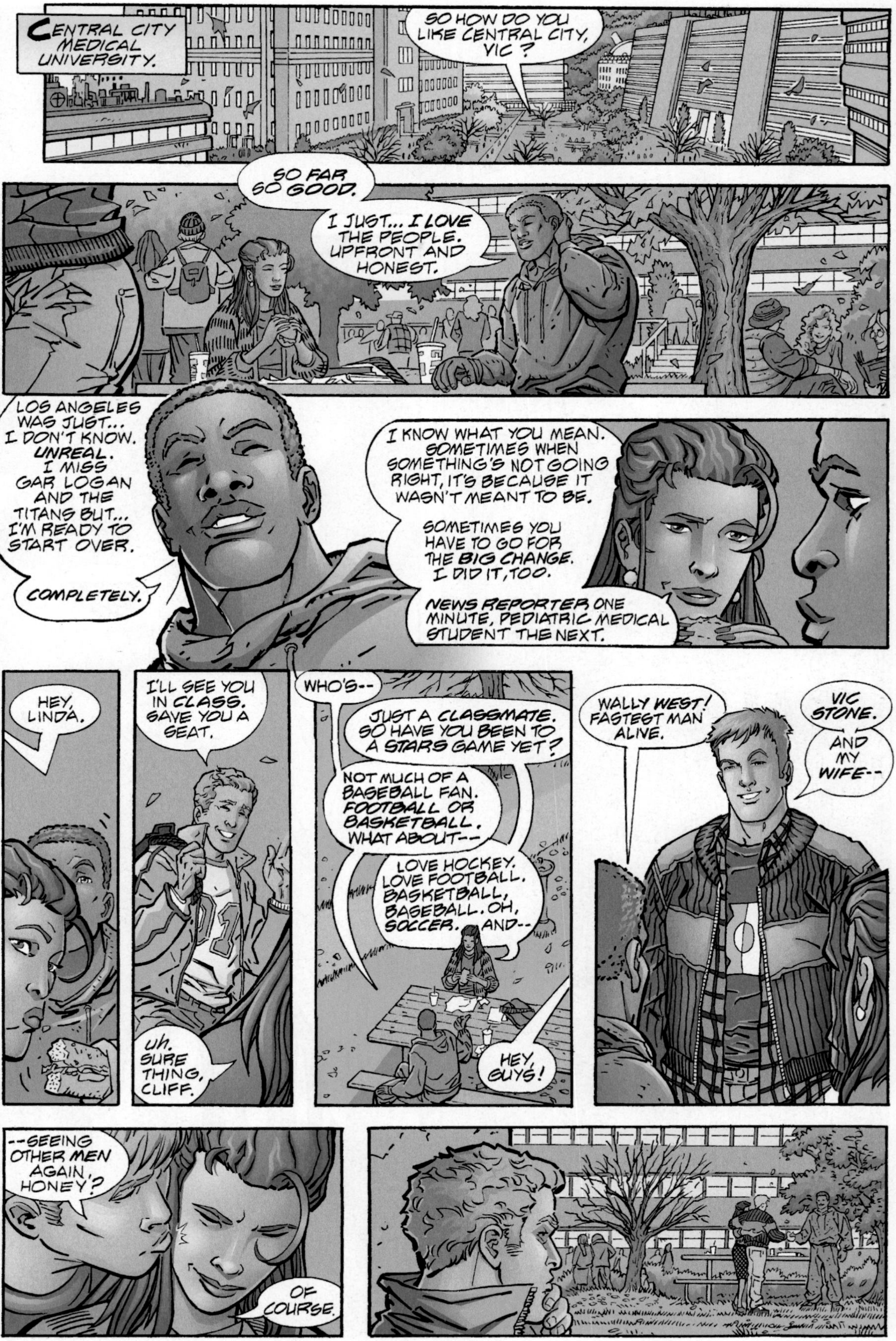
CENTRAL CITY MEDICAL UNIVERSITY.
SO HOW DO YOU LIKE CENTRAL CITY, VIC ?
SO FAR SO GOOD.
I JUST... I LOVE THE PEOPLE. UPFRONT AND HONEST.
LOS ANGELES WAS JUST... I DON'T KNOW. UNREAL. I MISS GAR LOGAN AND THE TITANS BUT... I'M READY TO START OVER.
COMPLETELY.
I KNOW WHAT YOU MEAN. SOMETIMES WHEN SOMETHING'S NOT GOING RIGHT, IT'S BECAUSE IT WASN'T MEANT TO BE.
SOMETIMES YOU HAVE TO GO FOR THE BIG CHANGE. I DID IT, TOO.
NEWS REPORTER ONE MINUTE, PEDIATRIC MEDICAL STUDENT THE NEXT.
HEY, LINDA.
I'LL SEE YOU IN CLASS. SAVE YOU A SEAT.
uh. SURE THING, CLIFF.
WHO'S--
JUST A CLASSMATE. SO HAVE YOU BEEN TO A STARS GAME YET?
NOT MUCH OF A BASEBALL FAN. FOOTBALL OR BASKETBALL. WHAT ABOUT--
LOVE HOCKEY. LOVE FOOTBALL. BASKETBALL, BASEBALL. OH, SOCCER. AND--
HEY, GUYS!
WALLY WEST! FASTEST MAN ALIVE.
VIC STONE.
AND MY WIFE--
--SEEING OTHER MEN AGAIN, HONEY?
OF COURSE.

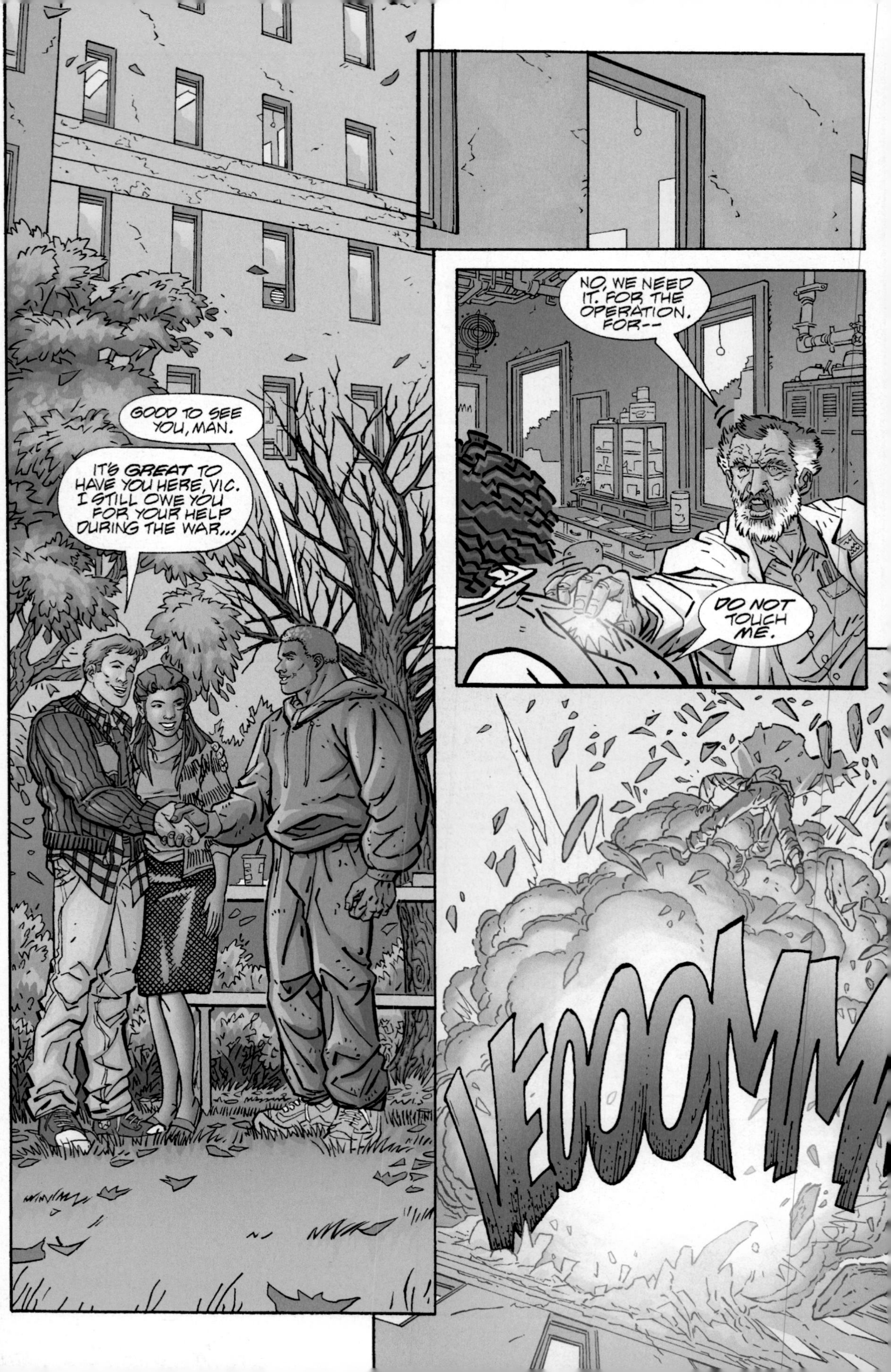
GOOD TO SEE YOU, MAN.
IT'S GREAT TO HAVE YOU HERE, VIC. I STILL OWE YOU FOR YOUR HELP DURING THE WAR...
NO, WE NEED IT. FOR THE OPERATION. FOR--
DO NOT TOUCH ME.
VEOOOMM

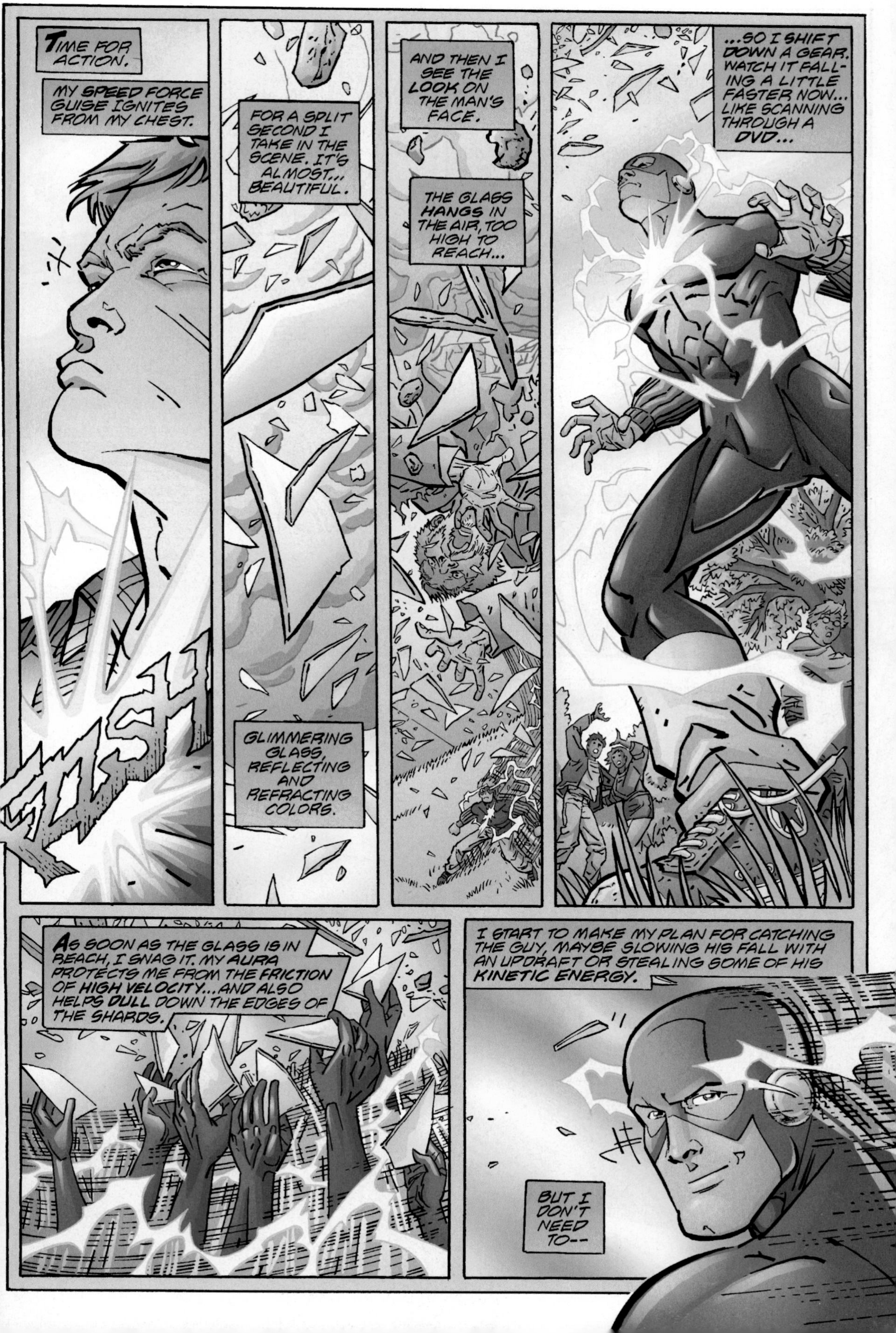
TIME FOR ACTION.
MY SPEED FORCE GUISE IGNITES FROM MY CHEST.
FOR A SPLIT SECOND I TAKE IN THE SCENE. IT'S ALMOST... BEAUTIFUL.
GLIMMERING GLASS, REFLECTING AND REFRACTING COLORS.
AND THEN I SEE THE LOOK ON THE MAN'S FACE.
THE GLASS HANGS IN THE AIR, TOO HIGH TO REACH...
...SO I SHIFT DOWN A GEAR. WATCH IT FALLING A LITTLE FASTER NOW... LIKE SCANNING THROUGH A DVD...
AS SOON AS THE GLASS IS IN REACH, I SNAG IT. MY AURA PROTECTS ME FROM THE FRICTION OF HIGH VELOCITY... AND ALSO HELPS DULL DOWN THE EDGES OF THE SHARDS.
I START TO MAKE MY PLAN FOR CATCHING THE GUY, MAYBE SLOWING HIS FALL WITH AN UPDRAFT OR STEALING SOME OF HIS KINETIC ENERGY.
BUT I DON'T NEED TO--

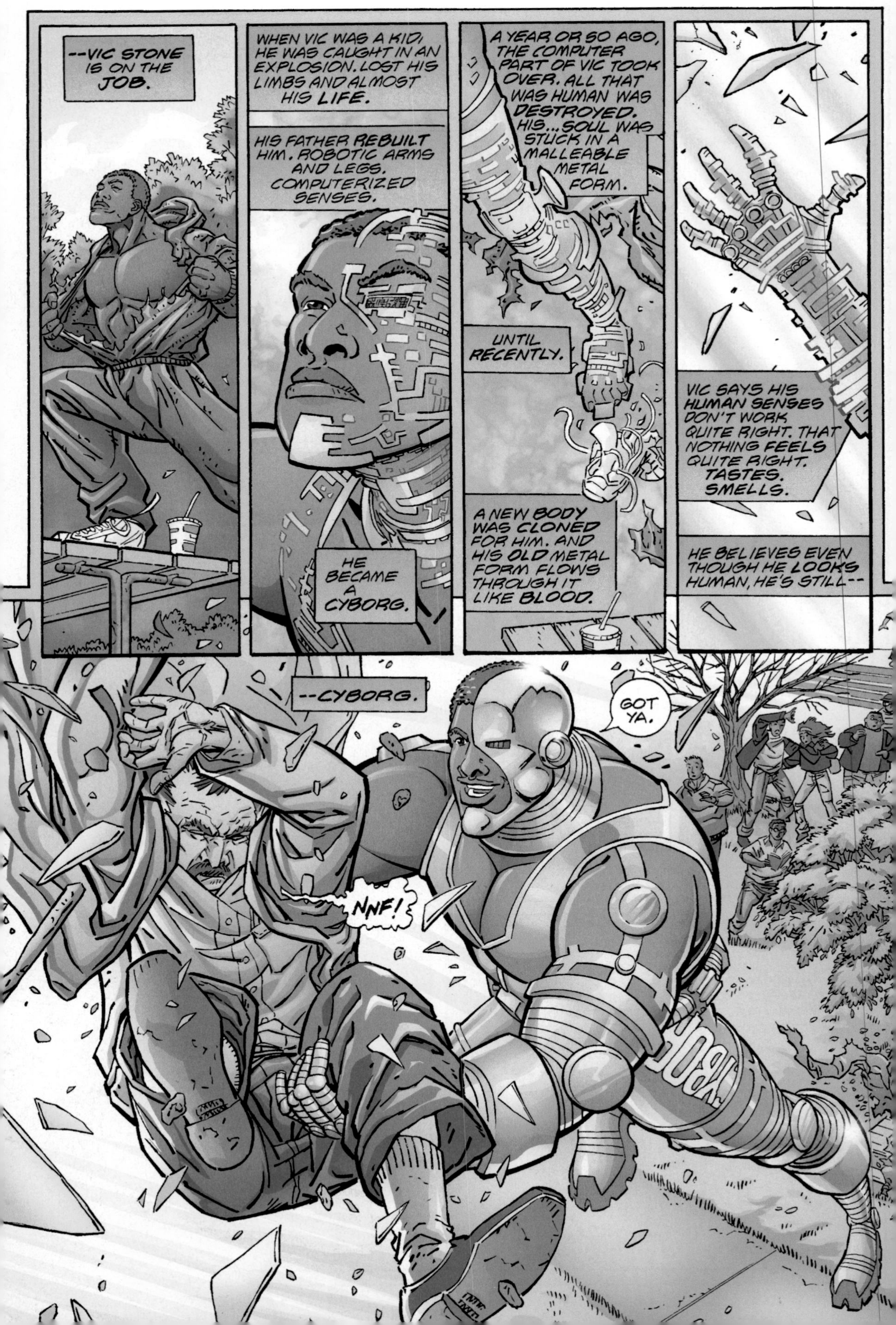
--VIC STONE IS ON THE JOB.
WHEN VIC WAS A KID, HE WAS CAUGHT IN AN EXPLOSION. LOST HIS LIMBS AND ALMOST HIS LIFE.
HIS FATHER REBUILT HIM. ROBOTIC ARMS AND LEGS. COMPUTERIZED SENSES.
HE BECAME A CYBORG.
A YEAR OR SO AGO, THE COMPUTER PART OF VIC TOOK OVER. ALL THAT WAS HUMAN WAS DESTROYED. HIS...SOUL WAS STUCK IN A MALLEABLE METAL FORM.
UNTIL RECENTLY.
A NEW BODY WAS CLONED FOR HIM. AND HIS OLD METAL FORM FLOWS THROUGH IT LIKE BLOOD.
VIC SAYS HIS HUMAN SENSES DON'T WORK QUITE RIGHT. THAT NOTHING FEELS QUITE RIGHT. TASTES. SMELLS.
HE BELIEVES EVEN THOUGH HE LOOKS HUMAN, HE'S STILL--
--CYBORG.
GOT YA.
NNF!

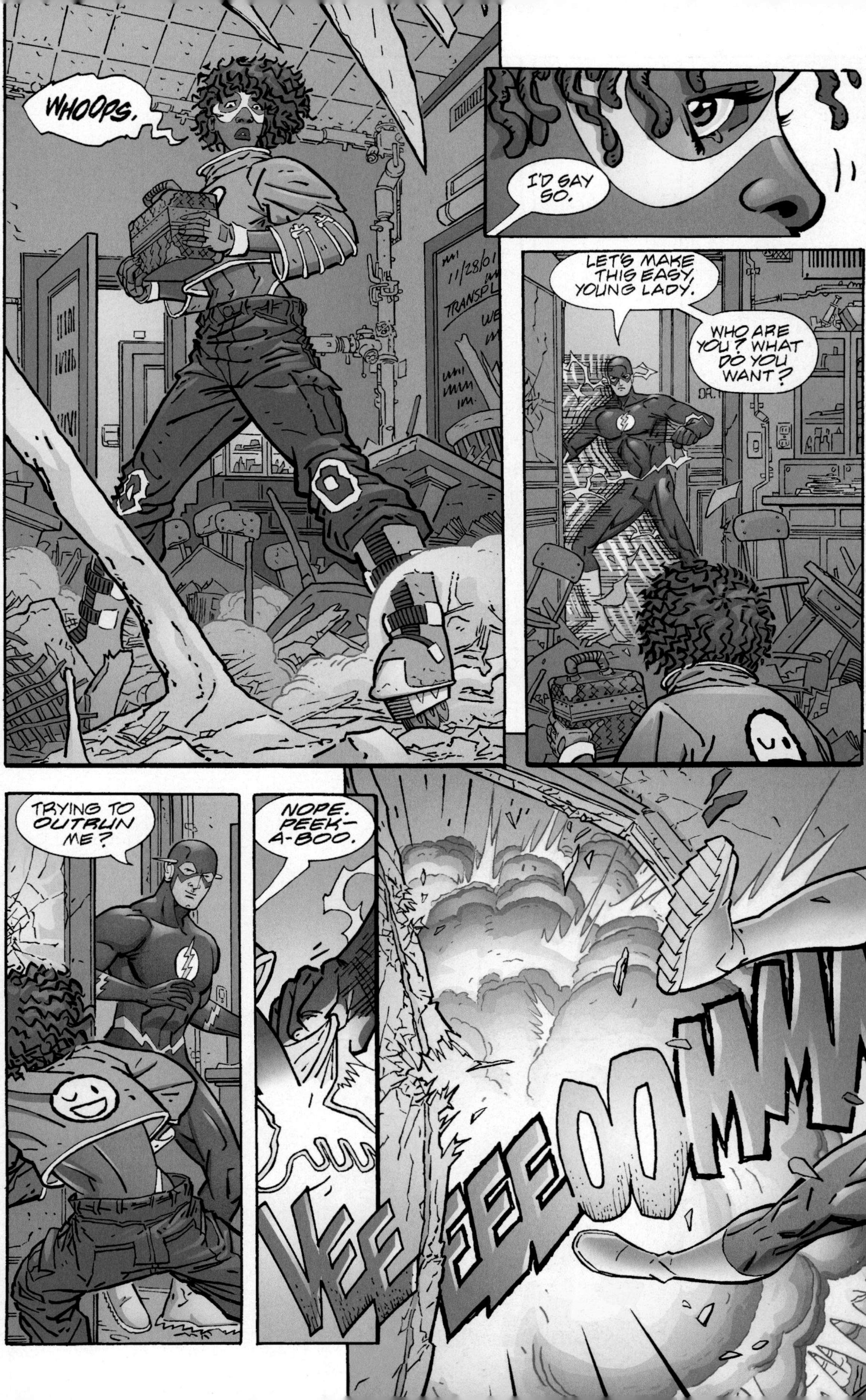
WHOOPS.
I'D SAY SO.
LET'S MAKE THIS EASY, YOUNG LADY.
WHO ARE YOU? WHAT DO YOU WANT?
TRYING TO OUTRUN ME?
NOPE. PEEK-A-BOO.
WEEEEEOOOMMMM

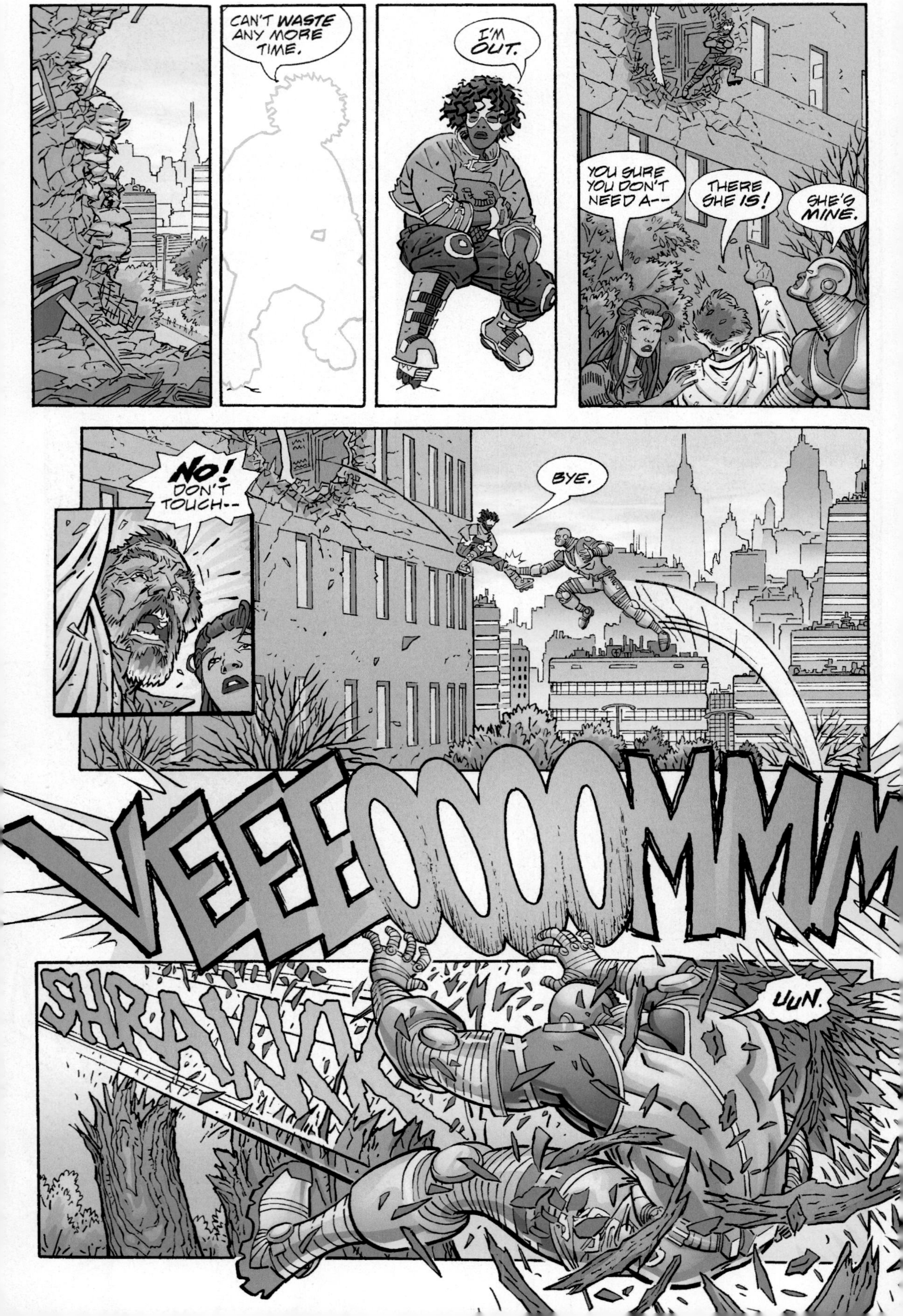
CAN'T WASTE ANY MORE TIME.
I'M OUT.
YOU SURE YOU DON'T NEED A--
THERE SHE IS!
SHE'S MINE.
NO! DON'T TOUCH--
BYE.
VEEEOOOOMMMM
SHRAKKA
UUN.

BBBKKK

SFKK! SFKK! SFKK!

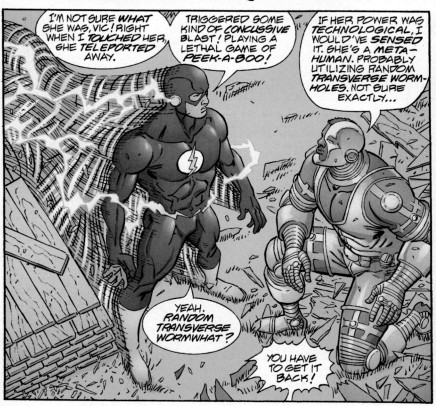

I'M NOT SURE *WHAT* SHE WAS, *VIC!* RIGHT WHEN I *TOUCHED* HER, SHE *TELEPORTED* AWAY.

TRIGGERED SOME KIND OF *CONCUSSIVE* BLAST! PLAYING A LETHAL GAME OF *PEEK-A-BOO!*

IF HER POWER WAS *TECHNOLOGICAL,* I WOULD'VE *SENSED* IT. SHE'S A *META-HUMAN.* PROBABLY UTILIZING *RANDOM TRANSVERSE WORM-HOLES.* NOT SURE EXACTLY...

YEAH. *RANDOM TRANSVERSE WORMWHAT?*

YOU HAVE TO GET IT BACK!

GET *WHAT BACK?* WHAT DID MS. *"PEEK-A-BOO"* TAKE?

A HUMAN *KIDNEY.*

THERE'S A WOMAN *SCHEDULED* FOR TRANSPLANT SURGERY *TONIGHT.* HER CREATINE LEVEL IS AT POINT SIX. SHE'S BEEN WAITING FOR MONTHS.

IF SHE DOESN'T *RECEIVE* THIS *KIDNEY,* SHE WILL *DIE.*

I WAS JUST DOING SOME *FINAL* CHECKING. OH, GOD, NOW IT'S GONE... WITHOUT A TRACE.

...NOT EXACTLY. I GOT HER *GLOVE.* TURN IT INSIDE OUT.

I JUST NEED TO *RUN* THESE *PRINTS.* SEE WHO--

LET ME *SCAN* THEM.

AND DIAL UP AN INTERNET CONNECTION.

WORRR

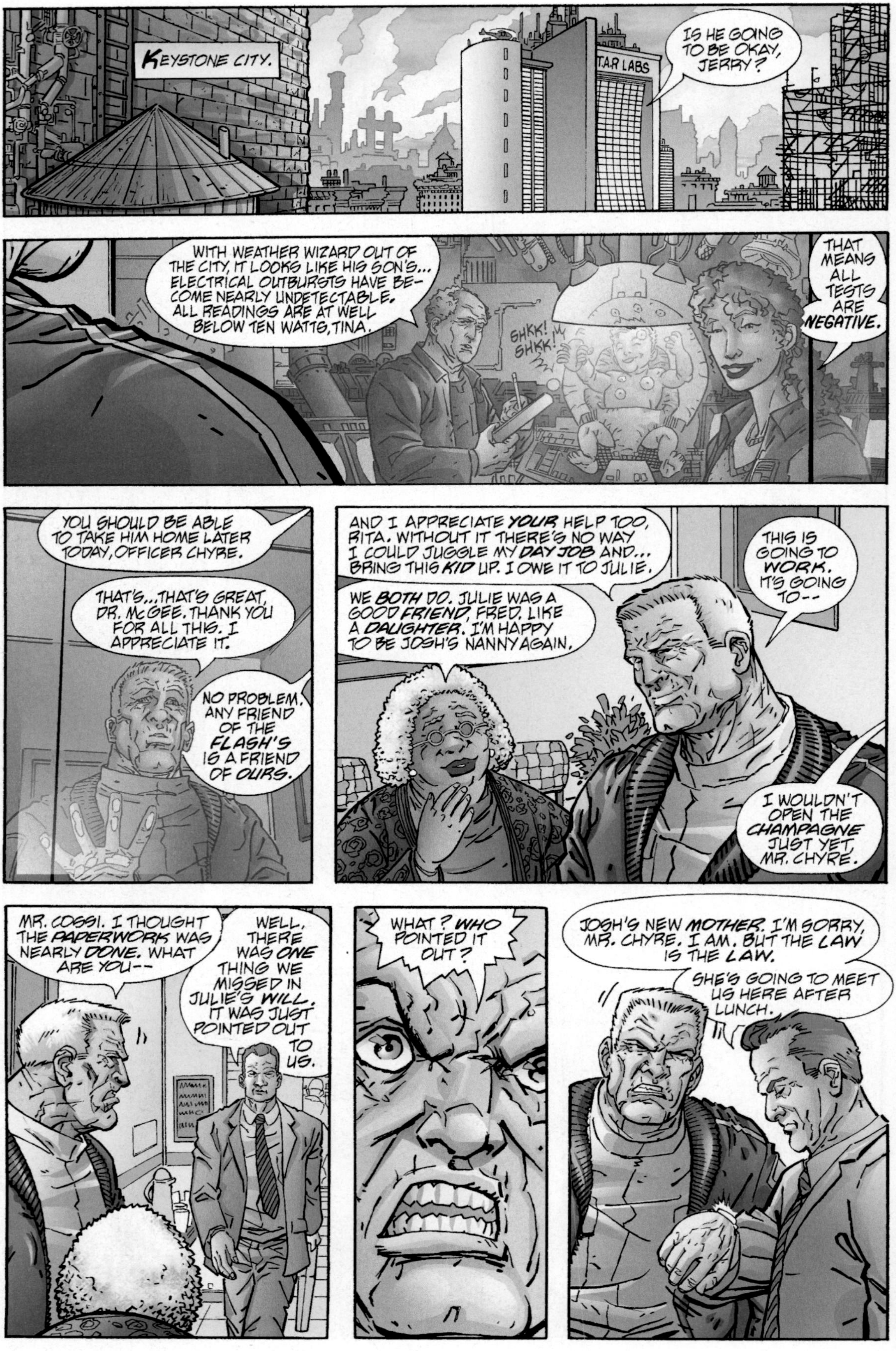
KEYSTONE CITY.
S.T.A.R LABS
IS HE GOING TO BE OKAY, JERRY?
WITH WEATHER WIZARD OUT OF THE CITY, IT LOOKS LIKE HIS SON'S... ELECTRICAL OUTBURSTS HAVE BECOME NEARLY UNDETECTABLE. ALL READINGS ARE AT WELL BELOW TEN WATTS, TINA.
SHKK! SHKK!
THAT MEANS ALL TESTS ARE NEGATIVE.
YOU SHOULD BE ABLE TO TAKE HIM HOME LATER TODAY, OFFICER CHYRE.
THAT'S...THAT'S GREAT, DR. McGEE. THANK YOU FOR ALL THIS. I APPRECIATE IT.
NO PROBLEM. ANY FRIEND OF THE FLASH'S IS A FRIEND OF OURS.
AND I APPRECIATE YOUR HELP TOO, RITA. WITHOUT IT THERE'S NO WAY I COULD JUGGLE MY DAY JOB AND... BRING THIS KID UP. I OWE IT TO JULIE.
WE BOTH DO. JULIE WAS A GOOD FRIEND, FRED. LIKE A DAUGHTER. I'M HAPPY TO BE JOSH'S NANNY AGAIN.
THIS IS GOING TO WORK. IT'S GOING TO--
I WOULDN'T OPEN THE CHAMPAGNE JUST YET, MR. CHYRE.
MR. COSSI. I THOUGHT THE PAPERWORK WAS NEARLY DONE. WHAT ARE YOU--
WELL, THERE WAS ONE THING WE MISSED IN JULIE'S WILL. IT WAS JUST POINTED OUT TO US.
WHAT? WHO POINTED IT OUT?
JOSH'S NEW MOTHER. I'M SORRY, MR. CHYRE. I AM. BUT THE LAW IS THE LAW.
SHE'S GOING TO MEET US HERE AFTER LUNCH.

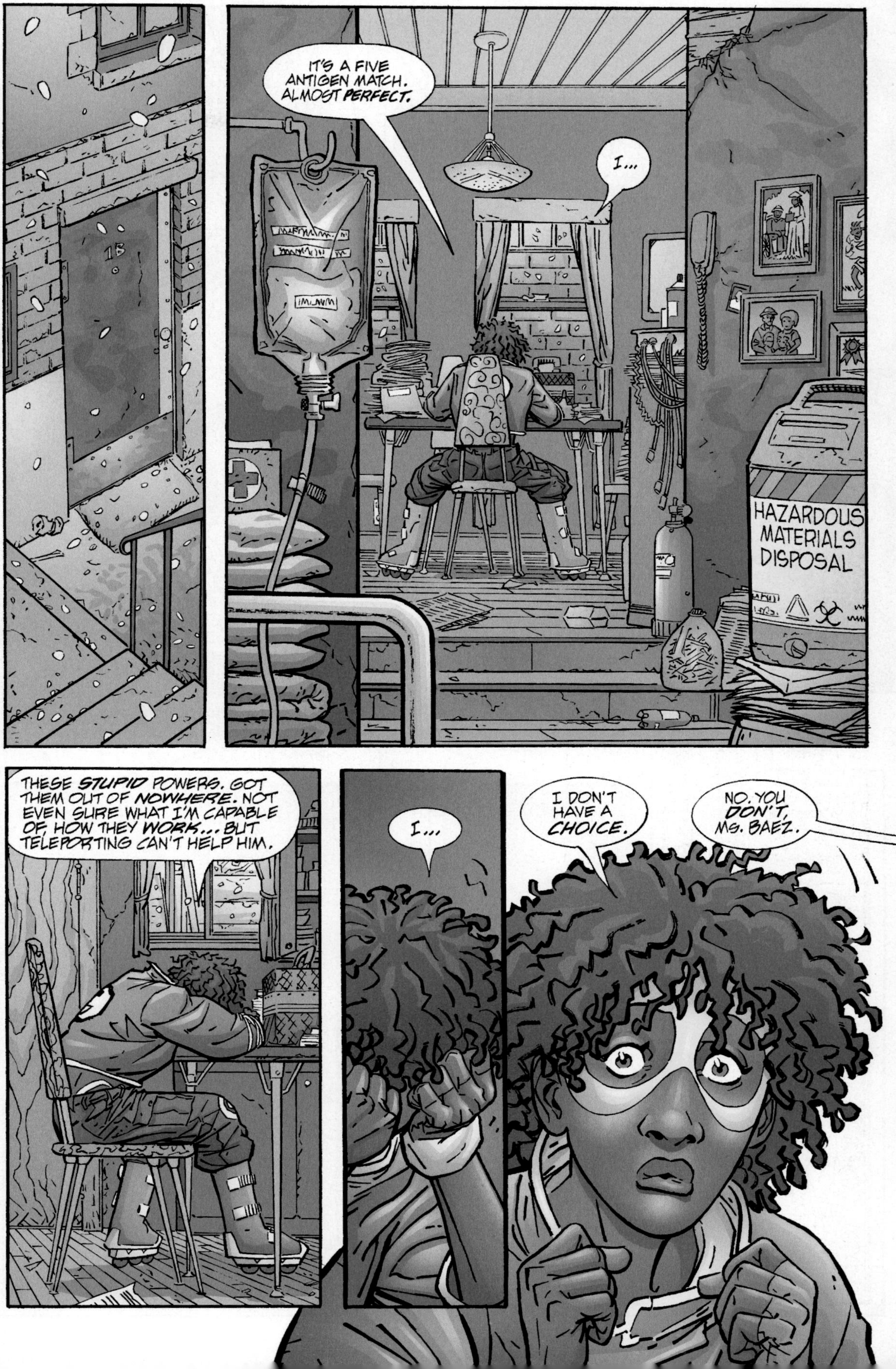

1B
IT'S A FIVE ANTIGEN MATCH. ALMOST PERFECT.
I...
HAZARDOUS MATERIALS DISPOSAL
THESE STUPID POWERS. GOT THEM OUT OF NOWHERE. NOT EVEN SURE WHAT I'M CAPABLE OF, HOW THEY WORK... BUT TELEPORTING CAN'T HELP HIM.
I...
I DON'T HAVE A CHOICE.
NO, YOU DON'T, MS. BAEZ.

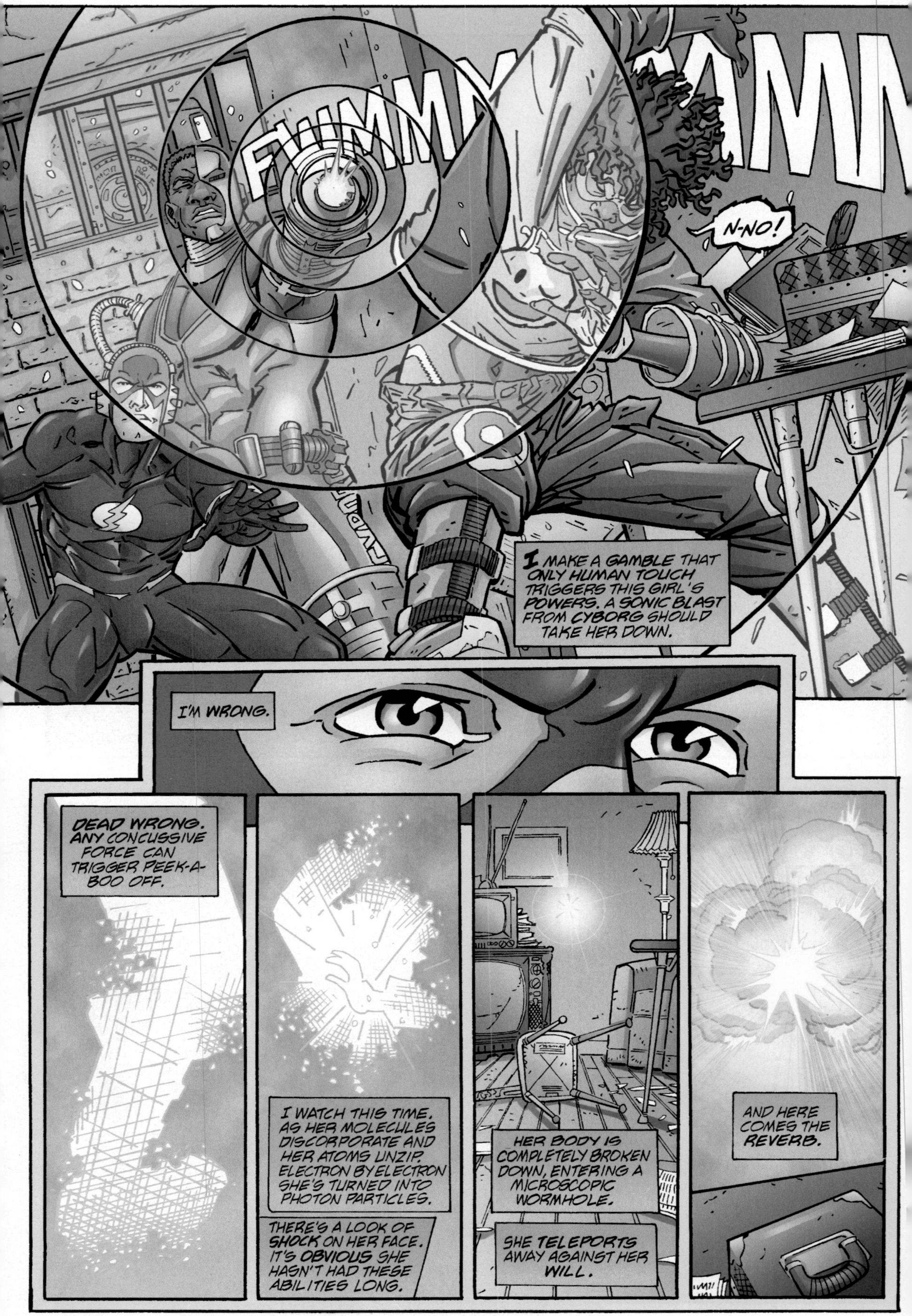
FWMMMMMMMMM
N-NO!
I MAKE A GAMBLE THAT ONLY HUMAN TOUCH TRIGGERS THIS GIRL'S POWERS. A SONIC BLAST FROM CYBORG SHOULD TAKE HER DOWN.
I'M WRONG.
DEAD WRONG. ANY CONCUSSIVE FORCE CAN TRIGGER PEEK-A-BOO OFF.
I WATCH THIS TIME, AS HER MOLECULES DISCORPORATE AND HER ATOMS UNZIP. ELECTRON BY ELECTRON SHE'S TURNED INTO PHOTON PARTICLES.
THERE'S A LOOK OF SHOCK ON HER FACE. IT'S OBVIOUS SHE HASN'T HAD THESE ABILITIES LONG.
HER BODY IS COMPLETELY BROKEN DOWN, ENTERING A MICROSCOPIC WORMHOLE.
SHE TELEPORTS AWAY AGAINST HER WILL.
AND HERE COMES THE REVERB.

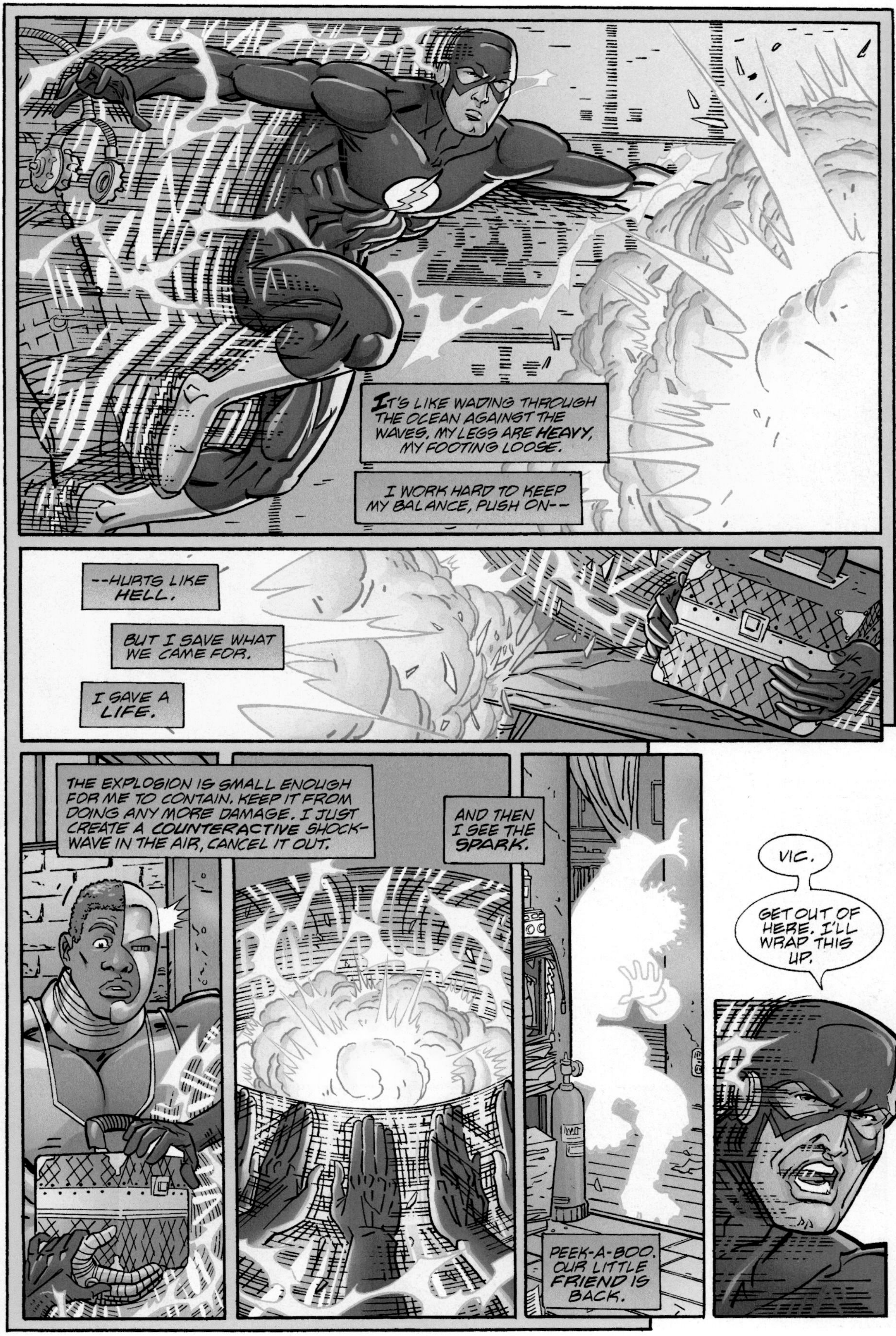

IT'S LIKE WADING THROUGH THE OCEAN AGAINST THE WAVES. MY LEGS ARE HEAVY, MY FOOTING LOOSE.
I WORK HARD TO KEEP MY BALANCE, PUSH ON--
--HURTS LIKE HELL.
BUT I SAVE WHAT WE CAME FOR.
I SAVE A LIFE.
THE EXPLOSION IS SMALL ENOUGH FOR ME TO CONTAIN. KEEP IT FROM DOING ANY MORE DAMAGE. I JUST CREATE A COUNTERACTIVE SHOCK-WAVE IN THE AIR, CANCEL IT OUT.
AND THEN I SEE THE SPARK.
PEEK-A-BOO. OUR LITTLE FRIEND IS BACK.
VIC.
GET OUT OF HERE. I'LL WRAP THIS UP.

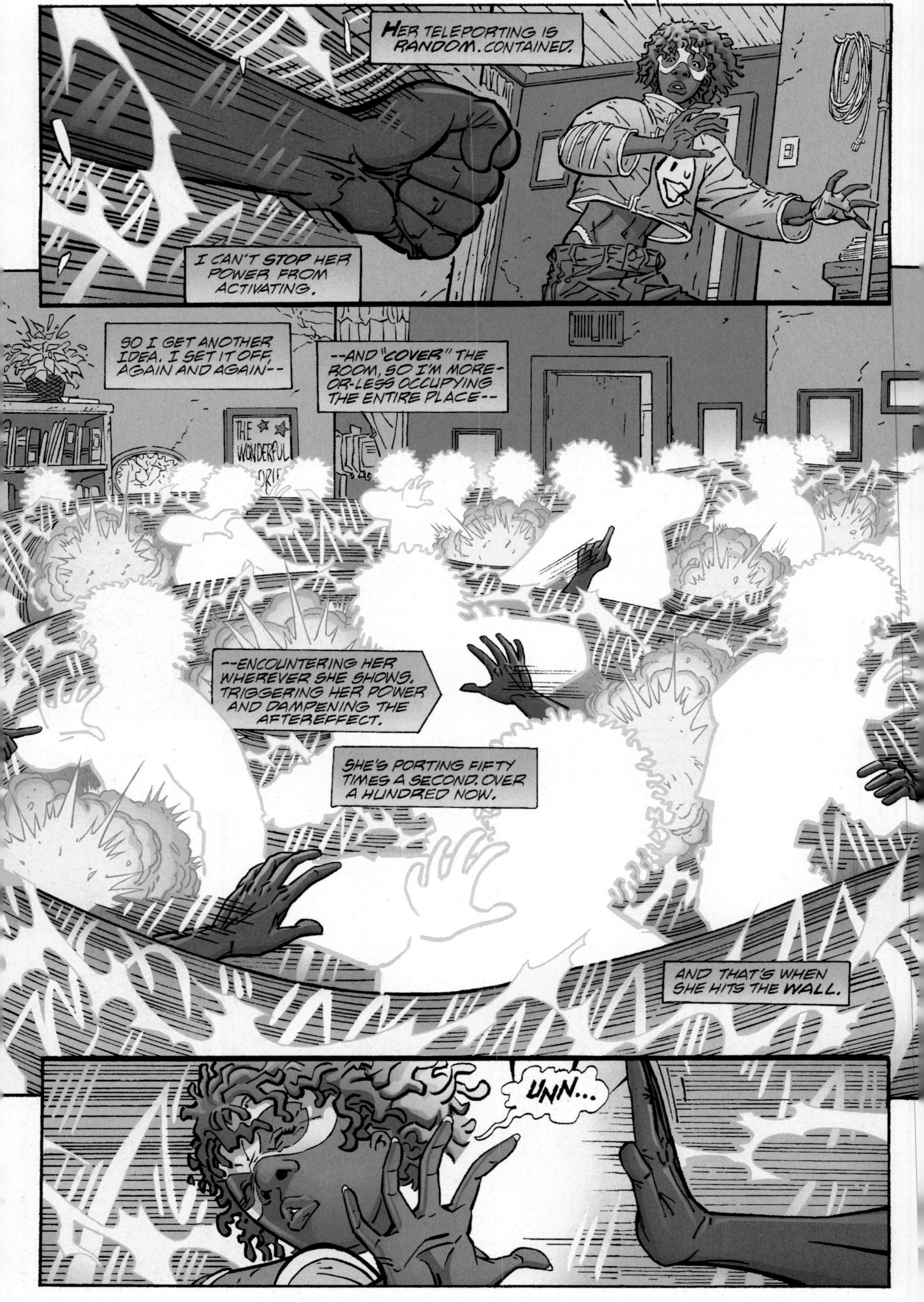
HER TELEPORTING IS RANDOM. CONTAINED.
I CAN'T STOP HER POWER FROM ACTIVATING.
SO I GET ANOTHER IDEA. I SET IT OFF, AGAIN AND AGAIN--
--AND "COVER" THE ROOM, SO I'M MORE-OR-LESS OCCUPYING THE ENTIRE PLACE--
THE WONDERFUL
--ENCOUNTERING HER WHEREVER SHE SHOWS. TRIGGERING HER POWER AND DAMPENING THE AFTEREFFECT.
SHE'S PORTING FIFTY TIMES A SECOND. OVER A HUNDRED NOW.
AND THAT'S WHEN SHE HITS THE WALL.
UNN...

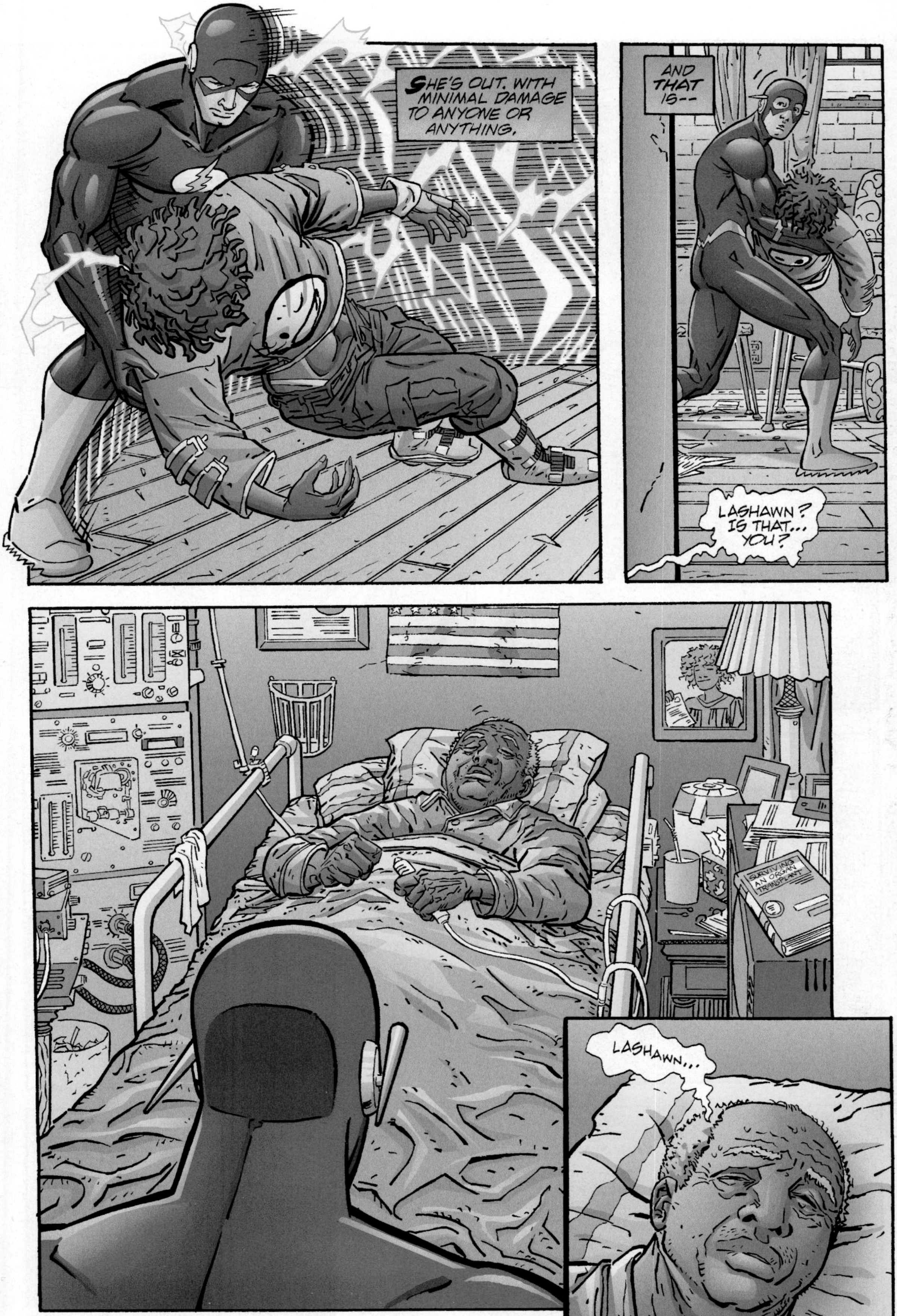
SHE'S OUT. WITH MINIMAL DAMAGE TO ANYONE OR ANYTHING.
AND THAT IS--
LASHAWN? IS THAT... YOU?
SURVIVING AN ORGAN TRANSPLANT
LASHAWN...

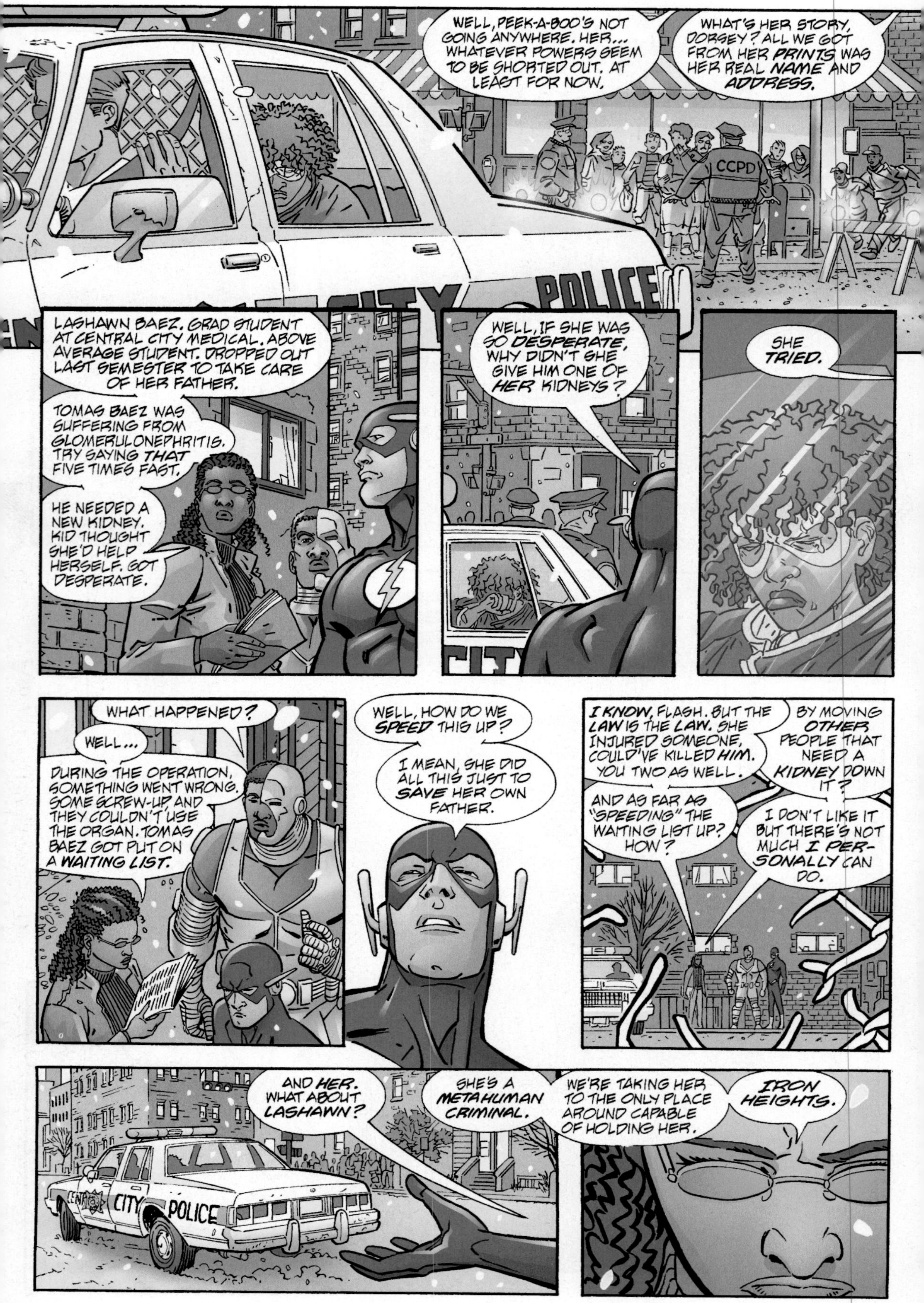
WELL, PEEK-A-BOO'S NOT GOING ANYWHERE. HER... WHATEVER POWERS SEEM TO BE SHORTED OUT. AT LEAST FOR NOW.
WHAT'S HER STORY, DORSEY? ALL WE GOT FROM HER PRINTS WAS HER REAL NAME AND ADDRESS.
CCPD
CITY POLICE
LASHAWN BAEZ. GRAD STUDENT AT CENTRAL CITY MEDICAL. ABOVE AVERAGE STUDENT. DROPPED OUT LAST SEMESTER TO TAKE CARE OF HER FATHER.
TOMAS BAEZ WAS SUFFERING FROM GLOMERULONEPHRITIS. TRY SAYING THAT FIVE TIMES FAST.
HE NEEDED A NEW KIDNEY. KID THOUGHT SHE'D HELP HERSELF. GOT DESPERATE.
WELL, IF SHE WAS SO DESPERATE, WHY DIDN'T SHE GIVE HIM ONE OF HER KIDNEYS?
SHE TRIED.
WHAT HAPPENED?
WELL...
DURING THE OPERATION, SOMETHING WENT WRONG. SOME SCREW-UP, AND THEY COULDN'T USE THE ORGAN. TOMAS BAEZ GOT PUT ON A WAITING LIST.
WELL, HOW DO WE SPEED THIS UP?
I MEAN, SHE DID ALL THIS JUST TO SAVE HER OWN FATHER.
I KNOW, FLASH. BUT THE LAW IS THE LAW. SHE INJURED SOMEONE, COULD'VE KILLED HIM. YOU TWO AS WELL.
AND AS FAR AS "SPEEDING" THE WAITING LIST UP? HOW?
BY MOVING OTHER PEOPLE THAT NEED A KIDNEY DOWN IT?
I DON'T LIKE IT BUT THERE'S NOT MUCH I PERSONALLY CAN DO.
AND HER. WHAT ABOUT LASHAWN?
SHE'S A METAHUMAN CRIMINAL.
WE'RE TAKING HER TO THE ONLY PLACE AROUND CAPABLE OF HOLDING HER.
IRON HEIGHTS.
CITY POLICE

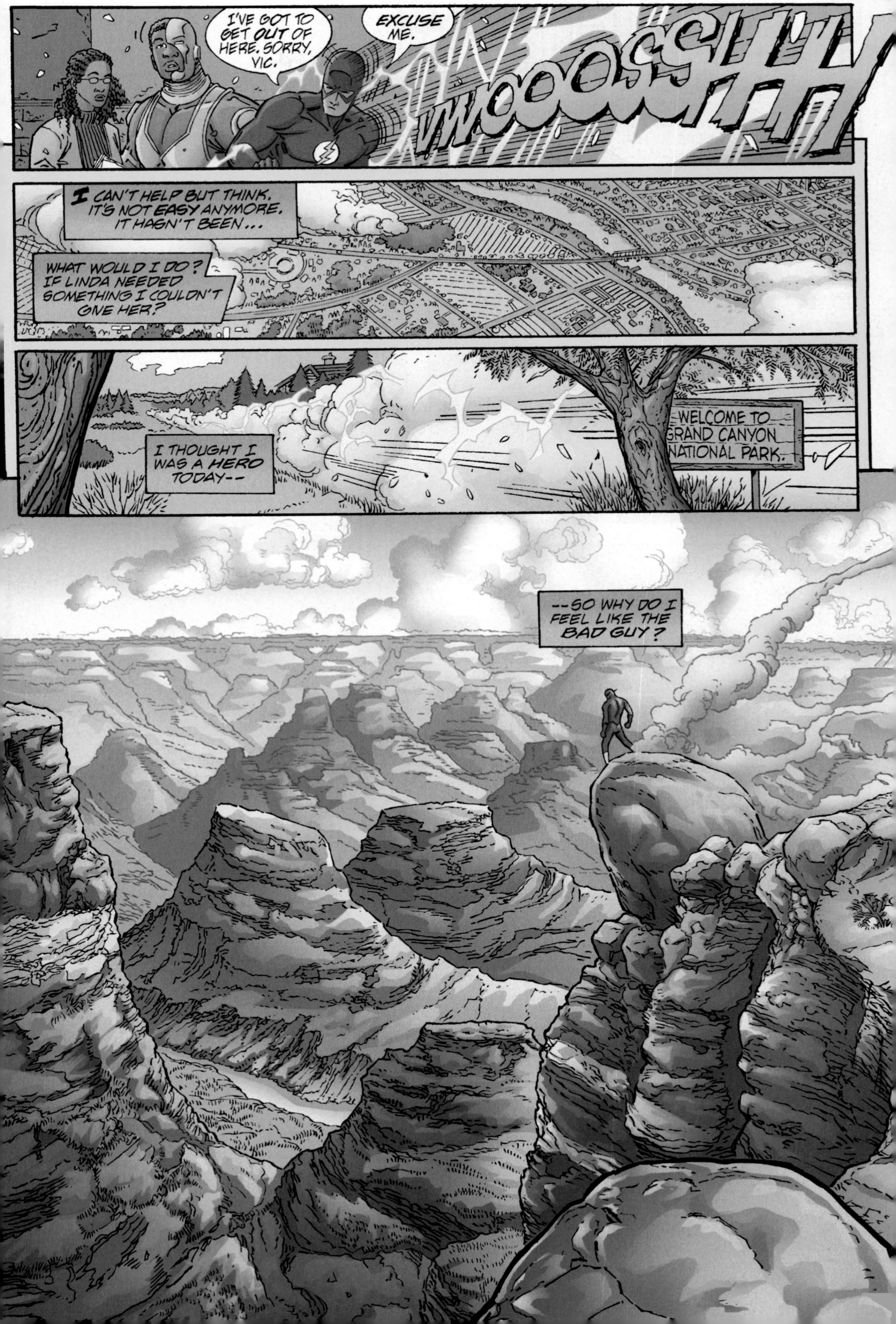
I'VE GOT TO GET OUT OF HERE. SORRY, VIC.
EXCUSE ME.
WOOOSSHH
I CAN'T HELP BUT THINK. IT'S NOT EASY ANYMORE. IT HASN'T BEEN...
WHAT WOULD I DO? IF LINDA NEEDED SOMETHING I COULDN'T GIVE HER?
WELCOME TO GRAND CANYON NATIONAL PARK.
I THOUGHT I WAS A HERO TODAY--
--SO WHY DO I FEEL LIKE THE BAD GUY?

EPILOGUE 1

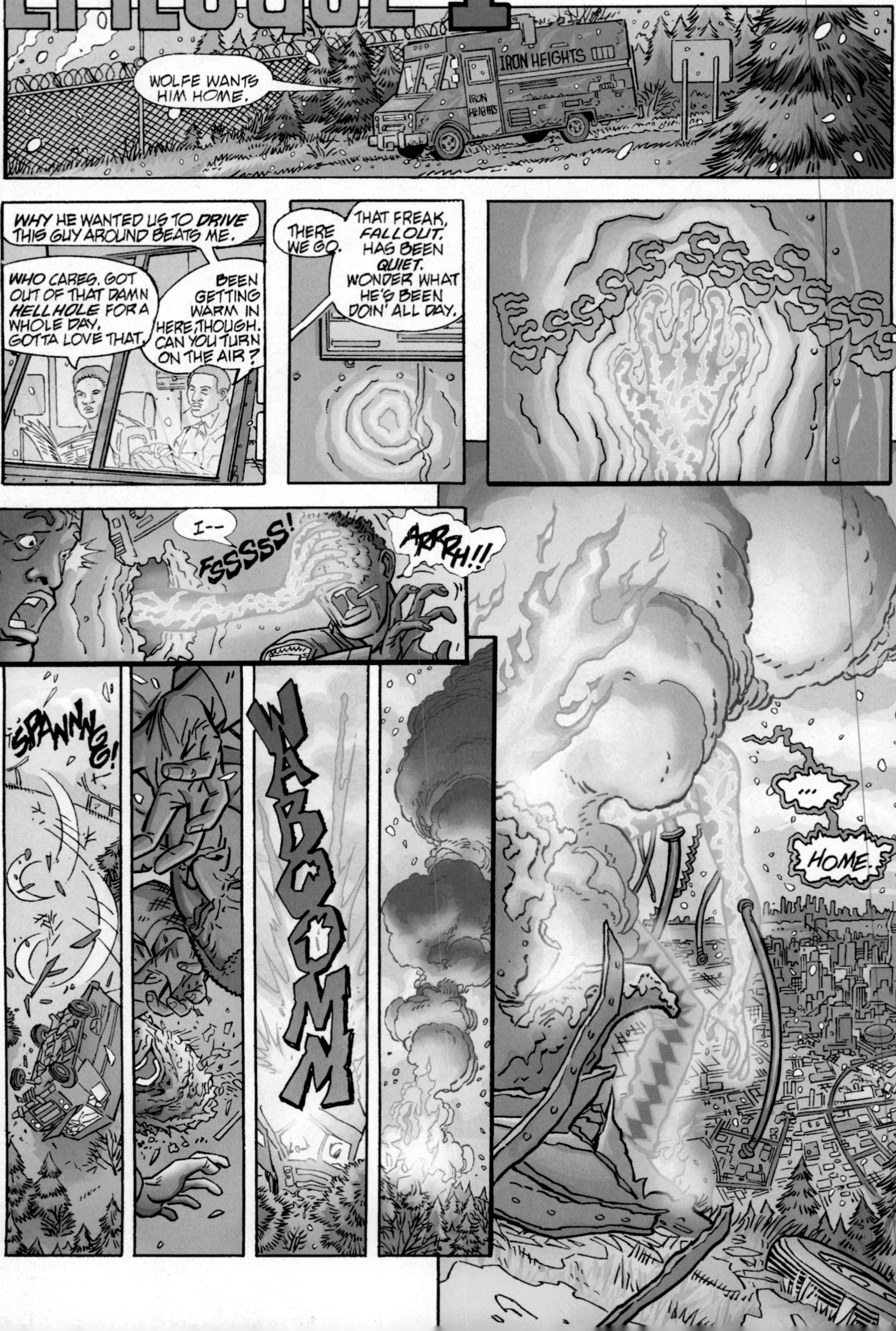
IRON HEIGHTS
IRON HEIGHTS
WOLFE WANTS HIM HOME.
WHY HE WANTED US TO DRIVE THIS GUY AROUND BEATS ME.
WHO CARES. GOT OUT OF THAT DAMN HELLHOLE FOR A WHOLE DAY. GOTTA LOVE THAT.
BEEN GETTING WARM IN HERE, THOUGH. CAN YOU TURN ON THE AIR?
THERE WE GO.
THAT FREAK, FALLOUT, HAS BEEN QUIET. WONDER WHAT HE'S BEEN DOIN' ALL DAY.
FSSSS-SSSSSSSSSSSSS
I--
FSSSSS!
ARRRGH!!
SPANNNGG!
WABOOMM
...
HOME.

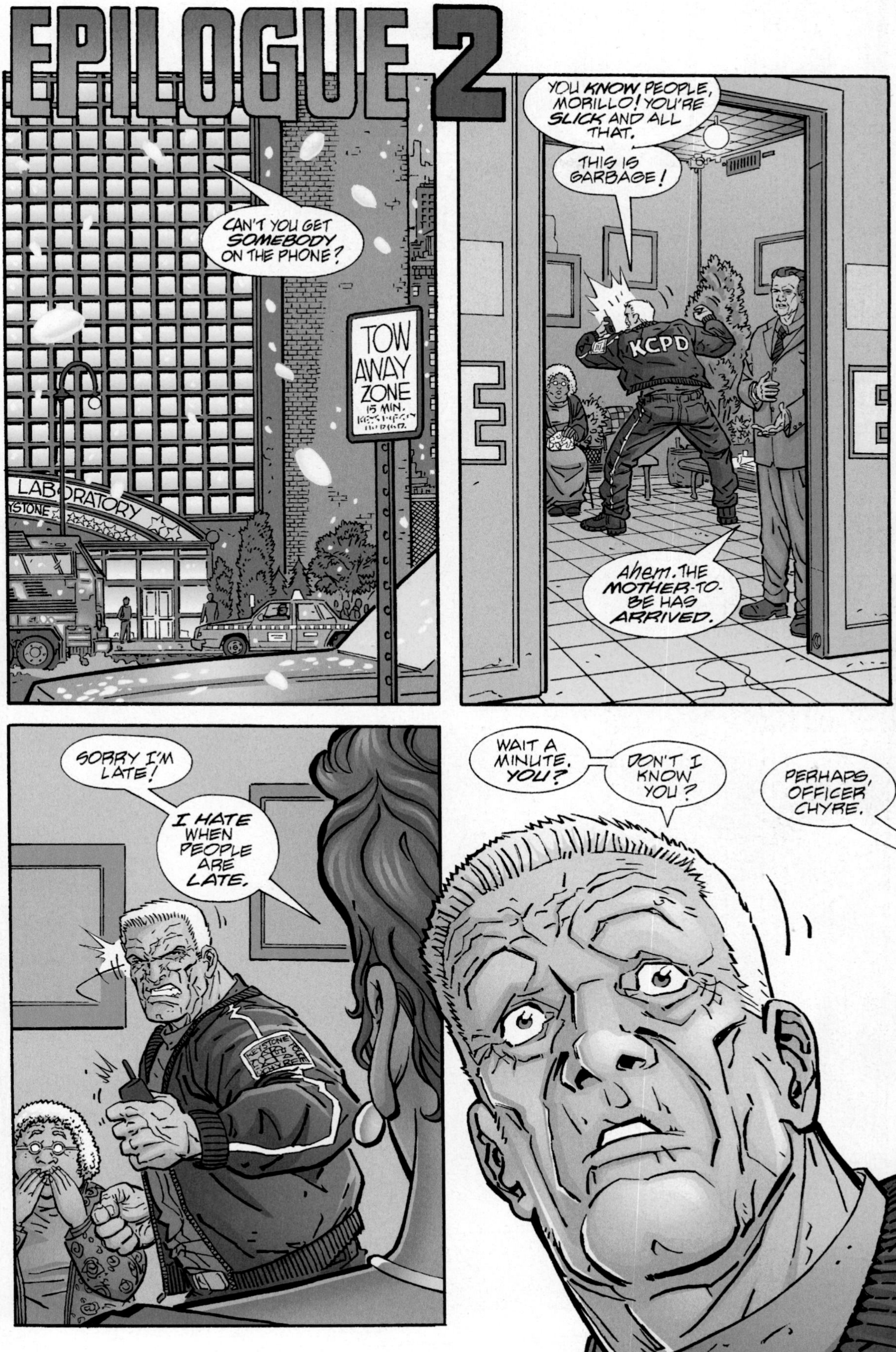
EPILOGUE 2
CAN'T YOU GET SOMEBODY ON THE PHONE?
TOW AWAY ZONE
15 MIN.
LABORATORY
YOU KNOW PEOPLE, MORILLO! YOU'RE SLICK AND ALL THAT.
THIS IS GARBAGE!
KCPD
Ahem. THE MOTHER-TO-BE HAS ARRIVED.
SORRY I'M LATE!
I HATE WHEN PEOPLE ARE LATE.
WAIT A MINUTE. YOU?
DON'T I KNOW YOU?
PERHAPS, OFFICER CHYRE.

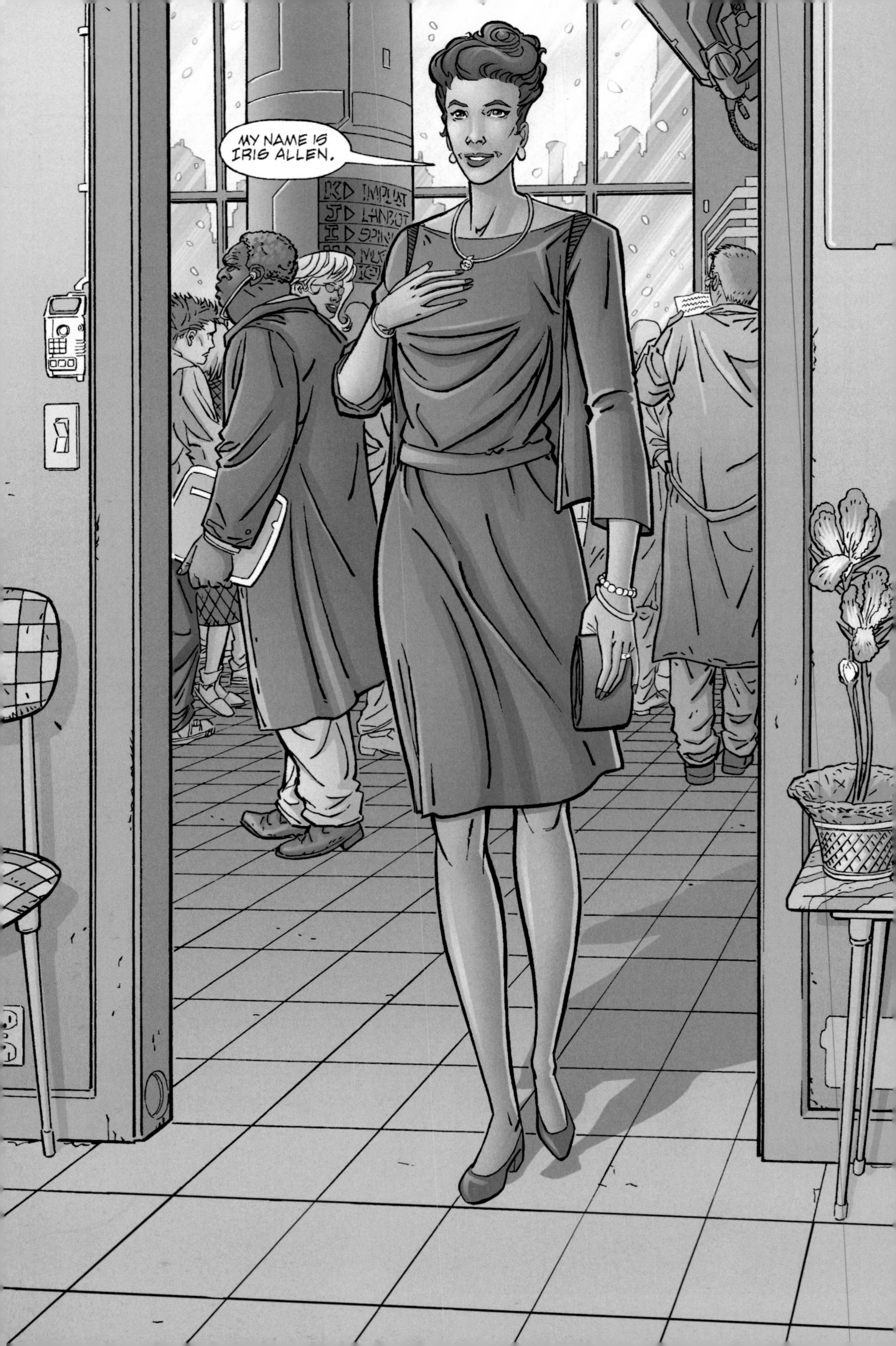
MY NAME IS IRIS ALLEN.

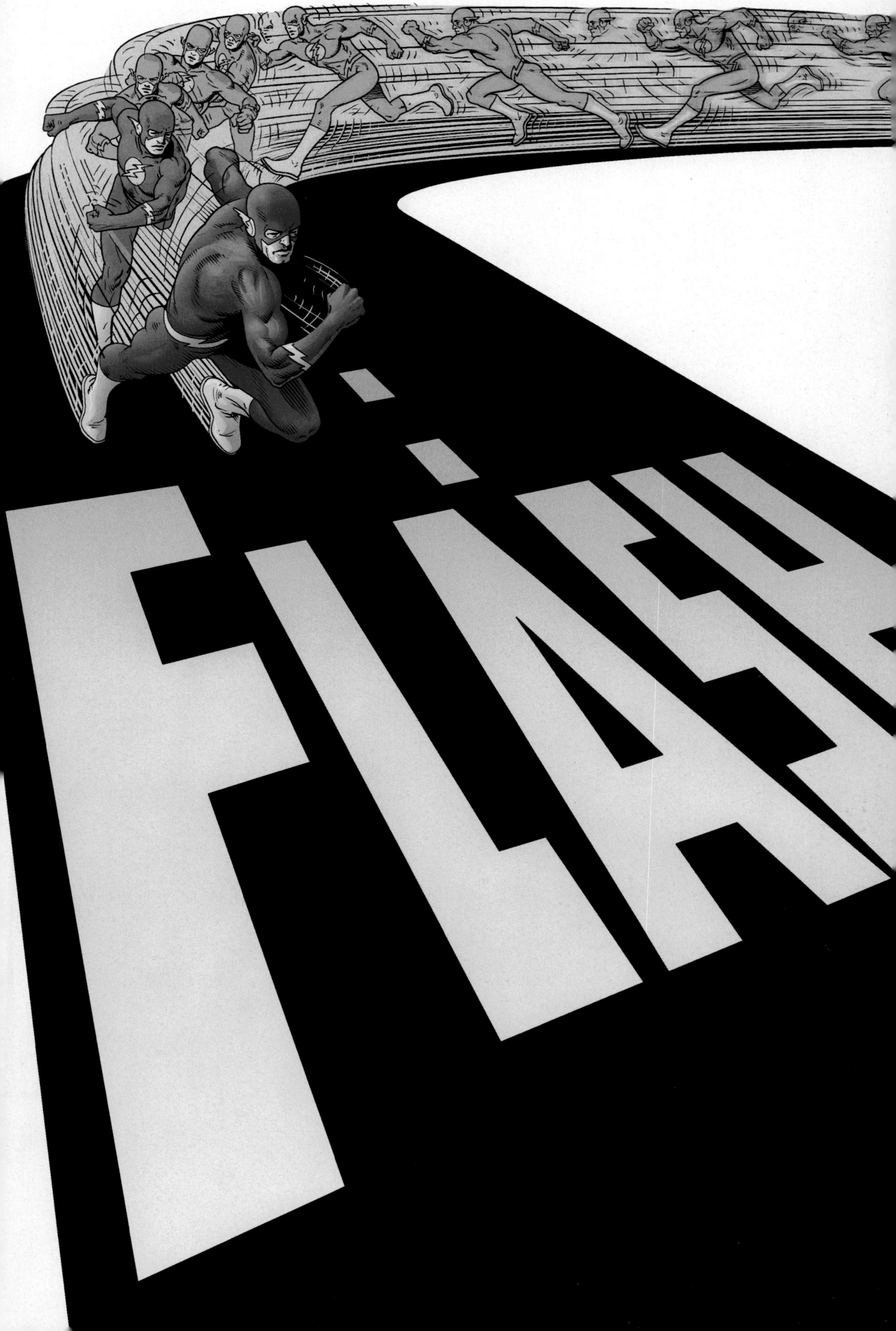

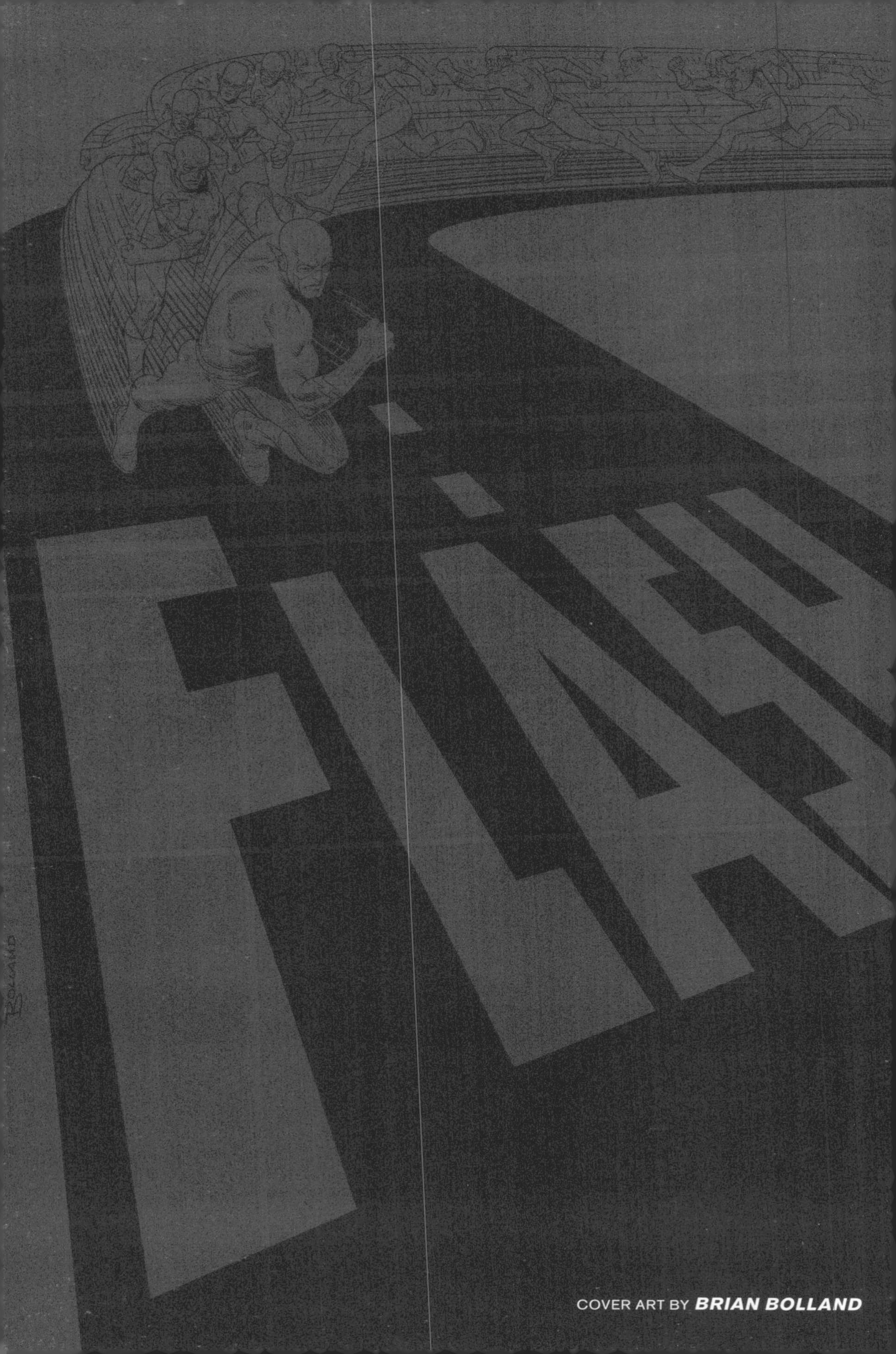

COVER ART BY **BRIAN BOLLAND**

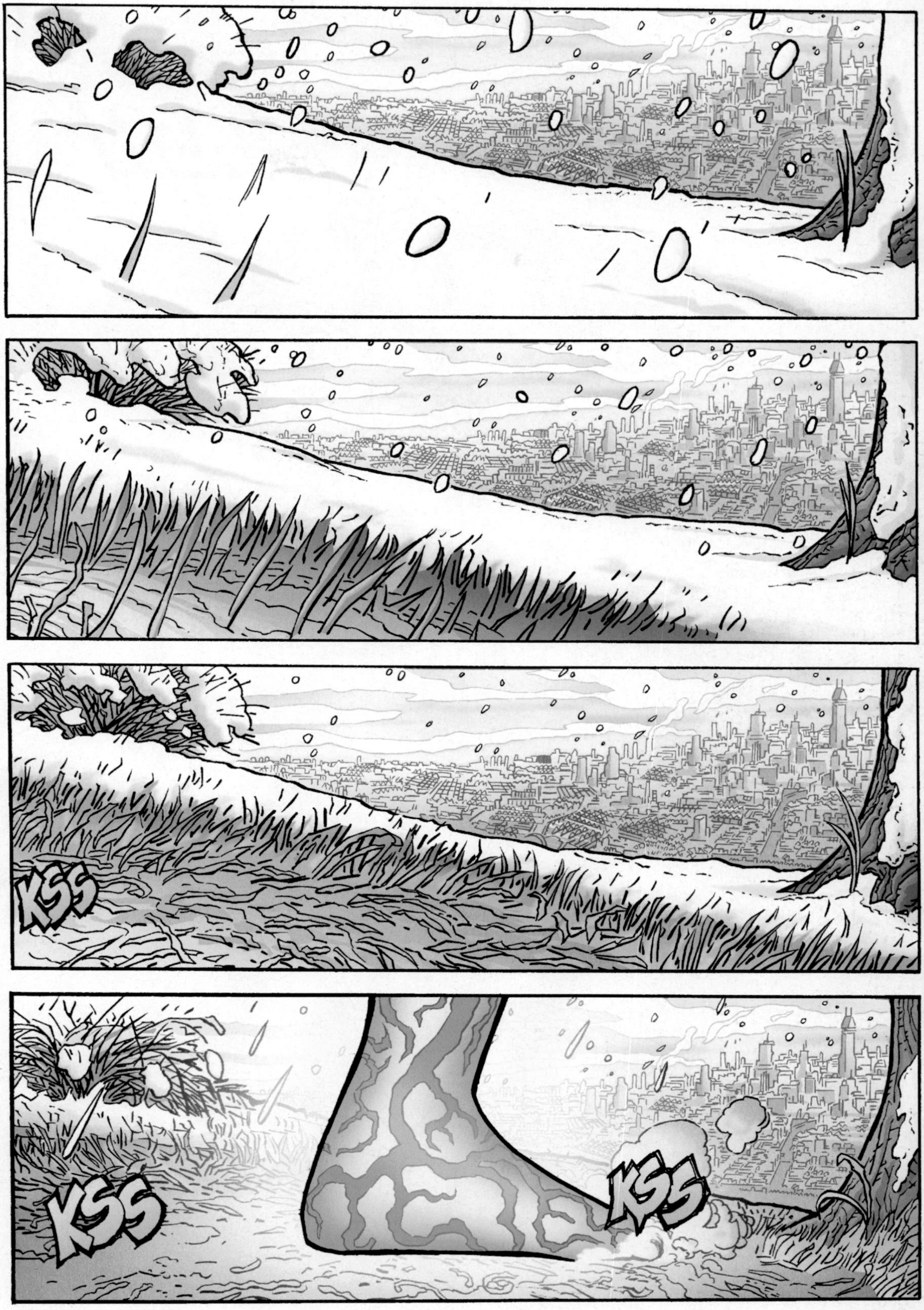
KSS
KSS
KSS

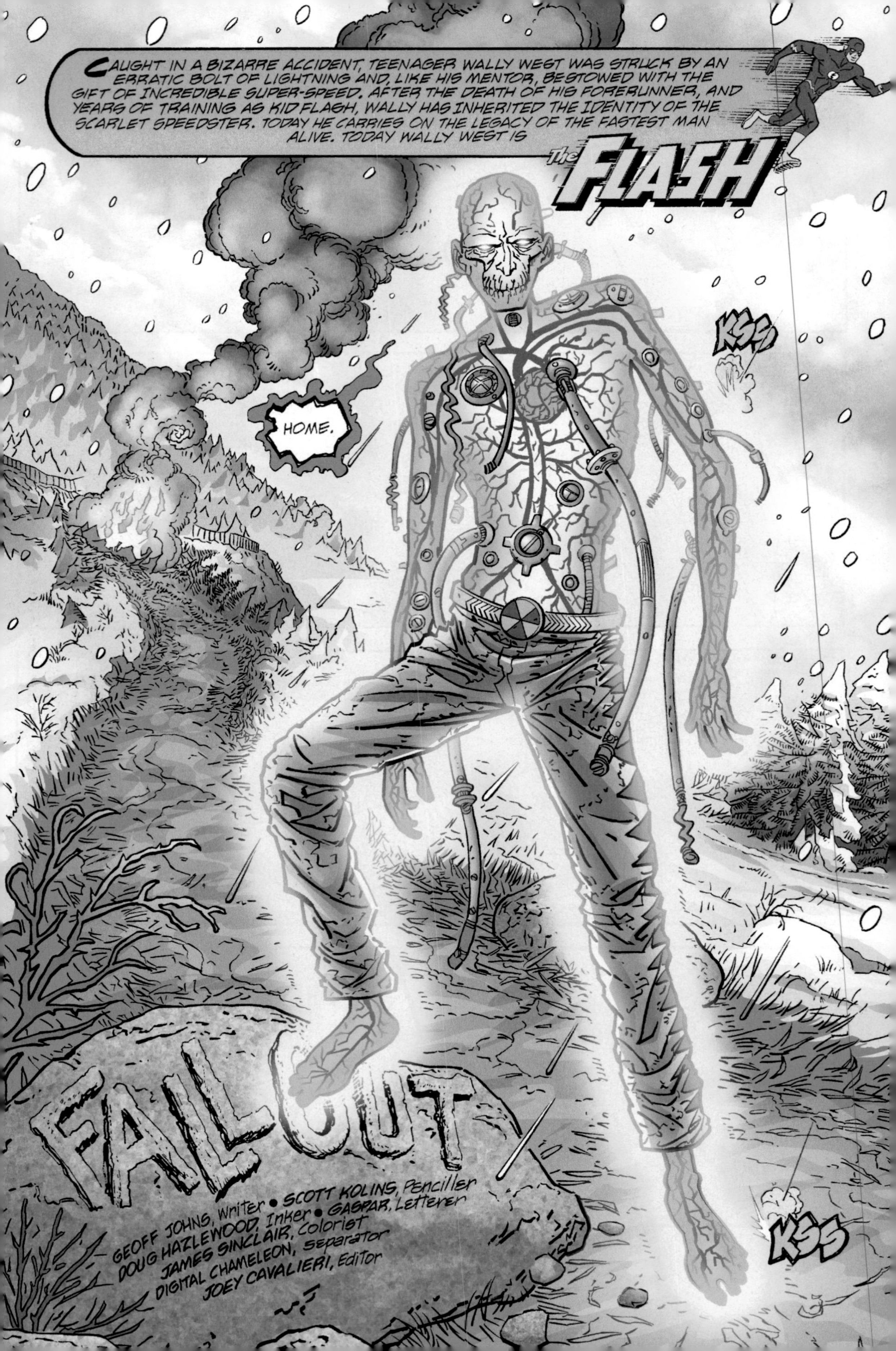

CAUGHT IN A BIZARRE ACCIDENT, TEENAGER WALLY WEST WAS STRUCK BY AN ERRATIC BOLT OF LIGHTNING AND, LIKE HIS MENTOR, BESTOWED WITH THE GIFT OF INCREDIBLE SUPER-SPEED. AFTER THE DEATH OF HIS FORERUNNER, AND YEARS OF TRAINING AS KID FLASH, WALLY HAS INHERITED THE IDENTITY OF THE SCARLET SPEEDSTER. TODAY HE CARRIES ON THE LEGACY OF THE FASTEST MAN ALIVE. TODAY WALLY WEST IS
The FLASH
KSS
HOME.
FALLOUT
GEOFF JOHNS, Writer • SCOTT KOLINS, Penciller
DOUG HAZLEWOOD, Inker • GASPAR, Letterer
JAMES SINCLAIR, Colorist
DIGITAL CHAMELEON, Separator
JOEY CAVALIERI, Editor
KSS

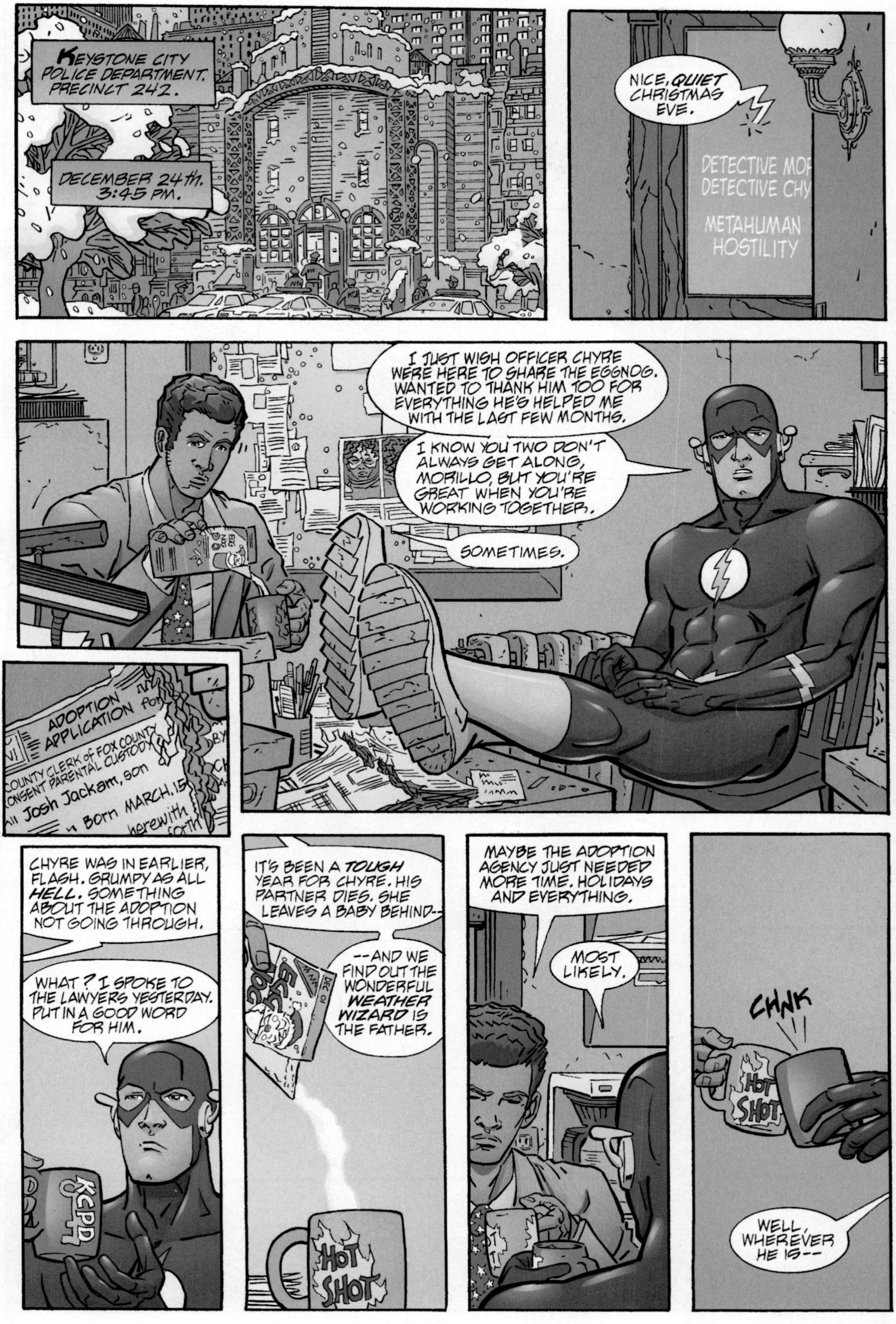
KEYSTONE CITY POLICE DEPARTMENT. PRECINCT 242.
DECEMBER 24th. 3:45 PM.
NICE, QUIET CHRISTMAS EVE.
DETECTIVE MOR
DETECTIVE CHY
METAHUMAN HOSTILITY
I JUST WISH OFFICER CHYRE WERE HERE TO SHARE THE EGGNOG. WANTED TO THANK HIM TOO FOR EVERYTHING HE'S HELPED ME WITH THE LAST FEW MONTHS.
I KNOW YOU TWO DON'T ALWAYS GET ALONG, MORILLO, BUT YOU'RE GREAT WHEN YOU'RE WORKING TOGETHER.
SOMETIMES.
ADOPTION APPLICATION for
COUNTY CLERK of FOX COUNTY
CONSENT PARENTAL CUSTODY
Josh Jackam, son
Born MARCH 15
herewith
CHYRE WAS IN EARLIER, FLASH. GRUMPY AS ALL HELL. SOMETHING ABOUT THE ADOPTION NOT GOING THROUGH.
WHAT? I SPOKE TO THE LAWYERS YESTERDAY. PUT IN A GOOD WORD FOR HIM.
KCPD
IT'S BEEN A TOUGH YEAR FOR CHYRE. HIS PARTNER DIES. SHE LEAVES A BABY BEHIND--
--AND WE FIND OUT THE WONDERFUL WEATHER WIZARD IS THE FATHER.
HOT SHOT
MAYBE THE ADOPTION AGENCY JUST NEEDED MORE TIME. HOLIDAYS AND EVERYTHING.
MOST LIKELY.
CHNK
HOT SHOT
WELL, WHEREVER HE IS--

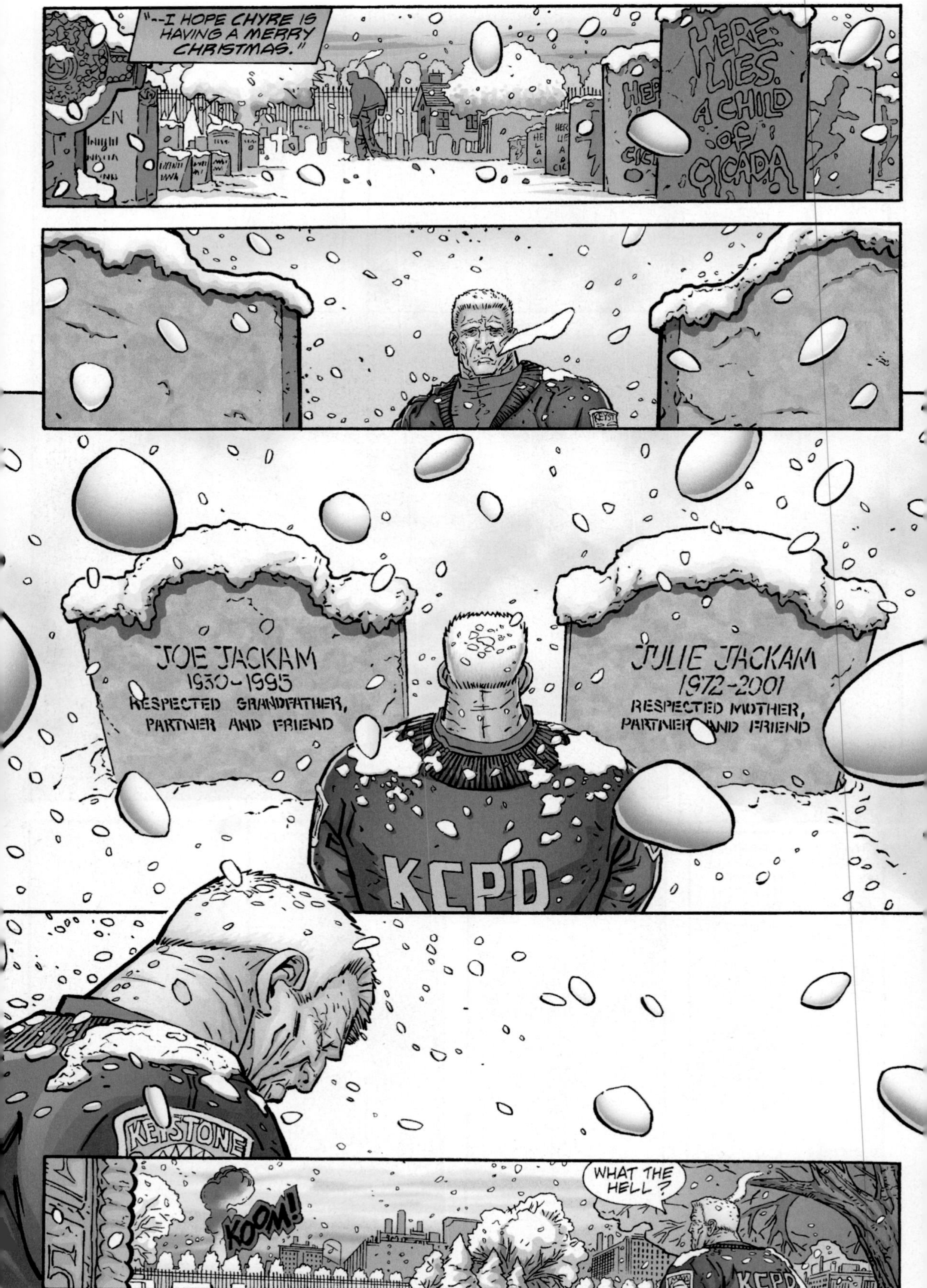
"--I HOPE CHYRE IS HAVING A MERRY CHRISTMAS."
HERE LIES. A CHILD of CICADA
JOE JACKAM
1930-1995
RESPECTED GRANDFATHER, PARTNER AND FRIEND
JULIE JACKAM
1972-2001
RESPECTED MOTHER, PARTNER AND FRIEND
KCPD
KEYSTONE
KOOM!
WHAT THE HELL?
KCPD

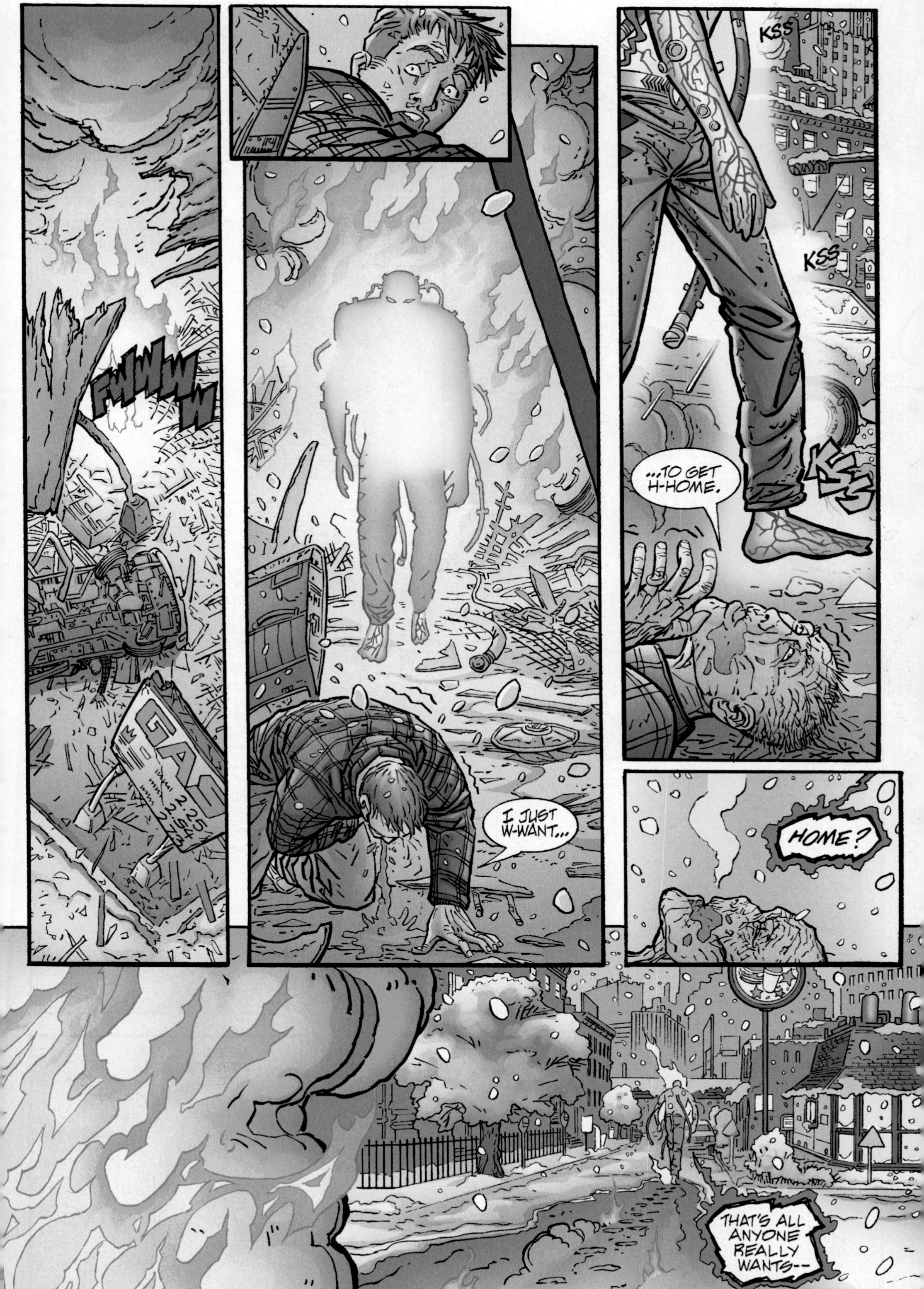
FWWWW
GAS
2.25
2.54
I JUST W-WANT...
KSS
KSS
KSS
...TO GET H-HOME.
HOME?
THAT'S ALL ANYONE REALLY WANTS--

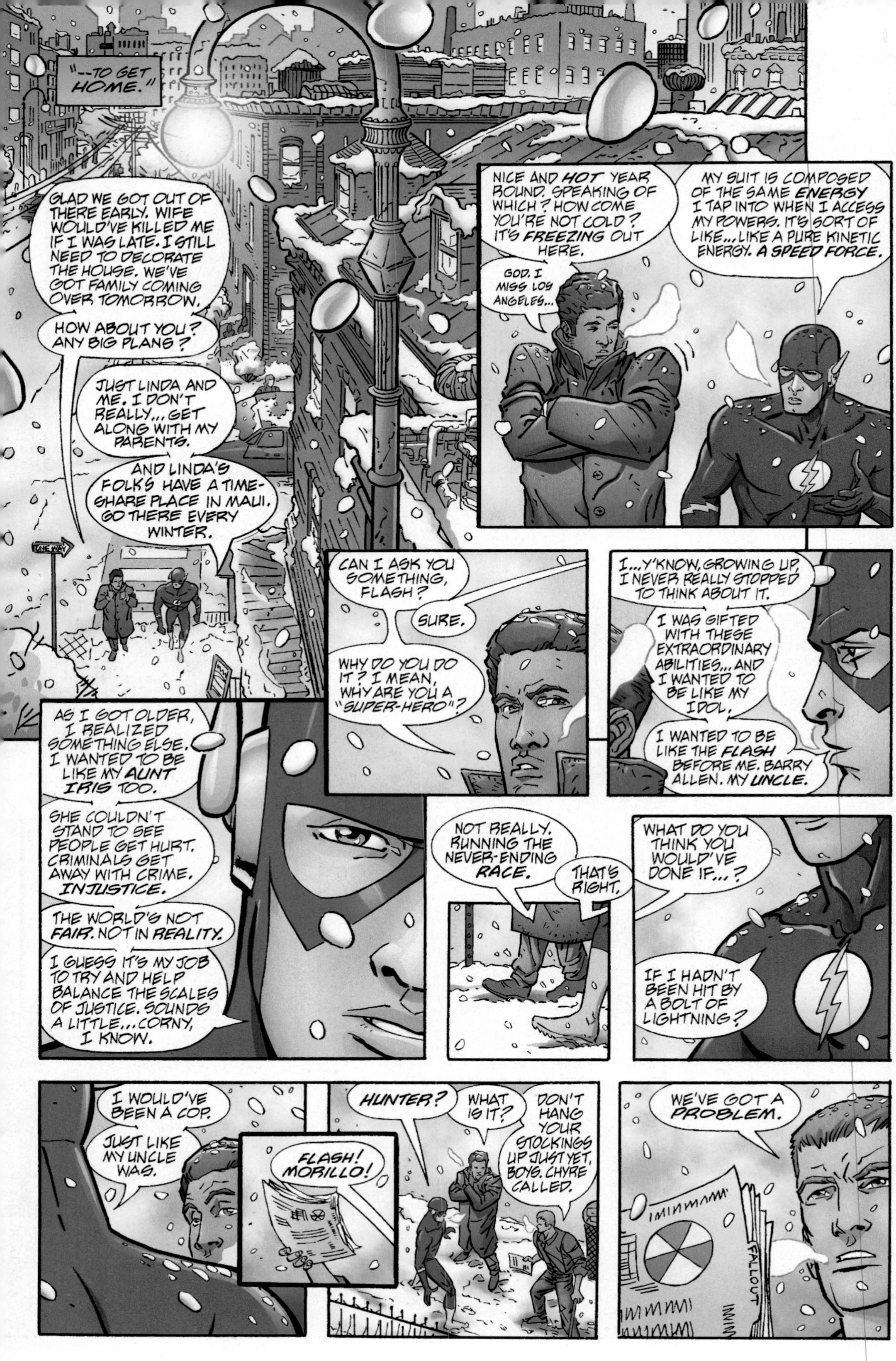
"--TO GET HOME."
GLAD WE GOT OUT OF THERE EARLY. WIFE WOULD'VE KILLED ME IF I WAS LATE. I STILL NEED TO DECORATE THE HOUSE. WE'VE GOT FAMILY COMING OVER TOMORROW.
HOW ABOUT YOU? ANY BIG PLANS?
JUST LINDA AND ME. I DON'T REALLY... GET ALONG WITH MY PARENTS.
AND LINDA'S FOLKS HAVE A TIME-SHARE PLACE IN MAUI. GO THERE EVERY WINTER.
ONE WAY
NICE AND HOT YEAR ROUND. SPEAKING OF WHICH? HOW COME YOU'RE NOT COLD? IT'S FREEZING OUT HERE.
GOD. I MISS LOS ANGELES...
MY SUIT IS COMPOSED OF THE SAME ENERGY I TAP INTO WHEN I ACCESS MY POWERS. IT'S SORT OF LIKE... LIKE A PURE KINETIC ENERGY. A SPEED FORCE.
CAN I ASK YOU SOMETHING, FLASH?
SURE.
WHY DO YOU DO IT? I MEAN, WHY ARE YOU A "SUPER-HERO"?
I... Y'KNOW, GROWING UP, I NEVER REALLY STOPPED TO THINK ABOUT IT.
I WAS GIFTED WITH THESE EXTRAORDINARY ABILITIES... AND I WANTED TO BE LIKE MY IDOL.
I WANTED TO BE LIKE THE FLASH BEFORE ME. BARRY ALLEN. MY UNCLE.
AS I GOT OLDER, I REALIZED SOMETHING ELSE. I WANTED TO BE LIKE MY AUNT IRIS TOO.
SHE COULDN'T STAND TO SEE PEOPLE GET HURT. CRIMINALS GET AWAY WITH CRIME. INJUSTICE.
THE WORLD'S NOT FAIR. NOT IN REALITY.
I GUESS IT'S MY JOB TO TRY AND HELP BALANCE THE SCALES OF JUSTICE. SOUNDS A LITTLE... CORNY, I KNOW.
NOT REALLY. RUNNING THE NEVER-ENDING RACE.
THAT'S RIGHT.
WHAT DO YOU THINK YOU WOULD'VE DONE IF...?
IF I HADN'T BEEN HIT BY A BOLT OF LIGHTNING?
I WOULD'VE BEEN A COP.
JUST LIKE MY UNCLE WAS.
FLASH! MORILLO!
HUNTER?
WHAT IS IT?
DON'T HANG YOUR STOCKINGS UP JUST YET, BOYS. CHYRE CALLED.
WE'VE GOT A PROBLEM.
FALLOUT

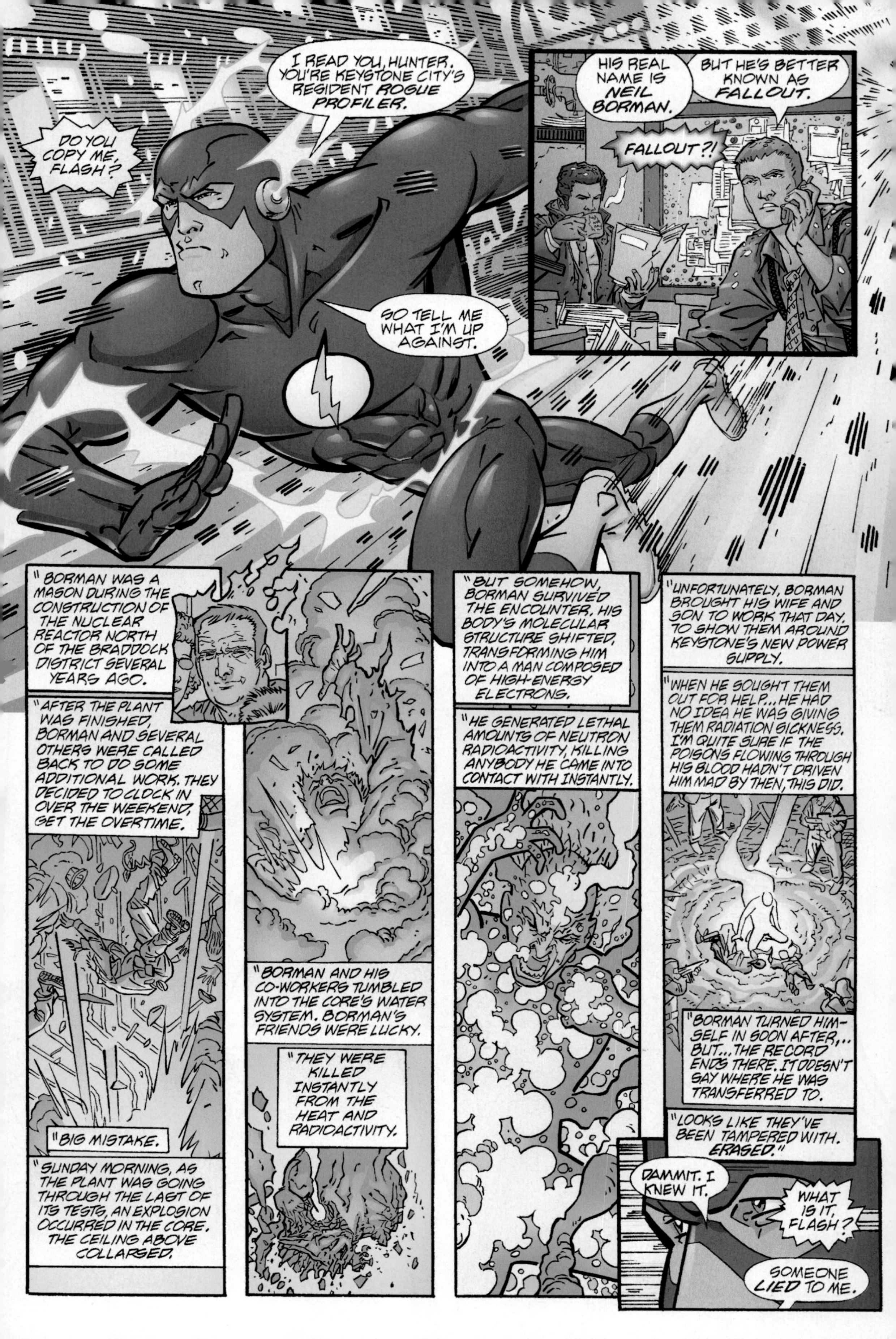
DO YOU COPY ME, FLASH?
I READ YOU, HUNTER. YOU'RE KEYSTONE CITY'S RESIDENT ROGUE PROFILER.
SO TELL ME WHAT I'M UP AGAINST.
HIS REAL NAME IS NEIL BORMAN.
BUT HE'S BETTER KNOWN AS FALLOUT.
FALLOUT?!
"BORMAN WAS A MASON DURING THE CONSTRUCTION OF THE NUCLEAR REACTOR NORTH OF THE BRADDOCK DISTRICT SEVERAL YEARS AGO.
"AFTER THE PLANT WAS FINISHED, BORMAN AND SEVERAL OTHERS WERE CALLED BACK TO DO SOME ADDITIONAL WORK. THEY DECIDED TO CLOCK IN OVER THE WEEKEND, GET THE OVERTIME.
"BIG MISTAKE.
"SUNDAY MORNING, AS THE PLANT WAS GOING THROUGH THE LAST OF ITS TESTS, AN EXPLOSION OCCURRED IN THE CORE. THE CEILING ABOVE COLLAPSED.
"BORMAN AND HIS CO-WORKERS TUMBLED INTO THE CORE'S WATER SYSTEM. BORMAN'S FRIENDS WERE LUCKY.
"THEY WERE KILLED INSTANTLY FROM THE HEAT AND RADIACTIVITY.
"BUT SOMEHOW, BORMAN SURVIVED THE ENCOUNTER. HIS BODY'S MOLECULAR STRUCTURE SHIFTED, TRANSFORMING HIM INTO A MAN COMPOSED OF HIGH-ENERGY ELECTRONS.
"HE GENERATED LETHAL AMOUNTS OF NEUTRON RADIOACTIVITY, KILLING ANYBODY HE CAME INTO CONTACT WITH INSTANTLY.
"UNFORTUNATELY, BORMAN BROUGHT HIS WIFE AND SON TO WORK THAT DAY, TO SHOW THEM AROUND KEYSTONE'S NEW POWER SUPPLY.
"WHEN HE SOUGHT THEM OUT FOR HELP... HE HAD NO IDEA HE WAS GIVING THEM RADIATION SICKNESS. I'M QUITE SURE IF THE POISONS FLOWING THROUGH HIS BLOOD HADN'T DRIVEN HIM MAD BY THEN, THIS DID.
"BORMAN TURNED HIMSELF IN SOON AFTER,... BUT... THE RECORD ENDS THERE. IT DOESN'T SAY WHERE HE WAS TRANSFERRED TO.
"LOOKS LIKE THEY'VE BEEN TAMPERED WITH. ERASED."
DAMMIT. I KNEW IT.
WHAT IS IT, FLASH?
SOMEONE LIED TO ME.

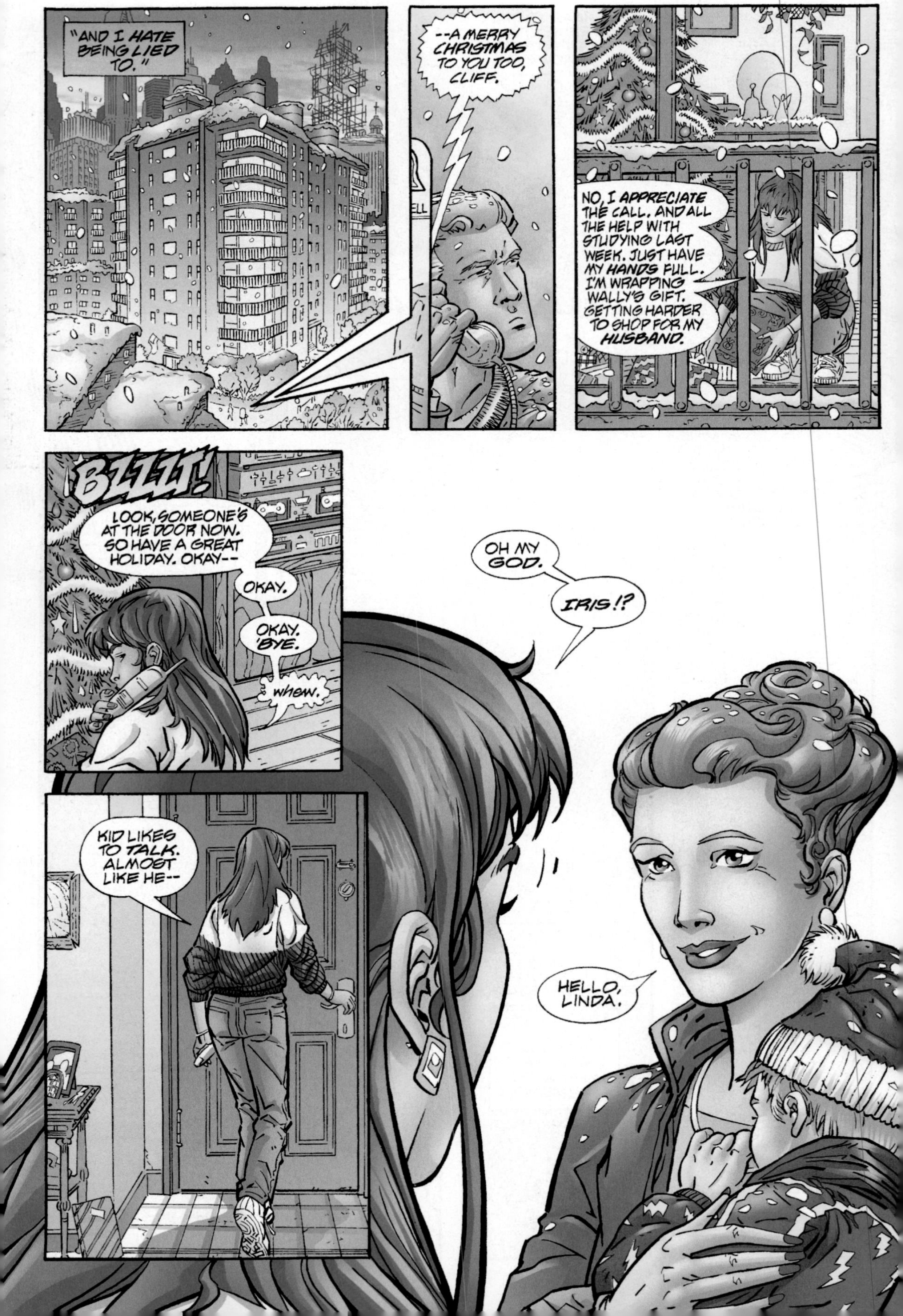
"AND I HATE BEING LIED TO."
--A MERRY CHRISTMAS TO YOU TOO, CLIFF.
NO, I APPRECIATE THE CALL. AND ALL THE HELP WITH STUDYING LAST WEEK. JUST HAVE MY HANDS FULL. I'M WRAPPING WALLY'S GIFT. GETTING HARDER TO SHOP FOR MY HUSBAND.
BZZZT!
LOOK, SOMEONE'S AT THE DOOR NOW. SO HAVE A GREAT HOLIDAY. OKAY--
OKAY.
OKAY. 'BYE.
whew.
KID LIKES TO TALK. ALMOST LIKE HE--
OH MY GOD.
IRIS!?
HELLO, LINDA.

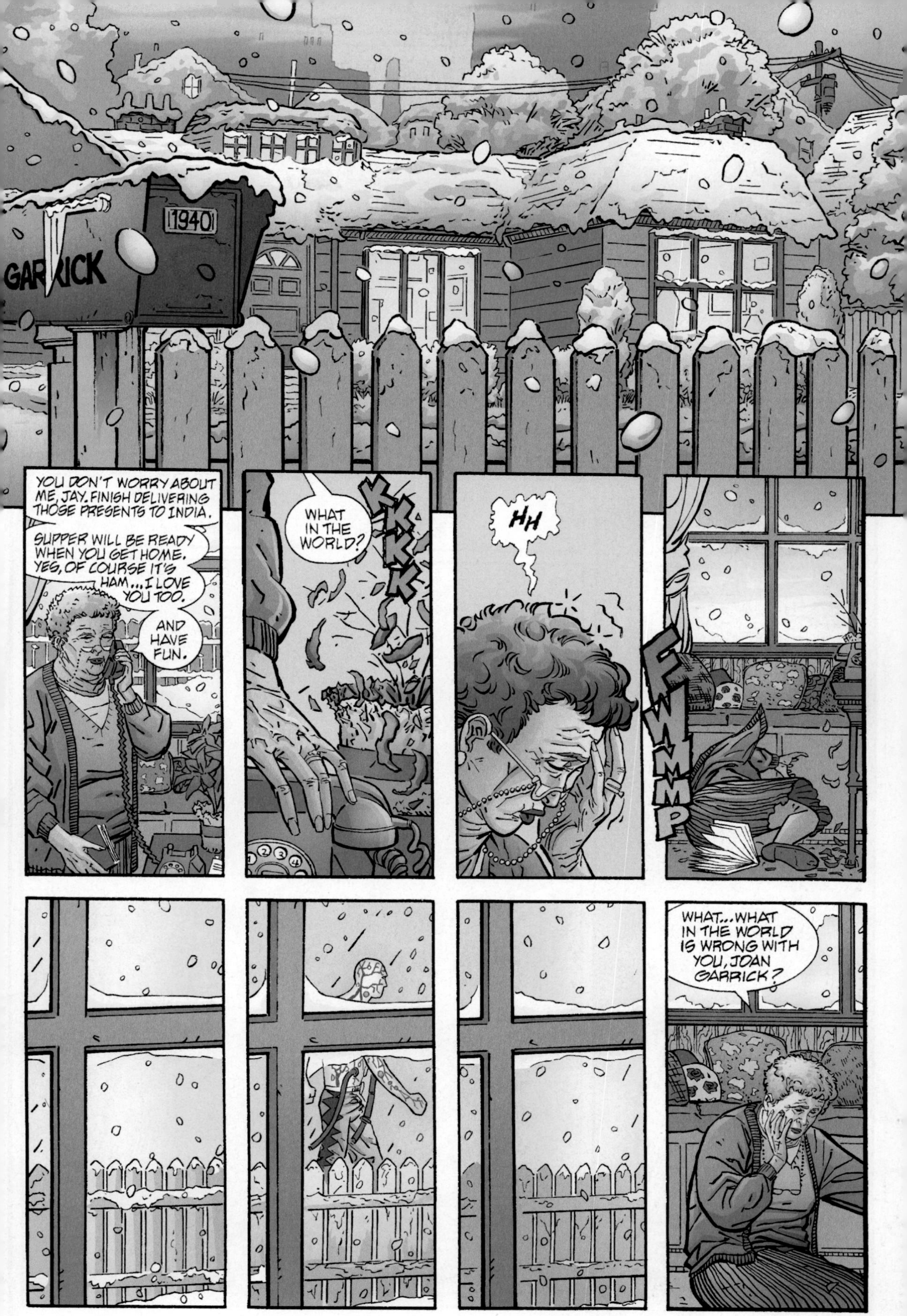
GARRICK
1940
YOU DON'T WORRY ABOUT ME, JAY. FINISH DELIVERING THOSE PRESENTS TO INDIA.
SUPPER WILL BE READY WHEN YOU GET HOME. YES, OF COURSE IT'S HAM... I LOVE YOU TOO.
AND HAVE FUN.
WHAT IN THE WORLD?
KKKKK
HH
FWMMP
WHAT... WHAT IN THE WORLD IS WRONG WITH YOU, JOAN GARRICK?

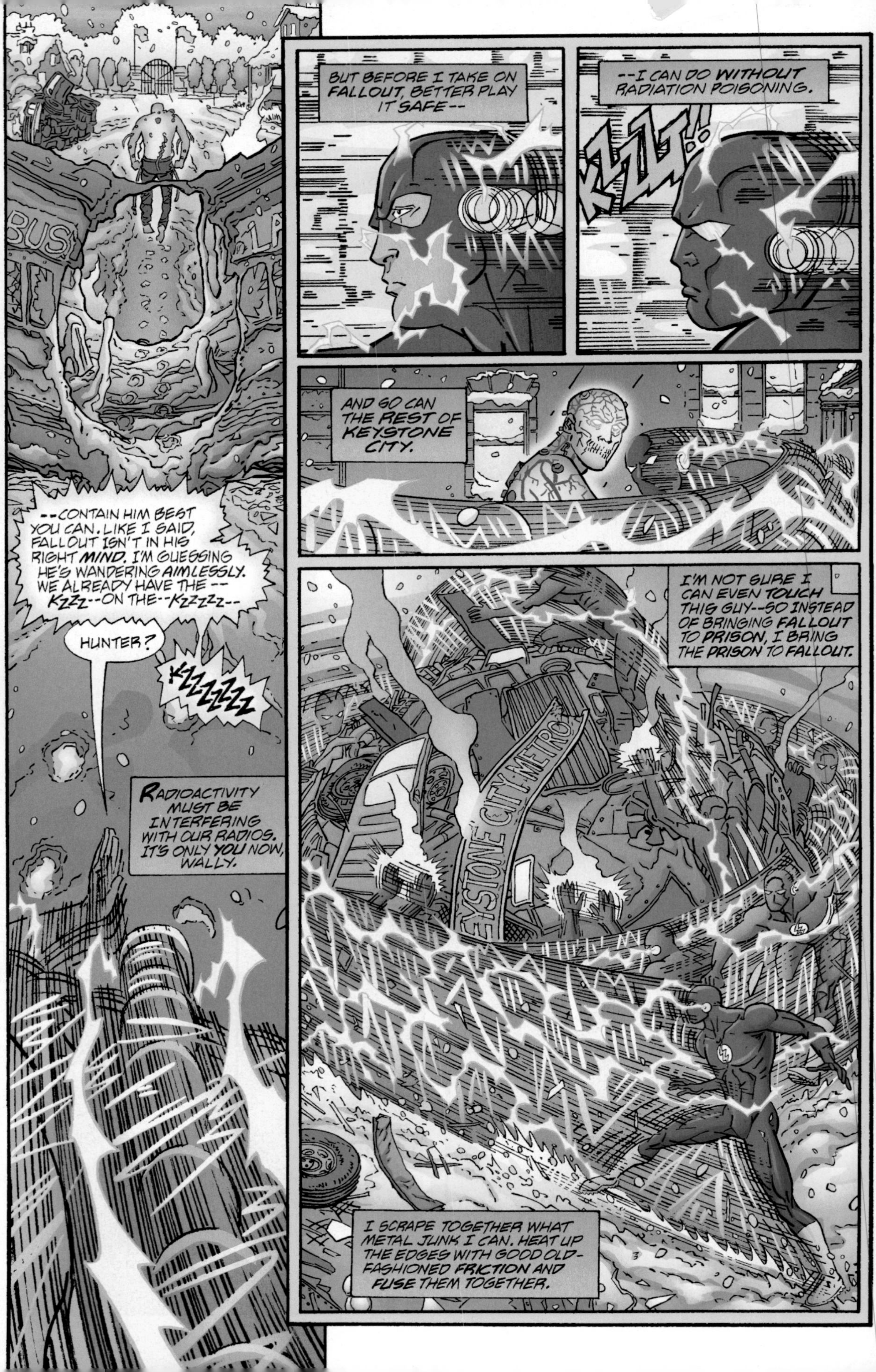
--CONTAIN HIM BEST YOU CAN. LIKE I SAID, FALLOUT ISN'T IN HIS RIGHT MIND. I'M GUESSING HE'S WANDERING AIMLESSLY. WE ALREADY HAVE THE --KZZZ--ON THE--KZZZZZ--
HUNTER?
KZZZZZZZ
RADIOACTIVITY MUST BE INTERFERING WITH OUR RADIOS. IT'S ONLY YOU NOW, WALLY.
BUT BEFORE I TAKE ON FALLOUT, BETTER PLAY IT SAFE--
--I CAN DO WITHOUT RADIATION POISONING.
KZZZT!!
AND SO CAN THE REST OF KEYSTONE CITY.
I'M NOT SURE I CAN EVEN TOUCH THIS GUY--SO INSTEAD OF BRINGING FALLOUT TO PRISON, I BRING THE PRISON TO FALLOUT.
KEYSTONE CITY METRO
I SCRAPE TOGETHER WHAT METAL JUNK I CAN. HEAT UP THE EDGES WITH GOOD OLD-FASHIONED FRICTION AND FUSE THEM TOGETHER.

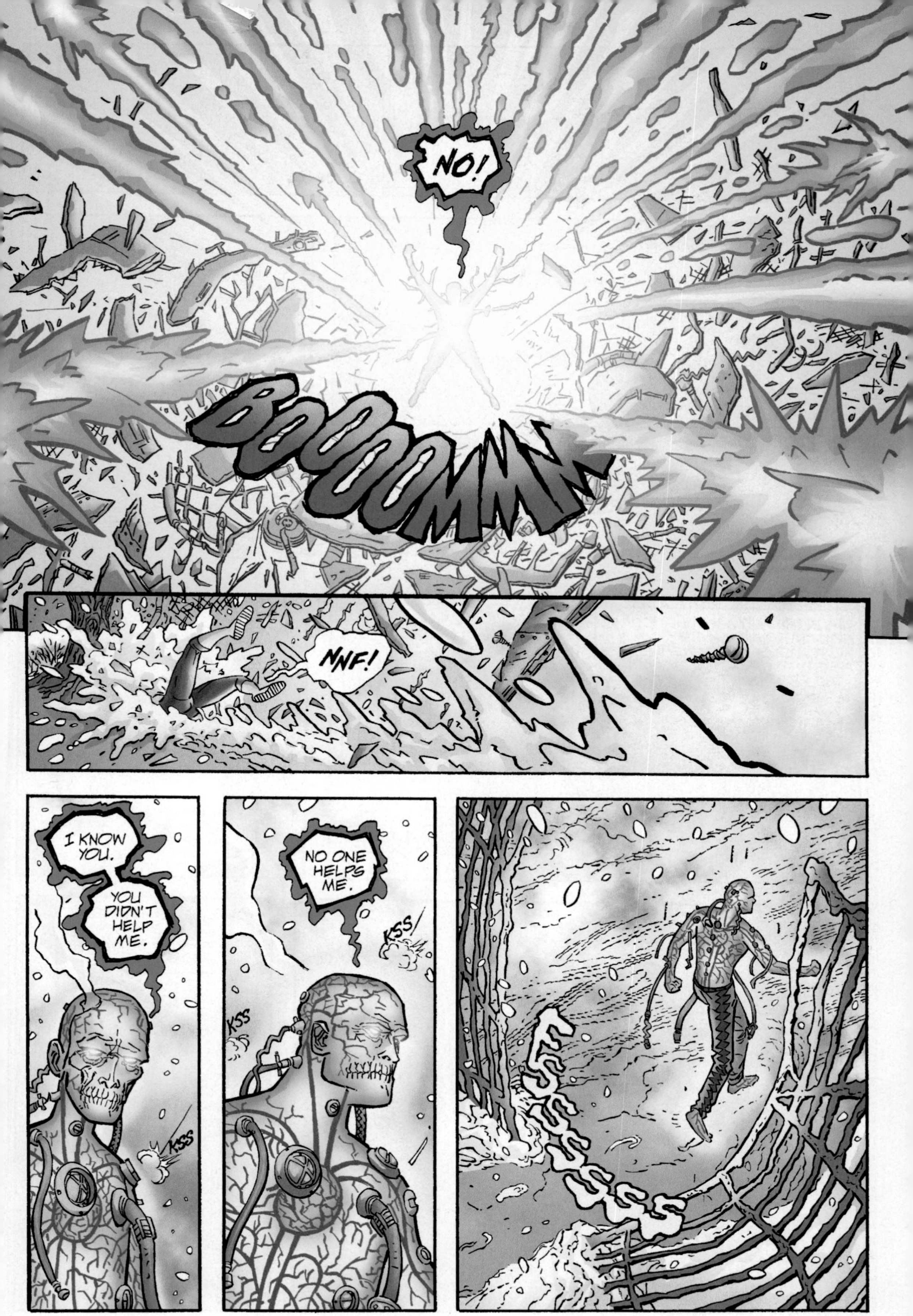
NO!
BOOOOMMM
NNF!
I KNOW YOU.
YOU DIDN'T HELP ME.
KSS
NO ONE HELPS ME.
KSS/
KSS
ESSSSSSS

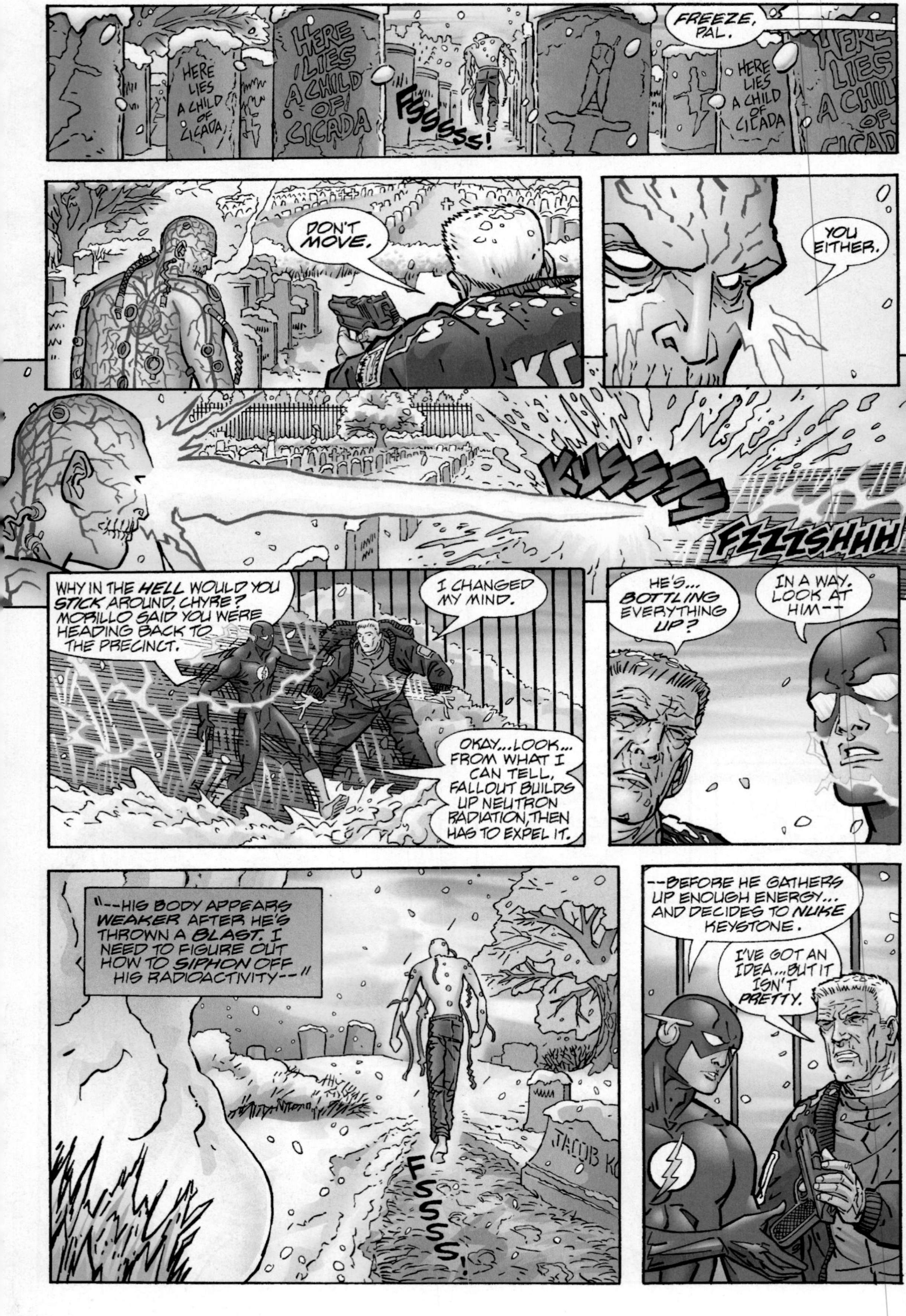

HERE LIES A CHILD OF CICADA
HERE LIES A CHILD OF CICADA
FSSSSSS!
FREEZE, PAL.
HERE LIES A CHILD OF CICADA
HERE LIES A CHILD OF CICADA
DON'T MOVE.
YOU EITHER.
KVSSSSS
FZZZSHHH
WHY IN THE HELL WOULD YOU STICK AROUND, CHYRE? MORILLO SAID YOU WERE HEADING BACK TO THE PRECINCT.
I CHANGED MY MIND.
OKAY...LOOK... FROM WHAT I CAN TELL, FALLOUT BUILDS UP NEUTRON RADIATION, THEN HAS TO EXPEL IT.
HE'S... BOTTLING EVERYTHING UP?
IN A WAY. LOOK AT HIM--
"--HIS BODY APPEARS WEAKER AFTER HE'S THROWN A BLAST. I NEED TO FIGURE OUT HOW TO SIPHON OFF HIS RADIOACTIVITY--"
FSSSS!
JACOB K
--BEFORE HE GATHERS UP ENOUGH ENERGY... AND DECIDES TO NUKE KEYSTONE.
I'VE GOT AN IDEA...BUT IT ISN'T PRETTY.

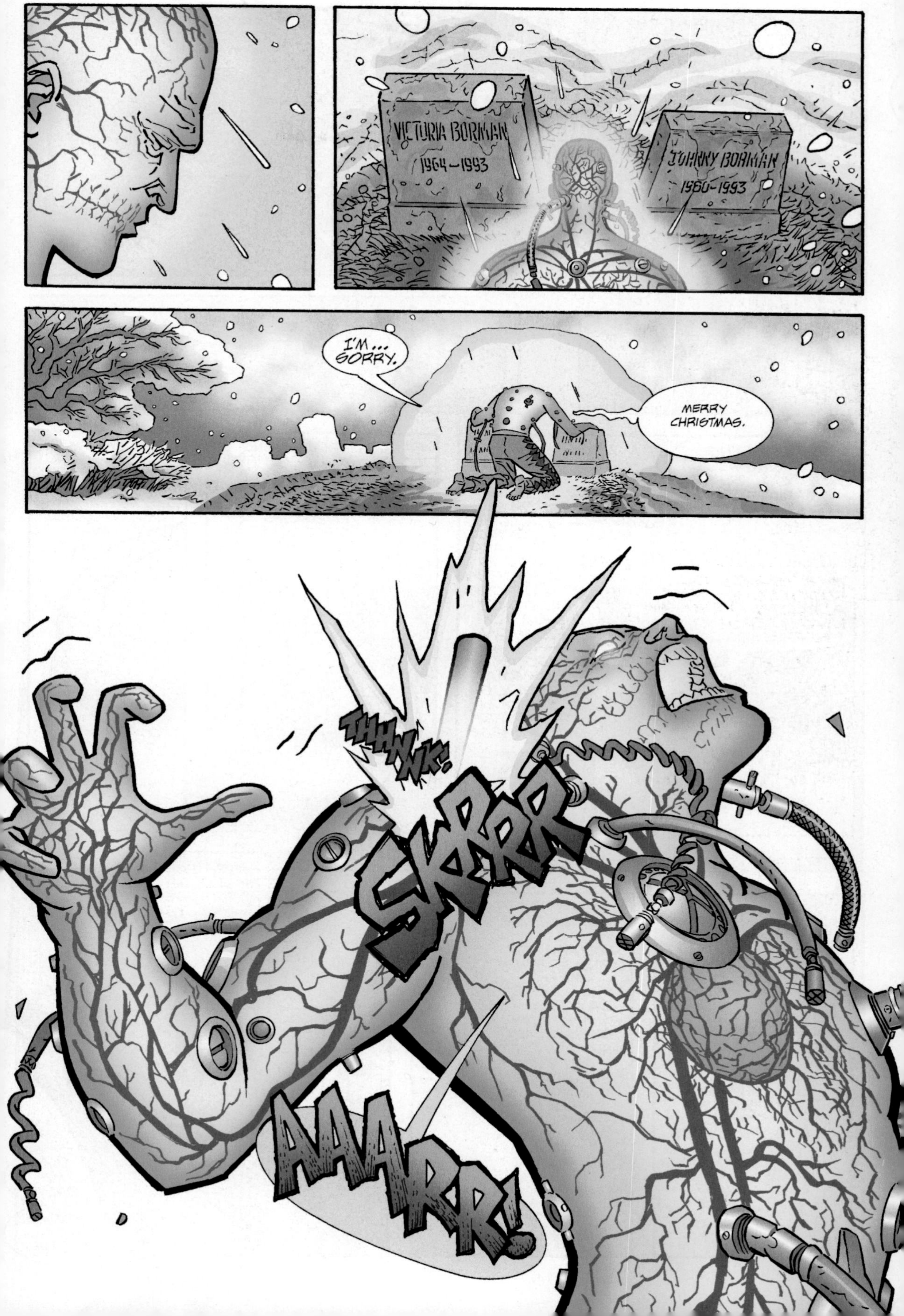
VICTORIA BORMAN
1964-1993
JOHNNY BORMAN
1980-1993
I'M... SORRY.
MERRY CHRISTMAS.
THHNNK!
SKRRR
AAARRR!

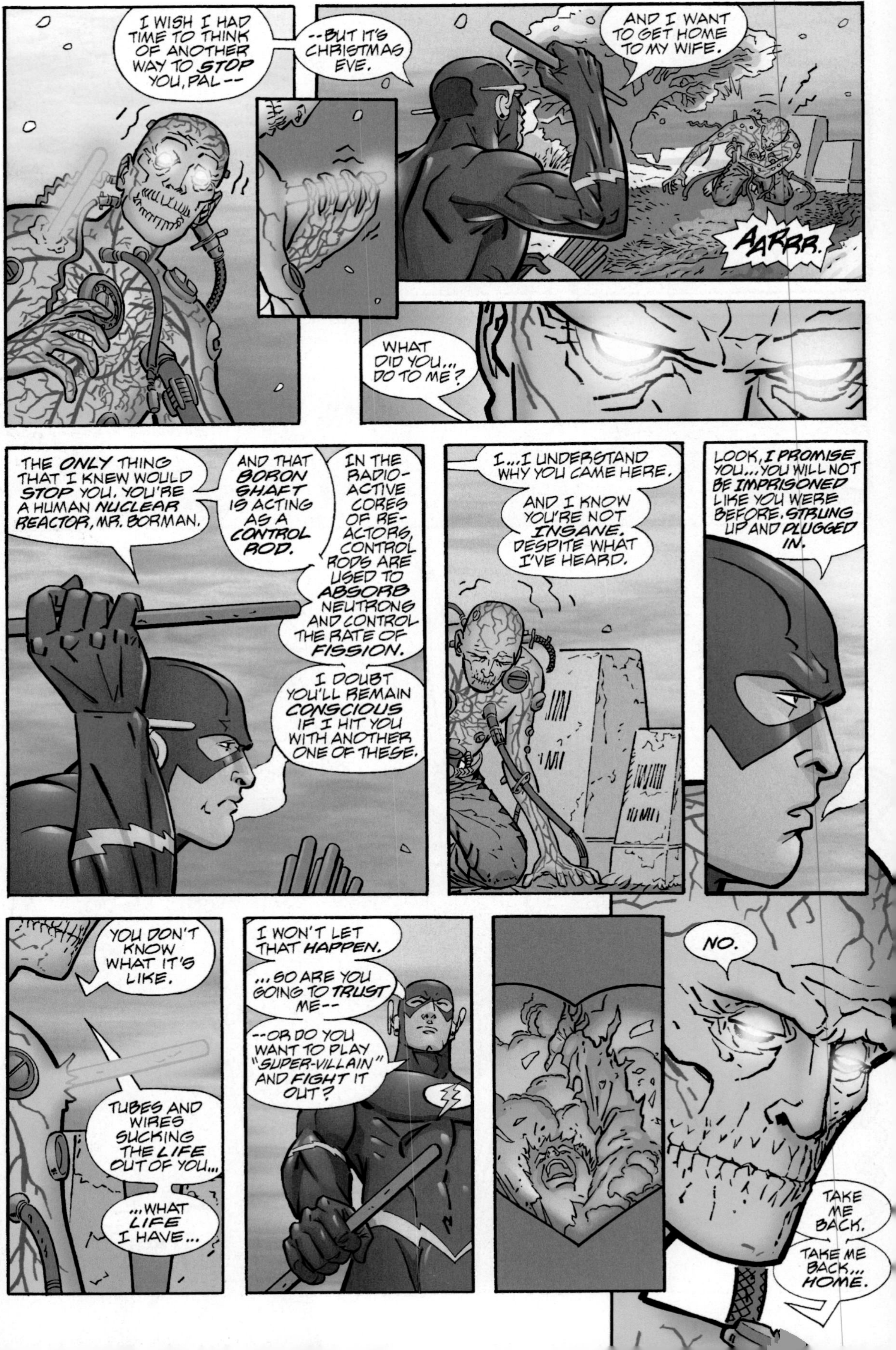
I WISH I HAD TIME TO THINK OF ANOTHER WAY TO STOP YOU, PAL--
--BUT IT'S CHRISTMAS EVE.
AND I WANT TO GET HOME TO MY WIFE.
AARRR.
WHAT DID YOU... DO TO ME?
THE ONLY THING THAT I KNEW WOULD STOP YOU. YOU'RE A HUMAN NUCLEAR REACTOR, MR. BORMAN.
AND THAT BORON SHAFT IS ACTING AS A CONTROL ROD.
IN THE RADIO-ACTIVE CORES OF RE-ACTORS, CONTROL RODS ARE USED TO ABSORB NEUTRONS AND CONTROL THE RATE OF FISSION.
I DOUBT YOU'LL REMAIN CONSCIOUS IF I HIT YOU WITH ANOTHER ONE OF THESE.
I... I UNDERSTAND WHY YOU CAME HERE.
AND I KNOW YOU'RE NOT INSANE. DESPITE WHAT I'VE HEARD.
LOOK, I PROMISE YOU... YOU WILL NOT BE IMPRISONED LIKE YOU WERE BEFORE, STRUNG UP AND PLUGGED IN.
YOU DON'T KNOW WHAT IT'S LIKE.
TUBES AND WIRES SUCKING THE LIFE OUT OF YOU...
...WHAT LIFE I HAVE...
I WON'T LET THAT HAPPEN.
...SO ARE YOU GOING TO TRUST ME--
--OR DO YOU WANT TO PLAY "SUPER-VILLAIN" AND FIGHT IT OUT?
NO.
TAKE ME BACK.
TAKE ME BACK... HOME.

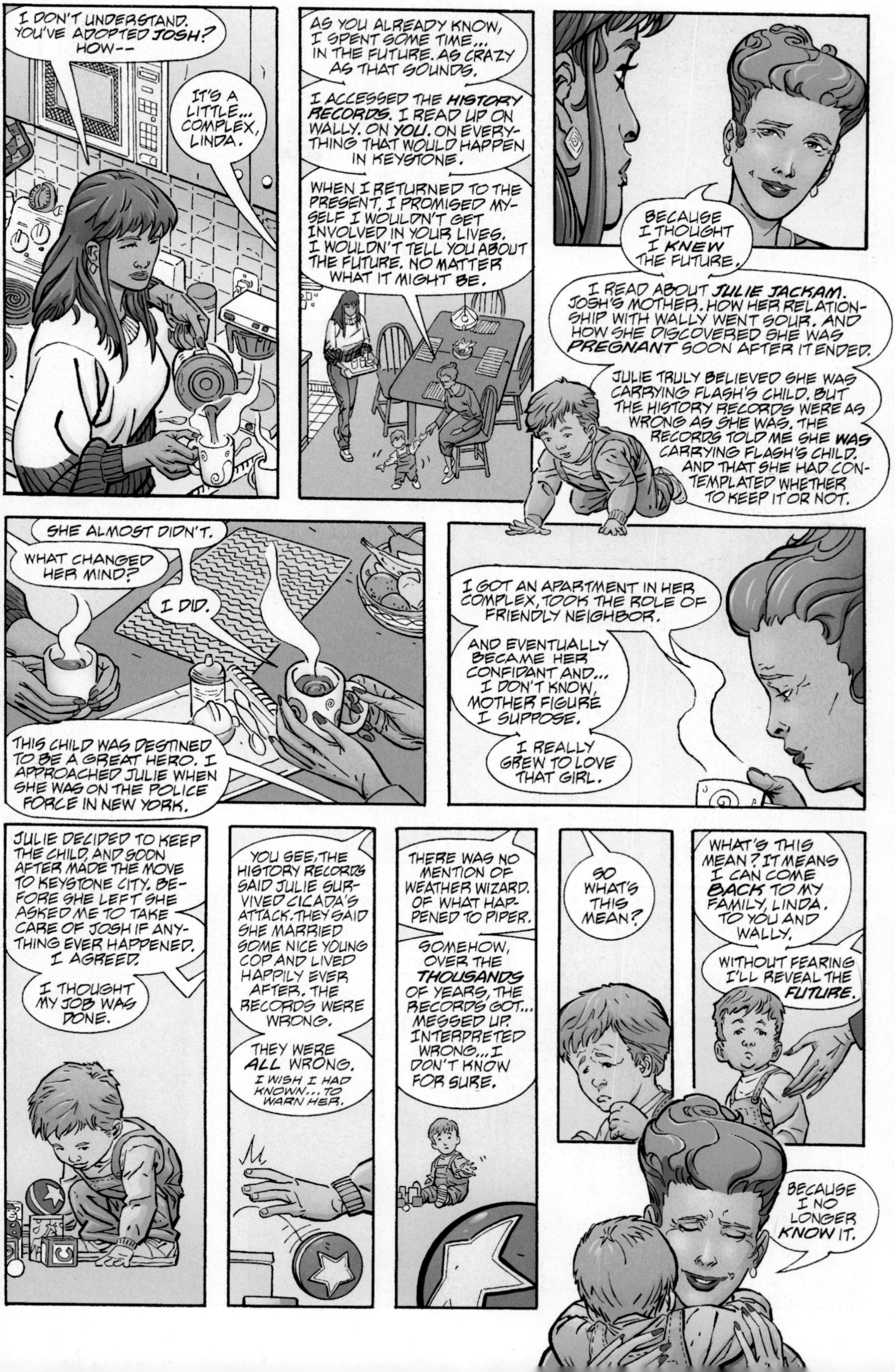
I DON'T UNDERSTAND. YOU'VE ADOPTED JOSH? HOW--
IT'S A LITTLE... COMPLEX, LINDA.
AS YOU ALREADY KNOW, I SPENT SOME TIME... IN THE FUTURE. AS CRAZY AS THAT SOUNDS.
I ACCESSED THE HISTORY RECORDS. I READ UP ON WALLY. ON YOU. ON EVERYTHING THAT WOULD HAPPEN IN KEYSTONE.
WHEN I RETURNED TO THE PRESENT, I PROMISED MYSELF I WOULDN'T GET INVOLVED IN YOUR LIVES. I WOULDN'T TELL YOU ABOUT THE FUTURE. NO MATTER WHAT IT MIGHT BE.
BECAUSE I THOUGHT I KNEW THE FUTURE.
I READ ABOUT JULIE JACKAM. JOSH'S MOTHER. HOW HER RELATIONSHIP WITH WALLY WENT SOUR. AND HOW SHE DISCOVERED SHE WAS PREGNANT SOON AFTER IT ENDED.
JULIE TRULY BELIEVED SHE WAS CARRYING FLASH'S CHILD. BUT THE HISTORY RECORDS WERE AS WRONG AS SHE WAS. THE RECORDS TOLD ME SHE WAS CARRYING FLASH'S CHILD. AND THAT SHE HAD CONTEMPLATED WHETHER TO KEEP IT OR NOT.
SHE ALMOST DIDN'T.
WHAT CHANGED HER MIND?
I DID.
THIS CHILD WAS DESTINED TO BE A GREAT HERO. I APPROACHED JULIE WHEN SHE WAS ON THE POLICE FORCE IN NEW YORK.
I GOT AN APARTMENT IN HER COMPLEX, TOOK THE ROLE OF FRIENDLY NEIGHBOR.
AND EVENTUALLY BECAME HER CONFIDANT AND... I DON'T KNOW, MOTHER FIGURE I SUPPOSE.
I REALLY GREW TO LOVE THAT GIRL.
JULIE DECIDED TO KEEP THE CHILD, AND SOON AFTER MADE THE MOVE TO KEYSTONE CITY. BEFORE SHE LEFT SHE ASKED ME TO TAKE CARE OF JOSH IF ANYTHING EVER HAPPENED. I AGREED.
I THOUGHT MY JOB WAS DONE.
YOU SEE, THE HISTORY RECORDS SAID JULIE SURVIVED CICADA'S ATTACK. THEY SAID SHE MARRIED SOME NICE YOUNG COP AND LIVED HAPPILY EVER AFTER. THE RECORDS WERE WRONG.
THEY WERE ALL WRONG. I WISH I HAD KNOWN... TO WARN HER.
THERE WAS NO MENTION OF WEATHER WIZARD. OF WHAT HAPPENED TO PIPER.
SOMEHOW, OVER THE THOUSANDS OF YEARS, THE RECORDS GOT... MESSED UP. INTERPRETED WRONG... I DON'T KNOW FOR SURE.
SO WHAT'S THIS MEAN?
WHAT'S THIS MEAN? IT MEANS I CAN COME BACK TO MY FAMILY, LINDA. TO YOU AND WALLY.
WITHOUT FEARING I'LL REVEAL THE FUTURE.
BECAUSE I NO LONGER KNOW IT.

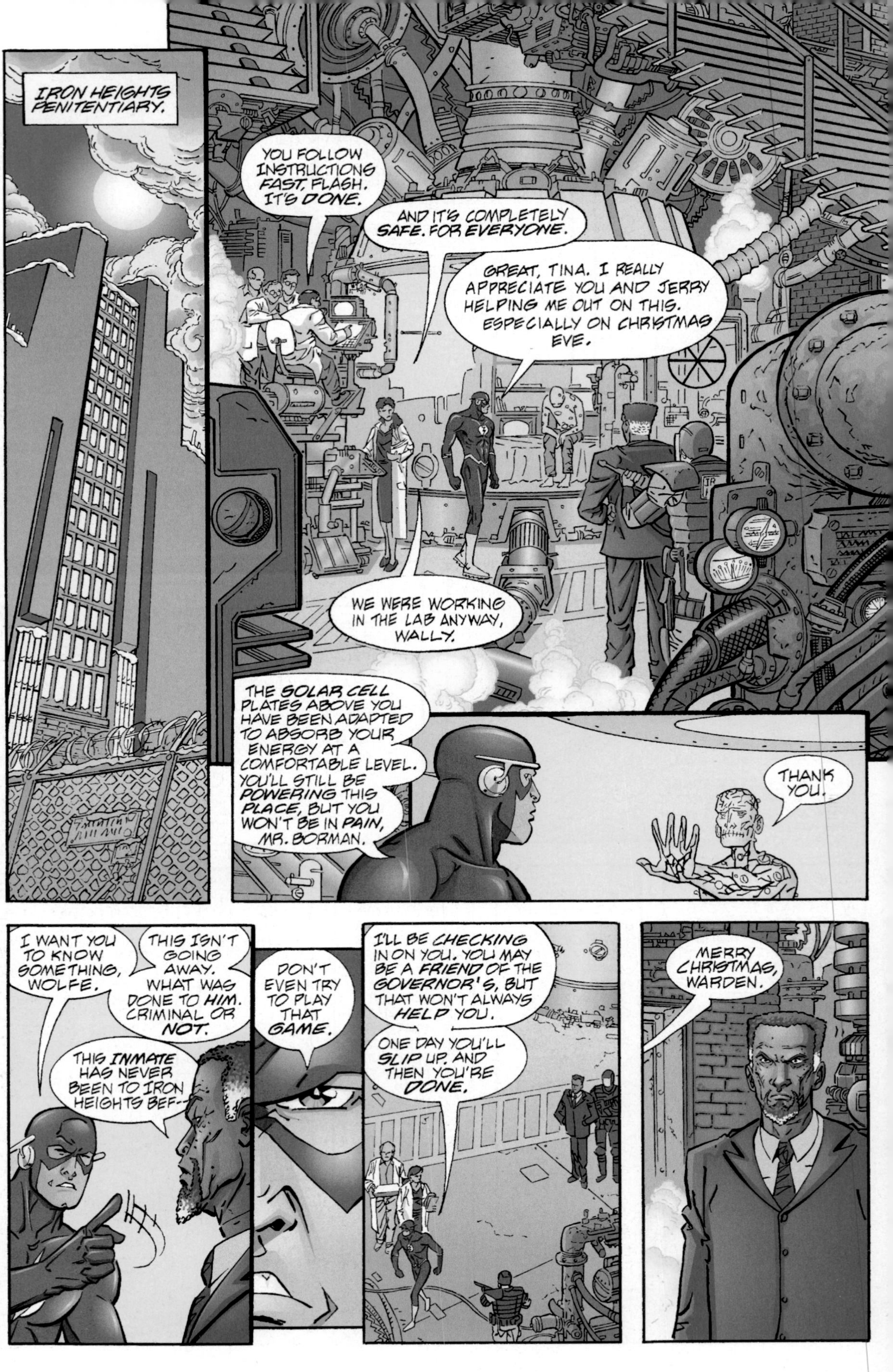
IRON HEIGHTS PENITENTIARY.
YOU FOLLOW INSTRUCTIONS FAST, FLASH. IT'S DONE.
AND IT'S COMPLETELY SAFE. FOR EVERYONE.
GREAT, TINA. I REALLY APPRECIATE YOU AND JERRY HELPING ME OUT ON THIS. ESPECIALLY ON CHRISTMAS EVE.
WE WERE WORKING IN THE LAB ANYWAY, WALLY.
THE SOLAR CELL PLATES ABOVE YOU HAVE BEEN ADAPTED TO ABSORB YOUR ENERGY AT A COMFORTABLE LEVEL. YOU'LL STILL BE POWERING THIS PLACE, BUT YOU WON'T BE IN PAIN, MR. BORMAN.
THANK YOU.
I WANT YOU TO KNOW SOMETHING, WOLFE.
THIS ISN'T GOING AWAY. WHAT WAS DONE TO HIM. CRIMINAL OR NOT.
THIS INMATE HAS NEVER BEEN TO IRON HEIGHTS BEF--
DON'T EVEN TRY TO PLAY THAT GAME.
I'LL BE CHECKING IN ON YOU. YOU MAY BE A FRIEND OF THE GOVERNOR'S, BUT THAT WON'T ALWAYS HELP YOU.
ONE DAY YOU'LL SLIP UP. AND THEN YOU'RE DONE.
MERRY CHRISTMAS, WARDEN.

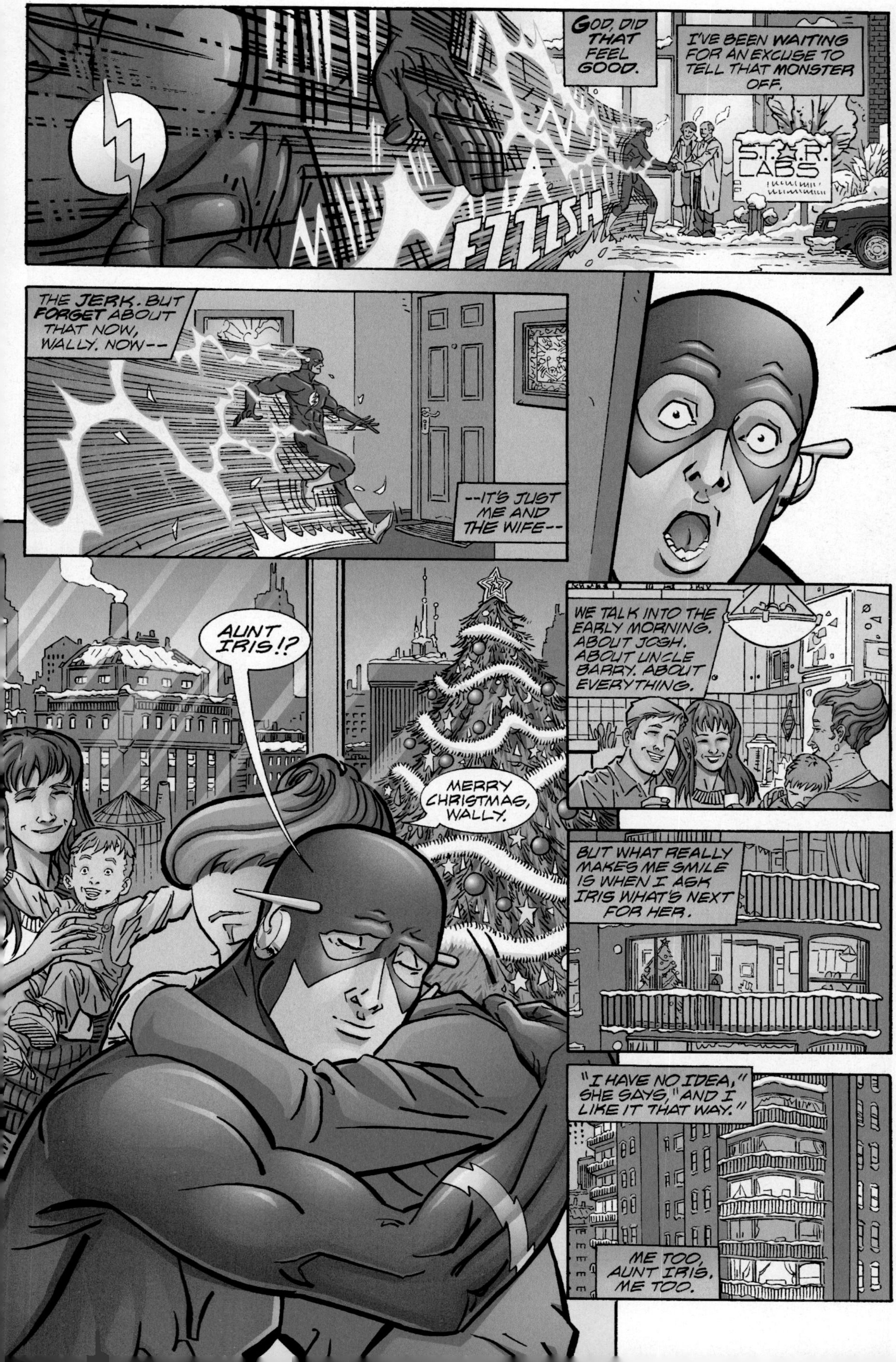
GOD, DID THAT FEEL GOOD.
I'VE BEEN WAITING FOR AN EXCUSE TO TELL THAT MONSTER OFF.
FZZZSH
S.T.A.R. LABS
THE JERK. BUT FORGET ABOUT THAT NOW, WALLY. NOW--
--IT'S JUST ME AND THE WIFE--
AUNT IRIS!?
MERRY CHRISTMAS, WALLY.
WE TALK INTO THE EARLY MORNING. ABOUT JOSH. ABOUT UNCLE BARRY. ABOUT EVERYTHING.
BUT WHAT REALLY MAKES ME SMILE IS WHEN I ASK IRIS WHAT'S NEXT FOR HER.
"I HAVE NO IDEA," SHE SAYS, "AND I LIKE IT THAT WAY."
ME TOO, AUNT IRIS. ME TOO.

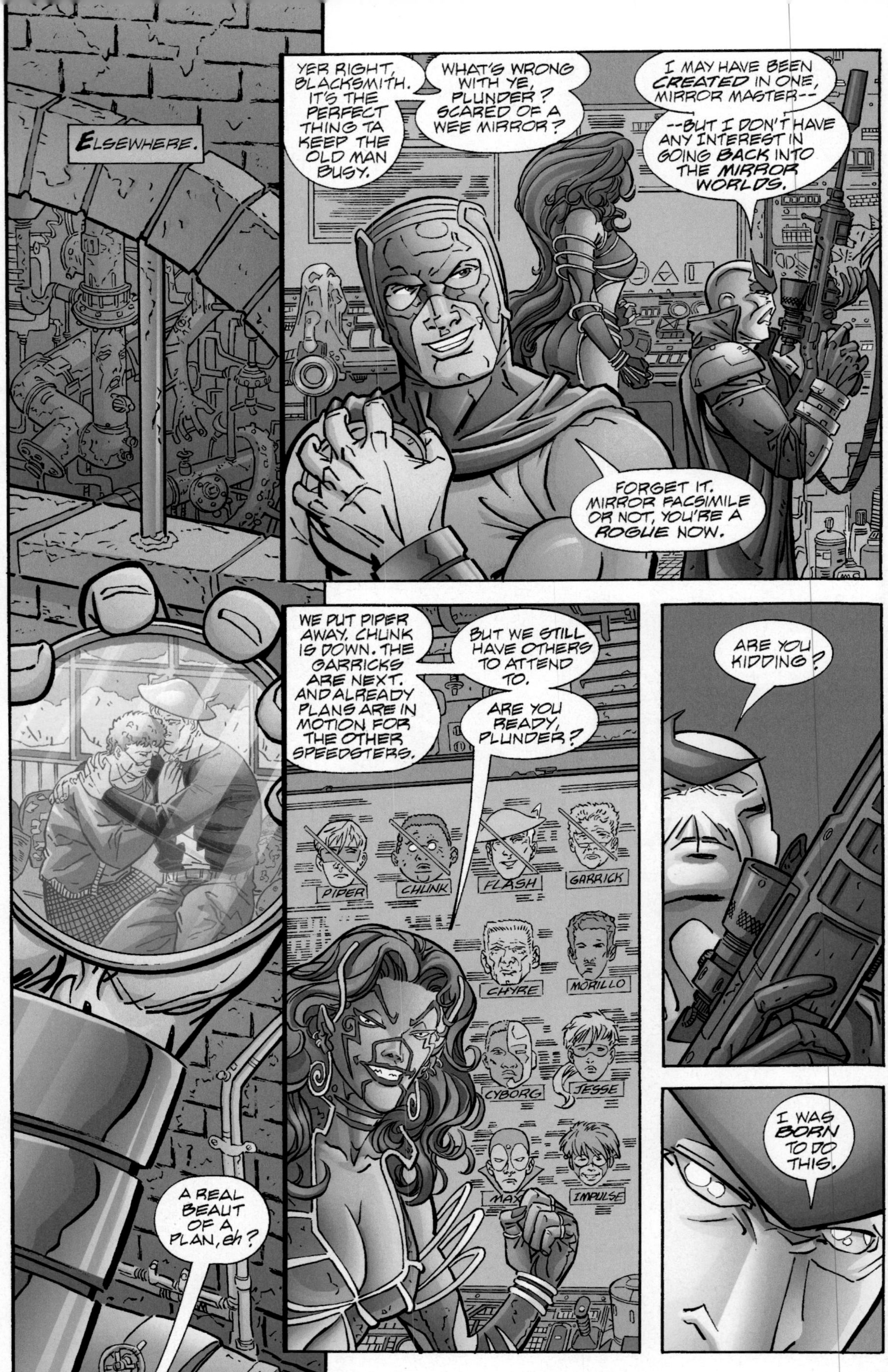
ELSEWHERE.
YER RIGHT, BLACKSMITH. IT'S THE PERFECT THING TA KEEP THE OLD MAN BUSY.
WHAT'S WRONG WITH YE, PLUNDER? SCARED OF A WEE MIRROR?
I MAY HAVE BEEN CREATED IN ONE, MIRROR MASTER--
--BUT I DON'T HAVE ANY INTEREST IN GOING BACK INTO THE MIRROR WORLDS.
FORGET IT. MIRROR FACSIMILE OR NOT, YOU'RE A ROGUE NOW.
A REAL BEAUT OF A PLAN, eh?
WE PUT PIPER AWAY. CHUNK IS DOWN. THE GARRICKS ARE NEXT. AND ALREADY PLANS ARE IN MOTION FOR THE OTHER SPEEDSTERS.
BUT WE STILL HAVE OTHERS TO ATTEND TO.
ARE YOU READY, PLUNDER?
PIPER
CHUNK
FLASH
GARRICK
CHYRE
MORILLO
CYBORG
JESSE
MAX
IMPULSE
ARE YOU KIDDING?
I WAS BORN TO DO THIS.

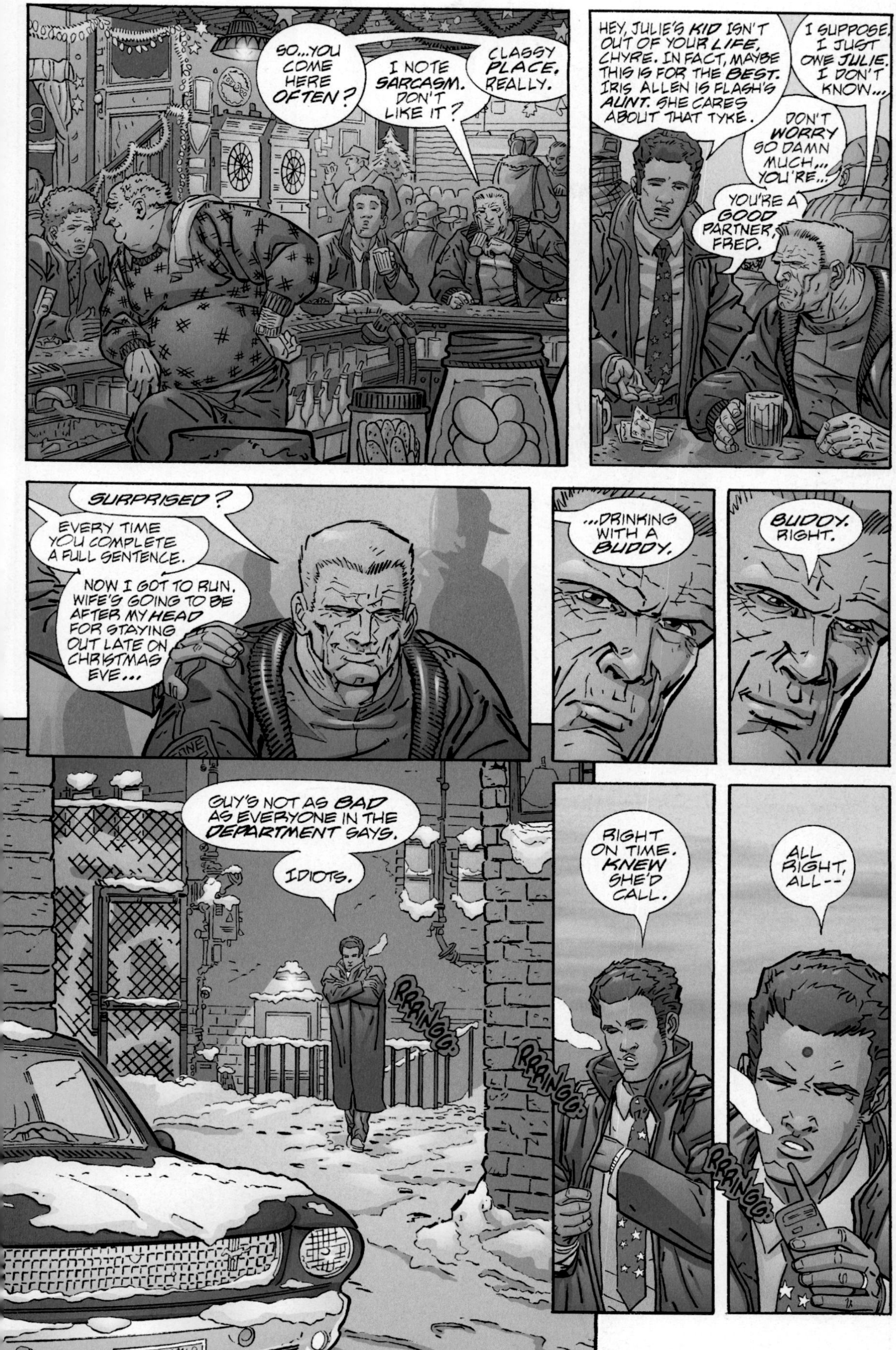
SO...YOU COME HERE OFTEN?
I NOTE SARCASM. DON'T LIKE IT?
CLASSY PLACE. REALLY.
HEY, JULIE'S KID ISN'T OUT OF YOUR LIFE, CHYRE. IN FACT, MAYBE THIS IS FOR THE BEST. IRIS ALLEN IS FLASH'S AUNT. SHE CARES ABOUT THAT TYKE.
I SUPPOSE. I JUST OWE JULIE. I DON'T KNOW...
DON'T WORRY SO DAMN MUCH... YOU'RE...
YOU'RE A GOOD PARTNER, FRED.
SURPRISED?
EVERY TIME YOU COMPLETE A FULL SENTENCE.
NOW I GOT TO RUN. WIFE'S GOING TO BE AFTER MY HEAD FOR STAYING OUT LATE ON CHRISTMAS EVE...
...DRINKING WITH A BUDDY.
BUDDY. RIGHT.
GUY'S NOT AS BAD AS EVERYONE IN THE DEPARTMENT SAYS.
IDIOTS.
RRRINGG.
RRRINGG.
RIGHT ON TIME. KNEW SHE'D CALL.
RRRINGG.
ALL RIGHT, ALL--

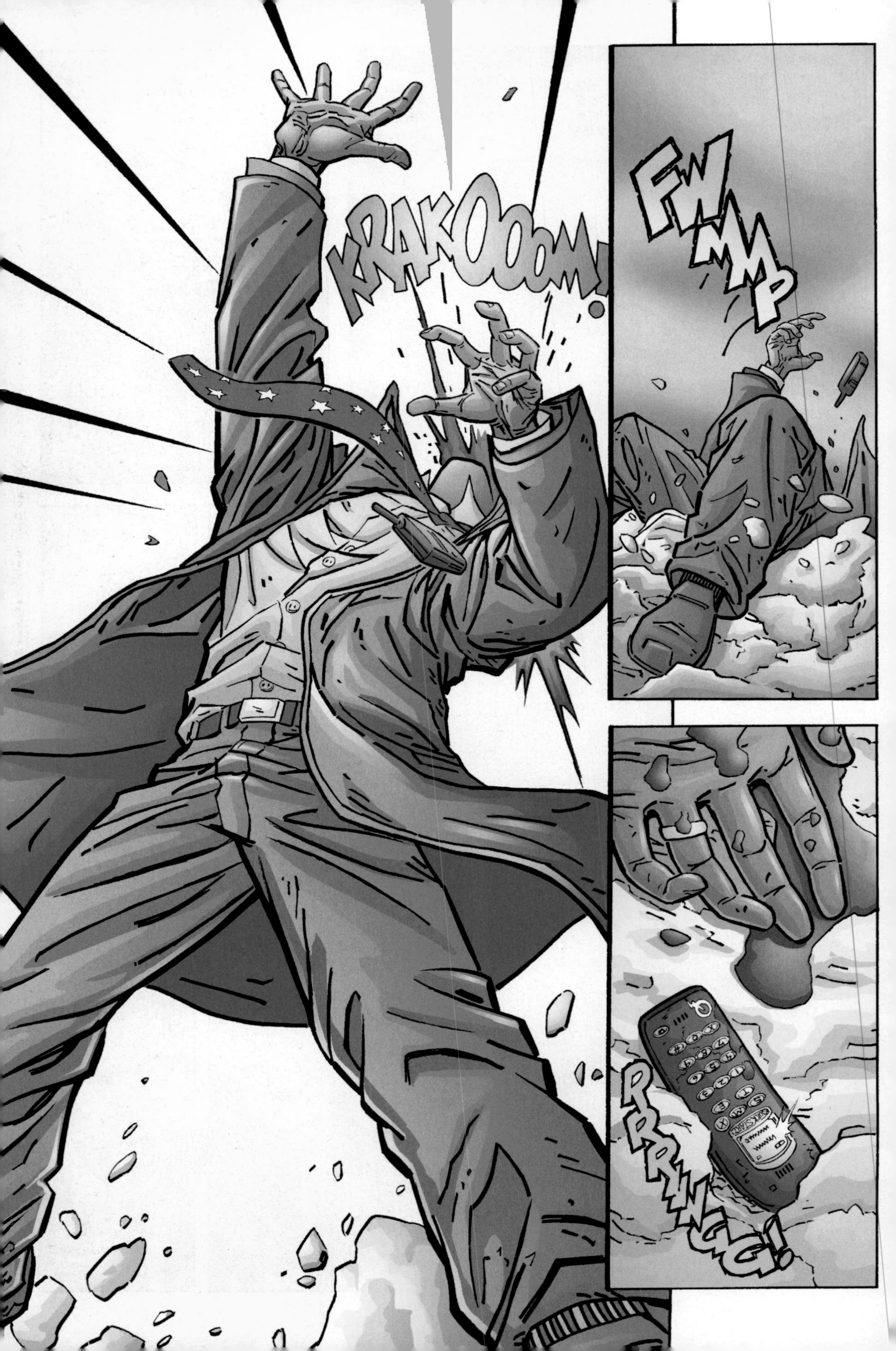
KRAKOOOOM!
FWMMP
RRRING!

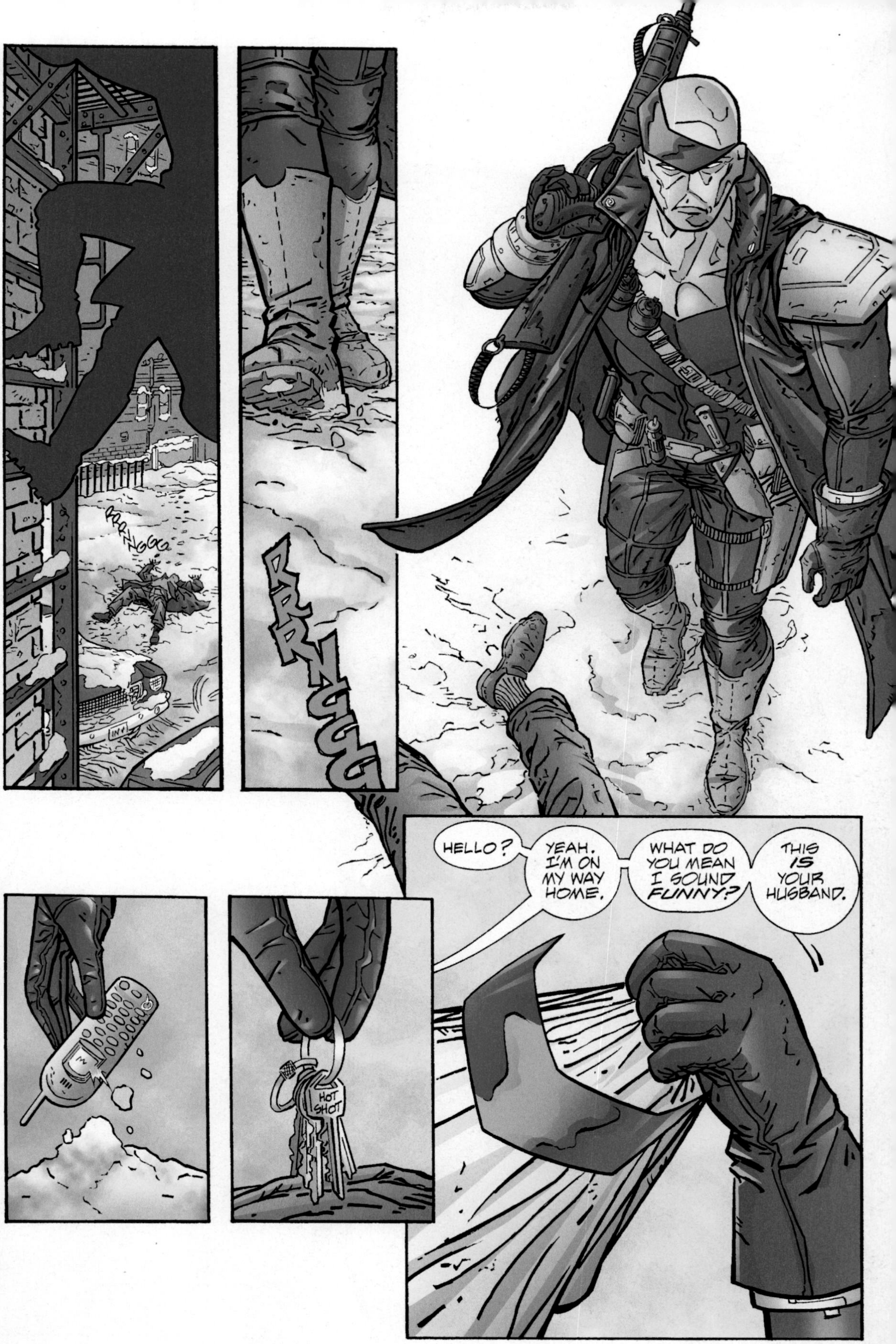

RRRRNGGG
RRRNGGG
HELLO?
YEAH. I'M ON MY WAY HOME.
WHAT DO YOU MEAN I SOUND *FUNNY?*
THIS *IS* YOUR HUSBAND.
HOT SHOT

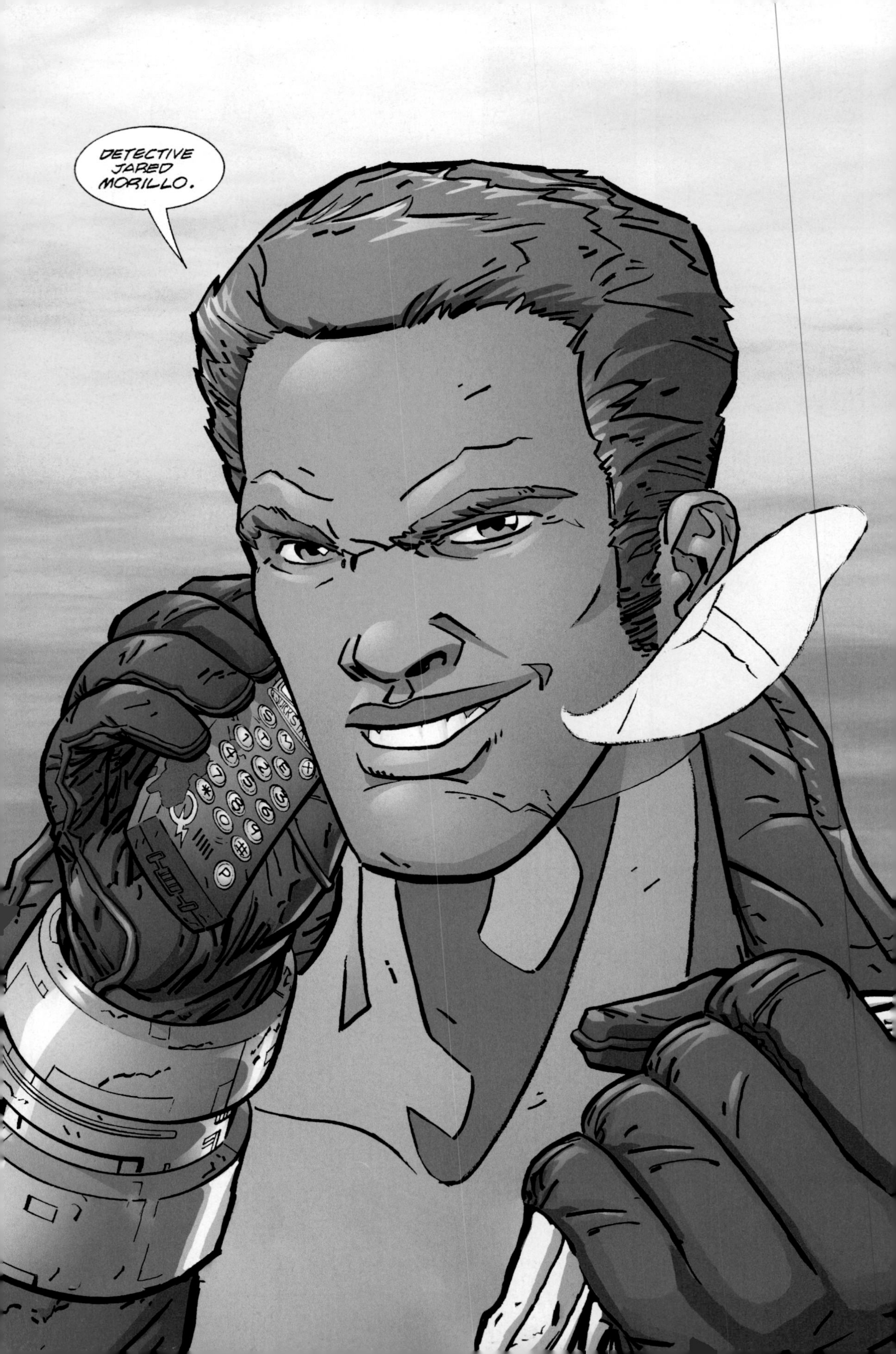
DETECTIVE JARED MORILLO.

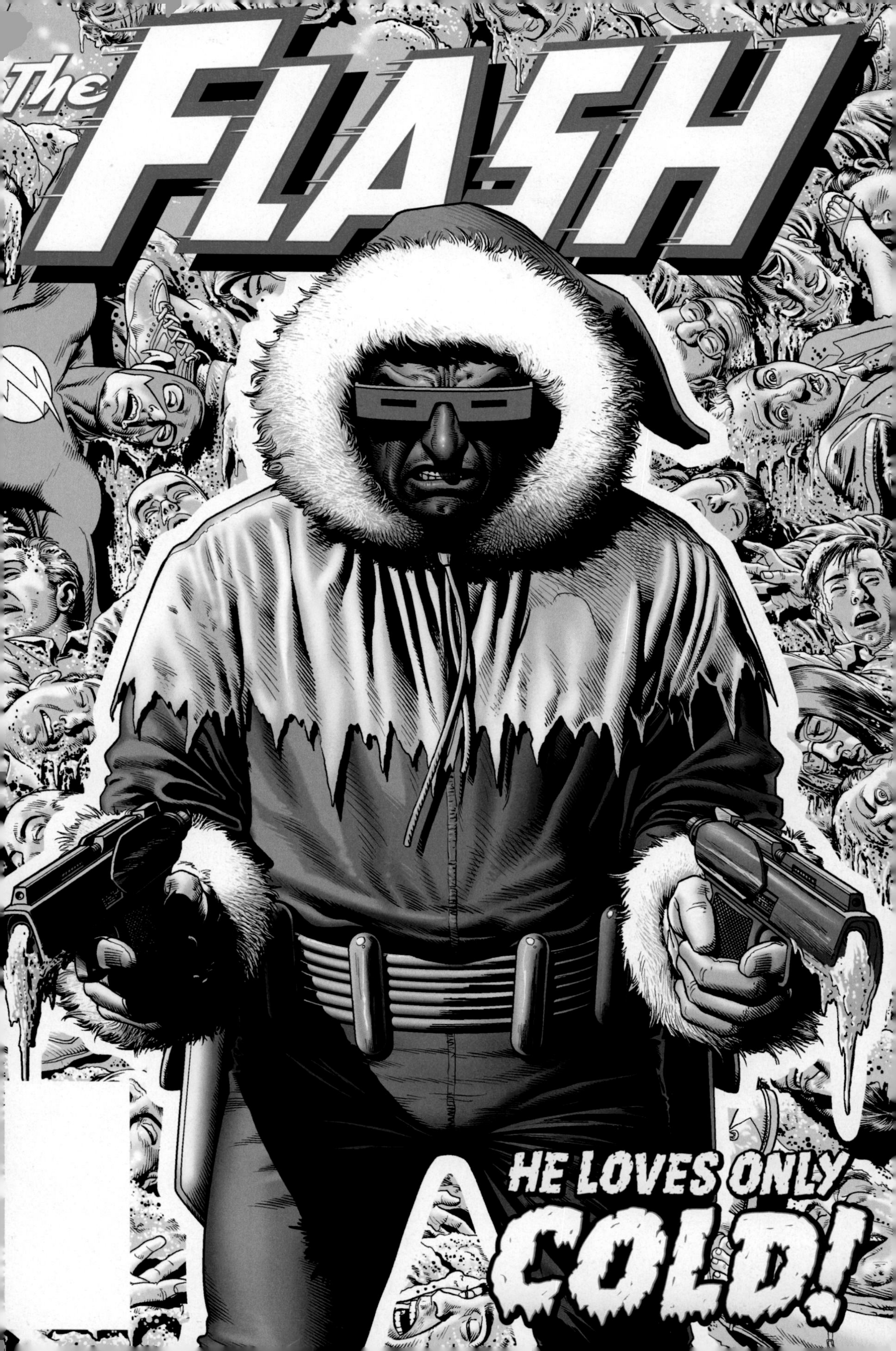
The FLASH
HE LOVES ONLY
COLD!

COVER ART BY **BRIAN BOLLAND**

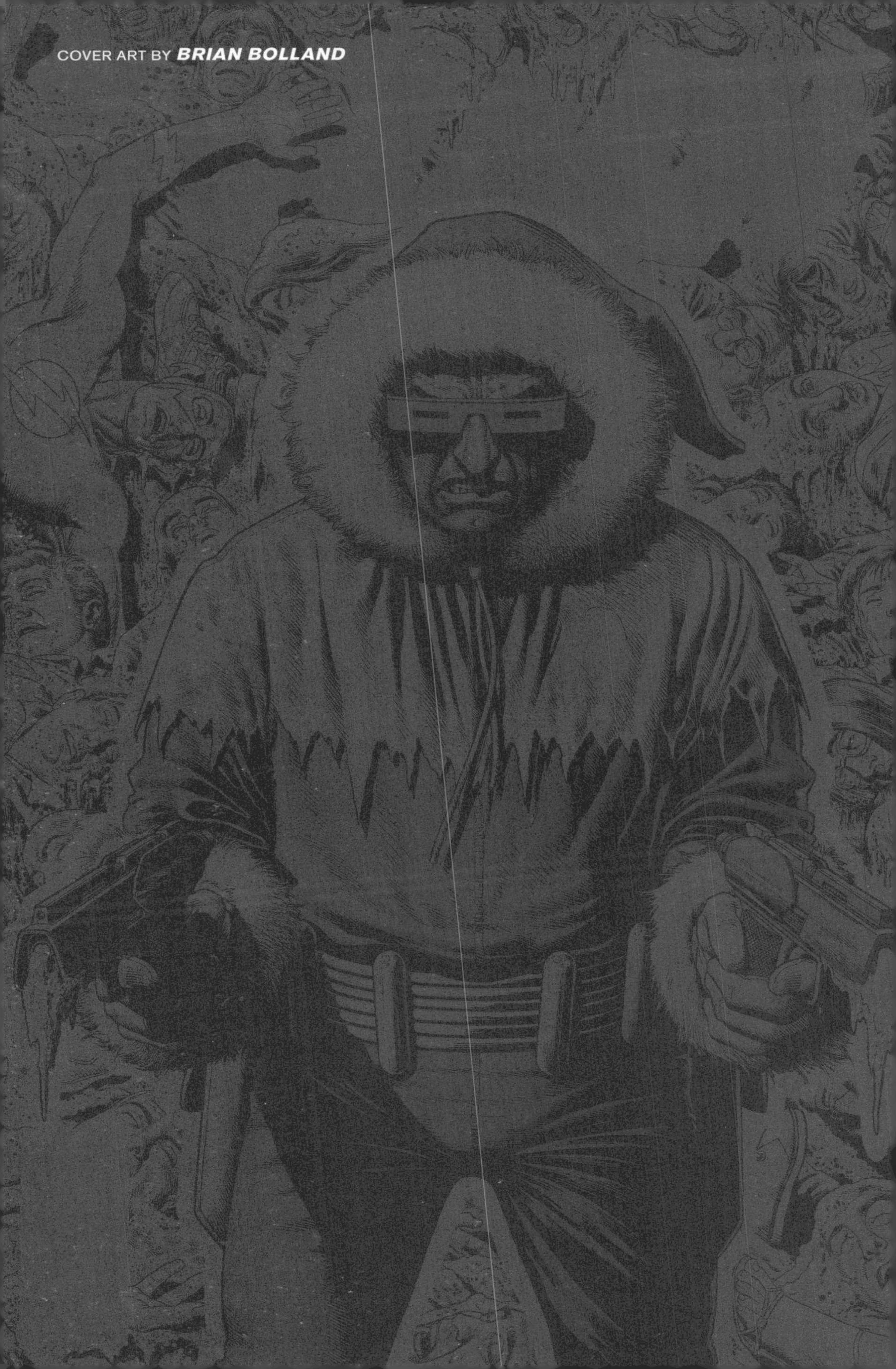

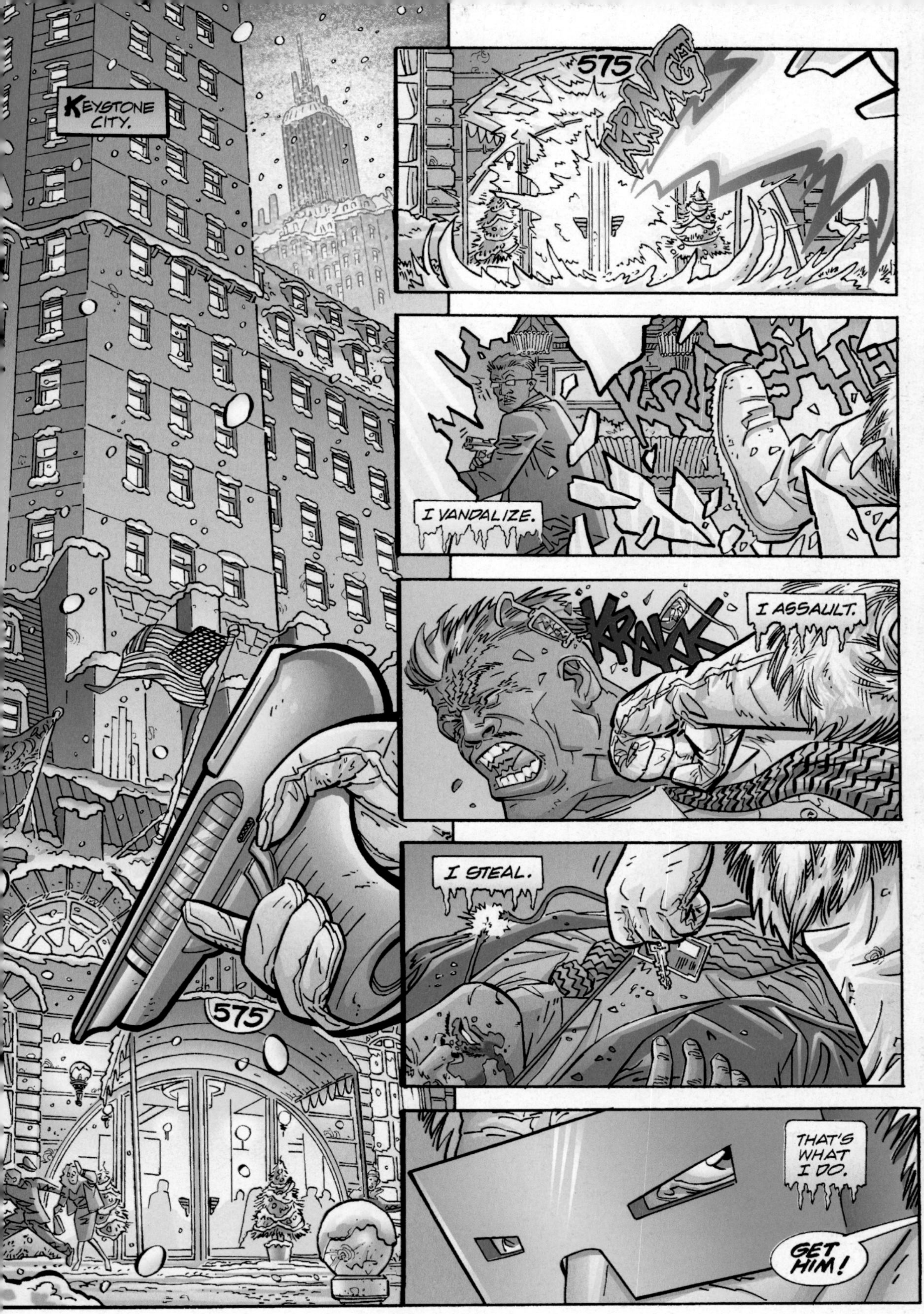
KEYSTONE CITY.
575
KRANG
I VANDALIZE.
KRESHH
KRAKK
I ASSAULT.
I STEAL.
575
THAT'S WHAT I DO.
GET HIM!

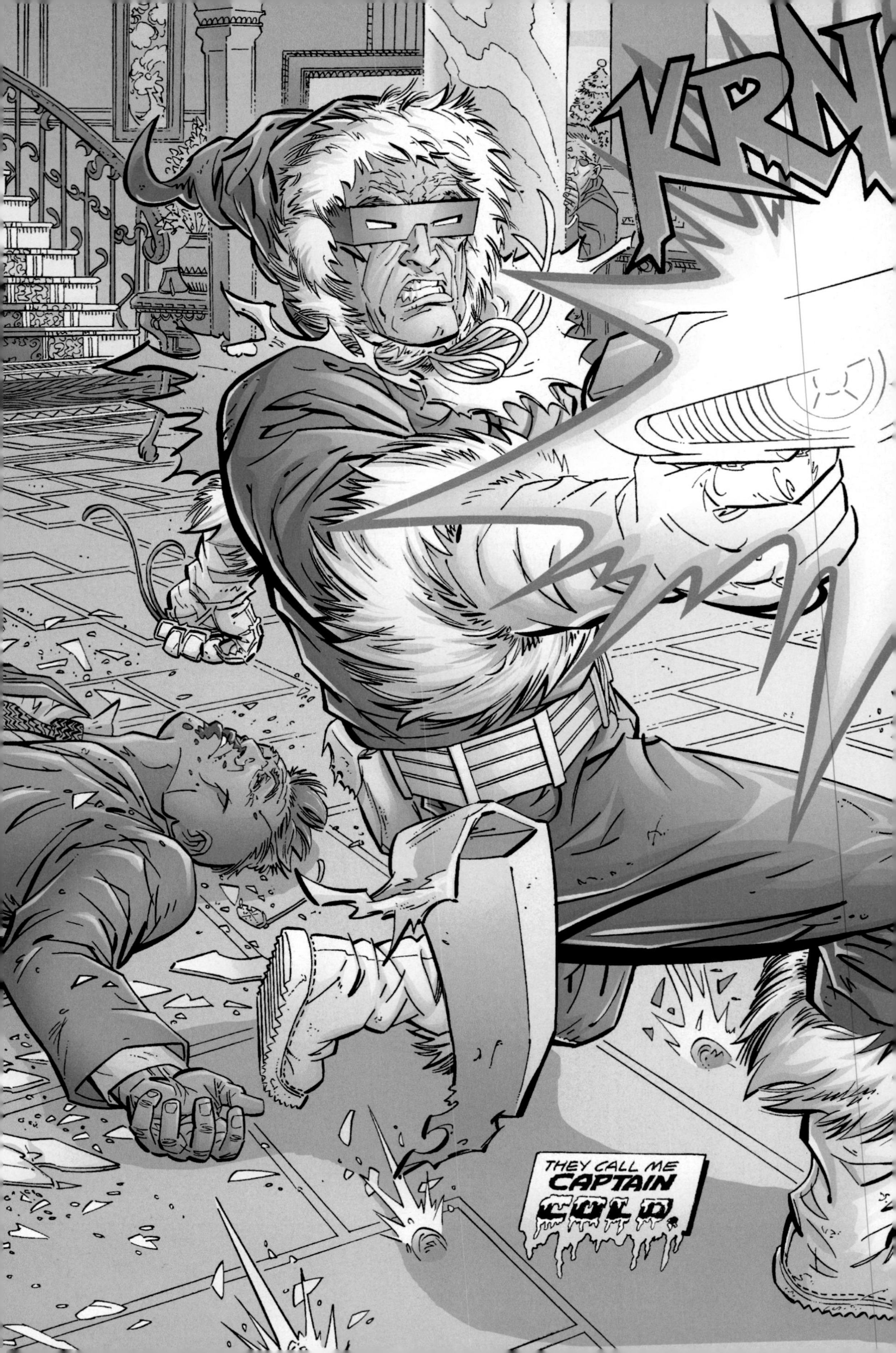
KRN
THEY CALL ME CAPTAIN COLD.

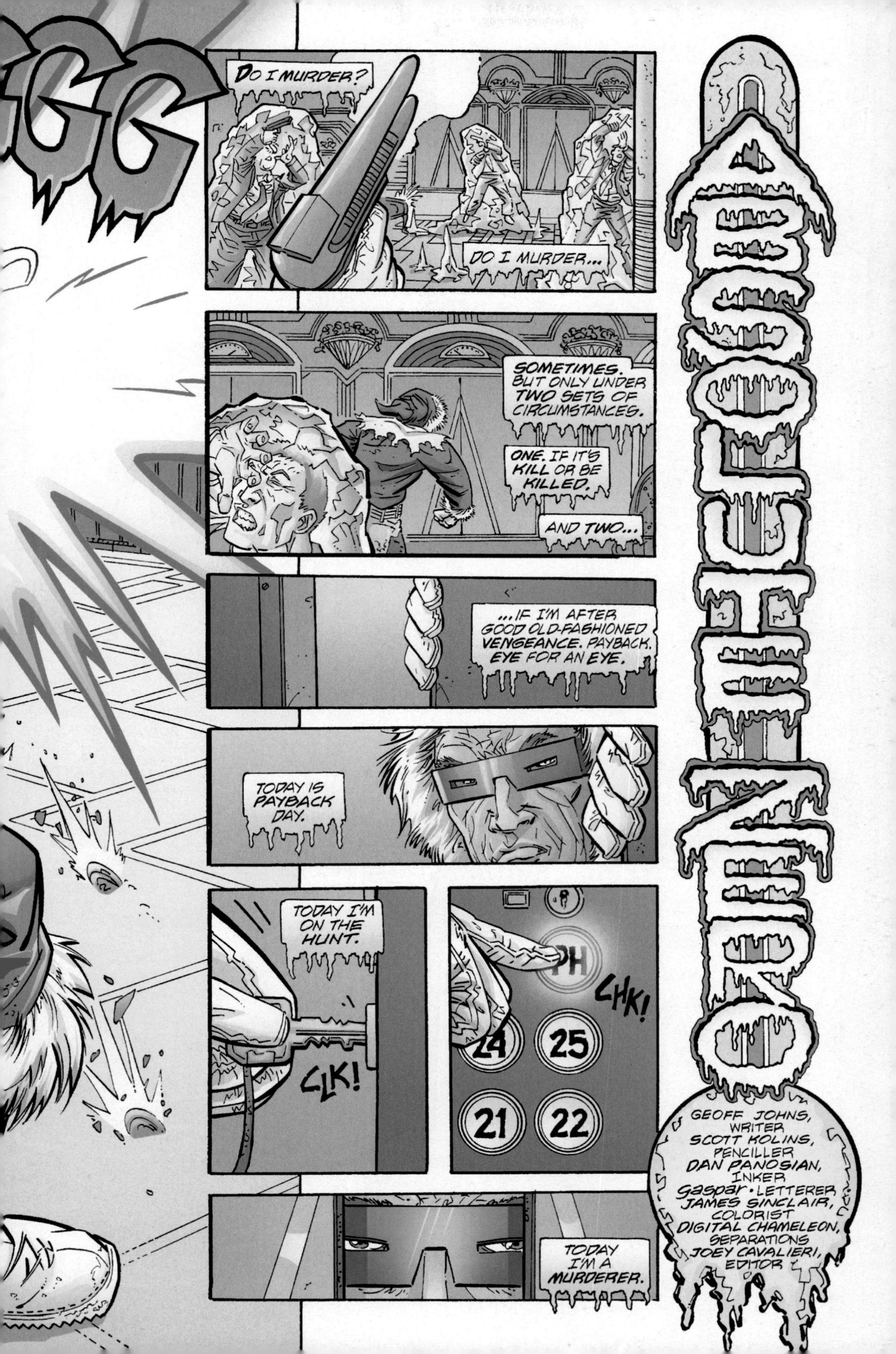
GG
DO I MURDER?
DO I MURDER...
SOMETIMES. BUT ONLY UNDER TWO SETS OF CIRCUMSTANCES.
ONE. IF IT'S KILL OR BE KILLED.
AND TWO...
...IF I'M AFTER GOOD OLD-FASHIONED VENGEANCE. PAYBACK. EYE FOR AN EYE.
TODAY IS PAYBACK DAY.
TODAY I'M ON THE HUNT.
CLK!
PH
CHK!
24
25
21
22
TODAY I'M A MURDERER.
A COLD CUT
GEOFF JOHNS, WRITER
SCOTT KOLINS, PENCILLER
DAN PANOSIAN, INKER
Gaspar • LETTERER
JAMES SINCLAIR, COLORIST
DIGITAL CHAMELEON, SEPARATIONS
JOEY CAVALIERI, EDITOR

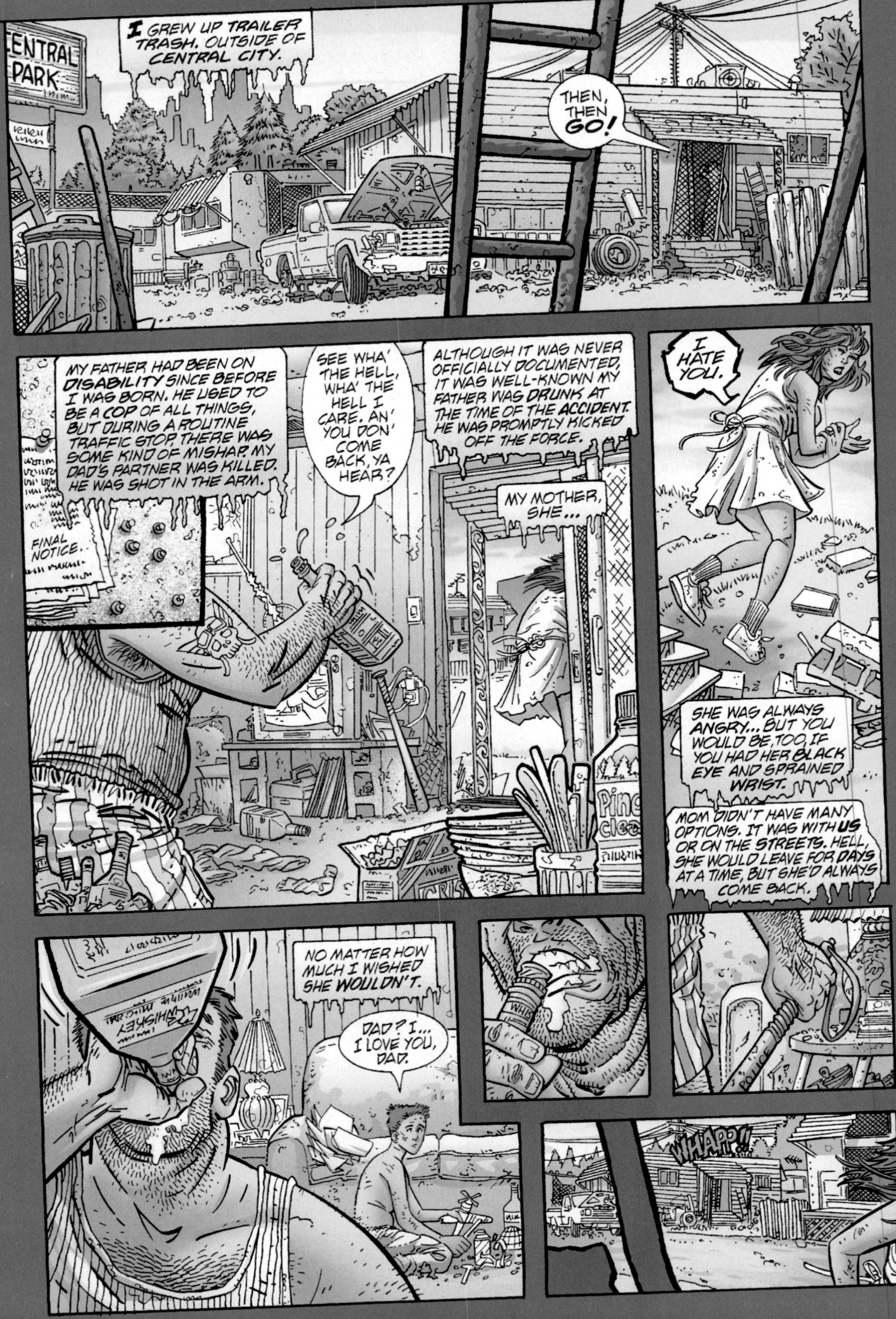

CENTRAL PARK
I GREW UP TRAILER TRASH. OUTSIDE OF CENTRAL CITY.
THEN, THEN GO!
MY FATHER HAD BEEN ON DISABILITY SINCE BEFORE I WAS BORN. HE USED TO BE A COP OF ALL THINGS, BUT DURING A ROUTINE TRAFFIC STOP, THERE WAS SOME KIND OF MISHAP. MY DAD'S PARTNER WAS KILLED. HE WAS SHOT IN THE ARM.
FINAL NOTICE
SEE WHA' THE HELL, WHA' THE HELL I CARE. AN' YOU DON' COME BACK, YA HEAR?
ALTHOUGH IT WAS NEVER OFFICIALLY DOCUMENTED, IT WAS WELL-KNOWN MY FATHER WAS DRUNK AT THE TIME OF THE ACCIDENT. HE WAS PROMPTLY KICKED OFF THE FORCE.
MY MOTHER, SHE...
I HATE YOU.
SHE WAS ALWAYS ANGRY... BUT YOU WOULD BE, TOO, IF YOU HAD HER BLACK EYE AND SPRAINED WRIST.
MOM DIDN'T HAVE MANY OPTIONS. IT WAS WITH US OR ON THE STREETS. HELL, SHE WOULD LEAVE FOR DAYS AT A TIME, BUT SHE'D ALWAYS COME BACK.
NO MATTER HOW MUCH I WISHED SHE WOULDN'T.
WHISKEY
DAD? I... I LOVE YOU, DAD.
POLICE
WHAPP!!

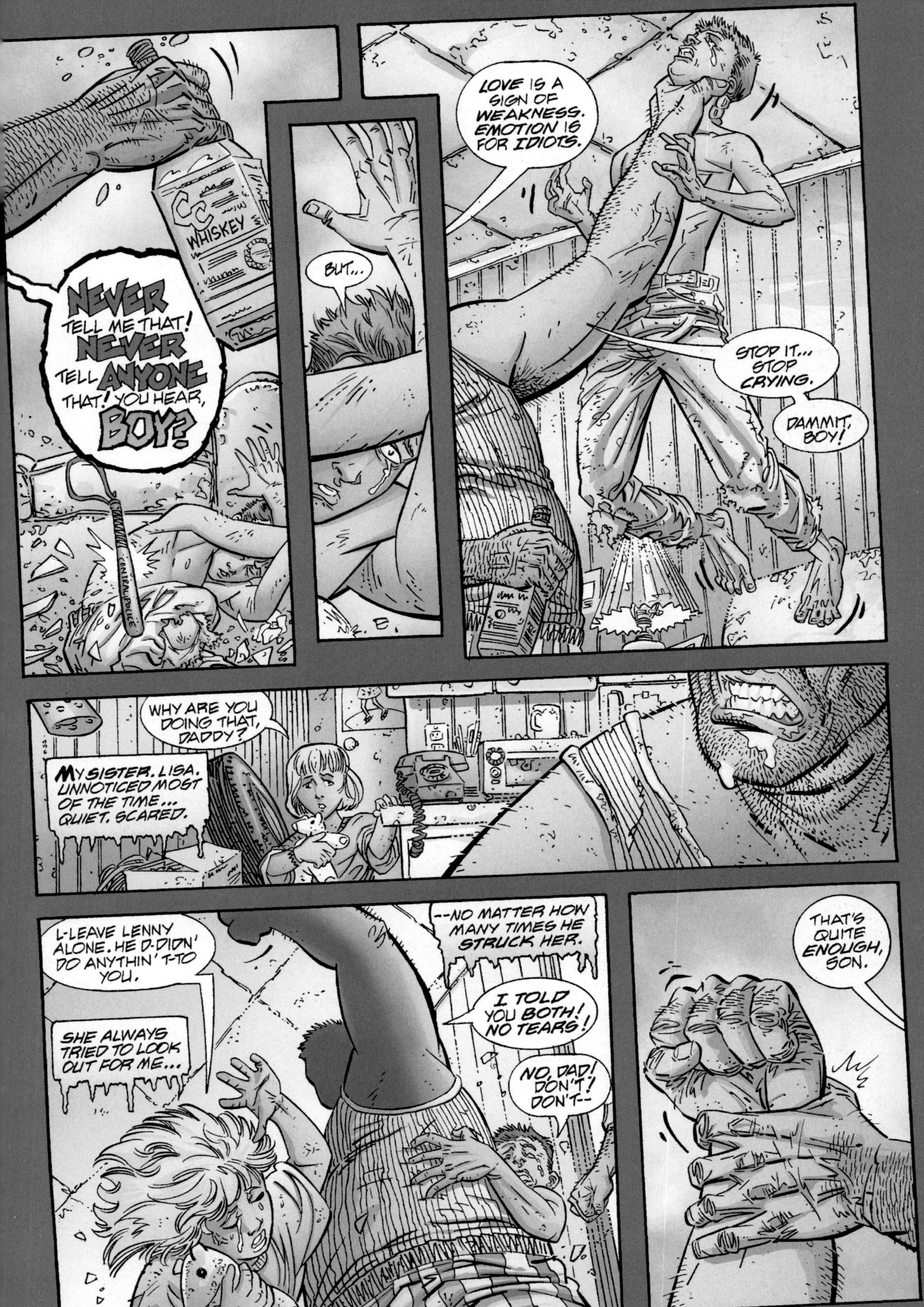
NEVER TELL ME THAT! NE-VER TELL ANYONE THAT! YOU HEAR, BOY?
WHISKEY
CENTRAL POLICE
BUT...
LOVE IS A SIGN OF WEAKNESS. EMOTION IS FOR IDIOTS.
STOP IT... STOP CRYING.
DAMMIT, BOY!
WHY ARE YOU DOING THAT, DADDY?
MY SISTER. LISA. UNNOTICED MOST OF THE TIME... QUIET. SCARED.
L-LEAVE LENNY ALONE. HE D-DIDN' DO ANYTHIN' T-TO YOU.
SHE ALWAYS TRIED TO LOOK OUT FOR ME...
--NO MATTER HOW MANY TIMES HE STRUCK HER.
I TOLD YOU BOTH! NO TEARS!
NO, DAD! DON'T! DON'T--
THAT'S QUITE ENOUGH, SON.

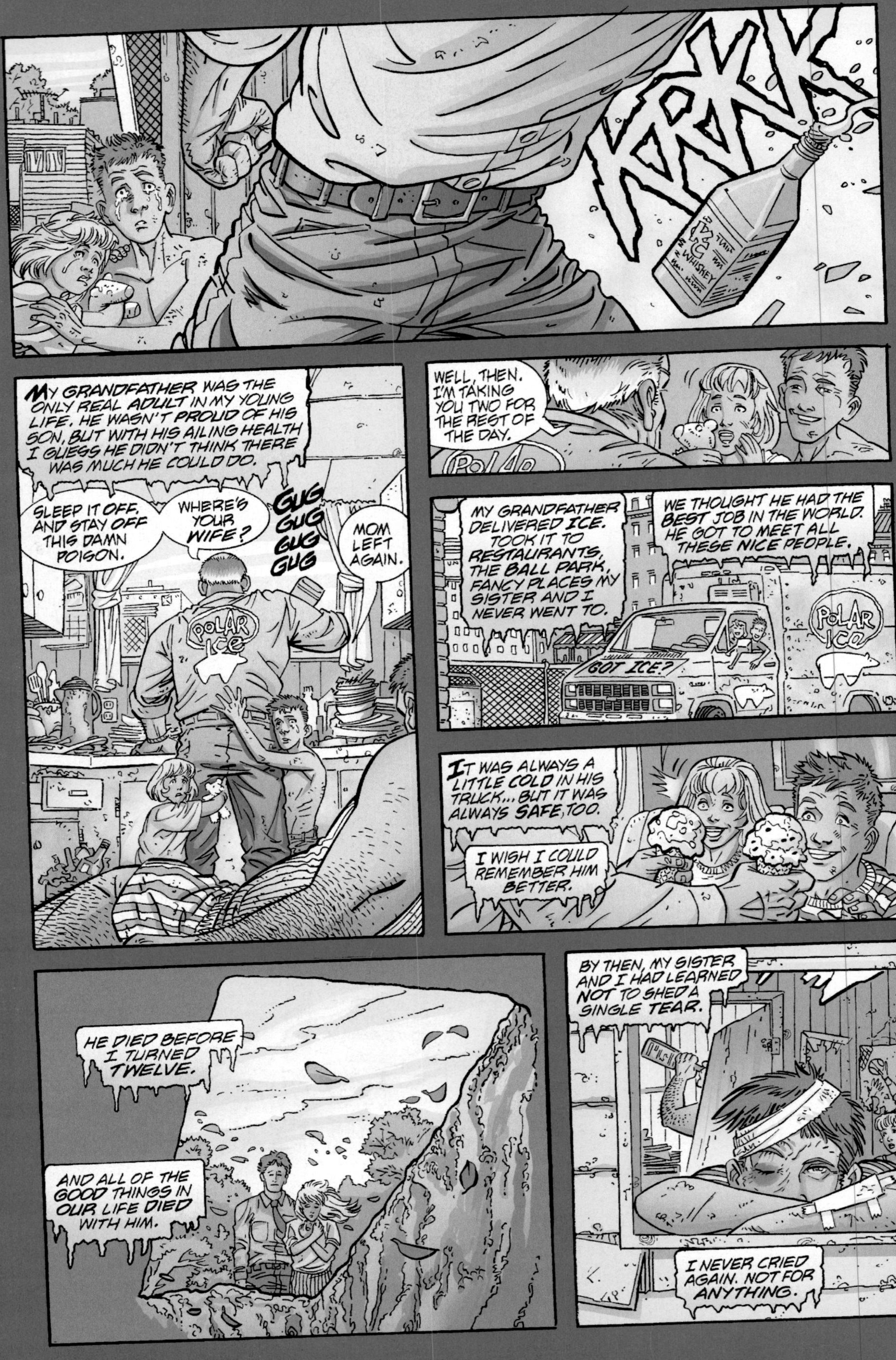
KRAKK
P&C WHISKEY
MY GRANDFATHER WAS THE ONLY REAL ADULT IN MY YOUNG LIFE. HE WASN'T PROUD OF HIS SON, BUT WITH HIS AILING HEALTH I GUESS HE DIDN'T THINK THERE WAS MUCH HE COULD DO.
SLEEP IT OFF. AND STAY OFF THIS DAMN POISON.
WHERE'S YOUR WIFE?
GUG GUG GUG GUG
MOM LEFT AGAIN.
POLAR ICE
WELL, THEN. I'M TAKING YOU TWO FOR THE REST OF THE DAY.
MY GRANDFATHER DELIVERED ICE. TOOK IT TO RESTAURANTS, THE BALL PARK, FANCY PLACES MY SISTER AND I NEVER WENT TO.
WE THOUGHT HE HAD THE BEST JOB IN THE WORLD. HE GOT TO MEET ALL THESE NICE PEOPLE.
GOT ICE?
POLAR ICE
IT WAS ALWAYS A LITTLE COLD IN HIS TRUCK... BUT IT WAS ALWAYS SAFE, TOO.
I WISH I COULD REMEMBER HIM BETTER.
HE DIED BEFORE I TURNED TWELVE.
AND ALL OF THE GOOD THINGS IN OUR LIFE DIED WITH HIM.
BY THEN, MY SISTER AND I HAD LEARNED NOT TO SHED A SINGLE TEAR.
I NEVER CRIED AGAIN. NOT FOR ANYTHING.

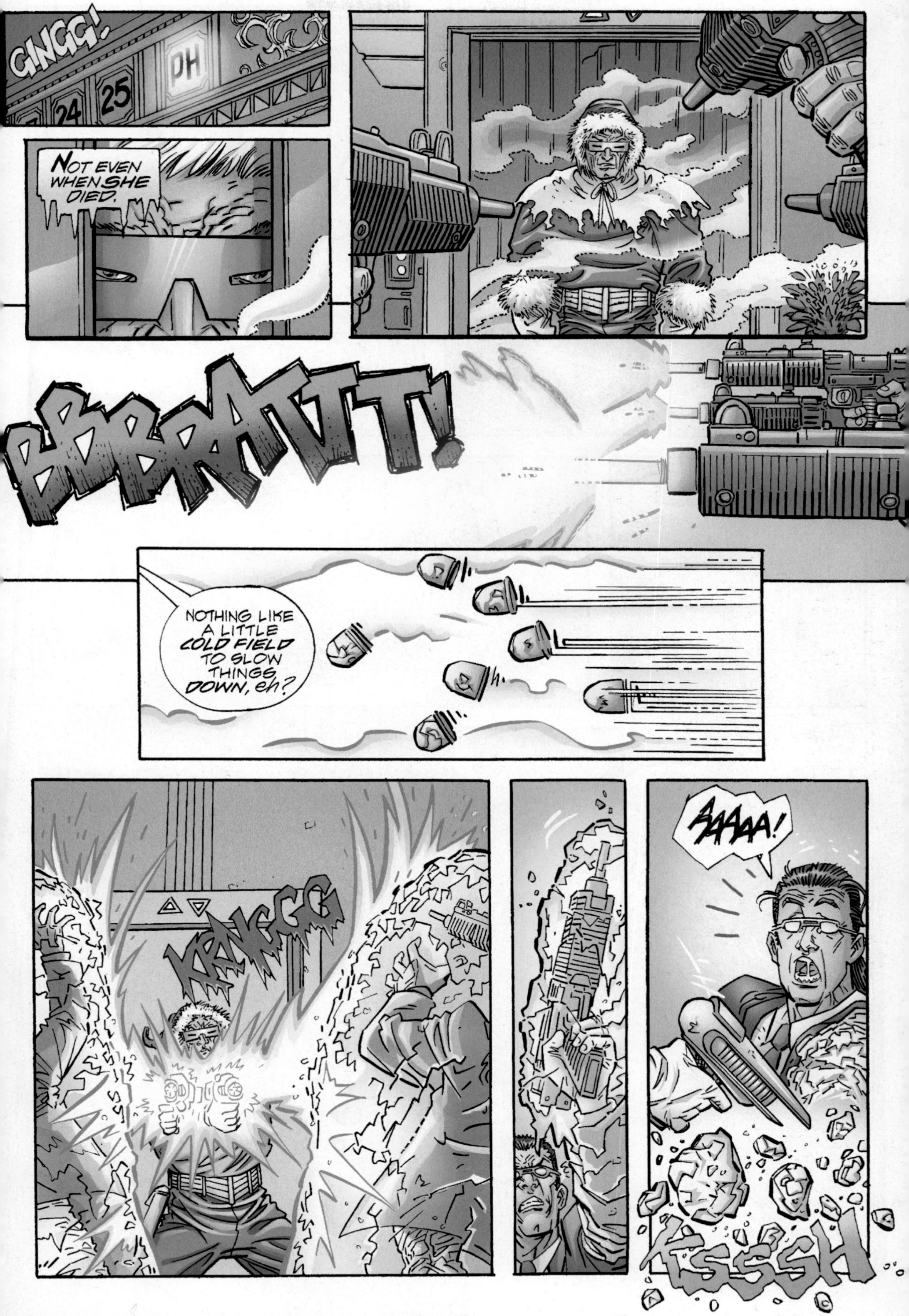
GNGG!
PH
25
24
NOT EVEN WHEN SHE DIED.
BBBRAAT!
NOTHING LIKE A LITTLE COLD FIELD TO SLOW THINGS DOWN, eh?
KRAKGG
AAAAA!
KSSSH

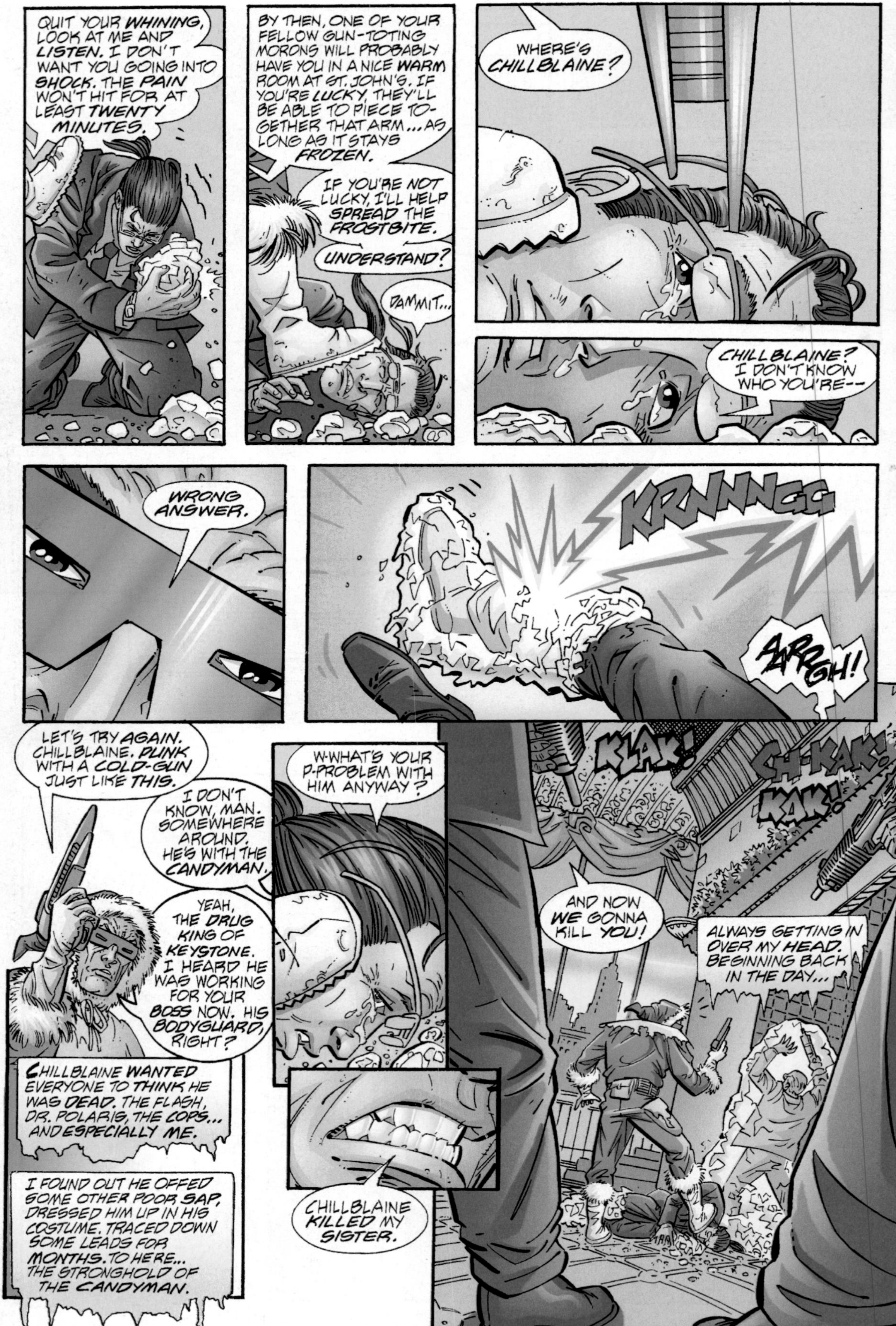
QUIT YOUR WHINING, LOOK AT ME AND LISTEN. I DON'T WANT YOU GOING INTO SHOCK. THE PAIN WON'T HIT FOR AT LEAST TWENTY MINUTES.
BY THEN, ONE OF YOUR FELLOW GUN-TOTING MORONS WILL PROBABLY HAVE YOU IN A NICE WARM ROOM AT ST. JOHN'S. IF YOU'RE LUCKY, THEY'LL BE ABLE TO PIECE TOGETHER THAT ARM... AS LONG AS IT STAYS FROZEN.
IF YOU'RE NOT LUCKY, I'LL HELP SPREAD THE FROSTBITE.
UNDERSTAND?
DAMMIT...
WHERE'S CHILLBLAINE?
CHILLBLAINE? I DON'T KNOW WHO YOU'RE--
WRONG ANSWER.
KRNNNGG
AARRGH!
LET'S TRY AGAIN. CHILLBLAINE. PUNK WITH A COLD-GUN JUST LIKE THIS.
I DON'T KNOW, MAN. SOMEWHERE AROUND. HE'S WITH THE CANDYMAN.
YEAH, THE DRUG KING OF KEYSTONE. I HEARD HE WAS WORKING FOR YOUR BOSS NOW. HIS BODYGUARD, RIGHT?
W-WHAT'S YOUR P-PROBLEM WITH HIM ANYWAY?
CHILLBLAINE KILLED MY SISTER.
CHILLBLAINE WANTED EVERYONE TO THINK HE WAS DEAD. THE FLASH, DR. POLARIS, THE COPS... AND ESPECIALLY ME.
I FOUND OUT HE OFFED SOME OTHER POOR SAP, DRESSED HIM UP IN HIS COSTUME. TRACED DOWN SOME LEADS FOR MONTHS. TO HERE... THE STRONGHOLD OF THE CANDYMAN.
KLAK!
CH-KAK!
KAK!
AND NOW WE GONNA KILL YOU!
ALWAYS GETTING IN OVER MY HEAD. BEGINNING BACK IN THE DAY...

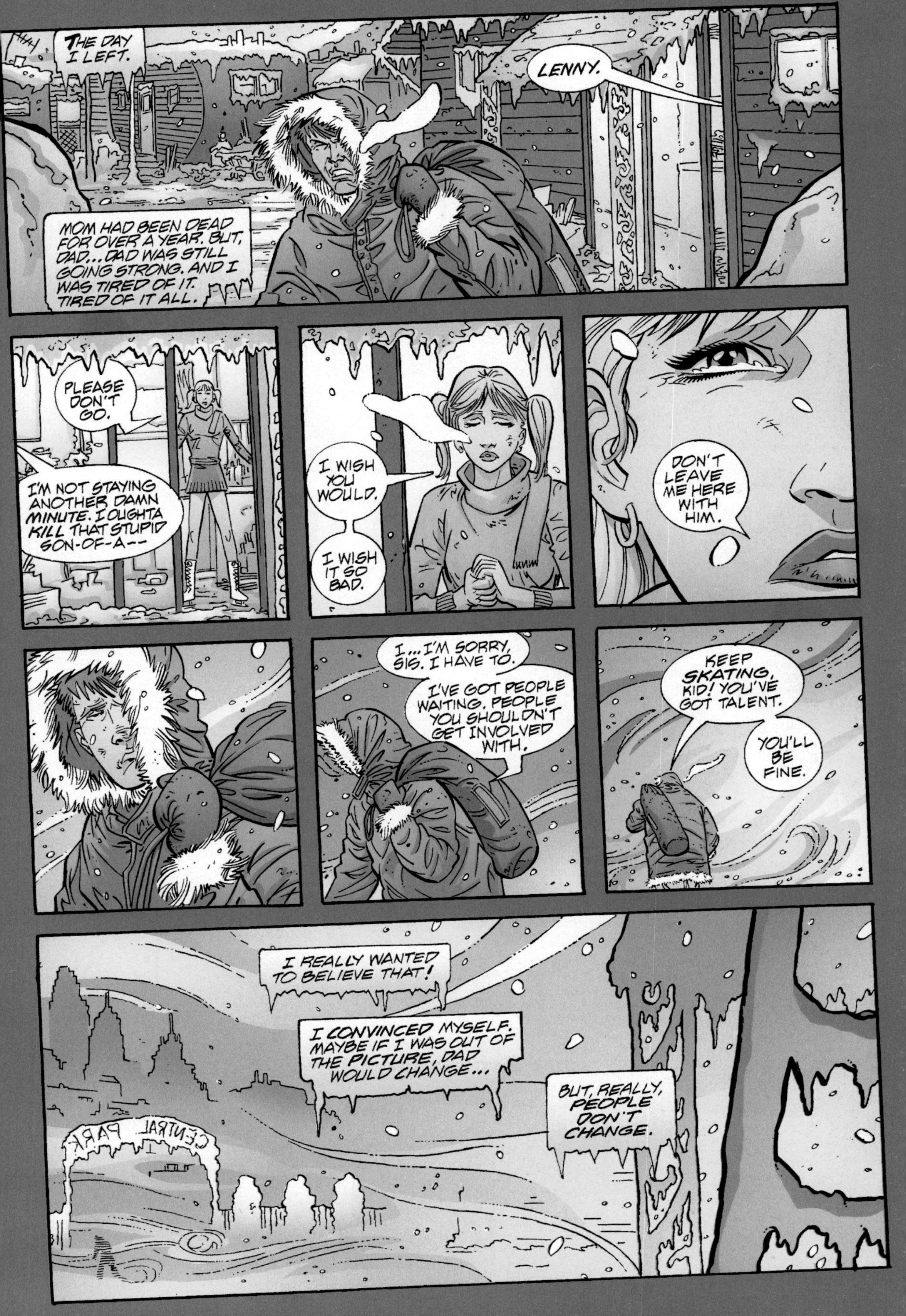
THE DAY I LEFT.
LENNY.
MOM HAD BEEN DEAD FOR OVER A YEAR. BUT, DAD... DAD WAS STILL GOING STRONG. AND I WAS TIRED OF IT. TIRED OF IT ALL.
PLEASE DON'T GO.
I'M NOT STAYING ANOTHER DAMN MINUTE. I OUGHTA KILL THAT STUPID SON-OF-A--
I WISH YOU WOULD.
I WISH IT SO BAD.
DON'T LEAVE ME HERE WITH HIM.
I... I'M SORRY, SIS. I HAVE TO.
I'VE GOT PEOPLE WAITING. PEOPLE YOU SHOULDN'T GET INVOLVED WITH.
KEEP SKATING, KID! YOU'VE GOT TALENT.
YOU'LL BE FINE.
I REALLY WANTED TO BELIEVE THAT!
I CONVINCED MYSELF. MAYBE IF I WAS OUT OF THE PICTURE, DAD WOULD CHANGE...
BUT, REALLY, PEOPLE DON'T CHANGE.
CENTRAL PARK

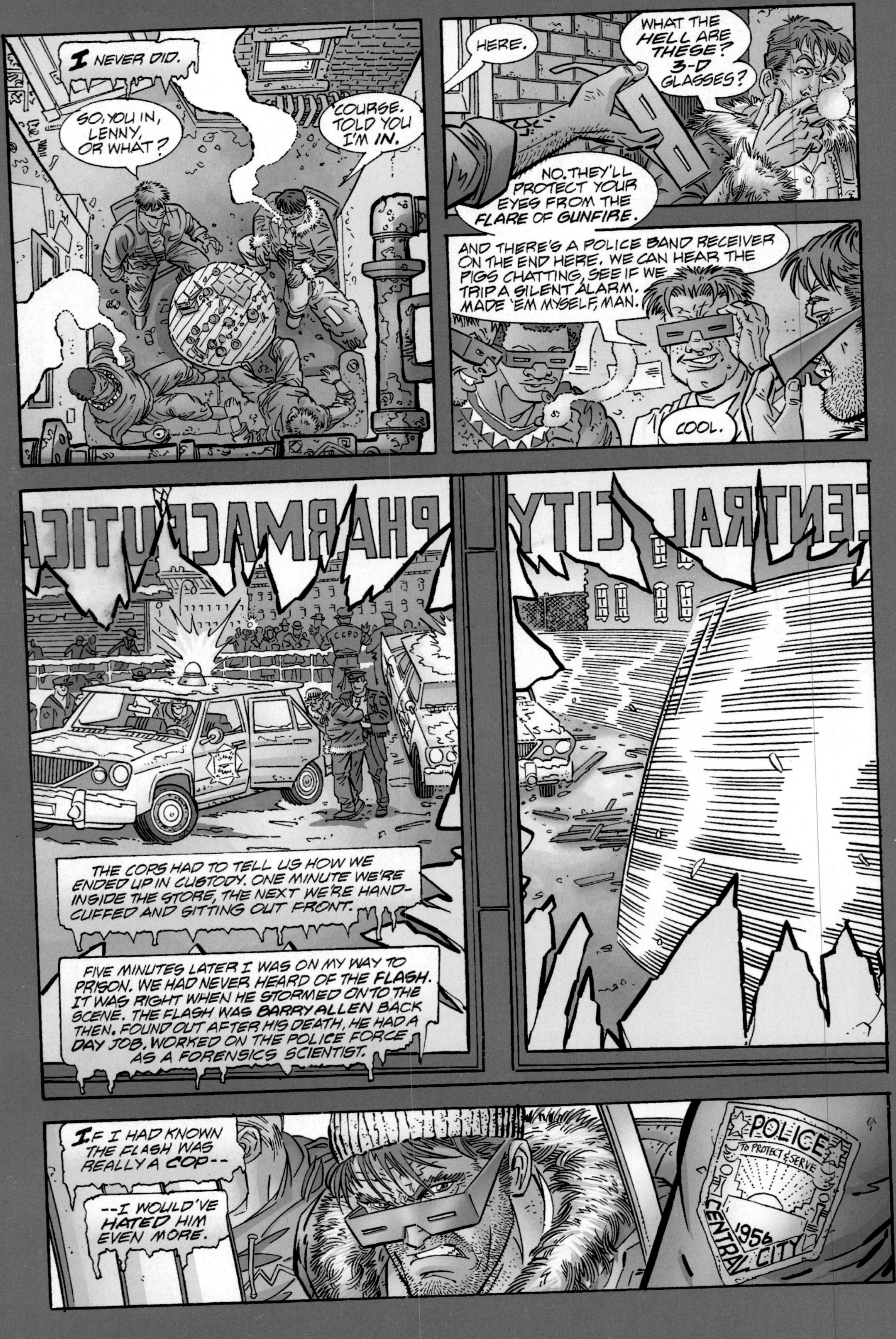
I NEVER DID.
SO, YOU IN, LENNY, OR WHAT?
COURSE. TOLD YOU I'M IN.
HERE.
WHAT THE HELL ARE THESE? 3-D GLASSES?
NO. THEY'LL PROTECT YOUR EYES FROM THE FLARE OF GUNFIRE.
AND THERE'S A POLICE BAND RECEIVER ON THE END HERE. WE CAN HEAR THE PIGS CHATTING, SEE IF WE TRIP A SILENT ALARM. MADE 'EM MYSELF, MAN.
COOL.
CENTRAL CITY PHARMACEUTICA
CCPD
THE COPS HAD TO TELL US HOW WE ENDED UP IN CUSTODY. ONE MINUTE WE'RE INSIDE THE STORE, THE NEXT WE'RE HAND-CUFFED AND SITTING OUT FRONT.
FIVE MINUTES LATER I WAS ON MY WAY TO PRISON. WE HAD NEVER HEARD OF THE FLASH. IT WAS RIGHT WHEN HE STORMED ONTO THE SCENE. THE FLASH WAS BARRY ALLEN BACK THEN. FOUND OUT AFTER HIS DEATH, HE HAD A DAY JOB. WORKED ON THE POLICE FORCE AS A FORENSICS SCIENTIST.
IF I HAD KNOWN THE FLASH WAS REALLY A COP--
--I WOULD'VE HATED HIM EVEN MORE.
POLICE
TO PROTECT & SERVE
CENTRAL CITY
1956

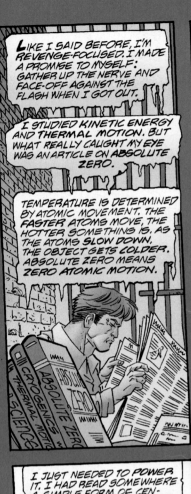

LIKE I SAID BEFORE, I'M REVENGE-FOCUSED. I MADE A PROMISE TO MYSELF: GATHER UP THE NERVE AND FACE-OFF AGAINST THE FLASH WHEN I GOT OUT.
I STUDIED KINETIC ENERGY AND THERMAL MOTION. BUT WHAT REALLY CAUGHT MY EYE WAS AN ARTICLE ON ABSOLUTE ZERO.
TEMPERATURE IS DETERMINED BY ATOMIC MOVEMENT. THE FASTER ATOMS MOVE, THE HOTTER SOMETHING IS. AS THE ATOMS SLOW DOWN, THE OBJECT GETS COLDER. ABSOLUTE ZERO MEANS ZERO ATOMIC MOTION.
ABSOLUTE ZERO
CRYOGENICS
WHEN I GOT OUT ON PAROLE, I BROKE INTO ONE OF THE LABS I'D READ ABOUT. I NEVER WAS TOO GREAT AT ALL THE SCIENCE SO I NEEDED SOME HELP. I STOLE SOME BLUE-PRINTS.
Thermal Motion Negator Engine X
AND I MADE A WEAPON.
I JUST NEEDED TO POWER IT. I HAD READ SOMEWHERE A SIMPLE FORM OF CEN-TRALIZED RADIATION, LIKE THE MAGNETIC CIRCLES OF CYCLOTRON RADIATION, WOULD ACTIVATE THE ENGINE IN MY GUN INDEFINITELY.
ONCE ENERGIZED, IT WOULD NEGATE KINETIC ENERGY--
--AND SLOW ANYTHING, EVEN THE FLASH, DOWN TO A STANDSTILL.
I QUICKLY FOUND OUT MY "COLD-GUN" DID A WHOLE LOT MORE THAN SIMPLY SLOW THINGS DOWN.
IT ICED THINGS UP. BIG TIME.
THE GUN BLASTS WERE A LITTLE BRIGHT, SO THOSE GLASSES THAT IDIOT MADE CAME IN HANDY.
I WAS MORE THAN HAPPY TO TRADE IN MY REAL NAME FOR SOMETHING A BIT...DRAMATIC, I GUESS. SOMETHING I THOUGHT WOULD GRAB THE FLASH'S ATTENTION. I ALWAYS LOVED THE COLD. ADDED THE "CAPTAIN" PART TO GIVE ME THE ILLUSION OF AUTHORITY.
GOOD-BYE, LENNY SNART--

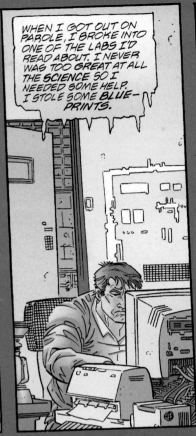

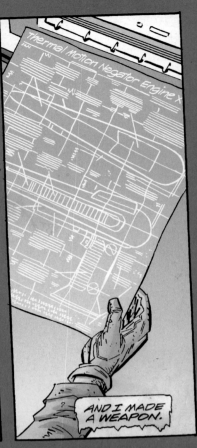

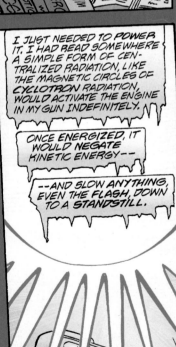

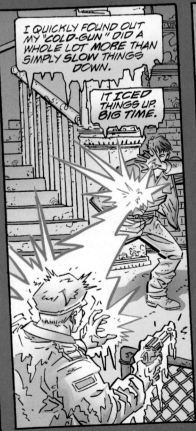

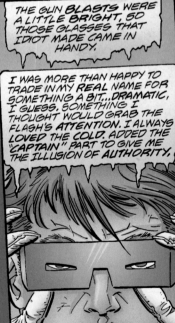

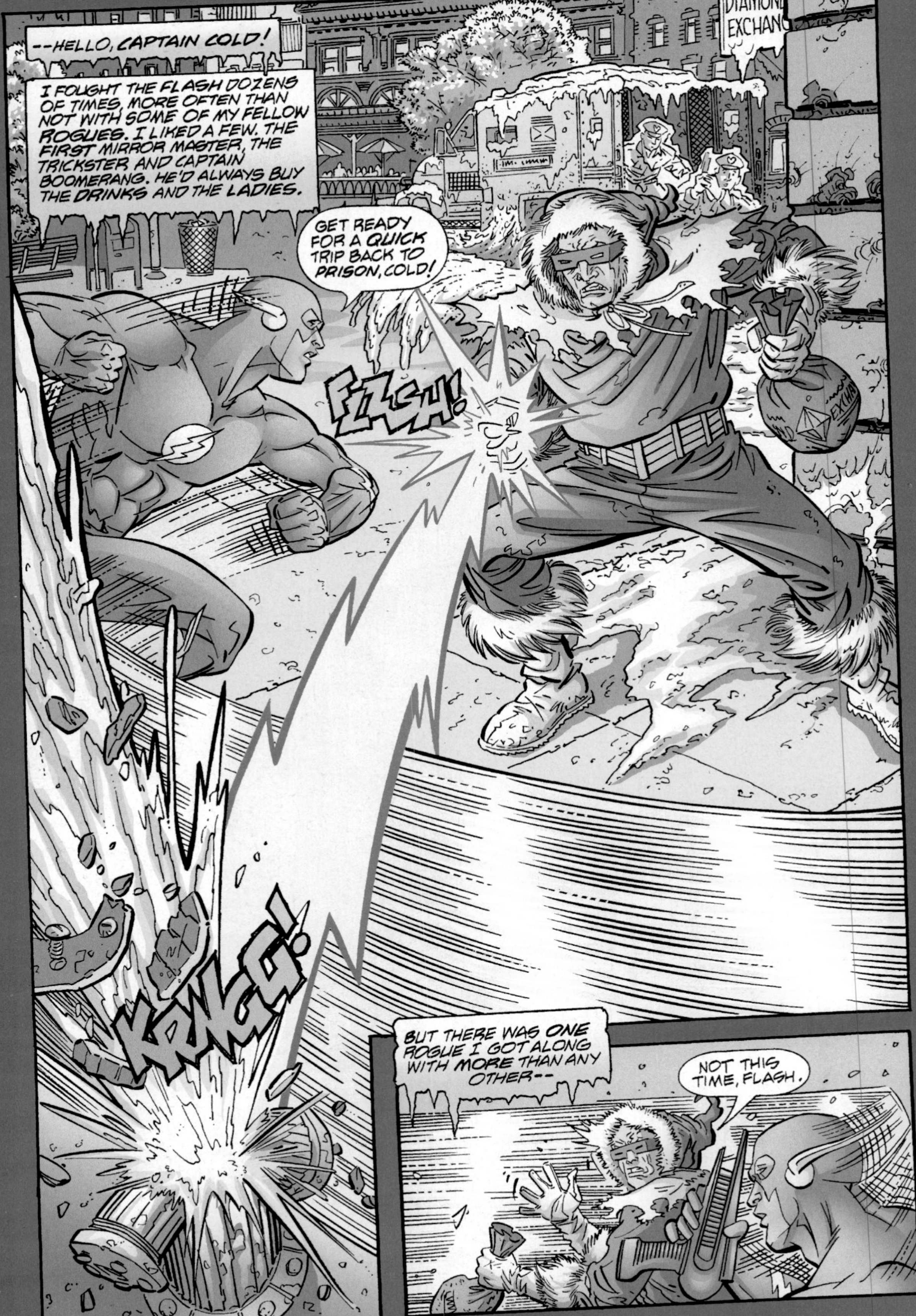

--HELLO, CAPTAIN COLD!
I FOUGHT THE FLASH DOZENS OF TIMES, MORE OFTEN THAN NOT WITH SOME OF MY FELLOW ROGUES. I LIKED A FEW. THE FIRST MIRROR MASTER, THE TRICKSTER AND CAPTAIN BOOMERANG. HE'D ALWAYS BUY THE DRINKS AND THE LADIES.
DIAMOND
EXCHANG
GET READY FOR A QUICK TRIP BACK TO PRISON, COLD!
FZZSH!
KRNGG!
BUT THERE WAS ONE ROGUE I GOT ALONG WITH MORE THAN ANY OTHER--
NOT THIS TIME, FLASH.

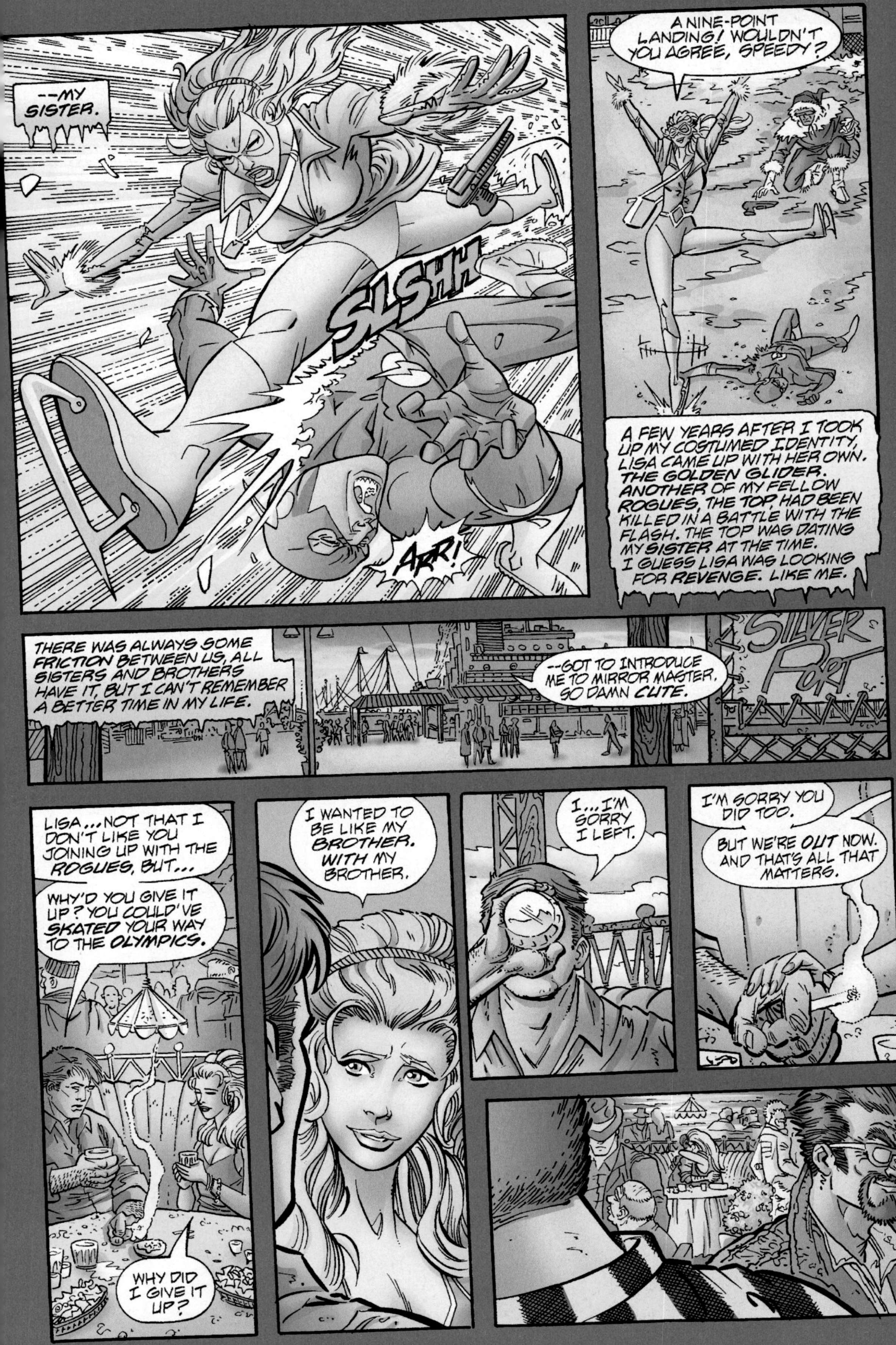
--MY SISTER.
SLSHH
ARR!
A NINE-POINT LANDING! WOULDN'T YOU AGREE, SPEEDY?
A FEW YEARS AFTER I TOOK UP MY COSTUMED IDENTITY, LISA CAME UP WITH HER OWN. THE GOLDEN GLIDER. ANOTHER OF MY FELLOW ROGUES, THE TOP, HAD BEEN KILLED IN A BATTLE WITH THE FLASH. THE TOP WAS DATING MY SISTER AT THE TIME. I GUESS LISA WAS LOOKING FOR REVENGE. LIKE ME.
THERE WAS ALWAYS SOME FRICTION BETWEEN US, ALL SISTERS AND BROTHERS HAVE IT, BUT I CAN'T REMEMBER A BETTER TIME IN MY LIFE.
--GOT TO INTRODUCE ME TO MIRROR MASTER, SO DAMN CUTE.
SILVER PORT
LISA... NOT THAT I DON'T LIKE YOU JOINING UP WITH THE ROGUES, BUT...
WHY'D YOU GIVE IT UP? YOU COULD'VE SKATED YOUR WAY TO THE OLYMPICS.
WHY DID I GIVE IT UP?
I WANTED TO BE LIKE MY BROTHER. WITH MY BROTHER.
I... I'M SORRY I LEFT.
I'M SORRY YOU DID TOO.
BUT WE'RE OUT NOW. AND THAT'S ALL THAT MATTERS.

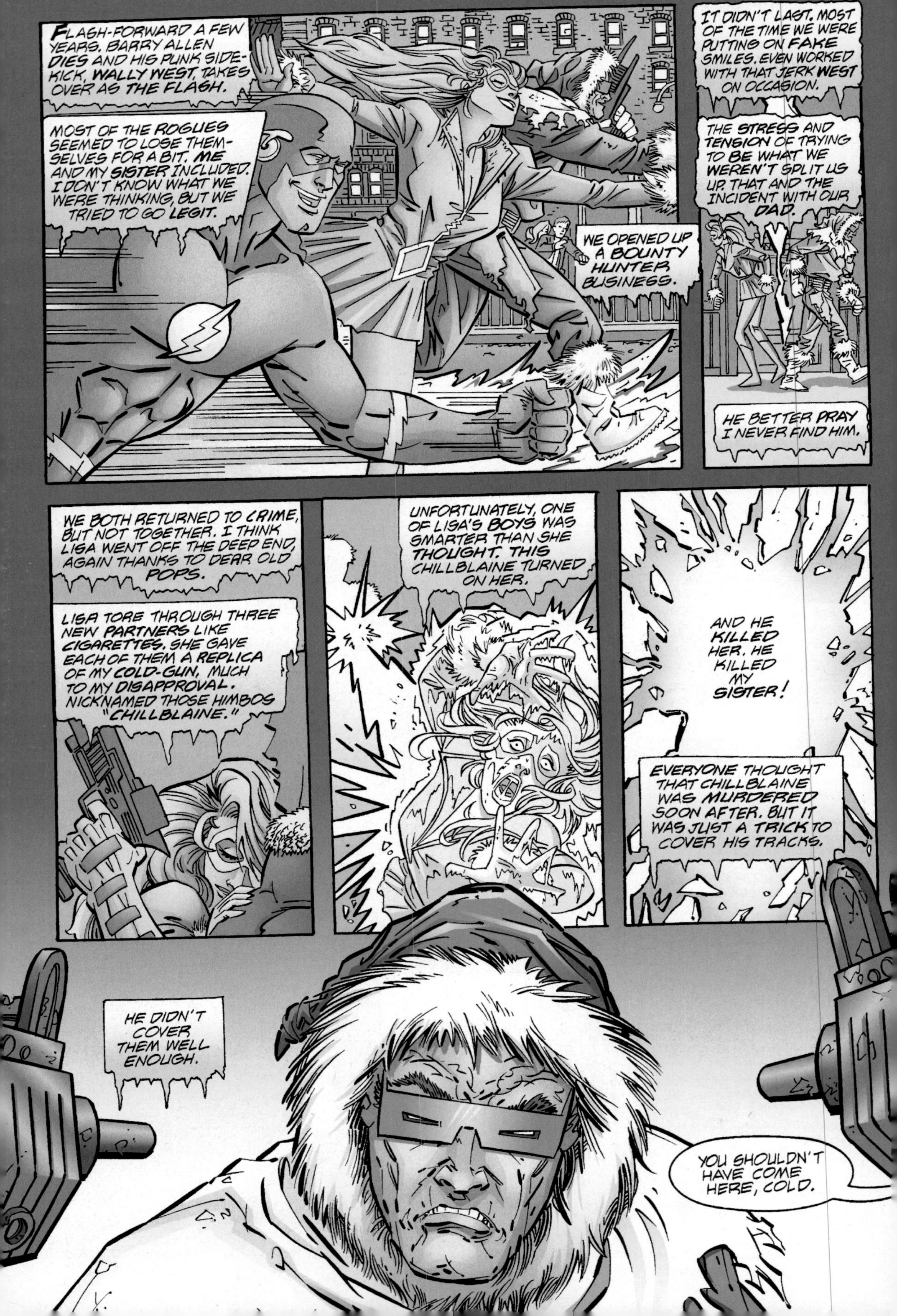

FLASH-FORWARD A FEW YEARS. BARRY ALLEN DIES AND HIS PUNK SIDE-KICK, WALLY WEST, TAKES OVER AS THE FLASH.
MOST OF THE ROGUES SEEMED TO LOSE THEMSELVES FOR A BIT. ME AND MY SISTER INCLUDED. I DON'T KNOW WHAT WE WERE THINKING, BUT WE TRIED TO GO LEGIT.
WE OPENED UP A BOUNTY HUNTER BUSINESS.
IT DIDN'T LAST. MOST OF THE TIME WE WERE PUTTING ON FAKE SMILES. EVEN WORKED WITH THAT JERK WEST ON OCCASION.
THE STRESS AND TENSION OF TRYING TO BE WHAT WE WEREN'T SPLIT US UP. THAT AND THE INCIDENT WITH OUR DAD.
HE BETTER PRAY I NEVER FIND HIM.
WE BOTH RETURNED TO CRIME, BUT NOT TOGETHER. I THINK LISA WENT OFF THE DEEP END, AGAIN THANKS TO DEAR OLD POPS.
LISA TORE THROUGH THREE NEW PARTNERS LIKE CIGARETTES. SHE GAVE EACH OF THEM A REPLICA OF MY COLD-GUN, MUCH TO MY DISAPPROVAL. NICKNAMED THOSE HIMBOS "CHILLBLAINE."
UNFORTUNATELY, ONE OF LISA'S BOYS WAS SMARTER THAN SHE THOUGHT. THIS CHILLBLAINE TURNED ON HER.
AND HE KILLED HER. HE KILLED MY SISTER!
EVERYONE THOUGHT THAT CHILLBLAINE WAS MURDERED SOON AFTER. BUT IT WAS JUST A TRICK TO COVER HIS TRACKS.
HE DIDN'T COVER THEM WELL ENOUGH.
YOU SHOULDN'T HAVE COME HERE, COLD.

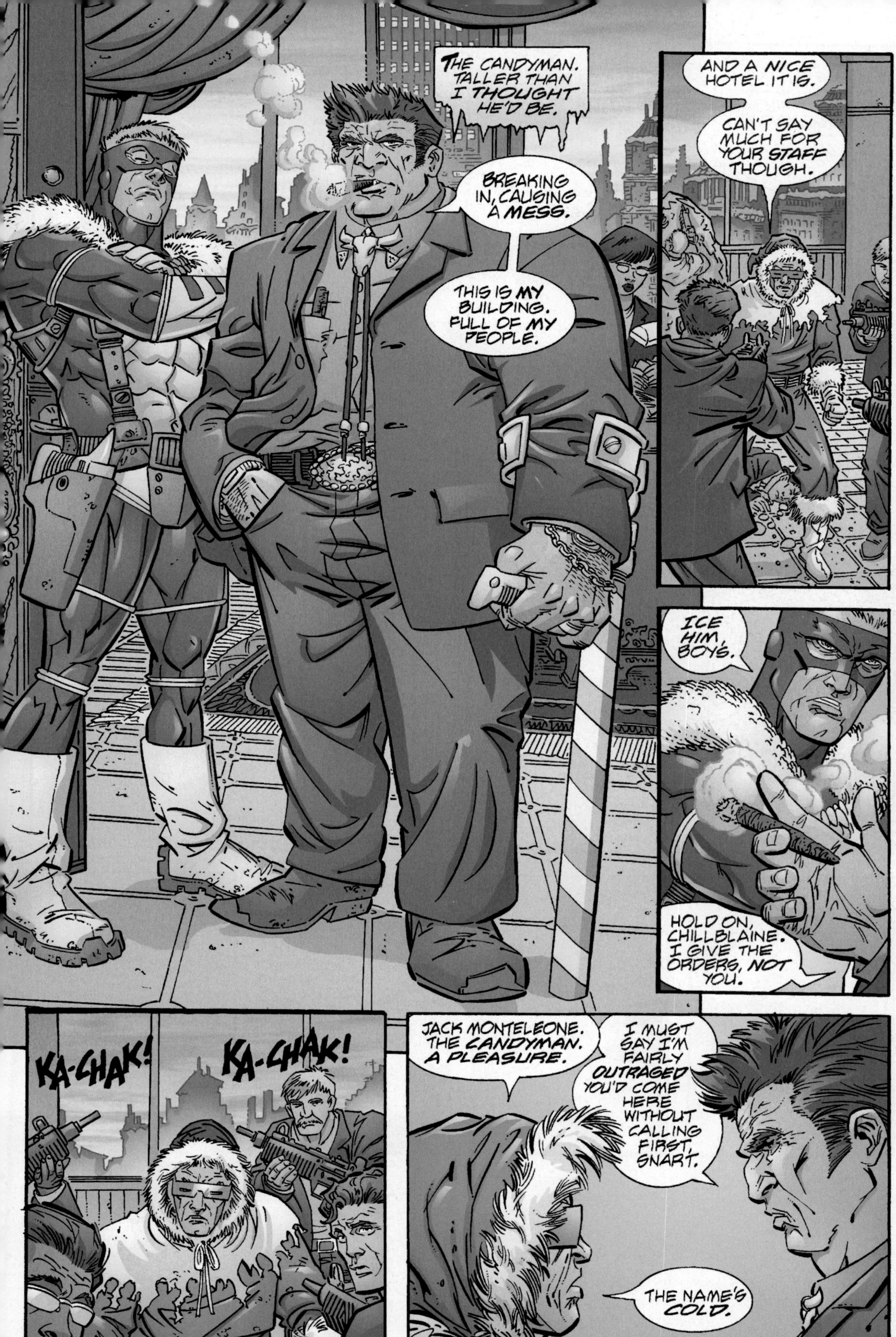
THE CANDYMAN. TALLER THAN I THOUGHT HE'D BE.
BREAKING IN, CAUSING A MESS.
THIS IS MY BUILDING. FULL OF MY PEOPLE.
AND A NICE HOTEL IT IS.
CAN'T SAY MUCH FOR YOUR STAFF THOUGH.
ICE HIM, BOYS.
HOLD ON, CHILLBLAINE. I GIVE THE ORDERS, NOT YOU.
KA-CHAK!
KA-CHAK!
JACK MONTELEONE. THE CANDYMAN. A PLEASURE.
I MUST SAY I'M FAIRLY OUTRAGED YOU'D COME HERE WITHOUT CALLING FIRST, SNART.
THE NAME'S COLD.

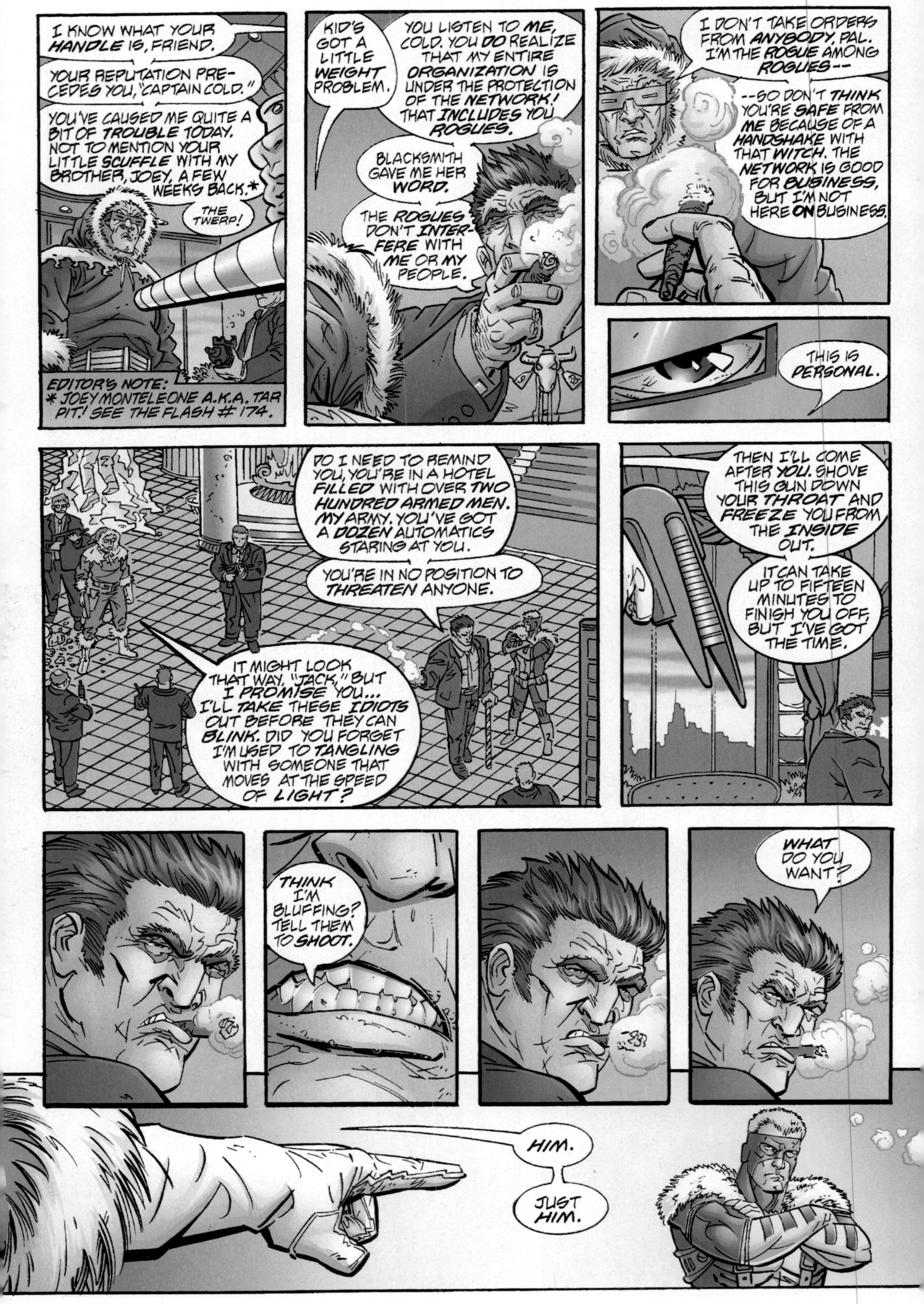
I KNOW WHAT YOUR HANDLE IS, FRIEND.
YOUR REPUTATION PRECEDES YOU, "CAPTAIN COLD."
YOU'VE CAUSED ME QUITE A BIT OF TROUBLE TODAY. NOT TO MENTION YOUR LITTLE SCUFFLE WITH MY BROTHER, JOEY, A FEW WEEKS BACK.*
THE TWERP!
EDITOR'S NOTE: * JOEY MONTELEONE A.K.A. TAR PIT! SEE THE FLASH # 174.
KID'S GOT A LITTLE WEIGHT PROBLEM.
YOU LISTEN TO ME, COLD. YOU DO REALIZE THAT MY ENTIRE ORGANIZATION IS UNDER THE PROTECTION OF THE NETWORK! THAT INCLUDES YOU ROGUES.
BLACKSMITH GAVE ME HER WORD.
THE ROGUES DON'T INTERFERE WITH ME OR MY PEOPLE.
I DON'T TAKE ORDERS FROM ANYBODY, PAL. I'M THE ROGUE AMONG ROGUES--
--SO DON'T THINK YOU'RE SAFE FROM ME BECAUSE OF A HANDSHAKE WITH THAT WITCH. THE NETWORK IS GOOD FOR BUSINESS, BUT I'M NOT HERE ON BUSINESS.
THIS IS PERSONAL.
DO I NEED TO REMIND YOU, YOU'RE IN A HOTEL FILLED WITH OVER TWO HUNDRED ARMED MEN. MY ARMY. YOU'VE GOT A DOZEN AUTOMATICS STARING AT YOU.
YOU'RE IN NO POSITION TO THREATEN ANYONE.
IT MIGHT LOOK THAT WAY, "JACK," BUT I PROMISE YOU... I'LL TAKE THESE IDIOTS OUT BEFORE THEY CAN BLINK. DID YOU FORGET I'M USED TO TANGLING WITH SOMEONE THAT MOVES AT THE SPEED OF LIGHT?
THEN I'LL COME AFTER YOU. SHOVE THIS GUN DOWN YOUR THROAT AND FREEZE YOU FROM THE INSIDE OUT.
IT CAN TAKE UP TO FIFTEEN MINUTES TO FINISH YOU OFF, BUT I'VE GOT THE TIME.
THINK I'M BLUFFING? TELL THEM TO SHOOT.
WHAT DO YOU WANT?
HIM.
JUST HIM.

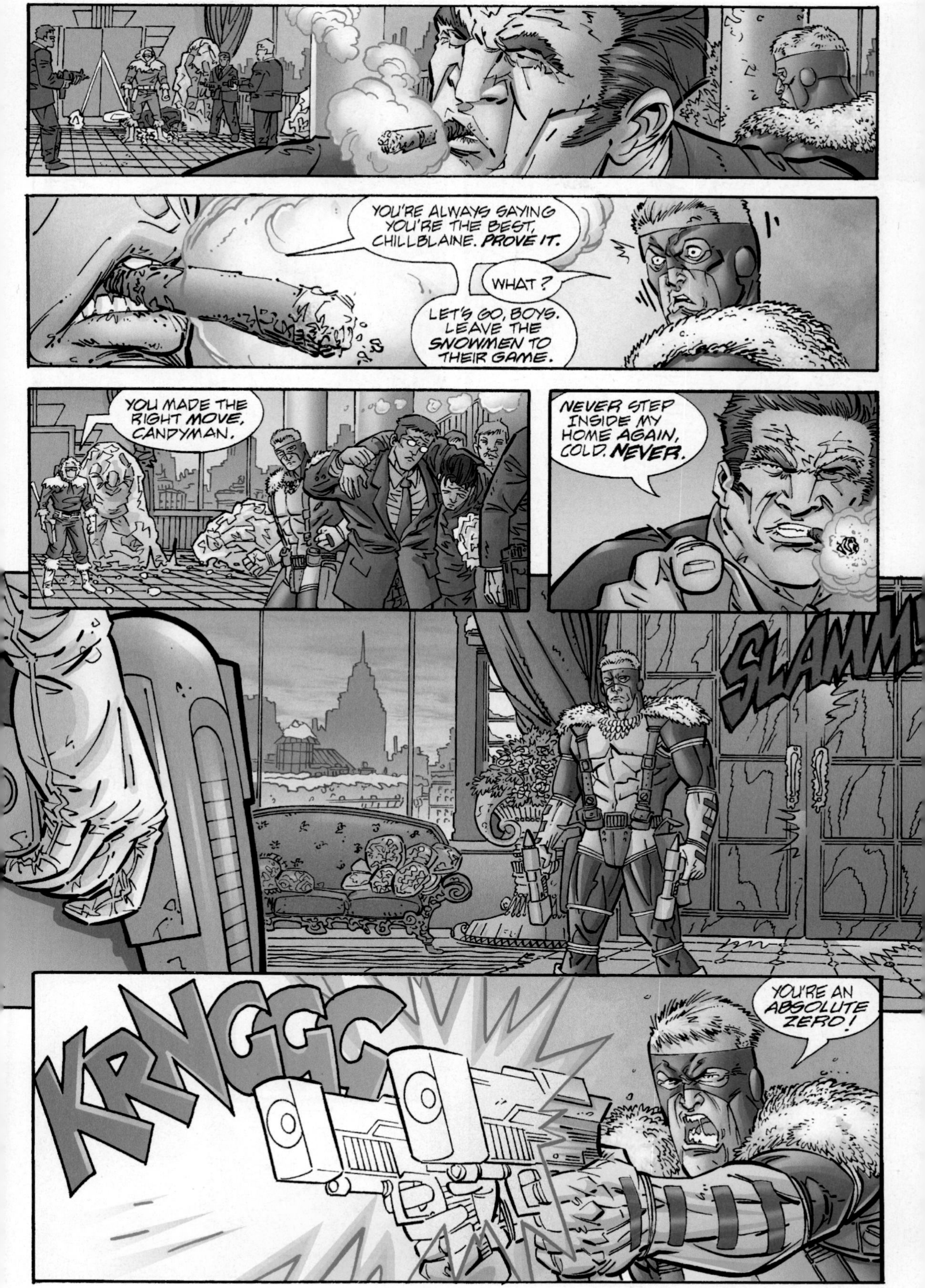
YOU'RE ALWAYS SAYING YOU'RE THE BEST, CHILLBLAINE. PROVE IT.
WHAT?
LET'S GO, BOYS. LEAVE THE SNOWMEN TO THEIR GAME.
YOU MADE THE RIGHT MOVE, CANDYMAN.
NEVER STEP INSIDE MY HOME AGAIN, COLD. NEVER.
SLAMM
KRNGGC
YOU'RE AN ABSOLUTE ZERO!

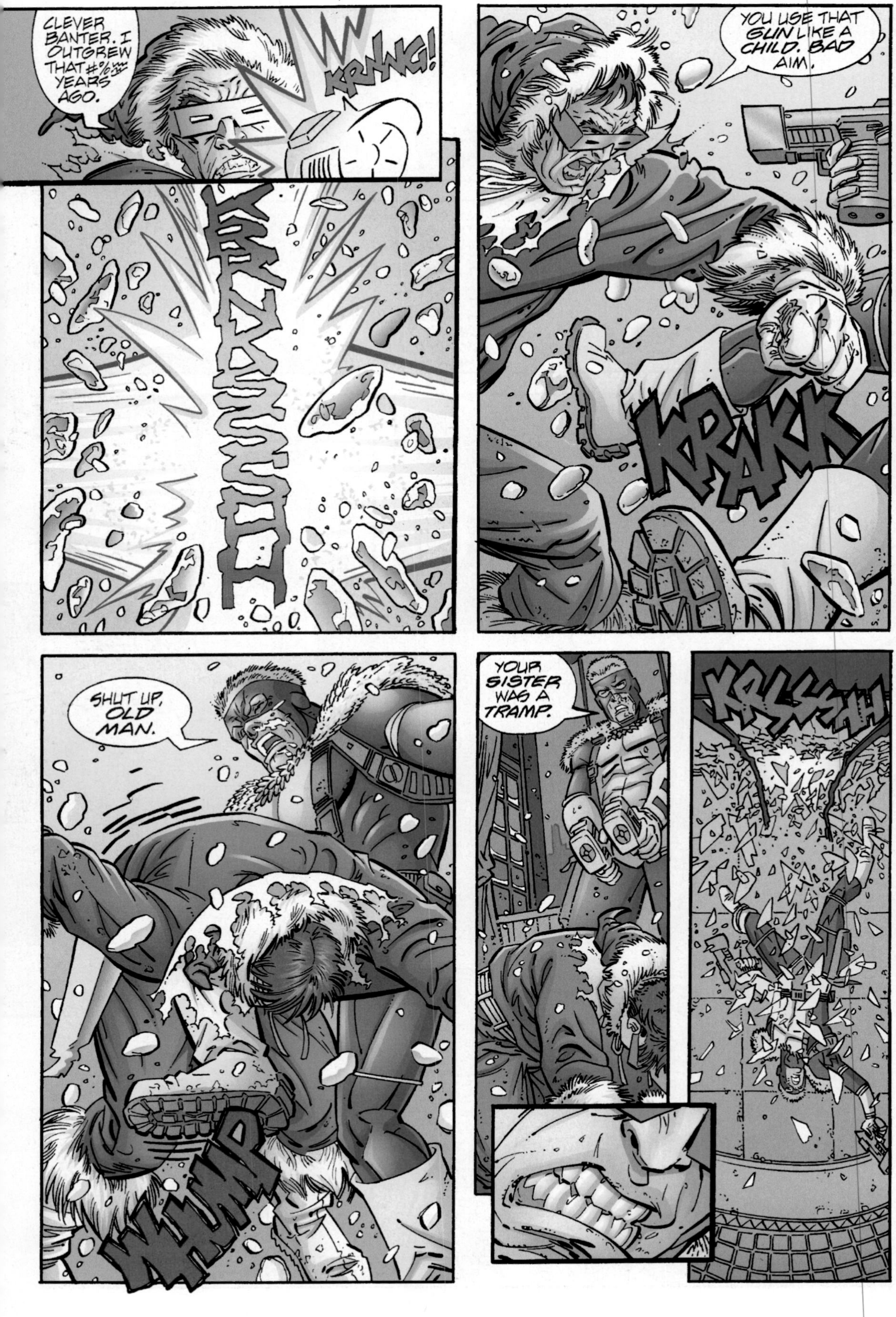

CLEVER BANTER. I OUTGREW THAT #%@ YEARS AGO.
KRNNG!
YOU USE THAT GUN LIKE A CHILD. BAD AIM.
KRAKK
SHUT UP, OLD MAN.
WHUMP
YOUR SISTER WAS A TRAMP.

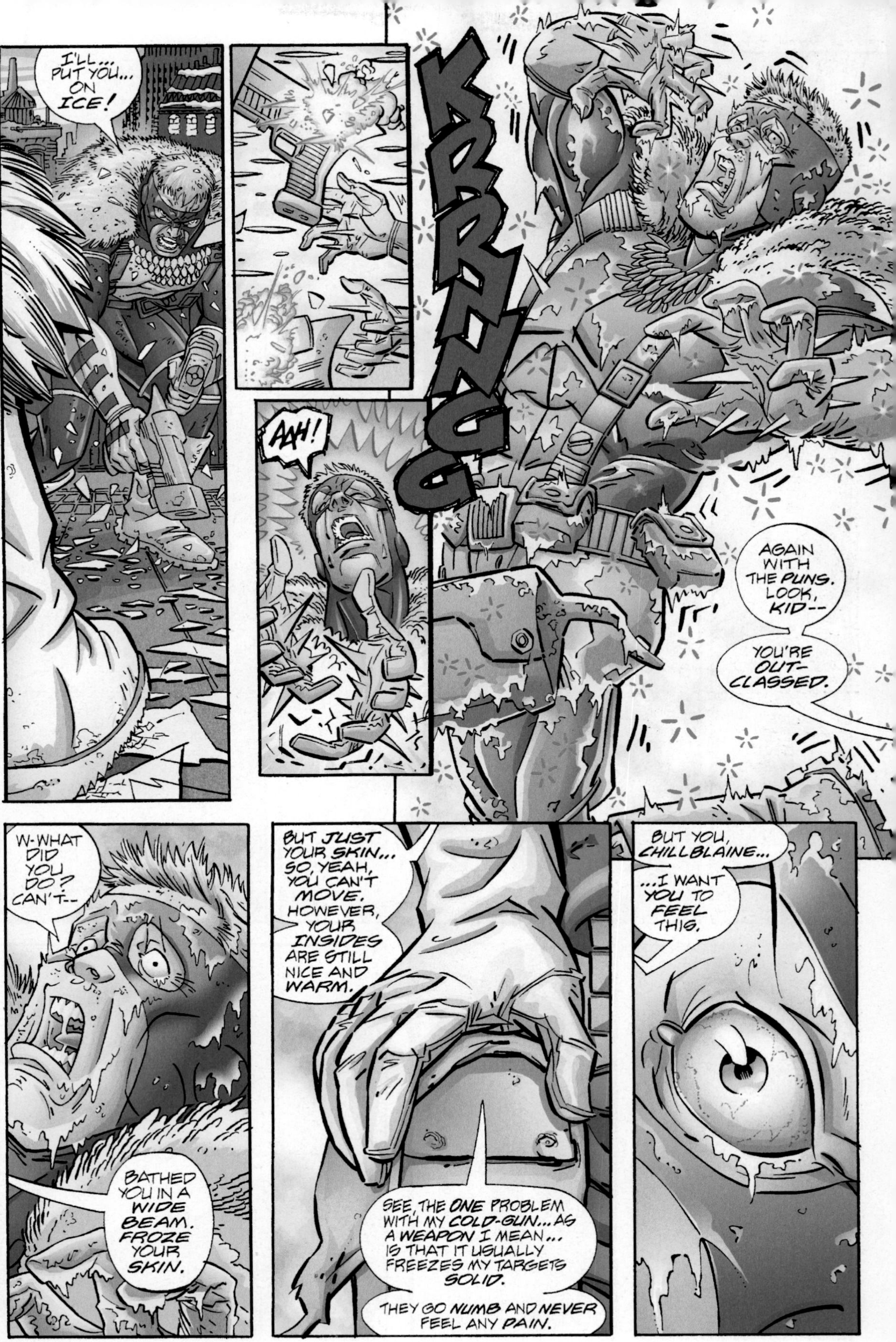
I'LL... PUT YOU... ON ICE!
KRRANG
AAH!
AGAIN WITH THE PUNS. LOOK, KID--
YOU'RE OUT-CLASSED.
W-WHAT DID YOU DO? CAN'T--
BATHED YOU IN A WIDE BEAM. FROZE YOUR SKIN.
BUT JUST YOUR SKIN... SO, YEAH, YOU CAN'T MOVE. HOWEVER, YOUR INSIDES ARE STILL NICE AND WARM.
SEE, THE ONE PROBLEM WITH MY COLD-GUN... AS A WEAPON I MEAN... IS THAT IT USUALLY FREEZES MY TARGETS SOLID.
THEY GO NUMB AND NEVER FEEL ANY PAIN.
BUT YOU, CHILLBLAINE...
...I WANT YOU TO FEEL THIS.

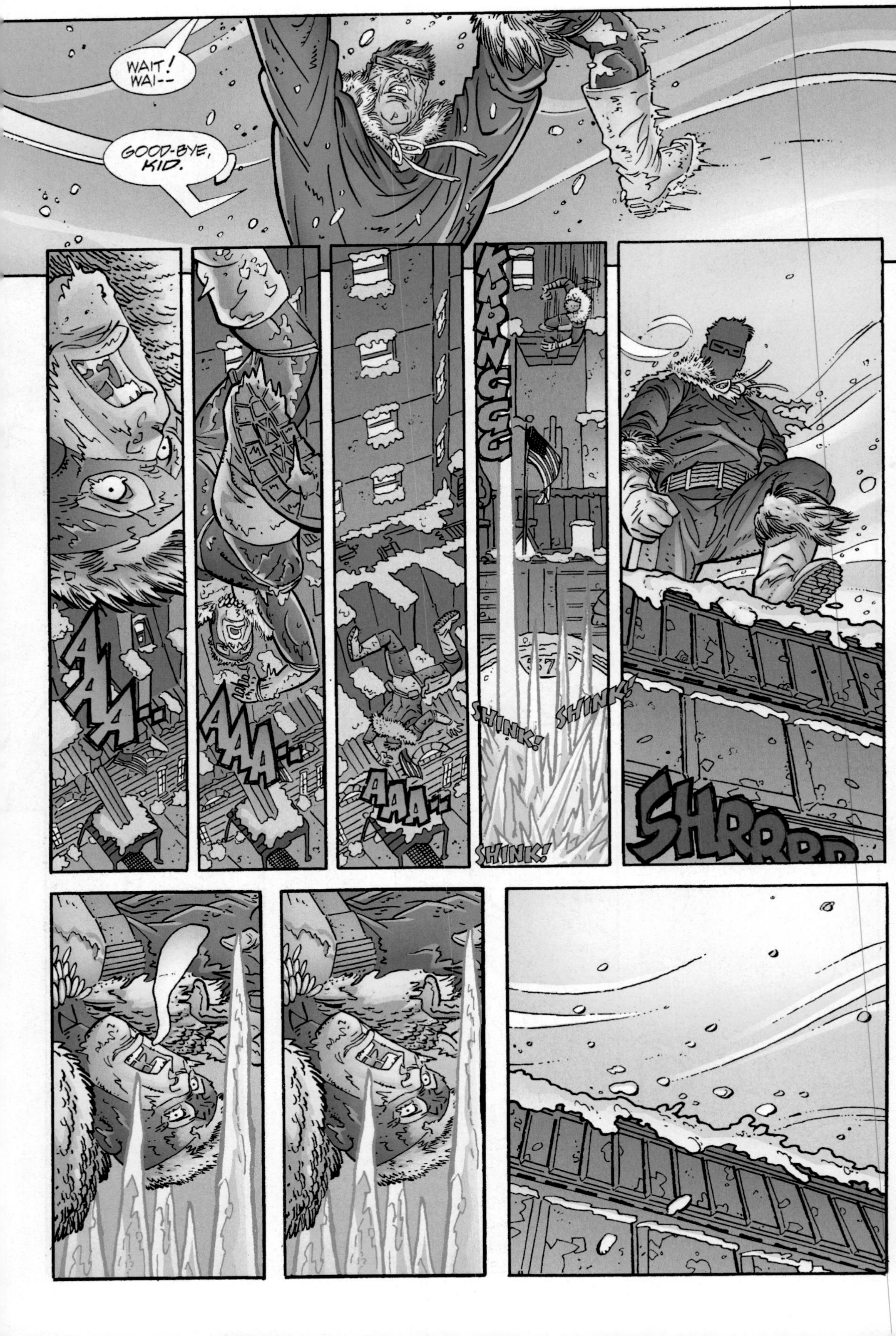
WAIT! WAI--
GOOD-BYE, KID.
AAA--
AAA--
AAA--
KRRNGGG
SHINK!
SHINK!
SHINK!
SHRRRRR

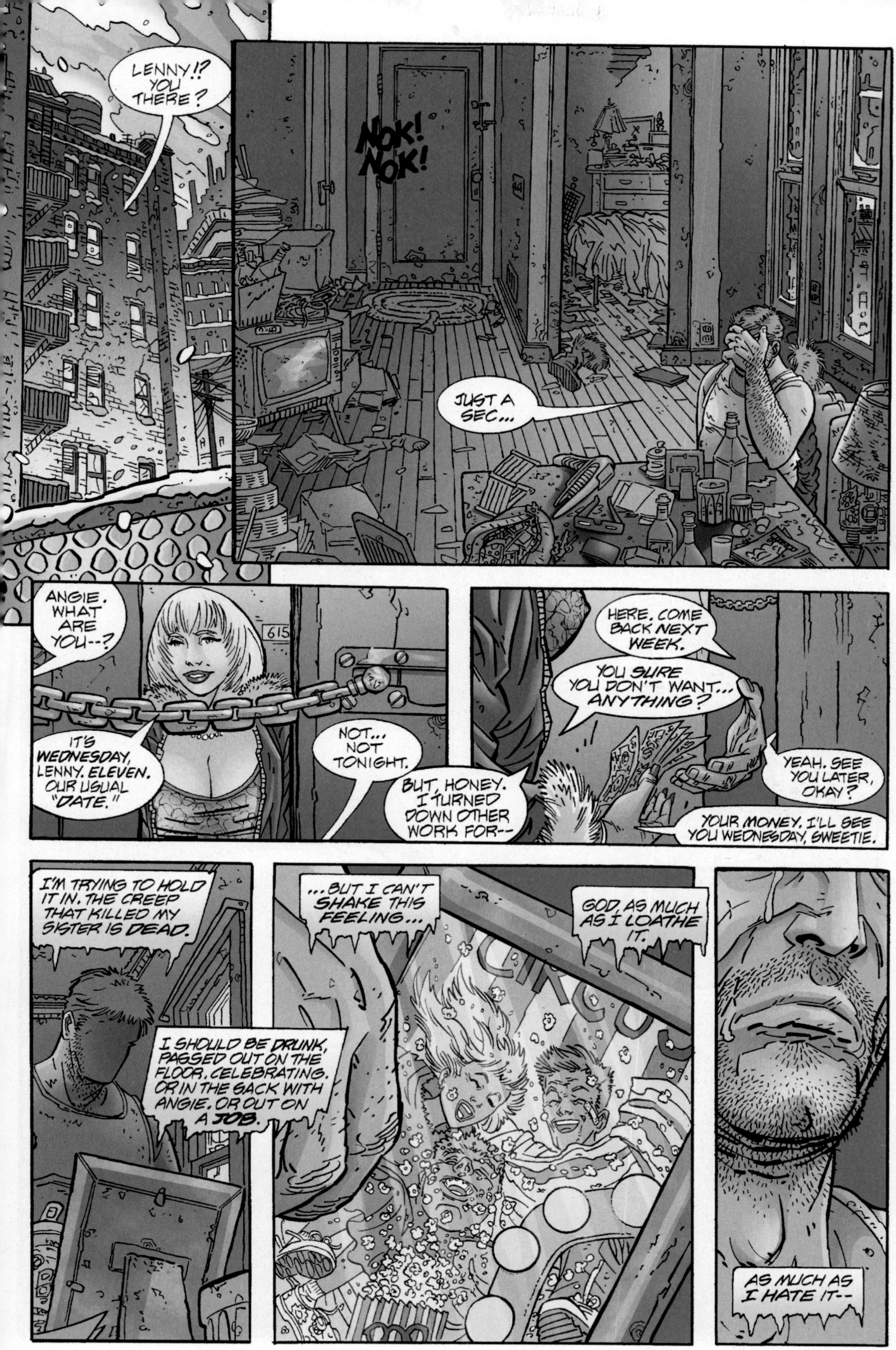
LENNY!? YOU THERE?
NOK! NOK!
JUST A SEC...
ANGIE. WHAT ARE YOU--?
IT'S WEDNESDAY, LENNY. ELEVEN. OUR USUAL "DATE."
NOT... NOT TONIGHT.
BUT, HONEY. I TURNED DOWN OTHER WORK FOR--
HERE. COME BACK NEXT WEEK.
YOU SURE YOU DON'T WANT... ANYTHING?
YEAH. SEE YOU LATER, OKAY?
YOUR MONEY. I'LL SEE YOU WEDNESDAY, SWEETIE.
I'M TRYING TO HOLD IT IN. THE CREEP THAT KILLED MY SISTER IS DEAD.
I SHOULD BE DRUNK, PASSED OUT ON THE FLOOR. CELEBRATING. OR IN THE SACK WITH ANGIE. OR OUT ON A JOB.
...BUT I CAN'T SHAKE THIS FEELING...
GOD, AS MUCH AS I LOATHE IT.
AS MUCH AS I HATE IT--

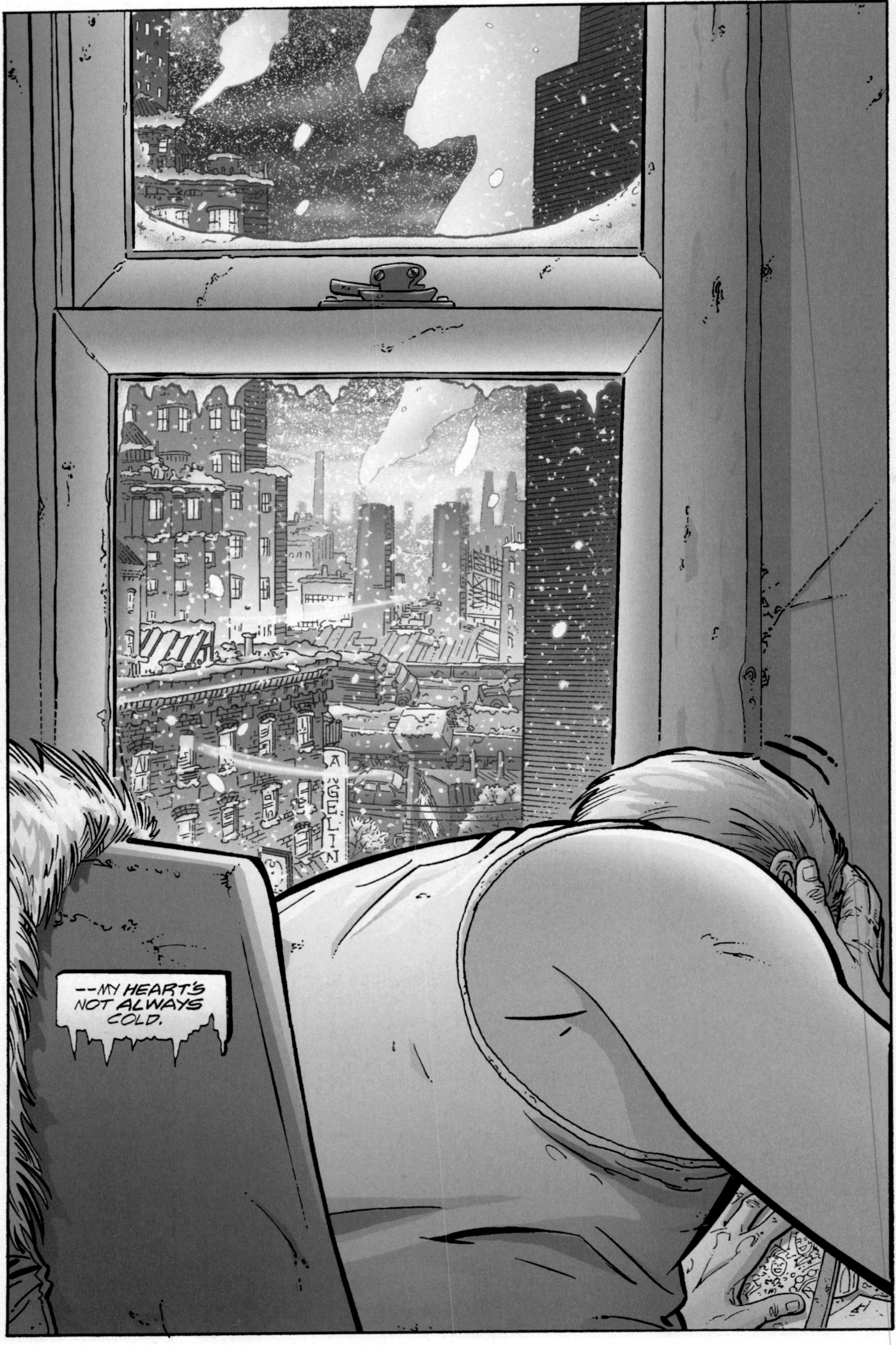
--MY HEART'S NOT ALWAYS COLD.
ANGELIN

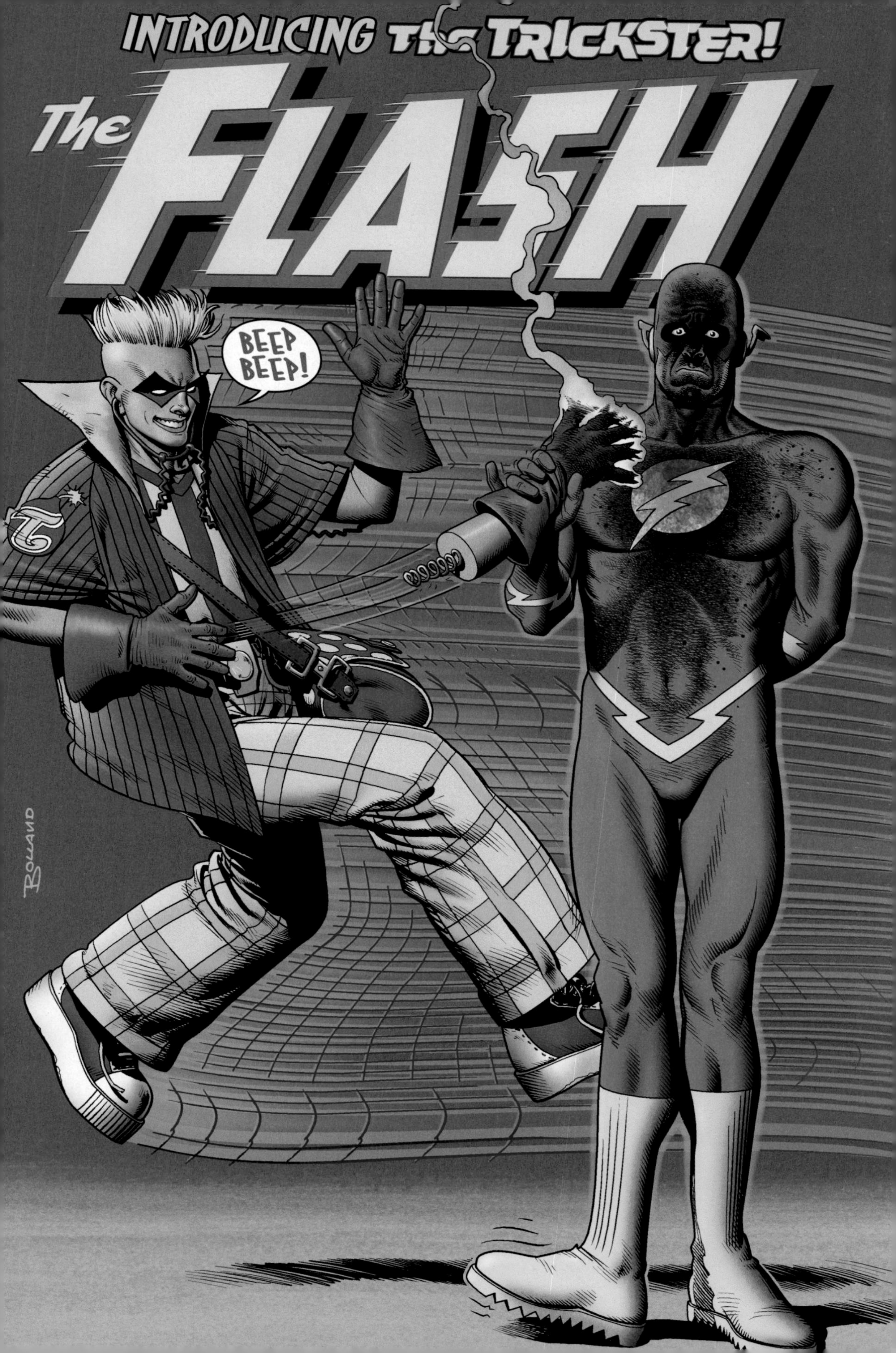

INTRODUCING the TRICKSTER!
The FLASH
BEEP BEEP!
BOLLAND

COVER ART BY **BRIAN BOLLAND**

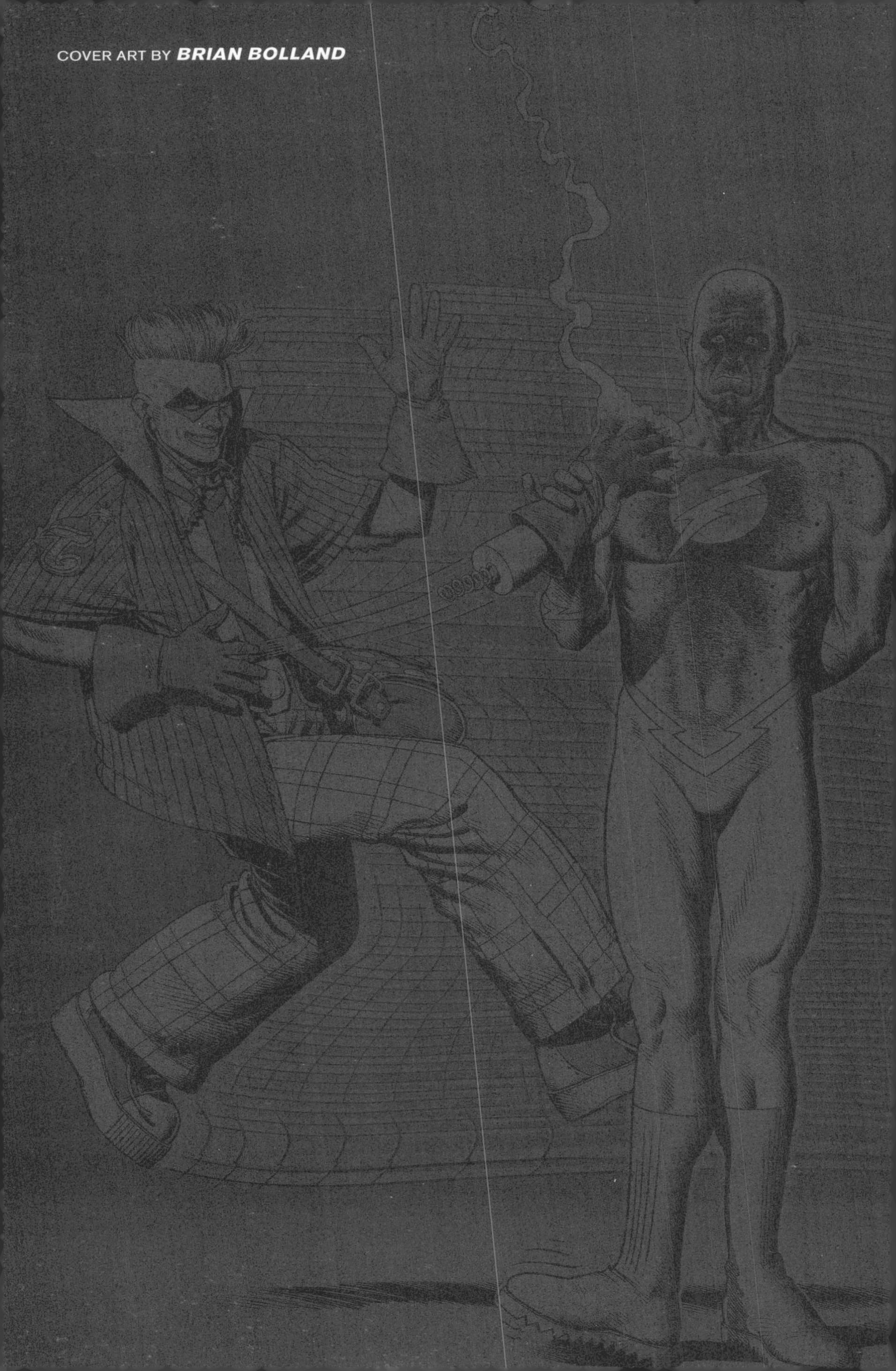

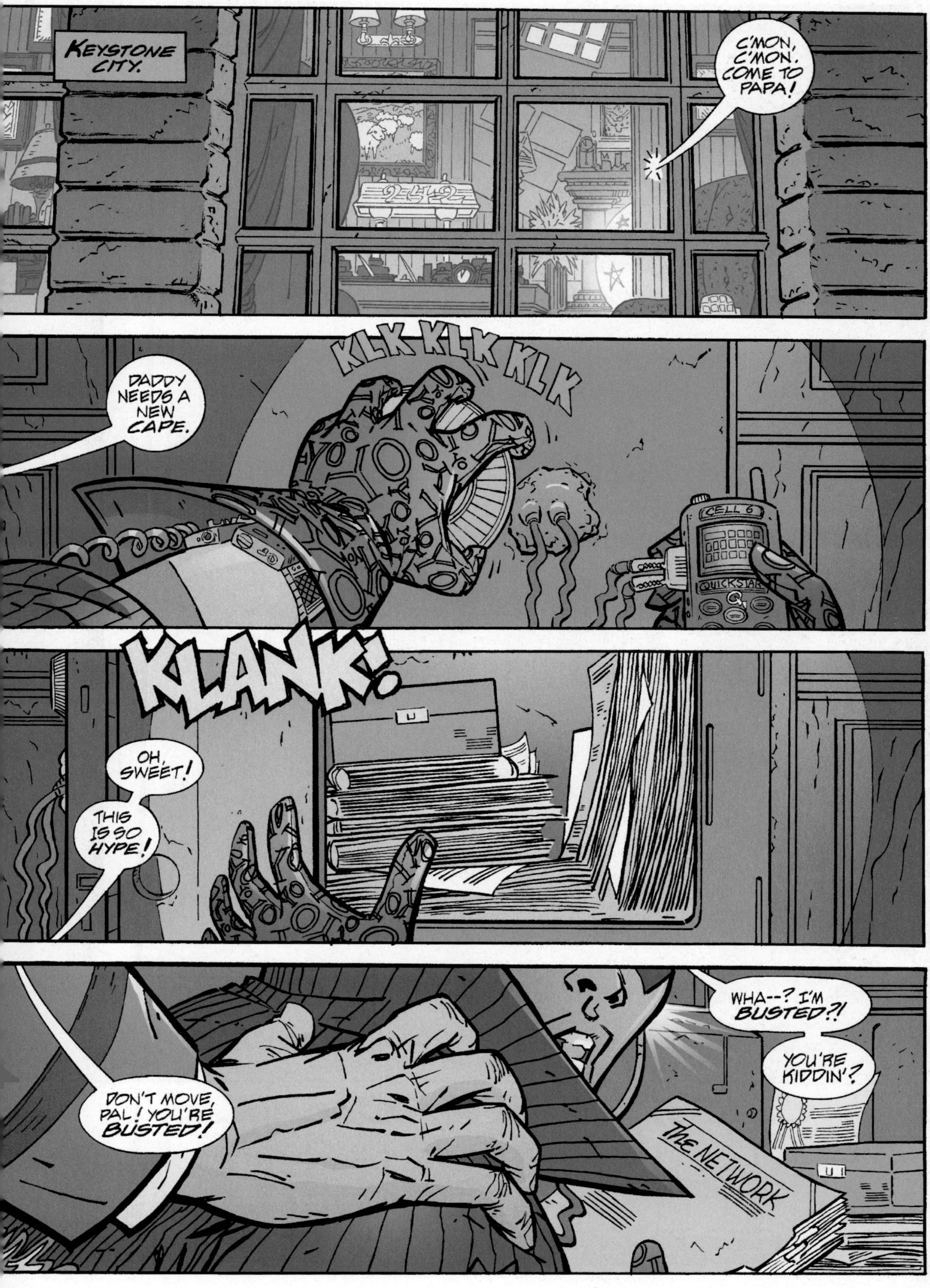
KEYSTONE CITY.
C'MON, C'MON. COME TO PAPA!
KLK KLK KLK
DADDY NEEDS A NEW CAPE.
CELL 6
QUICKSTAR
KLANK!
OH, SWEET!
THIS IS SO HYPE!
DON'T MOVE, PAL! YOU'RE BUSTED!
WHA--? I'M BUSTED?!
YOU'RE KIDDIN'?
The NETWORK

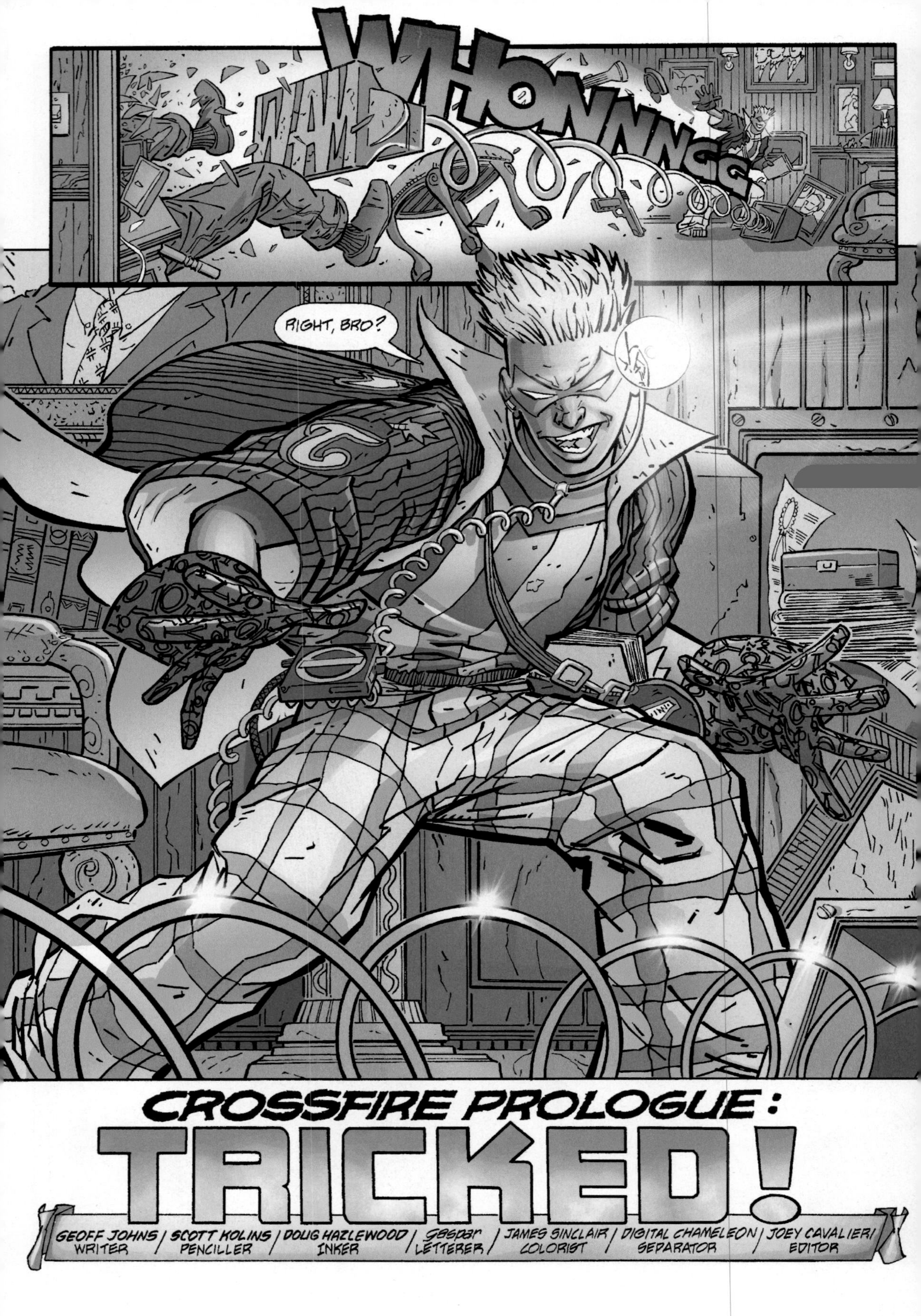
WAM
WHONNNGG
RIGHT, BRO?
CROSSFIRE PROLOGUE:
TRICKED!
GEOFF JOHNS WRITER
SCOTT KOLINS PENCILLER
DOUG HAZLEWOOD INKER
Gaspar LETTERER
JAMES SINCLAIR COLORIST
DIGITAL CHAMELEON SEPARATOR
JOEY CAVALIERI EDITOR

CLICK!

STOP OR WE'LL SHOOT!

OH, COME ON! I'M WAY OUT-NUMBERED!

HOW ABOUT WE CALL A *TRUCE*, FELLAHS? BREAK BREAD?

KENYON UNION 242

HERE.

HAVE SOME GUM.

SSSHRRB

NASTY!

THIS IS DEFINITELY *NOT* WORTH MY SIX BUCKS AN HOUR...

MMMFF!

BLAMM! BLAMM!

DAMN! Y'ALL ARE SO SENSITIVE!

I GUESS I'LL JUST TAKE MY STUFF AND GO HOME!

DON'T WORRY ABOUT ME THOUGH, RENT-A-COPS--

KSH!

KSH!

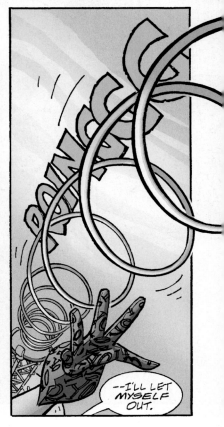

--I'LL LET MYSELF OUT.

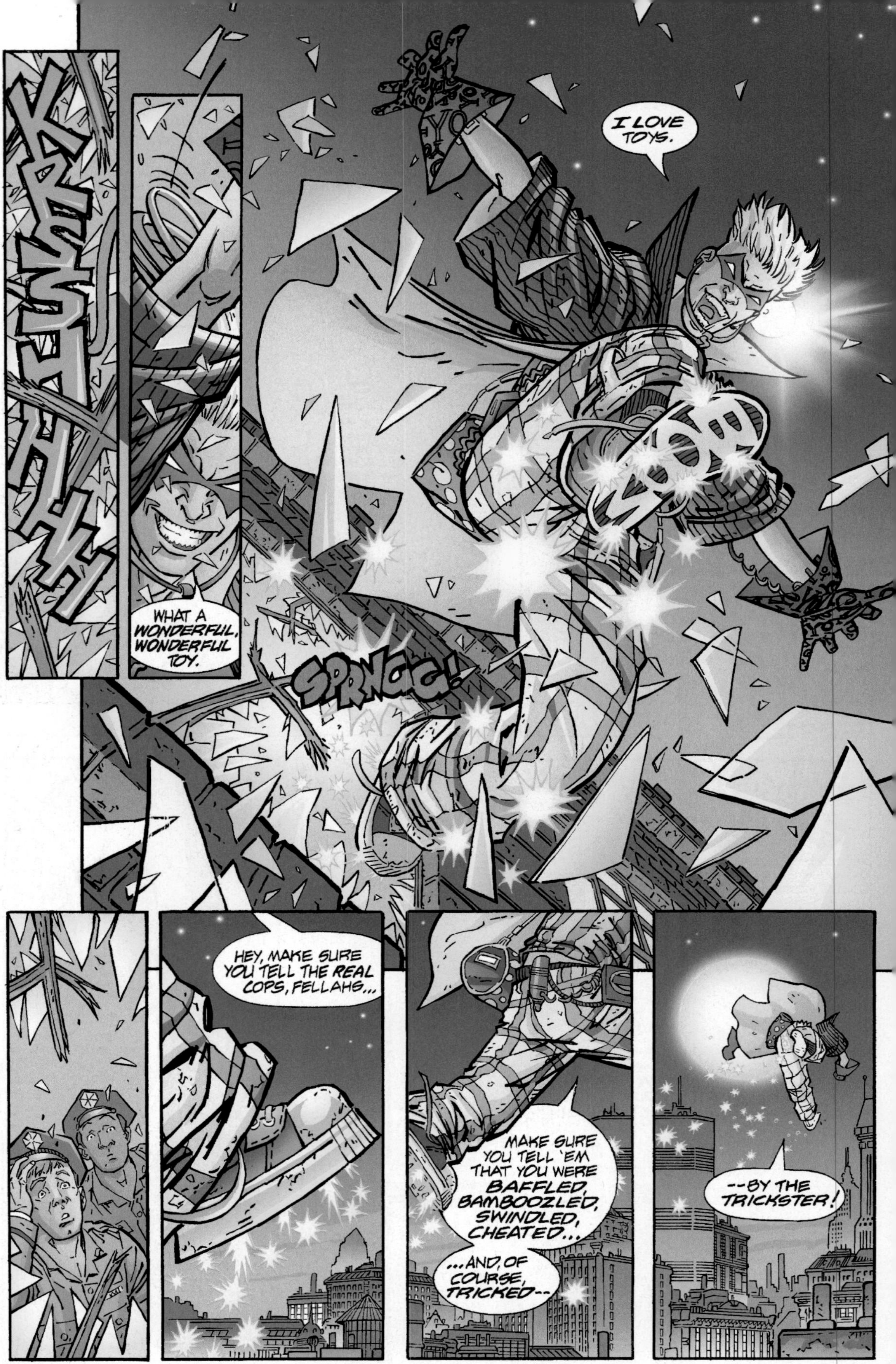

KRSSHH!
I LOVE TOYS.
WHAT A WONDERFUL, WONDERFUL TOY.
SPRNGG!
HEY, MAKE SURE YOU TELL THE REAL COPS, FELLAHS...
MAKE SURE YOU TELL 'EM THAT YOU WERE BAFFLED, BAMBOOZLED, SWINDLED, CHEATED...
...AND, OF COURSE, TRICKED--
--BY THE TRICKSTER!

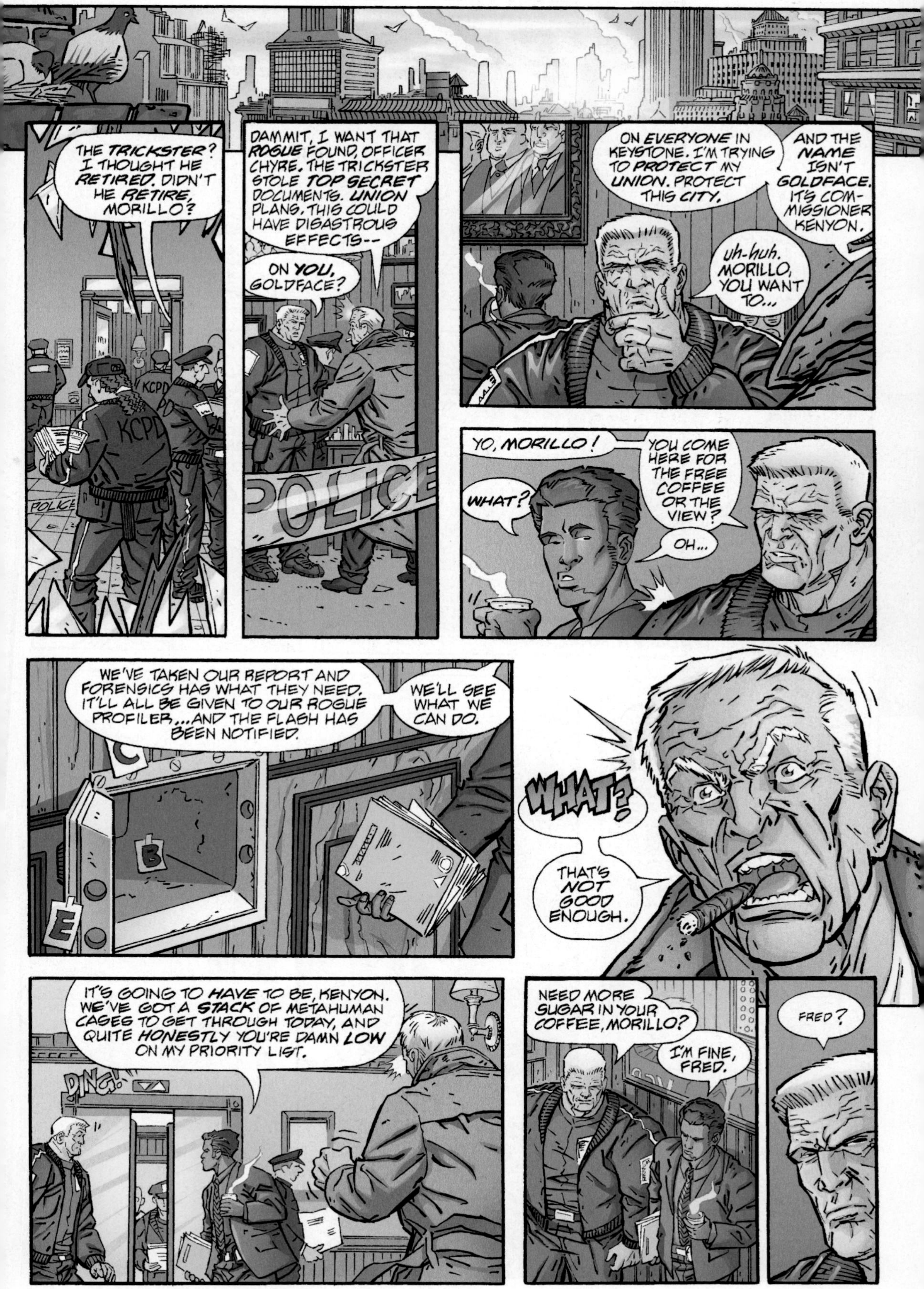
THE TRICKSTER? I THOUGHT HE RETIRED. DIDN'T HE RETIRE, MORILLO?
POLICE
DAMMIT, I WANT THAT ROGUE FOUND, OFFICER CHYRE. THE TRICKSTER STOLE TOP SECRET DOCUMENTS. UNION PLANS. THIS COULD HAVE DISASTROUS EFFECTS--
ON YOU, GOLDFACE?
POLICE
ON EVERYONE IN KEYSTONE. I'M TRYING TO PROTECT MY UNION. PROTECT THIS CITY.
AND THE NAME ISN'T GOLDFACE. IT'S COMMISSIONER KENYON.
uh-huh. MORILLO, YOU WANT TO...
YO, MORILLO!
YOU COME HERE FOR THE FREE COFFEE OR THE VIEW?
WHAT?
OH...
WE'VE TAKEN OUR REPORT AND FORENSICS HAS WHAT THEY NEED. IT'LL ALL BE GIVEN TO OUR ROGUE PROFILER...AND THE FLASH HAS BEEN NOTIFIED.
WE'LL SEE WHAT WE CAN DO.
WHAT?
THAT'S NOT GOOD ENOUGH.
IT'S GOING TO HAVE TO BE, KENYON. WE'VE GOT A STACK OF METAHUMAN CASES TO GET THROUGH TODAY, AND QUITE HONESTLY YOU'RE DAMN LOW ON MY PRIORITY LIST.
DING!
NEED MORE SUGAR IN YOUR COFFEE, MORILLO?
I'M FINE, FRED.
FRED?

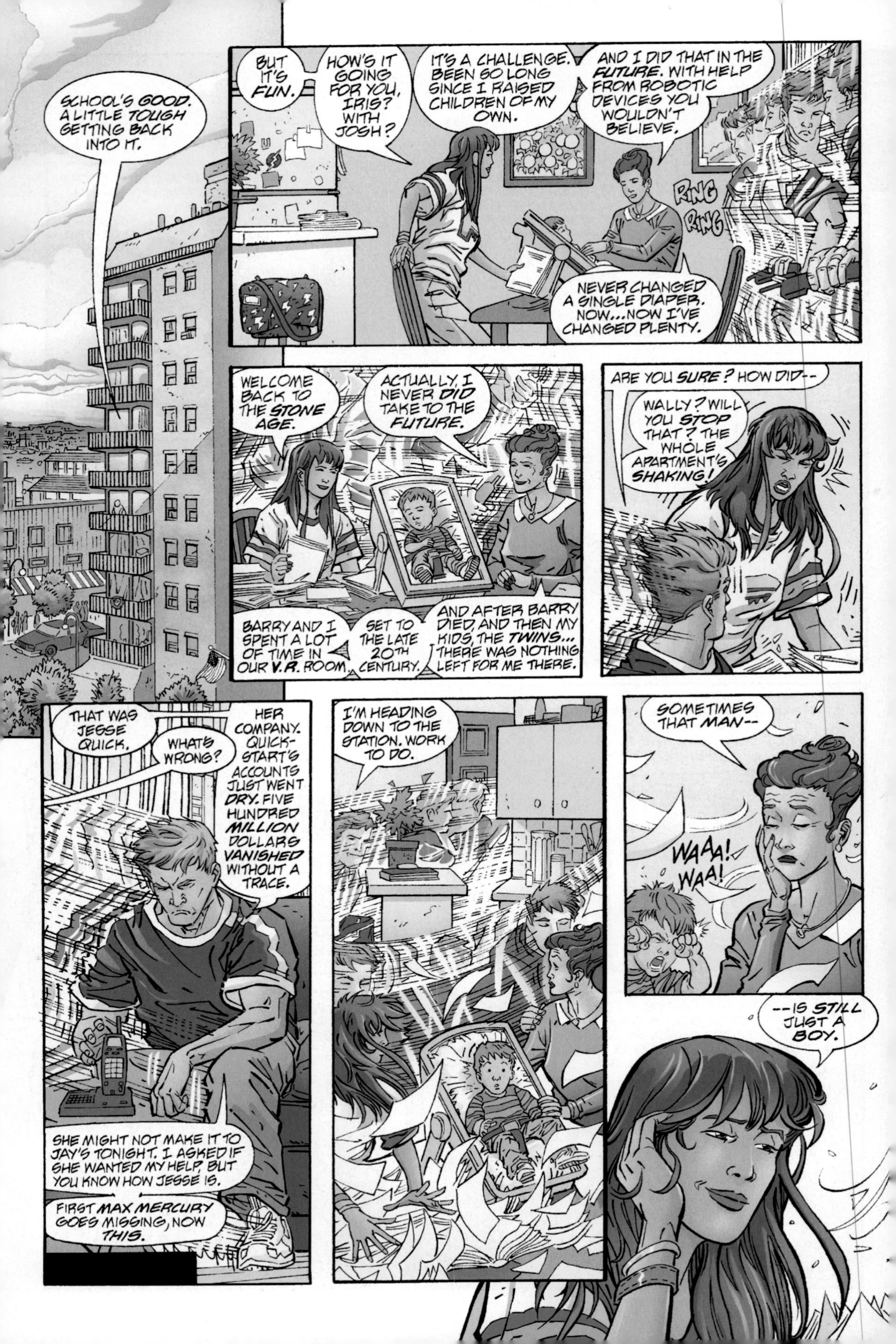
SCHOOL'S GOOD. A LITTLE TOUGH GETTING BACK INTO IT.
BUT IT'S FUN.
HOW'S IT GOING FOR YOU, IRIS? WITH JOSH?
IT'S A CHALLENGE. BEEN SO LONG SINCE I RAISED CHILDREN OF MY OWN.
AND I DID THAT IN THE FUTURE. WITH HELP FROM ROBOTIC DEVICES YOU WOULDN'T BELIEVE.
RING RING
NEVER CHANGED A SINGLE DIAPER. NOW...NOW I'VE CHANGED PLENTY.
WELCOME BACK TO THE STONE AGE.
ACTUALLY, I NEVER DID TAKE TO THE FUTURE.
BARRY AND I SPENT A LOT OF TIME IN OUR V.R. ROOM
SET TO THE LATE 20TH CENTURY.
AND AFTER BARRY DIED, AND THEN MY KIDS, THE TWINS... THERE WAS NOTHING LEFT FOR ME THERE.
ARE YOU SURE? HOW DID--
WALLY? WILL YOU STOP THAT? THE WHOLE APARTMENT'S SHAKING!
THAT WAS JESSE QUICK.
WHAT'S WRONG?
HER COMPANY. QUICKSTART'S ACCOUNTS JUST WENT DRY. FIVE HUNDRED MILLION DOLLARS VANISHED WITHOUT A TRACE.
SHE MIGHT NOT MAKE IT TO JAY'S TONIGHT. I ASKED IF SHE WANTED MY HELP, BUT YOU KNOW HOW JESSE IS.
FIRST MAX MERCURY GOES MISSING, NOW THIS.
[redacted]
I'M HEADING DOWN TO THE STATION. WORK TO DO.
SOMETIMES THAT MAN--
WAAA! WAA!
--IS STILL JUST A BOY.

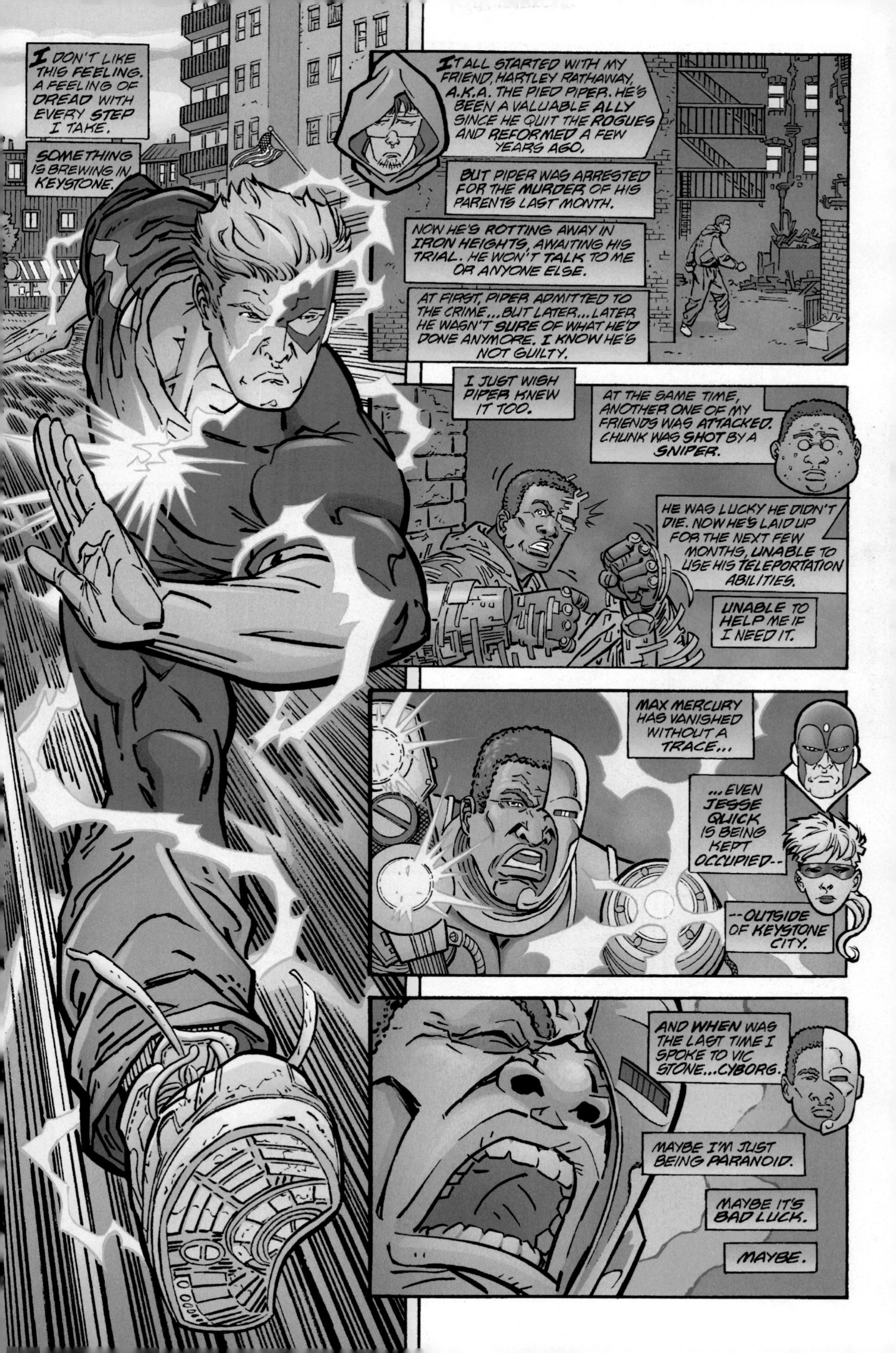
I DON'T LIKE THIS FEELING. A FEELING OF DREAD WITH EVERY STEP I TAKE.
SOMETHING IS BREWING IN KEYSTONE.
IT ALL STARTED WITH MY FRIEND, HARTLEY RATHAWAY, A.K.A. THE PIED PIPER. HE'S BEEN A VALUABLE ALLY SINCE HE QUIT THE ROGUES AND REFORMED A FEW YEARS AGO.
BUT PIPER WAS ARRESTED FOR THE MURDER OF HIS PARENTS LAST MONTH.
NOW HE'S ROTTING AWAY IN IRON HEIGHTS, AWAITING HIS TRIAL. HE WON'T TALK TO ME OR ANYONE ELSE.
AT FIRST, PIPER ADMITTED TO THE CRIME...BUT LATER...LATER HE WASN'T SURE OF WHAT HE'D DONE ANYMORE. I KNOW HE'S NOT GUILTY.
I JUST WISH PIPER KNEW IT TOO.
AT THE SAME TIME, ANOTHER ONE OF MY FRIENDS WAS ATTACKED. CHUNK WAS SHOT BY A SNIPER.
HE WAS LUCKY HE DIDN'T DIE. NOW HE'S LAID UP FOR THE NEXT FEW MONTHS, UNABLE TO USE HIS TELEPORTATION ABILITIES.
UNABLE TO HELP ME IF I NEED IT.
MAX MERCURY HAS VANISHED WITHOUT A TRACE...
...EVEN JESSE QUICK IS BEING KEPT OCCUPIED--
--OUTSIDE OF KEYSTONE CITY.
AND WHEN WAS THE LAST TIME I SPOKE TO VIC STONE...CYBORG.
MAYBE I'M JUST BEING PARANOID.
MAYBE IT'S BAD LUCK.
MAYBE.

THANK YOU, JAMES. THAT'S ALL I--

FT ZOTZ! *SSHZH!*

SORRY 'BOUT THAT, HUNTER.

TAKEN FROM A **SECURITY CAMERA** LAST NIGHT.

SO IT IS A NEW **TRICKSTER,**

HAS TO BE. THE ORIGINAL TRICKSTER, JAMES JESSE, GAVE UP HIS CON GAME A FEW MONTHS AGO. HE'S BEEN WORKING FOR THE BUREAU.

TESTING SECURITY. DAMN **FOOLS** WILL HIRE EX-CONS, BUT LET **ME** GO BE-CAUSE OF A **BAD** KNEE.

THEIR **LOSS,** HUNTER. I COULDN'T DO MY JOB HALF AS WELL WITHOUT YOUR HELP.

THANKS, FLASH. JAMES JESSE TOLD ME THERE WAS A BREAK-IN AT HIS OLD KEYSTONE STORAGE UNIT TWO WEEKS AGO. HIS COSTUME, HIS PATENTED AIR-WALKING SHOES, HIS COMPLETE BAG OF TRICKS WAS STOLEN.

SOME PRINTS WERE TAKEN...

...AND A WARRANT WAS ISSUED FOR THIS BOY'S ARREST.

DAMN. MUST BE THE NEW DETERGENT.

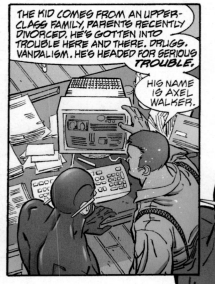

THE KID COMES FROM AN UPPER-CLASS FAMILY, PARENTS RECENTLY DIVORCED. HE'S GOTTEN INTO TROUBLE HERE AND THERE. DRUGS. VANDALISM. HE'S HEADED FOR SERIOUS **TROUBLE.**

HIS NAME IS AXEL WALKER.

BUT MY ENEMIES CALL ME--

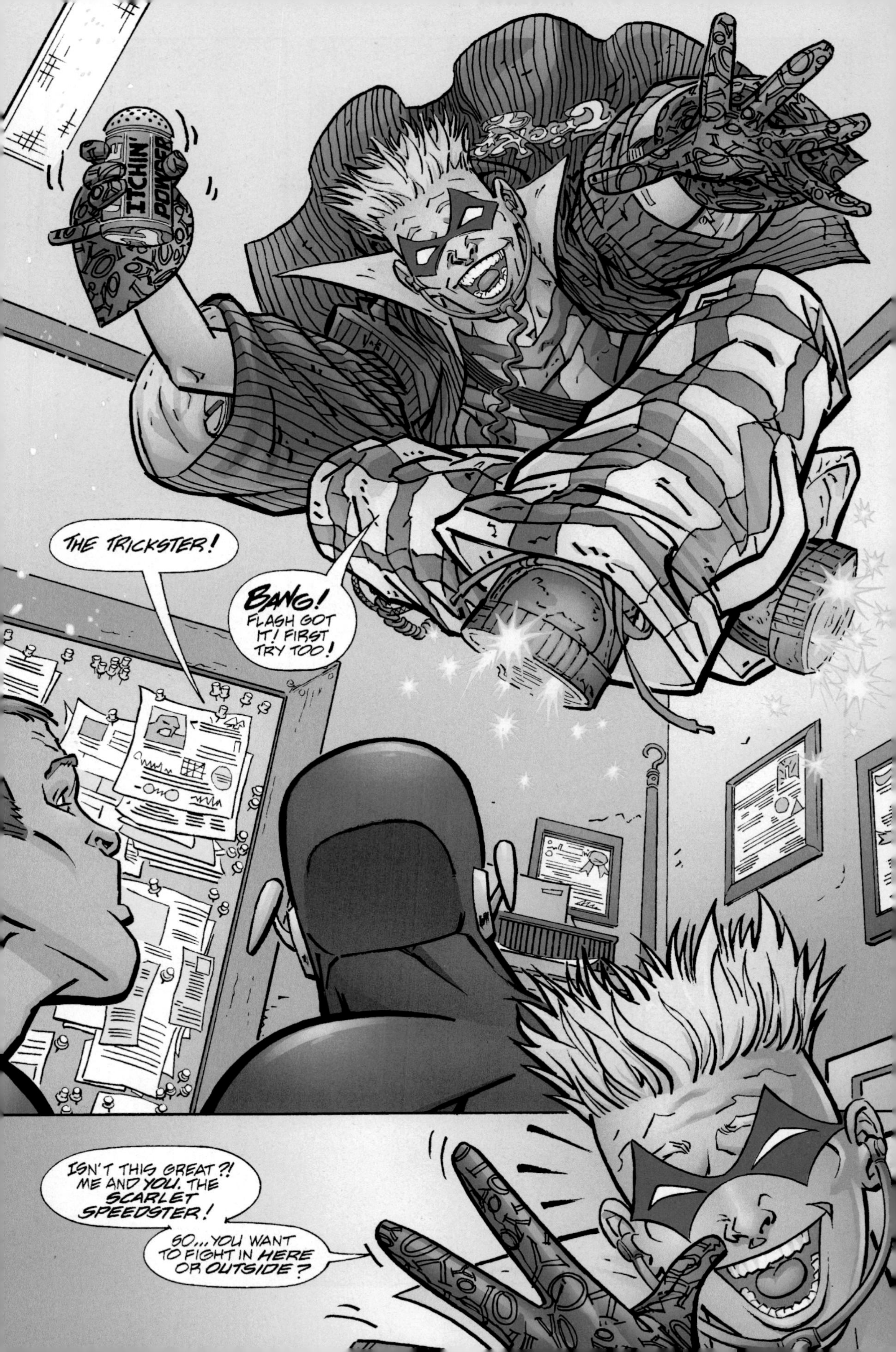
ITCHIN' POWDER
THE TRICKSTER!
BANG! FLASH GOT IT! FIRST TRY TOO!
ISN'T THIS GREAT?! ME AND YOU. THE SCARLET SPEEDSTER!
SO...YOU WANT TO FIGHT IN HERE OR OUTSIDE?

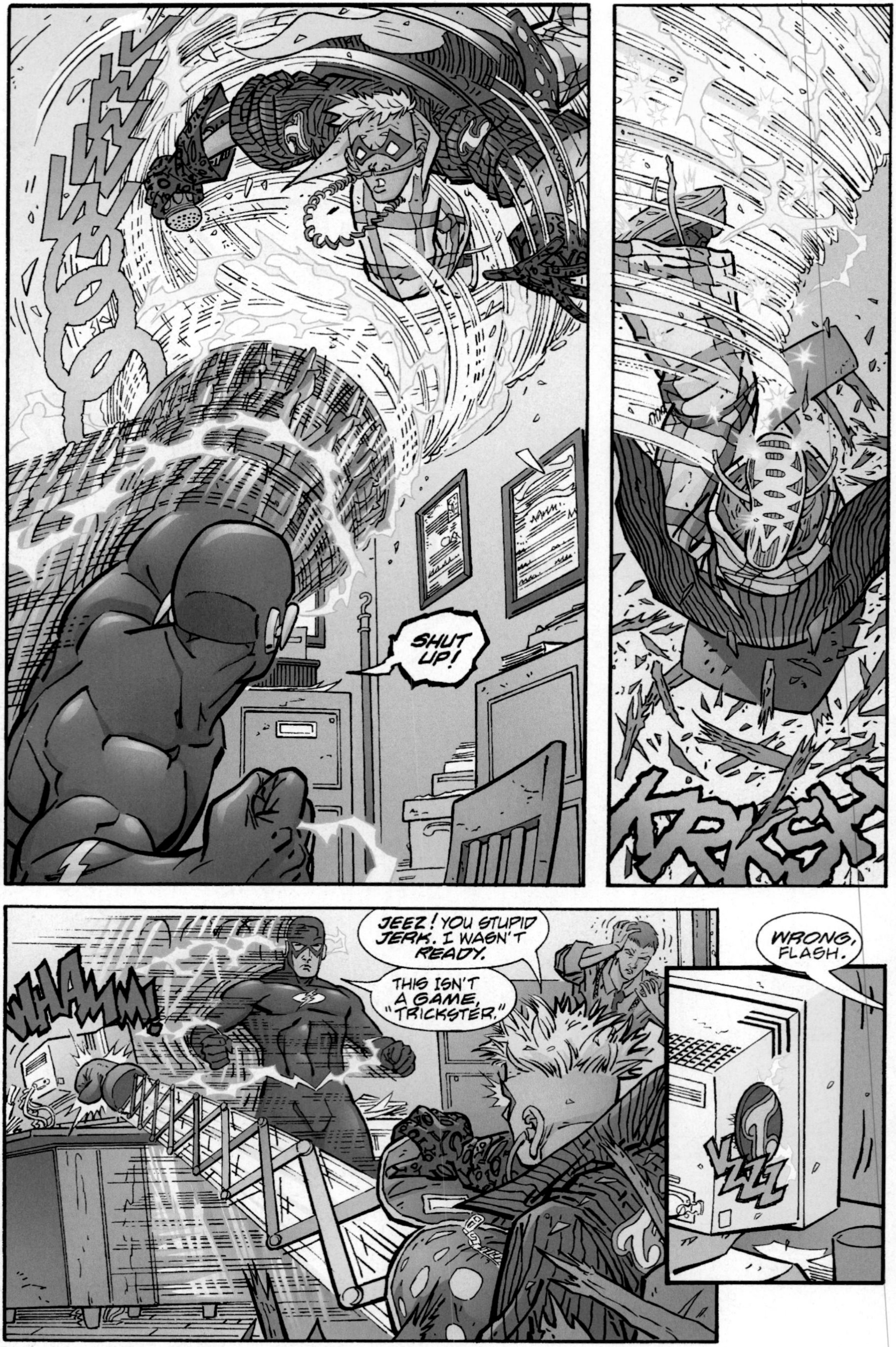
SHUT UP!
WHAMM!
JEEZ! YOU STUPID JERK. I WASN'T READY.
THIS ISN'T A GAME, "TRICKSTER."
WRONG, FLASH.

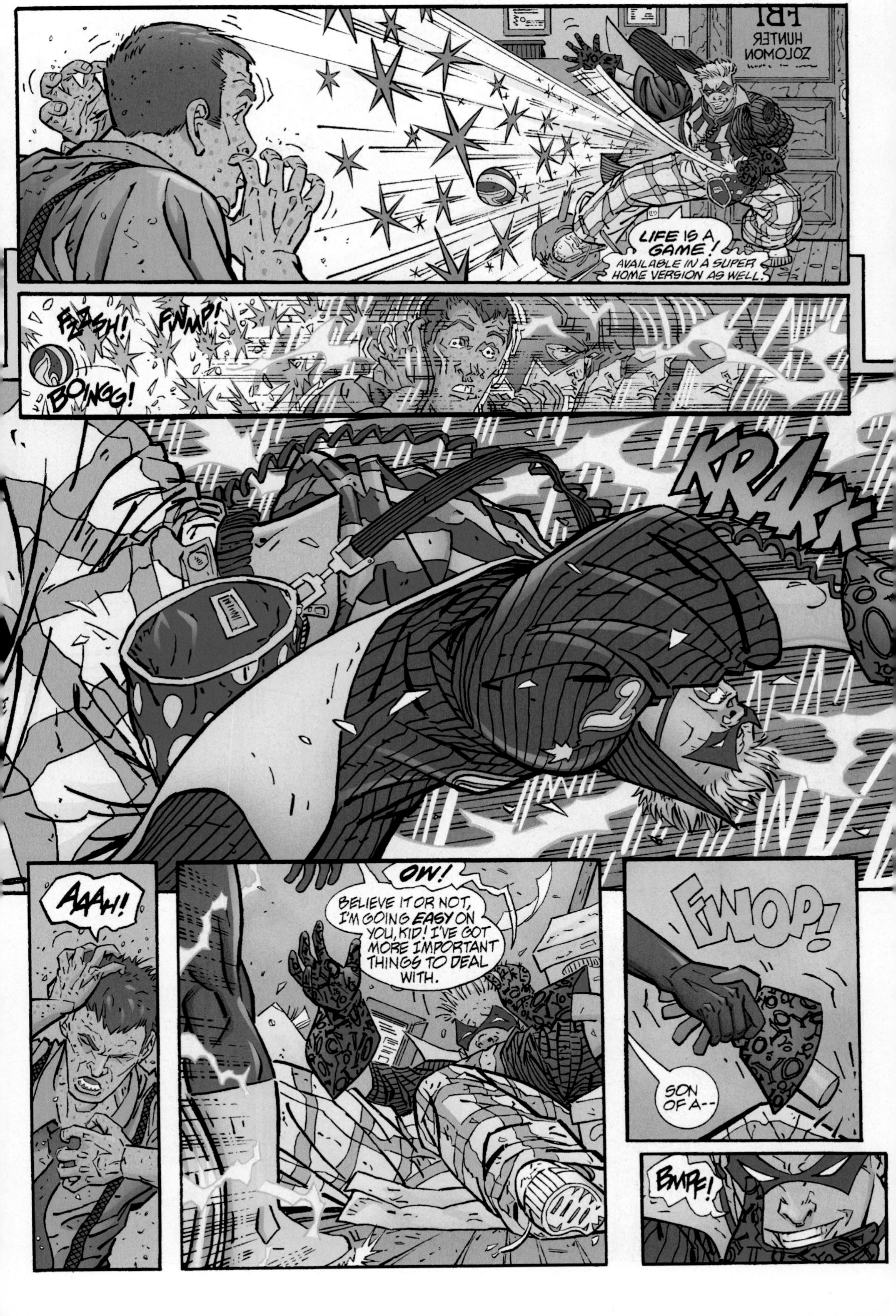
FBI
HUNTER
SOLOMON
LIFE IS A GAME! AVAILABLE IN A SUPER HOME VERSION AS WELL.
FZZASH!
FWMP!
BOINGG!
KRAKK
AAAH!
OW!
BELIEVE IT OR NOT, I'M GOING EASY ON YOU, KID! I'VE GOT MORE IMPORTANT THINGS TO DEAL WITH.
FWOP!
SON OF A--
BMPF!

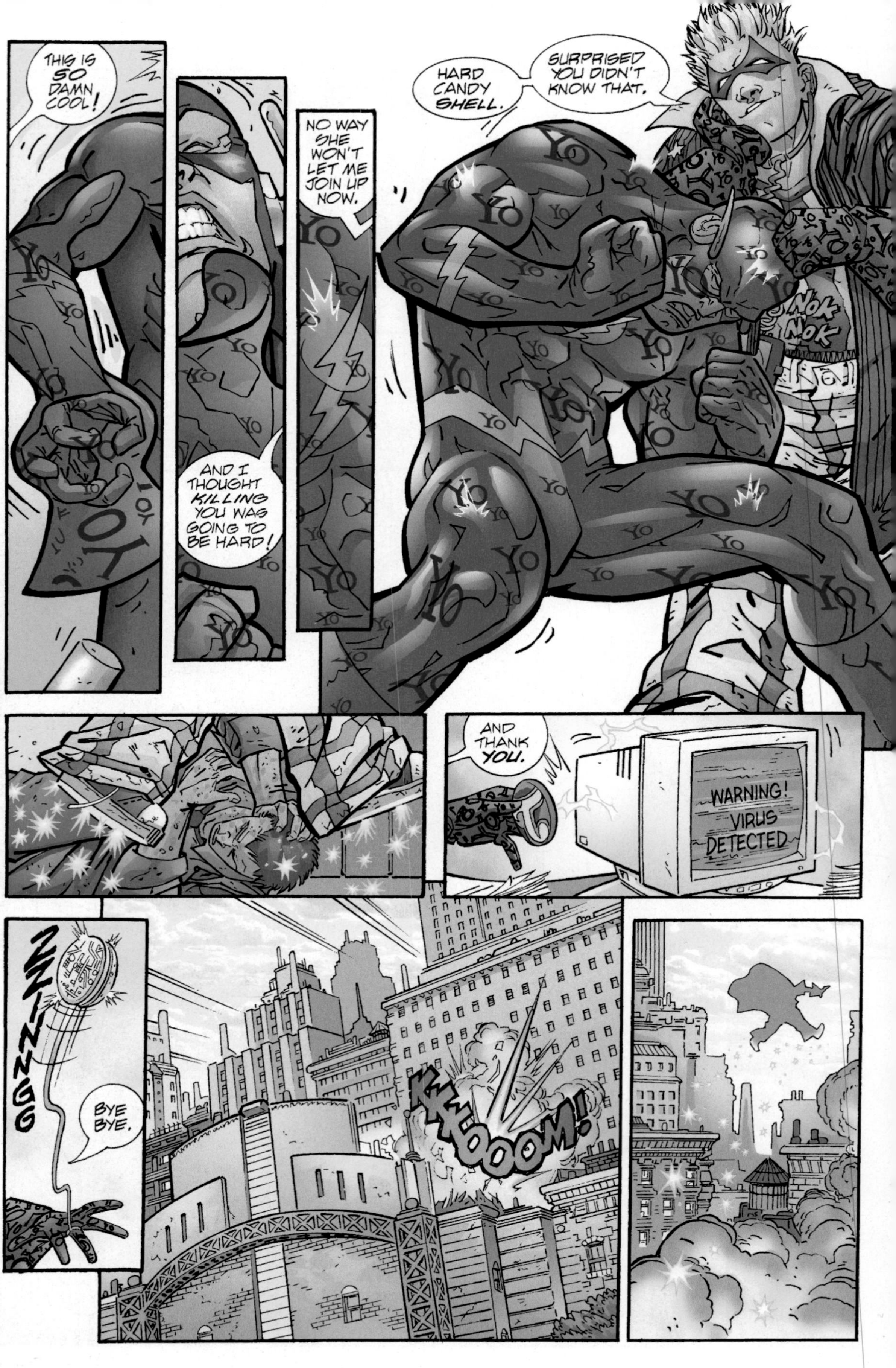
THIS IS *SO* DAMN COOL!
NO WAY SHE WON'T LET ME JOIN UP NOW.
HARD CANDY *SHELL*.
SURPRISED YOU DIDN'T KNOW THAT.
YO
NOK NOK
AND I THOUGHT *KILLING* YOU WAS GOING TO BE HARD!
AND THANK *YOU*.
WARNING! VIRUS DETECTED
ZZINNGG
BYE BYE.
KKAFOOOM!

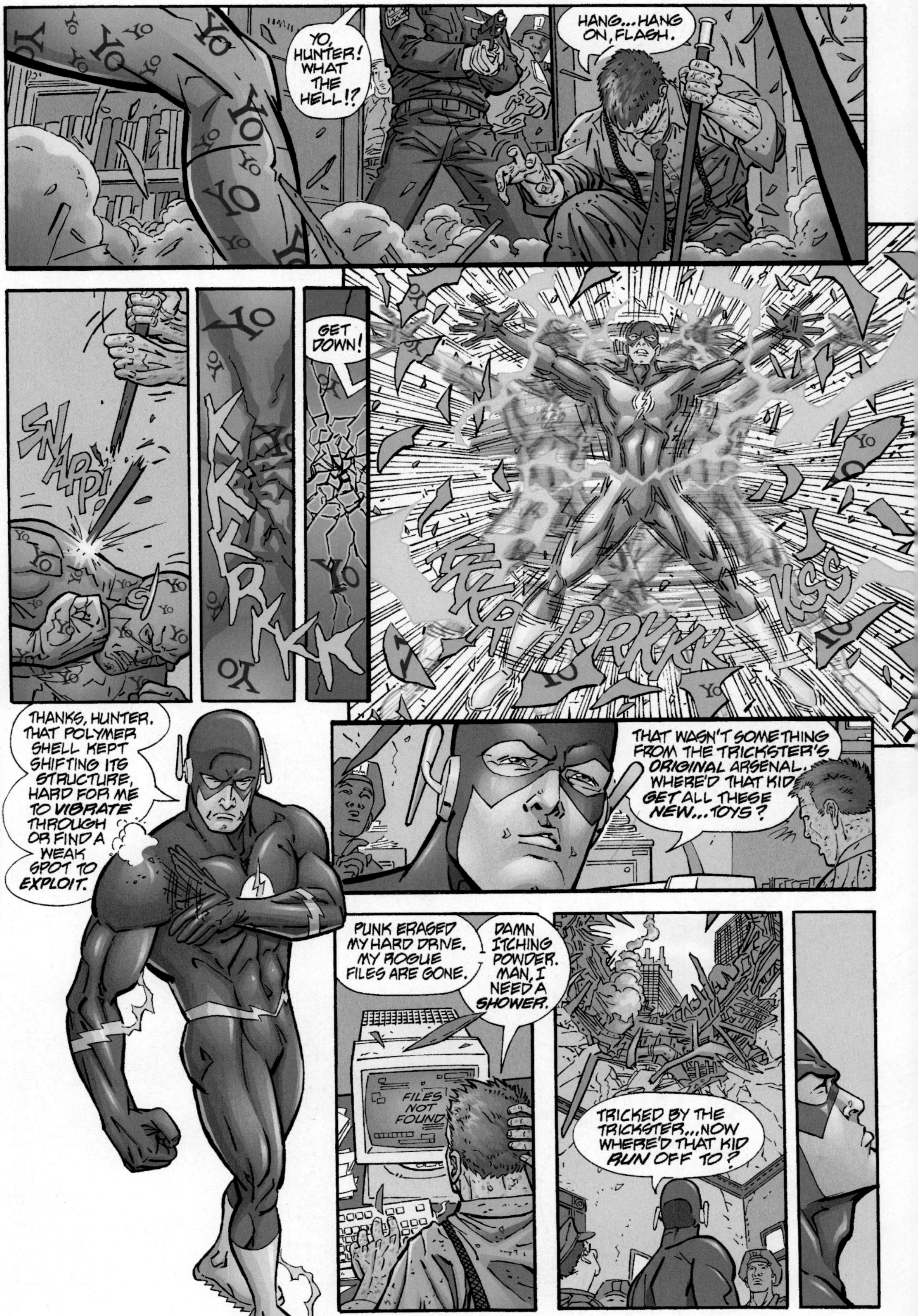
YO, HUNTER! WHAT THE HELL!?
HANG... HANG ON, FLASH.
SNAP!
GET DOWN!
KKRRKKK
KKKR RRKKKK KSS
THANKS, HUNTER. THAT POLYMER SHELL KEPT SHIFTING ITS STRUCTURE, HARD FOR ME TO VIBRATE THROUGH OR FIND A WEAK SPOT TO EXPLOIT.
THAT WASN'T SOMETHING FROM THE TRICKSTER'S ORIGINAL ARSENAL. WHERE'D THAT KID GET ALL THESE NEW... TOYS?
PUNK ERASED MY HARD DRIVE. MY ROGUE FILES ARE GONE.
DAMN ITCHING POWDER. MAN, I NEED A SHOWER.
FILES NOT FOUND
TRICKED BY THE TRICKSTER... NOW WHERE'D THAT KID RUN OFF TO?

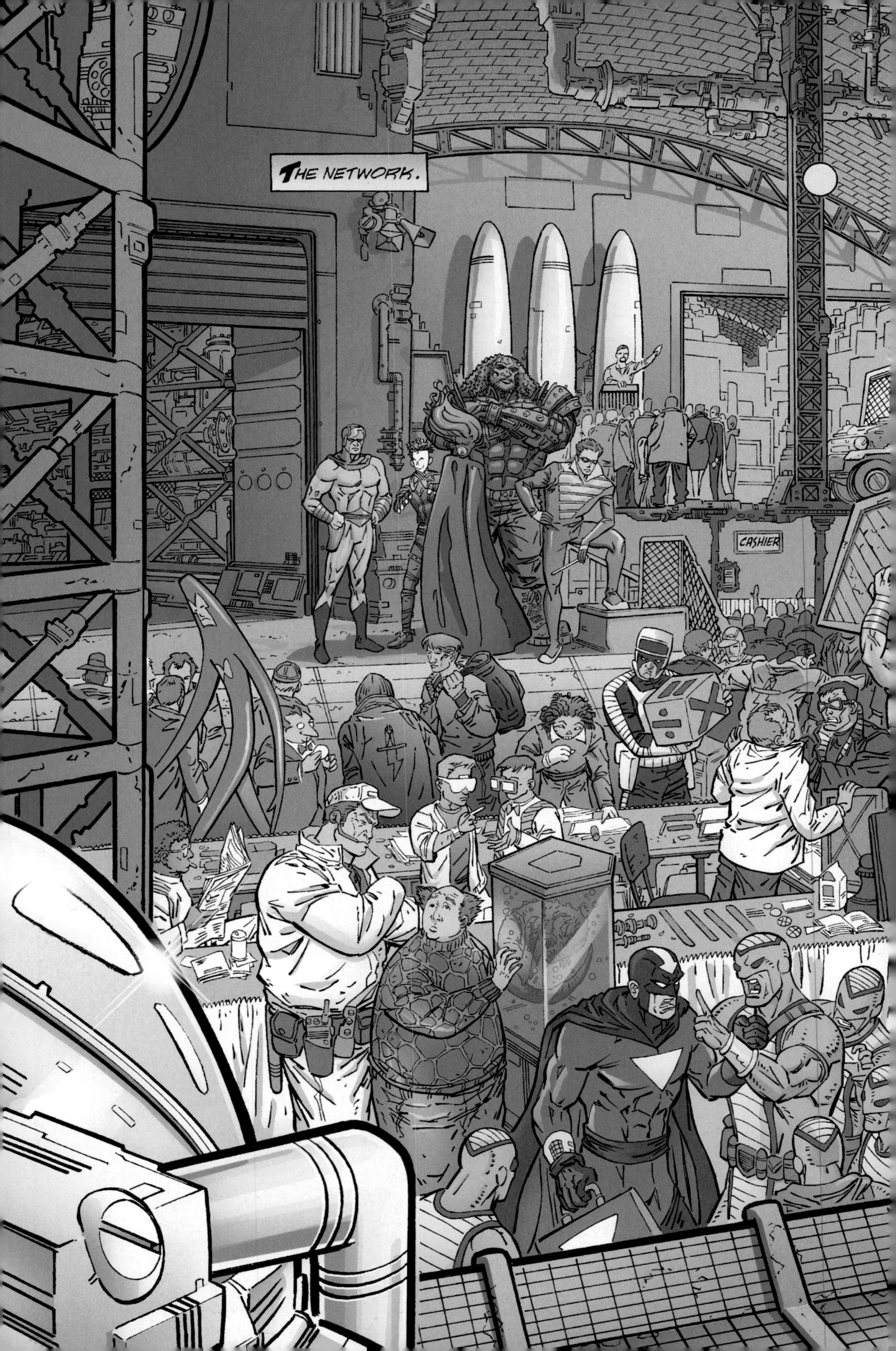
THE NETWORK.
CASHIER

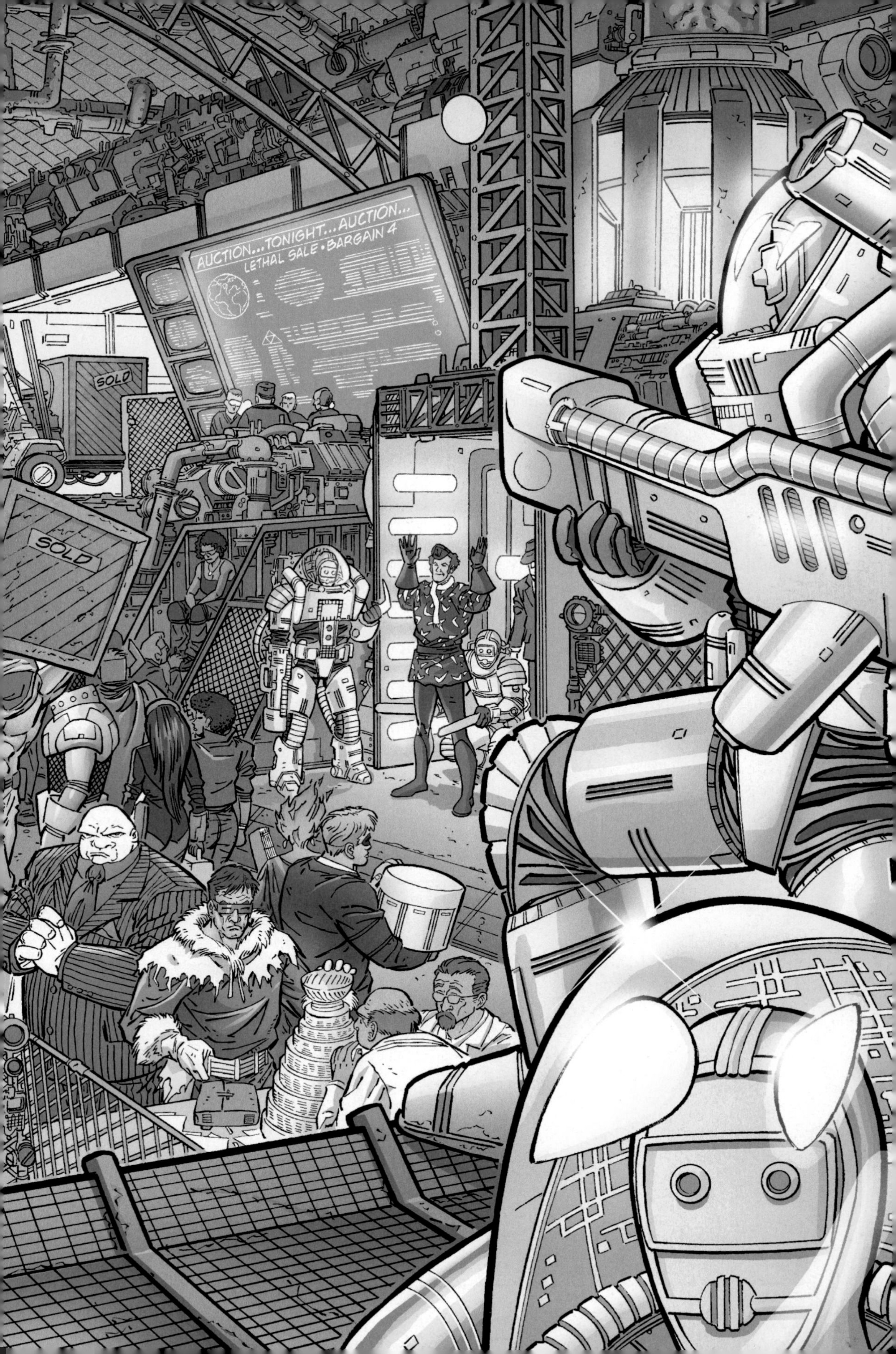
AUCTION...TONIGHT...AUCTION...
LETHAL SALE • BARGAIN 4
SOLD
SOLD

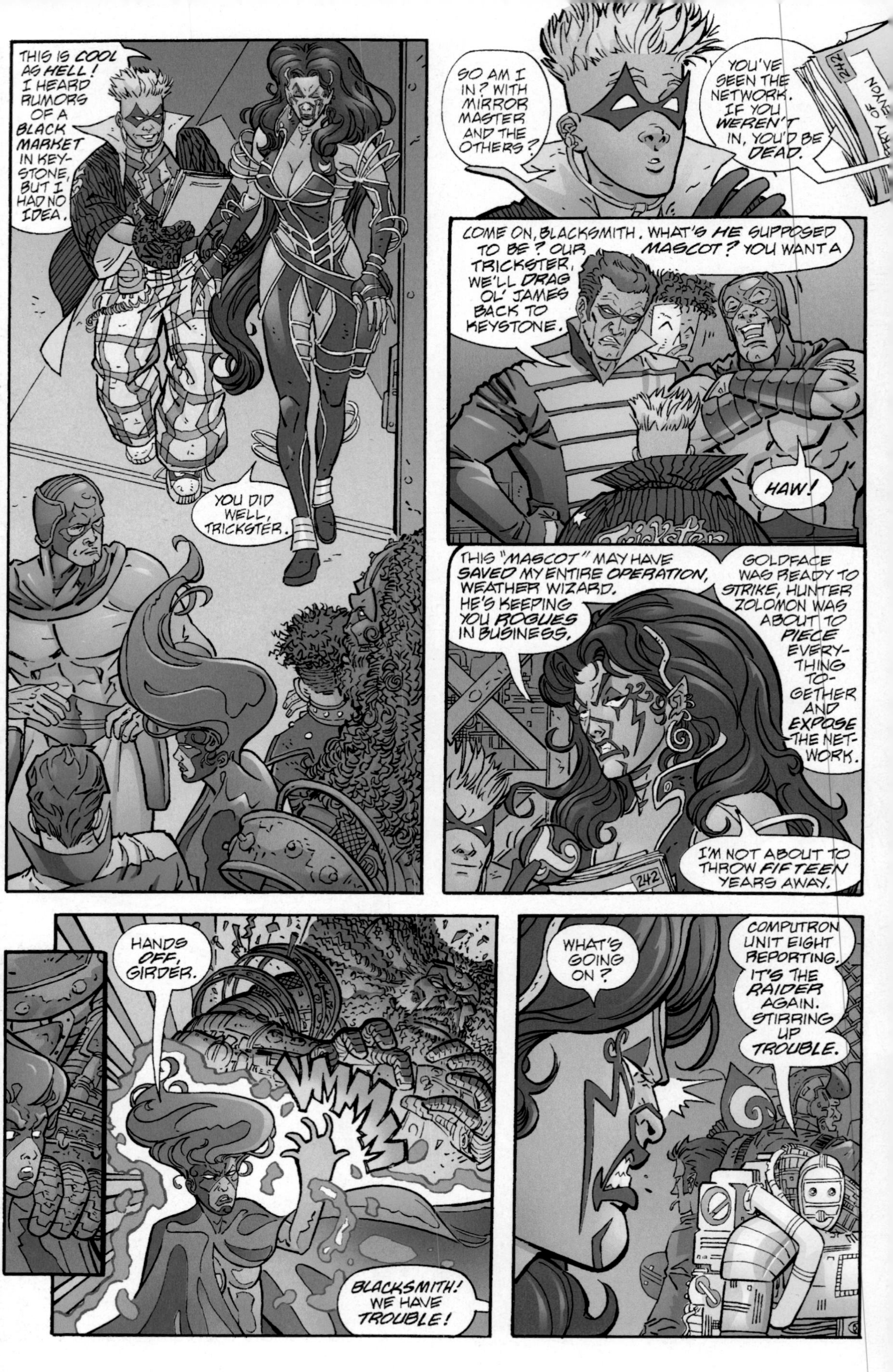
THIS IS COOL AS HELL! I HEARD RUMORS OF A BLACK MARKET IN KEYSTONE, BUT I HAD NO IDEA.
YOU DID WELL, TRICKSTER.
SO AM I IN? WITH MIRROR MASTER AND THE OTHERS?
YOU'VE SEEN THE NETWORK. IF YOU WEREN'T IN, YOU'D BE DEAD.
COME ON, BLACKSMITH. WHAT'S HE SUPPOSED TO BE? OUR MASCOT? YOU WANT A TRICKSTER, WE'LL DRAG OL' JAMES BACK TO KEYSTONE.
HAW!
THIS "MASCOT" MAY HAVE SAVED MY ENTIRE OPERATION, WEATHER WIZARD. HE'S KEEPING YOU ROGUES IN BUSINESS.
GOLDFACE WAS READY TO STRIKE, HUNTER ZOLOMON WAS ABOUT TO PIECE EVERYTHING TOGETHER AND EXPOSE THE NETWORK.
I'M NOT ABOUT TO THROW FIFTEEN YEARS AWAY.
HANDS OFF, GIRDER.
BLACKSMITH! WE HAVE TROUBLE!
WHAT'S GOING ON?
COMPUTRON UNIT EIGHT REPORTING. IT'S THE RAIDER AGAIN. STIRRING UP TROUBLE.

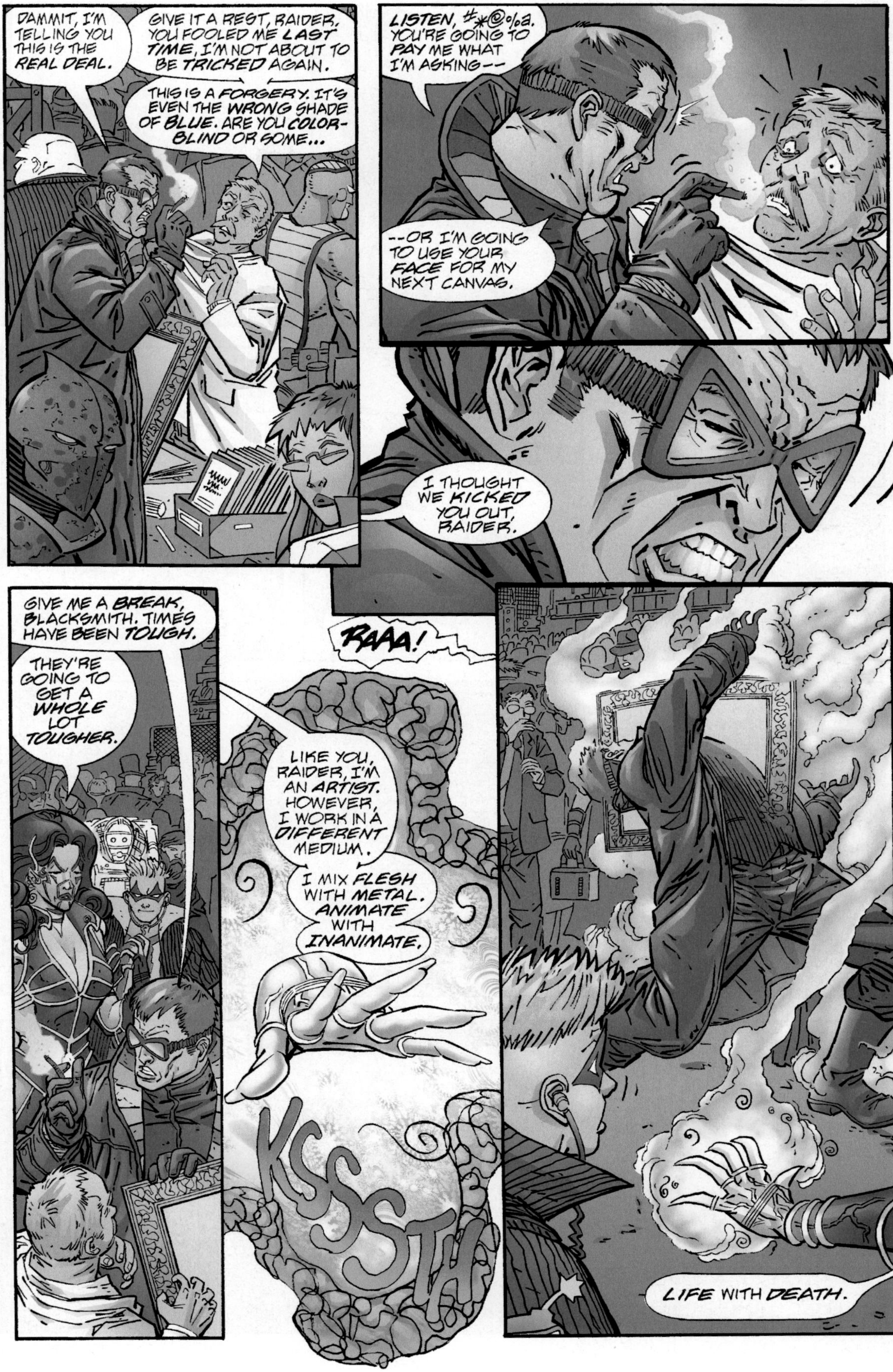
DAMMIT, I'M TELLING YOU THIS IS THE REAL DEAL.
GIVE IT A REST, RAIDER. YOU FOOLED ME LAST TIME, I'M NOT ABOUT TO BE TRICKED AGAIN.
THIS IS A FORGERY. IT'S EVEN THE WRONG SHADE OF BLUE. ARE YOU COLOR-BLIND OR SOME...
LISTEN, #*@%a. YOU'RE GOING TO PAY ME WHAT I'M ASKING--
--OR I'M GOING TO USE YOUR FACE FOR MY NEXT CANVAS.
I THOUGHT WE KICKED YOU OUT, RAIDER.
GIVE ME A BREAK, BLACKSMITH. TIMES HAVE BEEN TOUGH.
THEY'RE GOING TO GET A WHOLE LOT TOUGHER.
RAAA!
LIKE YOU, RAIDER, I'M AN ARTIST. HOWEVER, I WORK IN A DIFFERENT MEDIUM.
I MIX FLESH WITH METAL. ANIMATE WITH INANIMATE.
KSSSTH
LIFE WITH DEATH.

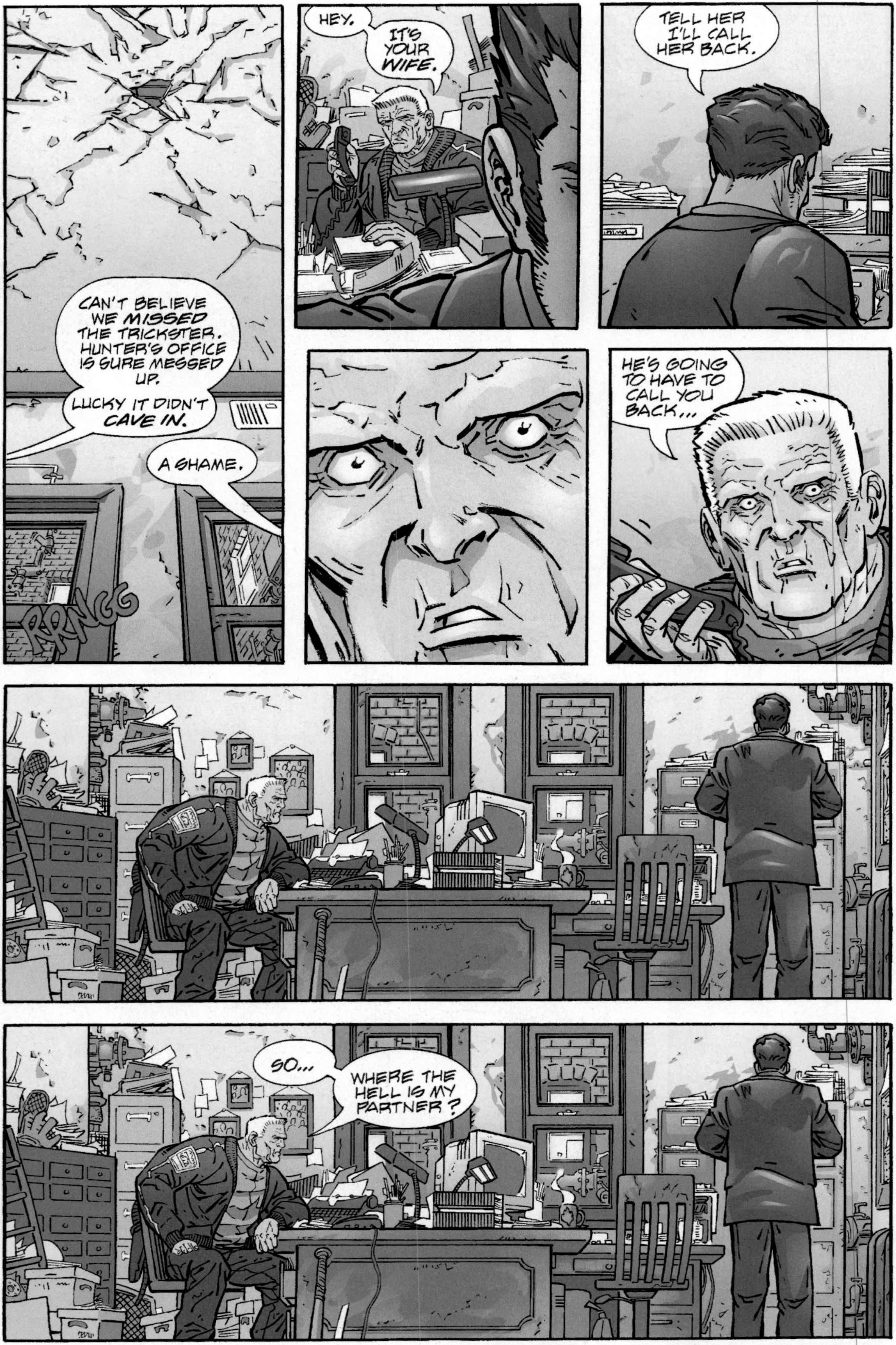
CAN'T BELIEVE WE MISSED THE TRICKSTER. HUNTER'S OFFICE IS SURE MESSED UP.
LUCKY IT DIDN'T CAVE IN.
A SHAME.
RRNGG
HEY.
IT'S YOUR WIFE.
TELL HER I'LL CALL HER BACK.
HE'S GOING TO HAVE TO CALL YOU BACK...
SO...
WHERE THE HELL IS MY PARTNER?

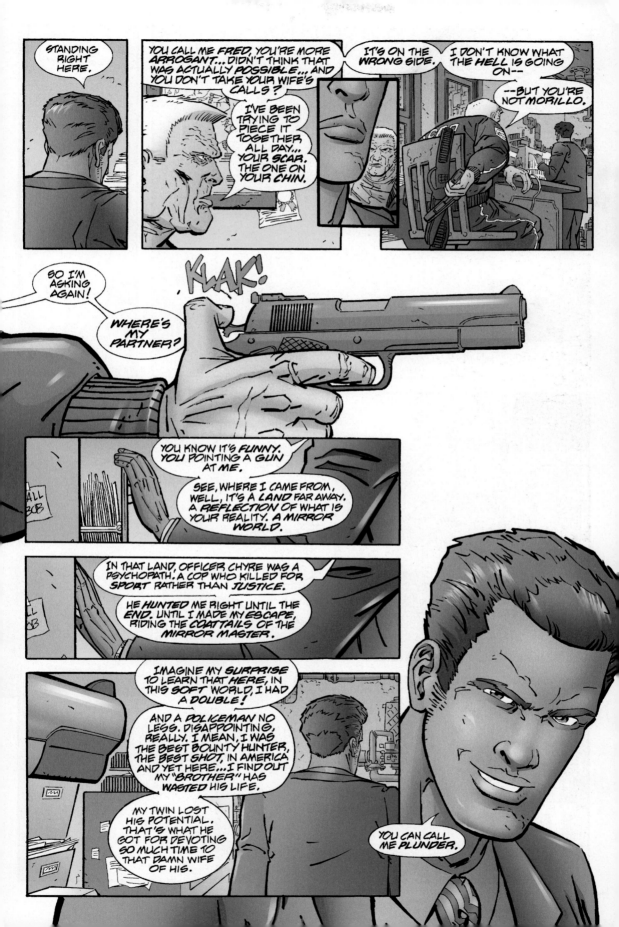

STANDING RIGHT HERE.

YOU CALL ME *FRED*. YOU'RE MORE *ARROGANT*... DIDN'T THINK THAT WAS ACTUALLY *POSSIBLE*... AND YOU DON'T TAKE YOUR WIFE'S CALLS?

I'VE BEEN TRYING TO PIECE IT TOGETHER ALL DAY... YOUR *SCAR*. THE ONE ON YOUR CHIN.

IT'S ON THE *WRONG SIDE*.

I DON'T KNOW WHAT THE *HELL* IS GOING ON--

--BUT YOU'RE *NOT MORILLO*.

SO I'M ASKING AGAIN!

WHERE'S MY *PARTNER*?

KWAK!

YOU KNOW IT'S *FUNNY*. YOU POINTING A GUN AT ME.

SEE, WHERE I CAME FROM, WELL, IT'S A *LAND* FAR AWAY. A *REFLECTION* OF WHAT IS YOUR REALITY. A *MIRROR WORLD*.

ALL BOB

IN THAT LAND, OFFICER *CHYRE* WAS A *PSYCHOPATH*. A COP WHO KILLED FOR *SPORT* RATHER THAN *JUSTICE*.

HE HUNTED ME RIGHT UNTIL THE *END*. UNTIL I MADE MY *ESCAPE*, RIDING THE *COATTAILS* OF THE *MIRROR MASTER*.

IMAGINE MY *SURPRISE* TO LEARN THAT *HERE*, IN THIS *SOFT WORLD*, I HAD A *DOUBLE*!

AND A *POLICEMAN* NO LESS. DISAPPOINTING, REALLY. I MEAN, I WAS THE BEST *BOUNTY HUNTER*, THE BEST *SHOT*, IN AMERICA AND YET HERE... I FIND OUT MY "BROTHER" HAS *WASTED* HIS LIFE.

MY *TWIN* LOST HIS *POTENTIAL*. THAT'S WHAT HE GOT FOR DEVOTING SO MUCH TIME TO THAT *DAMN WIFE* OF HIS.

YOU CAN CALL ME *PLUNDER*.

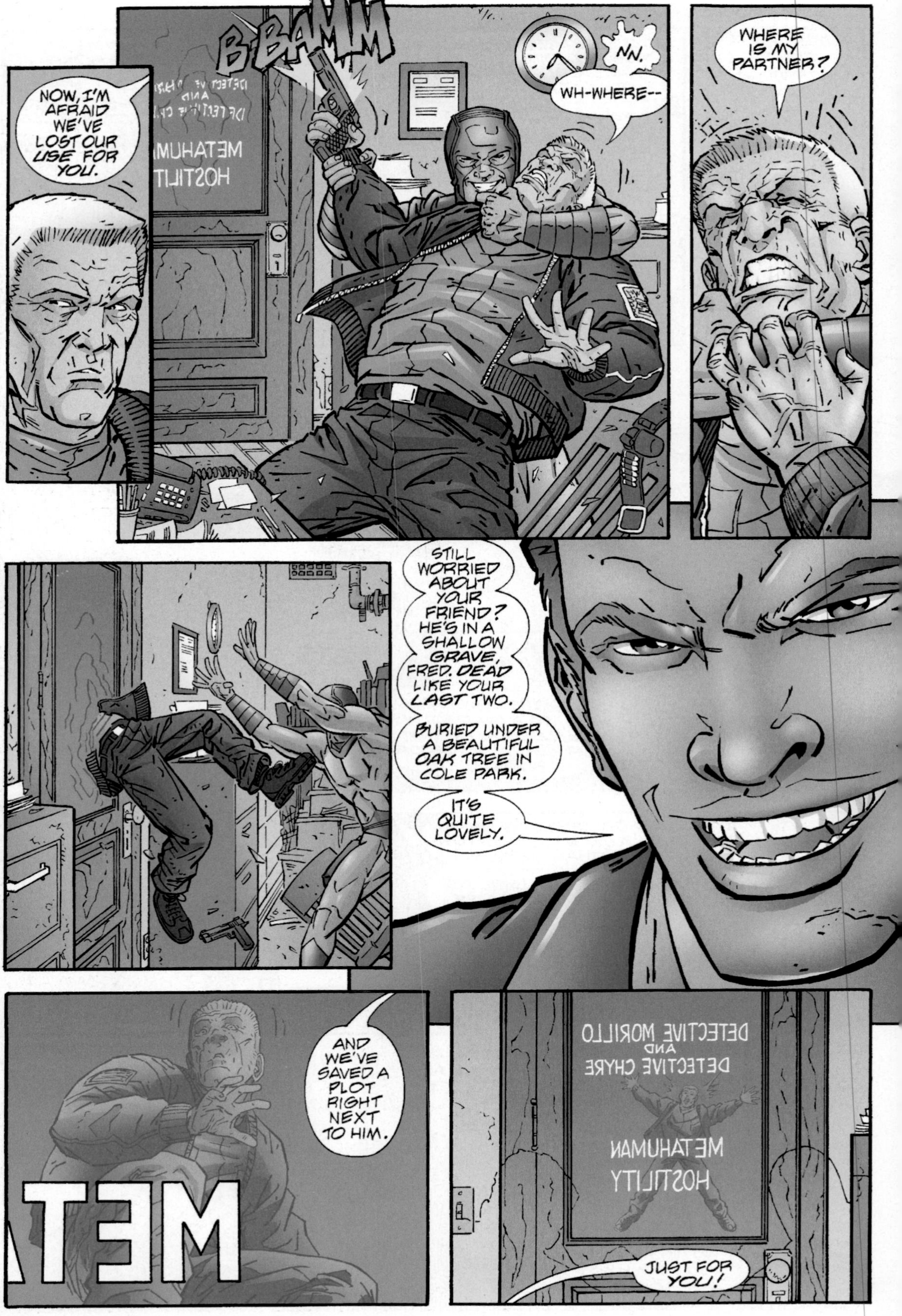
NOW, I'M AFRAID WE'VE LOST OUR USE FOR YOU.
B-BAMM
NN.
WH-WHERE--
WHERE IS MY PARTNER?
STILL WORRIED ABOUT YOUR FRIEND? HE'S IN A SHALLOW GRAVE, FRED. DEAD LIKE YOUR LAST TWO.
BURIED UNDER A BEAUTIFUL OAK TREE IN COLE PARK.
IT'S QUITE LOVELY.
AND WE'VE SAVED A PLOT RIGHT NEXT TO HIM.
DETECTIVE MORILLO AND DETECTIVE CHYRE
METAHUMAN HOSTILITY
JUST FOR YOU!

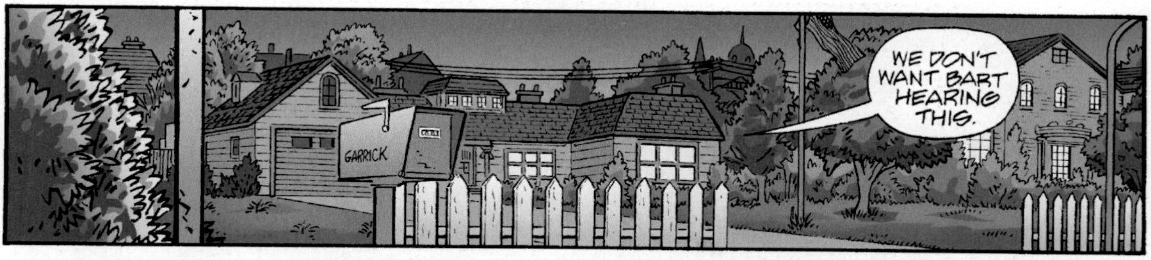
GARRICK
WE DON'T WANT BART HEARING THIS.

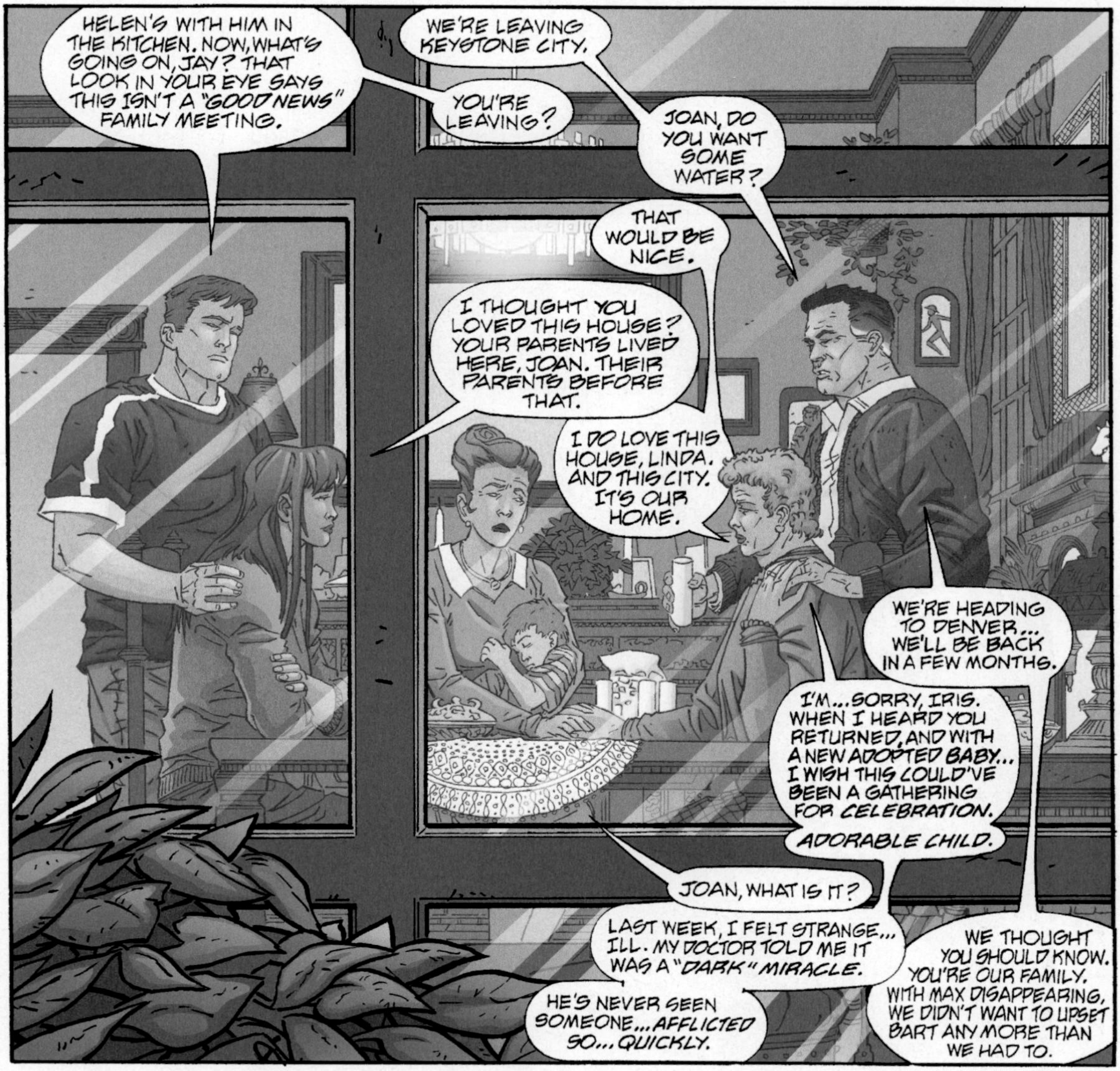
HELEN'S WITH HIM IN THE KITCHEN. NOW, WHAT'S GOING ON, JAY? THAT LOOK IN YOUR EYE SAYS THIS ISN'T A "GOOD NEWS" FAMILY MEETING.
WE'RE LEAVING KEYSTONE CITY.
YOU'RE LEAVING?
JOAN, DO YOU WANT SOME WATER?
THAT WOULD BE NICE.
I THOUGHT YOU LOVED THIS HOUSE? YOUR PARENTS LIVED HERE, JOAN. THEIR PARENTS BEFORE THAT.
I DO LOVE THIS HOUSE, LINDA. AND THIS CITY. IT'S OUR HOME.
WE'RE HEADING TO DENVER... WE'LL BE BACK IN A FEW MONTHS.
I'M... SORRY, IRIS. WHEN I HEARD YOU RETURNED, AND WITH A NEW ADOPTED BABY... I WISH THIS COULD'VE BEEN A GATHERING FOR CELEBRATION.
ADORABLE CHILD.
JOAN, WHAT IS IT?
LAST WEEK, I FELT STRANGE... ILL. MY DOCTOR TOLD ME IT WAS A "DARK" MIRACLE.
HE'S NEVER SEEN SOMEONE... AFFLICTED SO... QUICKLY.
WE THOUGHT YOU SHOULD KNOW. YOU'RE OUR FAMILY. WITH MAX DISAPPEARING, WE DIDN'T WANT TO UPSET BART ANY MORE THAN WE HAD TO.

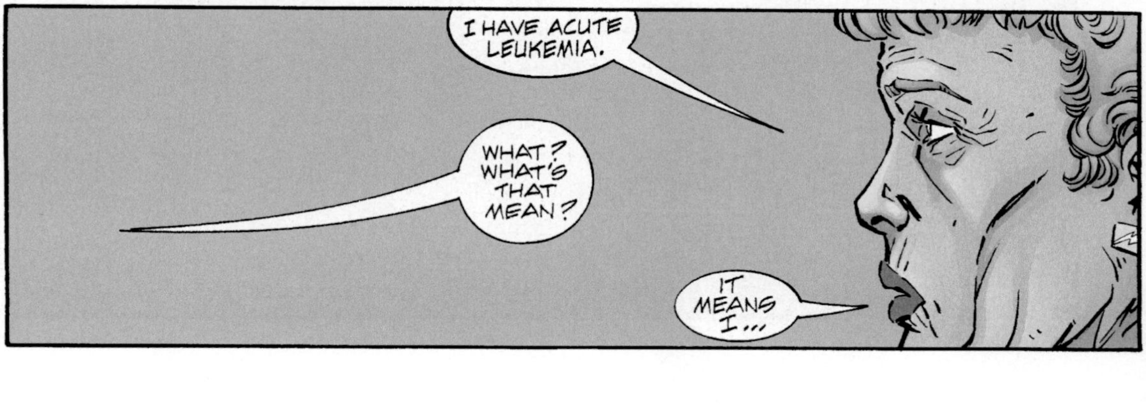
I HAVE ACUTE LEUKEMIA.
WHAT? WHAT'S THAT MEAN?
IT MEANS I...

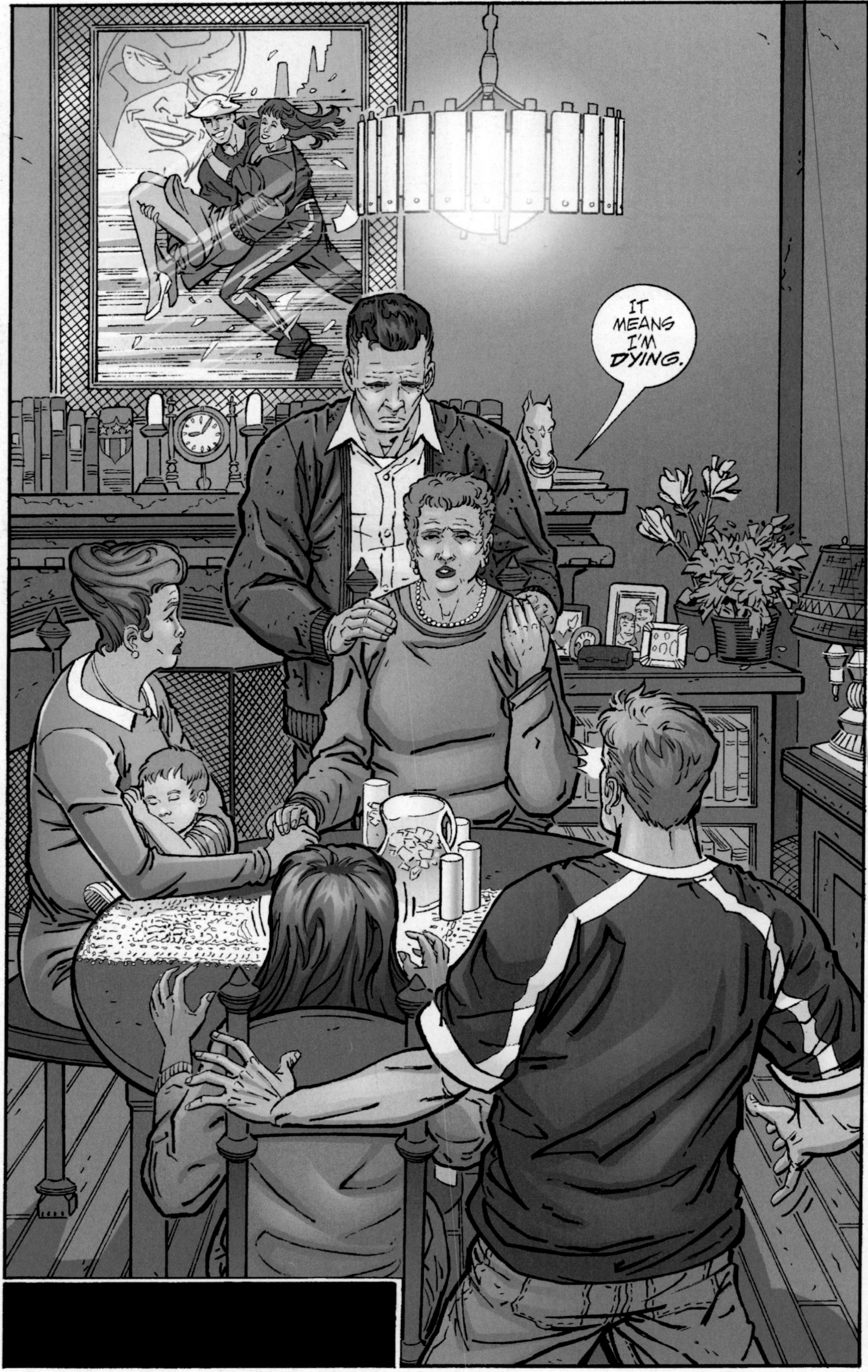
IT MEANS I'M DYING.

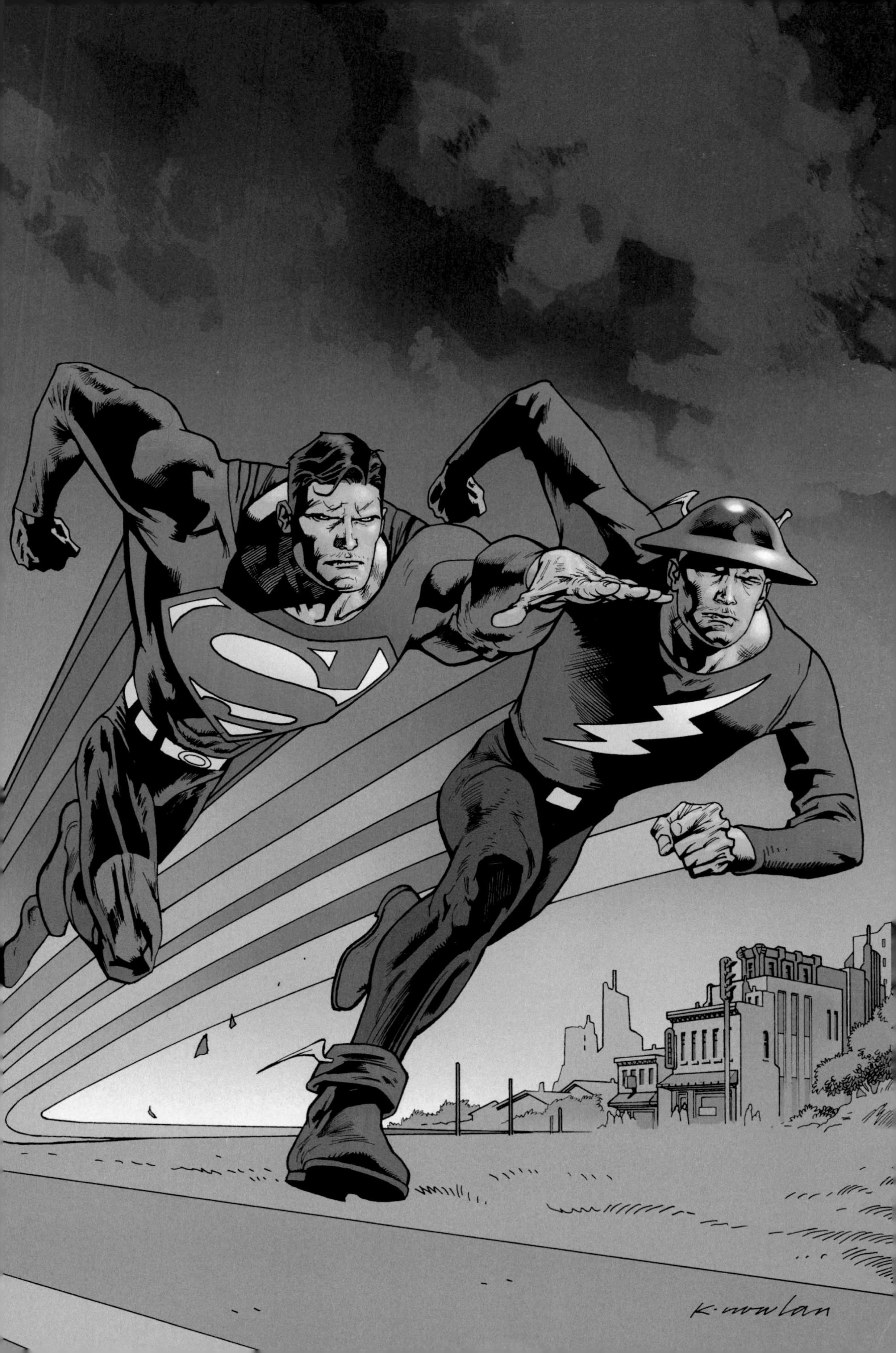
K·nowlan

COVER ART BY **KEVIN NOWLAN**

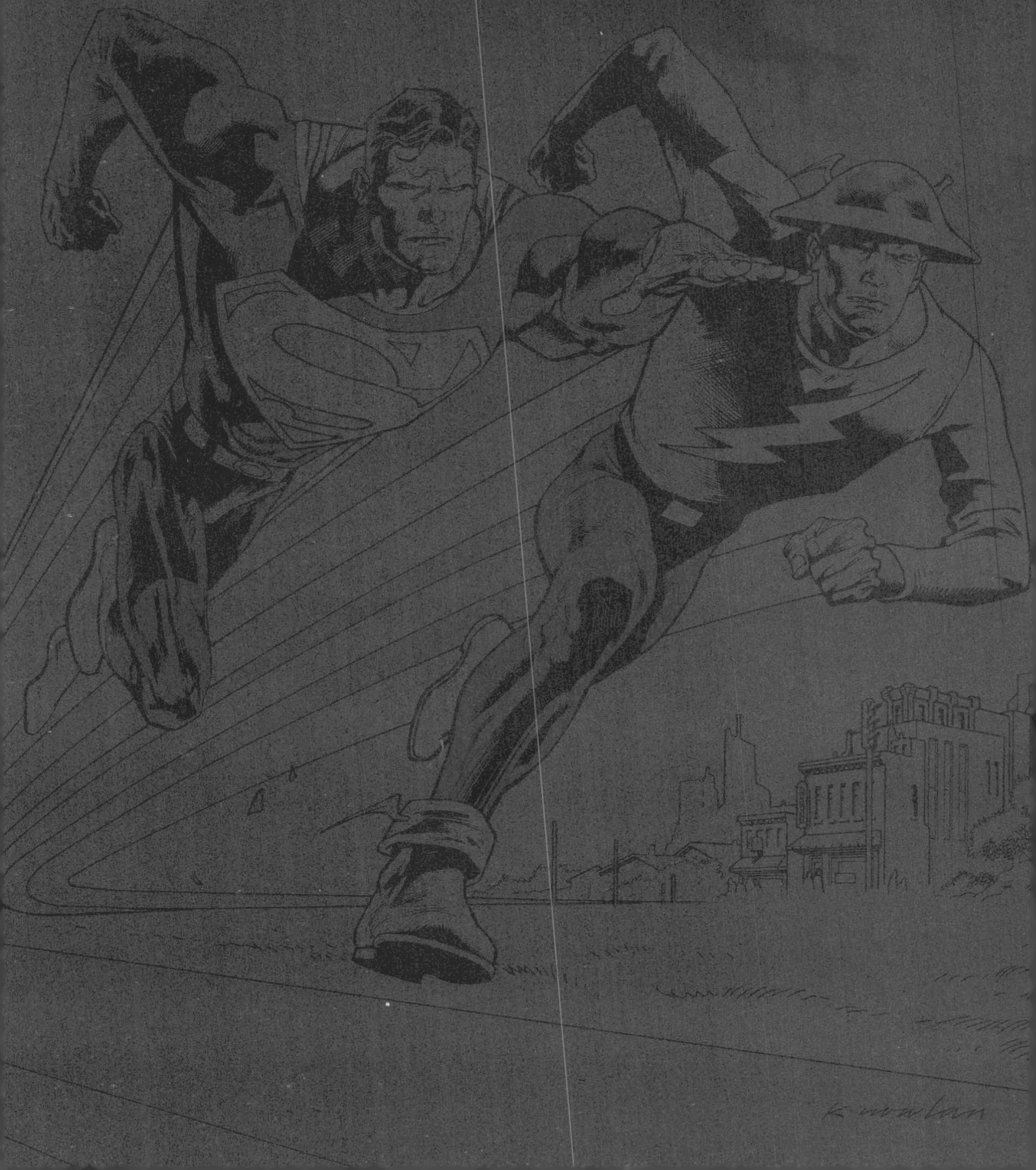

k nowlan

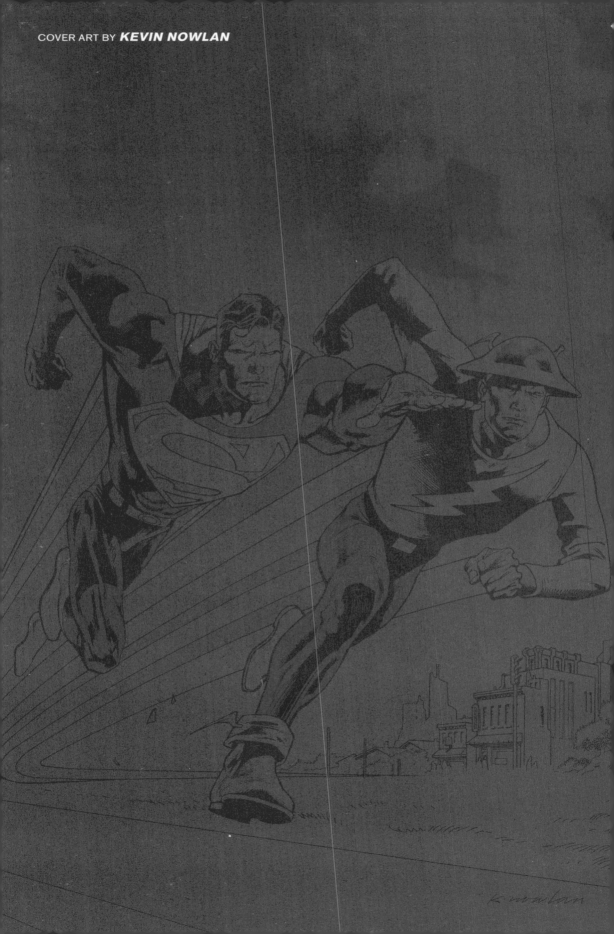

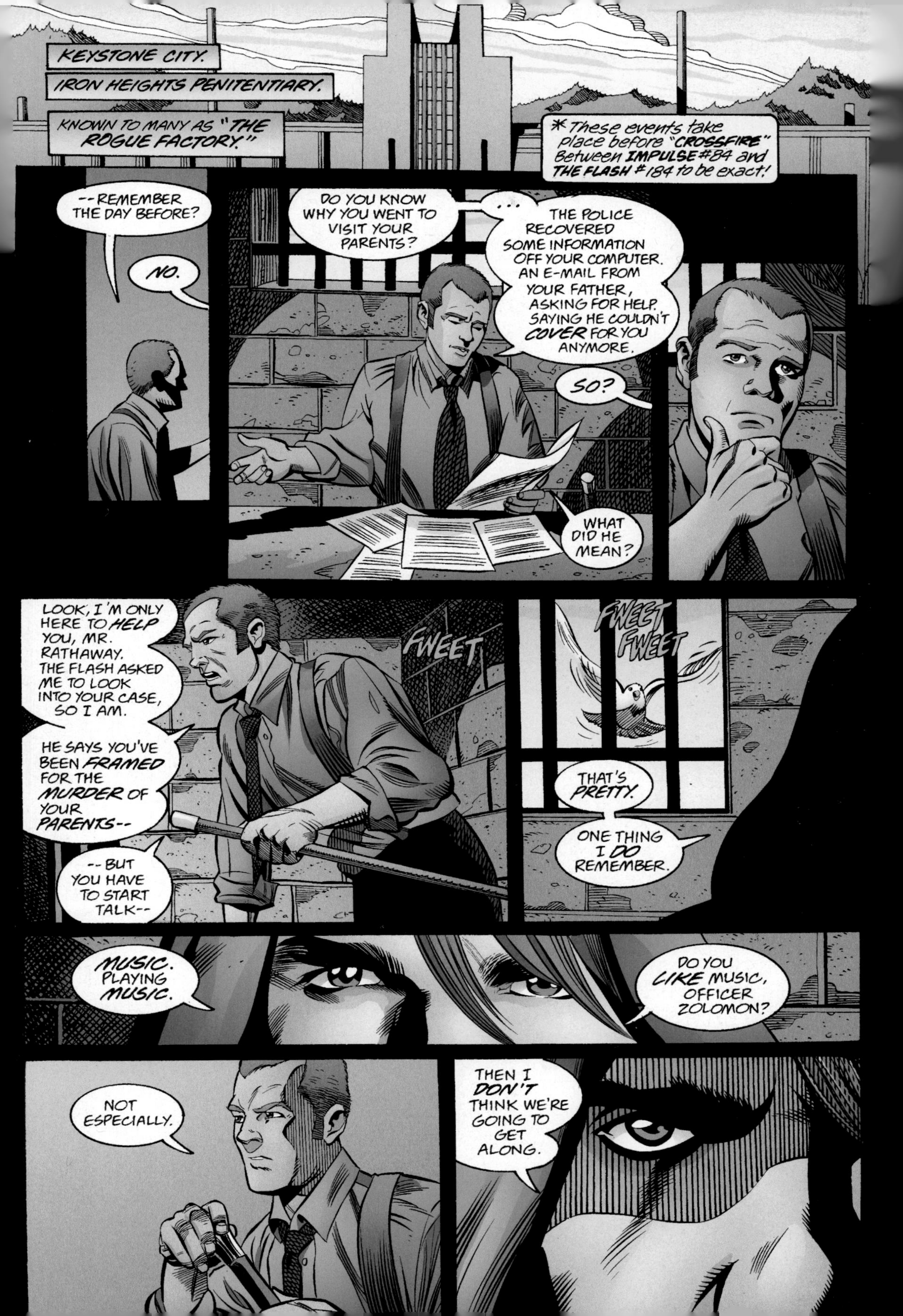

KEYSTONE CITY.
IRON HEIGHTS PENITENTIARY.
KNOWN TO MANY AS "THE ROGUE FACTORY."
* These events take place before "CROSSFIRE" Between IMPULSE #84 and THE FLASH #184 to be exact!
--REMEMBER THE DAY BEFORE?
NO.
DO YOU KNOW WHY YOU WENT TO VISIT YOUR PARENTS?
...
THE POLICE RECOVERED SOME INFORMATION OFF YOUR COMPUTER. AN E-MAIL FROM YOUR FATHER, ASKING FOR HELP. SAYING HE COULDN'T COVER FOR YOU ANYMORE.
SO?
WHAT DID HE MEAN?
LOOK, I'M ONLY HERE TO HELP YOU, MR. RATHAWAY. THE FLASH ASKED ME TO LOOK INTO YOUR CASE, SO I AM.
HE SAYS YOU'VE BEEN FRAMED FOR THE MURDER OF YOUR PARENTS--
--BUT YOU HAVE TO START TALK--
FWEET
FWEET FWEET
THAT'S PRETTY.
ONE THING I DO REMEMBER.
MUSIC. PLAYING MUSIC.
DO YOU LIKE MUSIC, OFFICER ZOLOMON?
NOT ESPECIALLY.
THEN I DON'T THINK WE'RE GOING TO GET ALONG.

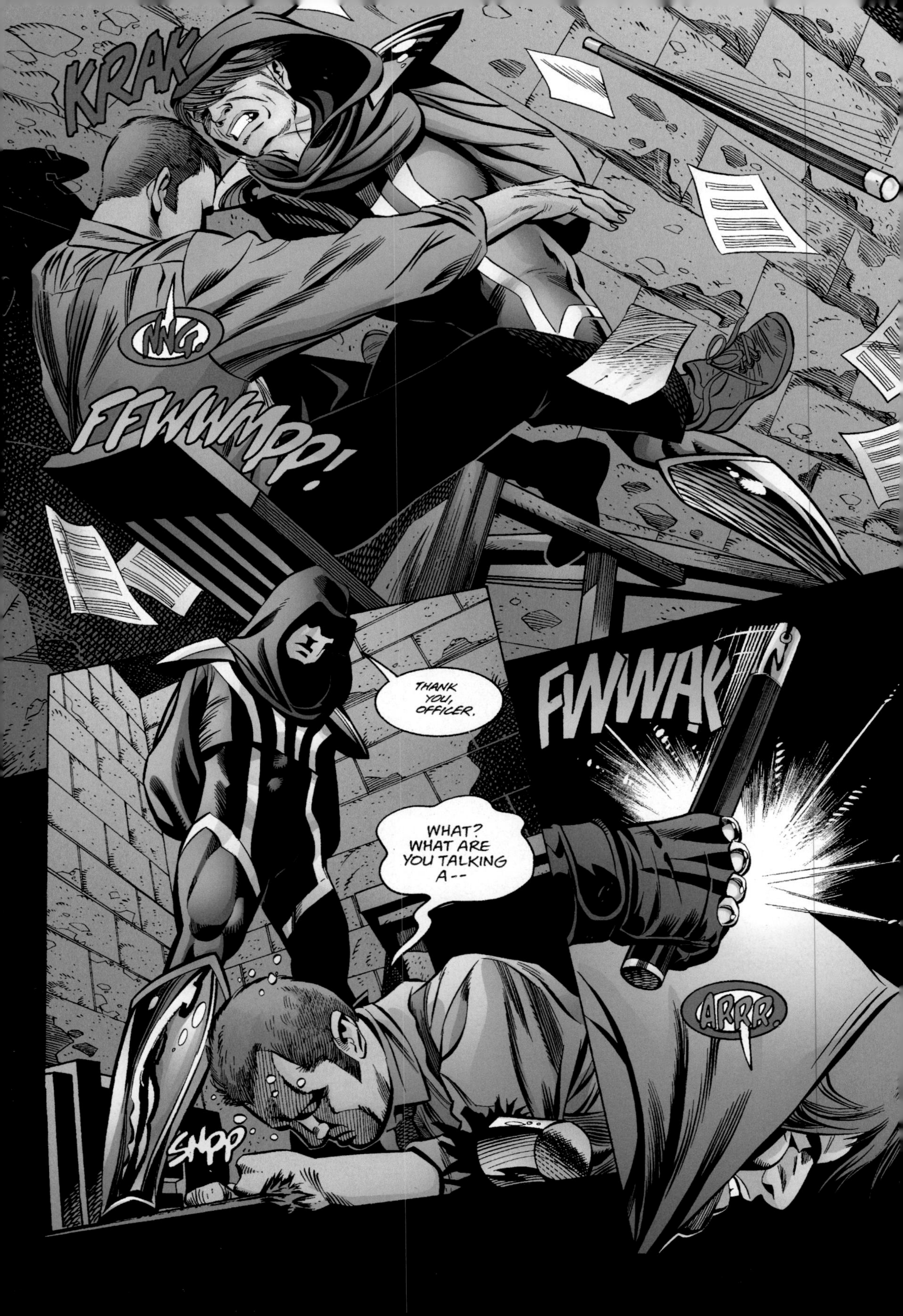
KRAK
NNG.
FFWWMPP!
THANK YOU, OFFICER.
FWWAK
WHAT? WHAT ARE YOU TALKING A--
ARRR.
SNPP

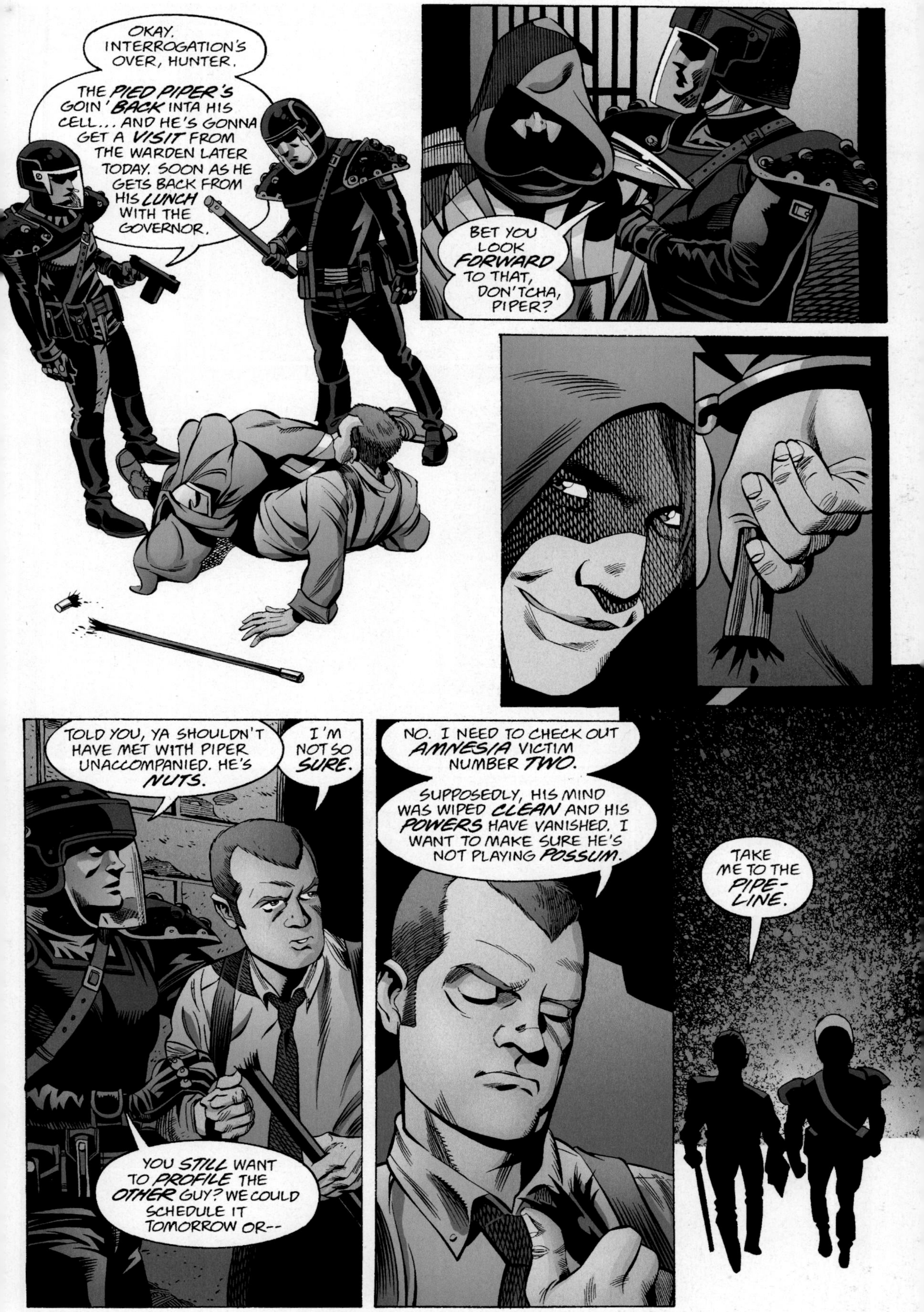
OKAY. INTERROGATION'S OVER, HUNTER.
THE PIED PIPER'S GOIN' BACK INTA HIS CELL... AND HE'S GONNA GET A VISIT FROM THE WARDEN LATER TODAY. SOON AS HE GETS BACK FROM HIS LUNCH WITH THE GOVERNOR.
BET YOU LOOK FORWARD TO THAT, DON'TCHA, PIPER?
TOLD YOU, YA SHOULDN'T HAVE MET WITH PIPER UNACCOMPANIED. HE'S NUTS.
I'M NOT SO SURE.
YOU STILL WANT TO PROFILE THE OTHER GUY? WE COULD SCHEDULE IT TOMORROW OR--
NO. I NEED TO CHECK OUT AMNESIA VICTIM NUMBER TWO.
SUPPOSEDLY, HIS MIND WAS WIPED CLEAN AND HIS POWERS HAVE VANISHED. I WANT TO MAKE SURE HE'S NOT PLAYING POSSUM.
TAKE ME TO THE PIPE-LINE.

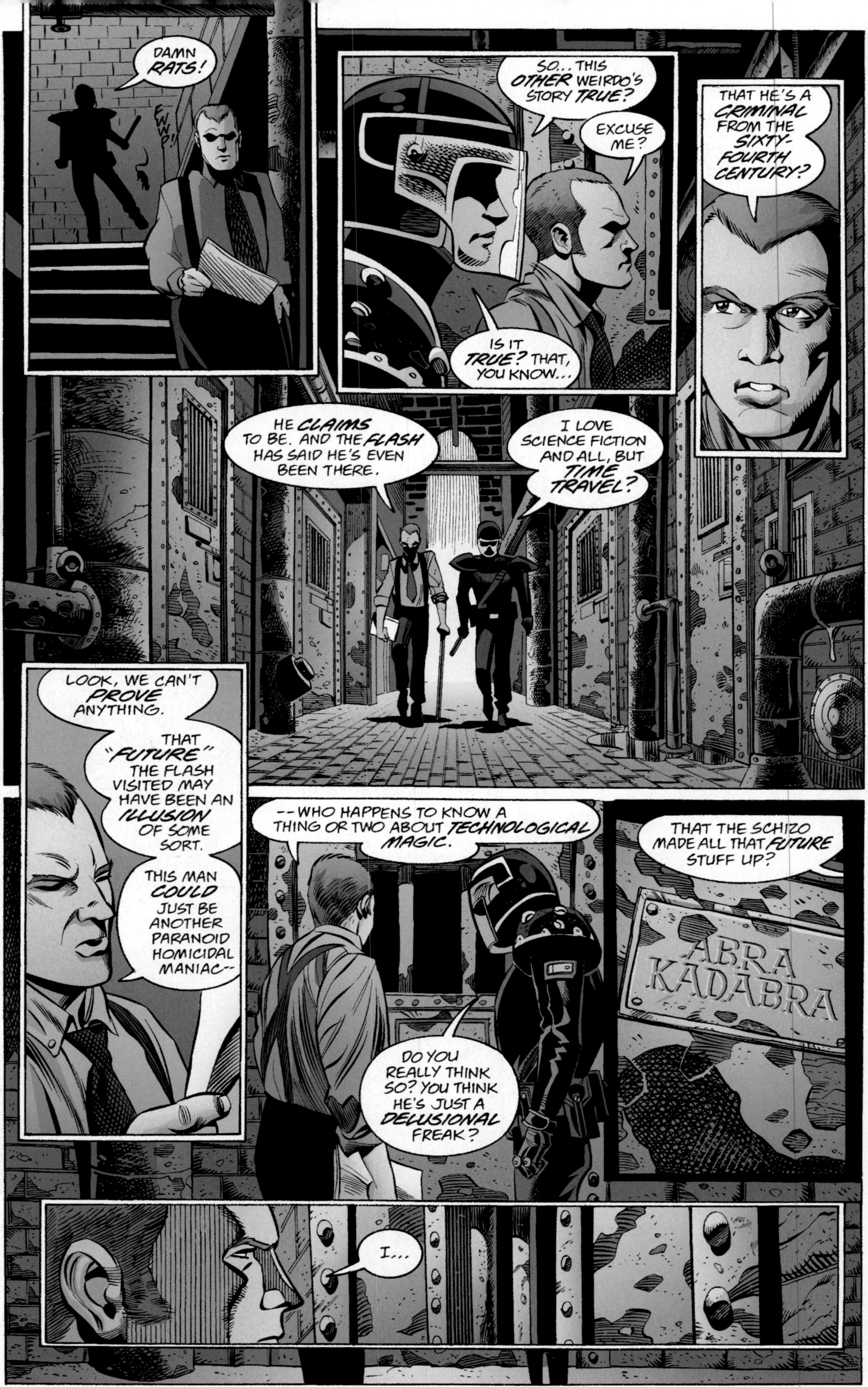
DAMN RATS!
FWWP!
SO... THIS OTHER WEIRDO'S STORY TRUE?
EXCUSE ME?
IS IT TRUE? THAT, YOU KNOW...
THAT HE'S A CRIMINAL FROM THE SIXTY-FOURTH CENTURY?
HE CLAIMS TO BE. AND THE FLASH HAS SAID HE'S EVEN BEEN THERE.
I LOVE SCIENCE FICTION AND ALL, BUT TIME TRAVEL?
LOOK, WE CAN'T PROVE ANYTHING.
THAT "FUTURE" THE FLASH VISITED MAY HAVE BEEN AN ILLUSION OF SOME SORT.
THIS MAN COULD JUST BE ANOTHER PARANOID HOMICIDAL MANIAC--
--WHO HAPPENS TO KNOW A THING OR TWO ABOUT TECHNOLOGICAL MAGIC.
DO YOU REALLY THINK SO? YOU THINK HE'S JUST A DELUSIONAL FREAK?
THAT THE SCHIZO MADE ALL THAT FUTURE STUFF UP?
ABRA KADABRA
I...

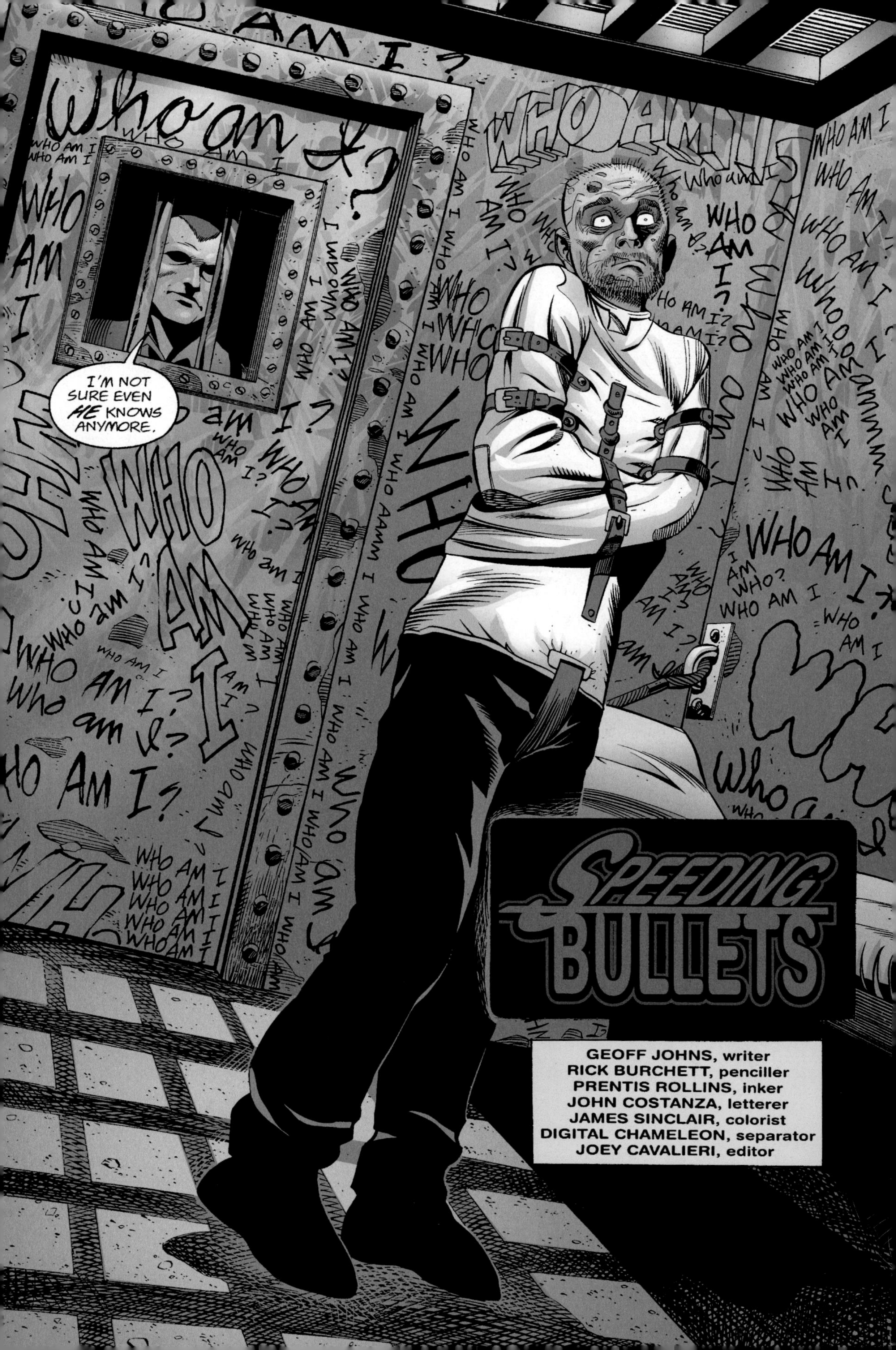
I'M NOT SURE EVEN HE KNOWS ANYMORE.
SPEEDING BULLETS
GEOFF JOHNS, writer
RICK BURCHETT, penciller
PRENTIS ROLLINS, inker
JOHN COSTANZA, letterer
JAMES SINCLAIR, colorist
DIGITAL CHAMELEON, separator
JOEY CAVALIERI, editor

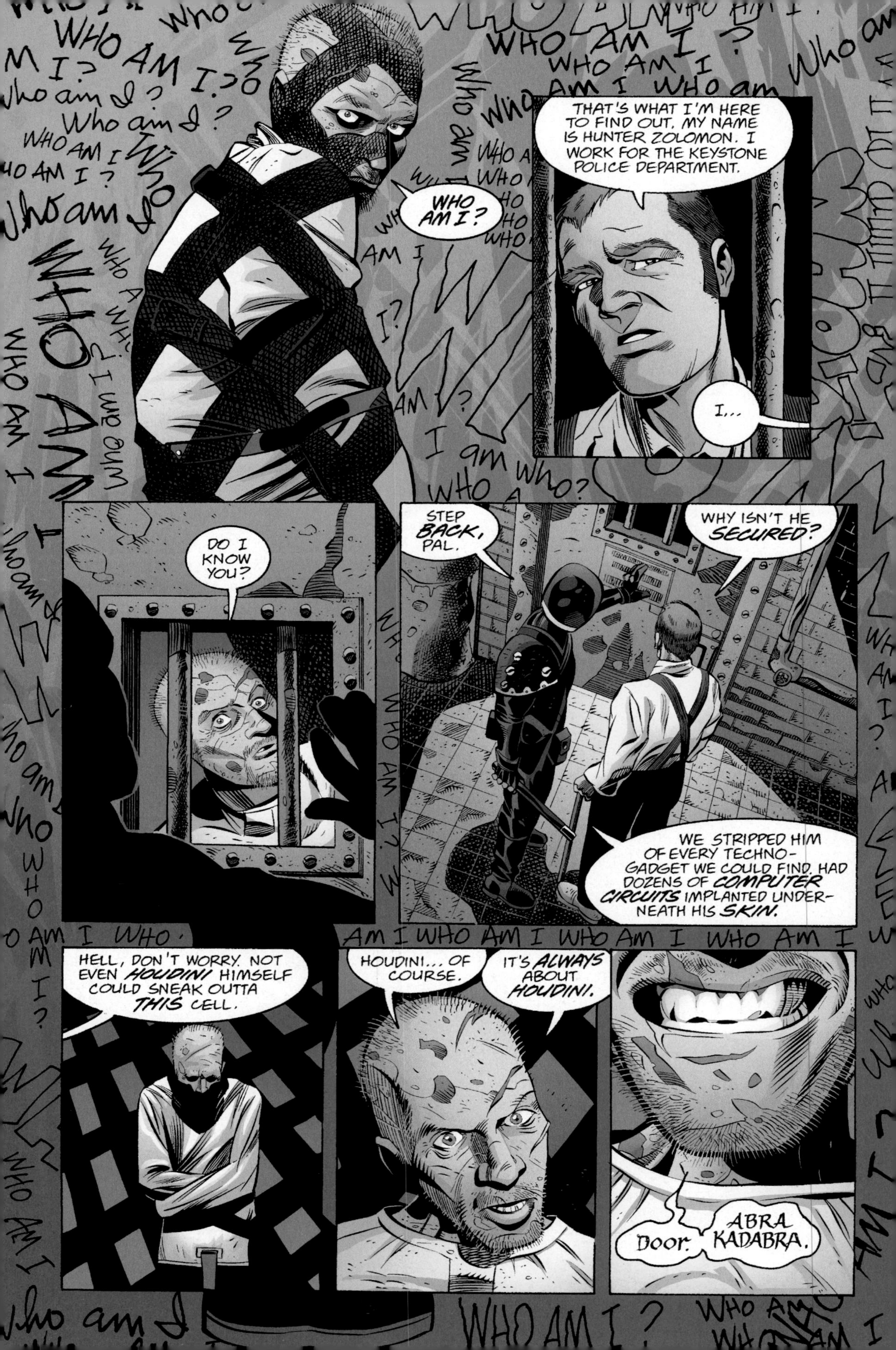
WHO AM I?
THAT'S WHAT I'M HERE TO FIND OUT. MY NAME IS HUNTER ZOLOMON. I WORK FOR THE KEYSTONE POLICE DEPARTMENT.
I...
DO I KNOW YOU?
STEP BACK, PAL.
WHY ISN'T HE SECURED?
WE STRIPPED HIM OF EVERY TECHNO-GADGET WE COULD FIND. HAD DOZENS OF COMPUTER CIRCUITS IMPLANTED UNDERNEATH HIS SKIN.
HELL, DON'T WORRY. NOT EVEN HOUDINI HIMSELF COULD SNEAK OUTTA THIS CELL.
HOUDINI... OF COURSE.
IT'S ALWAYS ABOUT HOUDINI.
ABRA KADABRA.
Door.
WHO AM I? WHO AM I WHO AM I WHO AM I WHO AM I

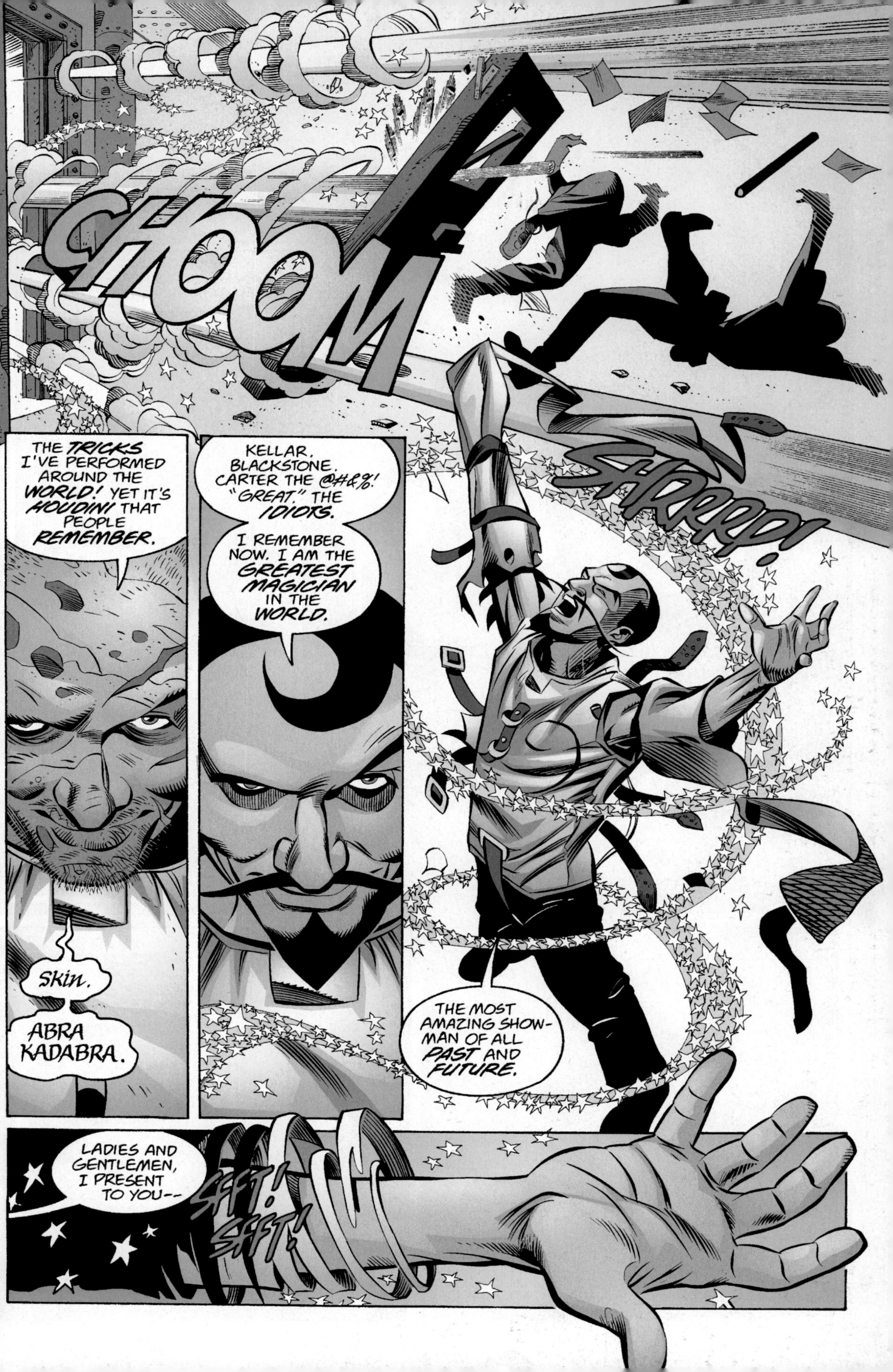
CHOOM!
SHRRRP!
THE TRICKS I'VE PERFORMED AROUND THE WORLD! YET IT'S HOUDINI THAT PEOPLE REMEMBER.
KELLAR. BLACKSTONE. CARTER THE @#&%! "GREAT." THE IDIOTS.
I REMEMBER NOW. I AM THE GREATEST MAGICIAN IN THE WORLD.
Skin.
ABRA KADABRA.
THE MOST AMAZING SHOWMAN OF ALL PAST AND FUTURE.
LADIES AND GENTLEMEN, I PRESENT TO YOU--
SFFT! SFFT!

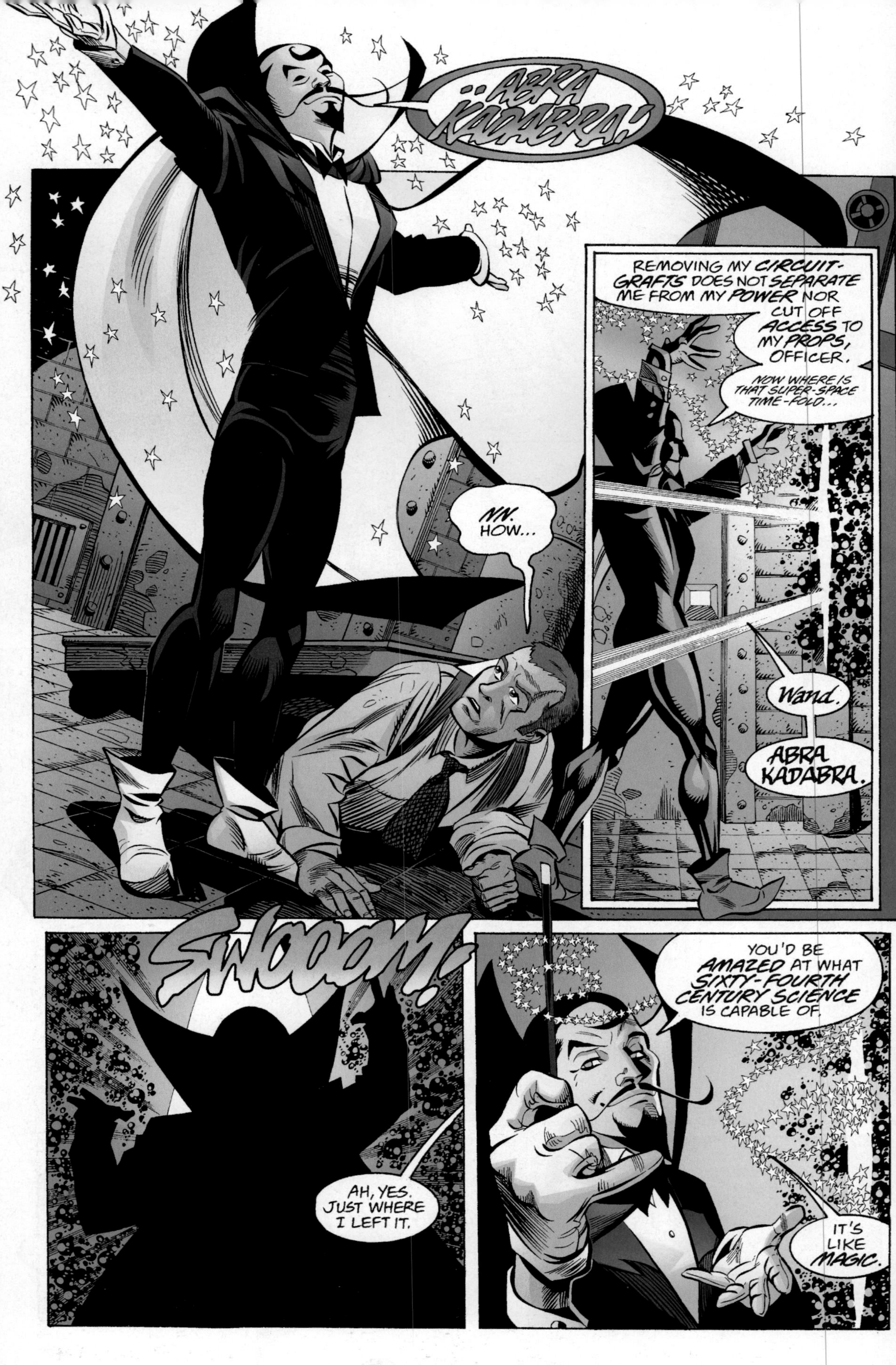
..ABRA KADABRA!
REMOVING MY CIRCUIT-GRAFTS DOES NOT SEPARATE ME FROM MY POWER NOR CUT OFF ACCESS TO MY PROPS, OFFICER.
NOW WHERE IS THAT SUPER-SPACE TIME-FOLD...
NN. HOW...
Wand.
ABRA KADABRA.
SWOOOM!
AH, YES. JUST WHERE I LEFT IT.
YOU'D BE AMAZED AT WHAT SIXTY-FOURTH CENTURY SCIENCE IS CAPABLE OF.
IT'S LIKE MAGIC.

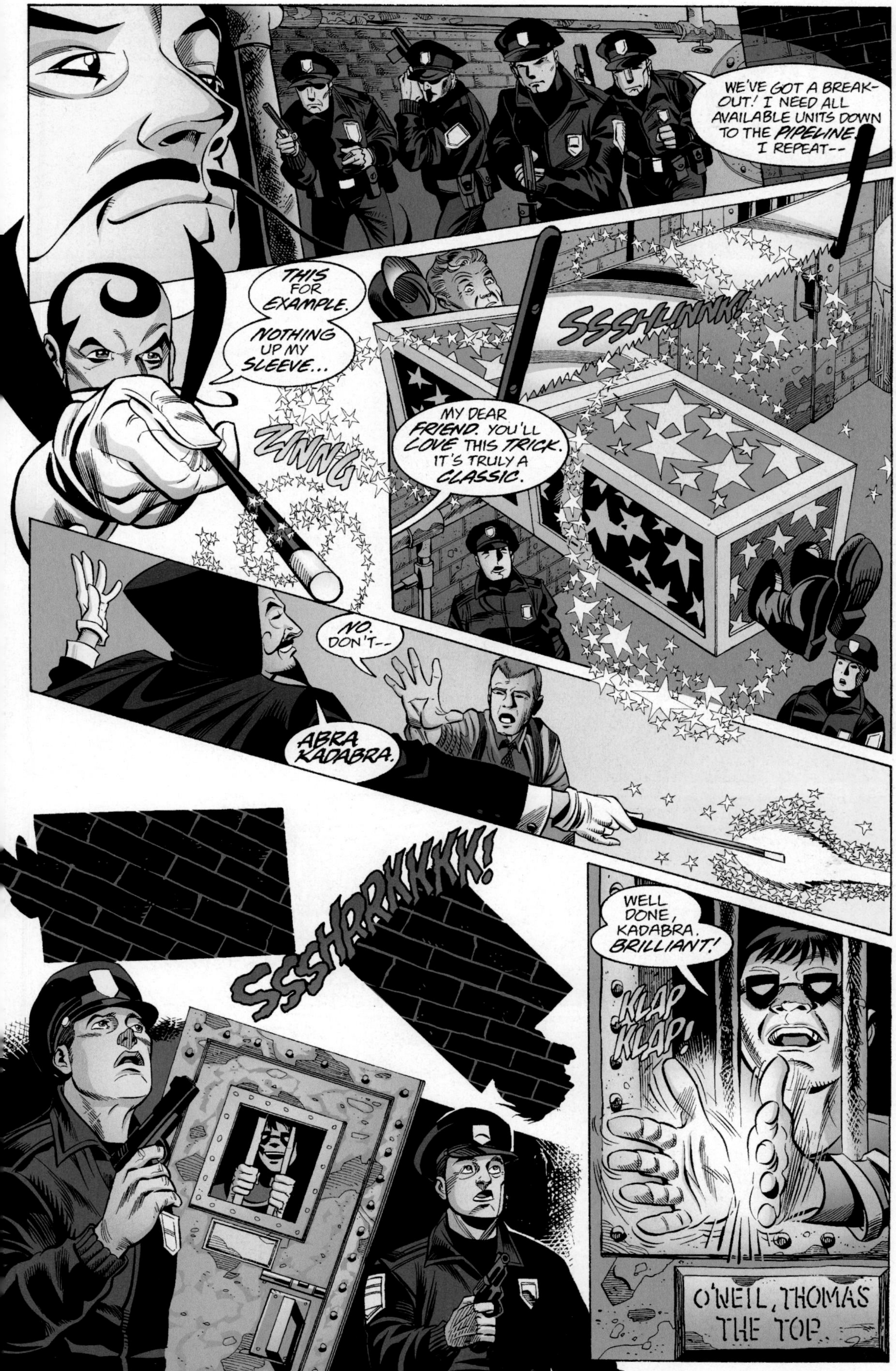

WE'VE GOT A BREAK-OUT! I NEED ALL AVAILABLE UNITS DOWN TO THE PIPELINE. I REPEAT--
THIS FOR EXAMPLE.
NOTHING UP MY SLEEVE...
ZINNG
SSSHUNNNK!
MY DEAR FRIEND. YOU'LL LOVE THIS TRICK. IT'S TRULY A CLASSIC.
NO. DON'T--
ABRA KADABRA.
SSSHRRKKKK!
WELL DONE, KADABRA. BRILLIANT!
KLAP KLAP!
O'NEIL, THOMAS
THE TOP

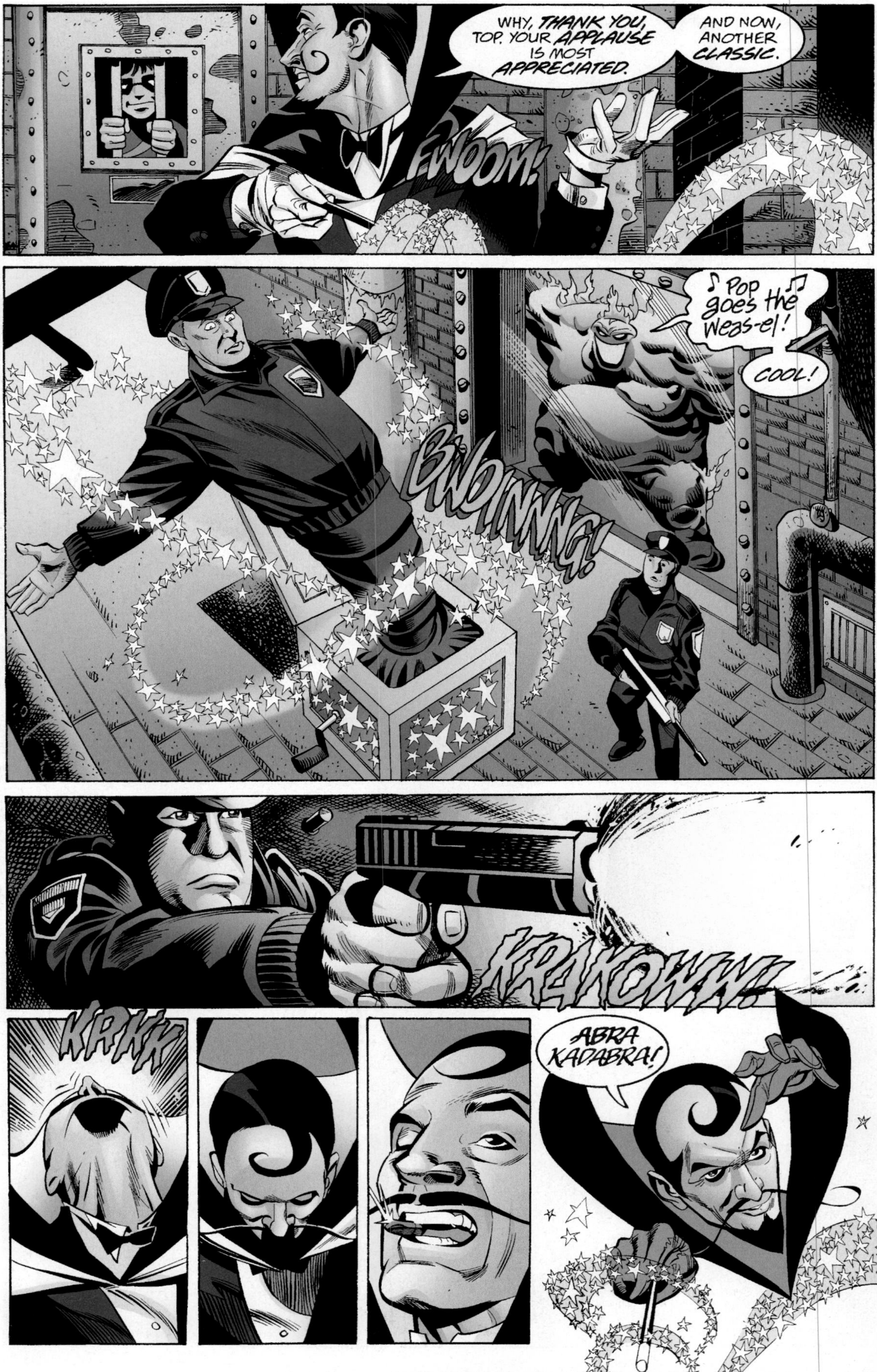
WHY, THANK YOU, TOP. YOUR APPLAUSE IS MOST APPRECIATED.
AND NOW, ANOTHER CLASSIC.
FWOOM!
♪ Pop goes the Weas-el! ♫
COOL!
BWOINNNG!
KRAKOWW!
KRKK
ABRA KADABRA!

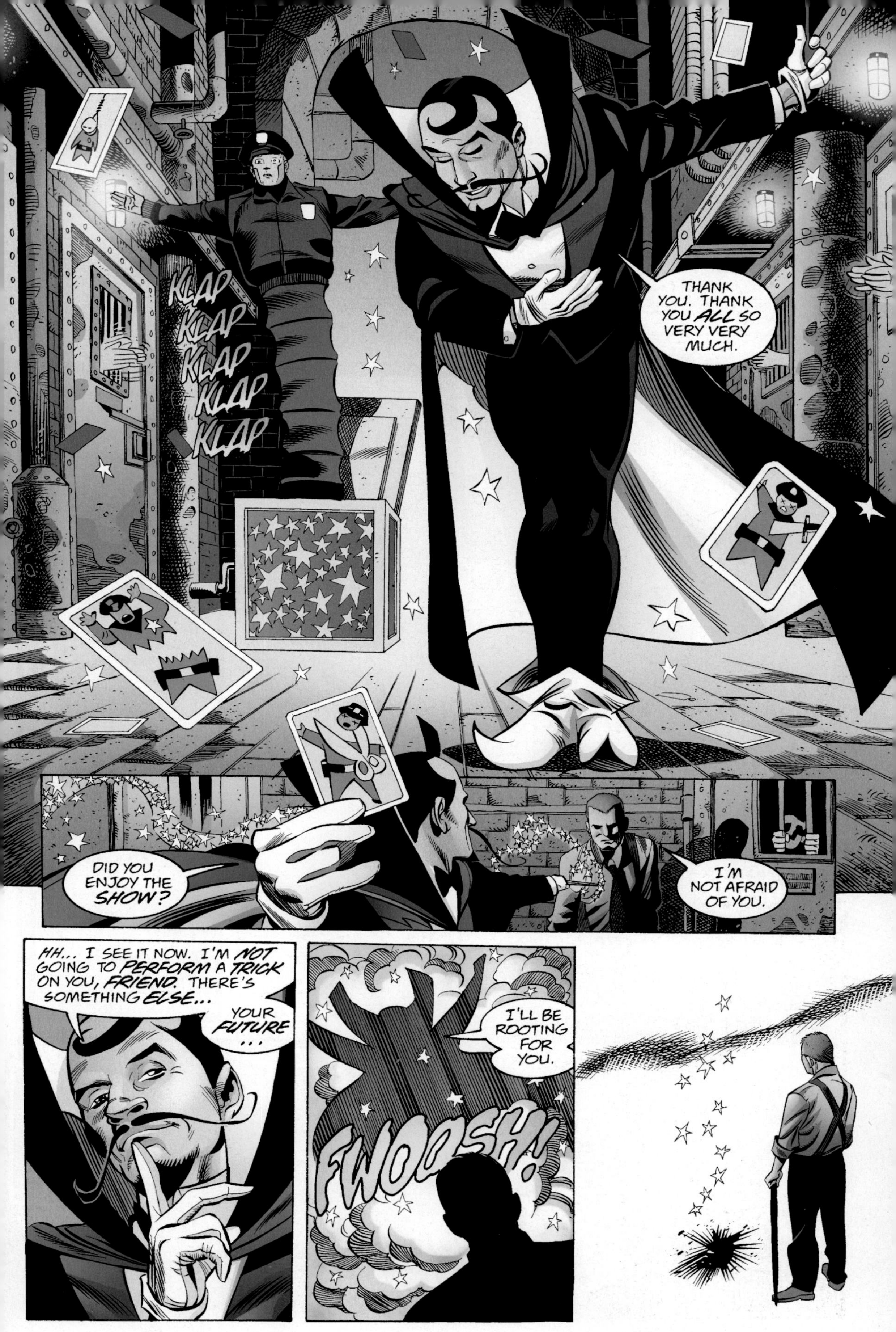
KLAP KLAP KLAP KLAP KLAP
THANK YOU. THANK YOU ALL SO VERY VERY MUCH.
DID YOU ENJOY THE SHOW?
I'M NOT AFRAID OF YOU.
HH... I SEE IT NOW. I'M NOT GOING TO PERFORM A TRICK ON YOU, FRIEND. THERE'S SOMETHING ELSE...
YOUR FUTURE...
I'LL BE ROOTING FOR YOU.
FWOOSH!

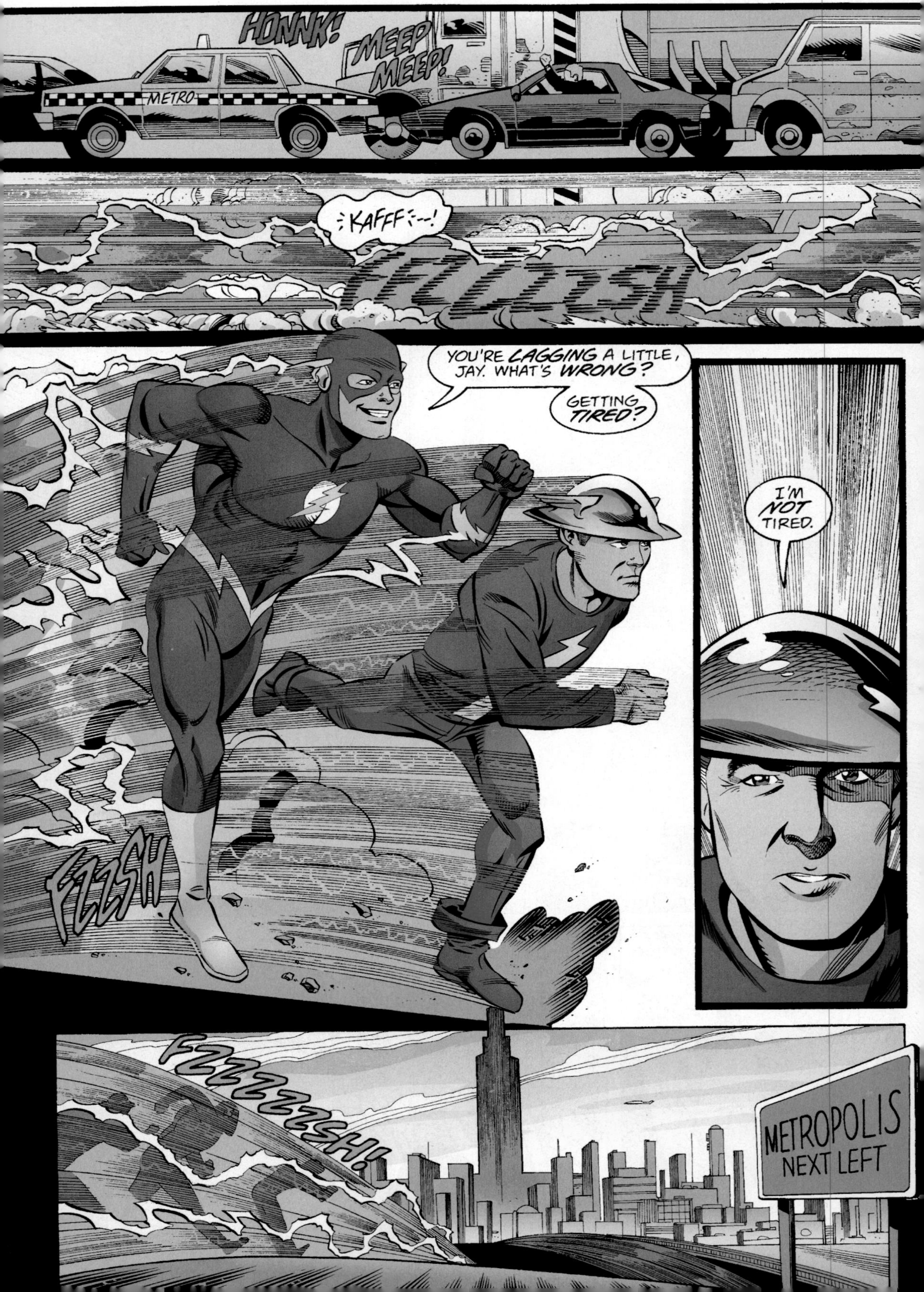
HONNK!
MEEP MEEP!
METRO
KAFFF--!
FFZZZSH
YOU'RE LAGGING A LITTLE, JAY. WHAT'S WRONG?
GETTING TIRED?
I'M NOT TIRED.
FZZSH
FZZZZZZSH!
METROPOLIS NEXT LEFT

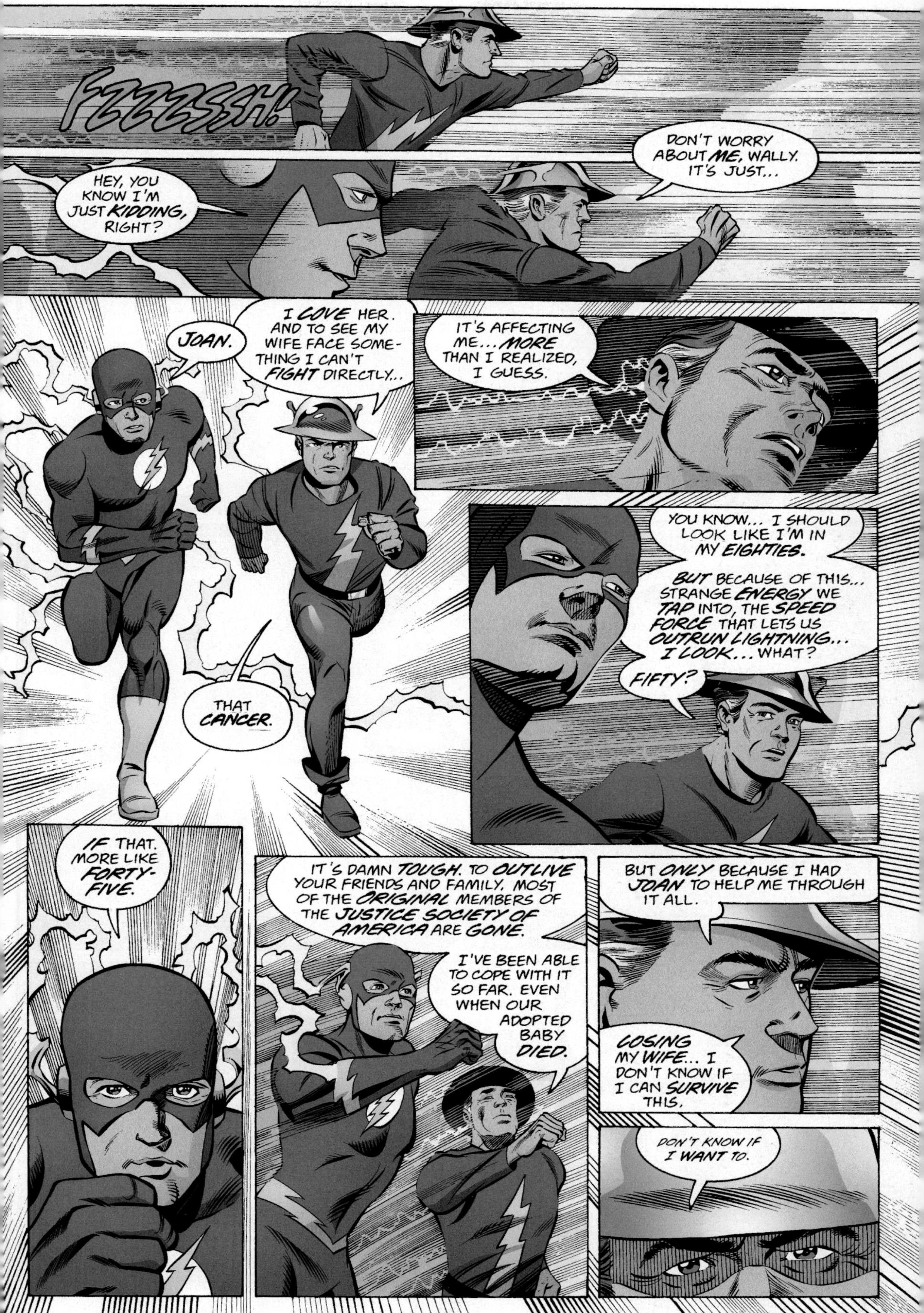
FZZZSSSH!
HEY, YOU KNOW I'M JUST KIDDING, RIGHT?
DON'T WORRY ABOUT ME, WALLY. IT'S JUST...
JOAN.
I LOVE HER. AND TO SEE MY WIFE FACE SOMETHING I CAN'T FIGHT DIRECTLY...
THAT CANCER.
IT'S AFFECTING ME... MORE THAN I REALIZED, I GUESS.
YOU KNOW... I SHOULD LOOK LIKE I'M IN MY EIGHTIES.
BUT BECAUSE OF THIS... STRANGE ENERGY WE TAP INTO, THE SPEED FORCE THAT LETS US OUTRUN LIGHTNING... I LOOK... WHAT?
FIFTY?
IF THAT. MORE LIKE FORTY-FIVE.
IT'S DAMN TOUGH. TO OUTLIVE YOUR FRIENDS AND FAMILY. MOST OF THE ORIGINAL MEMBERS OF THE JUSTICE SOCIETY OF AMERICA ARE GONE.
I'VE BEEN ABLE TO COPE WITH IT SO FAR. EVEN WHEN OUR ADOPTED BABY DIED.
BUT ONLY BECAUSE I HAD JOAN TO HELP ME THROUGH IT ALL.
LOSING MY WIFE... I DON'T KNOW IF I CAN SURVIVE THIS.
DON'T KNOW IF I WANT TO.

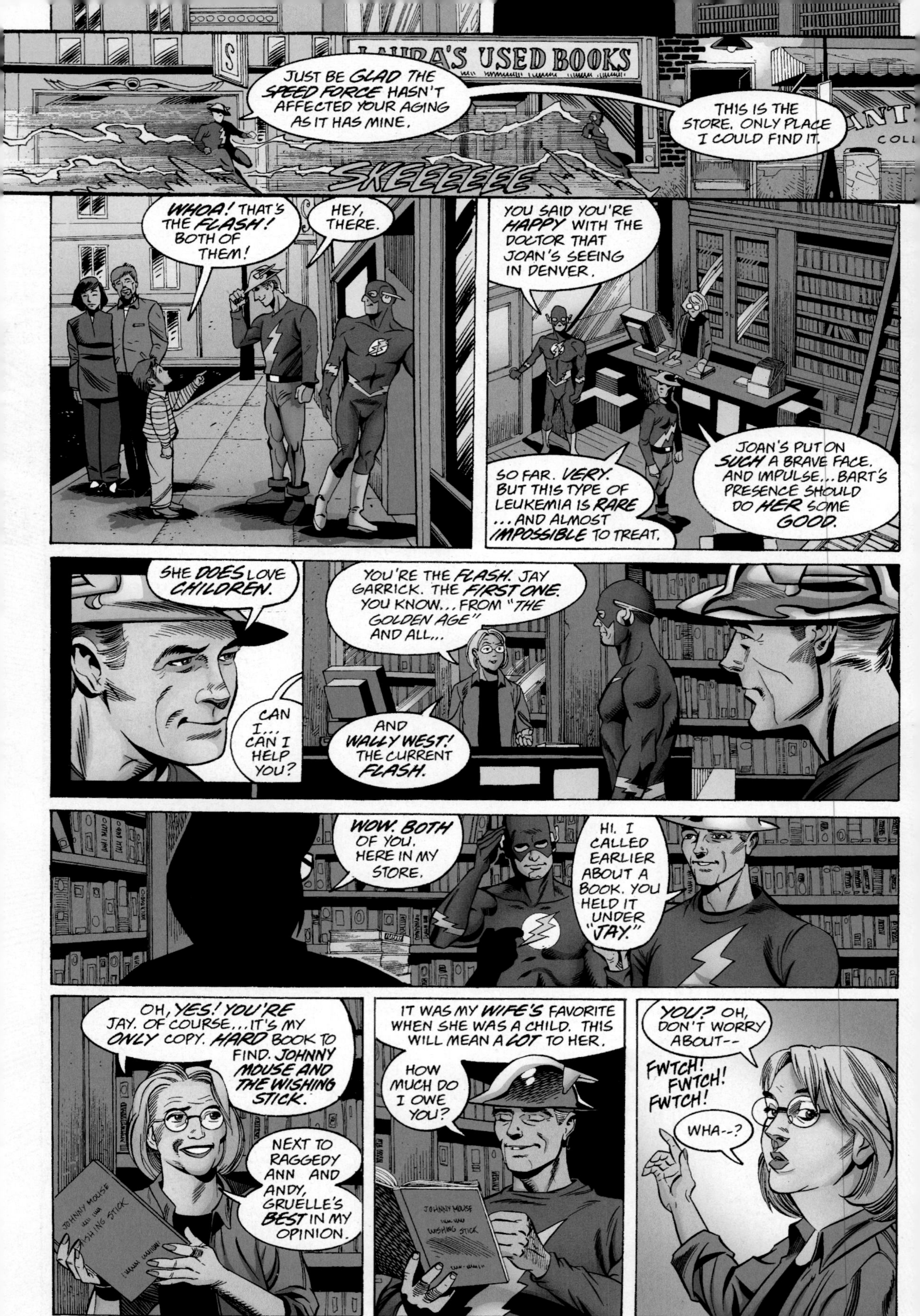
LAURA'S USED BOOKS
JUST BE GLAD THE SPEED FORCE HASN'T AFFECTED YOUR AGING AS IT HAS MINE.
THIS IS THE STORE. ONLY PLACE I COULD FIND IT.
SKEEEEEEE
WHOA! THAT'S THE FLASH! BOTH OF THEM!
HEY, THERE.
YOU SAID YOU'RE HAPPY WITH THE DOCTOR THAT JOAN'S SEEING IN DENVER.
SO FAR. VERY. BUT THIS TYPE OF LEUKEMIA IS RARE ...AND ALMOST IMPOSSIBLE TO TREAT.
JOAN'S PUT ON SUCH A BRAVE FACE. AND IMPULSE... BART'S PRESENCE SHOULD DO HER SOME GOOD.
SHE DOES LOVE CHILDREN.
CAN I... CAN I HELP YOU?
YOU'RE THE FLASH. JAY GARRICK. THE FIRST ONE. YOU KNOW... FROM "THE GOLDEN AGE" AND ALL...
AND WALLY WEST! THE CURRENT FLASH.
WOW. BOTH OF YOU. HERE IN MY STORE.
HI. I CALLED EARLIER ABOUT A BOOK. YOU HELD IT UNDER "JAY."
OH, YES! YOU'RE JAY. OF COURSE... IT'S MY ONLY COPY. HARD BOOK TO FIND. JOHNNY MOUSE AND THE WISHING STICK.
NEXT TO RAGGEDY ANN AND ANDY, GRUELLE'S BEST IN MY OPINION.
IT WAS MY WIFE'S FAVORITE WHEN SHE WAS A CHILD. THIS WILL MEAN A LOT TO HER.
HOW MUCH DO I OWE YOU?
YOU? OH, DON'T WORRY ABOUT--
FWTCH! FWTCH! FWTCH!
WHA--?

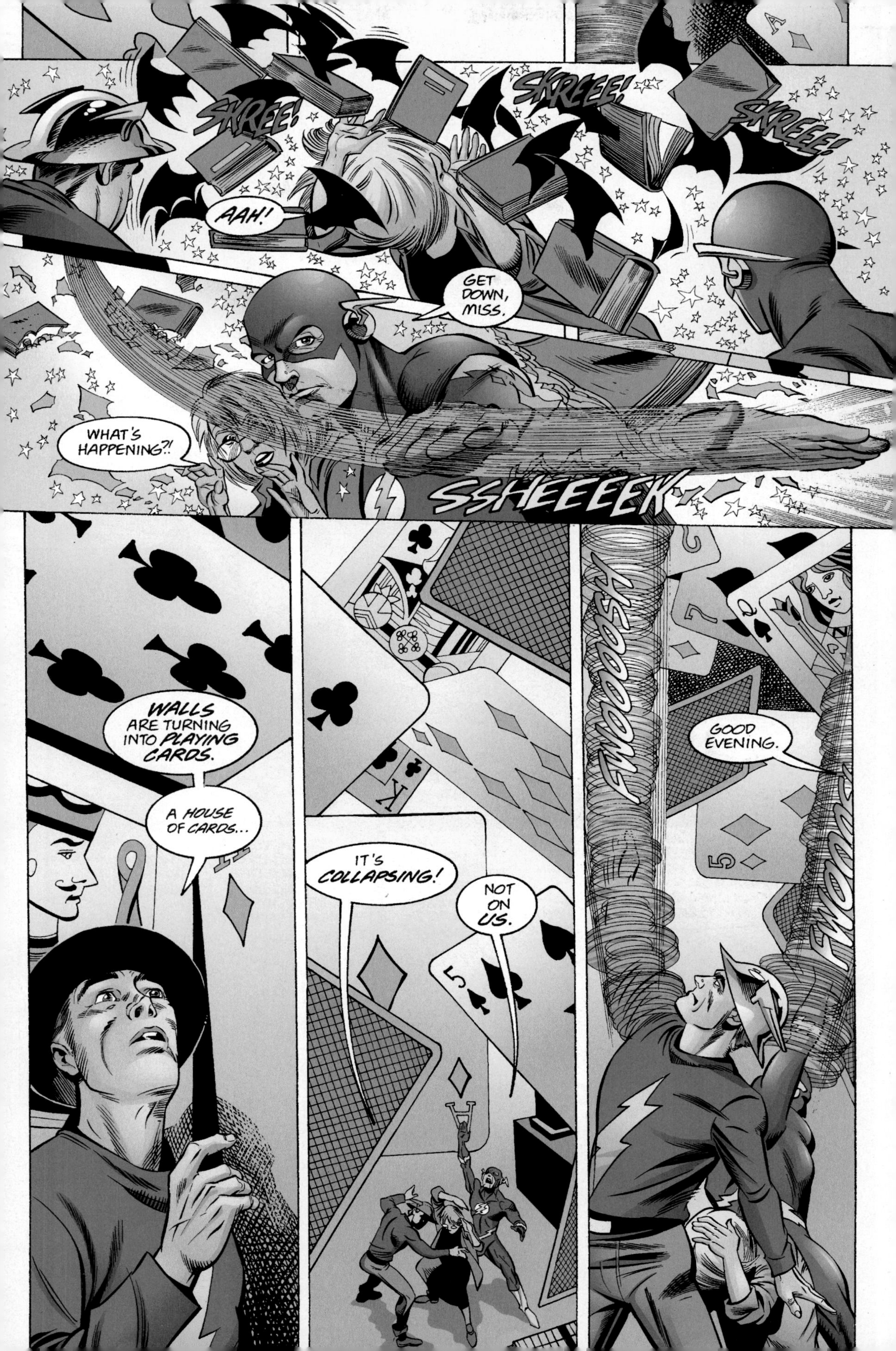
SKREE!
SKREEE!
SKREEE!
AAH!
GET DOWN, MISS.
WHAT'S HAPPENING?!
SSHEEEEK
WALLS ARE TURNING INTO PLAYING CARDS.
A HOUSE OF CARDS...
IT'S COLLAPSING!
NOT ON US.
GOOD EVENING.

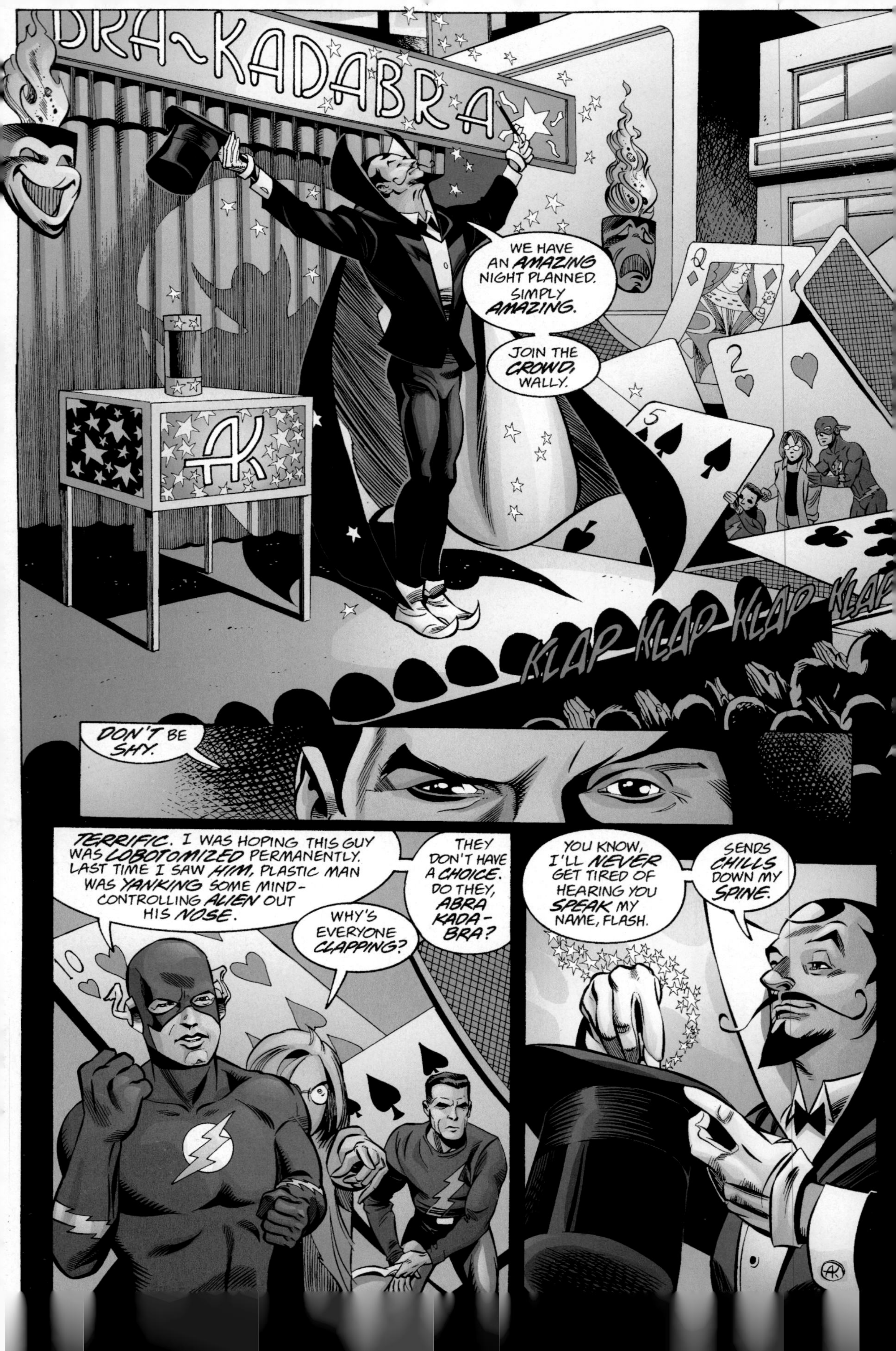

DRA~KADABRA
WE HAVE AN AMAZING NIGHT PLANNED. SIMPLY AMAZING.
JOIN THE CROWD, WALLY.
KLAP KLAP KLAP KLAP KLAP
DON'T BE SHY.
TERRIFIC. I WAS HOPING THIS GUY WAS LOBOTOMIZED PERMANENTLY. LAST TIME I SAW HIM, PLASTIC MAN WAS YANKING SOME MIND-CONTROLLING ALIEN OUT HIS NOSE.
WHY'S EVERYONE CLAPPING?
THEY DON'T HAVE A CHOICE. DO THEY, ABRA KADA-BRA?
YOU KNOW, I'LL NEVER GET TIRED OF HEARING YOU SPEAK MY NAME, FLASH.
SENDS CHILLS DOWN MY SPINE.

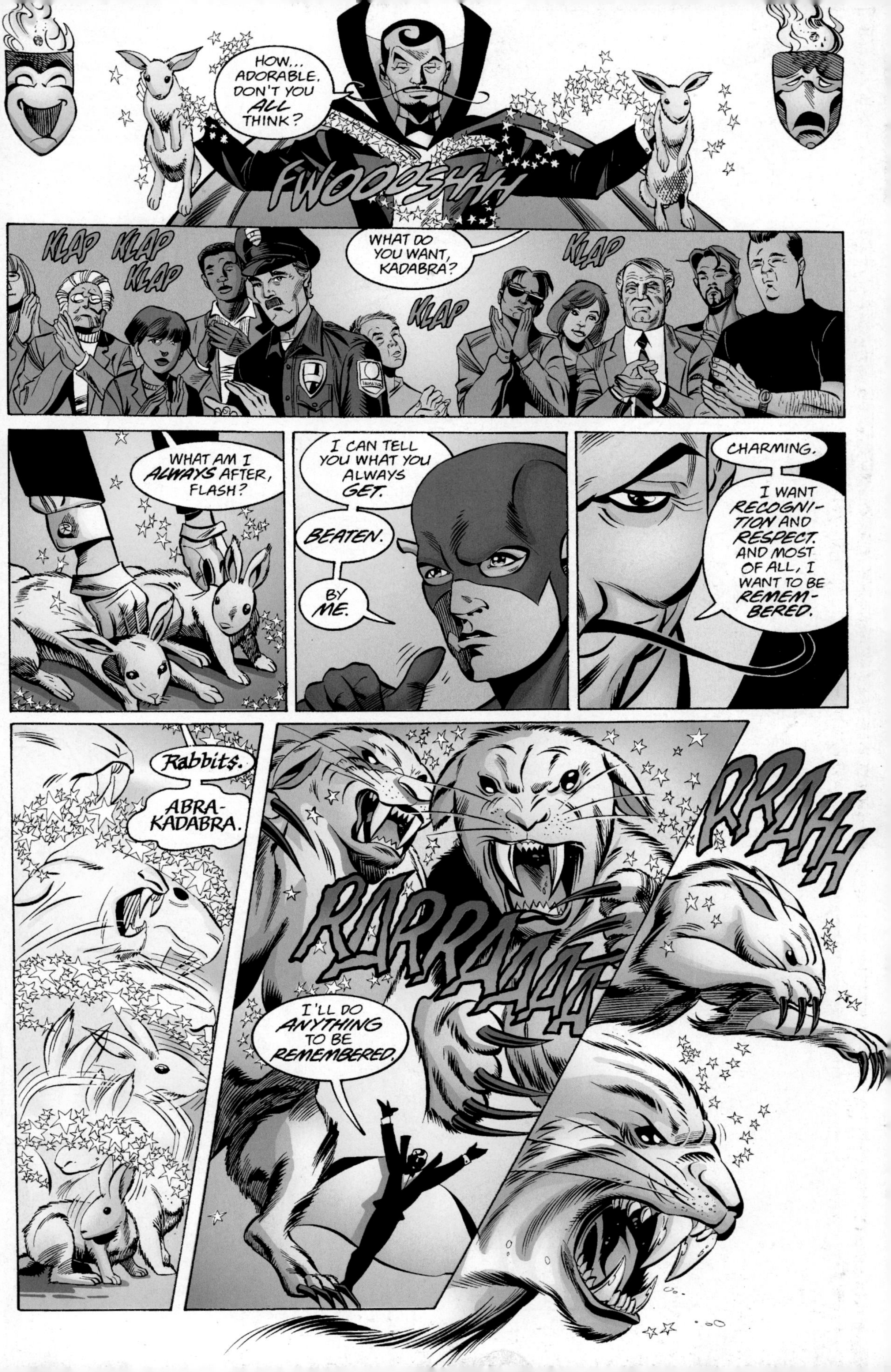
HOW... ADORABLE. DON'T YOU ALL THINK?
FWOOOSHH
KLAP KLAP KLAP
WHAT DO YOU WANT, KADABRA?
KLAP
KLAP
WHAT AM I ALWAYS AFTER, FLASH?
I CAN TELL YOU WHAT YOU ALWAYS GET.
BEATEN.
BY ME.
CHARMING.
I WANT RECOGNITION AND RESPECT. AND MOST OF ALL, I WANT TO BE REMEMBERED.
Rabbits.
ABRA-KADABRA.
RRAHH
RARRAAAT
I'LL DO ANYTHING TO BE REMEMBERED.

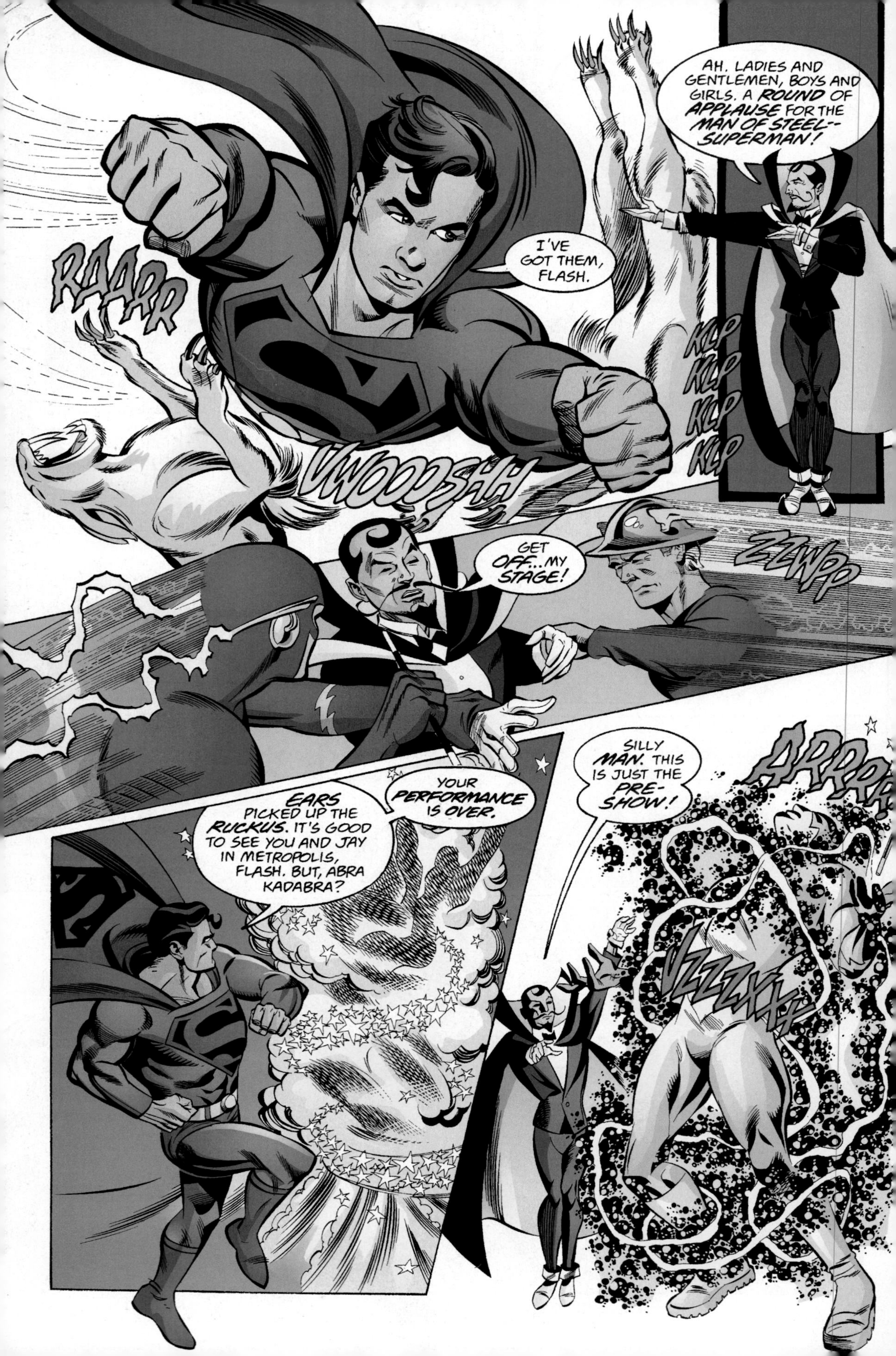

AH. LADIES AND GENTLEMEN, BOYS AND GIRLS. A ROUND OF APPLAUSE FOR THE MAN OF STEEL-- SUPERMAN!
RAARR
I'VE GOT THEM, FLASH.
KLP KLP KLP KLP
VWOOOSHH
GET OFF... MY STAGE!
ZZWPP
YOUR PERFORMANCE IS OVER.
EARS PICKED UP THE RUCKUS. IT'S GOOD TO SEE YOU AND JAY IN METROPOLIS, FLASH. BUT, ABRA KADABRA?
SILLY MAN. THIS IS JUST THE PRE-SHOW!
ARRRR
VZZZXX

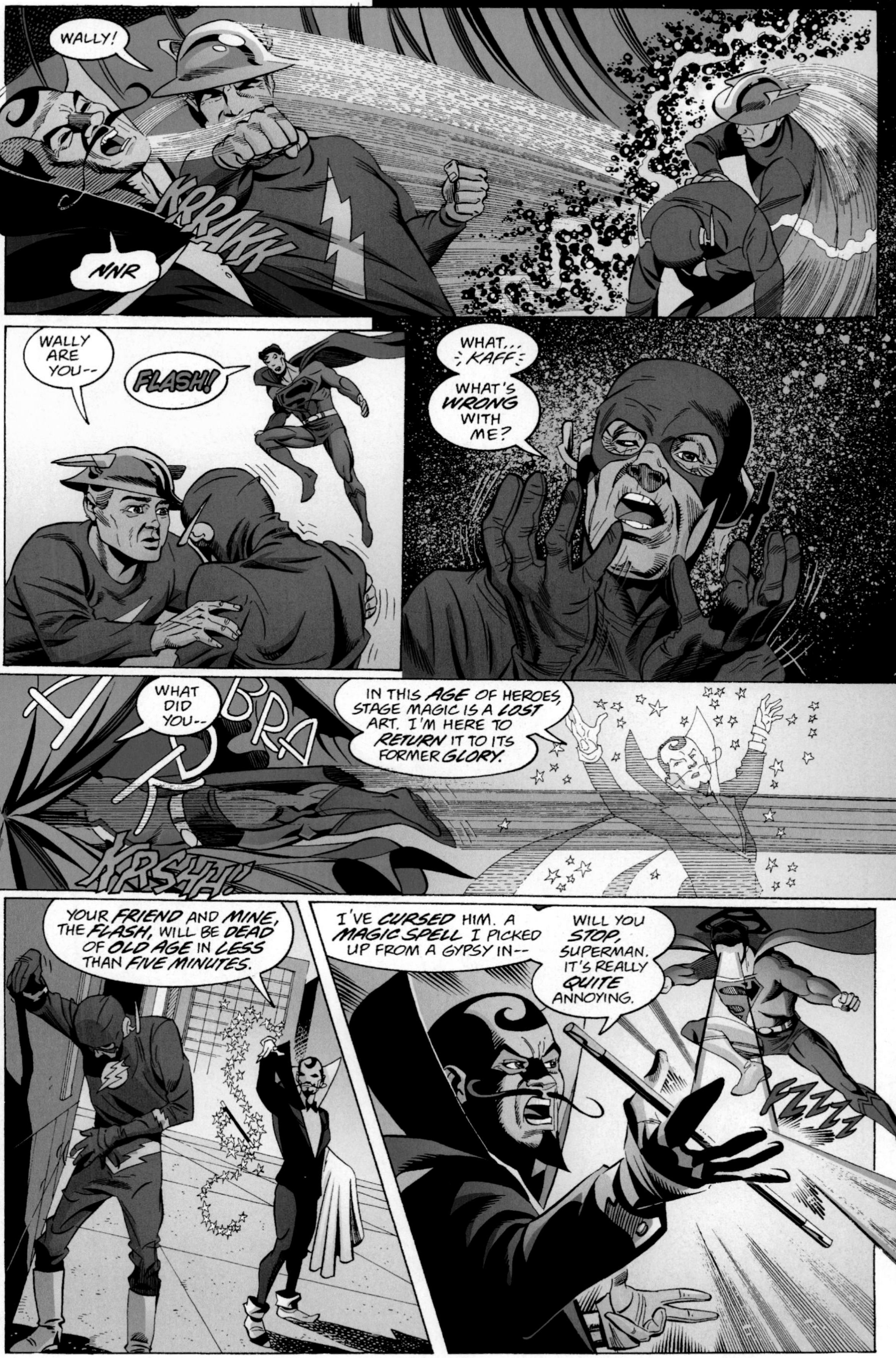
WALLY!
KRRAKK
NNR
WALLY ARE YOU--
FLASH!
WHAT... KAFF
WHAT'S WRONG WITH ME?
WHAT DID YOU--
IN THIS AGE OF HEROES, STAGE MAGIC IS A LOST ART. I'M HERE TO RETURN IT TO ITS FORMER GLORY.
KRSHH!
YOUR FRIEND AND MINE, THE FLASH, WILL BE DEAD OF OLD AGE IN LESS THAN FIVE MINUTES.
I'VE CURSED HIM. A MAGIC SPELL I PICKED UP FROM A GYPSY IN--
WILL YOU STOP, SUPERMAN. IT'S REALLY QUITE ANNOYING.
FZZZT

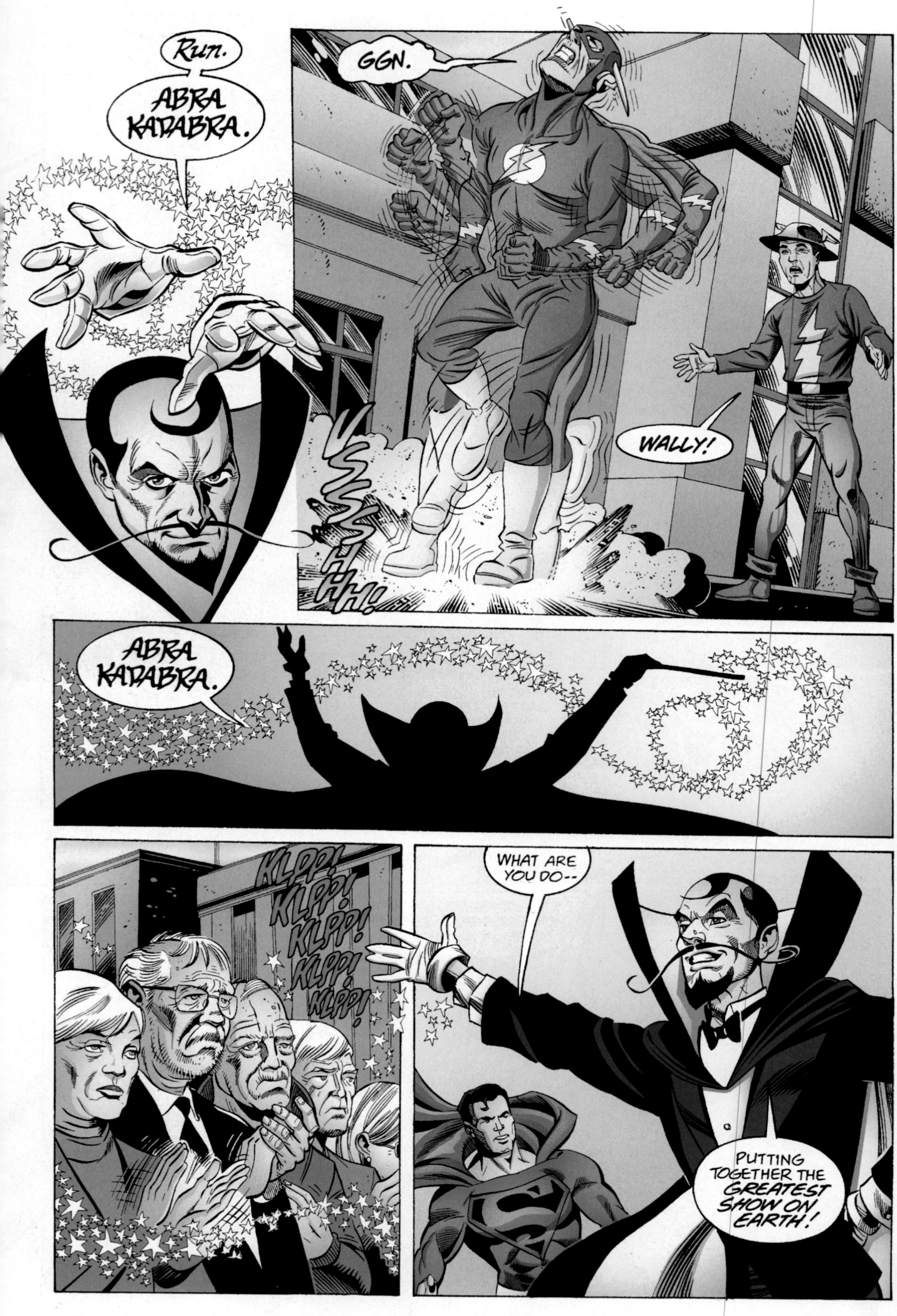
Run.
ABRA KADABRA.
GGN.
VSSSSHHH!
WALLY!
ABRA KADABRA.
KLPP! KLPP! KLPP! KLPP! KLPP!
WHAT ARE YOU DO--
PUTTING TOGETHER THE GREATEST SHOW ON EARTH!

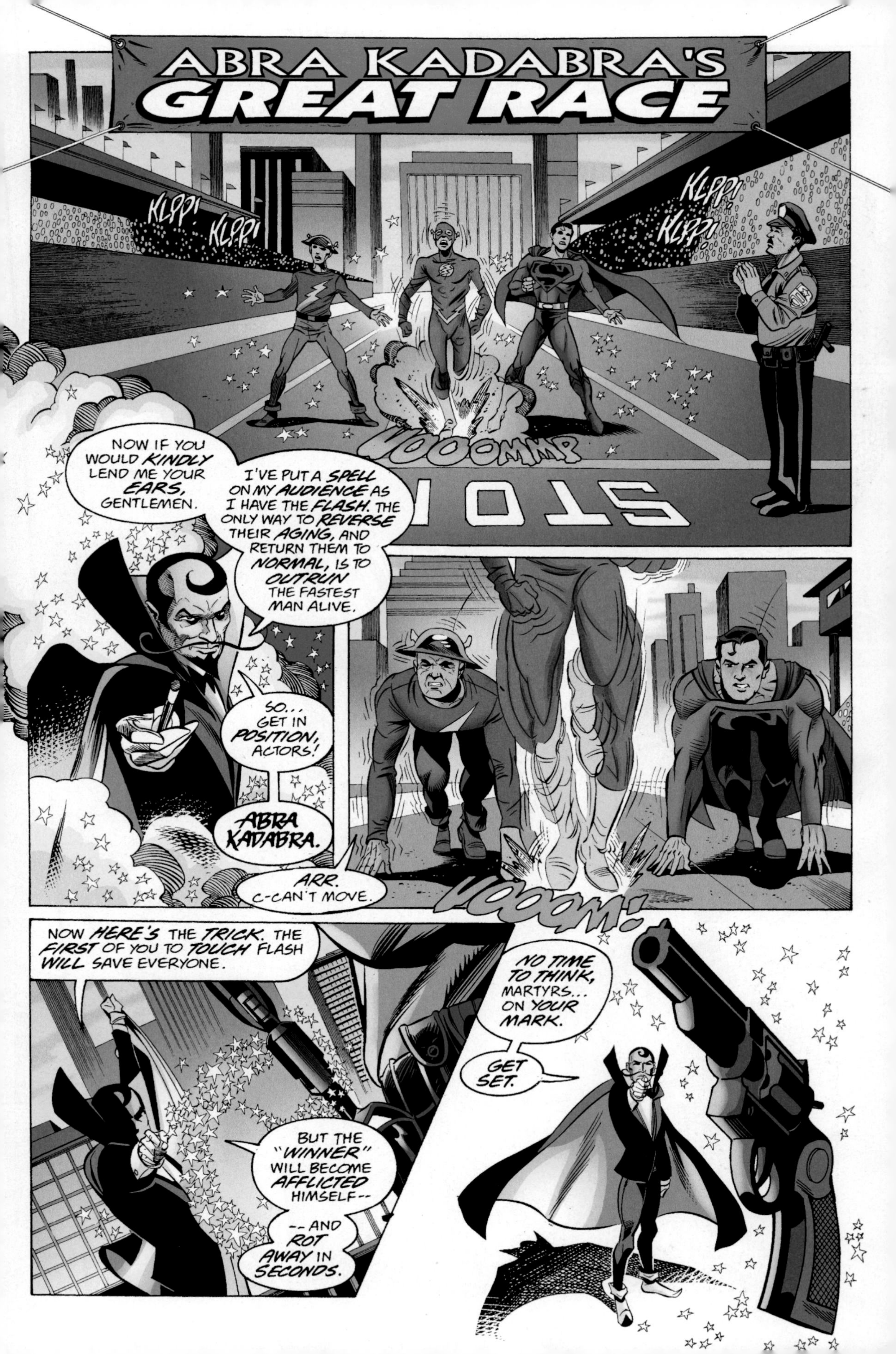

ABRA KADABRA'S GREAT RACE
KLPP! KLPP!
KLPP! KLPP!
VOOOMMP
STOP
NOW IF YOU WOULD *KINDLY* LEND ME YOUR *EARS,* GENTLEMEN.
I'VE PUT A *SPELL* ON MY *AUDIENCE* AS I HAVE THE *FLASH.* THE ONLY WAY TO *REVERSE* THEIR *AGING,* AND RETURN THEM TO *NORMAL,* IS TO *OUTRUN* THE FASTEST MAN ALIVE.
SO... GET IN *POSITION,* ACTORS!
ABRA KADABRA.
ARR. C-CAN'T MOVE.
VOOOM!
NOW *HERE'S* THE *TRICK.* THE *FIRST* OF YOU TO *TOUCH* FLASH *WILL* SAVE EVERYONE.
BUT THE "*WINNER*" WILL BECOME *AFFLICTED* HIMSELF--
-- AND *ROT AWAY* IN *SECONDS.*
NO TIME TO THINK, MARTYRS... ON *YOUR MARK.*
GET SET.

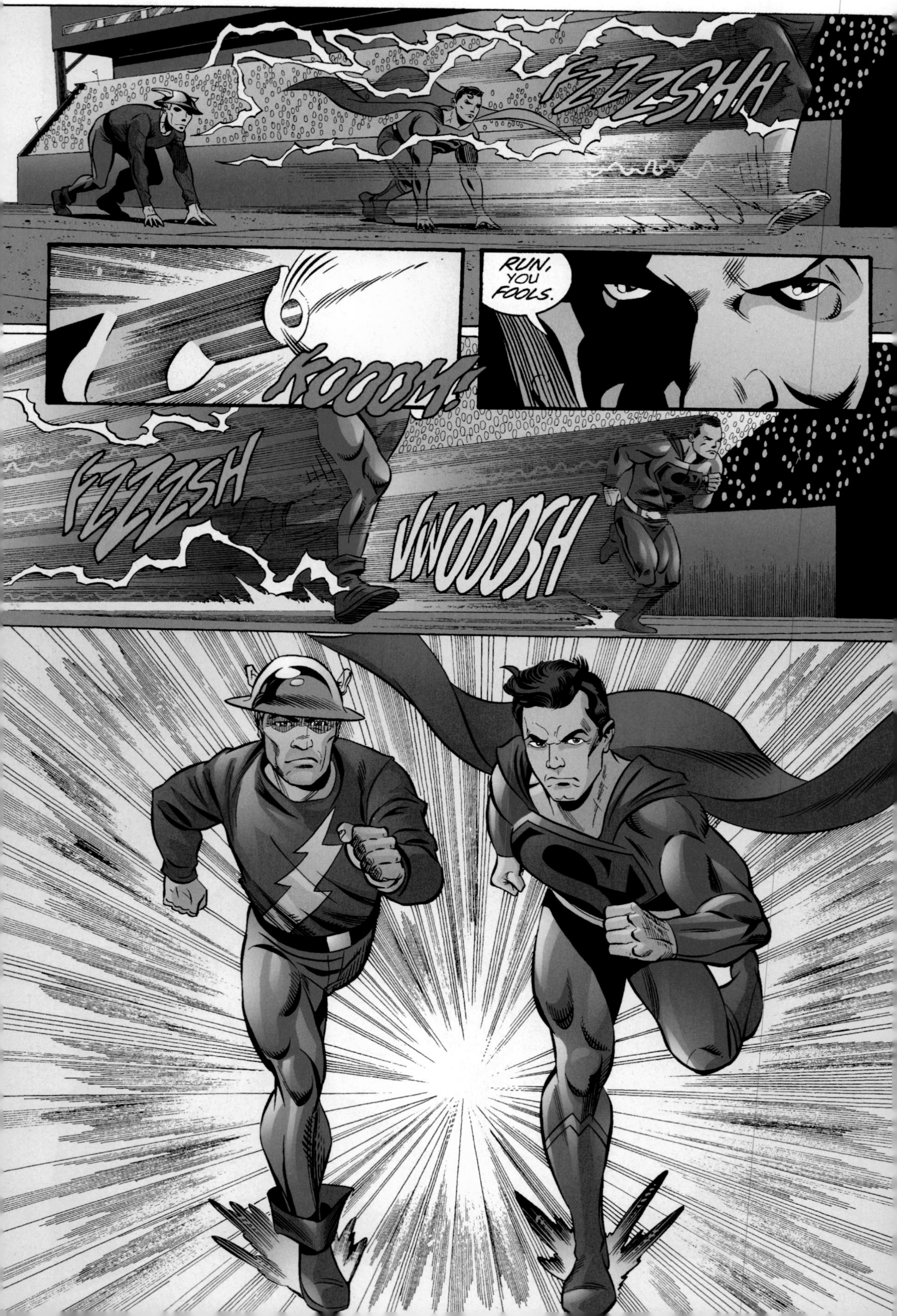

FZZZSHH
KOOOM!
RUN, YOU FOOLS.
FZZZSH
VWOOOSH

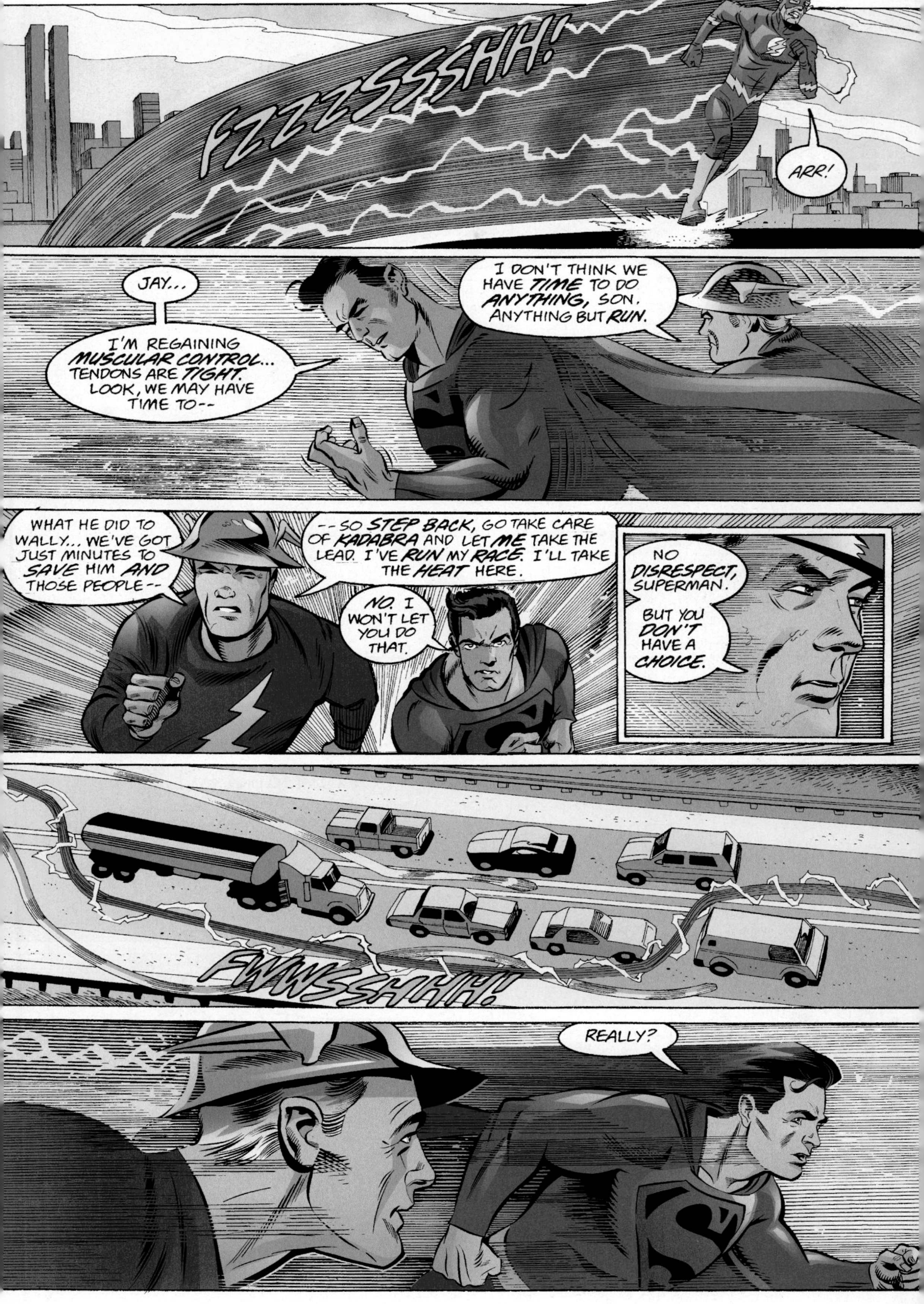
FZZZSSSSHH!
ARR!
JAY...
I'M REGAINING MUSCULAR CONTROL... TENDONS ARE TIGHT. LOOK, WE MAY HAVE TIME TO--
I DON'T THINK WE HAVE TIME TO DO ANYTHING, SON. ANYTHING BUT RUN.
WHAT HE DID TO WALLY... WE'VE GOT JUST MINUTES TO SAVE HIM AND THOSE PEOPLE--
--SO STEP BACK, GO TAKE CARE OF KADABRA AND LET ME TAKE THE LEAD. I'VE RUN MY RACE. I'LL TAKE THE HEAT HERE.
NO. I WON'T LET YOU DO THAT.
NO DISRESPECT, SUPERMAN.
BUT YOU DON'T HAVE A CHOICE.
FWWSSHHH!
REALLY?

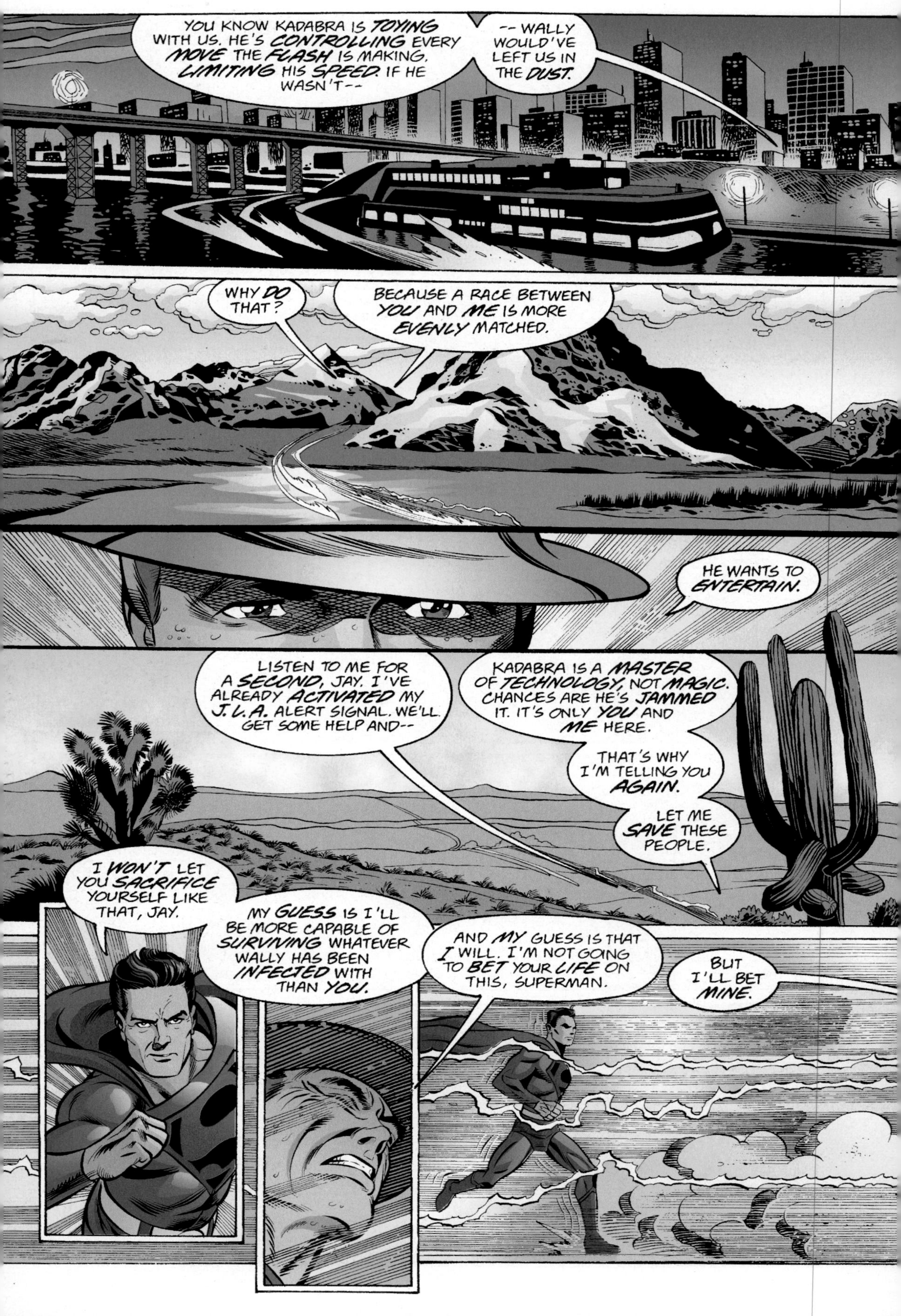
YOU KNOW KADABRA IS TOYING WITH US. HE'S CONTROLLING EVERY MOVE THE FLASH IS MAKING. LIMITING HIS SPEED. IF HE WASN'T--
--WALLY WOULD'VE LEFT US IN THE DUST.
WHY DO THAT?
BECAUSE A RACE BETWEEN YOU AND ME IS MORE EVENLY MATCHED.
HE WANTS TO ENTERTAIN.
LISTEN TO ME FOR A SECOND, JAY. I'VE ALREADY ACTIVATED MY J.L.A. ALERT SIGNAL. WE'LL GET SOME HELP AND--
KADABRA IS A MASTER OF TECHNOLOGY, NOT MAGIC. CHANCES ARE HE'S JAMMED IT. IT'S ONLY YOU AND ME HERE.
THAT'S WHY I'M TELLING YOU AGAIN.
LET ME SAVE THESE PEOPLE.
I WON'T LET YOU SACRIFICE YOURSELF LIKE THAT, JAY.
MY GUESS IS I'LL BE MORE CAPABLE OF SURVIVING WHATEVER WALLY HAS BEEN INFECTED WITH THAN YOU.
AND MY GUESS IS THAT I WILL. I'M NOT GOING TO BET YOUR LIFE ON THIS, SUPERMAN.
BUT I'LL BET MINE.

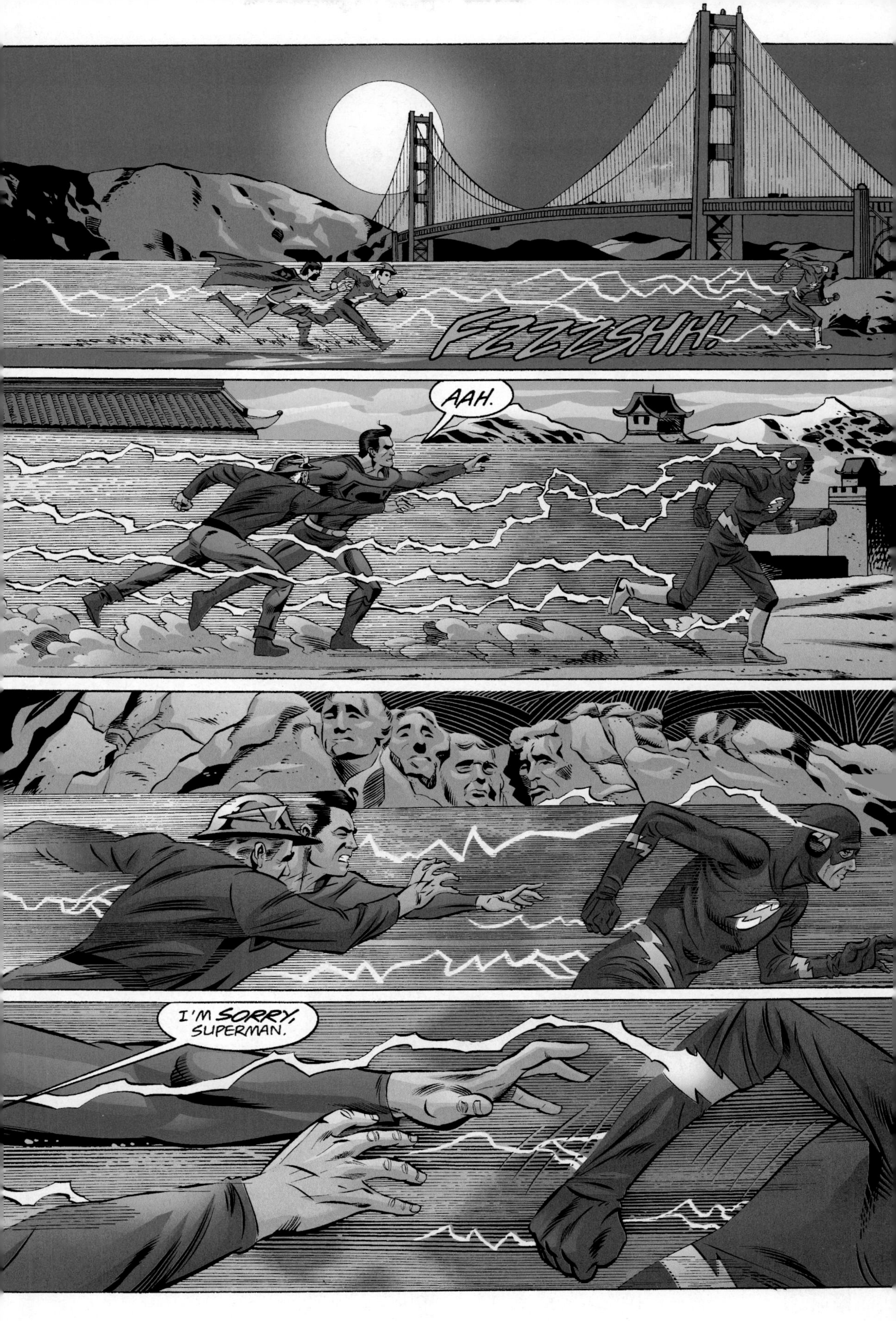
FZZZSHH!
AAH.
I'M SORRY, SUPERMAN.

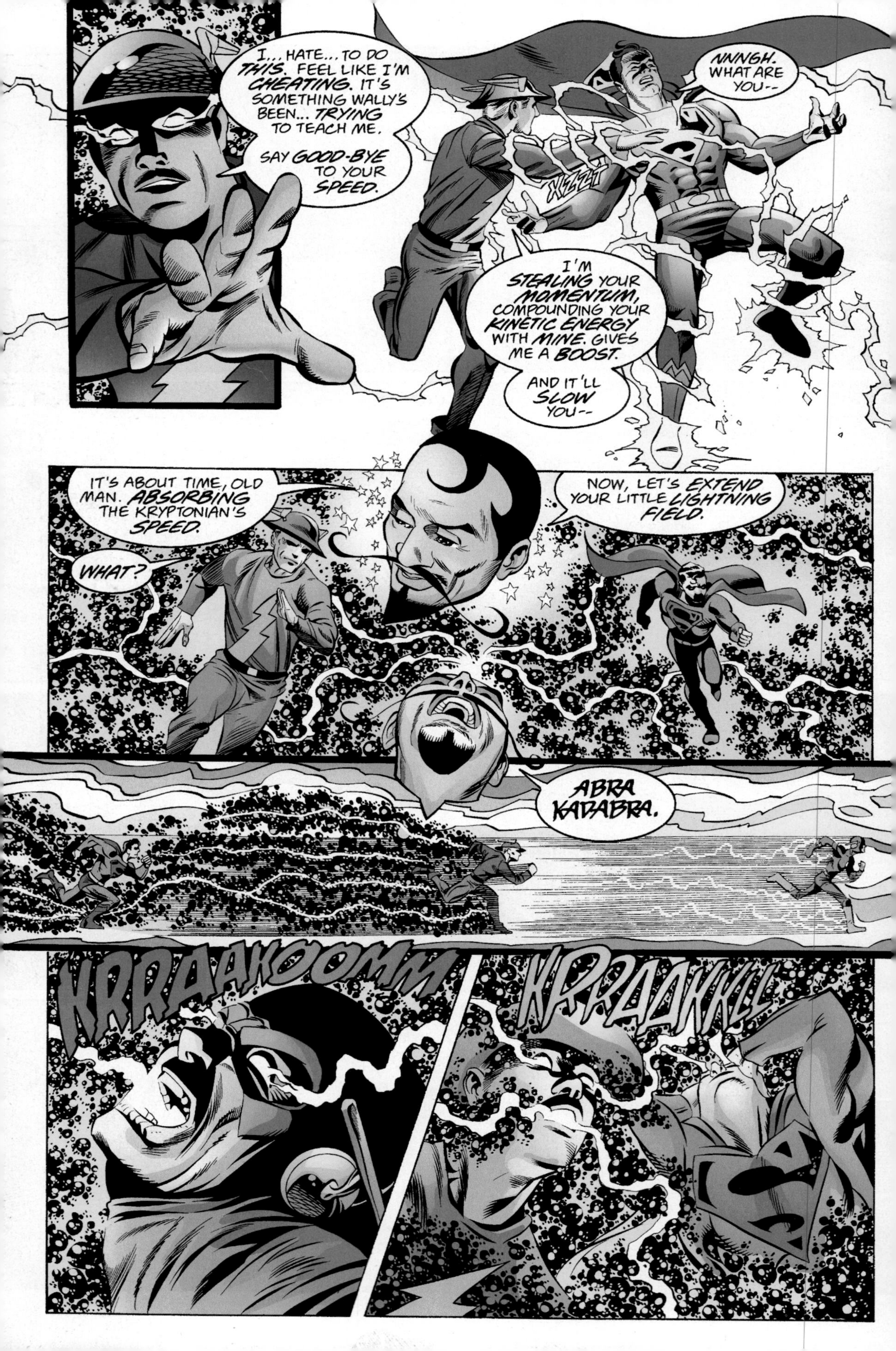

I... HATE... TO DO THIS. FEEL LIKE I'M CHEATING. IT'S SOMETHING WALLY'S BEEN... TRYING TO TEACH ME.
SAY GOOD-BYE TO YOUR SPEED.
NNNGH. WHAT ARE YOU--
XZZZT
I'M STEALING YOUR MOMENTUM, COMPOUNDING YOUR KINETIC ENERGY WITH MINE. GIVES ME A BOOST.
AND IT'LL SLOW YOU--
IT'S ABOUT TIME, OLD MAN. ABSORBING THE KRYPTONIAN'S SPEED.
WHAT?
NOW, LET'S EXTEND YOUR LITTLE LIGHTNING FIELD.
ABRA KADABRA.
KRRAAKOOMM
KRRAAKKLL

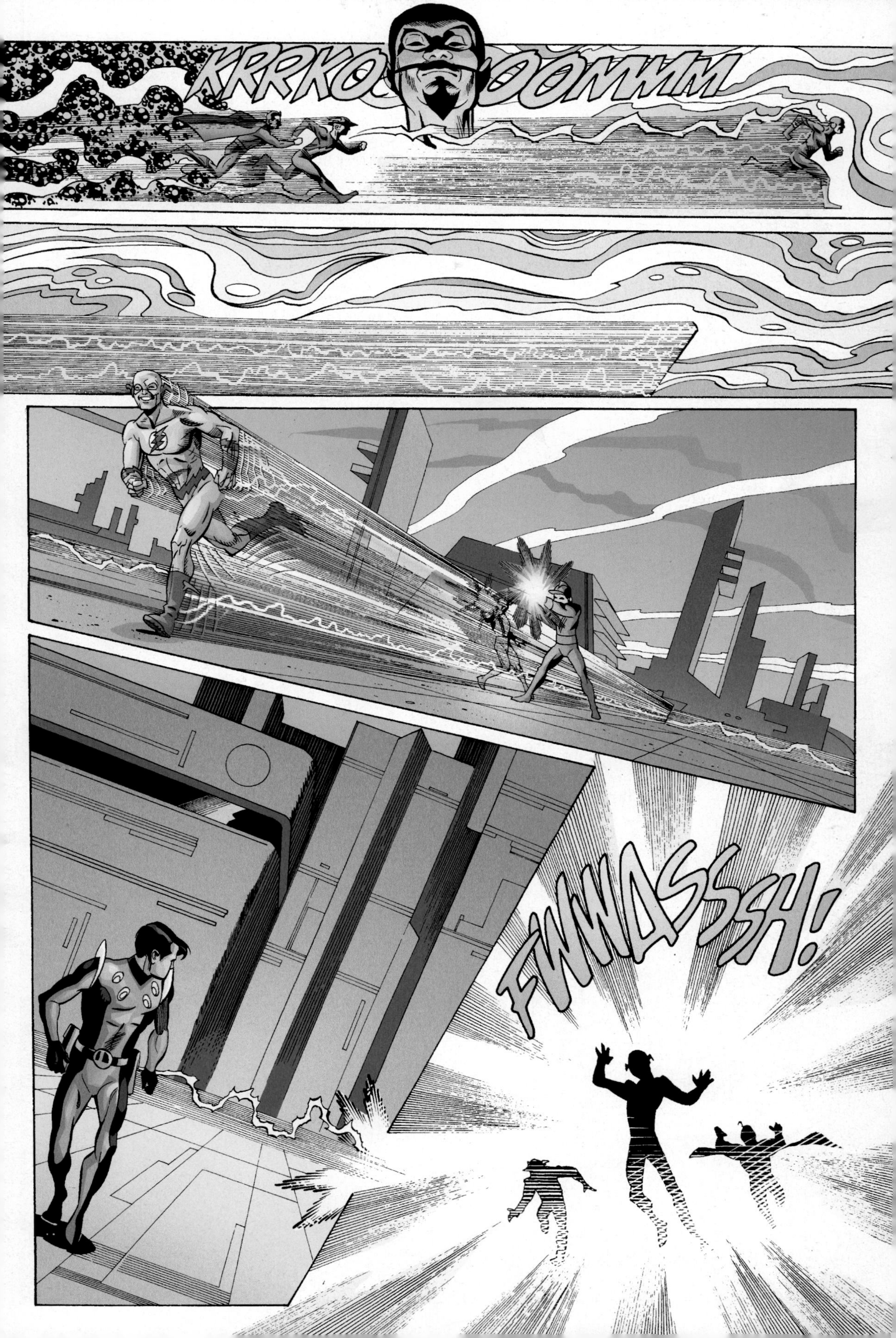
KRRKOOOONWM
FWWASSSH!

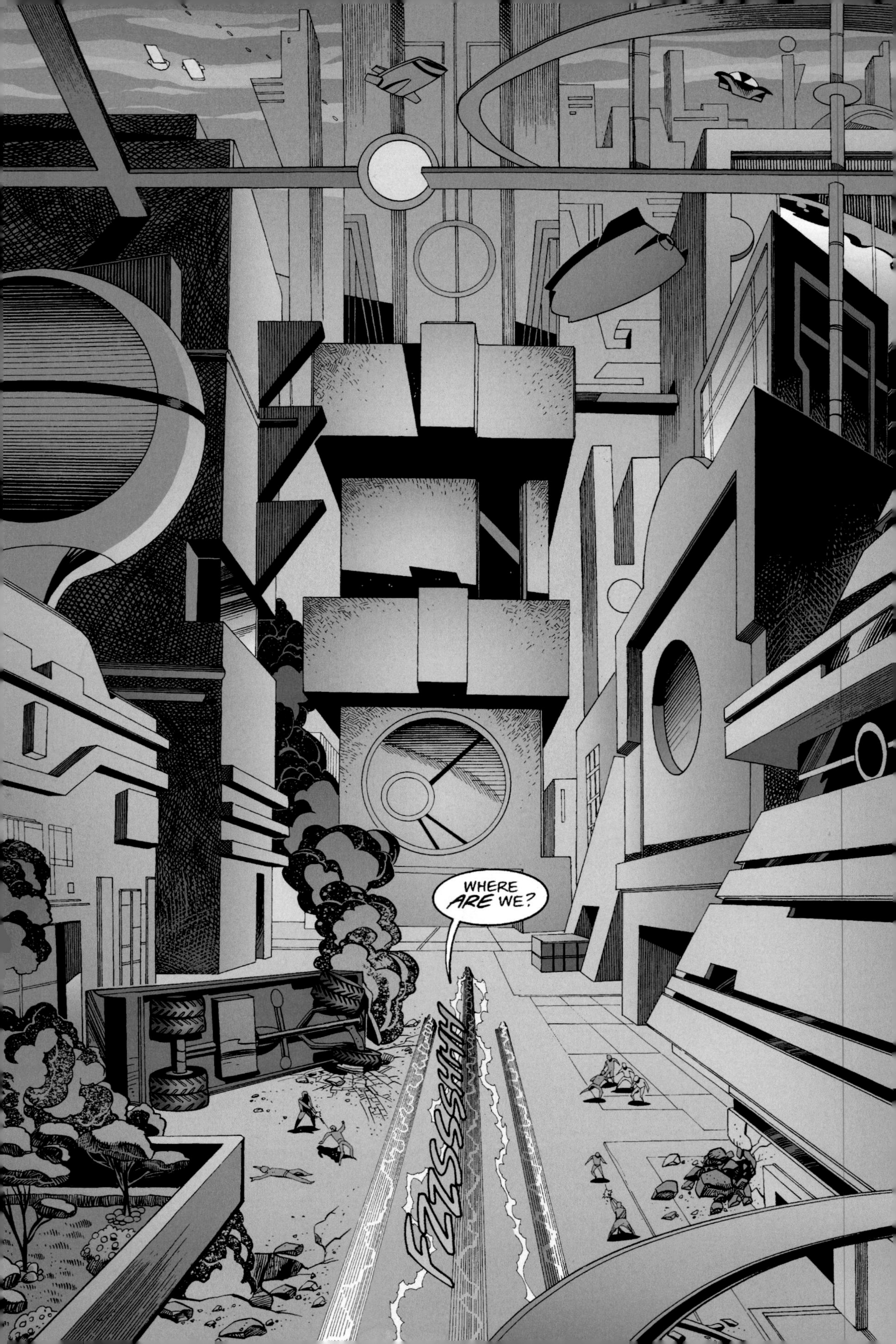
WHERE ARE WE?
FZZSSSHHH

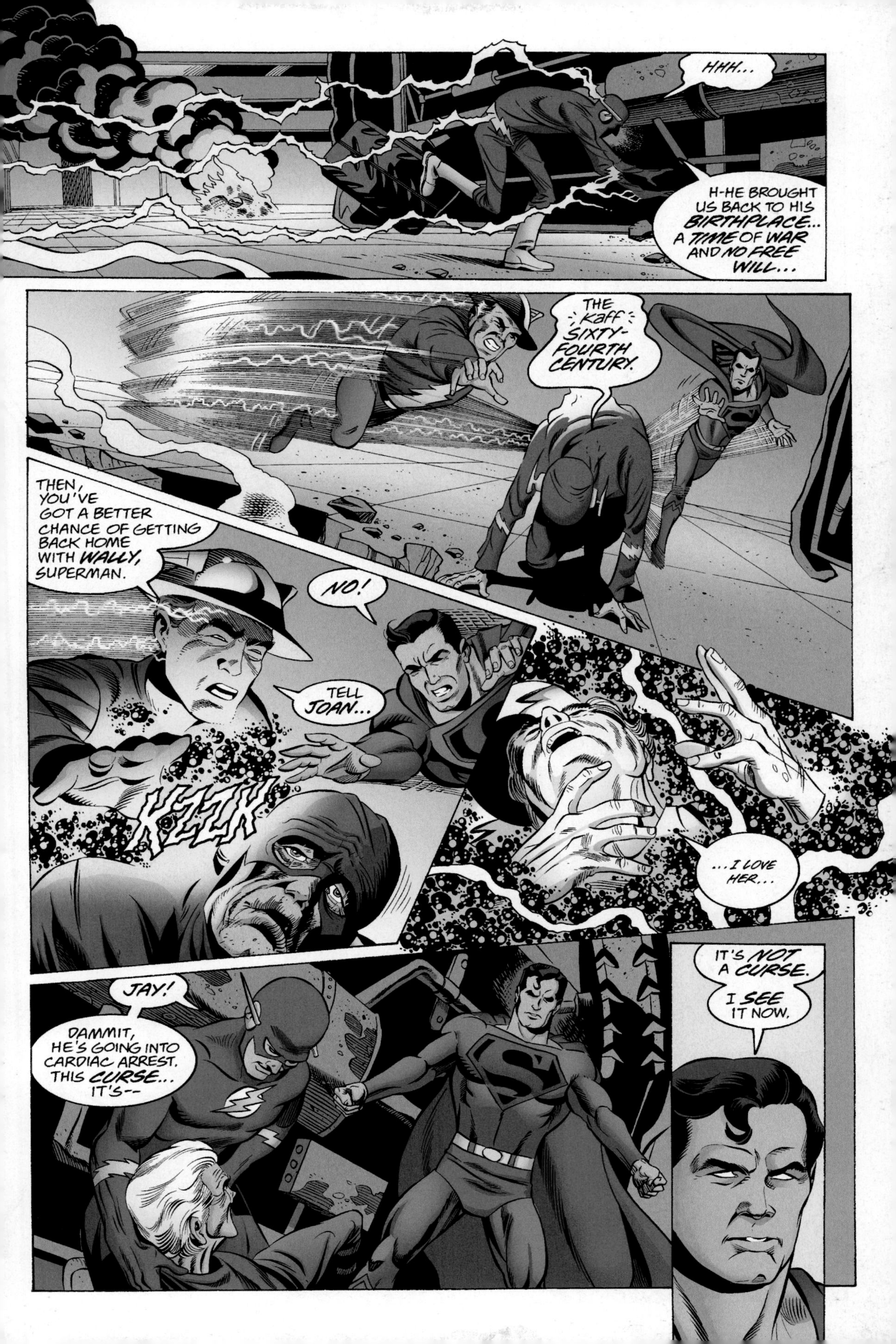
HHH...
H-HE BROUGHT US BACK TO HIS BIRTHPLACE... A TIME OF WAR AND NO FREE WILL...
THE *kaff* SIXTY-FOURTH CENTURY.
THEN, YOU'VE GOT A BETTER CHANCE OF GETTING BACK HOME WITH WALLY, SUPERMAN.
NO!
TELL JOAN...
KZZK
...I LOVE HER...
JAY!
DAMMIT, HE'S GOING INTO CARDIAC ARREST. THIS CURSE... IT'S--
IT'S NOT A CURSE.
I SEE IT NOW.

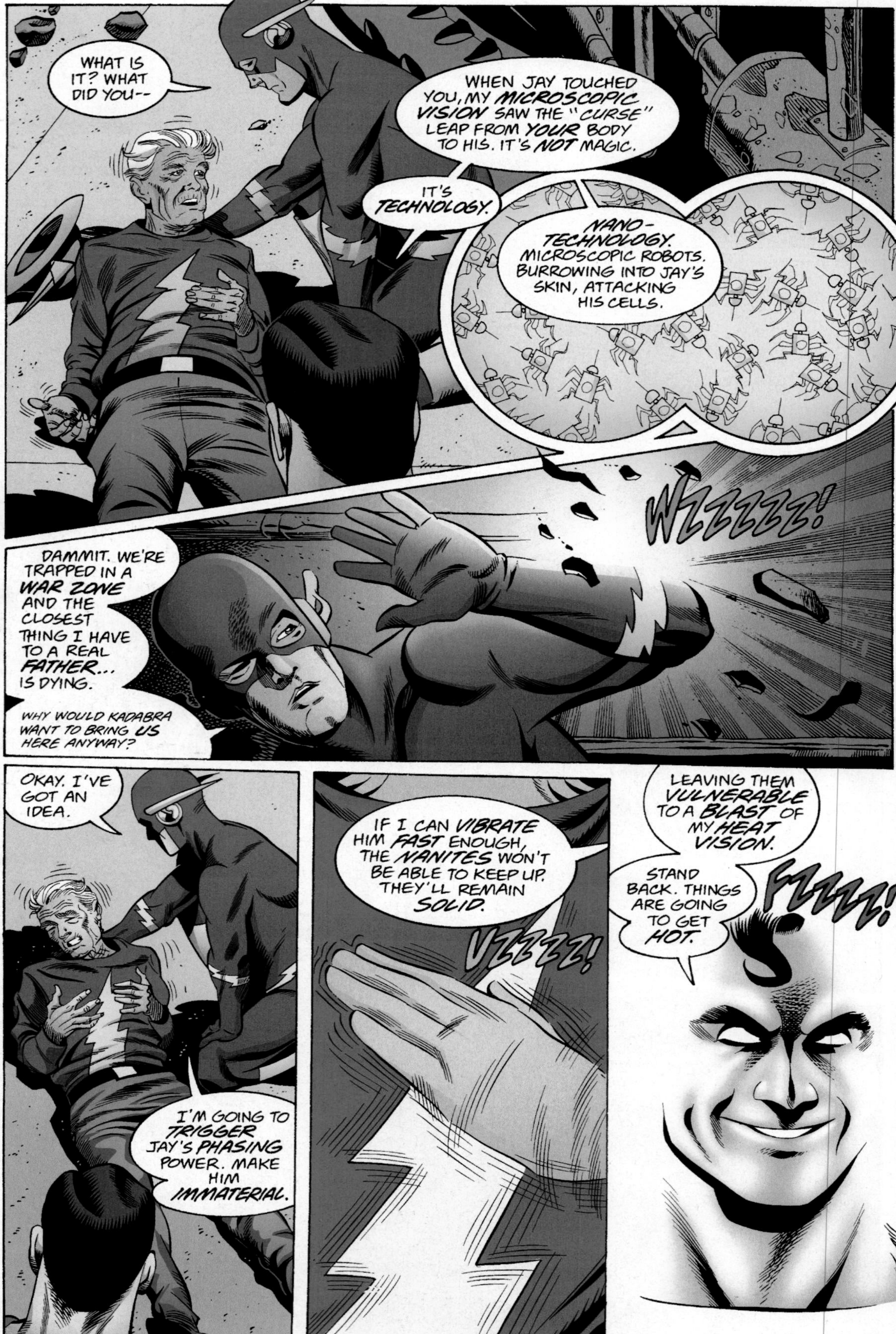
WHAT IS IT? WHAT DID YOU--
WHEN JAY TOUCHED YOU, MY MICROSCOPIC VISION SAW THE "CURSE" LEAP FROM YOUR BODY TO HIS. IT'S NOT MAGIC.
IT'S TECHNOLOGY.
NANO-TECHNOLOGY. MICROSCOPIC ROBOTS. BURROWING INTO JAY'S SKIN, ATTACKING HIS CELLS.
WZZZZZZ!
DAMMIT. WE'RE TRAPPED IN A WAR ZONE AND THE CLOSEST THING I HAVE TO A REAL FATHER... IS DYING.
WHY WOULD KADABRA WANT TO BRING US HERE ANYWAY?
OKAY. I'VE GOT AN IDEA.
I'M GOING TO TRIGGER JAY'S PHASING POWER. MAKE HIM IMMATERIAL.
IF I CAN VIBRATE HIM FAST ENOUGH, THE NANITES WON'T BE ABLE TO KEEP UP. THEY'LL REMAIN SOLID.
VZZZZZ!
LEAVING THEM VULNERABLE TO A BLAST OF MY HEAT VISION.
STAND BACK. THINGS ARE GOING TO GET HOT.
FZZZZ!

STEELWORKS
IMPLANT WEAPONS DIVISION 122

Y!!!

SHAKKA

I DON'T MISS THIS *TIME PERIOD.*

THE *ENDLESS* FIGHTING, THE *HOPELESS* CONFORMITY... AND THE *LACK OF ENTERTAINMENT.*

HOWEVER I *DO* MISS THE AVAILABILITY OF... *MAGICAL DEVICES.*

FANTASTIC.

I NEEDED TO *REPLENISH* MY *SUPPLY.*

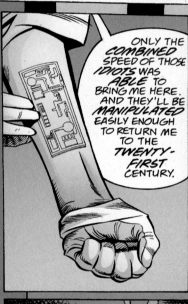

ONLY THE *COMBINED* SPEED OF THOSE *IDIOTS* WAS *ABLE* TO BRING ME HERE. AND THEY'LL BE *MANIPULATED* EASILY ENOUGH TO RETURN ME TO THE *TWENTY-FIRST* CENTURY.

KSSSSS!

:UHNN!: WHERE I WILL... AT *LAST* MAKE MY *MARK* IN *HISTORY!*

FIRE.

ABRA KADABRA.

MAGNIFICEN--

FWOOSH

FWOOOOO

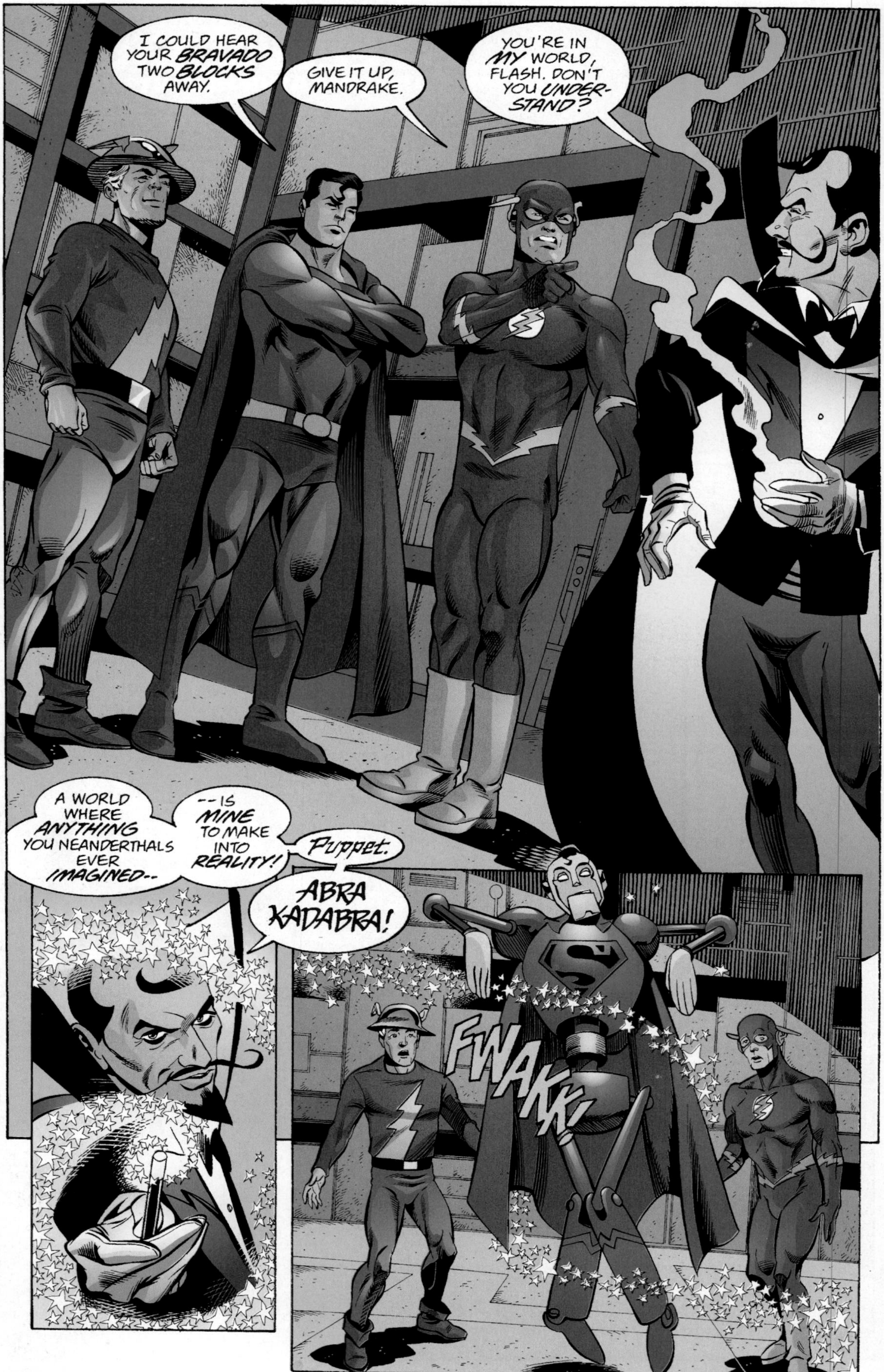
I COULD HEAR YOUR BRAVADO TWO BLOCKS AWAY.
GIVE IT UP, MANDRAKE.
YOU'RE IN MY WORLD, FLASH. DON'T YOU UNDER-STAND?
A WORLD WHERE ANYTHING YOU NEANDERTHALS EVER IMAGINED--
--IS MINE TO MAKE INTO REALITY!
Puppet.
ABRA KADABRA!
FWAKK!

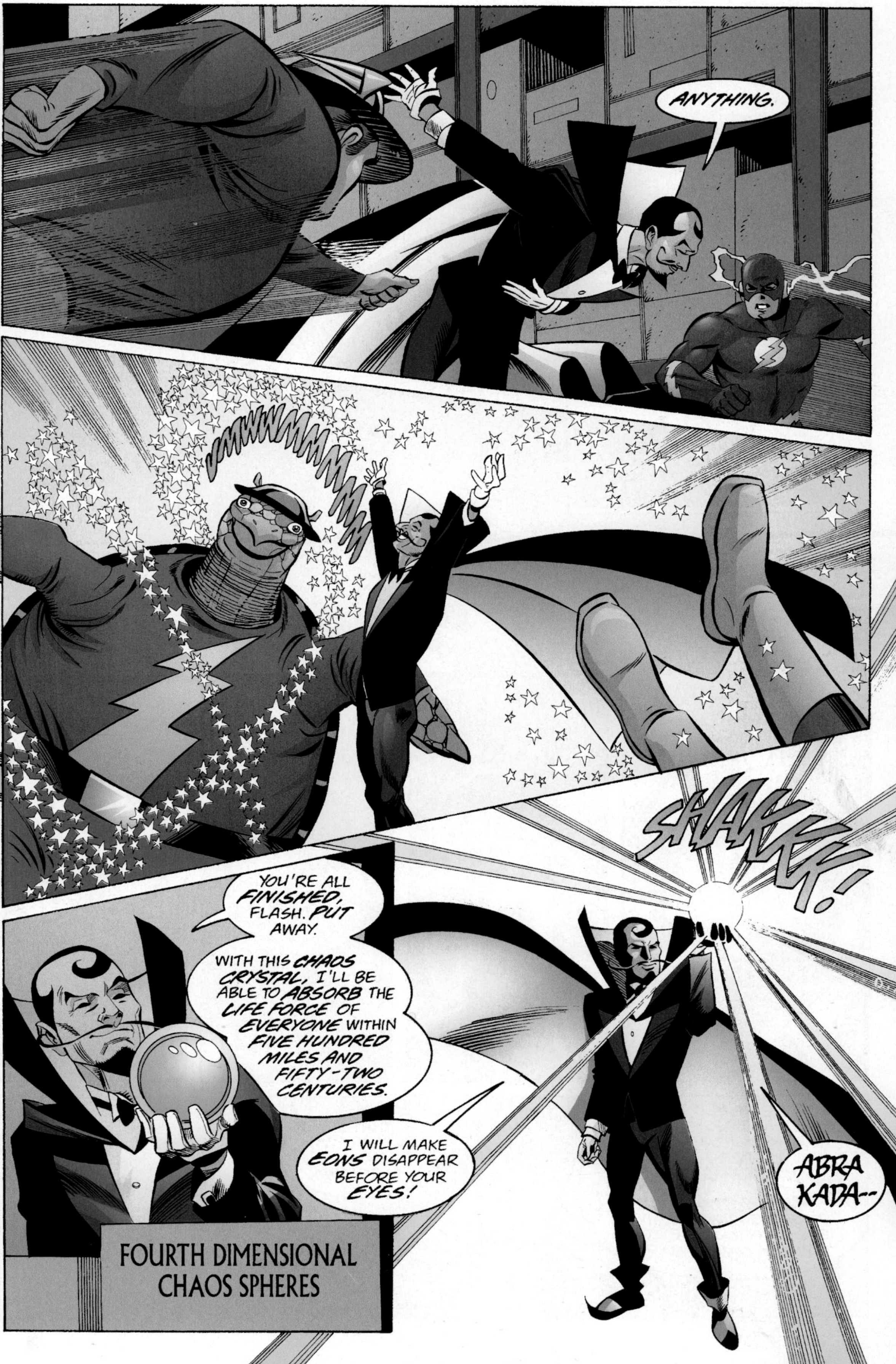
ANYTHING.
VMMMMMMMMM
SHAKKKK!
YOU'RE ALL FINISHED, FLASH. PUT AWAY.
WITH THIS CHAOS CRYSTAL, I'LL BE ABLE TO ABSORB THE LIFE FORCE OF EVERYONE WITHIN FIVE HUNDRED MILES AND FIFTY-TWO CENTURIES.
I WILL MAKE EONS DISAPPEAR BEFORE YOUR EYES!
ABRA KADA--
FOURTH DIMENSIONAL CHAOS SPHERES

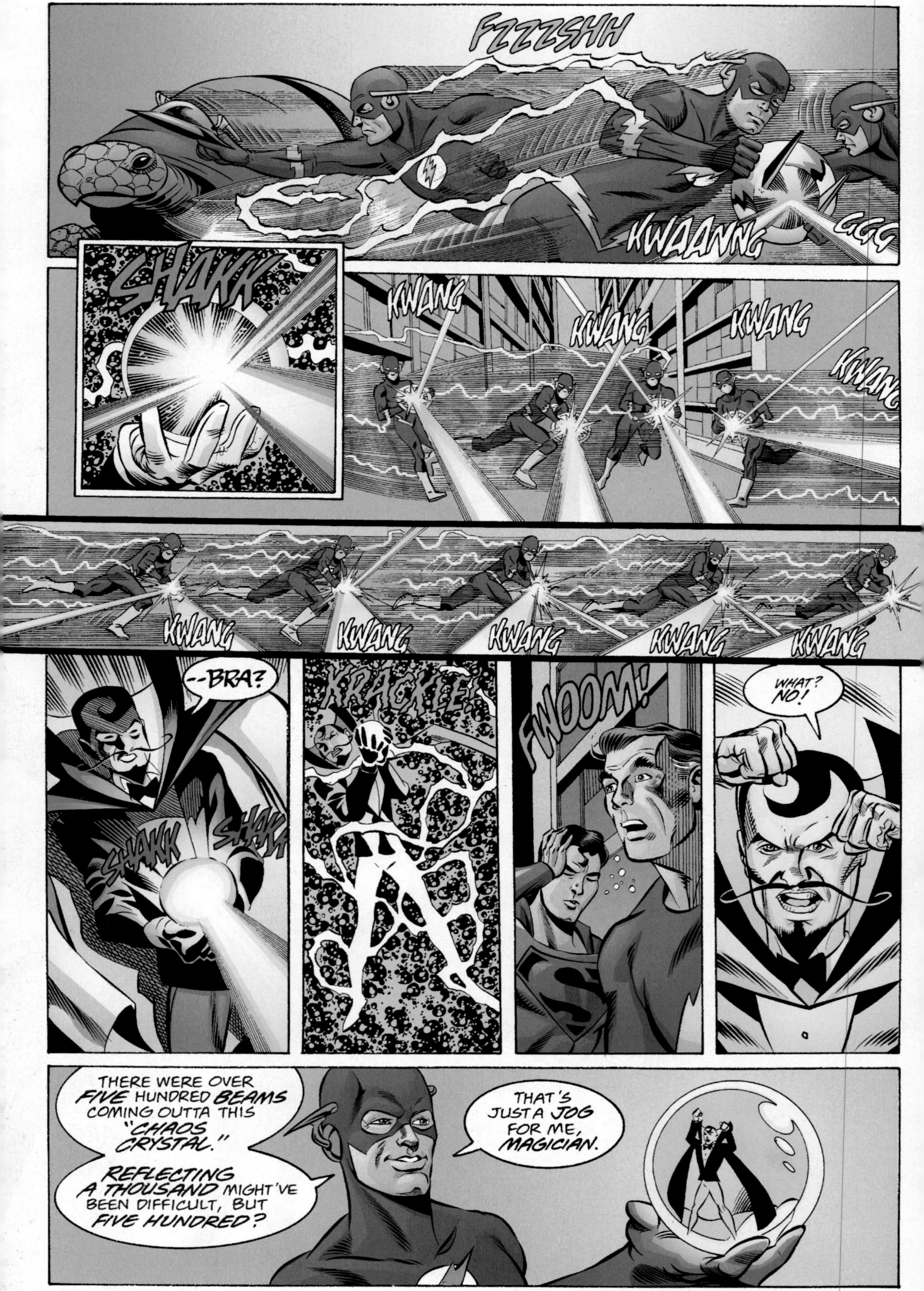
FZZZSHH
KWAANNG
GGG
SHAKK
KWANG
KWANG
KWANG
KWANG
KWANG
KWANG
KWANG
KWANG
KWANG
--BRA?
SHAKK
SHAKK
KRACKLE!
FWOOM!
WHAT? NO!
THERE WERE OVER FIVE HUNDRED BEAMS COMING OUTTA THIS "CHAOS CRYSTAL."
REFLECTING A THOUSAND MIGHT'VE BEEN DIFFICULT, BUT FIVE HUNDRED?
THAT'S JUST A JOG FOR ME, MAGICIAN.

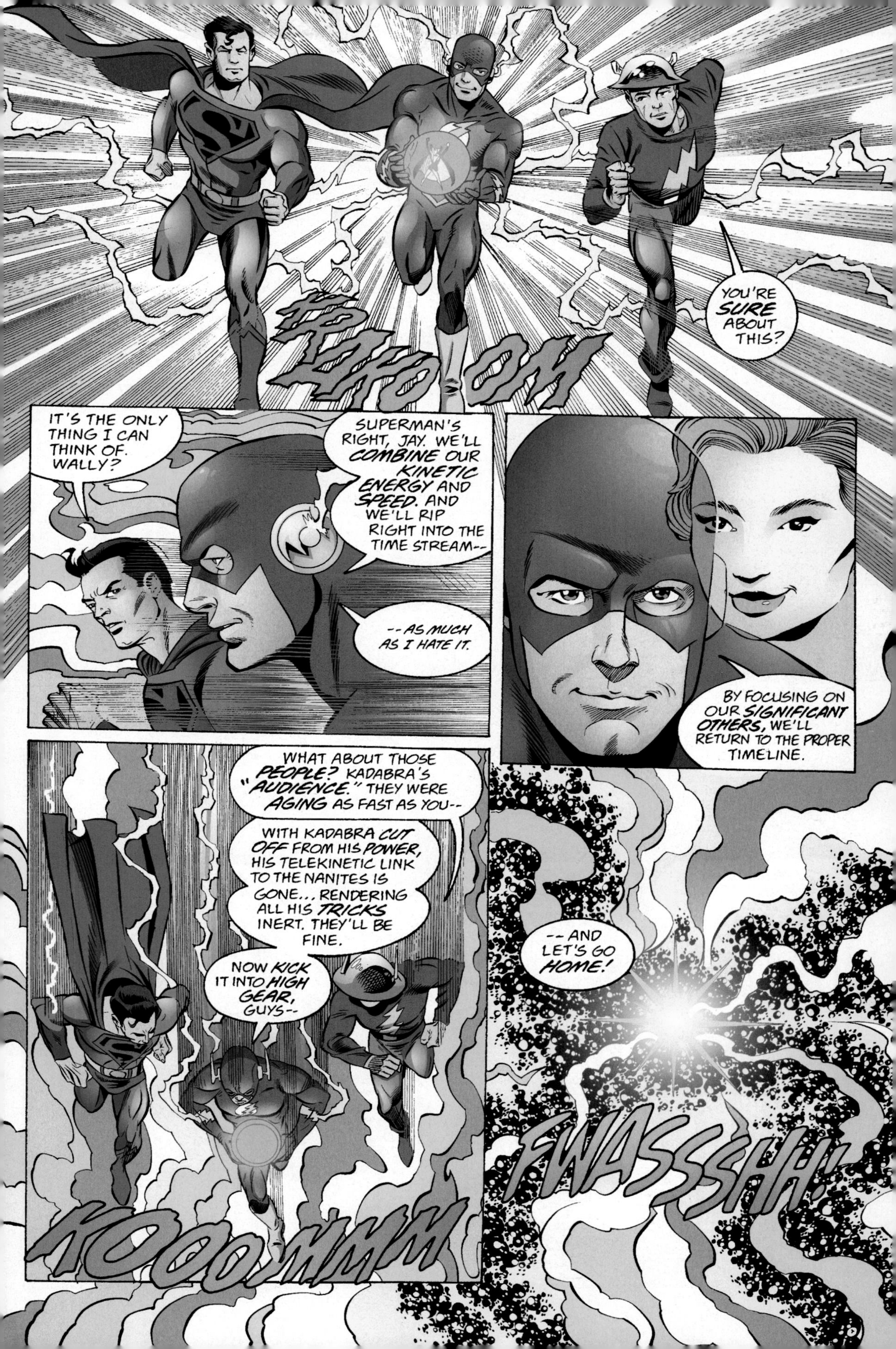
KRAKOOM
YOU'RE SURE ABOUT THIS?
IT'S THE ONLY THING I CAN THINK OF. WALLY?
SUPERMAN'S RIGHT, JAY. WE'LL COMBINE OUR KINETIC ENERGY AND SPEED, AND WE'LL RIP RIGHT INTO THE TIME STREAM--
--AS MUCH AS I HATE IT.
BY FOCUSING ON OUR SIGNIFICANT OTHERS, WE'LL RETURN TO THE PROPER TIMELINE.
WHAT ABOUT THOSE "PEOPLE?" KADABRA'S "AUDIENCE." THEY WERE AGING AS FAST AS YOU--
WITH KADABRA CUT OFF FROM HIS POWER, HIS TELEKINETIC LINK TO THE NANITES IS GONE... RENDERING ALL HIS TRICKS INERT. THEY'LL BE FINE.
NOW KICK IT INTO HIGH GEAR, GUYS--
KOOOMMM
--AND LET'S GO HOME!
FWASSSHH!

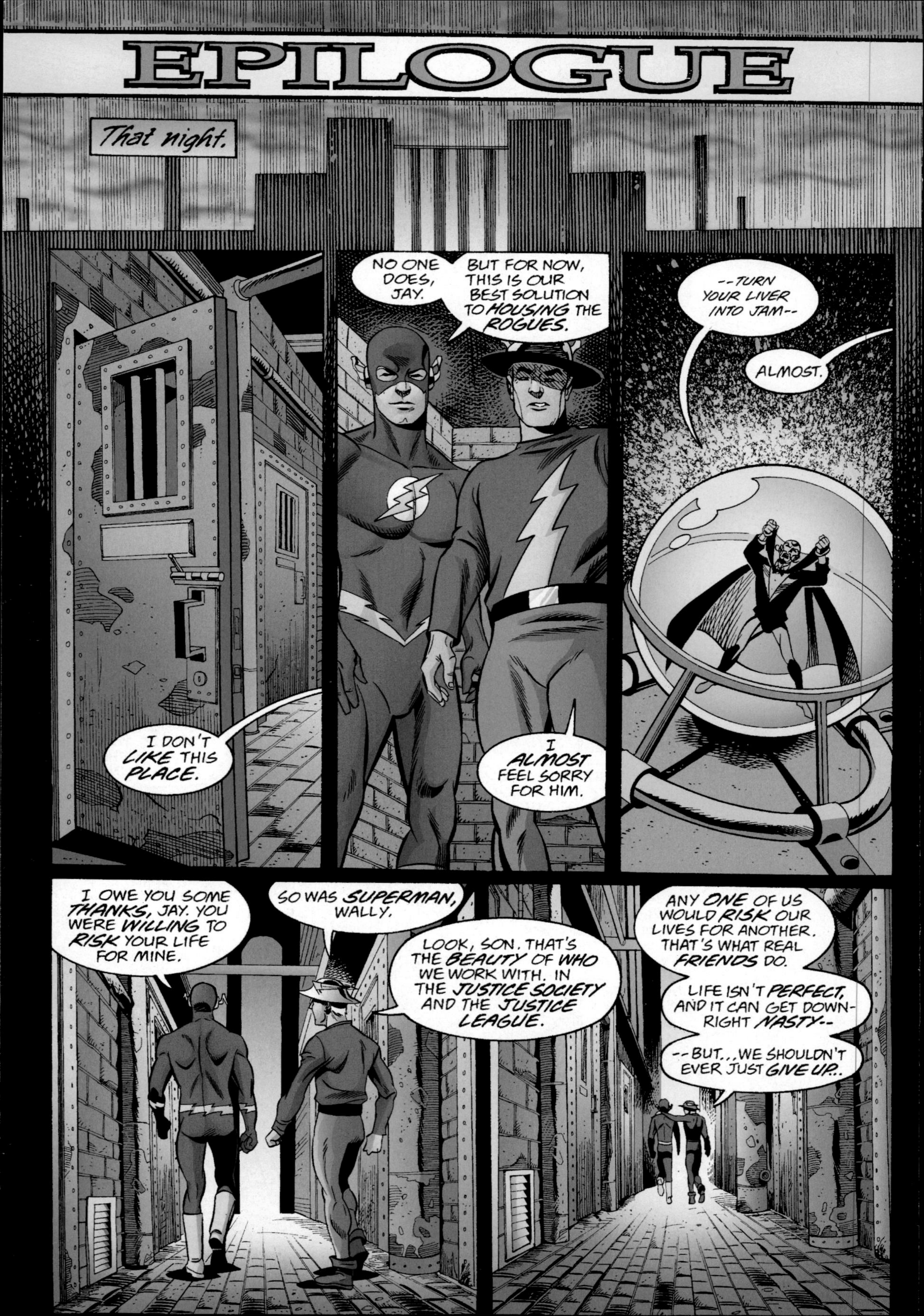
EPILOGUE
That night.
I DON'T LIKE THIS PLACE.
NO ONE DOES, JAY.
BUT FOR NOW, THIS IS OUR BEST SOLUTION TO HOUSING THE ROGUES.
I ALMOST FEEL SORRY FOR HIM.
--TURN YOUR LIVER INTO JAM--
ALMOST.
I OWE YOU SOME THANKS, JAY. YOU WERE WILLING TO RISK YOUR LIFE FOR MINE.
SO WAS SUPERMAN, WALLY.
LOOK, SON. THAT'S THE BEAUTY OF WHO WE WORK WITH. IN THE JUSTICE SOCIETY AND THE JUSTICE LEAGUE.
ANY ONE OF US WOULD RISK OUR LIVES FOR ANOTHER. THAT'S WHAT REAL FRIENDS DO.
LIFE ISN'T PERFECT, AND IT CAN GET DOWN-RIGHT NASTY--
--BUT...WE SHOULDN'T EVER JUST GIVE UP...

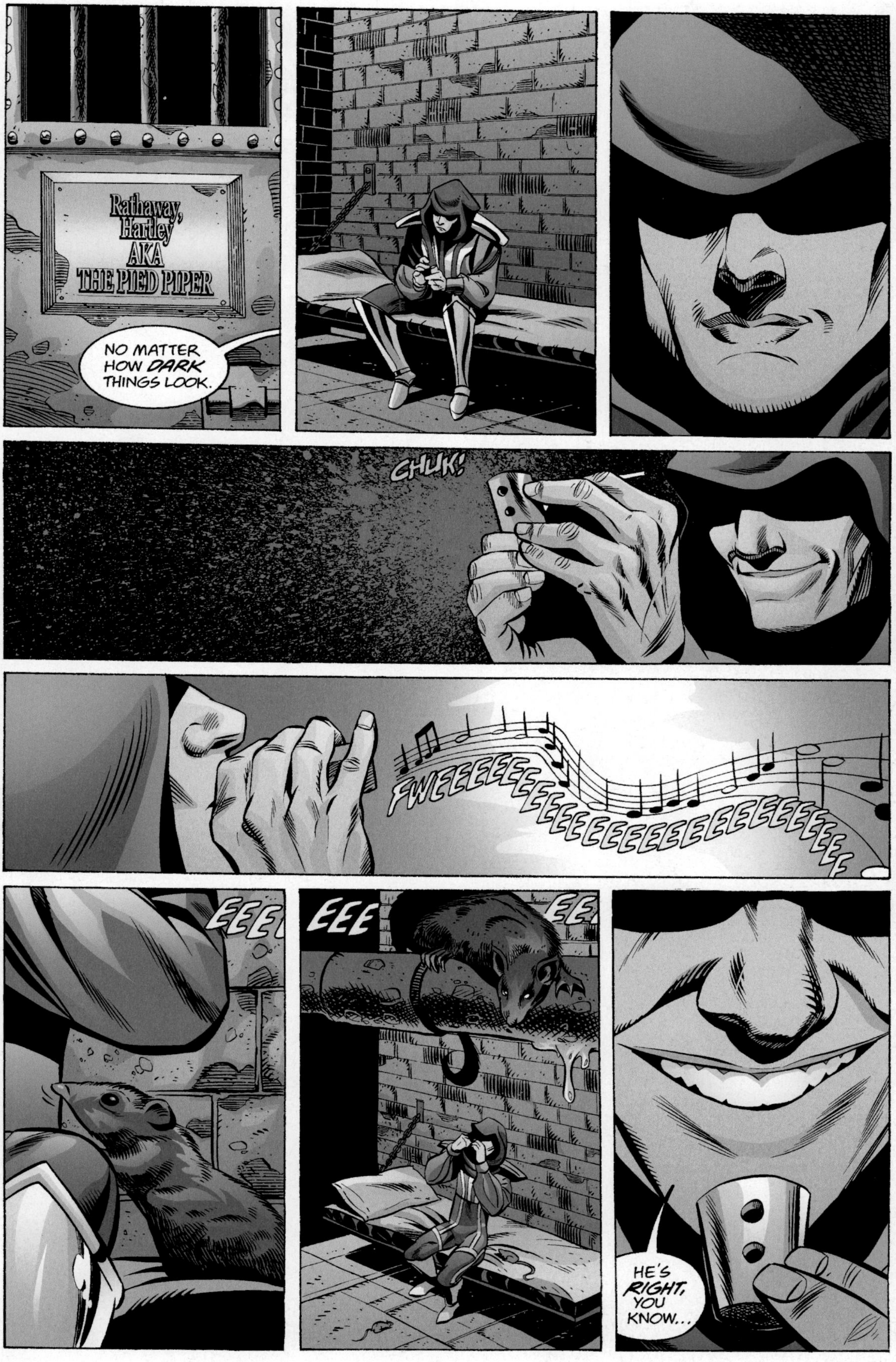

Rathaway, Hartley AKA THE PIED PIPER
NO MATTER HOW DARK THINGS LOOK.
CHUK!
FWEEEEEEEEEEEEEEEEEEEEEEEEEEEEEEEE
EEE
EEE
EE
HE'S RIGHT, YOU KNOW...

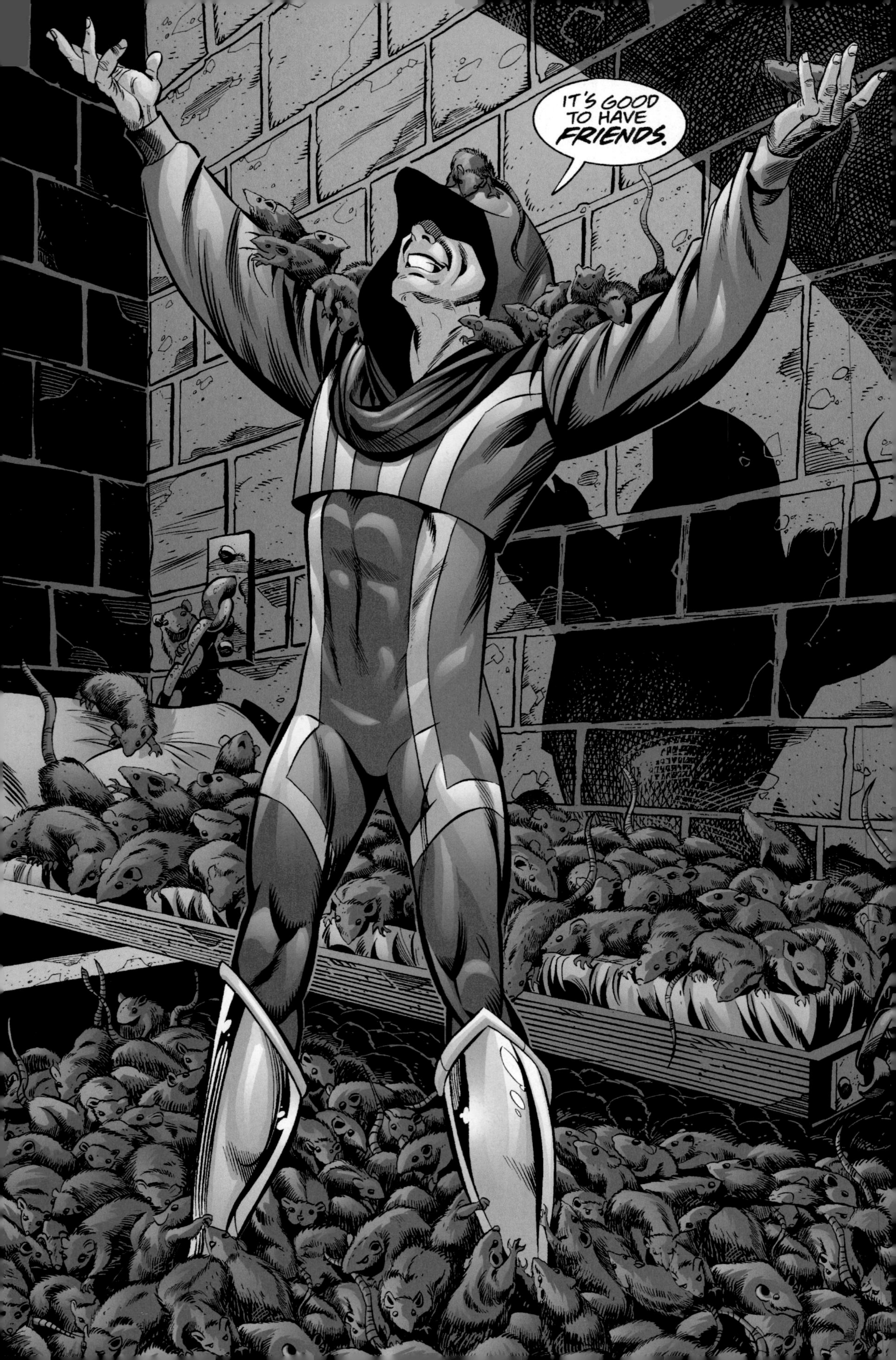
IT'S GOOD TO HAVE FRIENDS.

THE NEW ROGUES GALLERY!
The FLASH
KEYSTONE CHRONICLE
NEWS ROUNDUP
ECONOMIC REPORT
MIRROR MASTER'S MAGIC BULLET
SOCIETY
WEATHER AWFUL!
OBITUARIES
TRICKSTER'S BACK
KEYSTONE IN CHAOS
FLASH SAVES THE DAY
KEYSTONE CHRONICLE
FLASH SAVES CI

KEYSTONE CITY.

THE CITY OF INDUSTRY.

TIKA TIKA TAC TAC

BUILT IN KEYSTONE

AND HOME TO THE FLASH.

YOU'RE AWFULLY QUIET, WALLY.

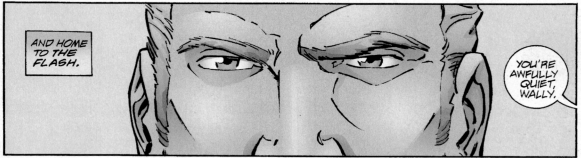

SO IS KEYSTONE.

I KNOW YOU'RE WORRIED ABOUT THE GARRICKS, BUT IRIS TALKED TO THEM THIS MORNING. JAY'S IMPRESSED WITH THE CANCER SPECIALIST JOAN'S SEEING.

IT'S MORE THAN THAT, LINDA.

THE GARRICKS AREN'T THE ONLY ONES TO BE HIT BY A STROKE OF BAD LUCK.

PIPER, CHUNK AND JESSE QUICK ARE OUT OF COMMISSION. MAX MERCURY IS STILL MISSING.

AND CYBORG... VIC HASN'T CALLED ME BACK, HAS HE?

NO. HE HASN'T.

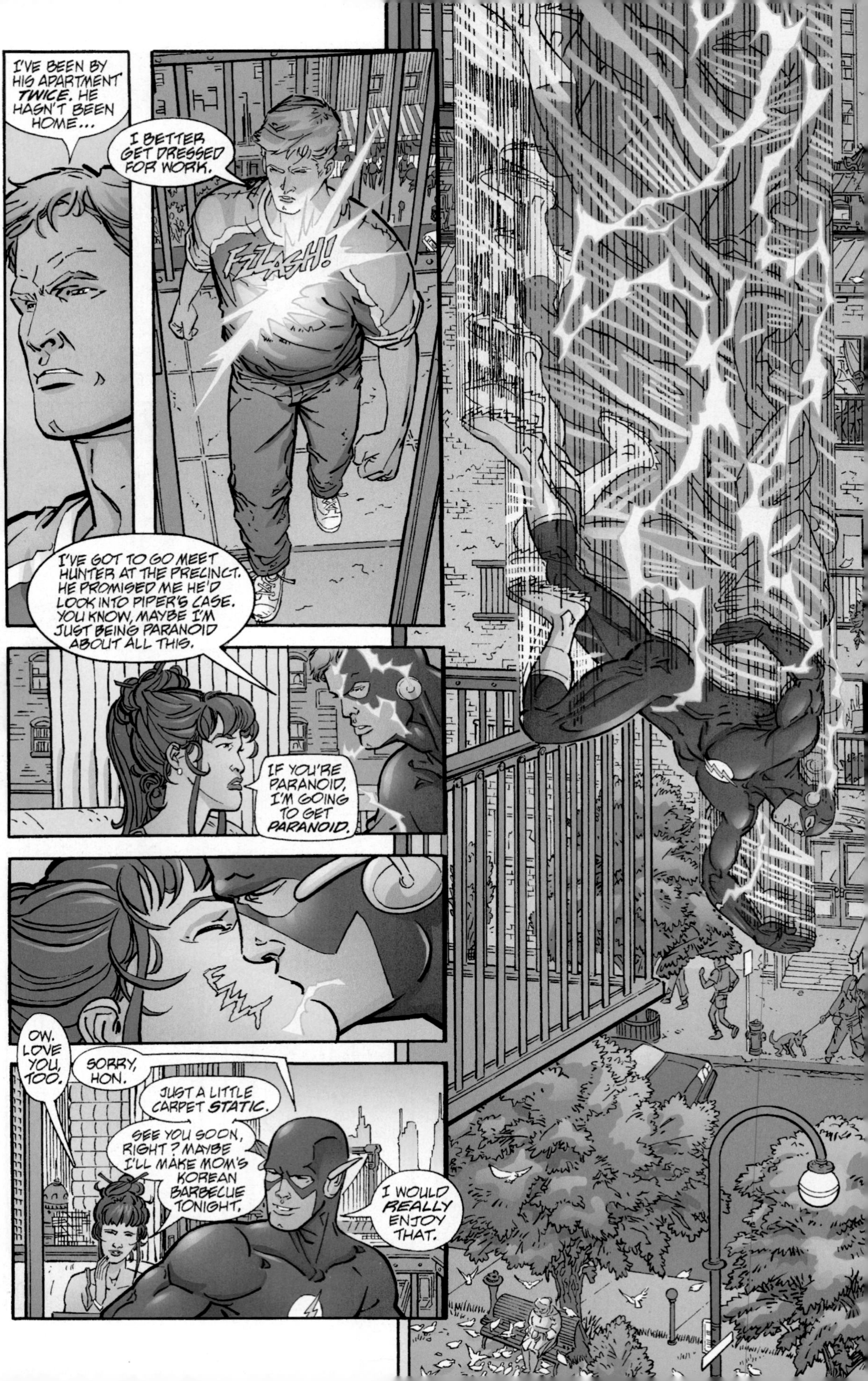
I'VE BEEN BY HIS APARTMENT TWICE. HE HASN'T BEEN HOME...
I BETTER GET DRESSED FOR WORK.
FLASH!
I'VE GOT TO GO MEET HUNTER AT THE PRECINCT. HE PROMISED ME HE'D LOOK INTO PIPER'S CASE. YOU KNOW, MAYBE I'M JUST BEING PARANOID ABOUT ALL THIS.
IF YOU'RE PARANOID, I'M GOING TO GET PARANOID.
OW. LOVE YOU, TOO.
SORRY, HON.
JUST A LITTLE CARPET STATIC.
SEE YOU SOON, RIGHT? MAYBE I'LL MAKE MOM'S KOREAN BARBECUE TONIGHT.
I WOULD REALLY ENJOY THAT.

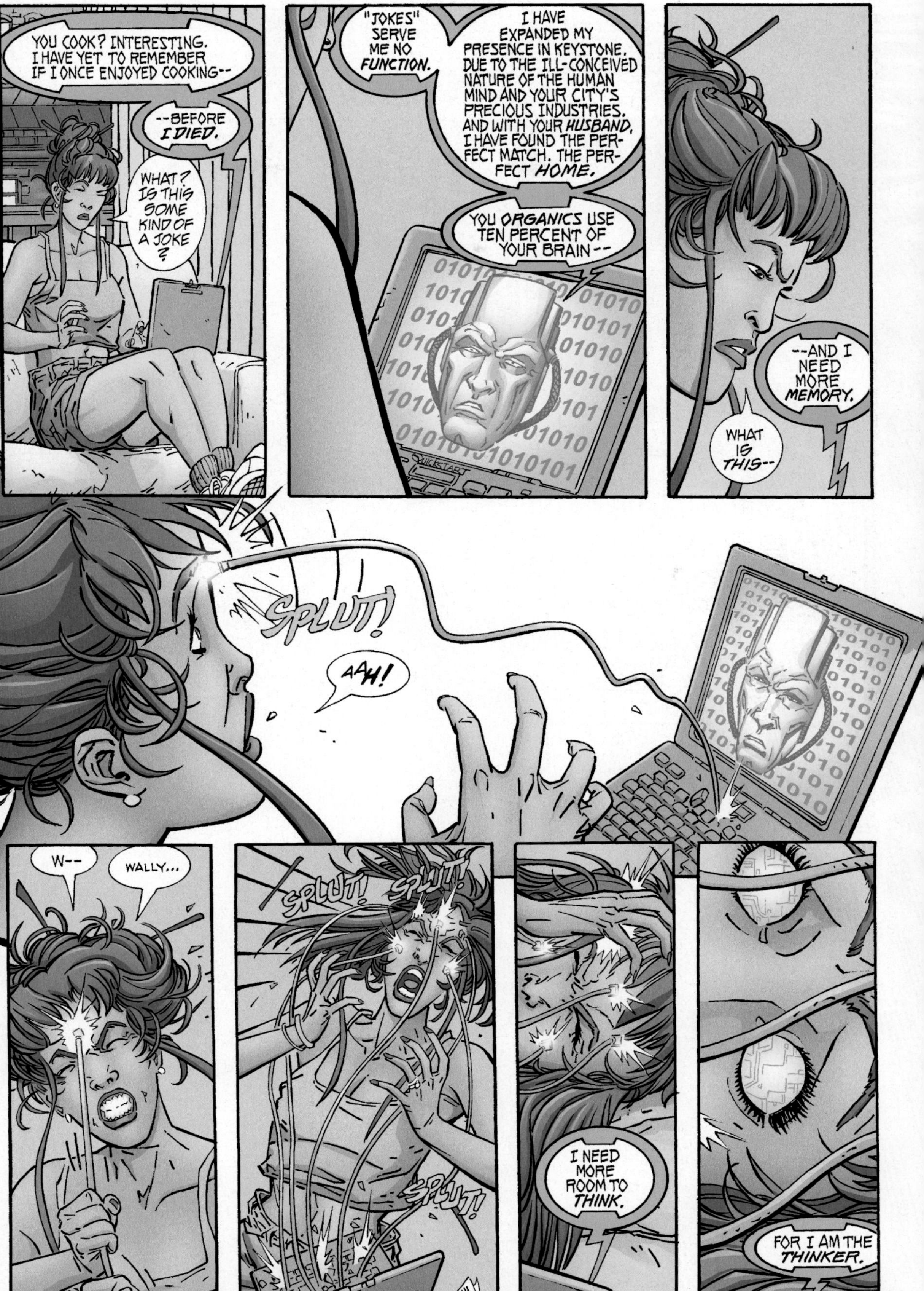
YOU COOK? INTERESTING. I HAVE YET TO REMEMBER IF I ONCE ENJOYED COOKING--
--BEFORE I DIED.
WHAT? IS THIS SOME KIND OF A JOKE?
"JOKES" SERVE ME NO FUNCTION.
I HAVE EXPANDED MY PRESENCE IN KEYSTONE. DUE TO THE ILL-CONCEIVED NATURE OF THE HUMAN MIND AND YOUR CITY'S PRECIOUS INDUSTRIES. AND WITH YOUR HUSBAND, I HAVE FOUND THE PERFECT MATCH. THE PERFECT HOME.
YOU ORGANICS USE TEN PERCENT OF YOUR BRAIN--
QUICKSTART
--AND I NEED MORE MEMORY.
WHAT IS THIS--
SPLUT!
AAH!
W--
WALLY...
SPLUT! SPLUT!
SPLUT!
I NEED MORE ROOM TO THINK.
FOR I AM THE THINKER.

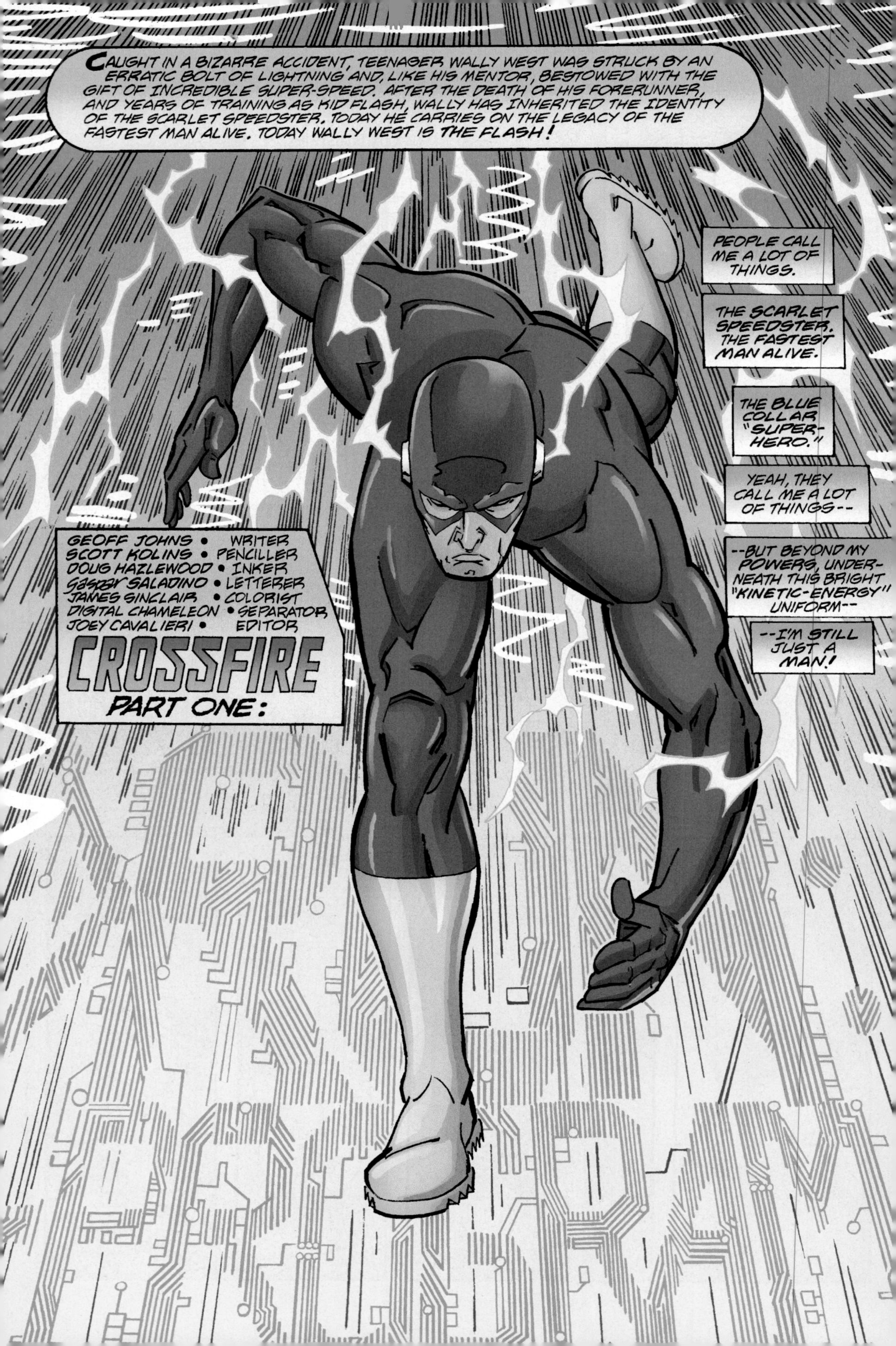
CAUGHT IN A BIZARRE ACCIDENT, TEENAGER WALLY WEST WAS STRUCK BY AN ERRATIC BOLT OF LIGHTNING AND, LIKE HIS MENTOR, BESTOWED WITH THE GIFT OF INCREDIBLE SUPER-SPEED. AFTER THE DEATH OF HIS FORERUNNER, AND YEARS OF TRAINING AS KID FLASH, WALLY HAS INHERITED THE IDENTITY OF THE SCARLET SPEEDSTER. TODAY HE CARRIES ON THE LEGACY OF THE FASTEST MAN ALIVE. TODAY WALLY WEST IS THE FLASH!
PEOPLE CALL ME A LOT OF THINGS.
THE SCARLET SPEEDSTER. THE FASTEST MAN ALIVE.
THE BLUE COLLAR "SUPER-HERO."
YEAH, THEY CALL ME A LOT OF THINGS--
--BUT BEYOND MY POWERS, UNDERNEATH THIS BRIGHT "KINETIC-ENERGY" UNIFORM--
--I'M STILL JUST A MAN!
GEOFF JOHNS • WRITER
SCOTT KOLINS • PENCILLER
DOUG HAZLEWOOD • INKER
Gaspar SALADINO • LETTERER
JAMES SINCLAIR • COLORIST
DIGITAL CHAMELEON • SEPARATOR
JOEY CAVALIERI • EDITOR
CROSSFIRE
PART ONE:

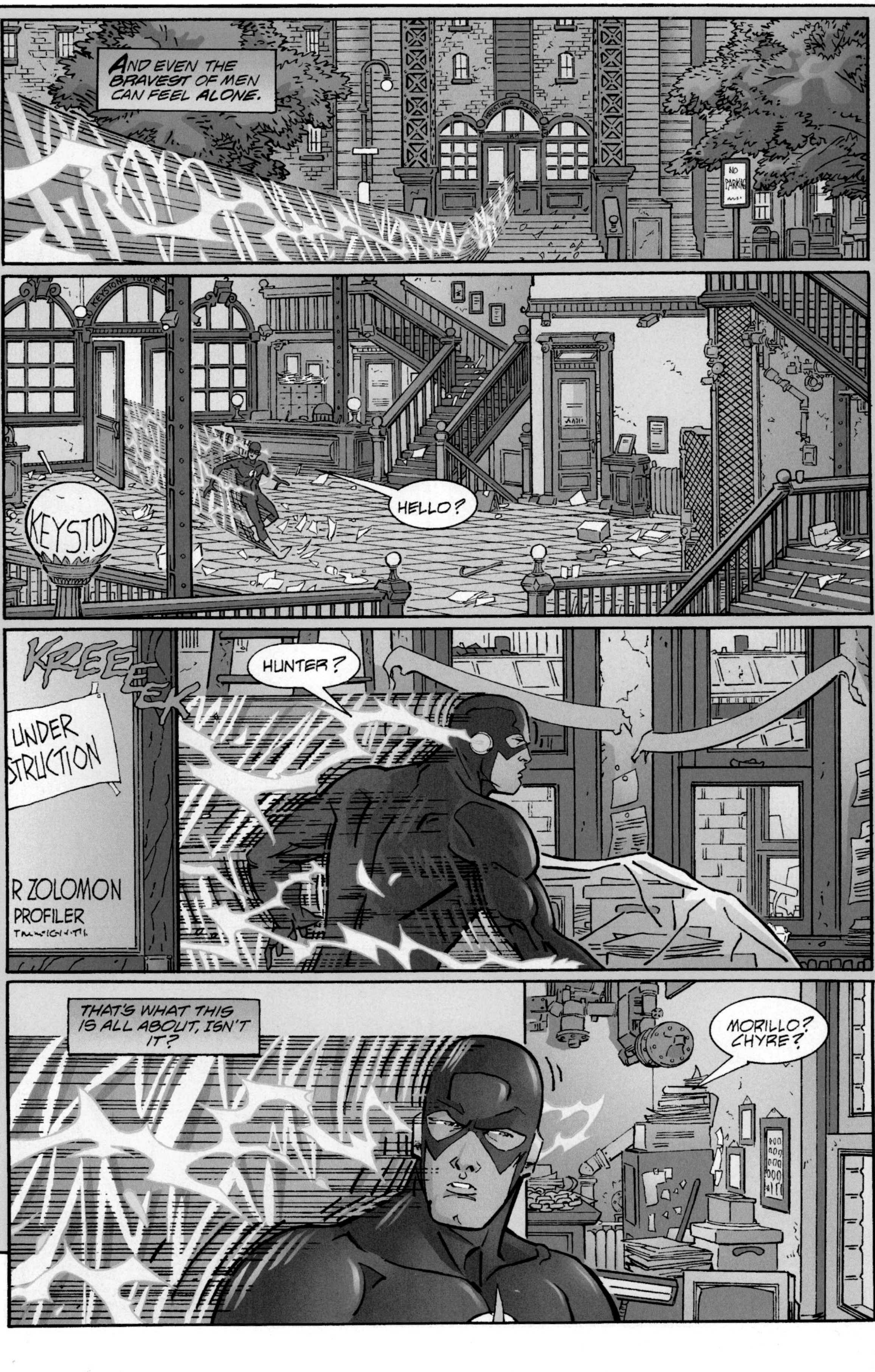
AND EVEN THE BRAVEST OF MEN CAN FEEL ALONE.
NO PARKING
HELLO?
KEYSTON
KREEEEEK
HUNTER?
UNDER
STRUCTION
R ZOLOMON
PROFILER
THAT'S WHAT THIS IS ALL ABOUT, ISN'T IT?
MORILLO? CHYRE?

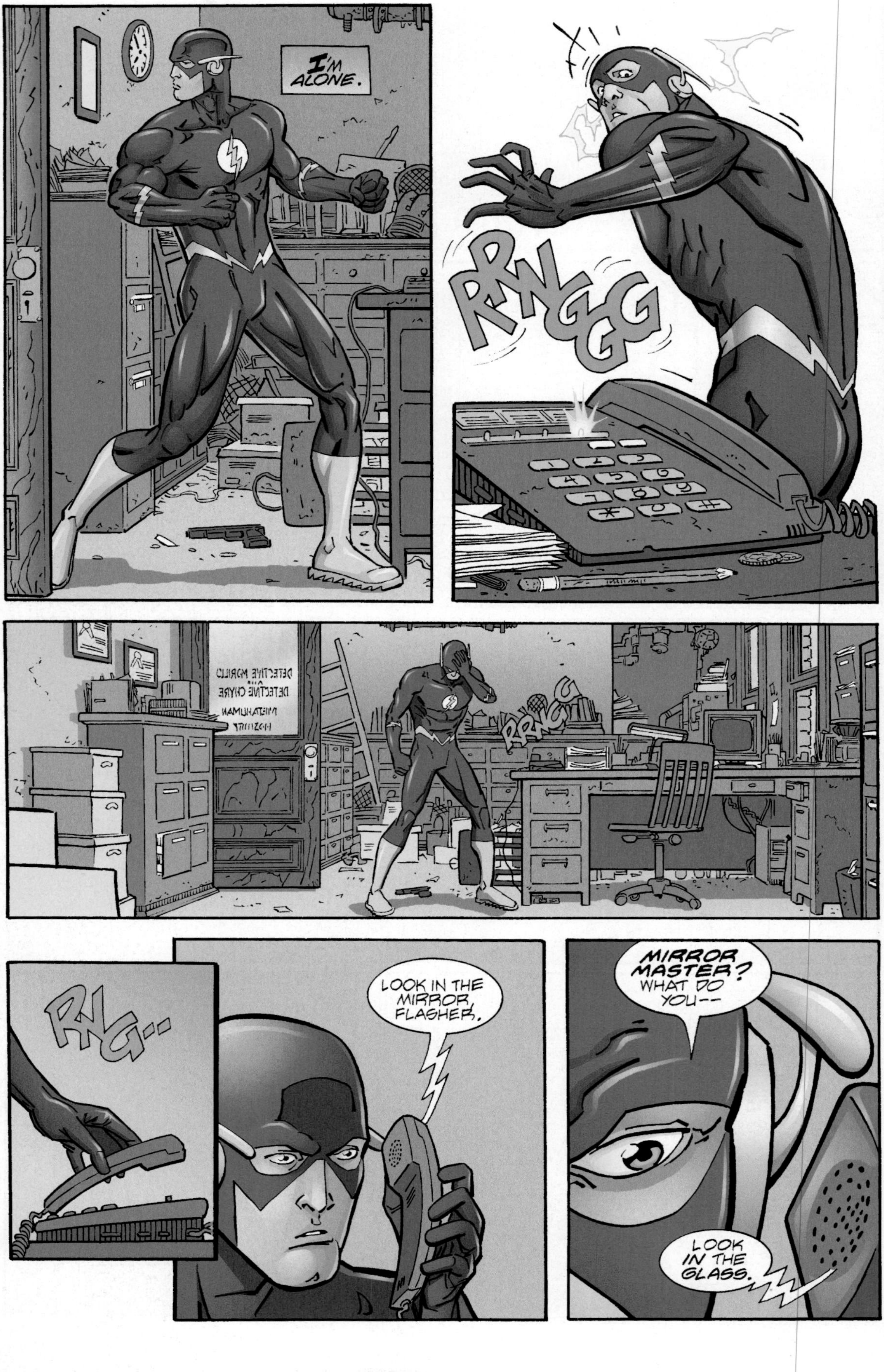
I'M ALONE.
RRNGGG
RRNG
RNG..
LOOK IN THE MIRROR, FLASHER.
MIRROR MASTER? WHAT DO YOU--
LOOK IN THE GLASS.

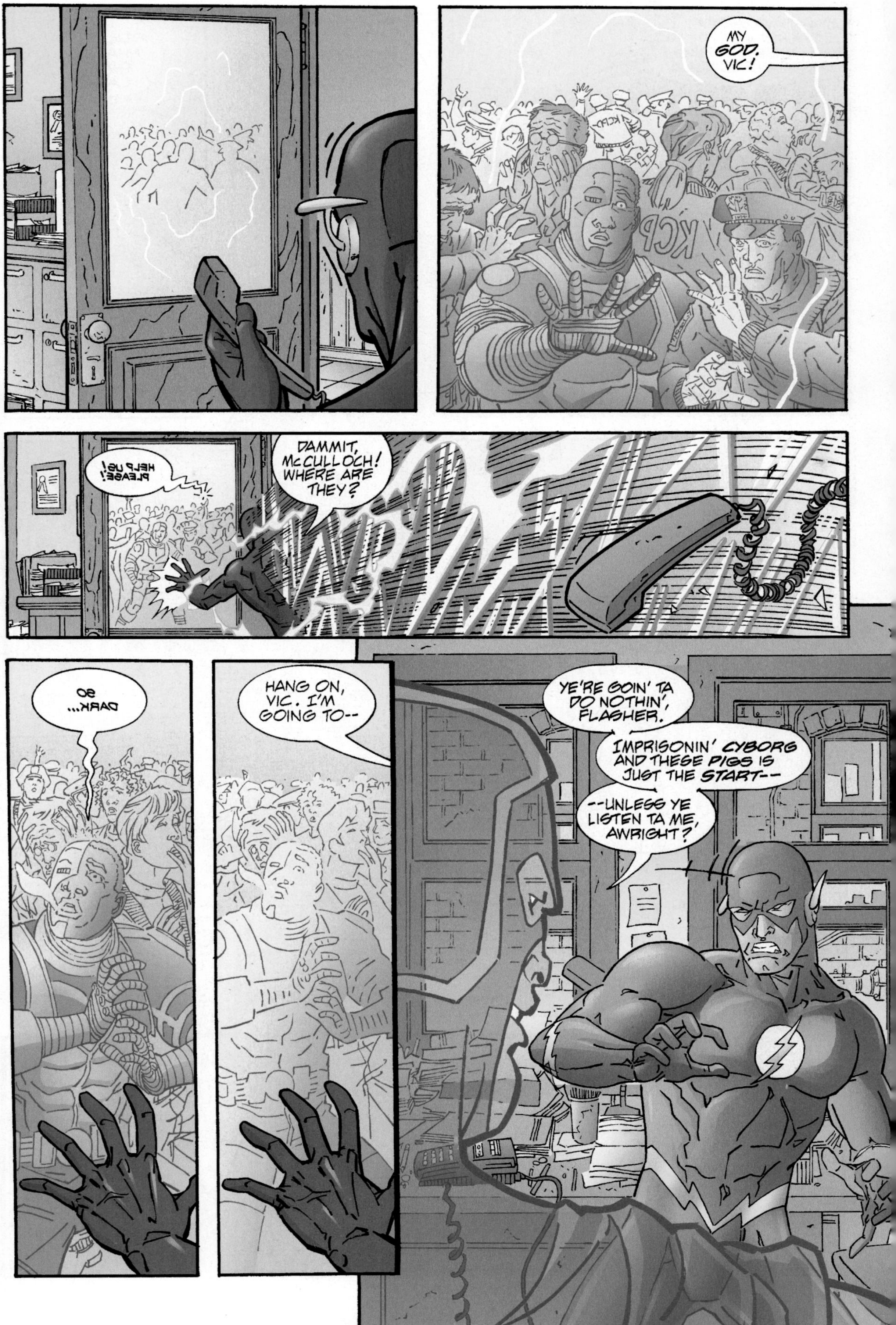
MY GOD. VIC!
HELP US! PLEASE!
DAMMIT, McCULLOCH! WHERE ARE THEY?
SO DARK...
HANG ON, VIC. I'M GOING TO--
YE'RE GOIN' TA DO NOTHIN', FLASHER.
IMPRISONIN' CYBORG AND THESE PIGS IS JUST THE START--
--UNLESS YE LISTEN TA ME, AWRIGHT?

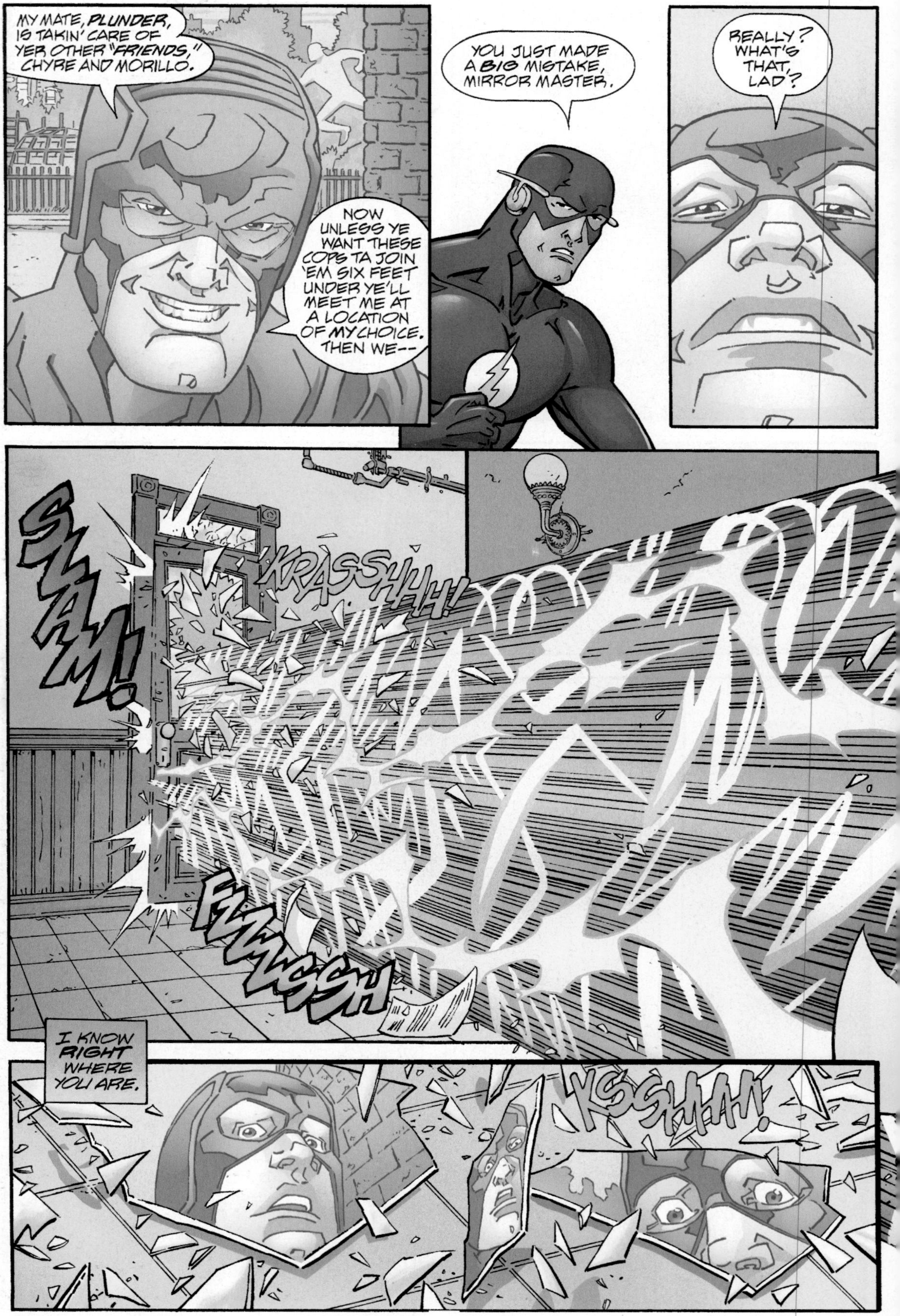

MY MATE, PLUNDER, IS TAKIN' CARE OF YER OTHER "FRIENDS," CHYRE AND MORILLO.
NOW UNLESS YE WANT THESE COPS TA JOIN 'EM SIX FEET UNDER YE'LL MEET ME AT A LOCATION OF MY CHOICE. THEN WE--
YOU JUST MADE A BIG MISTAKE, MIRROR MASTER.
REALLY? WHAT'S THAT, LAD?
SMAM!
KRASSHHH!
FWWSSH
I KNOW RIGHT WHERE YOU ARE.
YSSHAH!

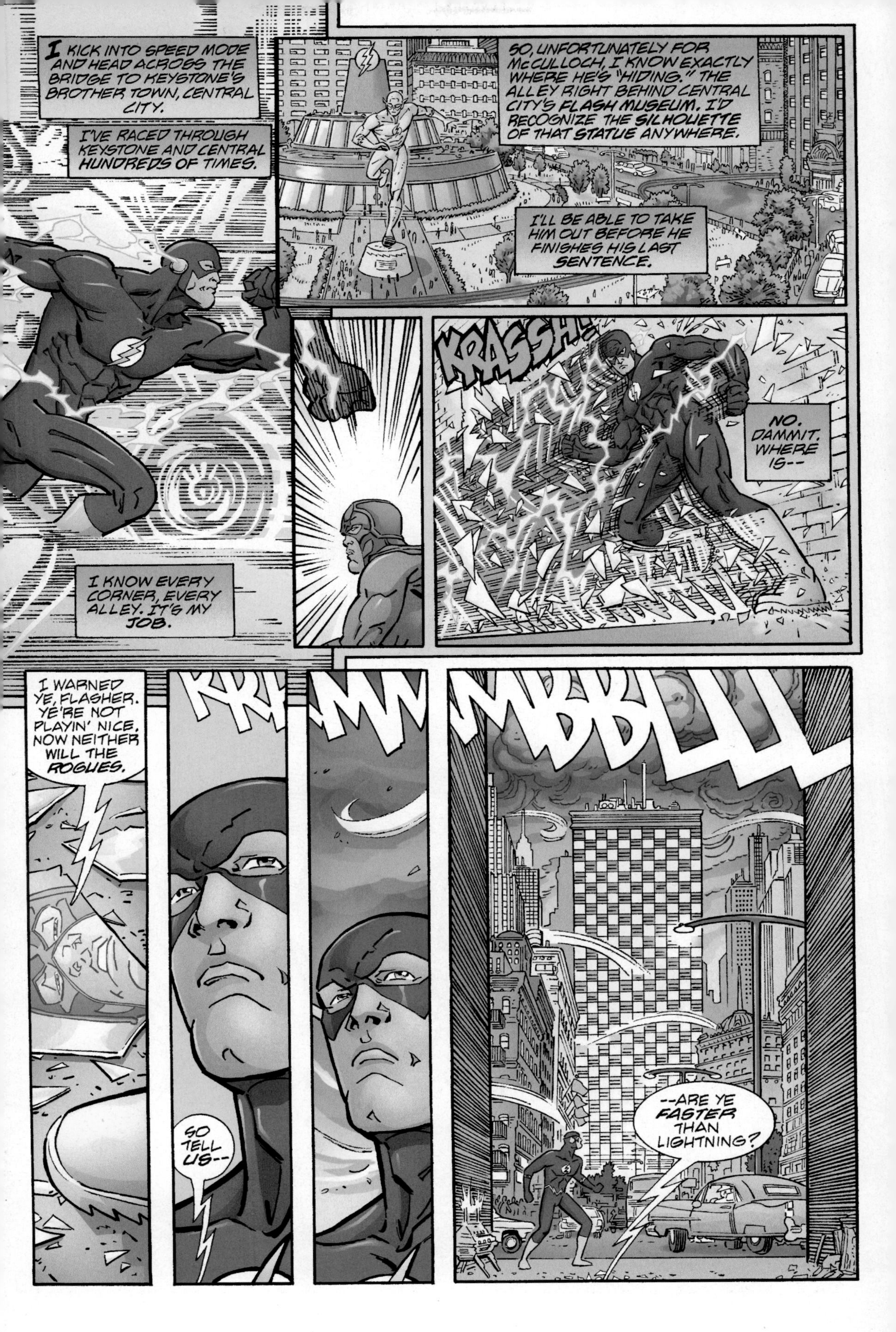
I KICK INTO SPEED MODE AND HEAD ACROSS THE BRIDGE TO KEYSTONE'S BROTHER TOWN, CENTRAL CITY.
I'VE RACED THROUGH KEYSTONE AND CENTRAL HUNDREDS OF TIMES.
SO, UNFORTUNATELY FOR McCULLOCH, I KNOW EXACTLY WHERE HE'S "HIDING." THE ALLEY RIGHT BEHIND CENTRAL CITY'S FLASH MUSEUM. I'D RECOGNIZE THE SILHOUETTE OF THAT STATUE ANYWHERE.
I'LL BE ABLE TO TAKE HIM OUT BEFORE HE FINISHES HIS LAST SENTENCE.
I KNOW EVERY CORNER, EVERY ALLEY. IT'S MY JOB.
KRASSH!
NO. DAMMIT. WHERE IS--
I WARNED YE, FLASHER. YE'RE NOT PLAYIN' NICE, NOW NEITHER WILL THE ROGUES.
KRRAMMBBLLL
SO TELL US--
--ARE YE FASTER THAN LIGHTNING?

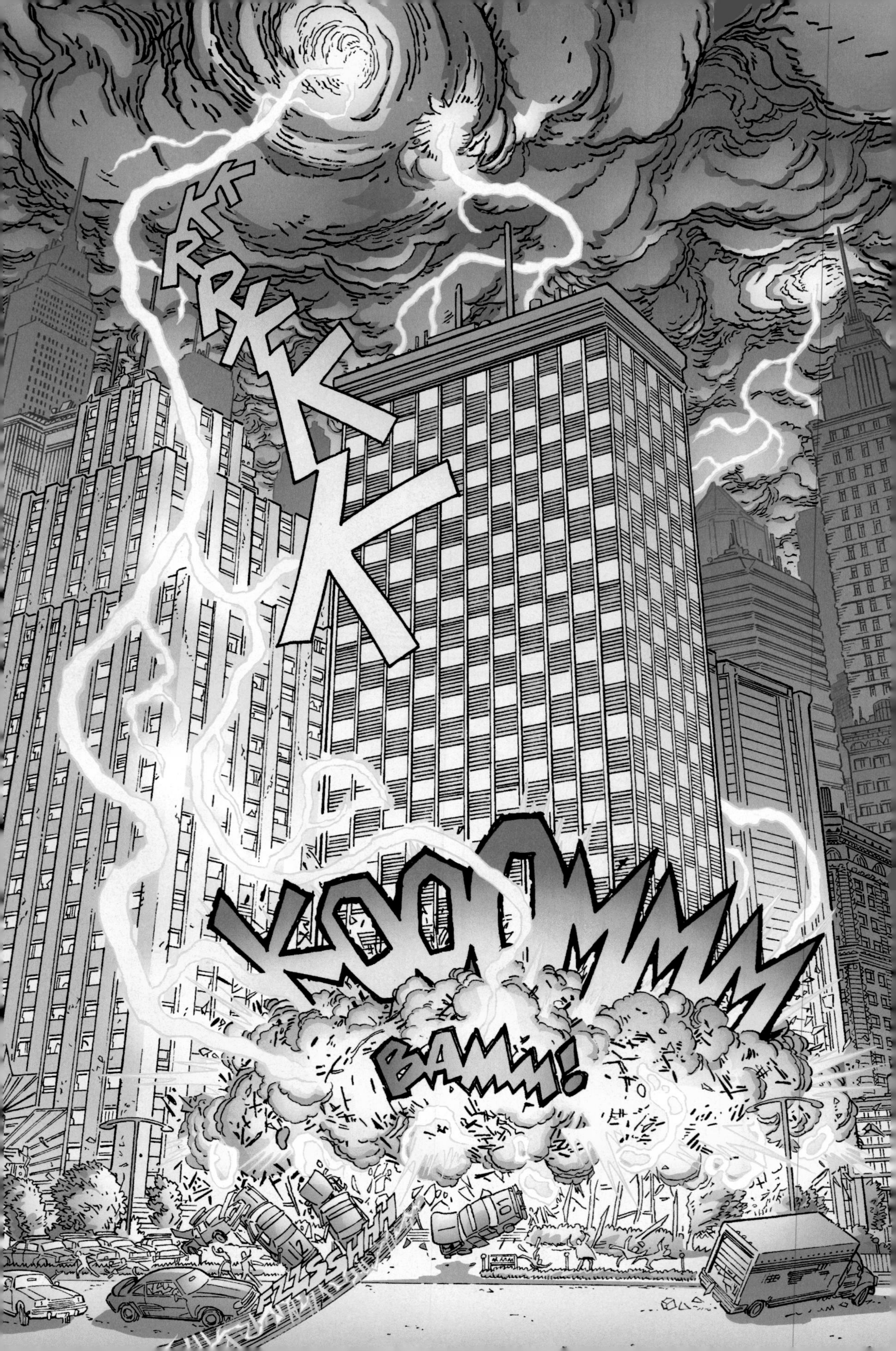

KRRKKK
KOOOMMM
BAMMM!
FZZZSSHHH

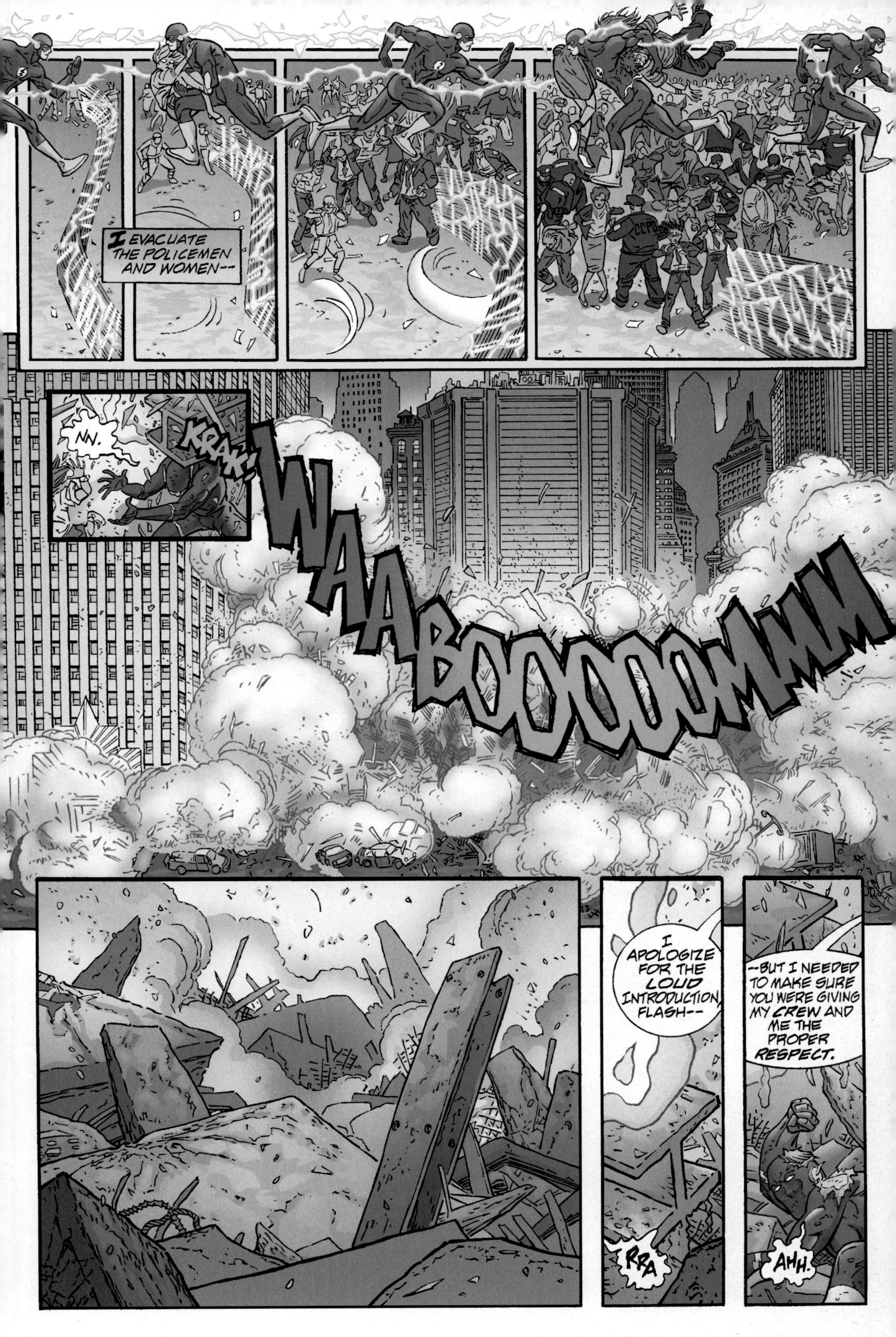
I EVACUATE THE POLICEMEN AND WOMEN--
NN.
KRAK!
WAABOOOOOMMM
I APOLOGIZE FOR THE LOUD INTRODUCTION, FLASH--
RRA
--BUT I NEEDED TO MAKE SURE YOU WERE GIVING MY CREW AND ME THE PROPER RESPECT.
AHH.

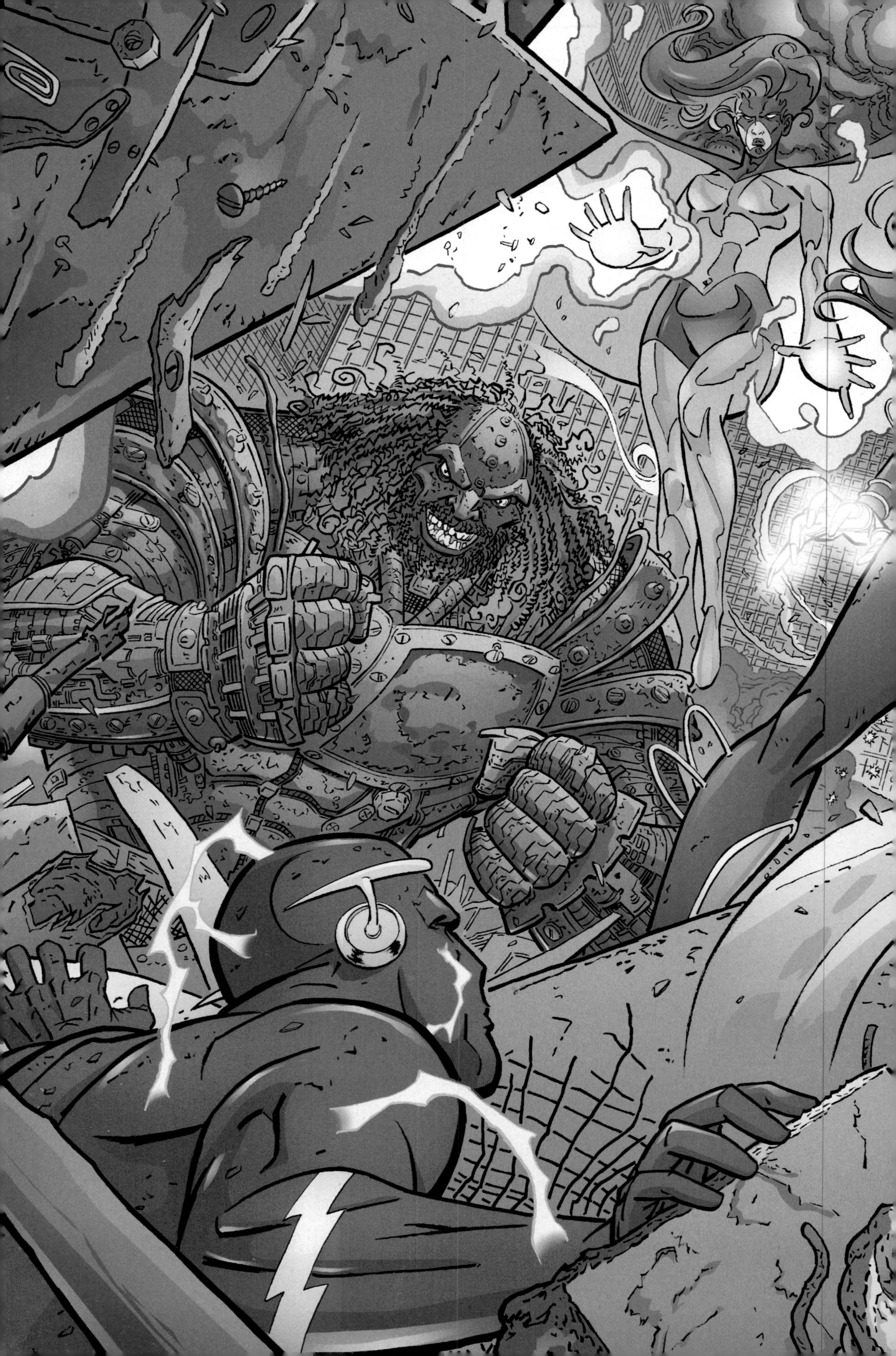

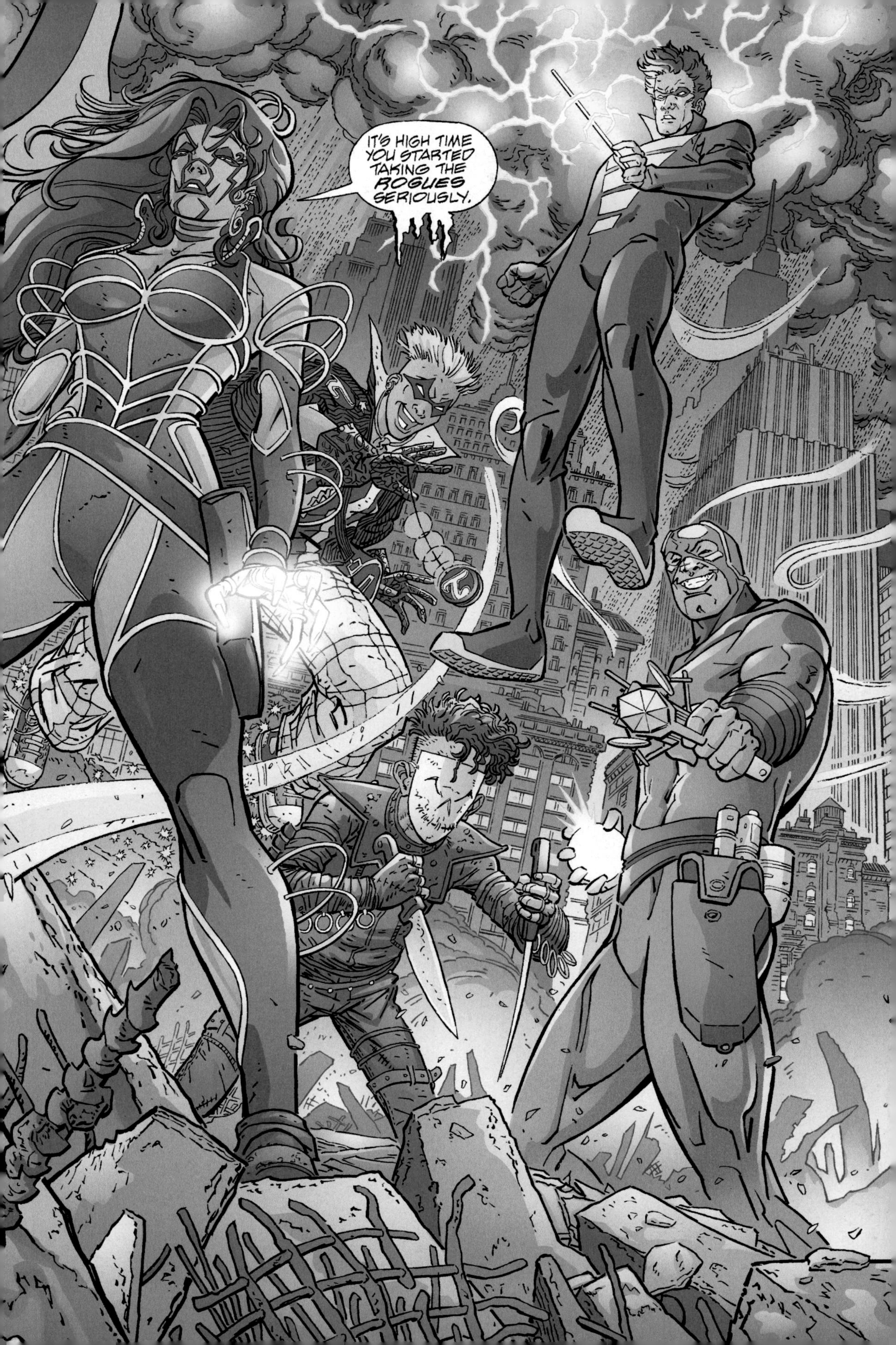
IT'S HIGH TIME YOU STARTED TAKING THE ROGUES SERIOUSLY.

KEYSTONE CITY.

THE OFFICE OF UNION COMMISSIONER KEITH "GOLDFACE" KENYON.

--NO DETAILS ON THE EXPLOSION IN CENTRAL CITY YET BUT... GOD, IT'S GETTING BAD UP HERE, LANCE. THE STORM IS-- KZZZ--BETTER--KZZZ-- LAND--KZZZ--NO--

IT'S STARTED EARLY. AND IT'S MY FAULT. TRICKSTER STOLE OUR DOCUMENTS ON THE NETWORK... AND BLACKSMITH.

THOUGHT I COULD TAKE CARE OF MY EX-WIFE MYSELF. THOUGHT I NEEDED TO. WHO'S GOING TO TRUST AN EX-SUPER-VILLAIN?... A COP KILLER.

KZZZZZZZZ

WE BETTER GATHER THE UNION UP, BOYS.

YOU HEAR...?

THMPP KATHMPP

YOUR BOYS...

YOUR BOYS ARE NOW STORAGE, "GOLDFACE."

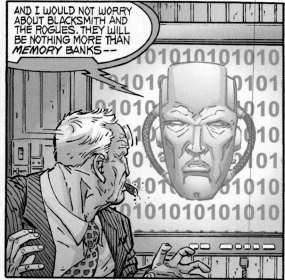

AND I WOULD NOT WORRY ABOUT BLACKSMITH AND THE ROGUES. THEY WILL BE NOTHING MORE THAN MEMORY BANKS--

1010101010
101010101
0101010
101
1010

--WHEN THEY JOIN MY BRAIN TRUST.

KRAK

WHPP!

WHPP!

LIKE EVERYONE IN KEYSTONE CITY.

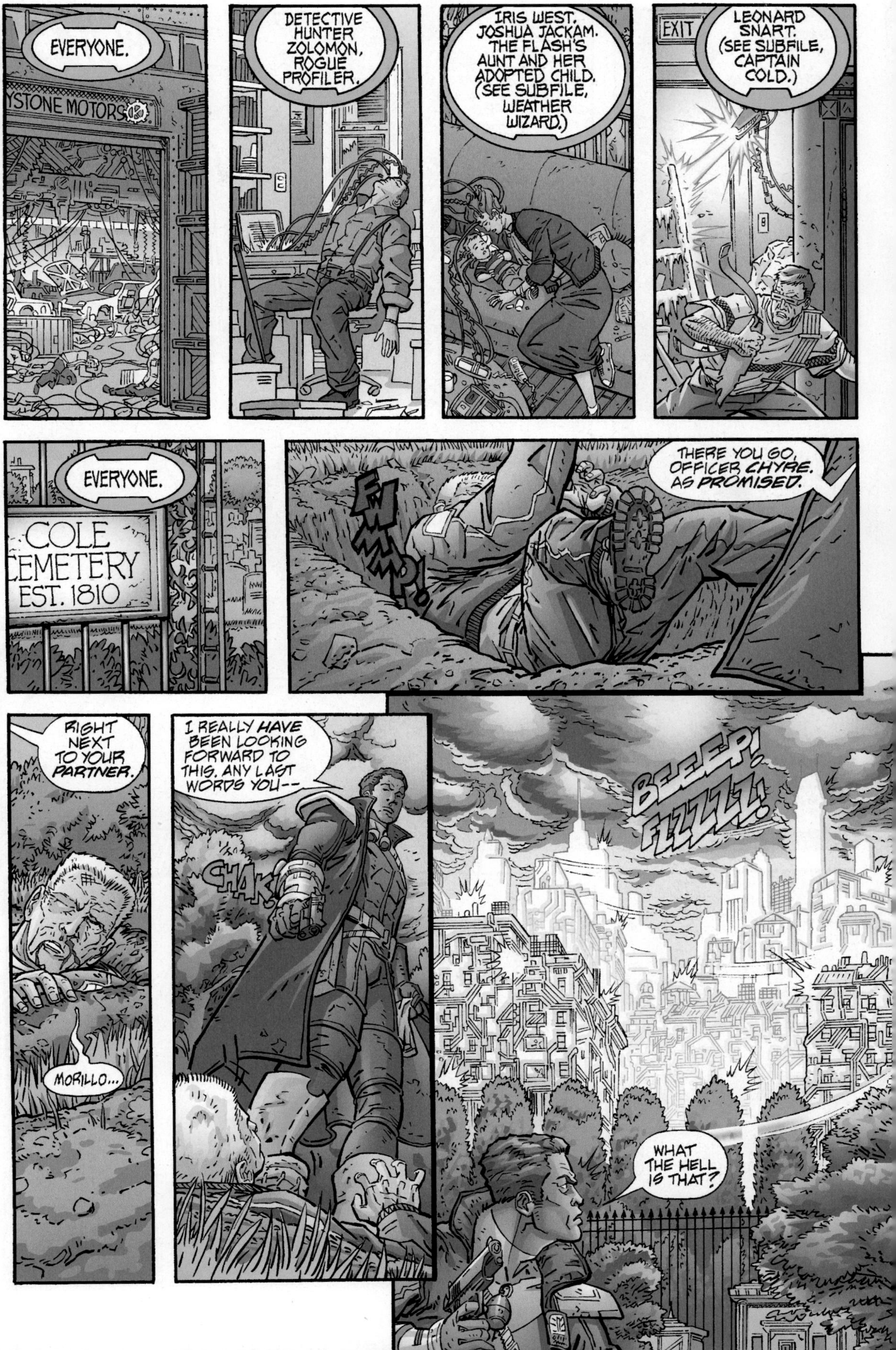
EVERYONE.
YSTONE MOTORS
DETECTIVE HUNTER ZOLOMON, ROGUE PROFILER.
IRIS WEST. JOSHUA JACKAM. THE FLASH'S AUNT AND HER ADOPTED CHILD. (SEE SUBFILE, WEATHER WIZARD.)
EXIT
LEONARD SNART. (SEE SUBFILE, CAPTAIN COLD.)
EVERYONE.
COLE CEMETERY EST. 1810
FWMMP!
THERE YOU GO, OFFICER CHYRE. AS PROMISED.
RIGHT NEXT TO YOUR PARTNER.
MORILLO...
I REALLY HAVE BEEN LOOKING FORWARD TO THIS. ANY LAST WORDS YOU--
CHAK
BEEEP! FIZZZZ!
WHAT THE HELL IS THAT?

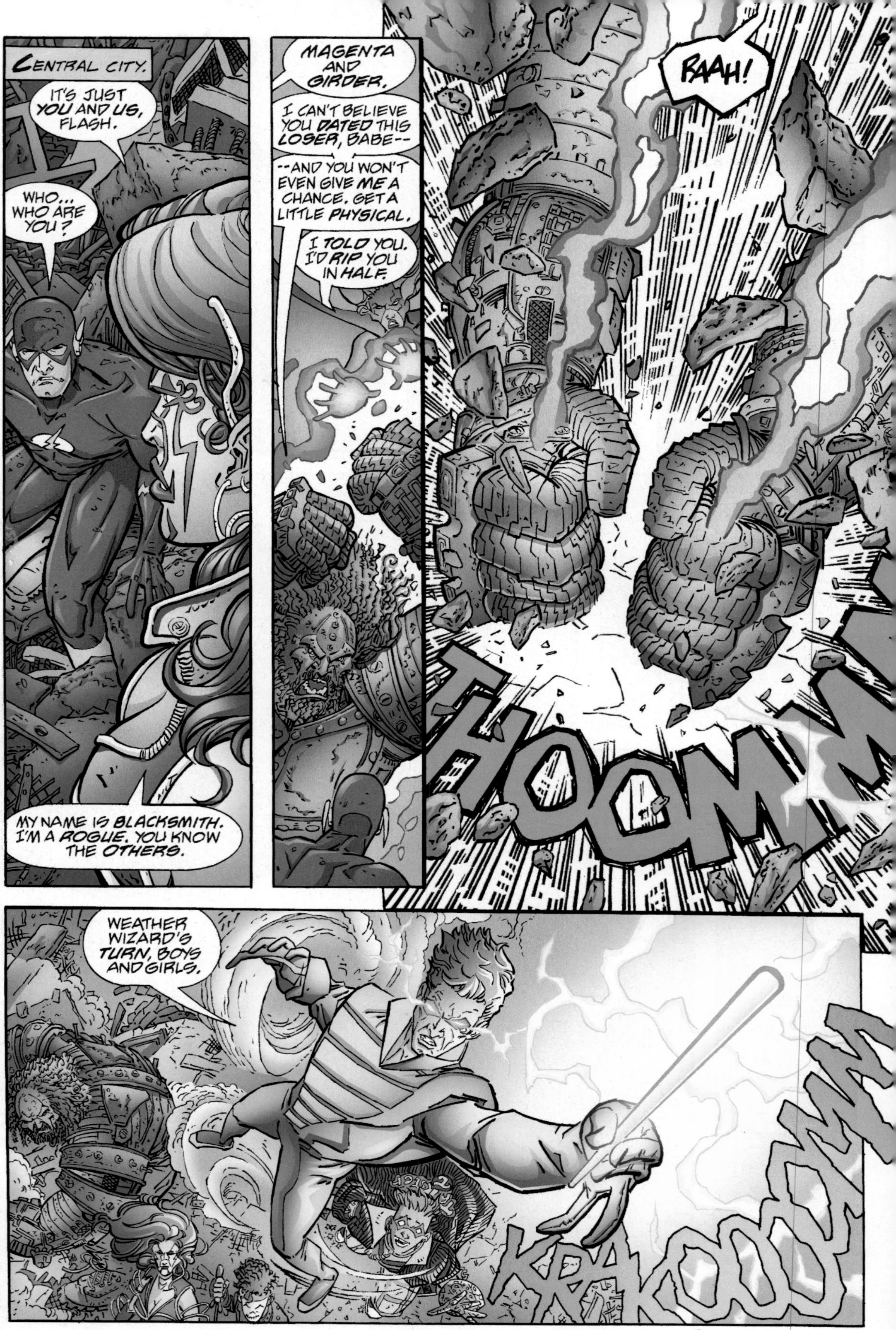
CENTRAL CITY.
IT'S JUST YOU AND US, FLASH.
WHO... WHO ARE YOU?
MY NAME IS BLACKSMITH. I'M A ROGUE. YOU KNOW THE OTHERS.
MAGENTA AND GIRDER.
I CAN'T BELIEVE YOU DATED THIS LOSER, BABE--
--AND YOU WON'T EVEN GIVE ME A CHANCE. GET A LITTLE PHYSICAL.
I TOLD YOU. I'D RIP YOU IN HALF.
RAAH!
THOOMM
WEATHER WIZARD'S TURN, BOYS AND GIRLS.
KRAKOOOM

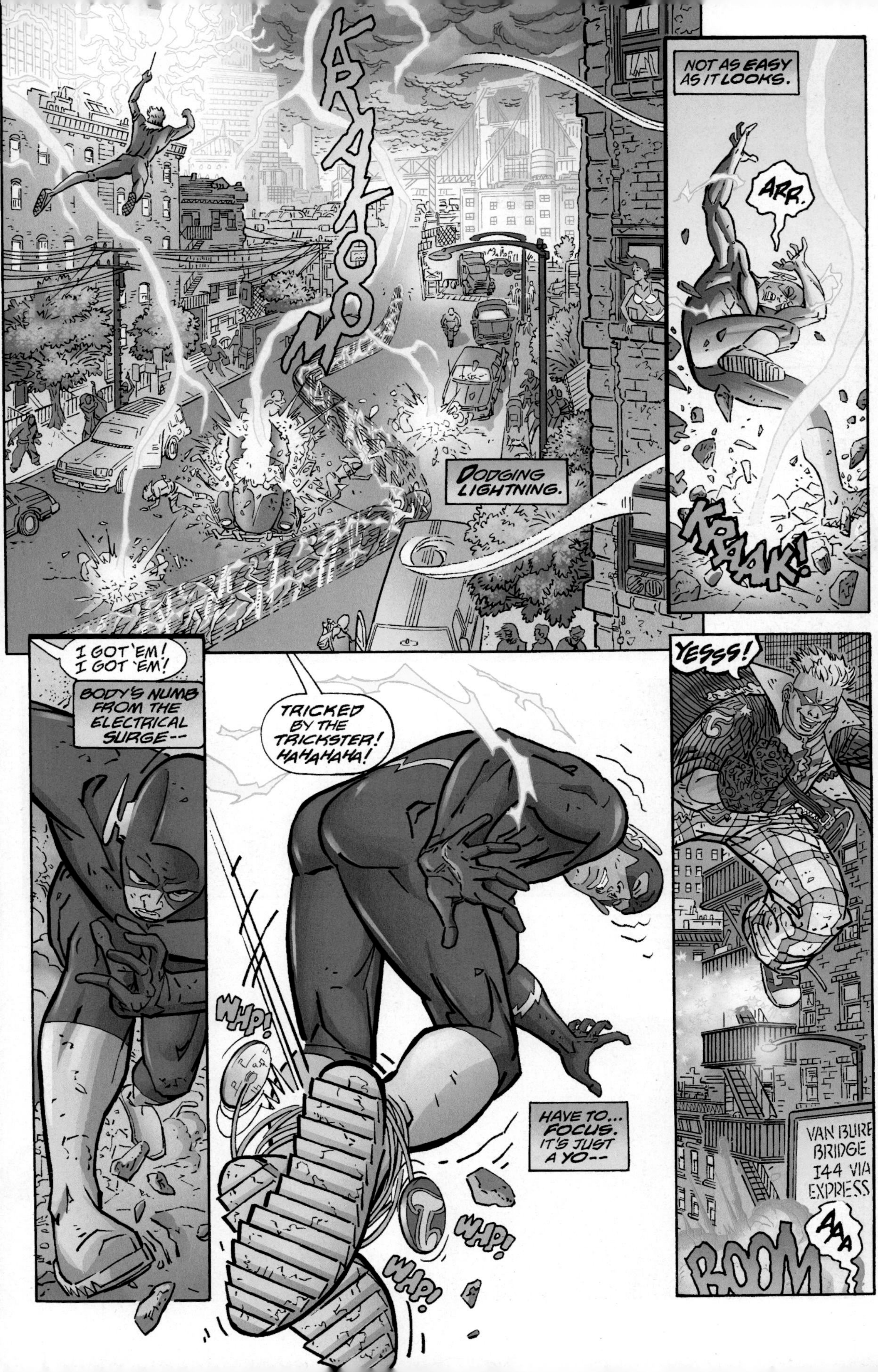
KRAKOOM
NOT AS EASY AS IT LOOKS.
ARR.
DODGING LIGHTNING.
KRAAK!
I GOT 'EM! I GOT 'EM!
BODY'S NUMB FROM THE ELECTRICAL SURGE--
TRICKED BY THE TRICKSTER! HAHAHAHA!
WHP!
HAVE TO... FOCUS. IT'S JUST A YO--
WHP!
WHP!
YESSS!
VAN BURE
BRIDGE
I44 VIA
EXPRESS
AAA
BOOM

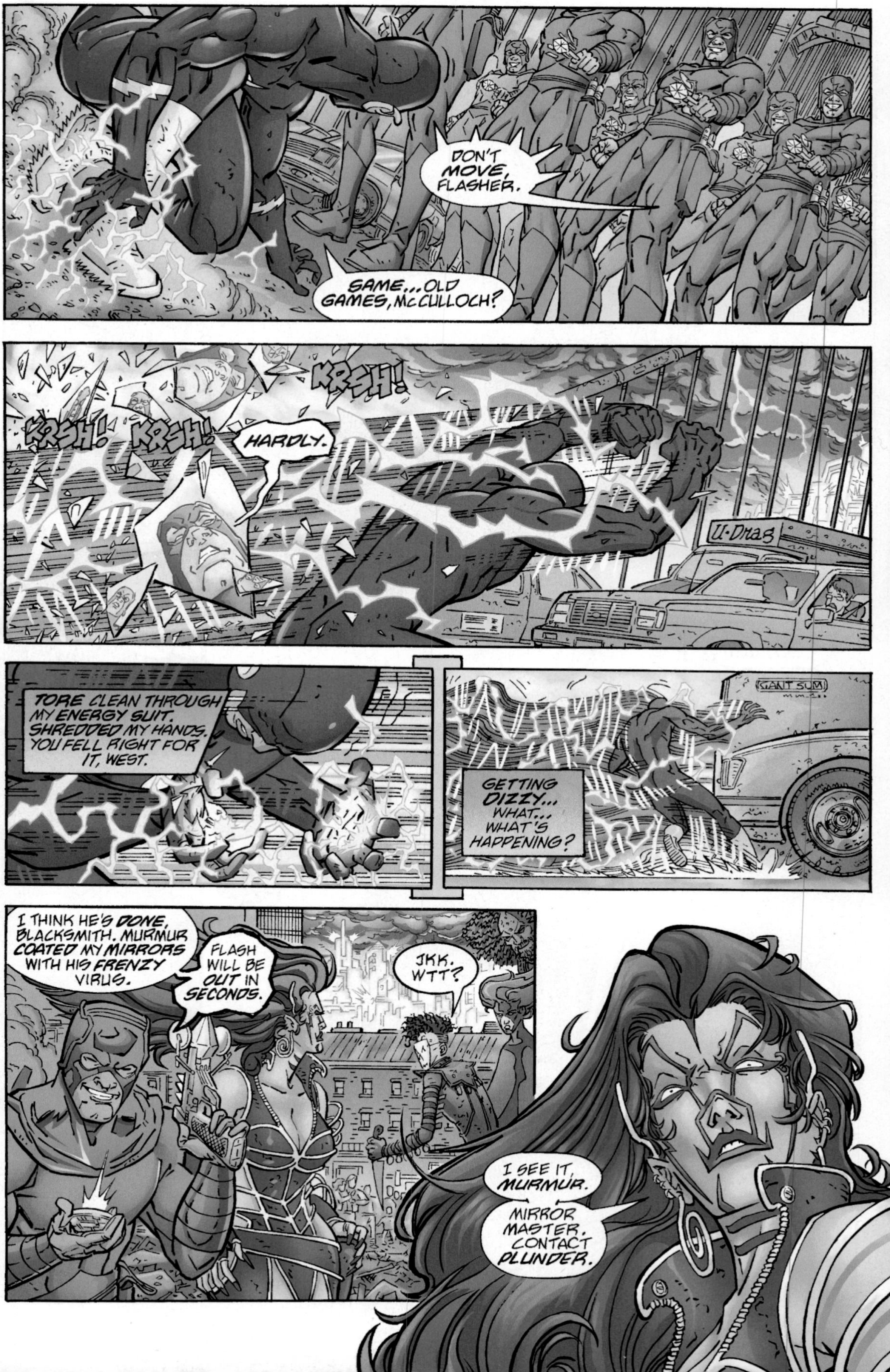
DON'T MOVE, FLASHER.
SAME... OLD GAMES, McCULLOCH?
KRSH!
KRSH!
KRSH!
HARDLY.
U-Drag
TORE CLEAN THROUGH MY ENERGY SUIT. SHREDDED MY HANDS. YOU FELL RIGHT FOR IT, WEST.
GETTING DIZZY... WHAT... WHAT'S HAPPENING?
I THINK HE'S DONE, BLACKSMITH. MURMUR COATED MY MIRRORS WITH HIS FRENZY VIRUS.
FLASH WILL BE OUT IN SECONDS.
JKK. WTT?
I SEE IT, MURMUR.
MIRROR MASTER, CONTACT PLUNDER.

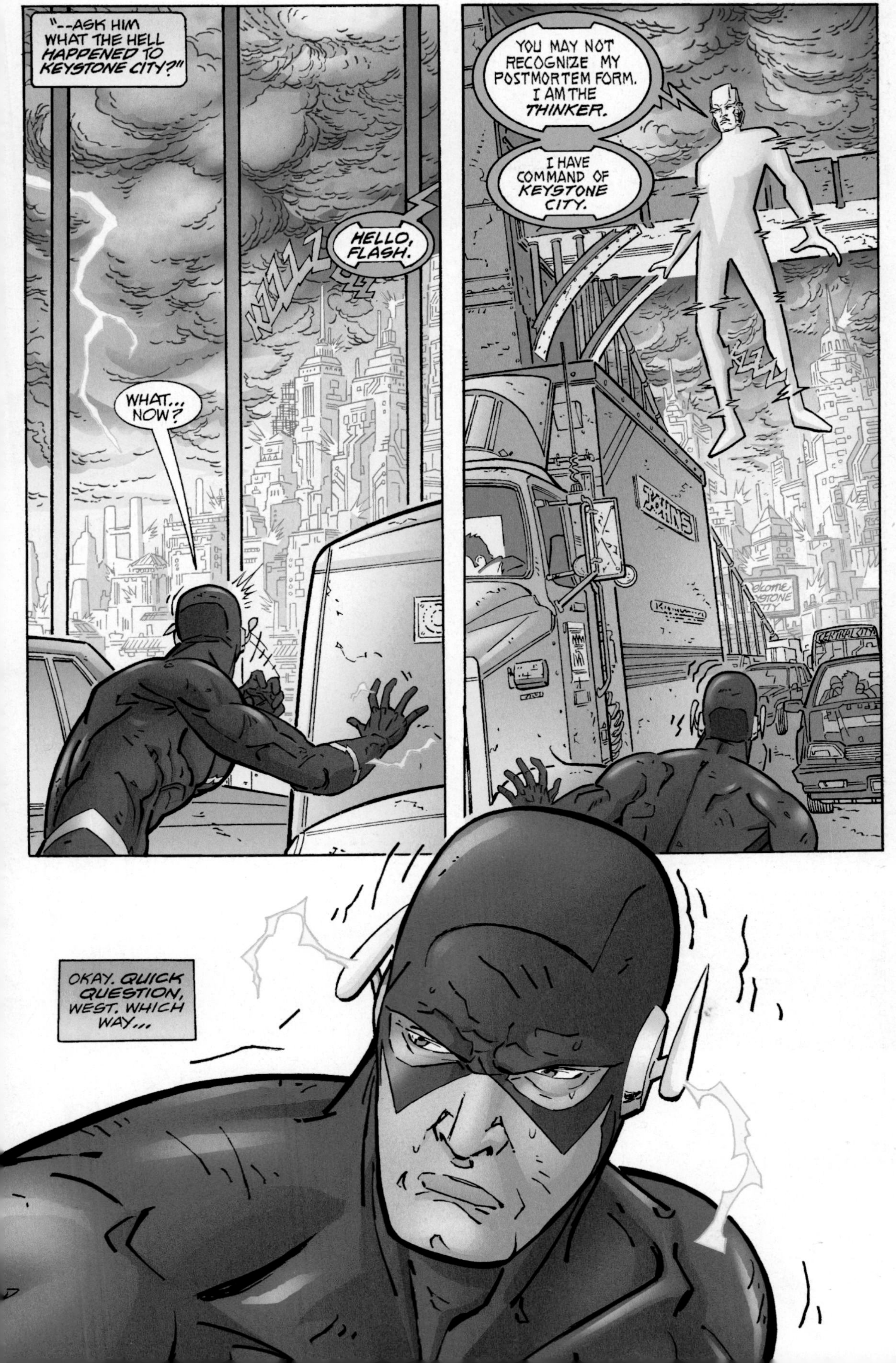
"--ASK HIM WHAT THE HELL HAPPENED TO KEYSTONE CITY?"
KZZZZT
HELLO, FLASH.
WHAT... NOW?
YOU MAY NOT RECOGNIZE MY POSTMORTEM FORM. I AM THE THINKER.
I HAVE COMMAND OF KEYSTONE CITY.
CENTRAL CITY
OKAY. QUICK QUESTION, WEST. WHICH WAY...

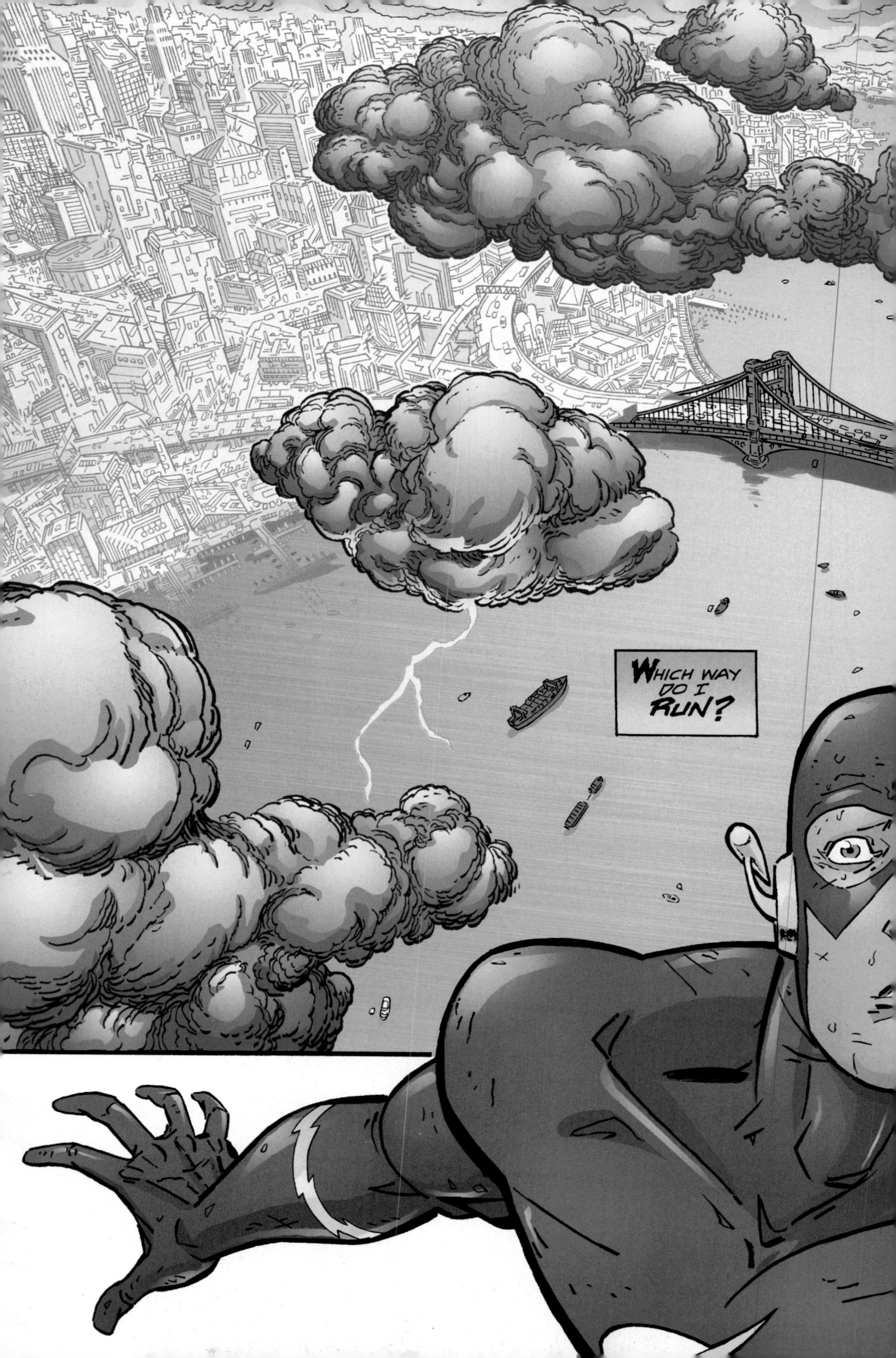
WHICH WAY DO I RUN?

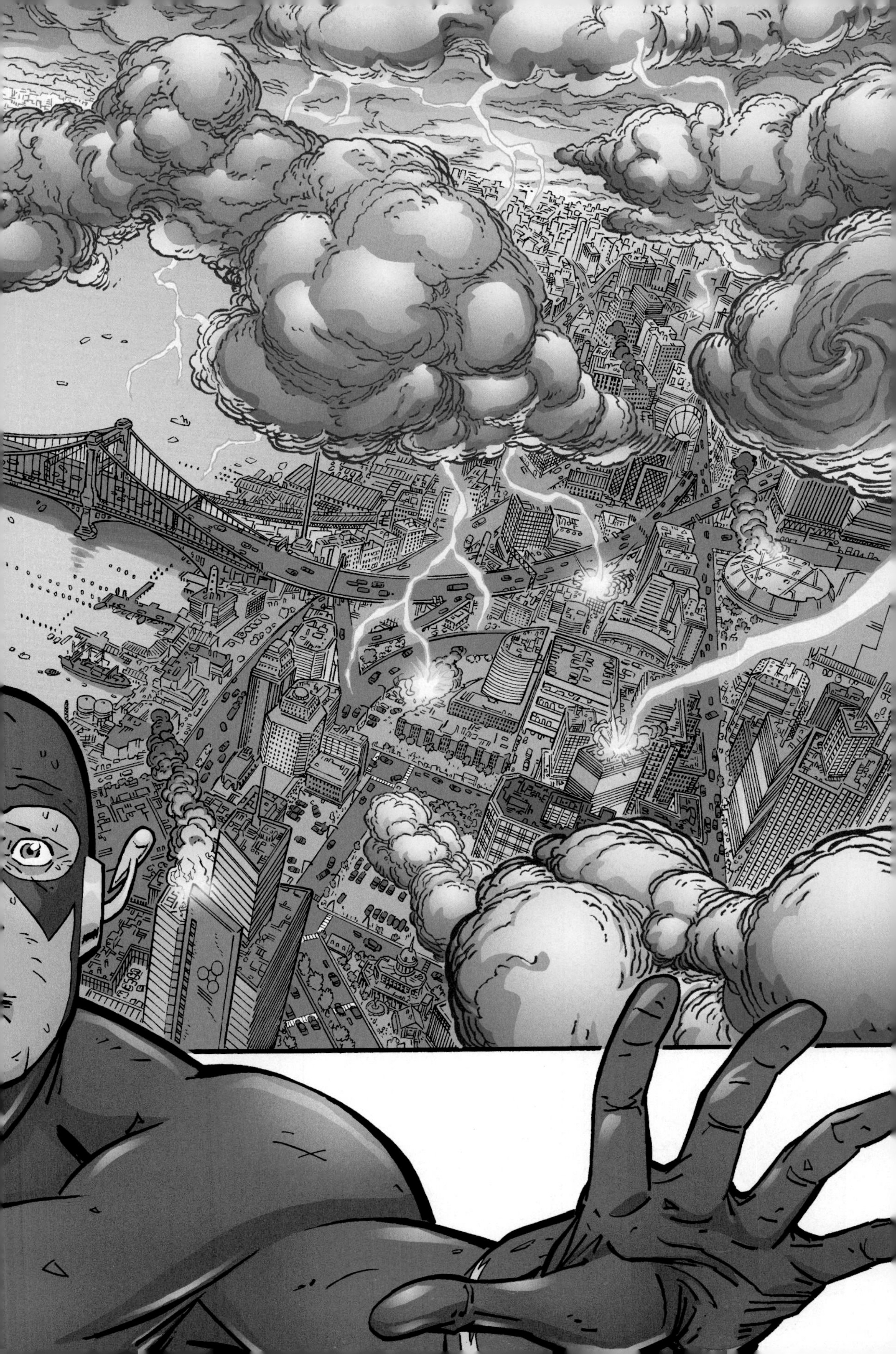

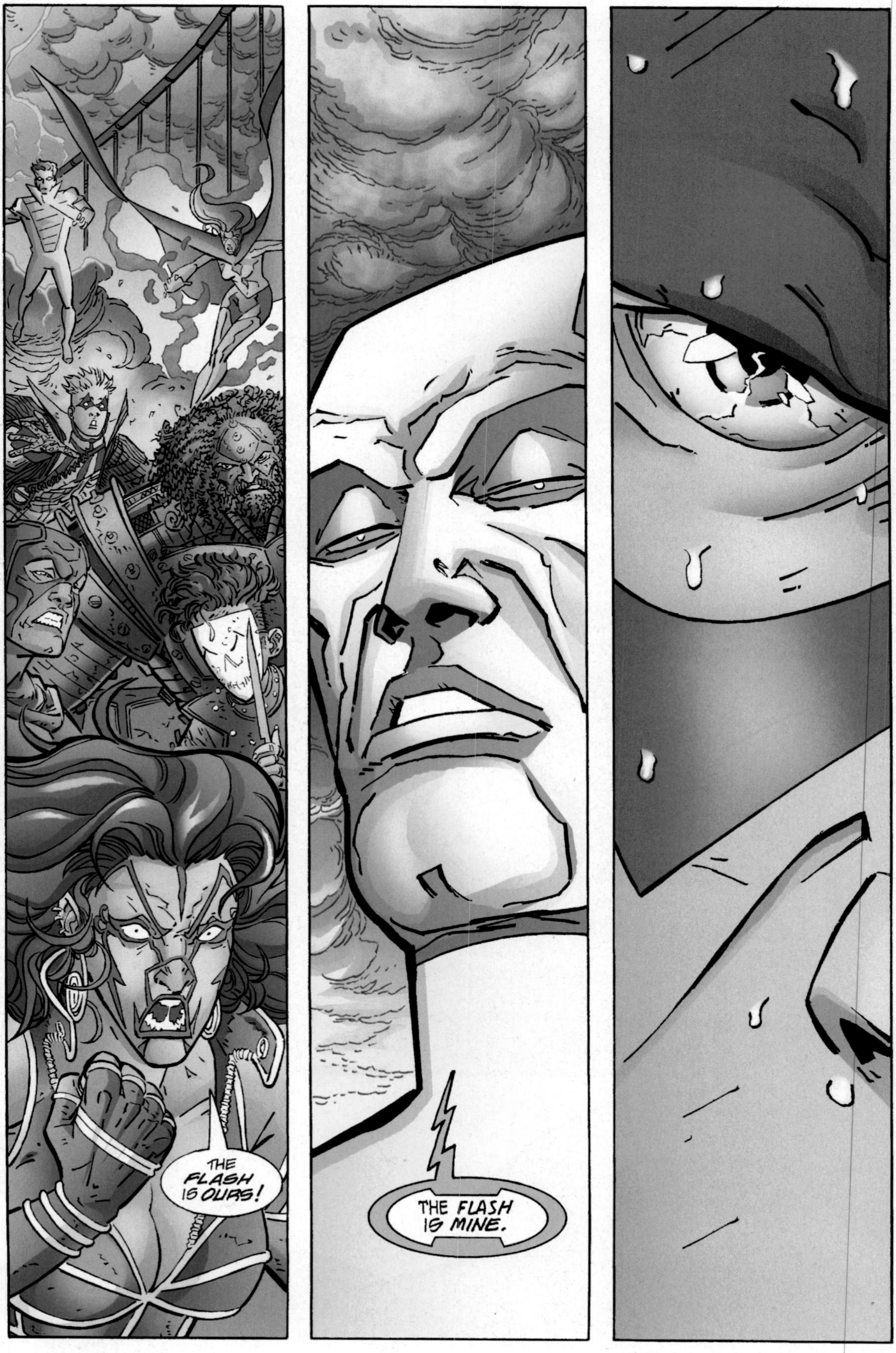
THE FLASH IS OURS!
THE FLASH IS MINE.

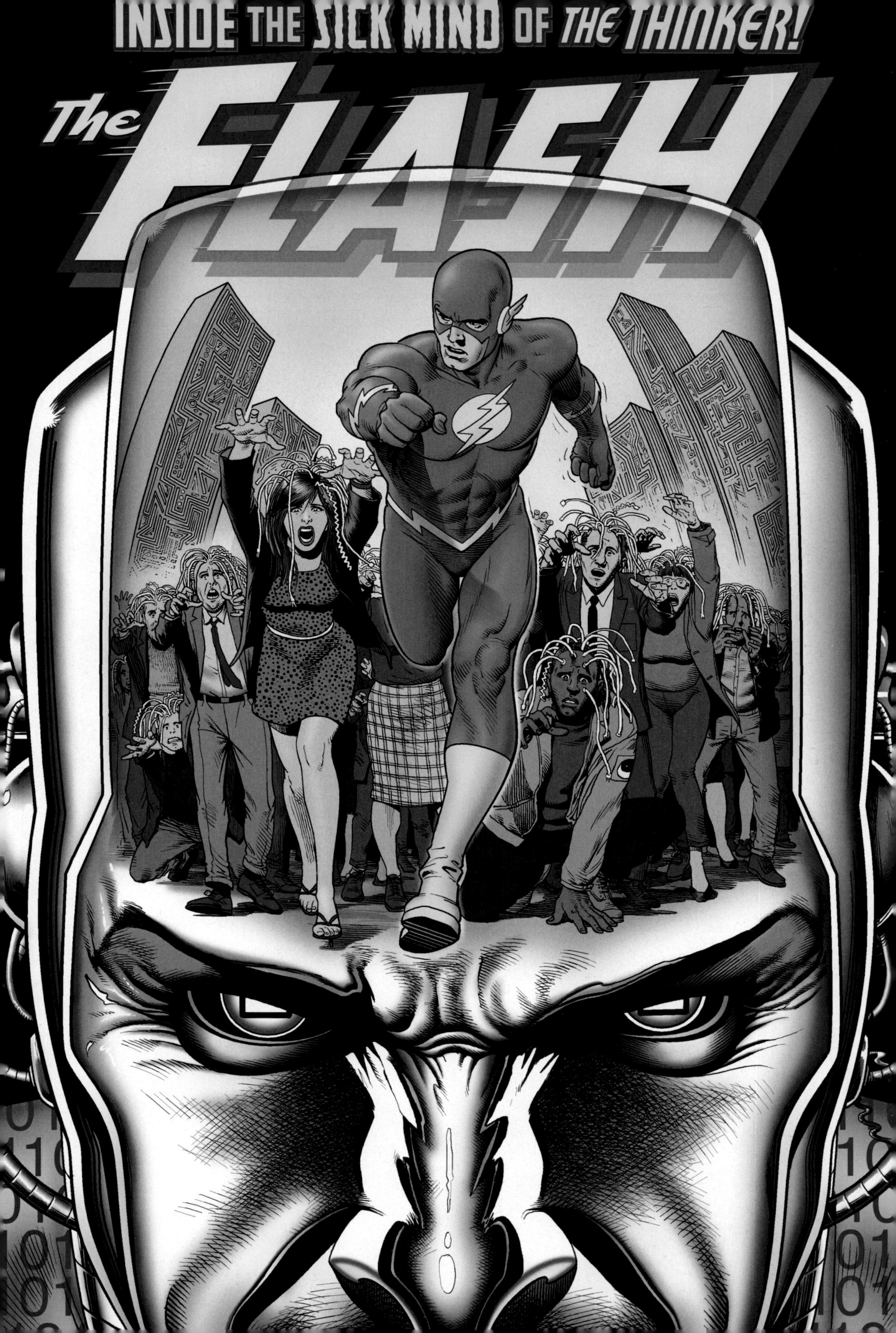
INSIDE THE SICK MIND OF THE THINKER!
The FLASH

COVER ART BY ***BRIAN BOLLAND***

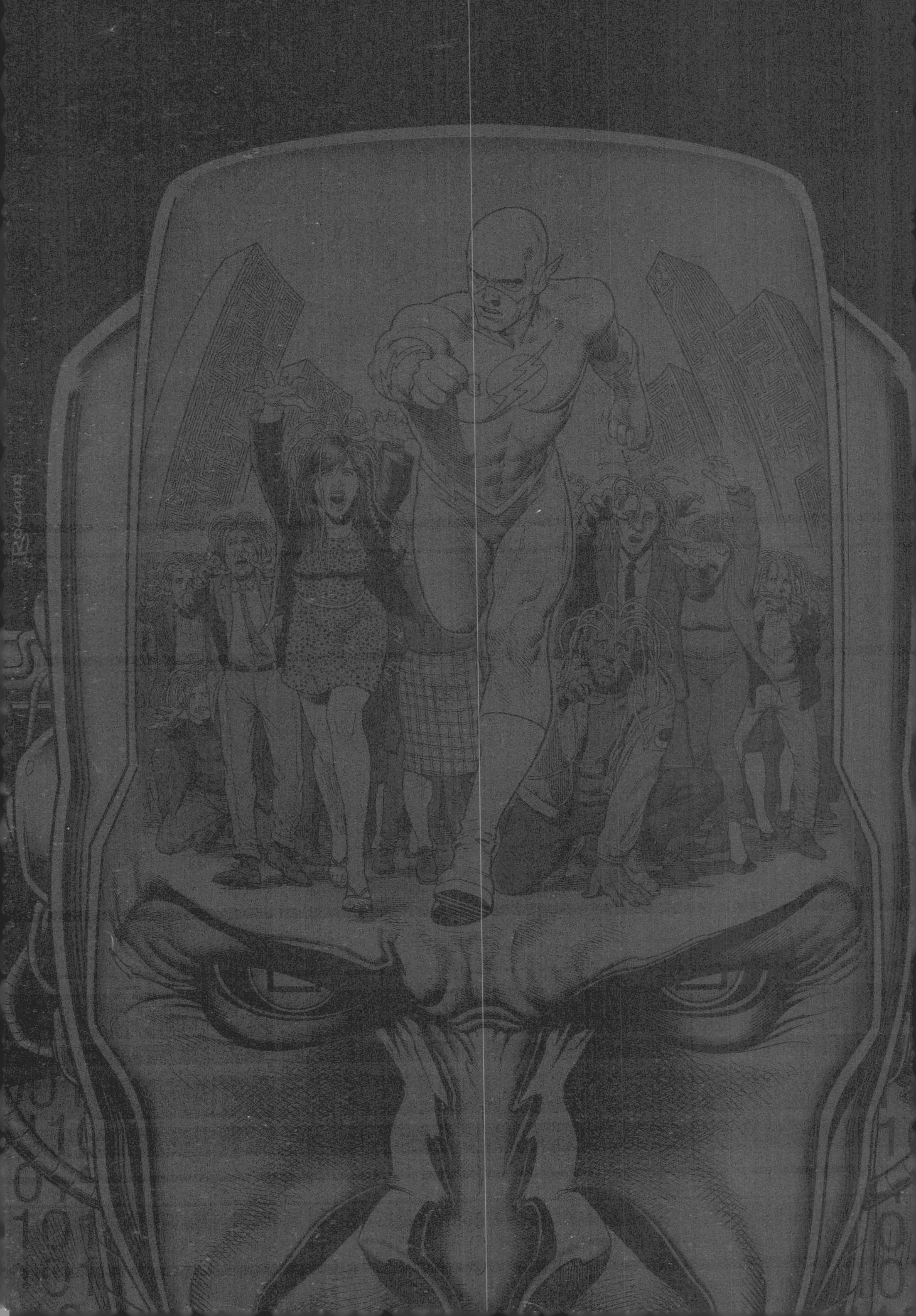

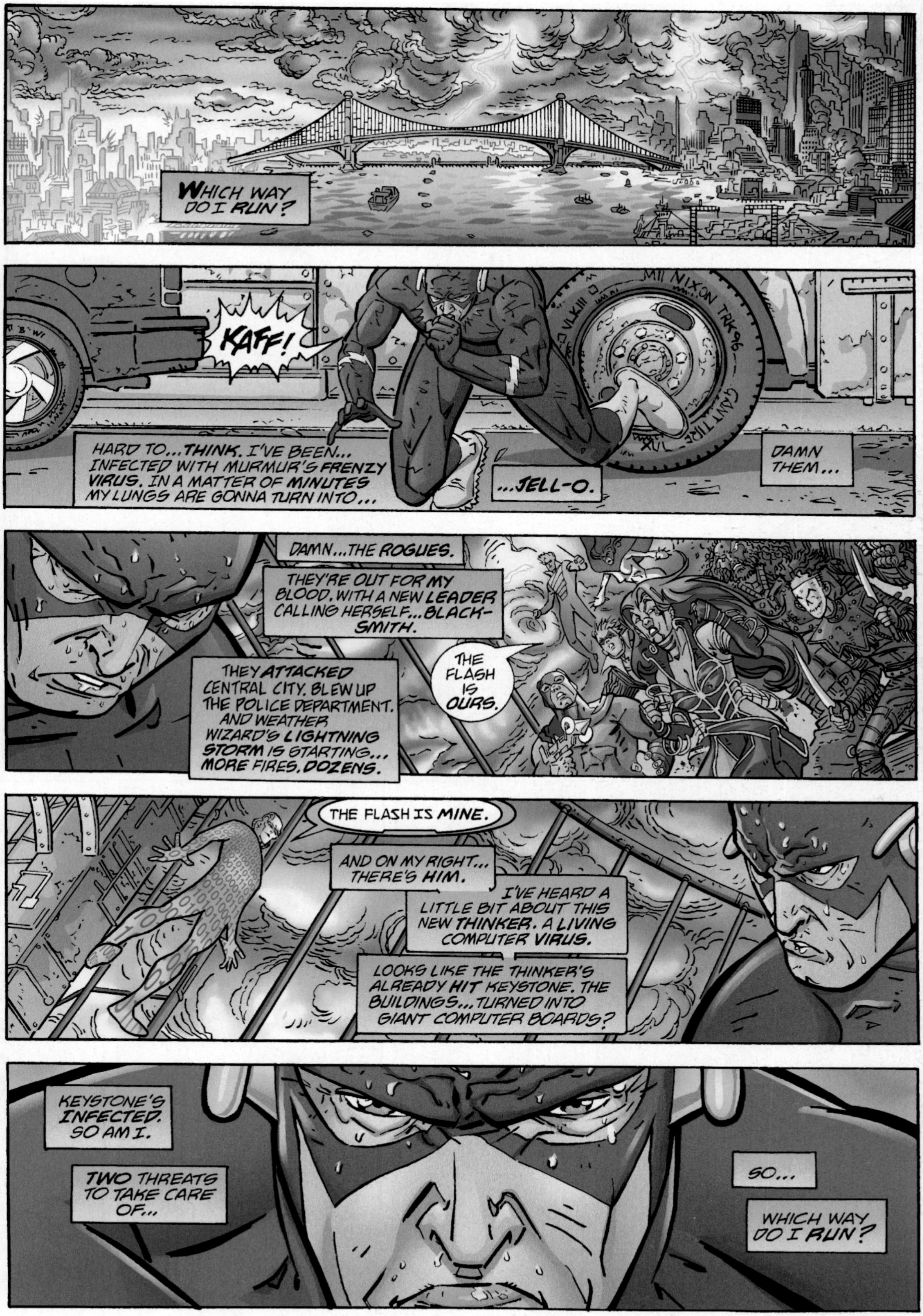
WHICH WAY DO I RUN?
KAFF!
HARD TO...THINK. I'VE BEEN... INFECTED WITH MURMUR'S FRENZY VIRUS. IN A MATTER OF MINUTES MY LUNGS ARE GONNA TURN INTO...
...JELL-O.
DAMN THEM...
DAMN...THE ROGUES.
THEY'RE OUT FOR MY BLOOD. WITH A NEW LEADER CALLING HERSELF...BLACKSMITH.
THEY ATTACKED CENTRAL CITY. BLEW UP THE POLICE DEPARTMENT. AND WEATHER WIZARD'S LIGHTNING STORM IS STARTING... MORE FIRES. DOZENS.
THE FLASH IS OURS.
THE FLASH IS MINE.
AND ON MY RIGHT... THERE'S HIM.
I'VE HEARD A LITTLE BIT ABOUT THIS NEW THINKER. A LIVING COMPUTER VIRUS.
LOOKS LIKE THE THINKER'S ALREADY HIT KEYSTONE. THE BUILDINGS...TURNED INTO GIANT COMPUTER BOARDS?
KEYSTONE'S INFECTED. SO AM I.
TWO THREATS TO TAKE CARE OF...
SO...
WHICH WAY DO I RUN?

RIGHT NOW I DON'T HAVE MUCH CHOICE.

I HEAD WEST.

I'M.... DYING.

AND IF I WANT TO STOP..THESE MONSTERS...

I'VE GOT TO... STAY ALIVE.

I SEE THE DAMAGE THE THINKER HAS DONE. EVERY LIVING THING HAS BEEN ENSNARED IN A WEB OF WIRES.

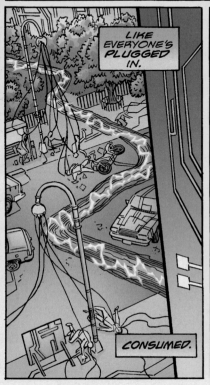

LIKE EVERYONE'S PLUGGED IN.

CONSUMED.

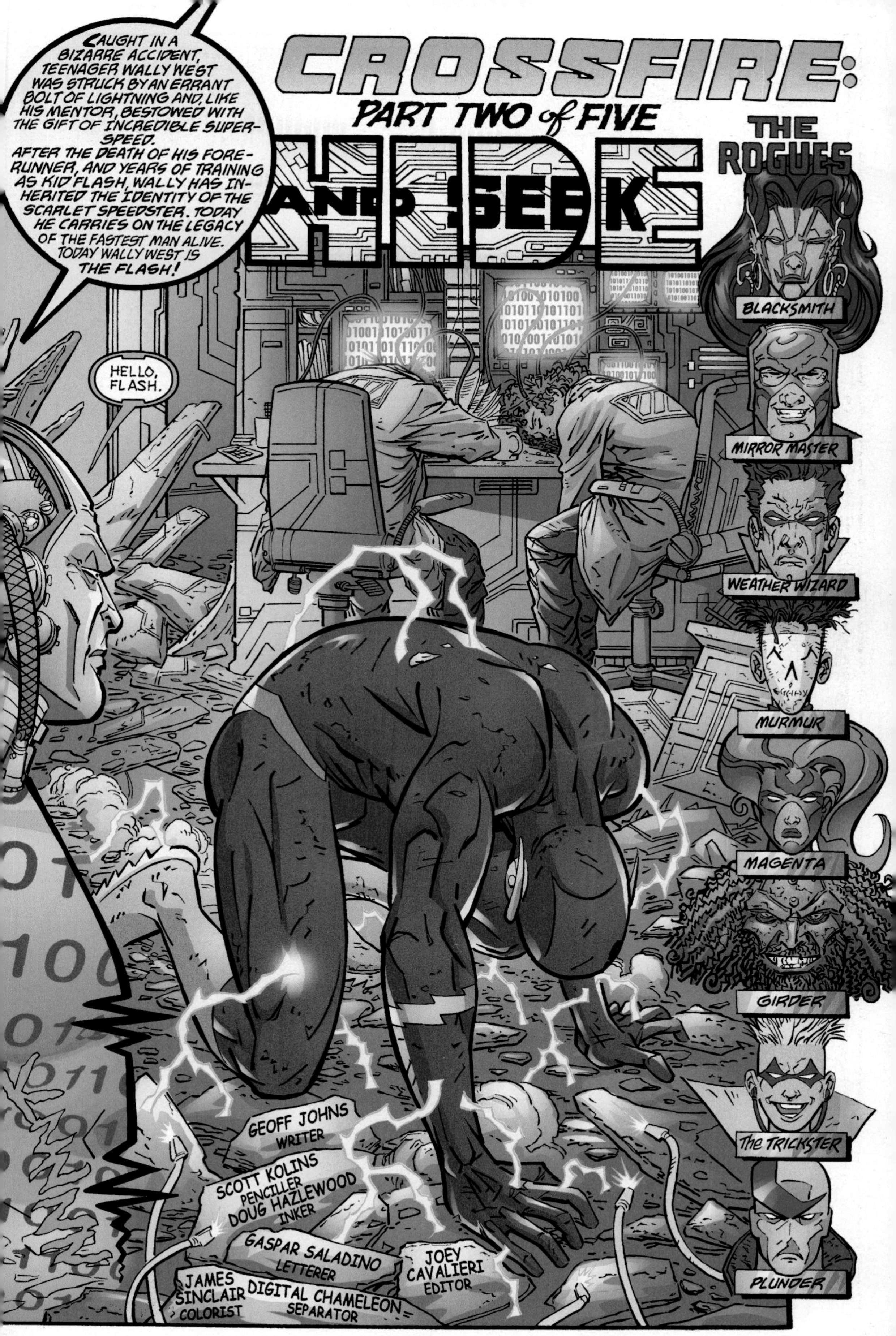

CAUGHT IN A BIZARRE ACCIDENT, TEENAGER WALLY WEST WAS STRUCK BY AN ERRANT BOLT OF LIGHTNING AND, LIKE HIS MENTOR, BESTOWED WITH THE GIFT OF INCREDIBLE SUPER-SPEED. AFTER THE DEATH OF HIS FORERUNNER, AND YEARS OF TRAINING AS KID FLASH, WALLY HAS INHERITED THE IDENTITY OF THE SCARLET SPEEDSTER. TODAY HE CARRIES ON THE LEGACY OF THE FASTEST MAN ALIVE. TODAY WALLY WEST IS THE FLASH!
CROSSFIRE:
PART TWO of FIVE
HIDE AND SEEK
THE ROGUES
BLACKSMITH
HELLO, FLASH.
MIRROR MASTER
WEATHER WIZARD
MURMUR
MAGENTA
GIRDER
The TRICKSTER
PLUNDER
GEOFF JOHNS WRITER
SCOTT KOLINS PENCILLER
DOUG HAZLEWOOD INKER
GASPAR SALADINO LETTERER
JOEY CAVALIERI EDITOR
JAMES SINCLAIR COLORIST
DIGITAL CHAMELEON SEPARATOR

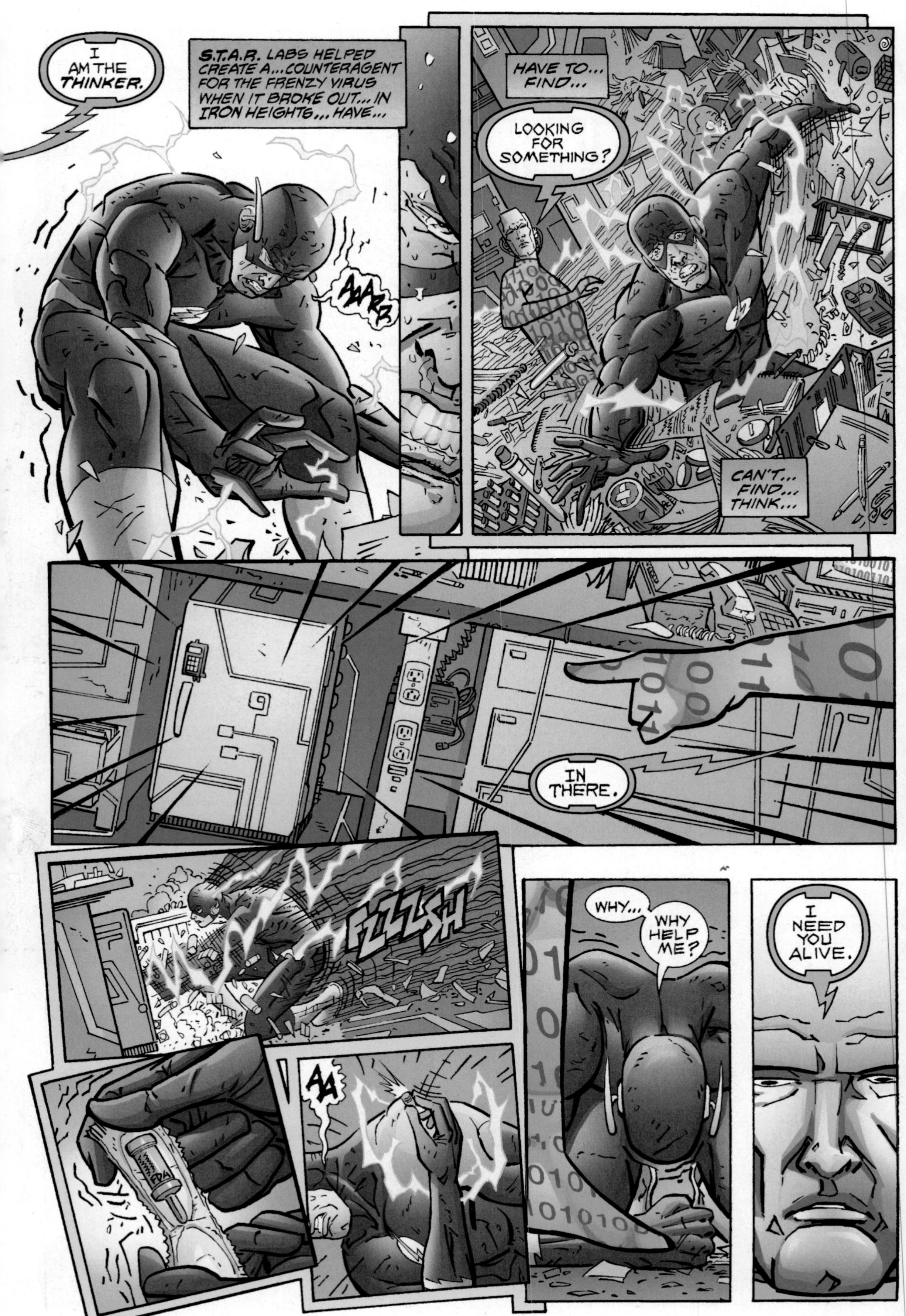
I AM THE THINKER.
S.T.A.R. LABS HELPED CREATE A... COUNTERAGENT FOR THE FRENZY VIRUS WHEN IT BROKE OUT... IN IRON HEIGHTS... HAVE...
AAARR
HAVE TO... FIND...
LOOKING FOR SOMETHING?
CAN'T... FIND... THINK...
IN THERE.
FZZZSH
AA
WHY...
WHY HELP ME?
I NEED YOU ALIVE.

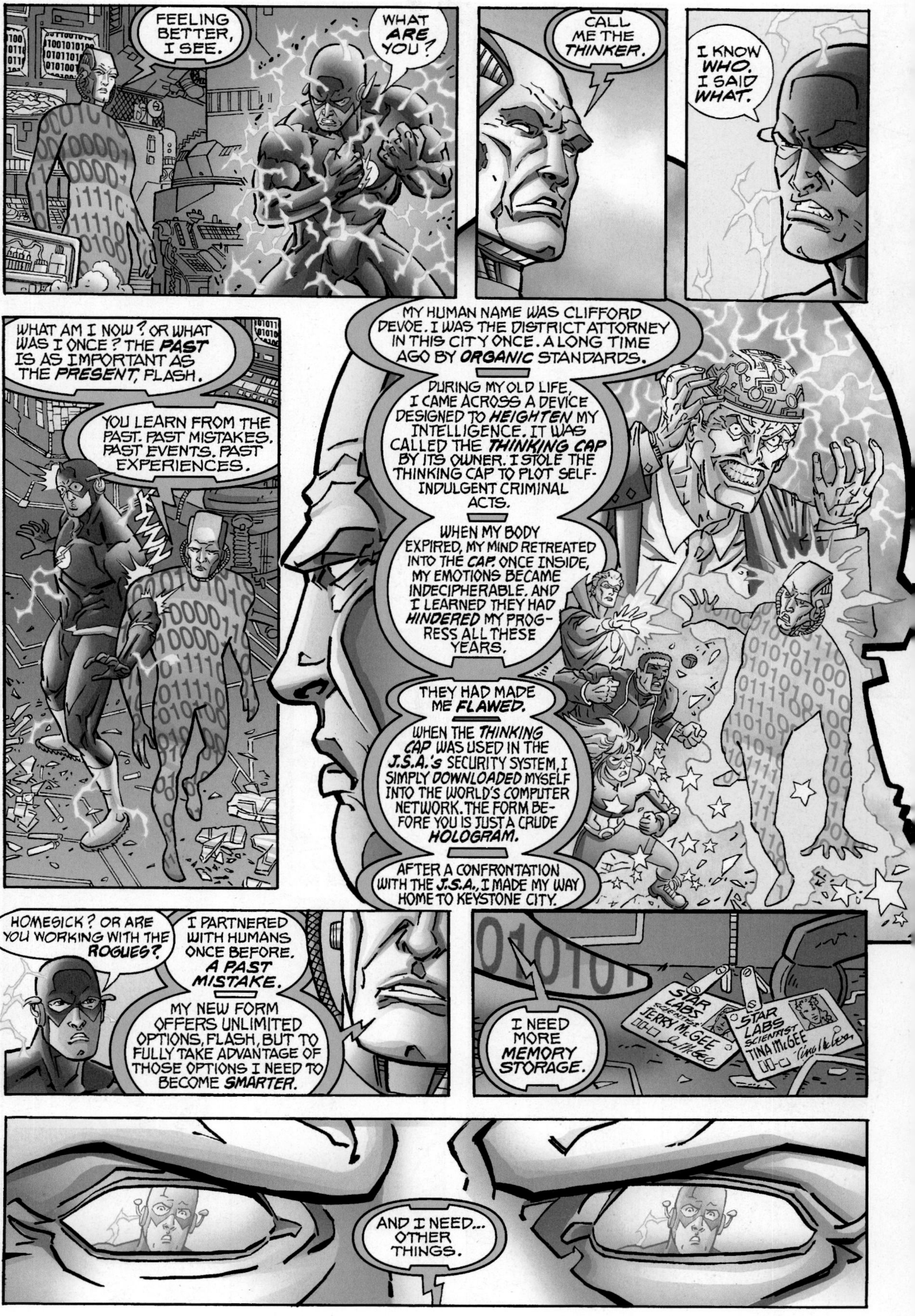

FEELING BETTER, I SEE.
WHAT ARE YOU?
CALL ME THE THINKER.
I KNOW WHO. I SAID WHAT.
WHAT AM I NOW? OR WHAT WAS I ONCE? THE PAST IS AS IMPORTANT AS THE PRESENT, FLASH.
YOU LEARN FROM THE PAST. PAST MISTAKES. PAST EVENTS. PAST EXPERIENCES.
MY HUMAN NAME WAS CLIFFORD DEVOE. I WAS THE DISTRICT ATTORNEY IN THIS CITY ONCE. A LONG TIME AGO BY ORGANIC STANDARDS.
DURING MY OLD LIFE, I CAME ACROSS A DEVICE DESIGNED TO HEIGHTEN MY INTELLIGENCE. IT WAS CALLED THE THINKING CAP BY ITS OWNER. I STOLE THE THINKING CAP TO PLOT SELF-INDULGENT CRIMINAL ACTS.
WHEN MY BODY EXPIRED, MY MIND RETREATED INTO THE CAP. ONCE INSIDE, MY EMOTIONS BECAME INDECIPHERABLE. AND I LEARNED THEY HAD HINDERED MY PROGRESS ALL THESE YEARS.
THEY HAD MADE ME FLAWED.
WHEN THE THINKING CAP WAS USED IN THE J.S.A.'s SECURITY SYSTEM, I SIMPLY DOWNLOADED MYSELF INTO THE WORLD'S COMPUTER NETWORK. THE FORM BEFORE YOU IS JUST A CRUDE HOLOGRAM.
AFTER A CONFRONTATION WITH THE J.S.A., I MADE MY WAY HOME TO KEYSTONE CITY.
HOMESICK? OR ARE YOU WORKING WITH THE ROGUES?
I PARTNERED WITH HUMANS ONCE BEFORE. A PAST MISTAKE.
MY NEW FORM OFFERS UNLIMITED OPTIONS, FLASH, BUT TO FULLY TAKE ADVANTAGE OF THOSE OPTIONS I NEED TO BECOME SMARTER.
I NEED MORE MEMORY STORAGE.
STAR LABS SCIENTIST JERRY McGEE
STAR LABS SCIENTIST TINA McGEE
AND I NEED... OTHER THINGS.

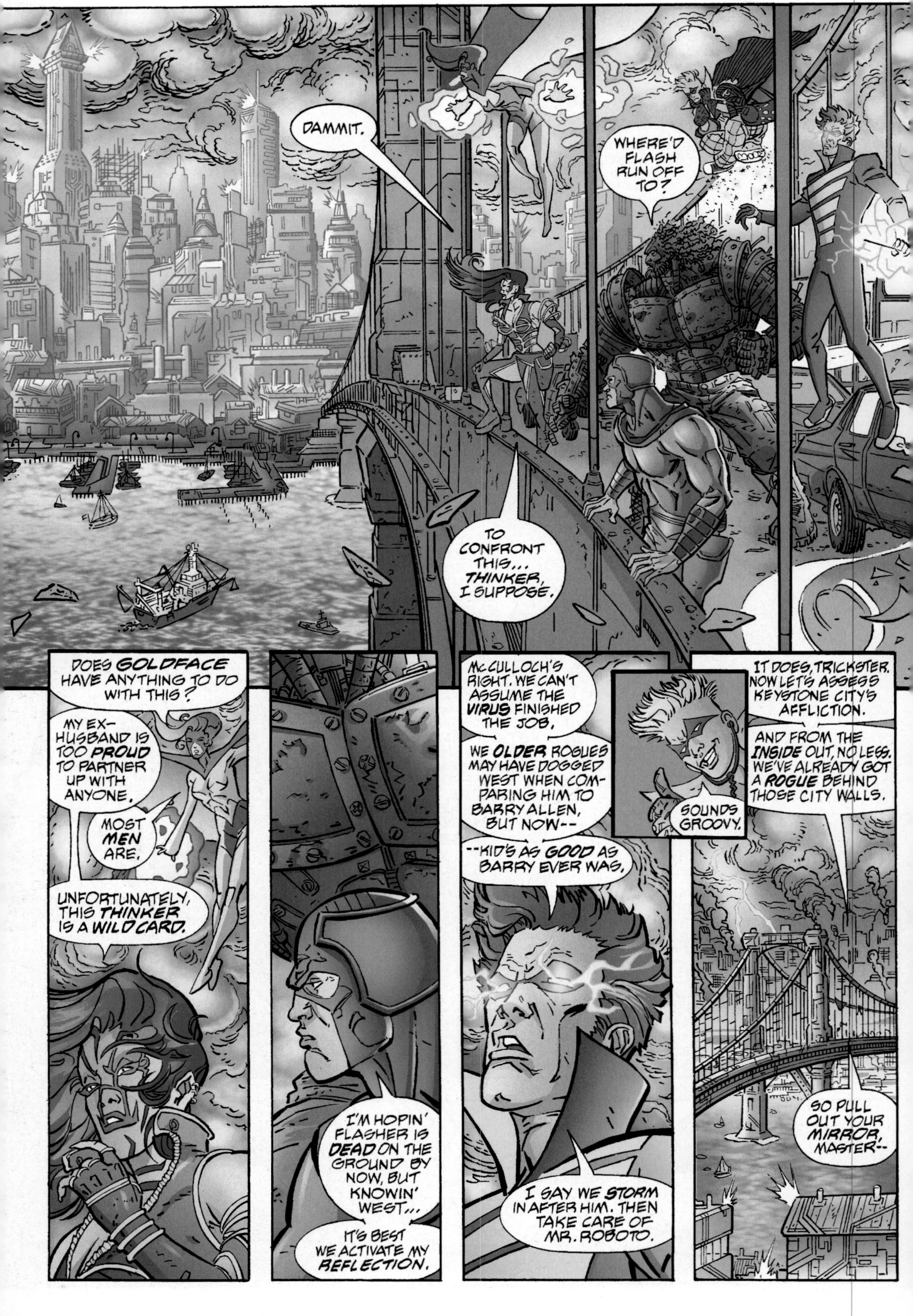
DAMMIT.
WHERE'D FLASH RUN OFF TO?
TO CONFRONT THIS... THINKER, I SUPPOSE.
DOES GOLDFACE HAVE ANYTHING TO DO WITH THIS?
MY EX-HUSBAND IS TOO PROUD TO PARTNER UP WITH ANYONE.
MOST MEN ARE.
UNFORTUNATELY, THIS THINKER IS A WILD CARD.
I'M HOPIN' FLASHER IS DEAD ON THE GROUND BY NOW, BUT KNOWIN' WEST...
IT'S BEST WE ACTIVATE MY REFLECTION.
McCULLOCH'S RIGHT. WE CAN'T ASSUME THE VIRUS FINISHED THE JOB.
WE OLDER ROGUES MAY HAVE DOGGED WEST WHEN COMPARING HIM TO BARRY ALLEN, BUT NOW--
--KID'S AS GOOD AS BARRY EVER WAS.
I SAY WE STORM IN AFTER HIM. THEN TAKE CARE OF MR. ROBOTO.
SOUNDS GROOVY.
IT DOES, TRICKSTER. NOW LET'S ASSESS KEYSTONE CITY'S AFFLICTION.
AND FROM THE INSIDE OUT, NO LESS. WE'VE ALREADY GOT A ROGUE BEHIND THOSE CITY WALLS.
SO PULL OUT YOUR MIRROR, MASTER--

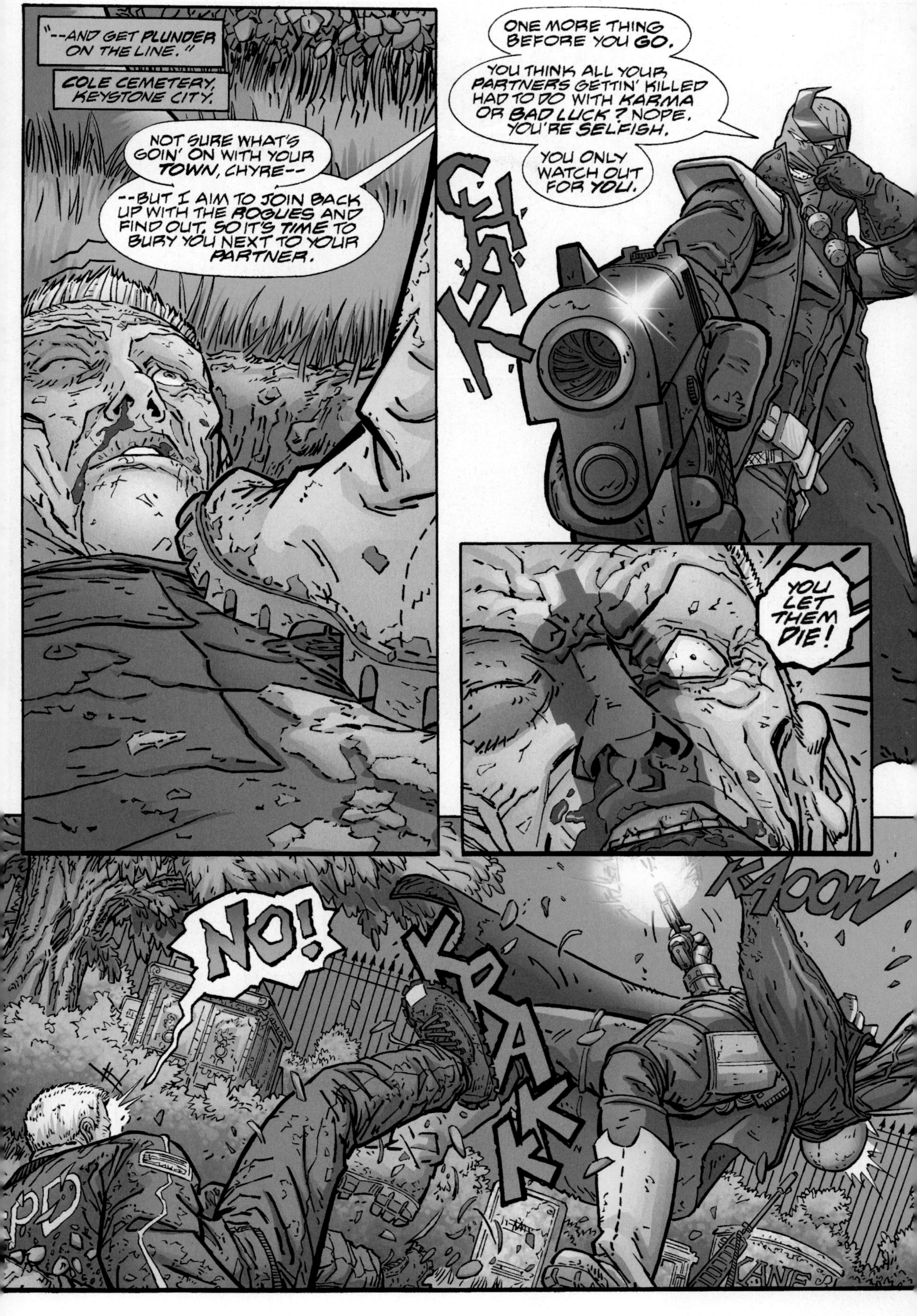
"--AND GET PLUNDER ON THE LINE."
COLE CEMETERY, KEYSTONE CITY.
NOT SURE WHAT'S GOIN' ON WITH YOUR TOWN, CHYRE--
--BUT I AIM TO JOIN BACK UP WITH THE ROGUES AND FIND OUT, SO IT'S TIME TO BURY YOU NEXT TO YOUR PARTNER.
ONE MORE THING BEFORE YOU GO.
YOU THINK ALL YOUR PARTNERS GETTIN' KILLED HAD TO DO WITH KARMA OR BAD LUCK? NOPE. YOU'RE SELFISH.
YOU ONLY WATCH OUT FOR YOU.
CHAK
YOU LET THEM DIE!
NO!
KRAKK
KAOOW

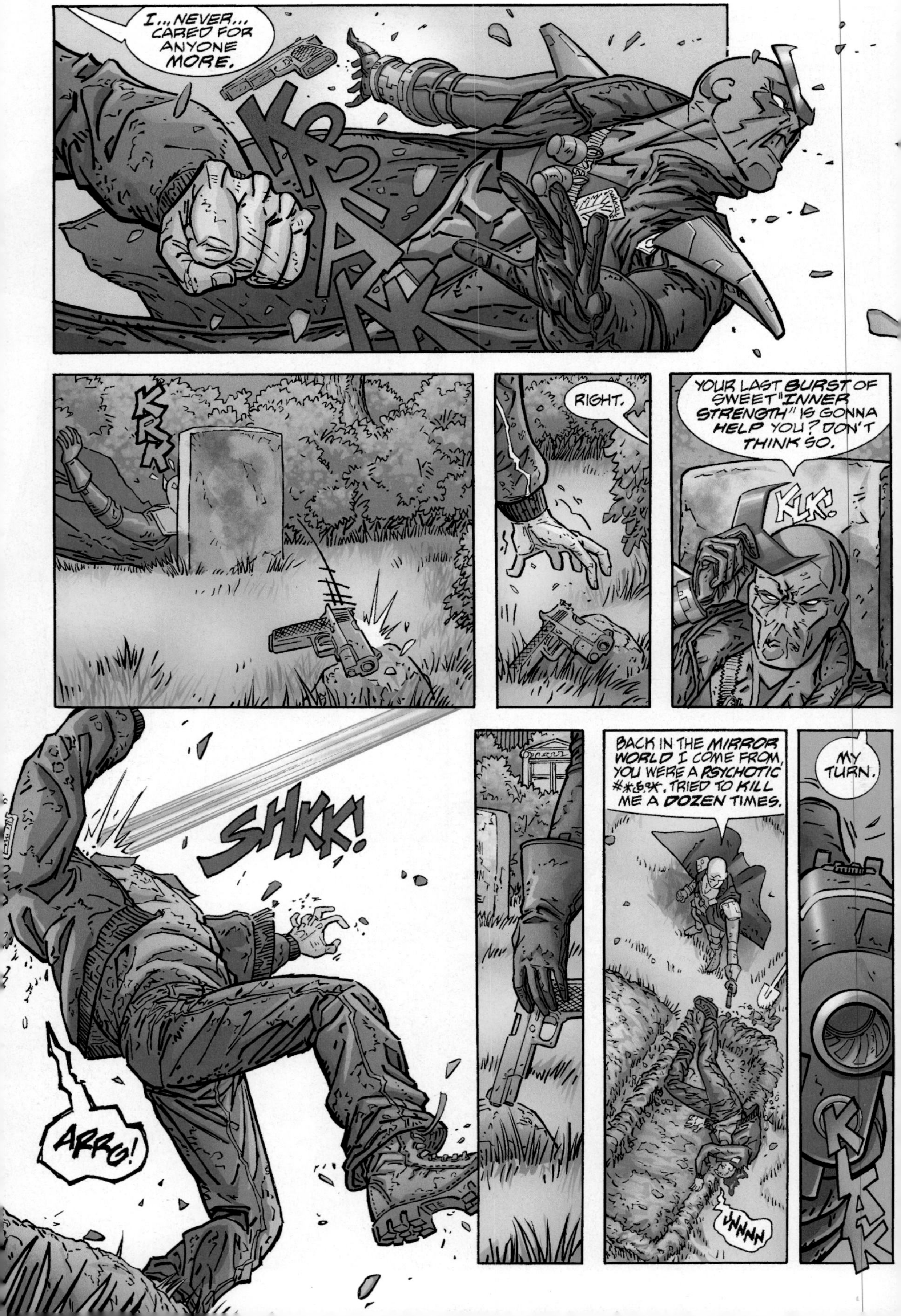
I... NEVER... CARED FOR ANYONE MORE.
KRRAKK
KRR
RIGHT.
YOUR LAST BURST OF SWEET "INNER STRENGTH" IS GONNA HELP YOU? DON'T THINK SO.
KLIK!
SHKK!
ARRG!
BACK IN THE MIRROR WORLD I COME FROM, YOU WERE A PSYCHOTIC #*&%. TRIED TO KILL ME A DOZEN TIMES.
UNNNN
MY TURN.
KLAK

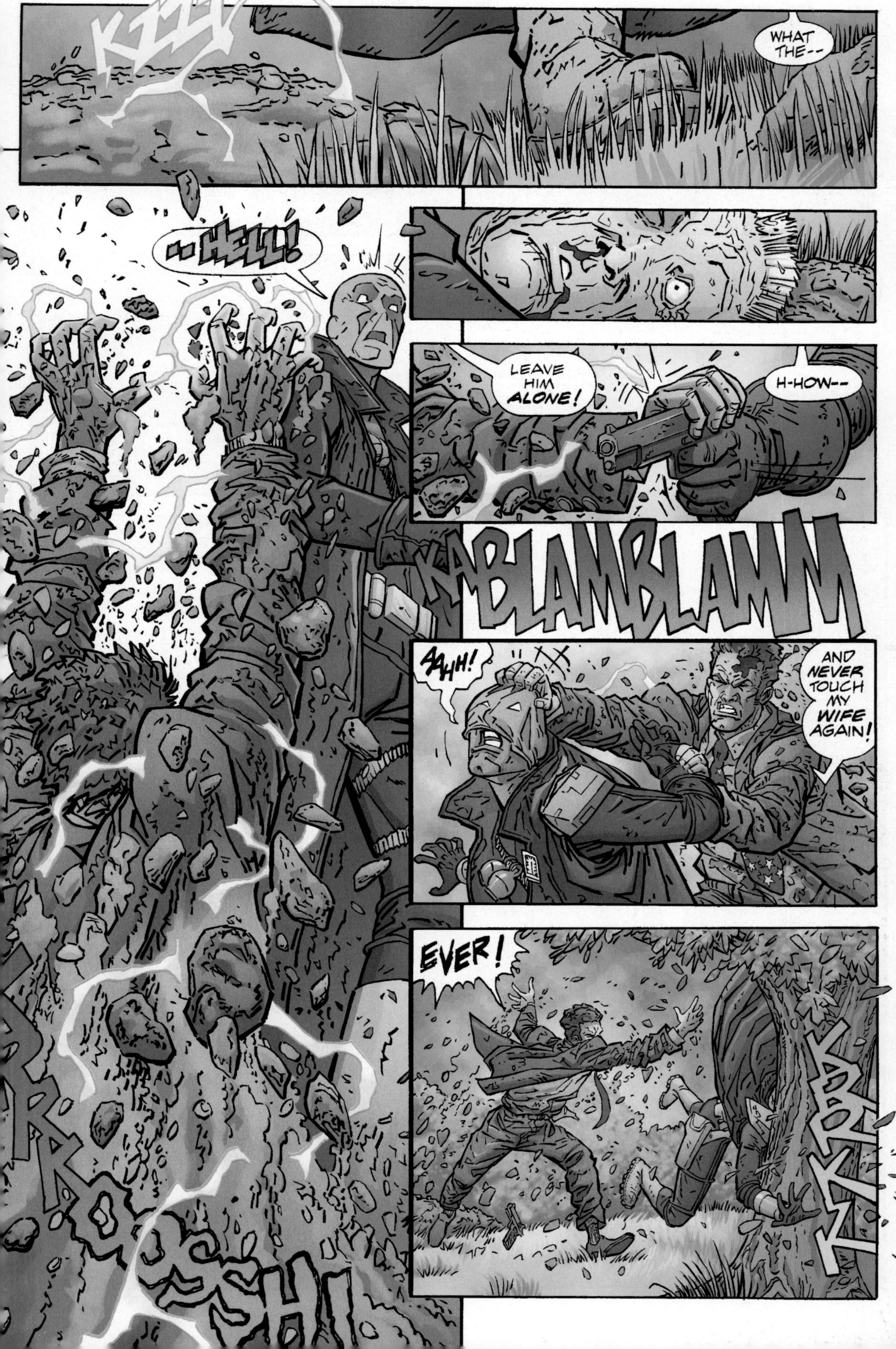
KZZT
WHAT THE--
--HELL!
LEAVE HIM ALONE!
H-HOW--
KABLAMBLAMM
AAHH!
AND NEVER TOUCH MY WIFE AGAIN!
EVER!
KRAK
KRROOSSH!

...

THIS'LL *NEVER* GET CLEAN, HAIR'S PROBABLY A *MESS*.

...

I...LOOK, I KNOW YOU'RE *PROBABLY* FREAKED OUT BY ALL THIS.

ME *TOO*. HELL, I SHOULD'VE TOLD YOU, CHYRE, ABOUT THAT LIFE-SUCKING *VAMPIRE*, CICADA.

STABBED ME WITH ONE OF HIS *ENERGY* KNIVES. NOW I HEAL, FROM ANY WOUND APPARENTLY.

EVEN A *GUNSHOT* TO THE HEAD.

EARS ARE *STILL* RINGING.

LOOK, CAN WE KEEP THIS BETWEEN *YOU* AND *ME*?

YOU DAMN *IDIOT*.

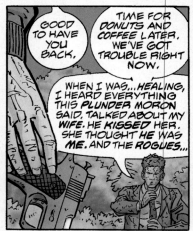

GOOD TO HAVE YOU BACK.

TIME FOR *DONUTS* AND *COFFEE* LATER. WE'VE GOT *TROUBLE* RIGHT NOW.

WHEN I WAS...*HEALING*, I HEARD EVERYTHING THIS *PLUNDER* MORON SAID, TALKED ABOUT MY *WIFE*. HE *KISSED* HER. SHE THOUGHT *HE* WAS *ME*. AND THE *ROGUES*...

THE *ROGUES* ARE--

YE READ ME, LAD?

WHERE ARE YE?

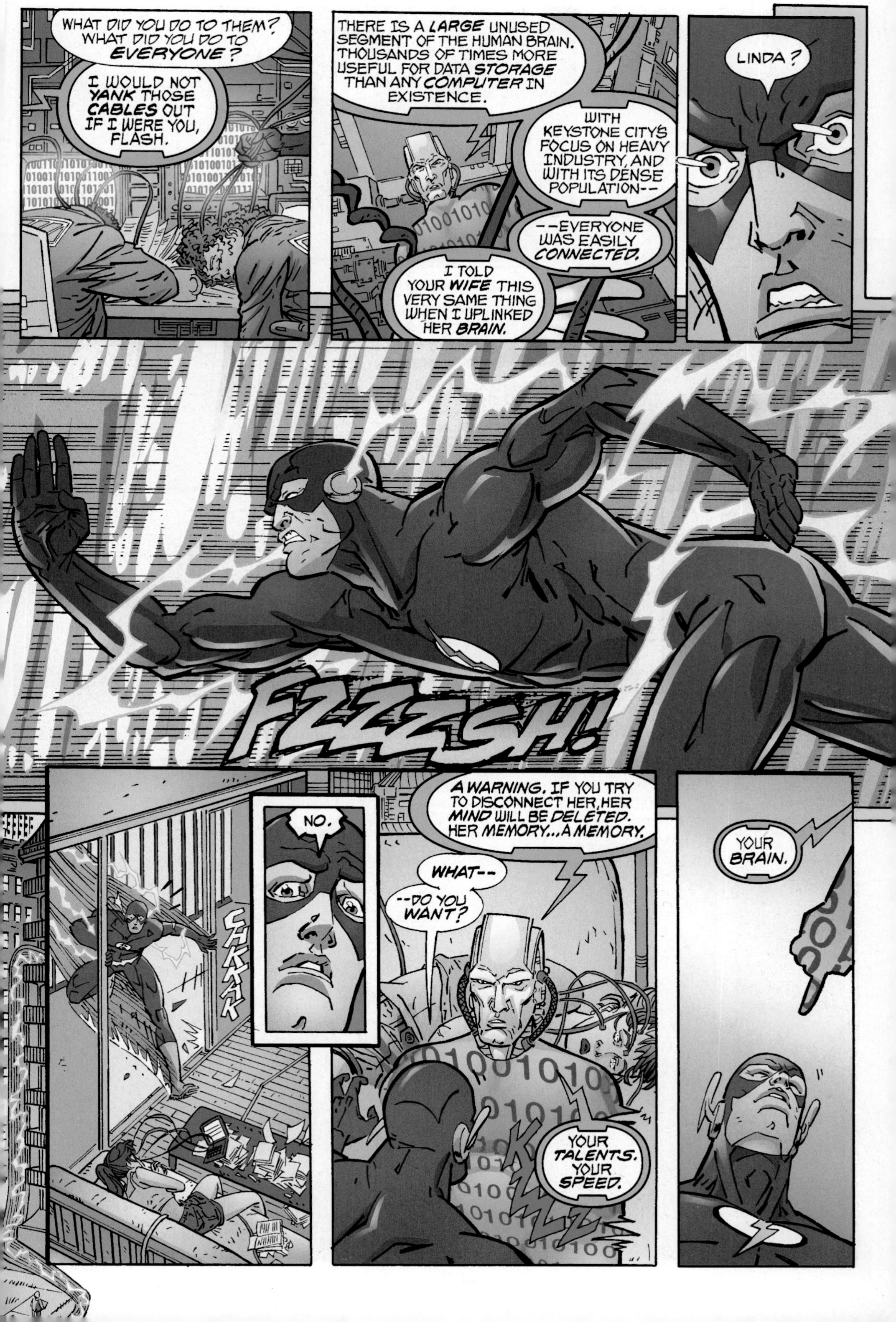
WHAT DID YOU DO TO THEM? WHAT DID YOU DO TO EVERYONE?
I WOULD NOT YANK THOSE CABLES OUT IF I WERE YOU, FLASH.
THERE IS A LARGE UNUSED SEGMENT OF THE HUMAN BRAIN. THOUSANDS OF TIMES MORE USEFUL FOR DATA STORAGE THAN ANY COMPUTER IN EXISTENCE.
WITH KEYSTONE CITY'S FOCUS ON HEAVY INDUSTRY, AND WITH ITS DENSE POPULATION--
--EVERYONE WAS EASILY CONNECTED.
I TOLD YOUR WIFE THIS VERY SAME THING WHEN I UPLINKED HER BRAIN.
LINDA?
FZZZSH!
CHKKKK
NO.
A WARNING. IF YOU TRY TO DISCONNECT HER, HER MIND WILL BE DELETED. HER MEMORY...A MEMORY.
WHAT--
--DO YOU WANT?
YOUR TALENTS. YOUR SPEED.
YOUR BRAIN.

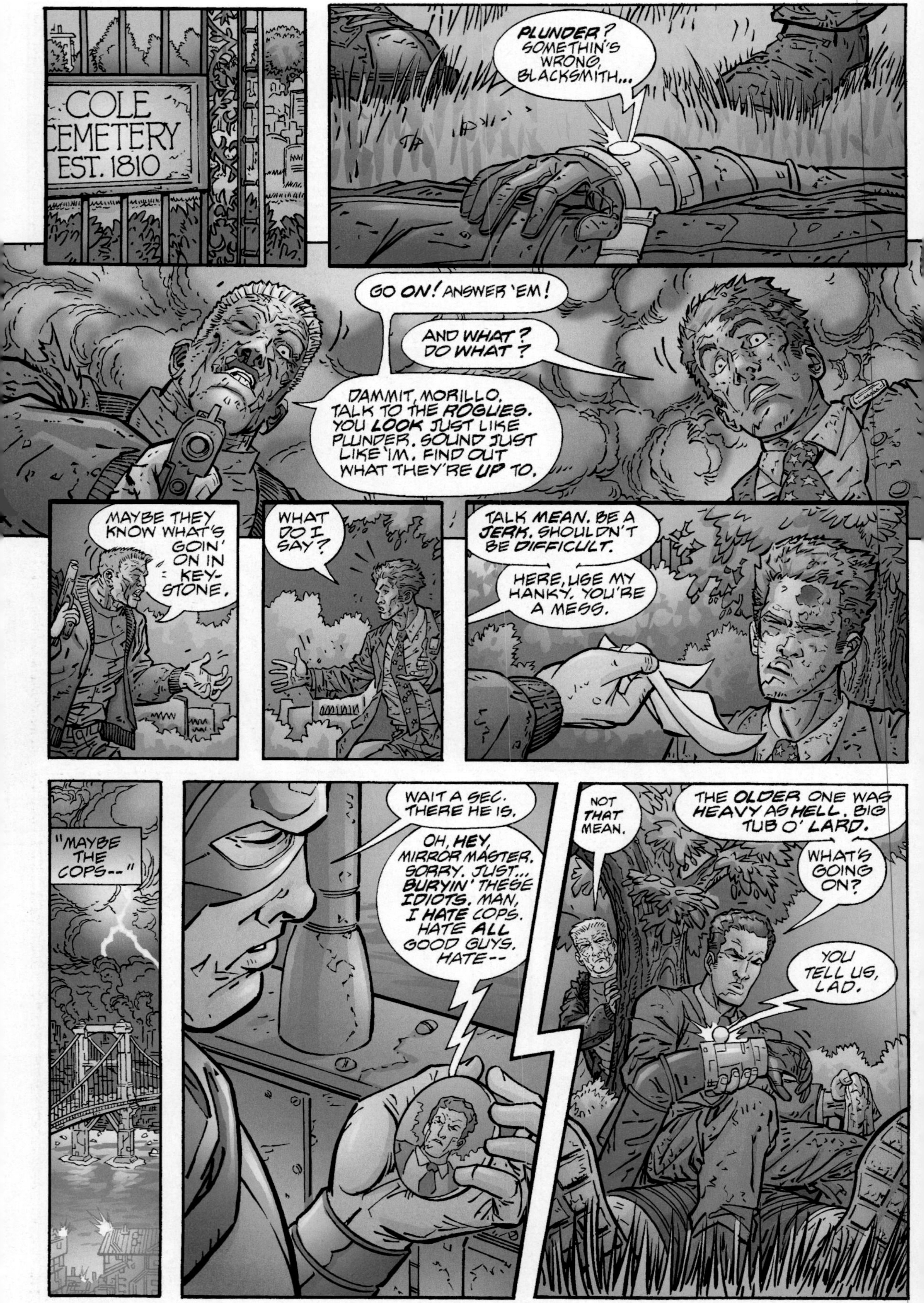
COLE CEMETERY EST. 1810
PLUNDER? SOMETHIN'S WRONG, BLACKSMITH...
GO ON! ANSWER 'EM!
AND WHAT? DO WHAT?
DAMMIT, MORILLO. TALK TO THE ROGUES. YOU LOOK JUST LIKE PLUNDER. SOUND JUST LIKE 'IM. FIND OUT WHAT THEY'RE UP TO.
MAYBE THEY KNOW WHAT'S GOIN' ON IN KEY-STONE.
WHAT DO I SAY?
TALK MEAN. BE A JERK. SHOULDN'T BE DIFFICULT.
HERE, USE MY HANKY. YOU'RE A MESS.
"MAYBE THE COPS--"
WAIT A SEC. THERE HE IS.
OH, HEY, MIRROR MASTER. SORRY. JUST... BURYIN' THESE IDIOTS. MAN, I HATE COPS. HATE ALL GOOD GUYS. HATE--
NOT THAT MEAN.
THE OLDER ONE WAS HEAVY AS HELL. BIG TUB O' LARD.
WHAT'S GOING ON?
YOU TELL US, LAD.

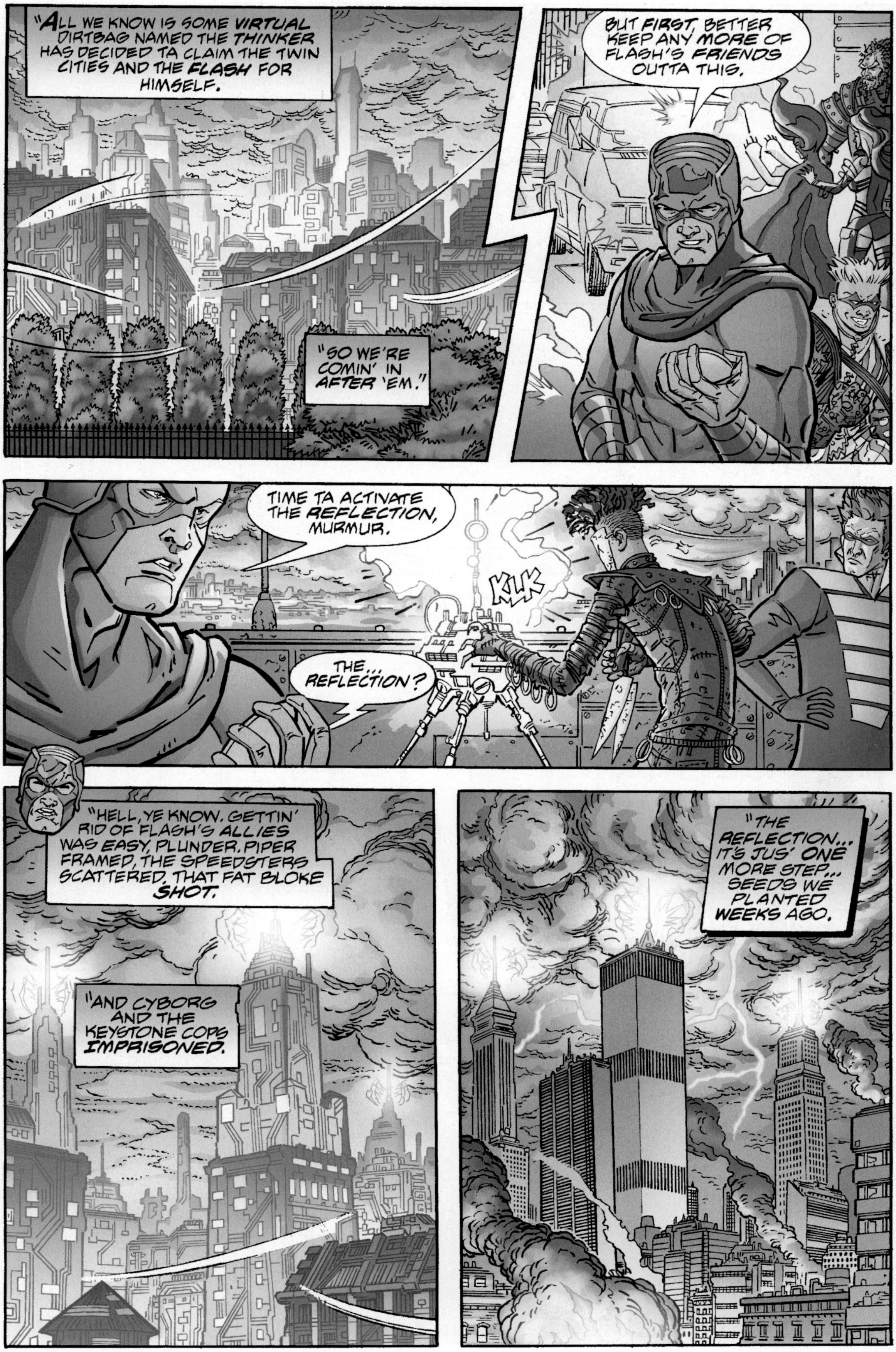
"ALL WE KNOW IS SOME VIRTUAL DIRTBAG NAMED THE THINKER HAS DECIDED TA CLAIM THE TWIN CITIES AND THE FLASH FOR HIMSELF.
"SO WE'RE COMIN' IN AFTER 'EM."
BUT FIRST, BETTER KEEP ANY MORE OF FLASH'S FRIENDS OUTTA THIS.
TIME TA ACTIVATE THE REFLECTION, MURMUR.
KLIK
THE... REFLECTION?
"HELL, YE KNOW. GETTIN' RID OF FLASH'S ALLIES WAS EASY. PLUNDER. PIPER FRAMED. THE SPEEDSTERS SCATTERED. THAT FAT BLOKE SHOT.
"AND CYBORG AND THE KEYSTONE COPS IMPRISONED.
"THE REFLECTION... IT'S JUS' ONE MORE STEP... SEEDS WE PLANTED WEEKS AGO.

" WHEN THE ROGUES ATTACKED THOSE RADIO TOWERS, WE ATTACHED SOME 'OPEN' MIRRORS ON THEIR ANTENNAS.

"ACTIVATE THE MIRRORS AND WE'RE PROTECTED.

" ANY PHONE CALL, ANY COMMUNICATION MADE TO KEYSTONE CITY WILL GET AN AUTOMATIC REPLY, SEEMINGLY REAL--

"--THANKS TA MY SILVER LIQUID TECH.

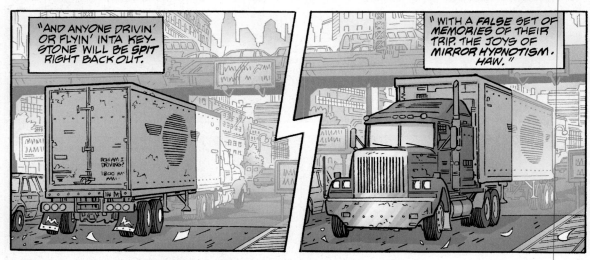

"AND ANYONE DRIVIN' OR FLYIN' INTA KEYSTONE WILL BE SPIT RIGHT BACK OUT.

" WITH A FALSE SET OF MEMORIES OF THEIR TRIP. THE JOYS OF MIRROR HYPNOTISM. HAW. "

HOW AM I DRIVING? 1800 M-MM

STAND YOUR GROUND, PLUNDER, I'LL CONTACT YE WHEN WE'RE IN THE CITY.

MIRROR MASTER OUT.

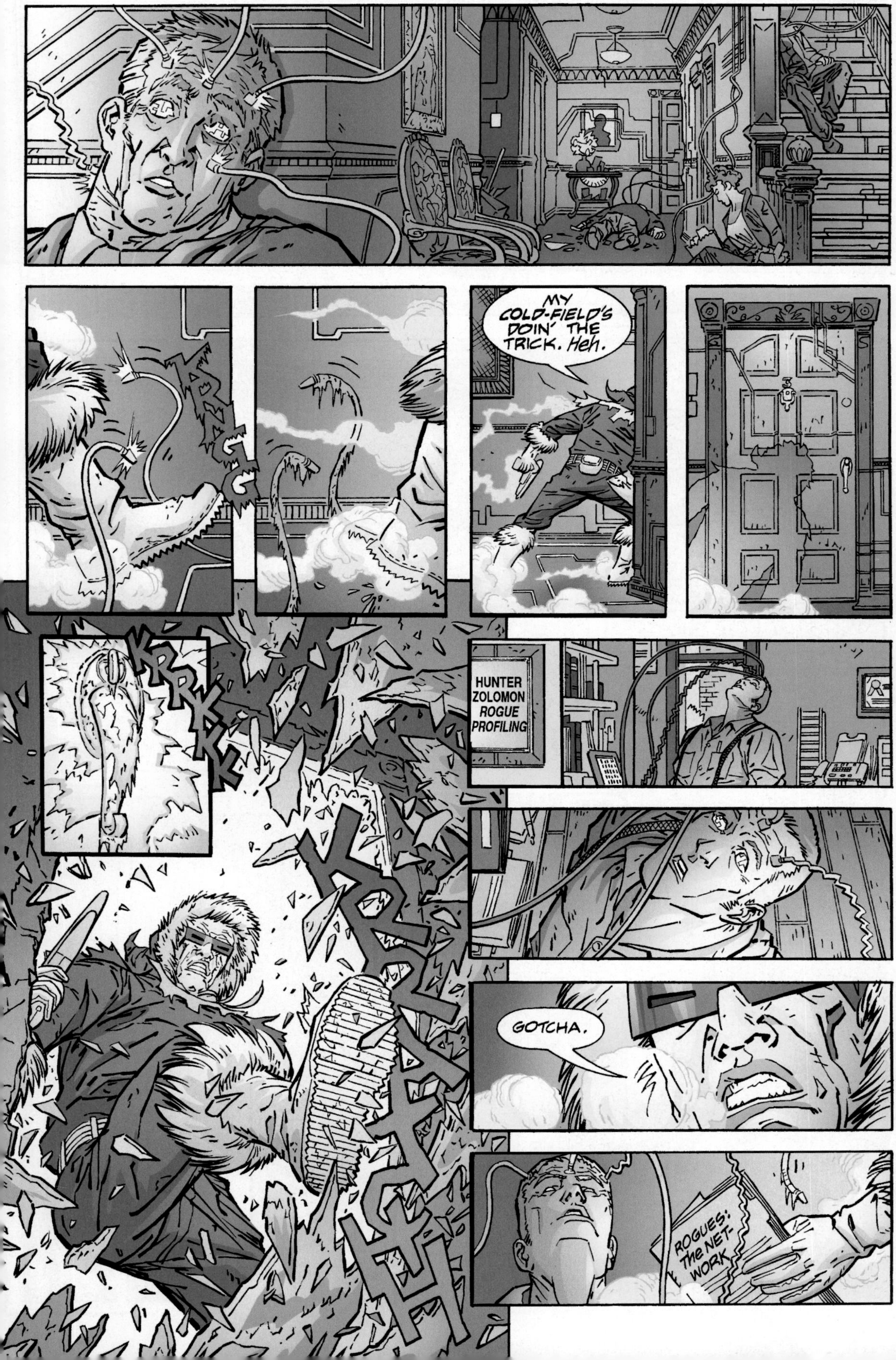
KRAGG
MY COLD-FIELD'S DOIN' THE TRICK. Heh.
KRRKKK
HUNTER ZOLOMON ROGUE PROFILING
KRRAKKH
GOTCHA.
ROGUES: THE NET-WORK

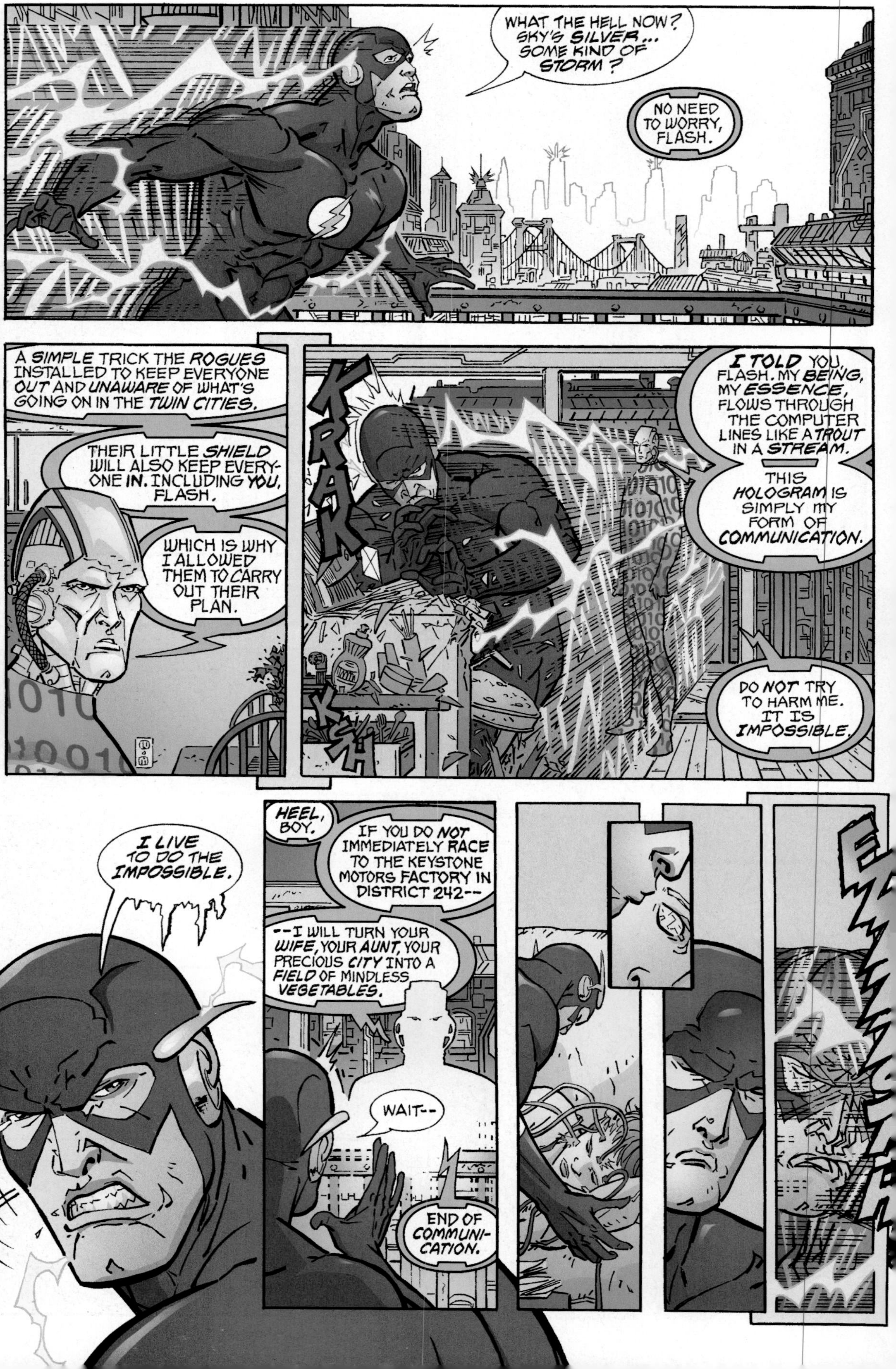
WHAT THE HELL NOW? SKY'S SILVER... SOME KIND OF STORM?
NO NEED TO WORRY, FLASH.
A SIMPLE TRICK THE ROGUES INSTALLED TO KEEP EVERYONE OUT AND UNAWARE OF WHAT'S GOING ON IN THE TWIN CITIES.
THEIR LITTLE SHIELD WILL ALSO KEEP EVERYONE IN. INCLUDING YOU, FLASH.
WHICH IS WHY I ALLOWED THEM TO CARRY OUT THEIR PLAN.
KRAK
KSSH
I TOLD YOU, FLASH. MY BEING, MY ESSENCE, FLOWS THROUGH THE COMPUTER LINES LIKE A TROUT IN A STREAM.
THIS HOLOGRAM IS SIMPLY MY FORM OF COMMUNICATION.
DO NOT TRY TO HARM ME. IT IS IMPOSSIBLE.
I LIVE TO DO THE IMPOSSIBLE.
HEEL, BOY.
IF YOU DO NOT IMMEDIATELY RACE TO THE KEYSTONE MOTORS FACTORY IN DISTRICT 242--
--I WILL TURN YOUR WIFE, YOUR AUNT, YOUR PRECIOUS CITY INTO A FIELD OF MINDLESS VEGETABLES.
WAIT--
END OF COMMUNICATION.

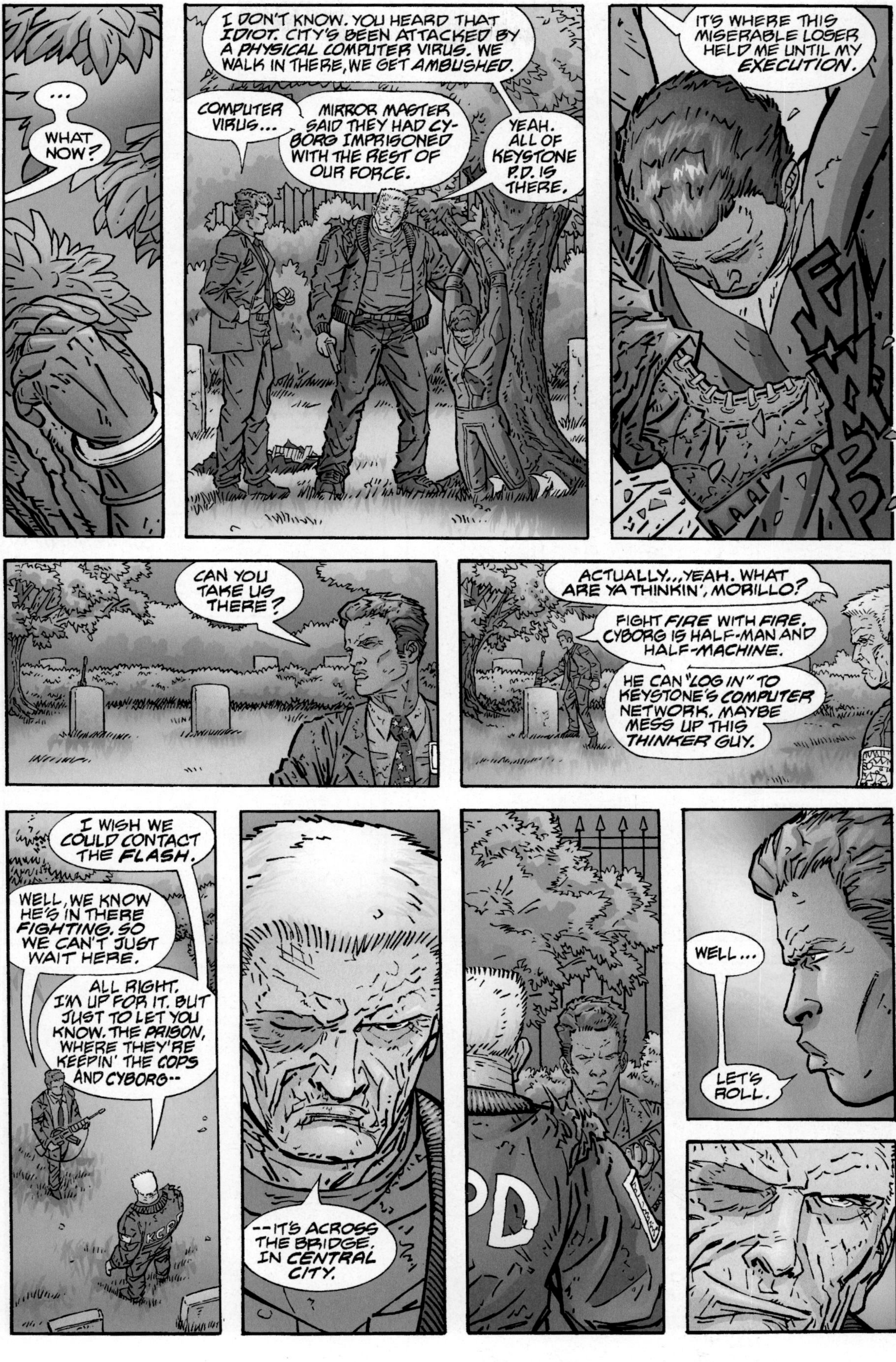
...
WHAT NOW?
I DON'T KNOW. YOU HEARD THAT IDIOT. CITY'S BEEN ATTACKED BY A PHYSICAL COMPUTER VIRUS. WE WALK IN THERE, WE GET AMBUSHED.
COMPUTER VIRUS...
MIRROR MASTER SAID THEY HAD CYBORG IMPRISONED WITH THE REST OF OUR FORCE.
YEAH. ALL OF KEYSTONE P.D. IS THERE.
IT'S WHERE THIS MISERABLE LOSER HELD ME UNTIL MY EXECUTION.
FWUMP
CAN YOU TAKE US THERE?
ACTUALLY... YEAH. WHAT ARE YA THINKIN', MORILLO?
FIGHT FIRE WITH FIRE. CYBORG IS HALF-MAN AND HALF-MACHINE.
HE CAN "LOG IN" TO KEYSTONE'S COMPUTER NETWORK. MAYBE MESS UP THIS THINKER GUY.
I WISH WE COULD CONTACT THE FLASH.
WELL, WE KNOW HE'S IN THERE FIGHTING. SO WE CAN'T JUST WAIT HERE.
ALL RIGHT. I'M UP FOR IT. BUT JUST TO LET YOU KNOW. THE PRISON, WHERE THEY'RE KEEPIN' THE COPS AND CYBORG--
--IT'S ACROSS THE BRIDGE. IN CENTRAL CITY.
WELL...
LET'S ROLL.

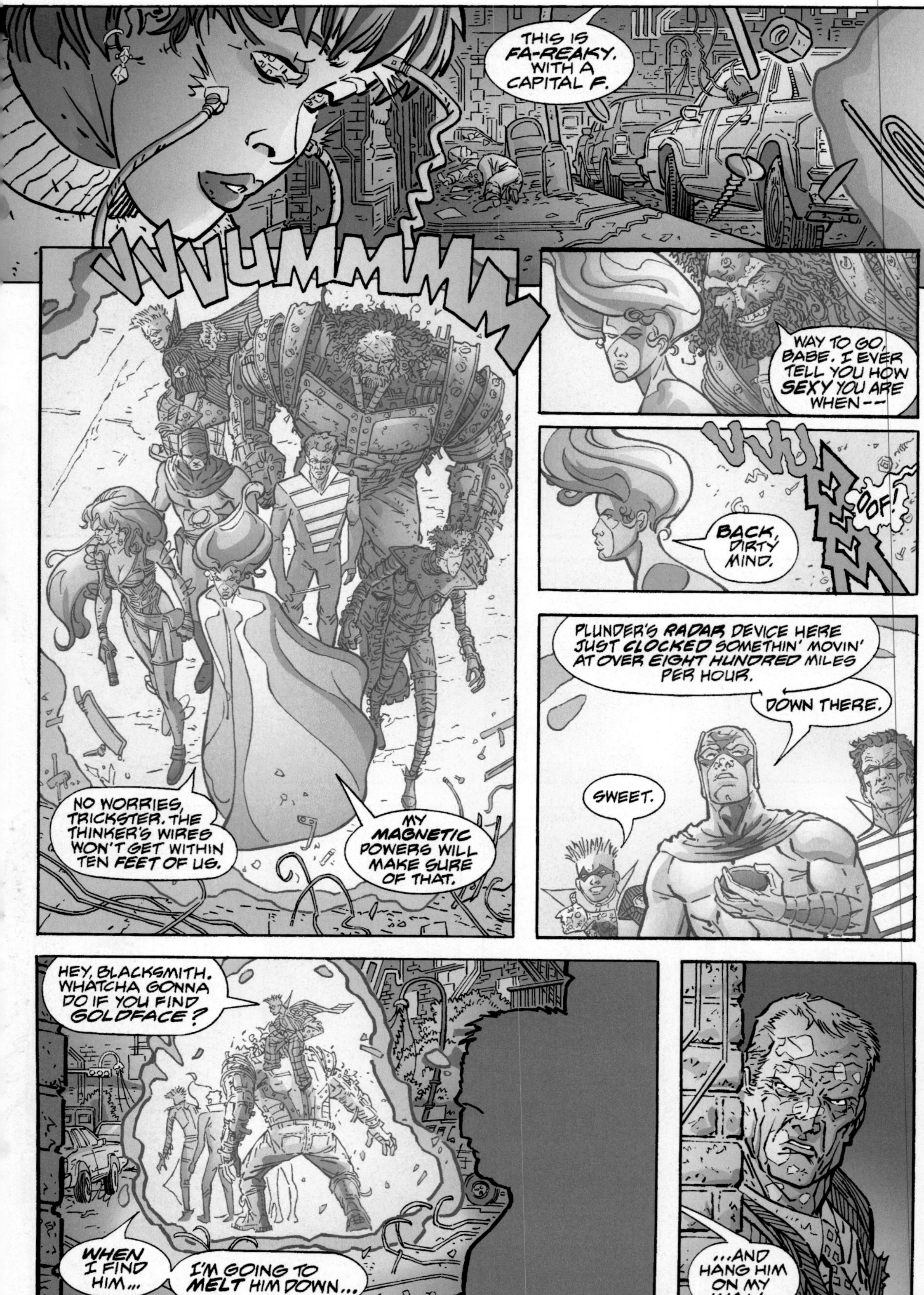
THIS IS FA-REAKY. WITH A CAPITAL F.
VVVUMMMM
NO WORRIES, TRICKSTER. THE THINKER'S WIRES WON'T GET WITHIN TEN FEET OF US.
MY MAGNETIC POWERS WILL MAKE SURE OF THAT.
WAY TO GO, BABE. I EVER TELL YOU HOW SEXY YOU ARE WHEN--
VVUD
OOF!
BACK, DIRTY MIND.
PLUNDER'S RADAR DEVICE HERE JUST CLOCKED SOMETHIN' MOVIN' AT OVER EIGHT HUNDRED MILES PER HOUR.
DOWN THERE.
SWEET.
HEY, BLACKSMITH. WHATCHA GONNA DO IF YOU FIND GOLDFACE?
WHEN I FIND HIM...
I'M GOING TO MELT HIM DOWN...
...AND HANG HIM ON MY WALL.

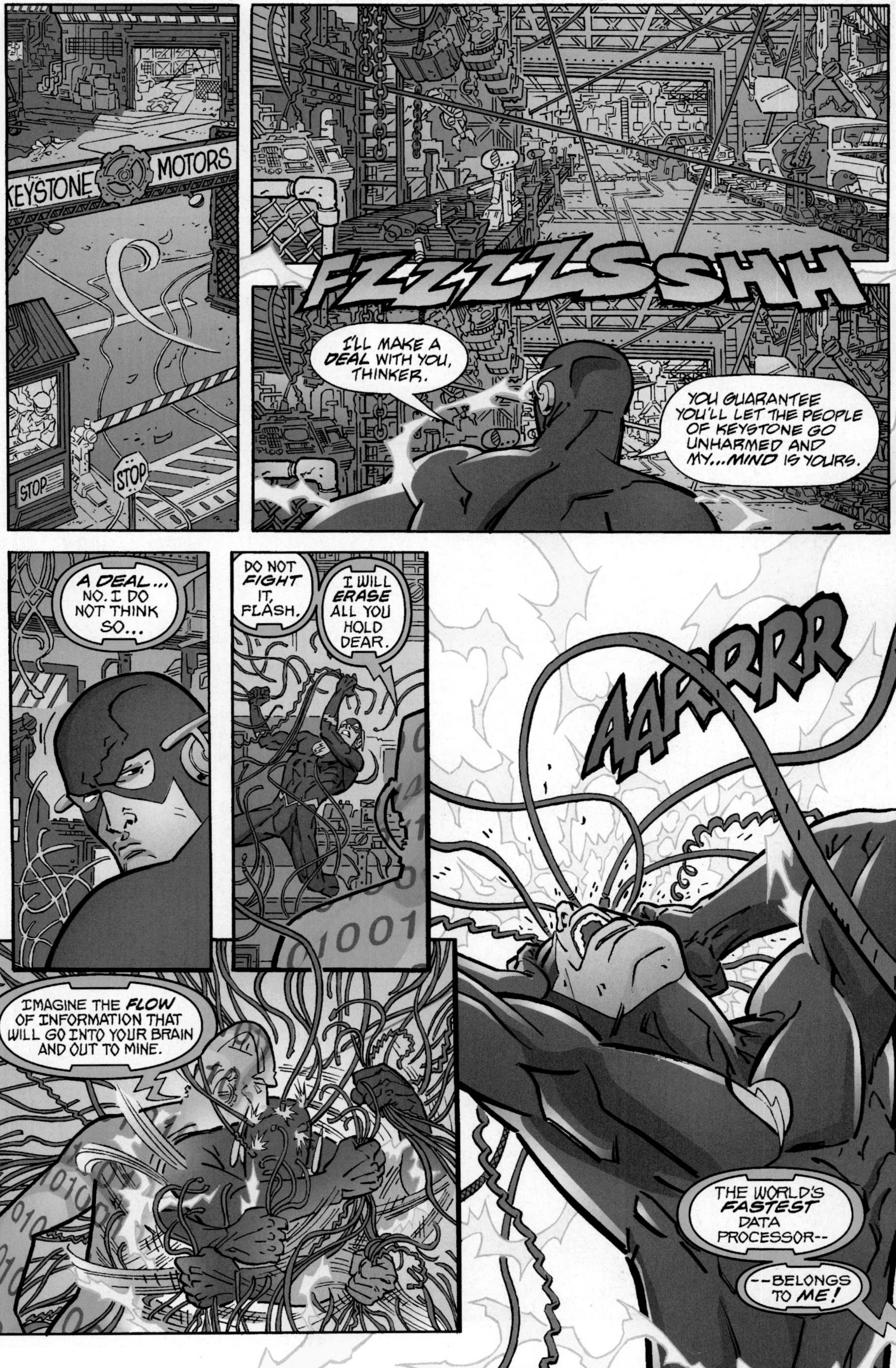
KEYSTONE MOTORS
STOP
STOP
FZZZZSSHH
I'LL MAKE A DEAL WITH YOU, THINKER.
YOU GUARANTEE YOU'LL LET THE PEOPLE OF KEYSTONE GO UNHARMED AND MY... MIND IS YOURS.
A DEAL... NO. I DO NOT THINK SO...
DO NOT FIGHT IT, FLASH.
I WILL ERASE ALL YOU HOLD DEAR.
AARRRR
IMAGINE THE FLOW OF INFORMATION THAT WILL GO INTO YOUR BRAIN AND OUT TO MINE.
THE WORLD'S FASTEST DATA PROCESSOR--
--BELONGS TO ME!

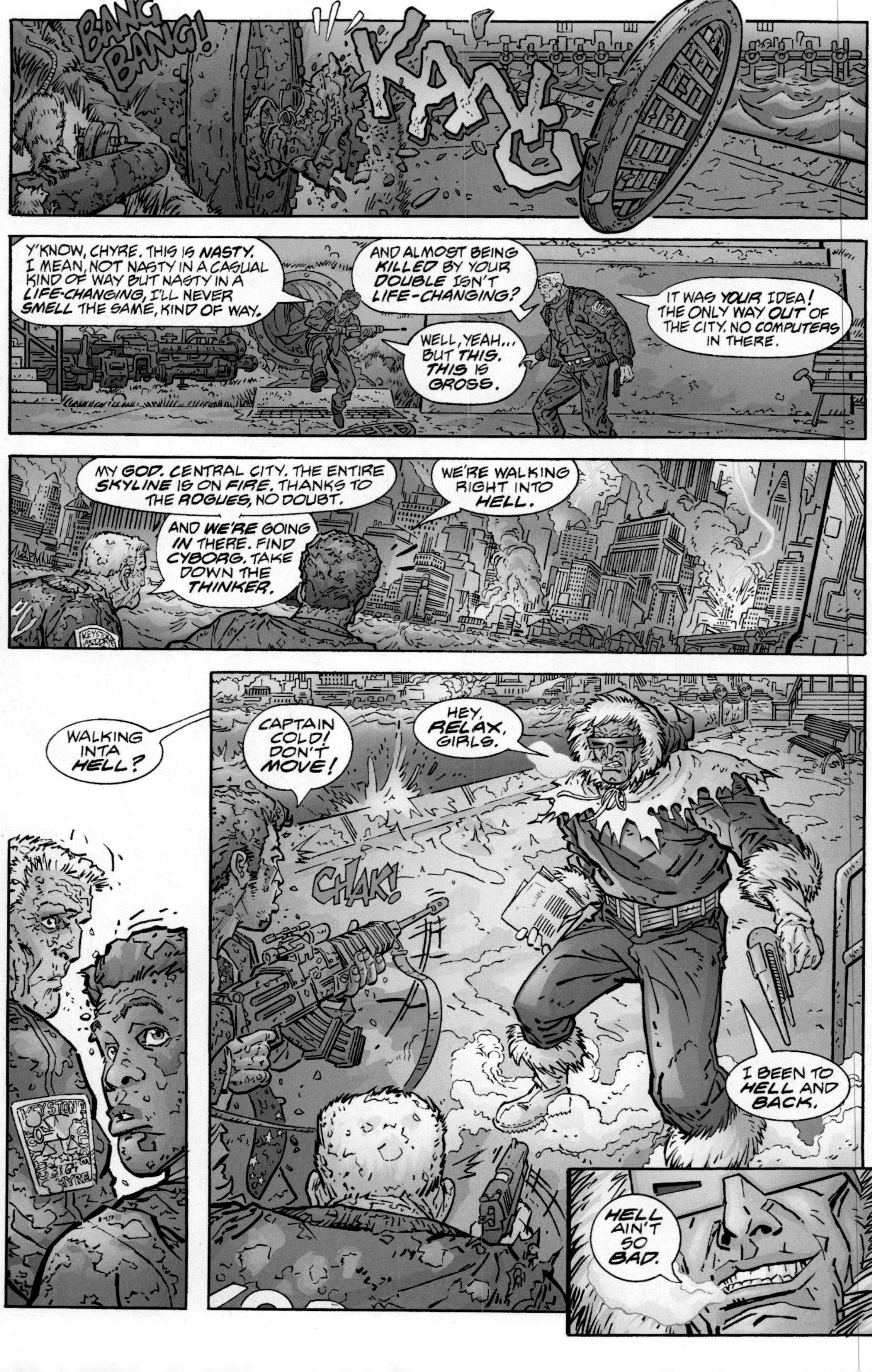
BANG BANG!
KA-KUNG
Y'KNOW, CHYRE, THIS IS NASTY. I MEAN, NOT NASTY IN A CASUAL KIND OF WAY BUT NASTY IN A LIFE-CHANGING, I'LL NEVER SMELL THE SAME, KIND OF WAY.
AND ALMOST BEING KILLED BY YOUR DOUBLE ISN'T LIFE-CHANGING?
WELL, YEAH... BUT THIS. THIS IS GROSS.
IT WAS YOUR IDEA! THE ONLY WAY OUT OF THE CITY. NO COMPUTERS IN THERE.
MY GOD. CENTRAL CITY. THE ENTIRE SKYLINE IS ON FIRE. THANKS TO THE ROGUES, NO DOUBT.
AND WE'RE GOING IN THERE. FIND CYBORG. TAKE DOWN THE THINKER.
WE'RE WALKING RIGHT INTO HELL.
WALKING INTA HELL?
CAPTAIN COLD! DON'T MOVE!
HEY, RELAX, GIRLS.
CHAK!
I BEEN TO HELL AND BACK.
HELL AIN'T SO BAD.

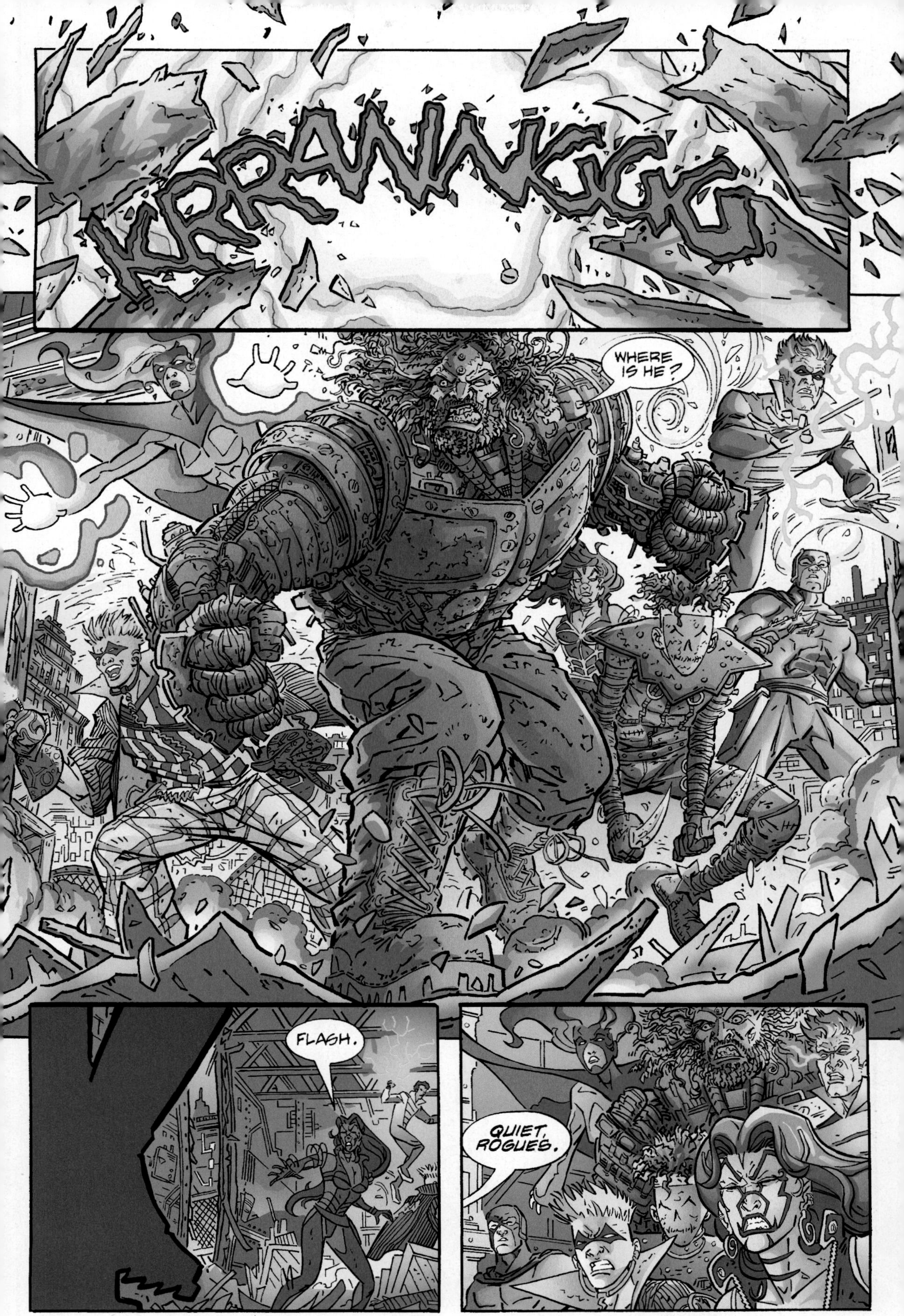
KRRANNGGG
WHERE IS HE?
FLASH.
QUIET, ROGUES.

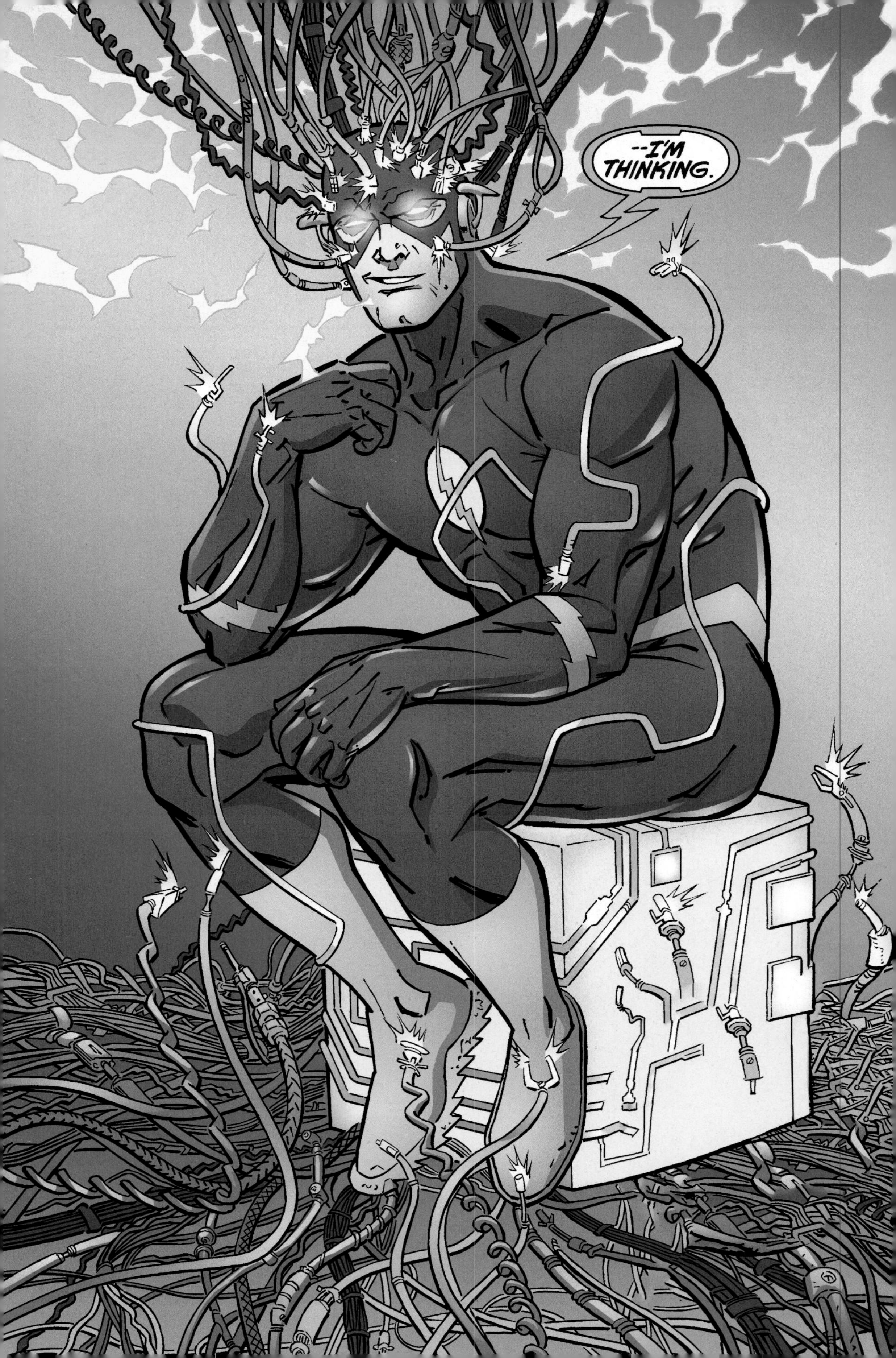
--I'M THINKING.

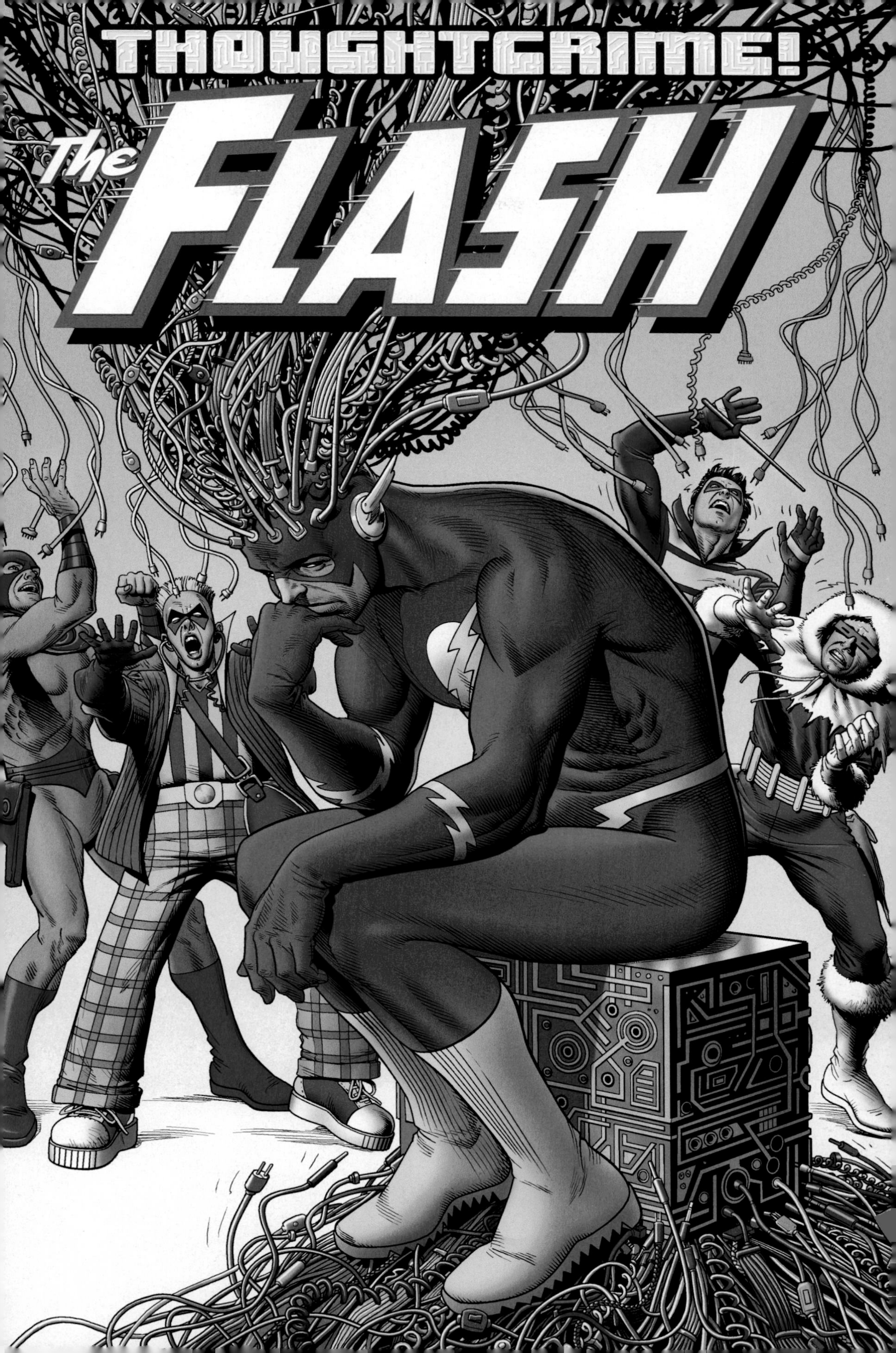
THOUGHTCRIME!
The FLASH

COVER ART BY ***BRIAN BOLLAND***

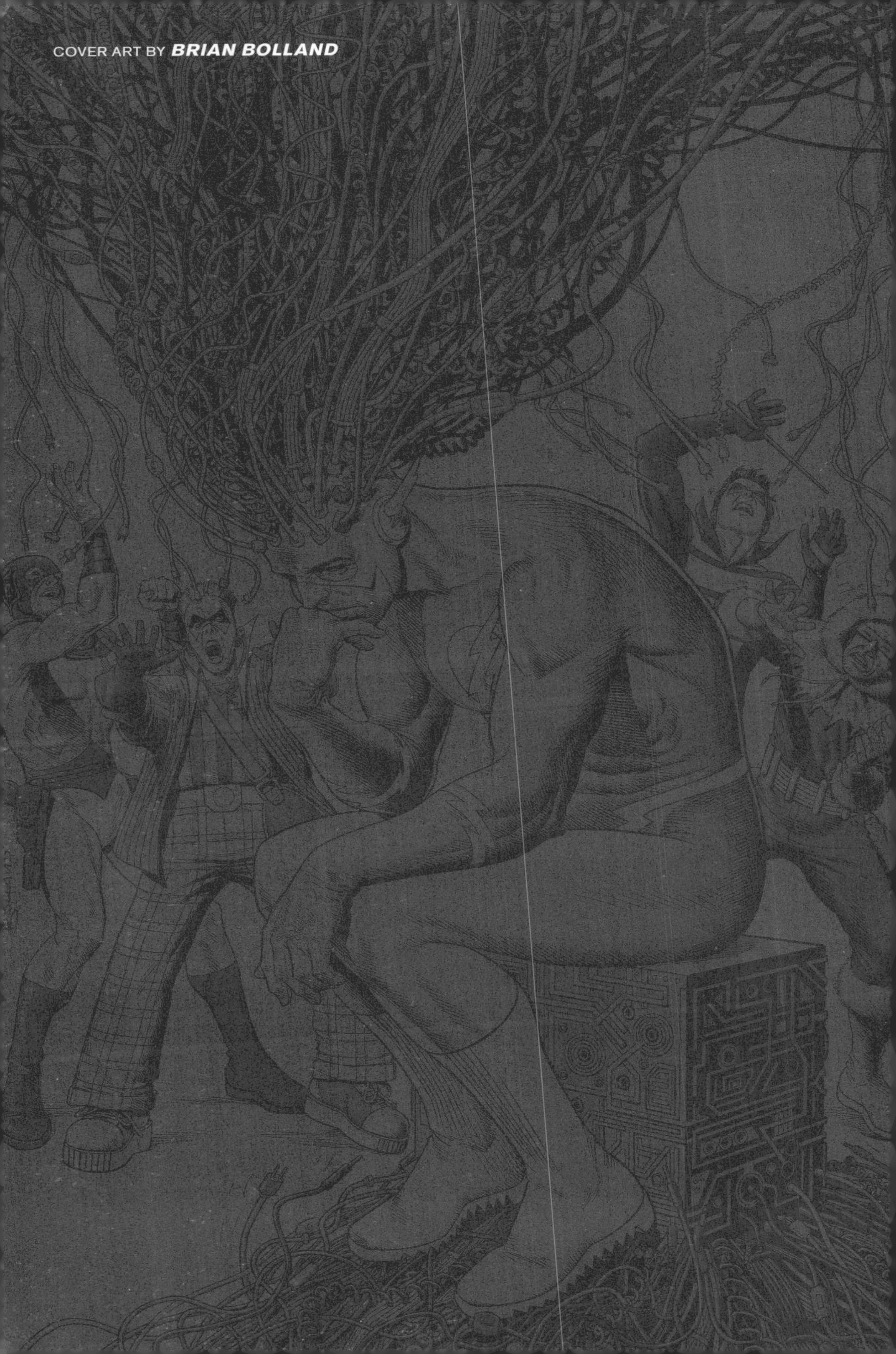

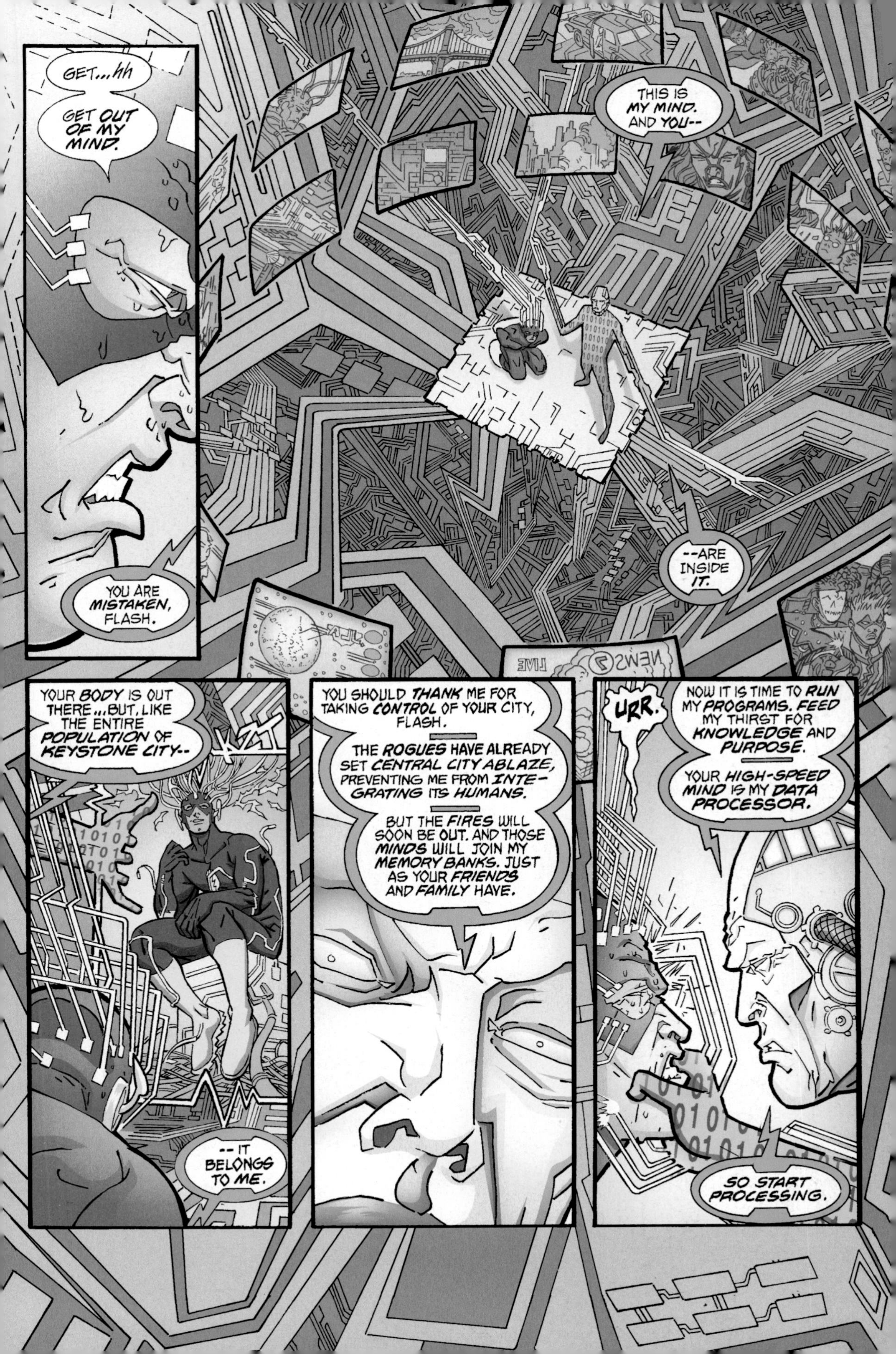
GET...hh
GET OUT OF MY MIND.
THIS IS MY MIND. AND YOU--
--ARE INSIDE IT.
YOU ARE MISTAKEN, FLASH.
YOUR BODY IS OUT THERE...BUT, LIKE THE ENTIRE POPULATION OF KEYSTONE CITY--
--IT BELONGS TO ME.
YOU SHOULD THANK ME FOR TAKING CONTROL OF YOUR CITY, FLASH.
THE ROGUES HAVE ALREADY SET CENTRAL CITY ABLAZE, PREVENTING ME FROM INTEGRATING ITS HUMANS.
BUT THE FIRES WILL SOON BE OUT. AND THOSE MINDS WILL JOIN MY MEMORY BANKS. JUST AS YOUR FRIENDS AND FAMILY HAVE.
URR.
NOW IT IS TIME TO RUN MY PROGRAMS. FEED MY THIRST FOR KNOWLEDGE AND PURPOSE.
YOUR HIGH-SPEED MIND IS MY DATA PROCESSOR.
SO START PROCESSING.

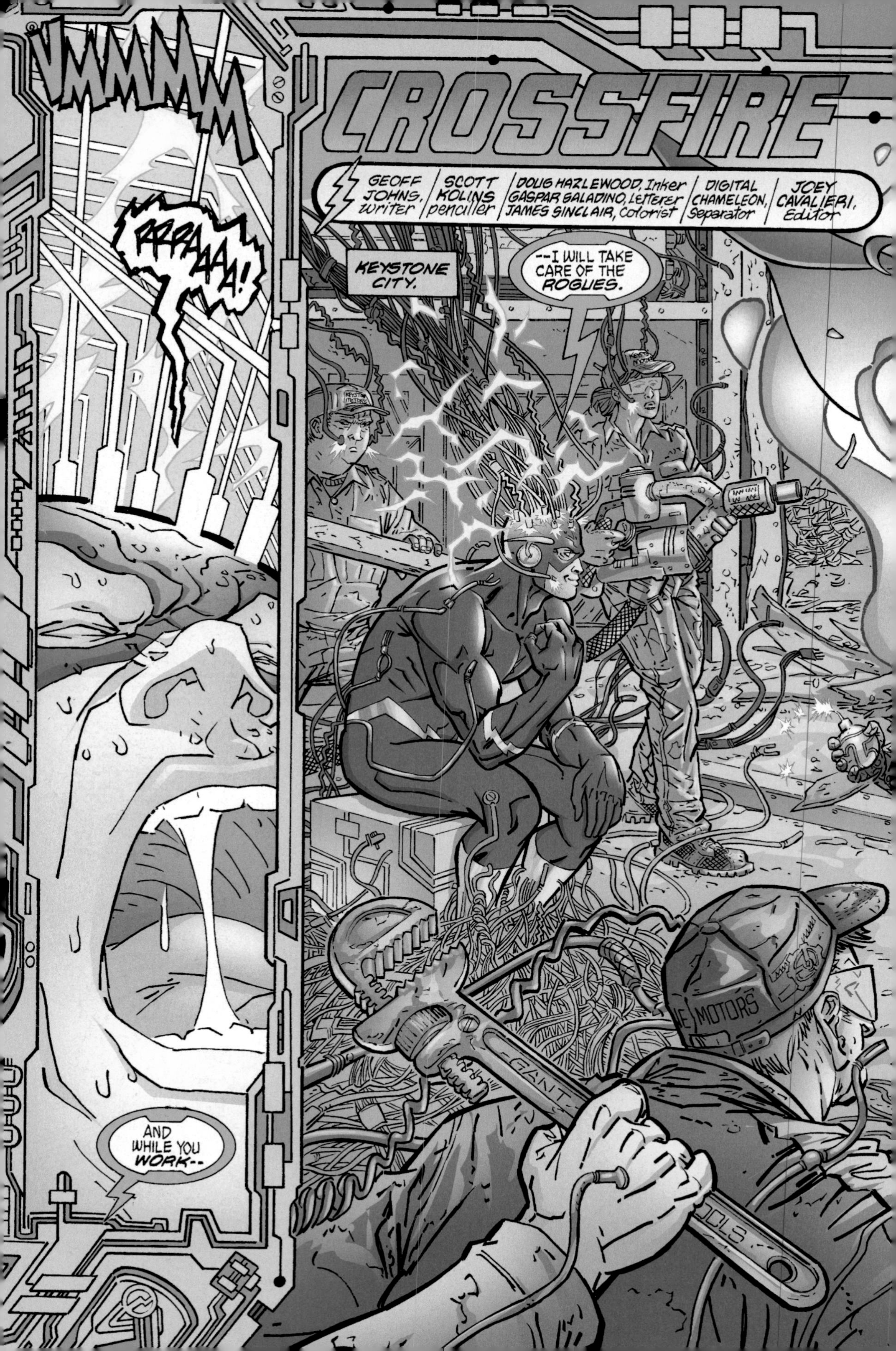
VMMMMM
PRRRAAAAA!
AND WHILE YOU WORK--
CROSSFIRE
GEOFF JOHNS, writer
SCOTT KOLINS penciller
DOUG HAZLEWOOD, Inker
GASPAR SALADINO, Letterer
JAMES SINCLAIR, Colorist
DIGITAL CHAMELEON, Separator
JOEY CAVALIERI, Editor
KEYSTONE CITY.
--I WILL TAKE CARE OF THE ROGUES.
MOTORS
GANT
OOLS

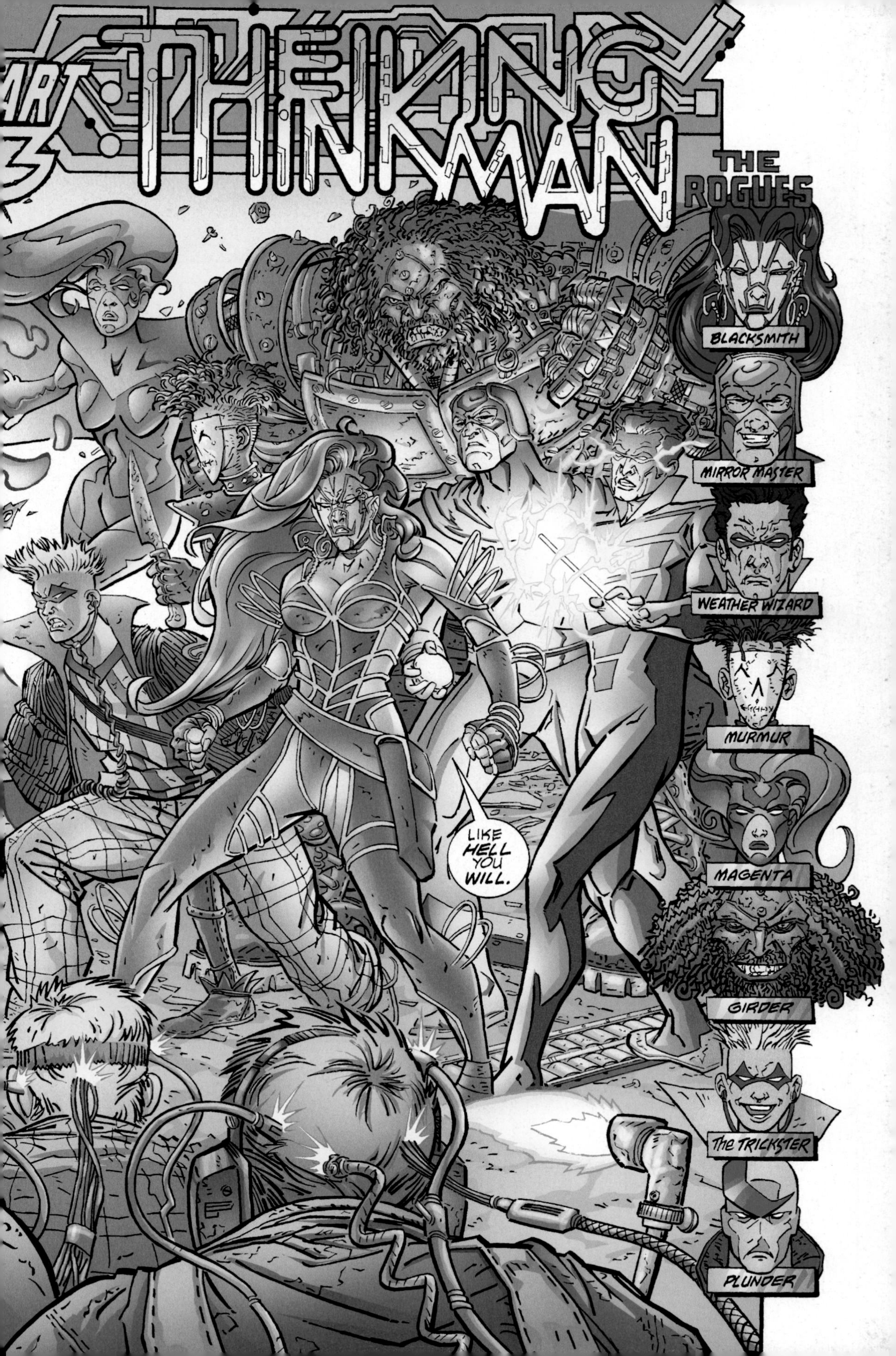
PART 3
THE FANCY
THINKMAN
THE ROGUES
BLACKSMITH
MIRROR MASTER
WEATHER WIZARD
MURMUR
MAGENTA
GIRDER
The TRICKSTER
PLUNDER
LIKE HELL YOU WILL.

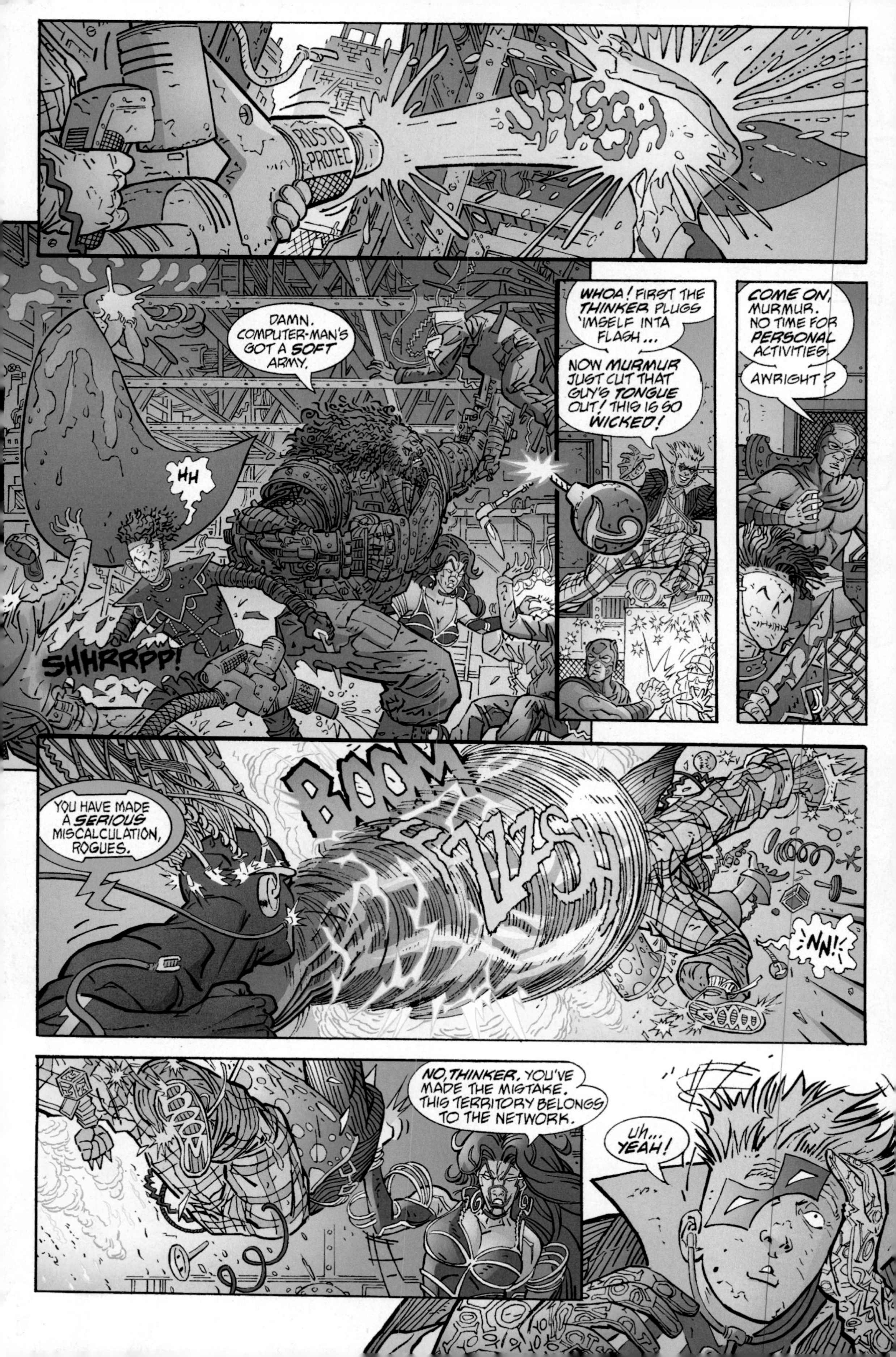
RUSTO PROTEC
SPSSSH
DAMN. COMPUTER-MAN'S GOT A SOFT ARMY.
HH
SHHRRPP!
WHOA! FIRST THE THINKER PLUGS 'IMSELF INTA FLASH...
NOW MURMUR JUST CUT THAT GUY'S TONGUE OUT! THIS IS SO WICKED!
COME ON, MURMUR. NO TIME FOR PERSONAL ACTIVITIES.
AWRIGHT?
YOU HAVE MADE A SERIOUS MISCALCULATION, ROGUES.
BOOM
FZZZSH
NN!
NO, THINKER, YOU'VE MADE THE MISTAKE. THIS TERRITORY BELONGS TO THE NETWORK.
Uh... YEAH!

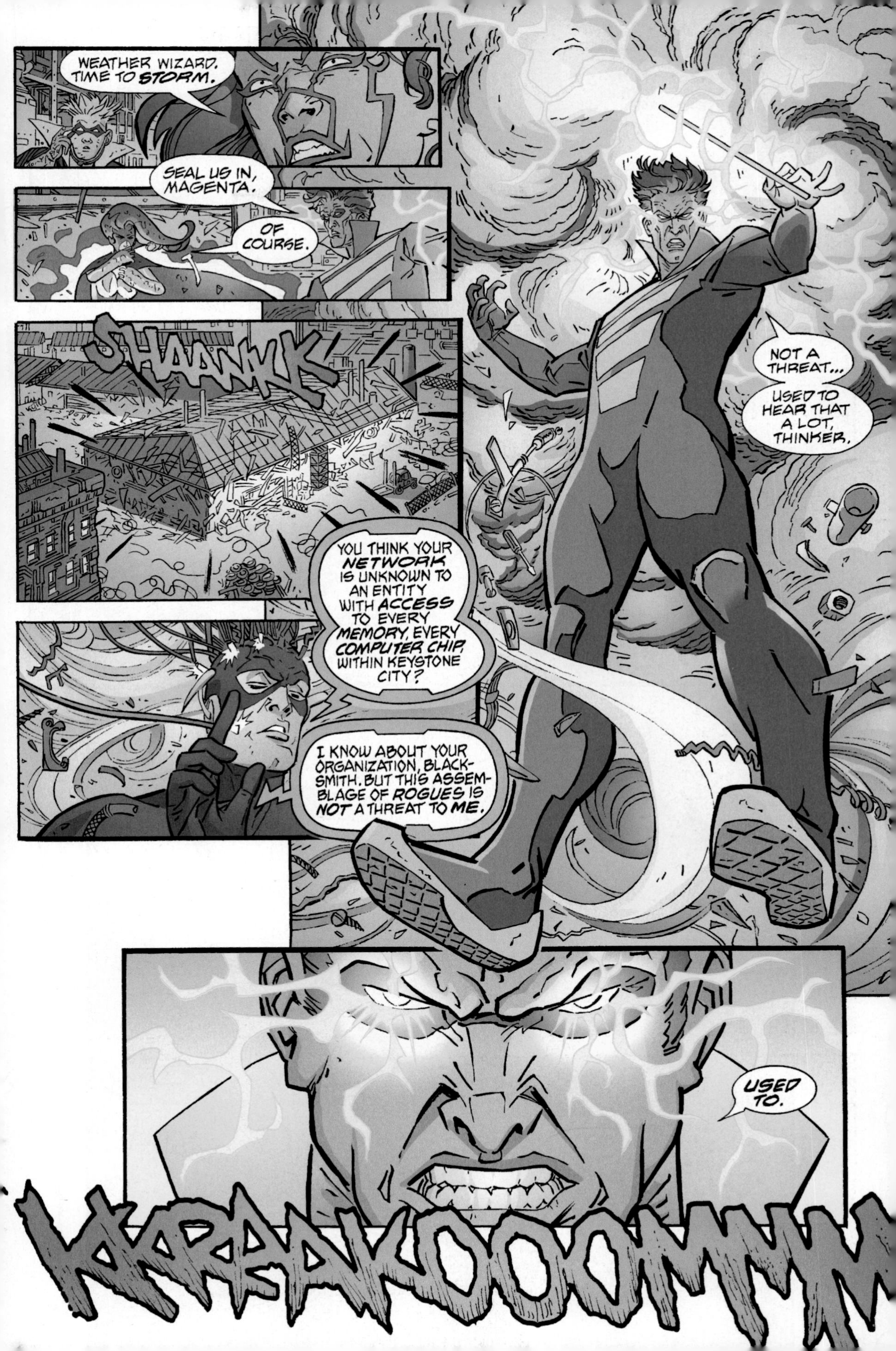
WEATHER WIZARD. TIME TO STORM.
SEAL US IN, MAGENTA.
OF COURSE.
SHAANKK!
NOT A THREAT...
USED TO HEAR THAT A LOT, THINKER.
YOU THINK YOUR NETWORK IS UNKNOWN TO AN ENTITY WITH ACCESS TO EVERY MEMORY, EVERY COMPUTER CHIP, WITHIN KEYSTONE CITY?
I KNOW ABOUT YOUR ORGANIZATION, BLACKSMITH. BUT THIS ASSEMBLAGE OF ROGUES IS NOT A THREAT TO ME.
USED TO.
KRRAKOOOMM

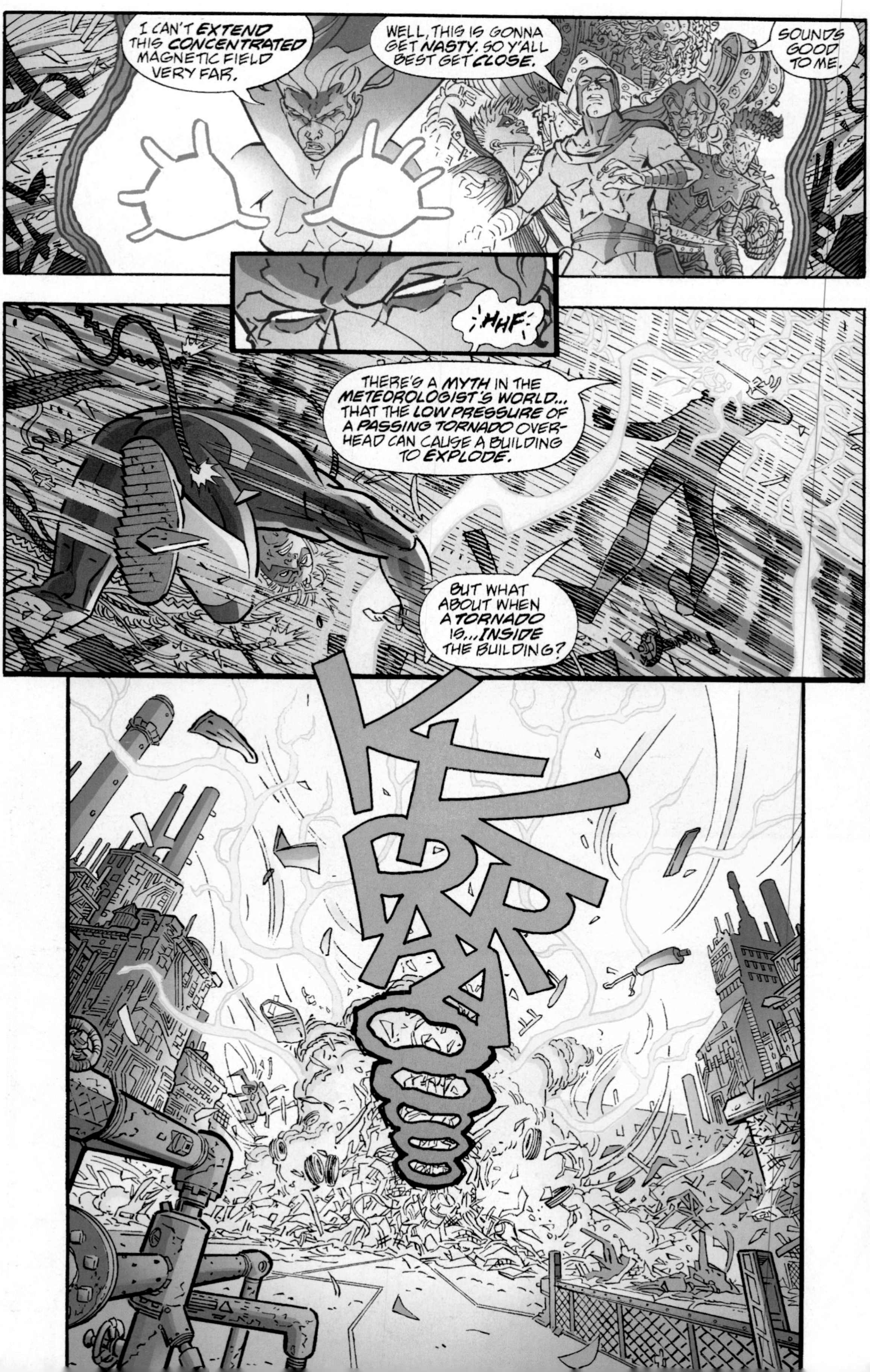
I CAN'T EXTEND THIS CONCENTRATED MAGNETIC FIELD VERY FAR.
WELL, THIS IS GONNA GET NASTY. SO Y'ALL BEST GET CLOSE.
SOUNDS GOOD TO ME.
HHF
THERE'S A MYTH IN THE METEOROLOGIST'S WORLD... THAT THE LOW PRESSURE OF A PASSING TORNADO OVER-HEAD CAN CAUSE A BUILDING TO EXPLODE.
BUT WHAT ABOUT WHEN A TORNADO IS... INSIDE THE BUILDING?
KRRBAROOOOO

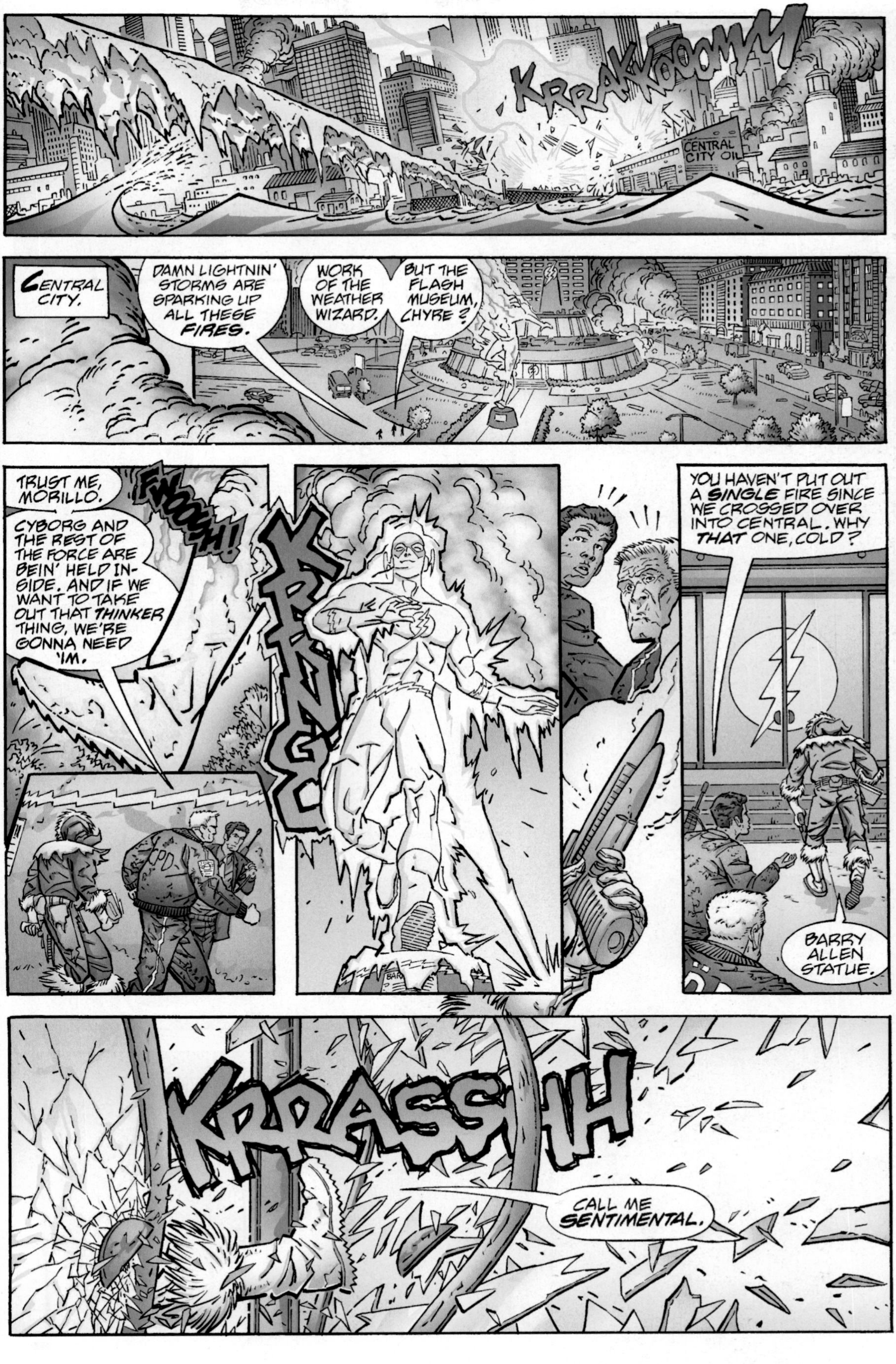
KRRAKOOOMM
CENTRAL CITY OIL
CENTRAL CITY.
DAMN LIGHTNIN' STORMS ARE SPARKING UP ALL THESE FIRES.
WORK OF THE WEATHER WIZARD.
BUT THE FLASH MUSEUM, CHYRE?
TRUST ME, MORILLO.
CYBORG AND THE REST OF THE FORCE ARE BEIN' HELD INSIDE. AND IF WE WANT TO TAKE OUT THAT THINKER THING, WE'RE GONNA NEED 'IM.
FWOOSH!
KRANG
YOU HAVEN'T PUT OUT A SINGLE FIRE SINCE WE CROSSED OVER INTO CENTRAL. WHY THAT ONE, COLD?
BARRY ALLEN STATUE.
KRRASSHH
CALL ME SENTIMENTAL.

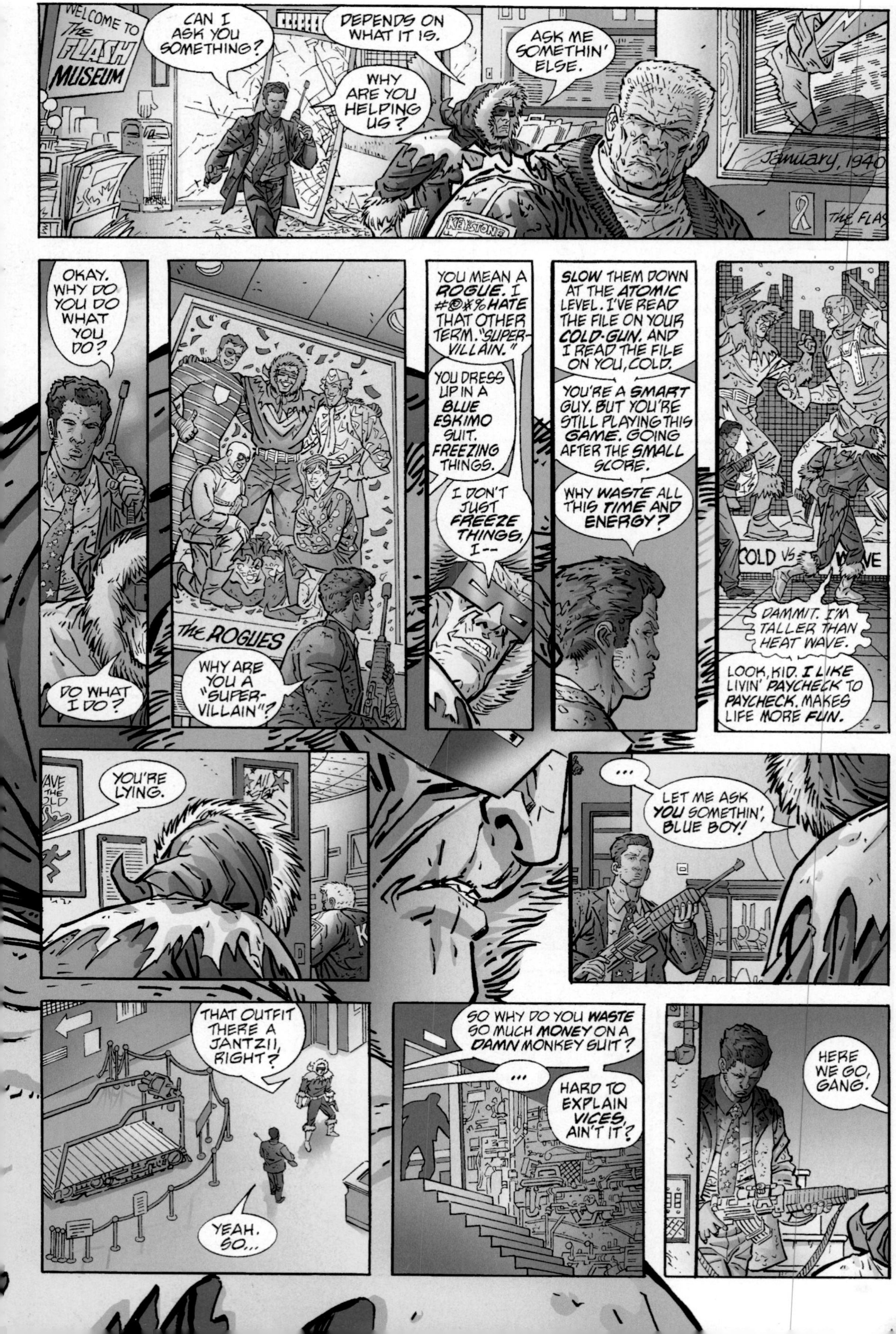

WELCOME TO The FLASH MUSEUM
CAN I ASK YOU SOMETHING?
DEPENDS ON WHAT IT IS.
WHY ARE YOU HELPING US?
ASK ME SOMETHIN' ELSE.
January, 1940
KEYSTONE
OKAY. WHY DO YOU DO WHAT YOU DO?
DO WHAT I DO?
THE ROGUES
WHY ARE YOU A "SUPER-VILLAIN"?
YOU MEAN A ROGUE. I #@*% HATE THAT OTHER TERM. "SUPER-VILLAIN."
YOU DRESS UP IN A BLUE ESKIMO SUIT. FREEZING THINGS.
I DON'T JUST FREEZE THINGS, I--
SLOW THEM DOWN AT THE ATOMIC LEVEL. I'VE READ THE FILE ON YOUR COLD-GUN. AND I READ THE FILE ON YOU, COLD.
YOU'RE A SMART GUY. BUT YOU'RE STILL PLAYING THIS GAME. GOING AFTER THE SMALL SCORE.
WHY WASTE ALL THIS TIME AND ENERGY?
COLD VS WAVE
DAMMIT. I'M TALLER THAN HEAT WAVE.
LOOK, KID. I LIKE LIVIN' PAYCHECK TO PAYCHECK. MAKES LIFE MORE FUN.
YOU'RE LYING.
...
LET ME ASK YOU SOMETHIN', BLUE BOY!
THAT OUTFIT THERE A JANTZII, RIGHT?
YEAH. SO...
SO WHY DO YOU WASTE SO MUCH MONEY ON A DAMN MONKEY SUIT?
...
HARD TO EXPLAIN VICES, AIN'T IT?
HERE WE GO, GANG.

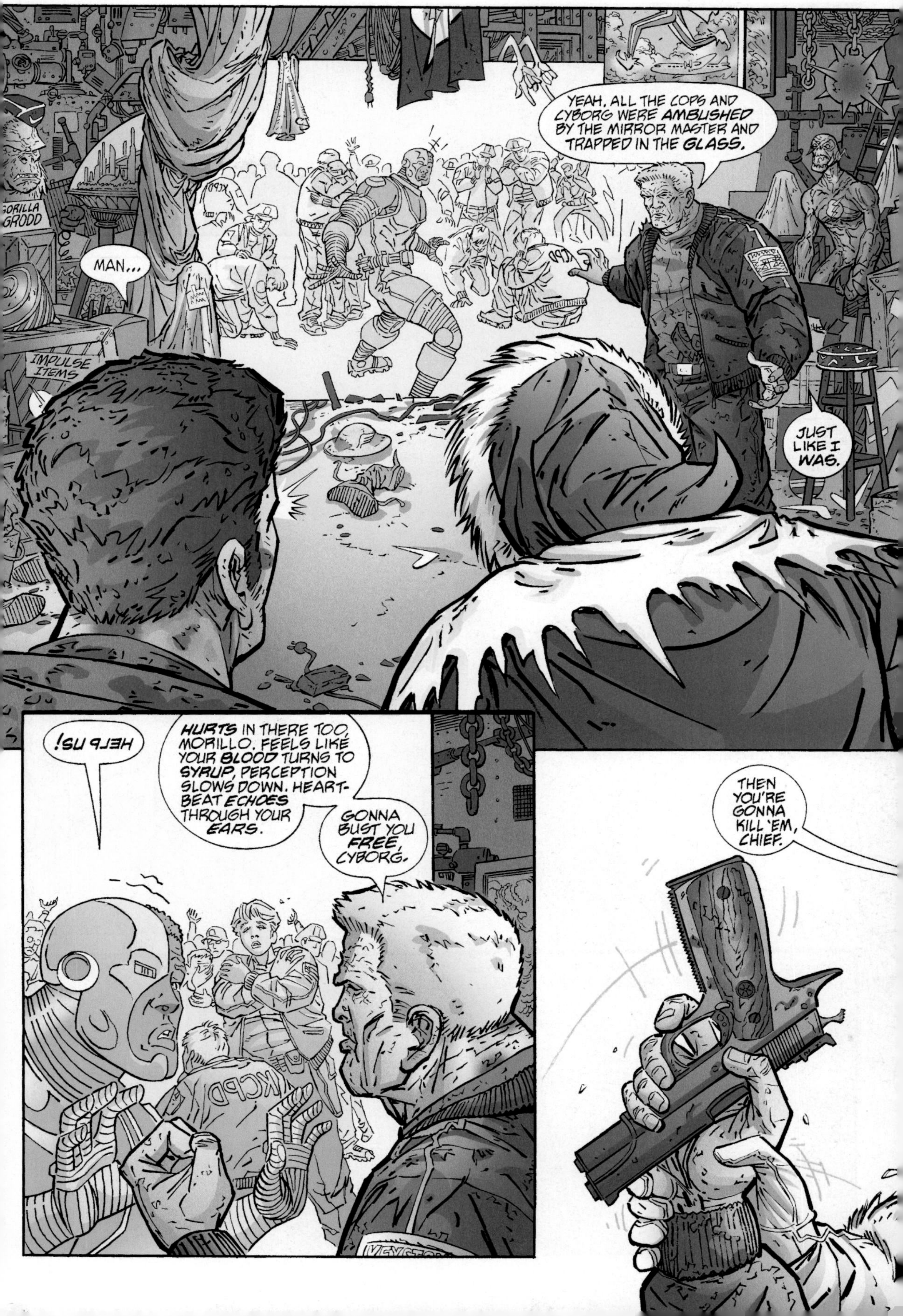
GORILLA GRODD
IMPULSE ITEMS
KCPD
MAN...
YEAH. ALL THE COPS AND CYBORG WERE AMBUSHED BY THE MIRROR MASTER AND TRAPPED IN THE GLASS.
JUST LIKE I WAS.
HELP US!
HURTS IN THERE TOO, MORILLO. FEELS LIKE YOUR BLOOD TURNS TO SYRUP, PERCEPTION SLOWS DOWN. HEART-BEAT ECHOES THROUGH YOUR EARS.
GONNA BUST YOU FREE, CYBORG.
KCPD
THEN YOU'RE GONNA KILL 'EM, CHIEF.

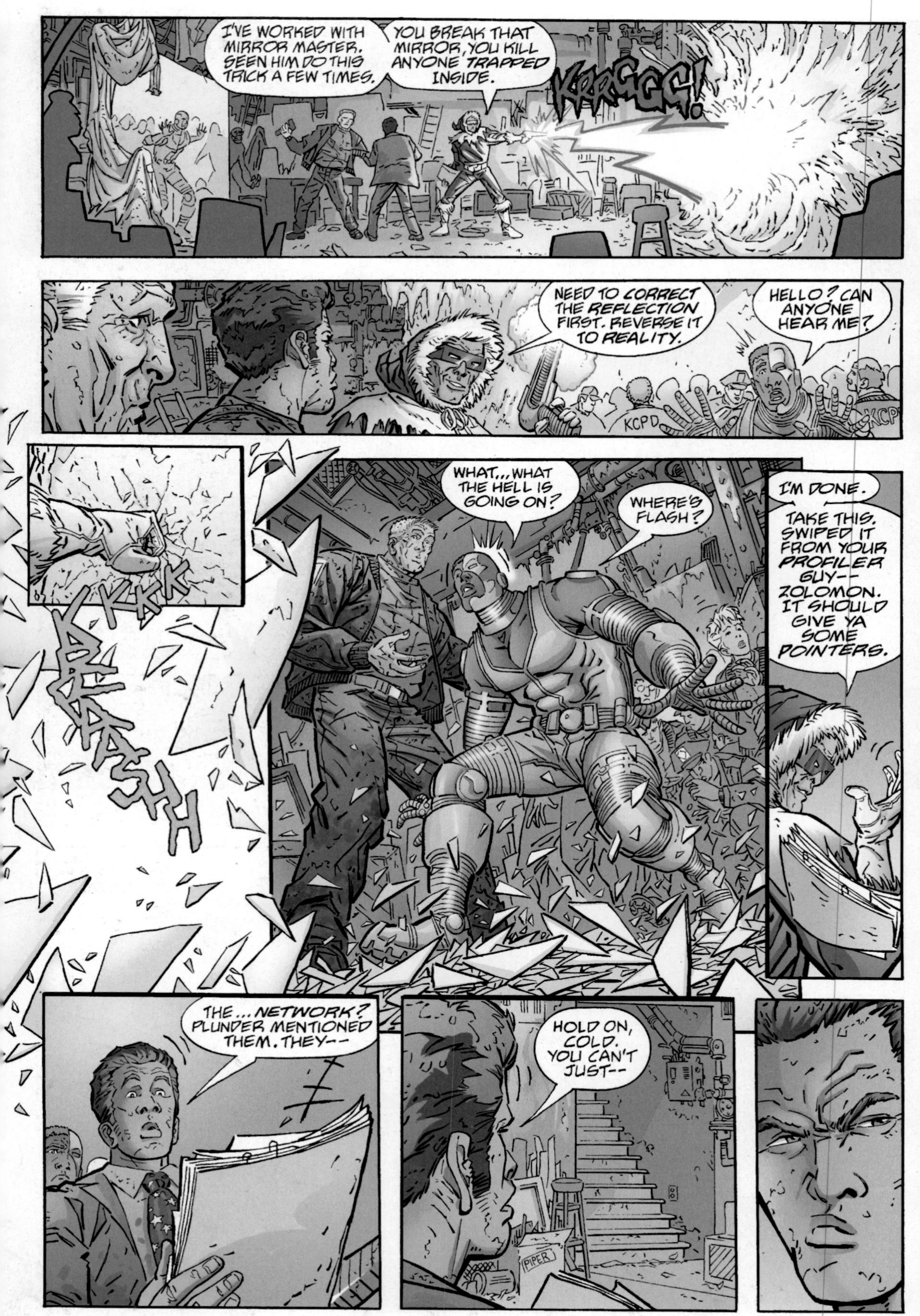
I'VE WORKED WITH MIRROR MASTER. SEEN HIM DO THIS TRICK A FEW TIMES.
YOU BREAK THAT MIRROR, YOU KILL ANYONE TRAPPED INSIDE.
KRRGGG!
NEED TO CORRECT THE REFLECTION FIRST. REVERSE IT TO REALITY.
HELLO? CAN ANYONE HEAR ME?
KCPD
KKKK
BKRASHH
WHAT... WHAT THE HELL IS GOING ON?
WHERE'S FLASH?
I'M DONE.
TAKE THIS. SWIPED IT FROM YOUR PROFILER GUY-- ZOLOMON. IT SHOULD GIVE YA SOME POINTERS.
THE... NETWORK? PLUNDER MENTIONED THEM. THEY--
HOLD ON, COLD. YOU CAN'T JUST--
PIPER

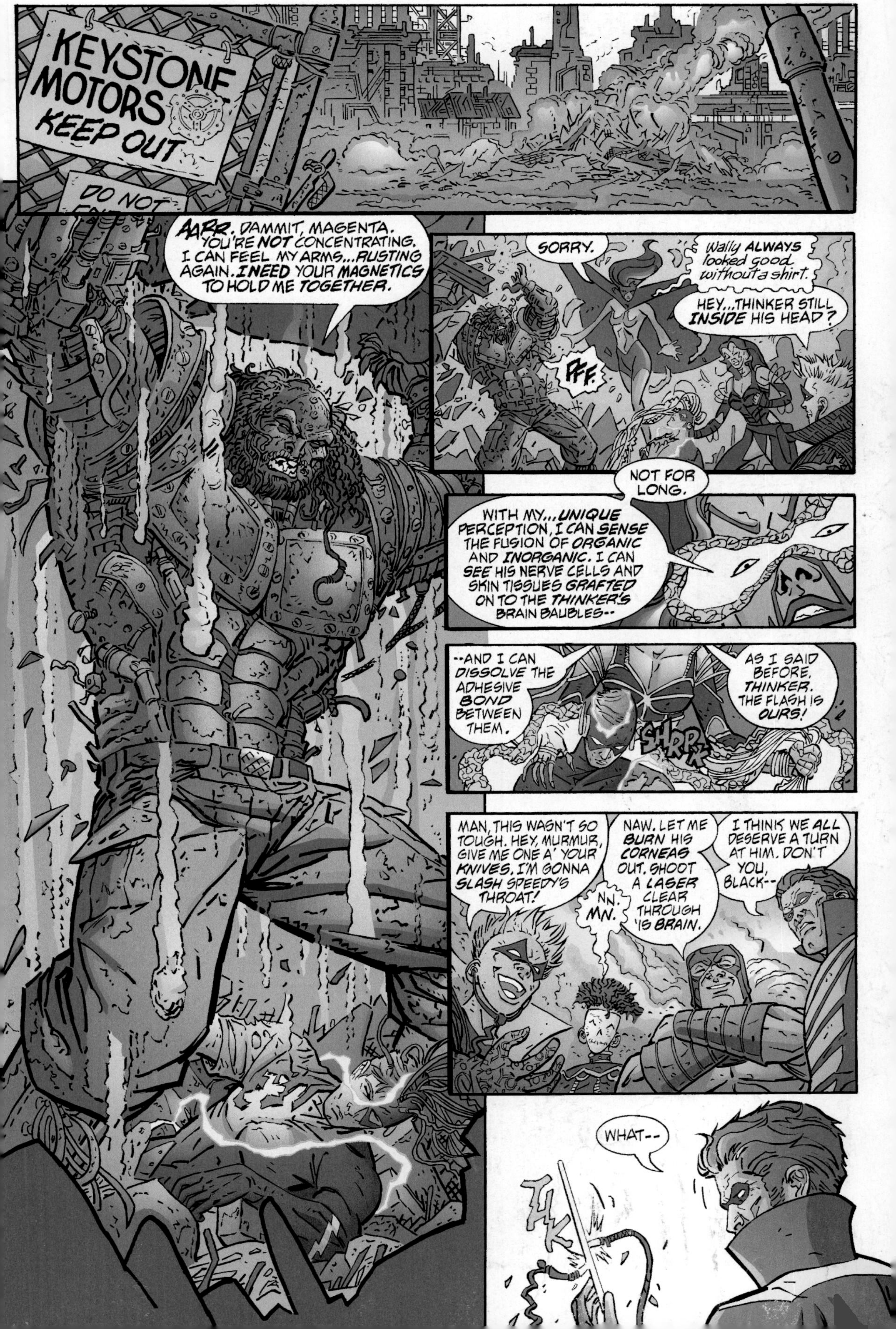
KEYSTONE MOTORS KEEP OUT
DO NOT
AARR. DAMMIT, MAGENTA. YOU'RE NOT CONCENTRATING. I CAN FEEL MY ARMS... RUSTING AGAIN. I NEED YOUR MAGNETICS TO HOLD ME TOGETHER.
SORRY.
Wally ALWAYS looked good without a shirt.
HEY... THINKER STILL INSIDE HIS HEAD?
PFFF.
NOT FOR LONG.
WITH MY... UNIQUE PERCEPTION, I CAN SENSE THE FUSION OF ORGANIC AND INORGANIC. I CAN SEE HIS NERVE CELLS AND SKIN TISSUES GRAFTED ON TO THE THINKER'S BRAIN BAUBLES--
--AND I CAN DISSOLVE THE ADHESIVE BOND BETWEEN THEM.
AS I SAID BEFORE, THINKER. THE FLASH IS OURS!
SHRPK
MAN, THIS WASN'T SO TOUGH. HEY, MURMUR, GIVE ME ONE A' YOUR KNIVES. I'M GONNA SLASH SPEEDY'S THROAT!
NN. MN.
NAW. LET ME BURN HIS CORNEAS OUT. SHOOT A LASER CLEAR THROUGH 'IS BRAIN.
I THINK WE ALL DESERVE A TURN AT HIM. DON'T YOU, BLACK--
WHAT--
THK

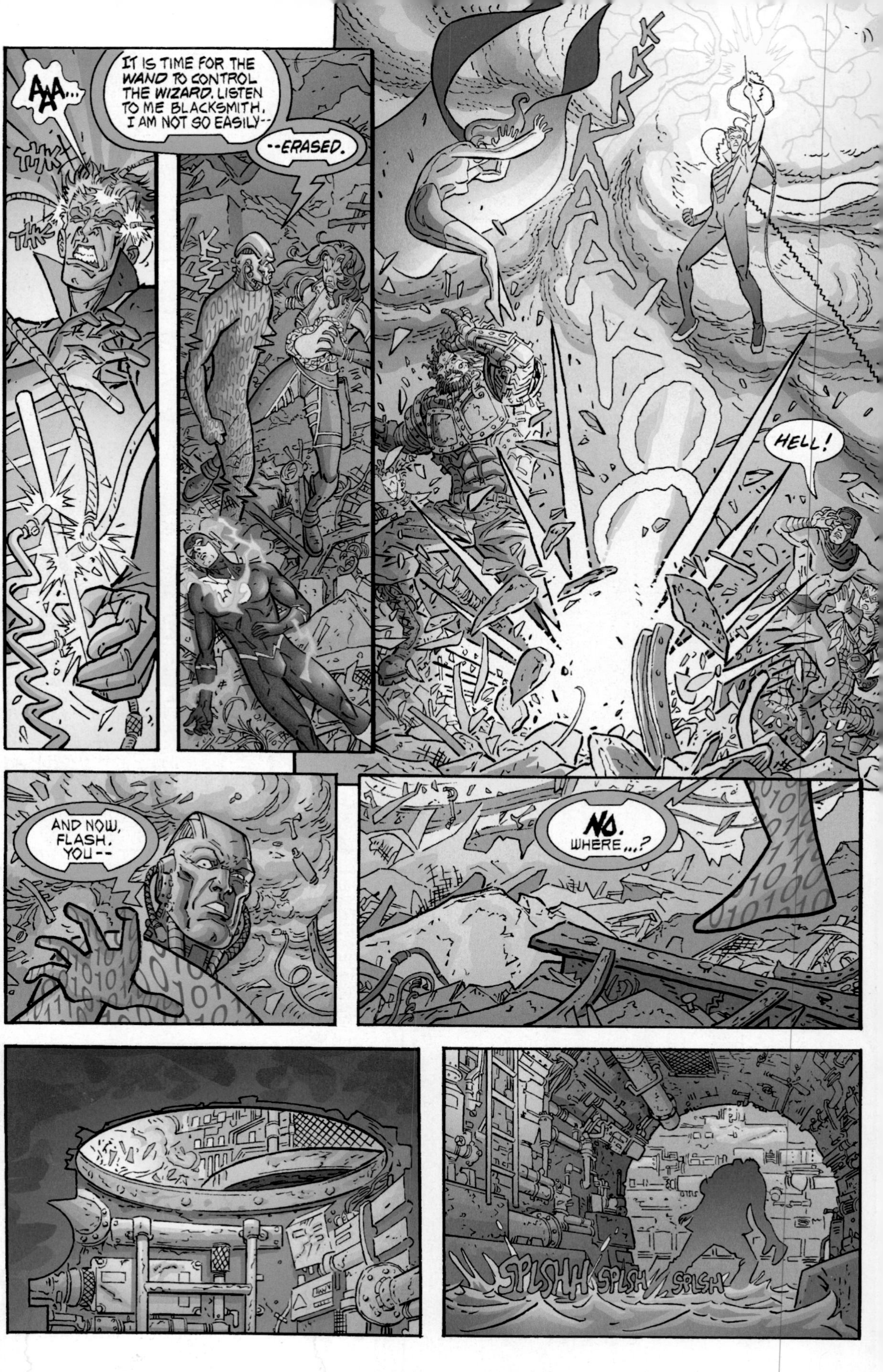
AAA...
THK
THK
IT IS TIME FOR THE WAND TO CONTROL THE WIZARD. LISTEN TO ME BLACKSMITH. I AM NOT SO EASILY--
--ERASED.
KAKKKK
KAAKOOO
HELL!
AND NOW, FLASH. YOU--
NO. WHERE...?
SPLSHH SPLSH SPLSH

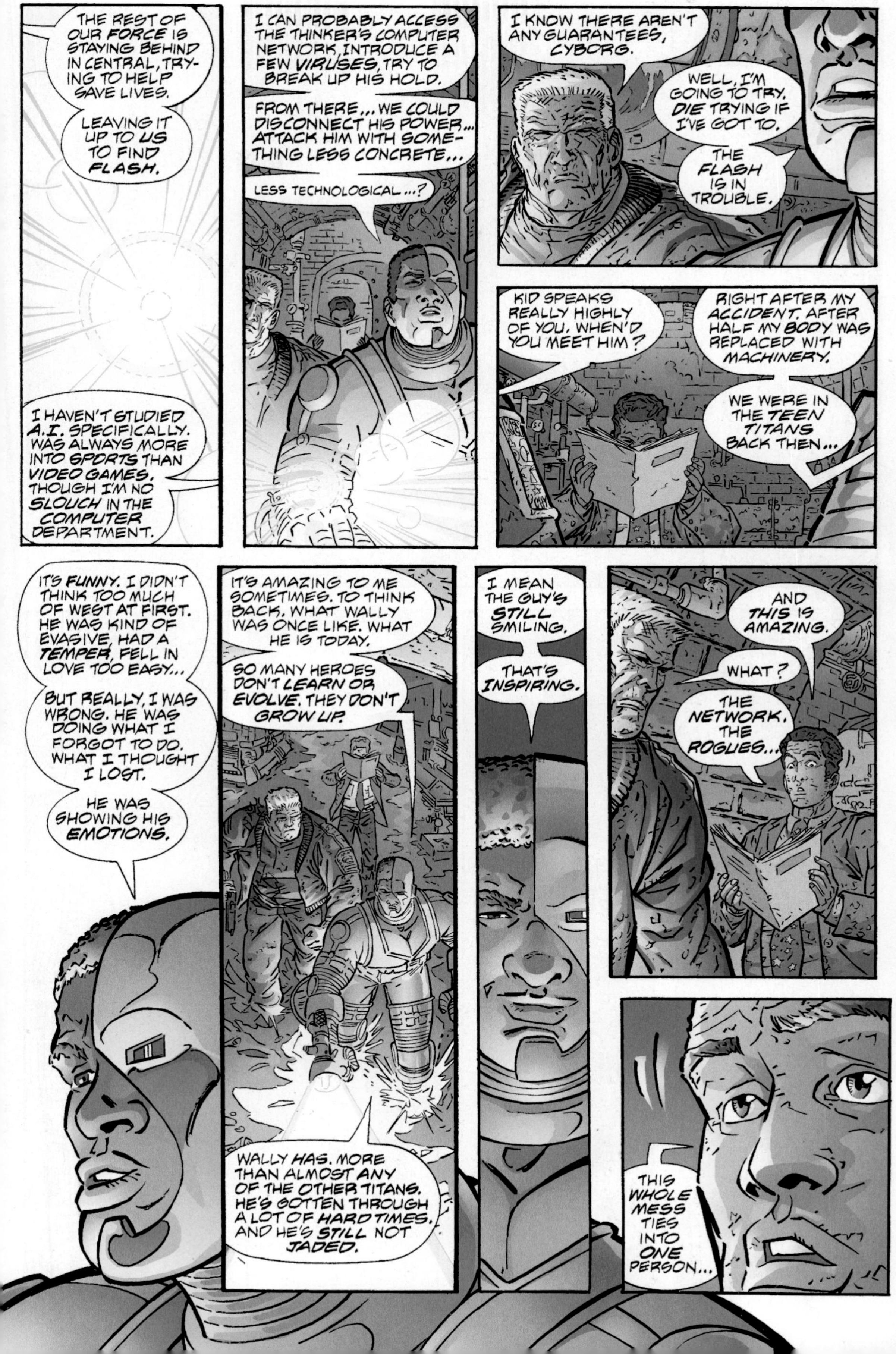
THE REST OF OUR FORCE IS STAYING BEHIND IN CENTRAL, TRYING TO HELP SAVE LIVES.
LEAVING IT UP TO US TO FIND FLASH.
I HAVEN'T STUDIED A.I. SPECIFICALLY. WAS ALWAYS MORE INTO SPORTS THAN VIDEO GAMES. THOUGH I'M NO SLOUCH IN THE COMPUTER DEPARTMENT.
I CAN PROBABLY ACCESS THE THINKER'S COMPUTER NETWORK, INTRODUCE A FEW VIRUSES, TRY TO BREAK UP HIS HOLD.
FROM THERE... WE COULD DISCONNECT HIS POWER... ATTACK HIM WITH SOMETHING LESS CONCRETE...
LESS TECHNOLOGICAL...?
I KNOW THERE AREN'T ANY GUARANTEES, CYBORG.
WELL, I'M GOING TO TRY. DIE TRYING IF I'VE GOT TO.
THE FLASH IS IN TROUBLE.
KID SPEAKS REALLY HIGHLY OF YOU. WHEN'D YOU MEET HIM?
RIGHT AFTER MY ACCIDENT. AFTER HALF MY BODY WAS REPLACED WITH MACHINERY.
WE WERE IN THE TEEN TITANS BACK THEN...
IT'S FUNNY. I DIDN'T THINK TOO MUCH OF WEST AT FIRST. HE WAS KIND OF EVASIVE, HAD A TEMPER, FELL IN LOVE TOO EASY...
BUT REALLY, I WAS WRONG. HE WAS DOING WHAT I FORGOT TO DO. WHAT I THOUGHT I LOST.
HE WAS SHOWING HIS EMOTIONS.
IT'S AMAZING TO ME SOMETIMES. TO THINK BACK. WHAT WALLY WAS ONCE LIKE. WHAT HE IS TODAY.
SO MANY HEROES DON'T LEARN OR EVOLVE. THEY DON'T GROW UP.
WALLY HAS. MORE THAN ALMOST ANY OF THE OTHER TITANS. HE'S GOTTEN THROUGH A LOT OF HARD TIMES. AND HE'S STILL NOT JADED.
I MEAN THE GUY'S STILL SMILING.
THAT'S INSPIRING.
AND THIS IS AMAZING.
WHAT?
THE NETWORK. THE ROGUES...
THIS WHOLE MESS TIES INTO ONE PERSON...

"--GOLDFACE."

...LINDA?

I'M AFRAID NOT, FLASH.

WHERE... WHERE AM I, KENYON?

IN THE SUBBASEMENT OF THE UNION HEADQUARTERS. AN OLD BOMB SHELTER. DON'T WORRY. YOU'RE SAFE.

I'M NOT WORRIED ABOUT ME. THE CITIES... CENTRAL AND KEYSTONE.

WHAT HAPPENED TO YOUR... SKIN?

I THINK IT'S TIME YOU FILLED ME IN, GOLDFACE.

WHAT ARE YOU DOING HERE?

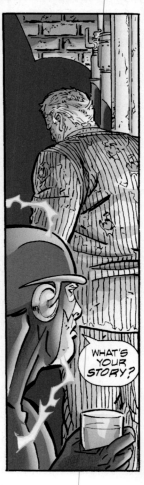

WHAT'S YOUR STORY?

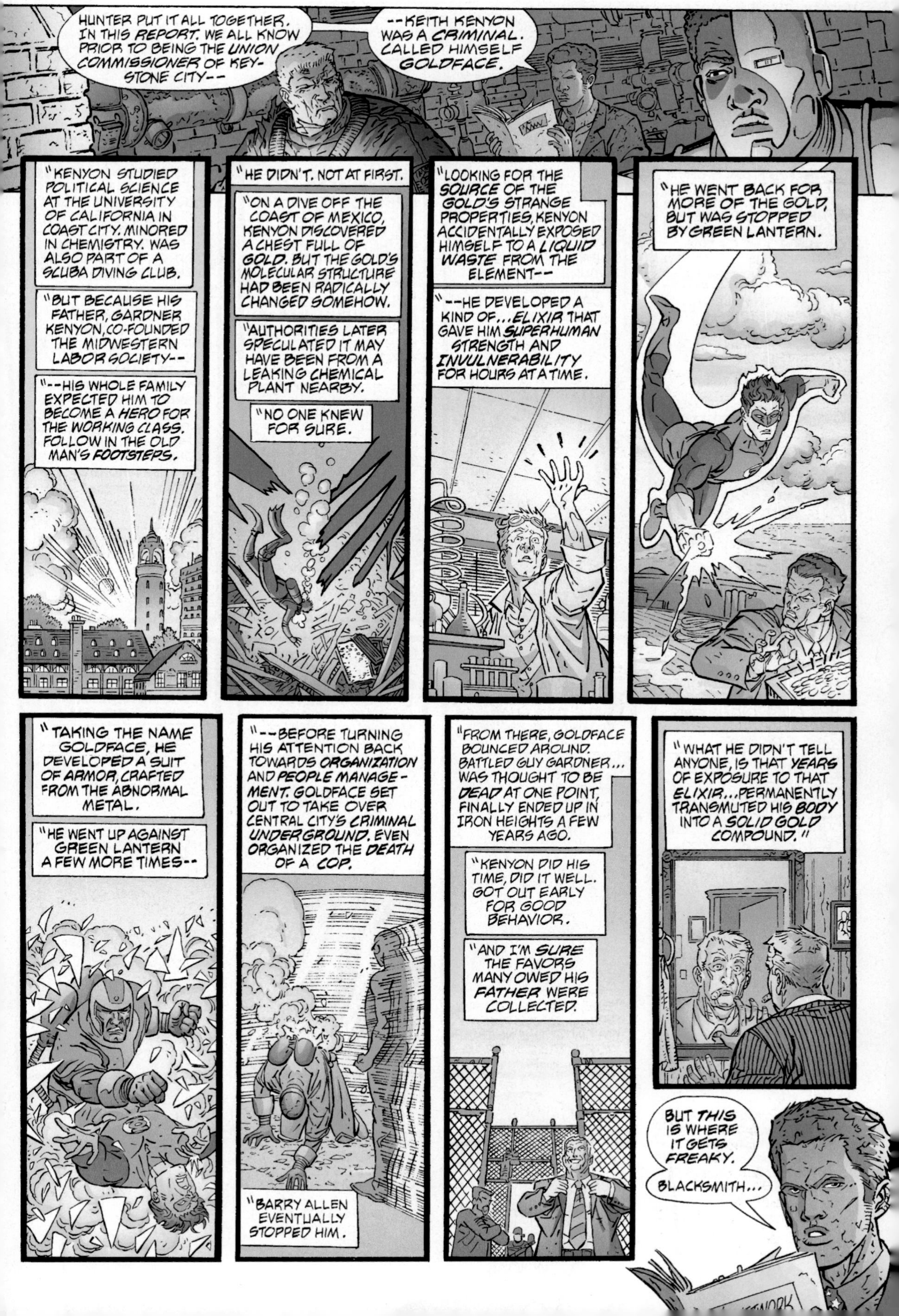
HUNTER PUT IT ALL TOGETHER. IN THIS REPORT. WE ALL KNOW PRIOR TO BEING THE UNION COMMISSIONER OF KEY-STONE CITY--
--KEITH KENYON WAS A CRIMINAL. CALLED HIMSELF GOLDFACE.
"KENYON STUDIED POLITICAL SCIENCE AT THE UNIVERSITY OF CALIFORNIA IN COAST CITY. MINORED IN CHEMISTRY. WAS ALSO PART OF A SCUBA DIVING CLUB.
"BUT BECAUSE HIS FATHER, GARDNER KENYON, CO-FOUNDED THE MIDWESTERN LABOR SOCIETY--
"--HIS WHOLE FAMILY EXPECTED HIM TO BECOME A HERO FOR THE WORKING CLASS. FOLLOW IN THE OLD MAN'S FOOTSTEPS.
"HE DIDN'T. NOT AT FIRST.
"ON A DIVE OFF THE COAST OF MEXICO, KENYON DISCOVERED A CHEST FULL OF GOLD. BUT THE GOLD'S MOLECULAR STRUCTURE HAD BEEN RADICALLY CHANGED SOMEHOW.
"AUTHORITIES LATER SPECULATED IT MAY HAVE BEEN FROM A LEAKING CHEMICAL PLANT NEARBY.
"NO ONE KNEW FOR SURE.
"LOOKING FOR THE SOURCE OF THE GOLD'S STRANGE PROPERTIES, KENYON ACCIDENTALLY EXPOSED HIMSELF TO A LIQUID WASTE FROM THE ELEMENT--
"--HE DEVELOPED A KIND OF...ELIXIR THAT GAVE HIM SUPERHUMAN STRENGTH AND INVULNERABILITY FOR HOURS AT A TIME.
"HE WENT BACK FOR MORE OF THE GOLD, BUT WAS STOPPED BY GREEN LANTERN.
"TAKING THE NAME GOLDFACE, HE DEVELOPED A SUIT OF ARMOR, CRAFTED FROM THE ABNORMAL METAL.
"HE WENT UP AGAINST GREEN LANTERN A FEW MORE TIMES--
"--BEFORE TURNING HIS ATTENTION BACK TOWARDS ORGANIZATION AND PEOPLE MANAGE-MENT. GOLDFACE SET OUT TO TAKE OVER CENTRAL CITY'S CRIMINAL UNDERGROUND. EVEN ORGANIZED THE DEATH OF A COP.
"BARRY ALLEN EVENTUALLY STOPPED HIM.
"FROM THERE, GOLDFACE BOUNCED AROUND. BATTLED GUY GARDNER... WAS THOUGHT TO BE DEAD AT ONE POINT, FINALLY ENDED UP IN IRON HEIGHTS A FEW YEARS AGO.
"KENYON DID HIS TIME, DID IT WELL. GOT OUT EARLY FOR GOOD BEHAVIOR.
"AND I'M SURE THE FAVORS MANY OWED HIS FATHER WERE COLLECTED.
"WHAT HE DIDN'T TELL ANYONE, IS THAT YEARS OF EXPOSURE TO THAT ELIXIR...PERMANENTLY TRANSMUTED HIS BODY INTO A SOLID GOLD COMPOUND."
BUT THIS IS WHERE IT GETS FREAKY.
BLACKSMITH...

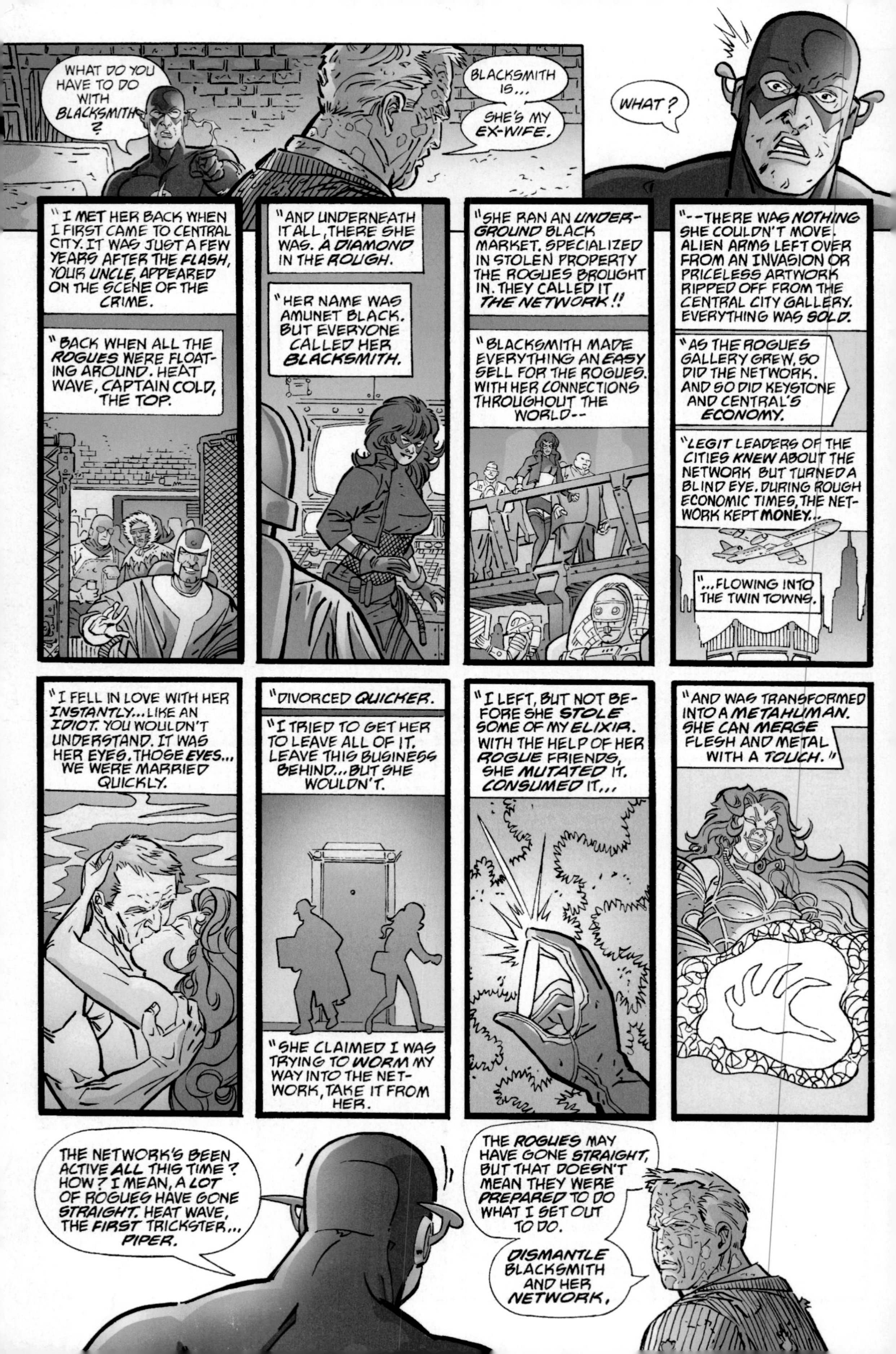

WHAT DO YOU HAVE TO DO WITH BLACKSMITH?
BLACKSMITH IS...
SHE'S MY EX-WIFE.
WHAT?
"I MET HER BACK WHEN I FIRST CAME TO CENTRAL CITY. IT WAS JUST A FEW YEARS AFTER THE FLASH, YOUR UNCLE, APPEARED ON THE SCENE OF THE CRIME.
"BACK WHEN ALL THE ROGUES WERE FLOATING AROUND. HEAT WAVE, CAPTAIN COLD, THE TOP.
"AND UNDERNEATH IT ALL, THERE SHE WAS. A DIAMOND IN THE ROUGH.
"HER NAME WAS AMUNET BLACK. BUT EVERYONE CALLED HER BLACKSMITH.
"SHE RAN AN UNDERGROUND BLACK MARKET. SPECIALIZED IN STOLEN PROPERTY THE ROGUES BROUGHT IN. THEY CALLED IT THE NETWORK!!
"BLACKSMITH MADE EVERYTHING AN EASY SELL FOR THE ROGUES. WITH HER CONNECTIONS THROUGHOUT THE WORLD--
"--THERE WAS NOTHING SHE COULDN'T MOVE. ALIEN ARMS LEFT OVER FROM AN INVASION OR PRICELESS ARTWORK RIPPED OFF FROM THE CENTRAL CITY GALLERY. EVERYTHING WAS SOLD.
"AS THE ROGUES GALLERY GREW, SO DID THE NETWORK. AND SO DID KEYSTONE AND CENTRAL'S ECONOMY.
"LEGIT LEADERS OF THE CITIES KNEW ABOUT THE NETWORK BUT TURNED A BLIND EYE. DURING ROUGH ECONOMIC TIMES, THE NETWORK KEPT MONEY...
"...FLOWING INTO THE TWIN TOWNS.
"I FELL IN LOVE WITH HER INSTANTLY... LIKE AN IDIOT. YOU WOULDN'T UNDERSTAND. IT WAS HER EYES. THOSE EYES... WE WERE MARRIED QUICKLY.
"DIVORCED QUICKER.
"I TRIED TO GET HER TO LEAVE ALL OF IT. LEAVE THIS BUSINESS BEHIND... BUT SHE WOULDN'T.
"SHE CLAIMED I WAS TRYING TO WORM MY WAY INTO THE NETWORK, TAKE IT FROM HER.
"I LEFT, BUT NOT BEFORE SHE STOLE SOME OF MY ELIXIR. WITH THE HELP OF HER ROGUE FRIENDS, SHE MUTATED IT. CONSUMED IT...
"AND WAS TRANSFORMED INTO A METAHUMAN. SHE CAN MERGE FLESH AND METAL WITH A TOUCH."
THE NETWORK'S BEEN ACTIVE ALL THIS TIME? HOW? I MEAN, A LOT OF ROGUES HAVE GONE STRAIGHT. HEAT WAVE, THE FIRST TRICKSTER... PIPER.
THE ROGUES MAY HAVE GONE STRAIGHT, BUT THAT DOESN'T MEAN THEY WERE PREPARED TO DO WHAT I SET OUT TO DO.
DISMANTLE BLACKSMITH AND HER NETWORK.

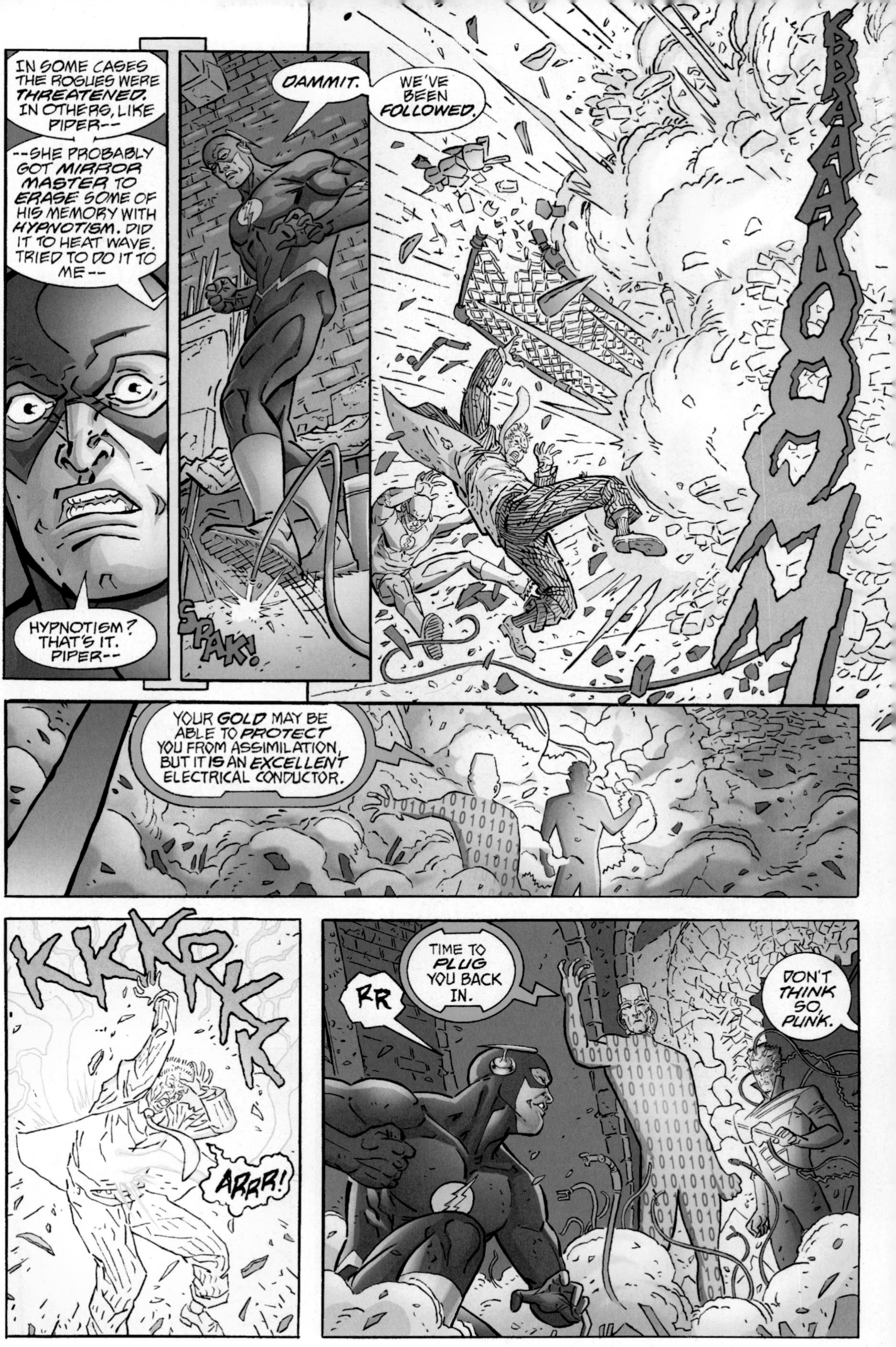
IN SOME CASES THE ROGUES WERE THREATENED. IN OTHERS, LIKE PIPER--
--SHE PROBABLY GOT MIRROR MASTER TO ERASE SOME OF HIS MEMORY WITH HYPNOTISM. DID IT TO HEAT WAVE. TRIED TO DO IT TO ME--
HYPNOTISM? THAT'S IT. PIPER--
DAMMIT.
WE'VE BEEN FOLLOWED.
SPAK!
KRAAAAABOOM
YOUR GOLD MAY BE ABLE TO PROTECT YOU FROM ASSIMILATION, BUT IT IS AN EXCELLENT ELECTRICAL CONDUCTOR.
KKKRKKK
ARRR!
TIME TO PLUG YOU BACK IN.
RR
DON'T THINK SO, PUNK.

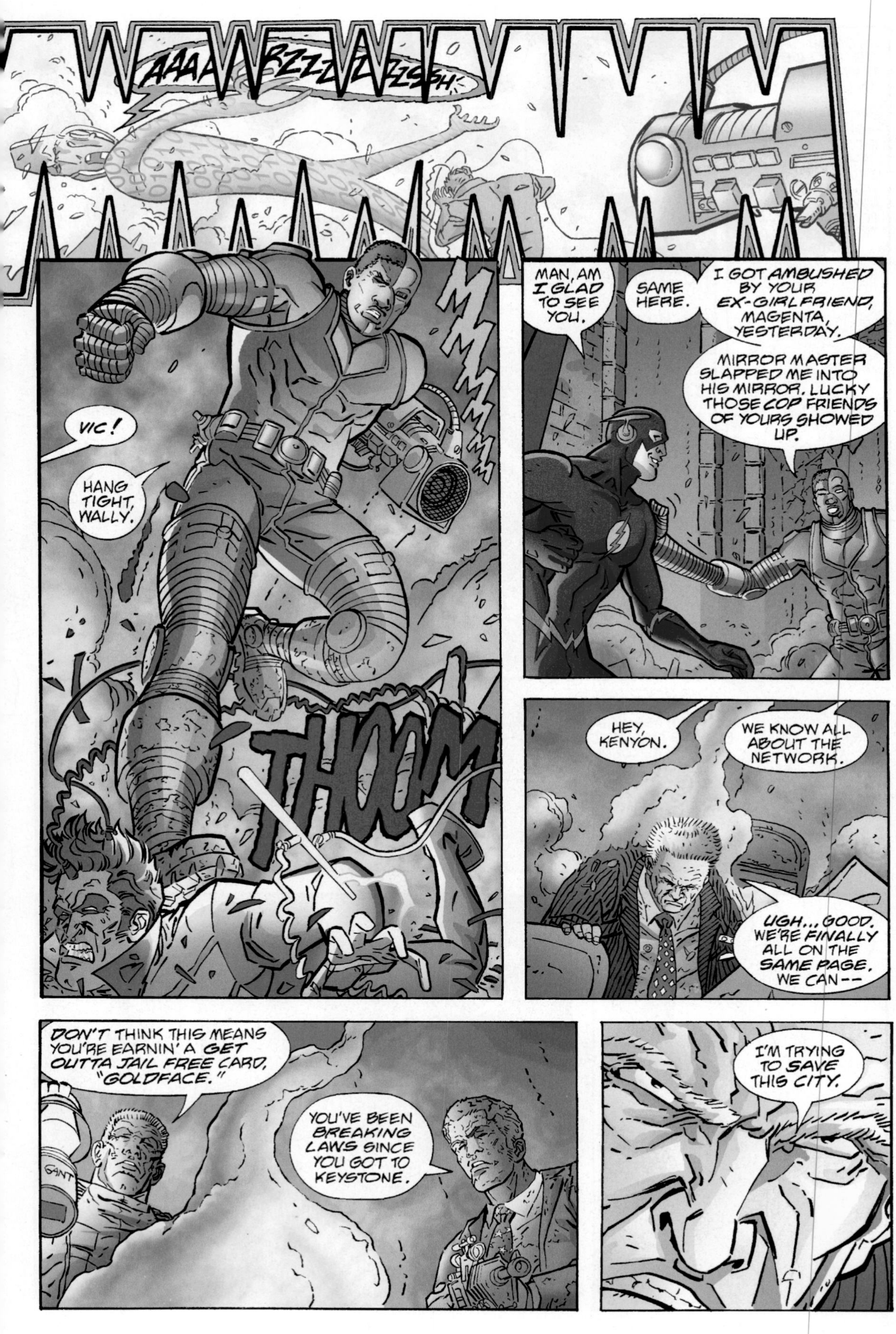
WWAAAAAAAAAAAAVVVVVVMMM
AAAARZZZZZZZZZSH
MMMMMMMM
VIC!
HANG TIGHT, WALLY.
THOOM
MAN, AM I GLAD TO SEE YOU.
SAME HERE.
I GOT AMBUSHED BY YOUR EX-GIRLFRIEND, MAGENTA, YESTERDAY.
MIRROR MASTER SLAPPED ME INTO HIS MIRROR. LUCKY THOSE COP FRIENDS OF YOURS SHOWED UP.
HEY, KENYON.
WE KNOW ALL ABOUT THE NETWORK.
UGH... GOOD. WE'RE FINALLY ALL ON THE SAME PAGE. WE CAN--
DON'T THINK THIS MEANS YOU'RE EARNIN' A GET OUTTA JAIL FREE CARD, "GOLDFACE."
YOU'VE BEEN BREAKING LAWS SINCE YOU GOT TO KEYSTONE.
I'M TRYING TO SAVE THIS CITY.

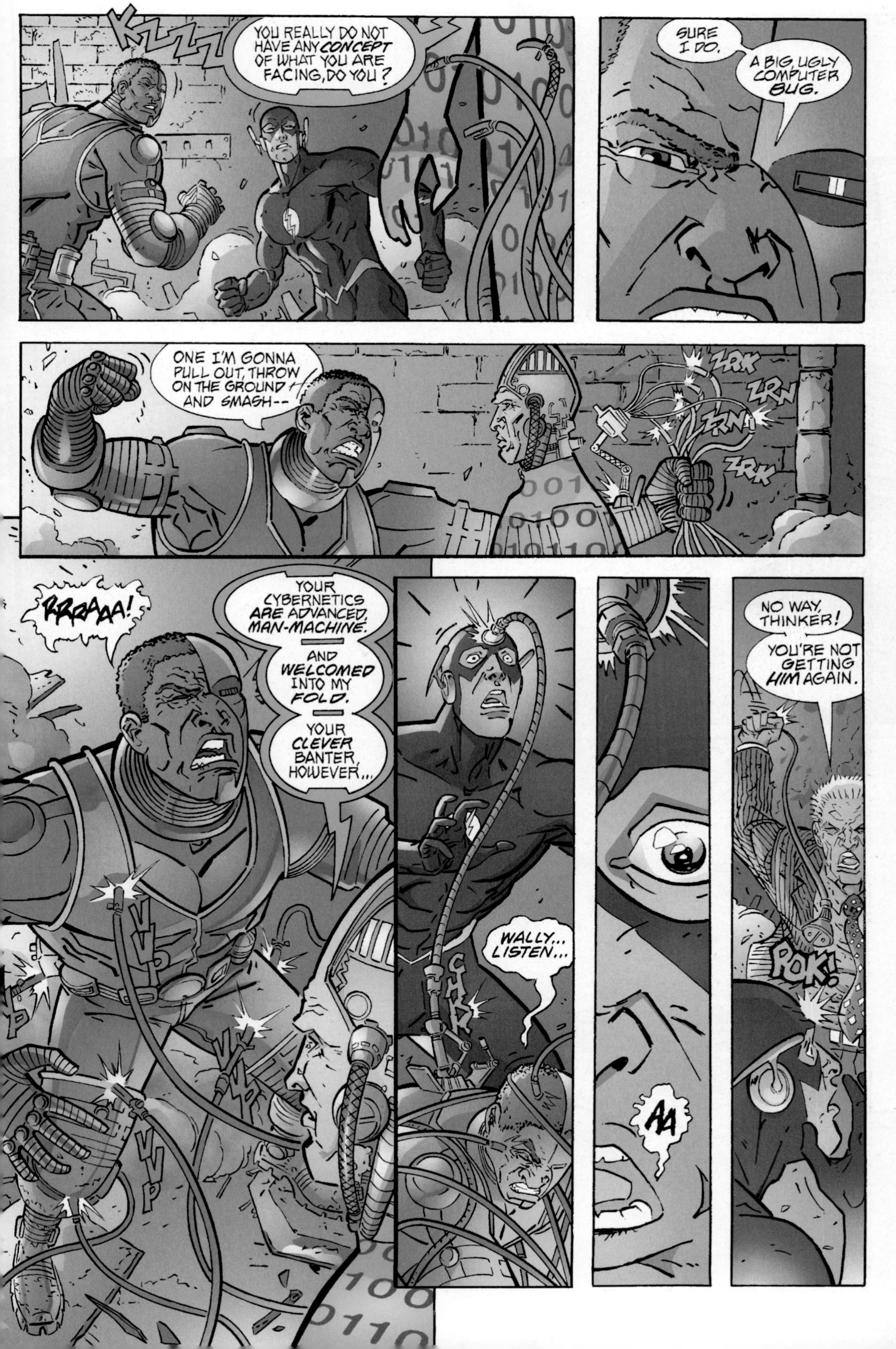
KZZZZ
YOU REALLY DO NOT HAVE ANY CONCEPT OF WHAT YOU ARE FACING, DO YOU?
SURE I DO.
A BIG, UGLY COMPUTER BUG.
ONE I'M GONNA PULL OUT, THROW ON THE GROUND AND SMASH--
ZRK
ZRN
ZRN
ZRK
RRRAAA!
YOUR CYBERNETICS ARE ADVANCED, MAN-MACHINE.
AND WELCOMED INTO MY FOLD.
YOUR CLEVER BANTER, HOWEVER...
WALLY... LISTEN...
CHK
AA
NO WAY, THINKER!
YOU'RE NOT GETTING HIM AGAIN.
POK!

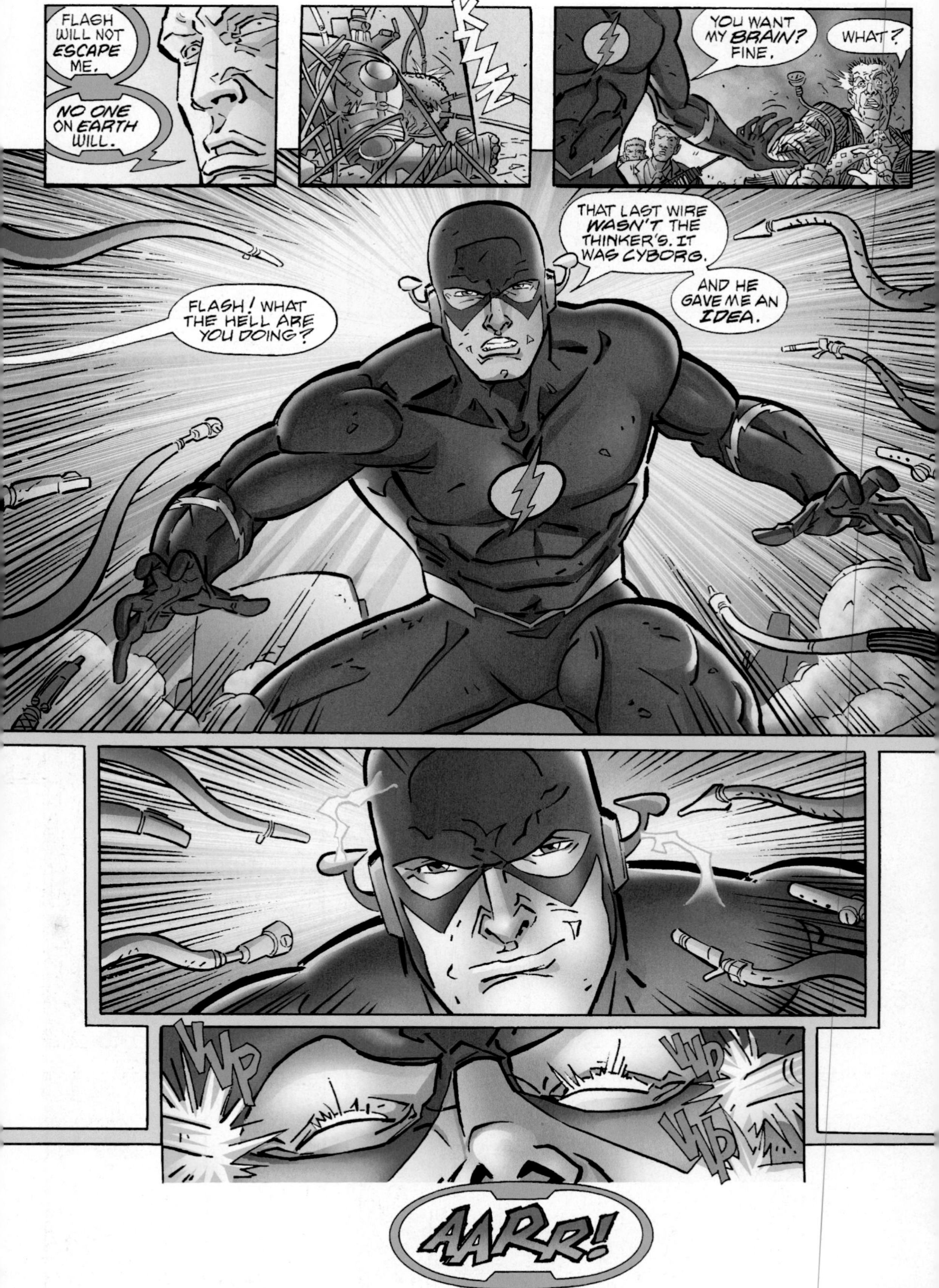
FLASH WILL NOT ESCAPE ME.
NO ONE ON EARTH WILL.
KZZZ
YOU WANT MY BRAIN? FINE.
WHAT?
THAT LAST WIRE WASN'T THE THINKER'S. IT WAS CYBORG.
AND HE GAVE ME AN IDEA.
FLASH! WHAT THE HELL ARE YOU DOING?
VWP
VWP
VWP
AARR!

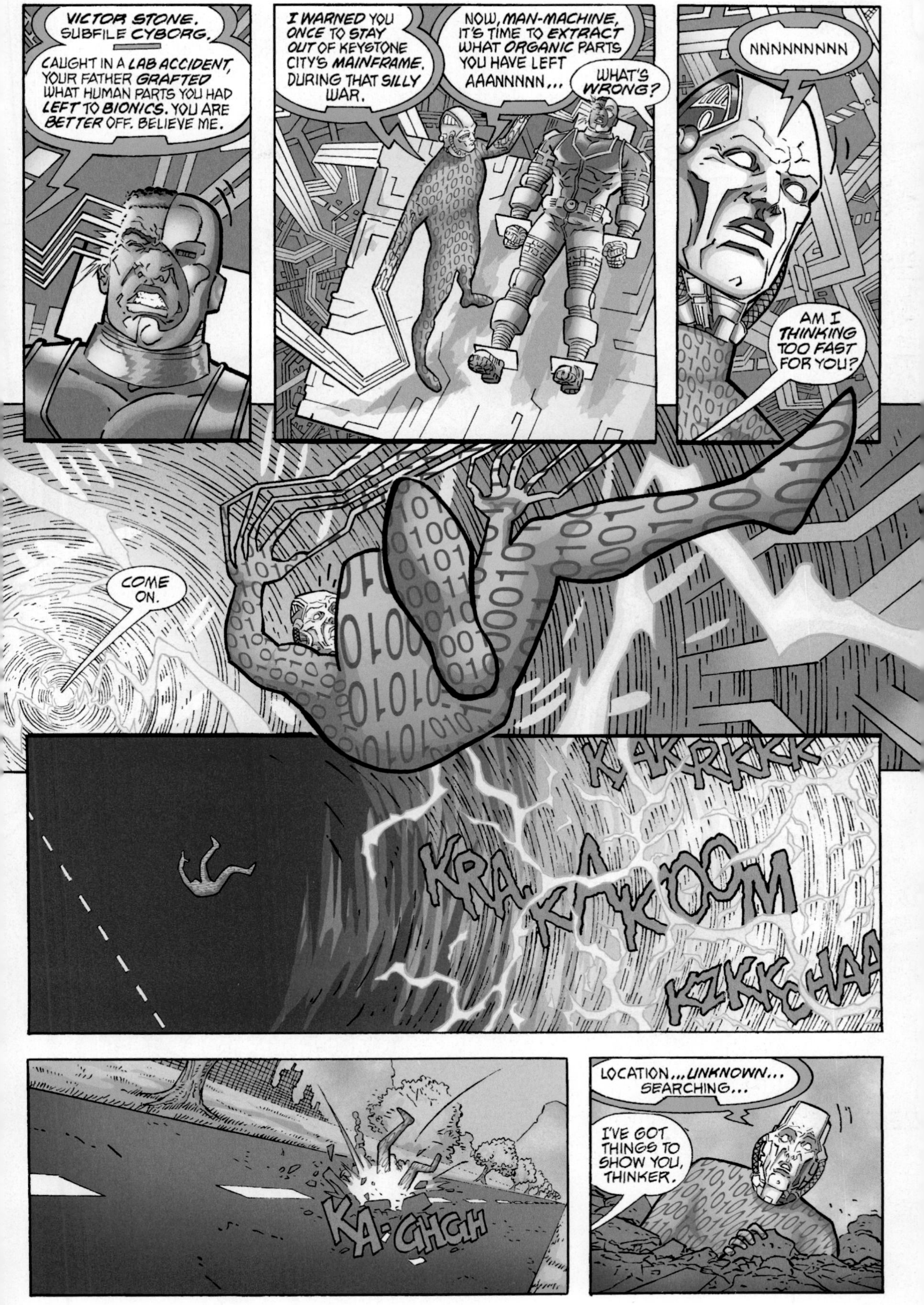
VICTOR STONE. SUBFILE CYBORG.
CAUGHT IN A LAB ACCIDENT, YOUR FATHER GRAFTED WHAT HUMAN PARTS YOU HAD LEFT TO BIONICS. YOU ARE BETTER OFF. BELIEVE ME.
I WARNED YOU ONCE TO STAY OUT OF KEYSTONE CITY'S MAINFRAME. DURING THAT SILLY WAR.
NOW, MAN-MACHINE, IT'S TIME TO EXTRACT WHAT ORGANIC PARTS YOU HAVE LEFT AAANNNNN...
WHAT'S WRONG?
NNNNNNNNN
AM I THINKING TOO FAST FOR YOU?
COME ON.
KAKRKKK
KRAKAKOOM
KZKKCHAA
KA-CHGH
LOCATION... UNKNOWN... SEARCHING...
I'VE GOT THINGS TO SHOW YOU, THINKER.

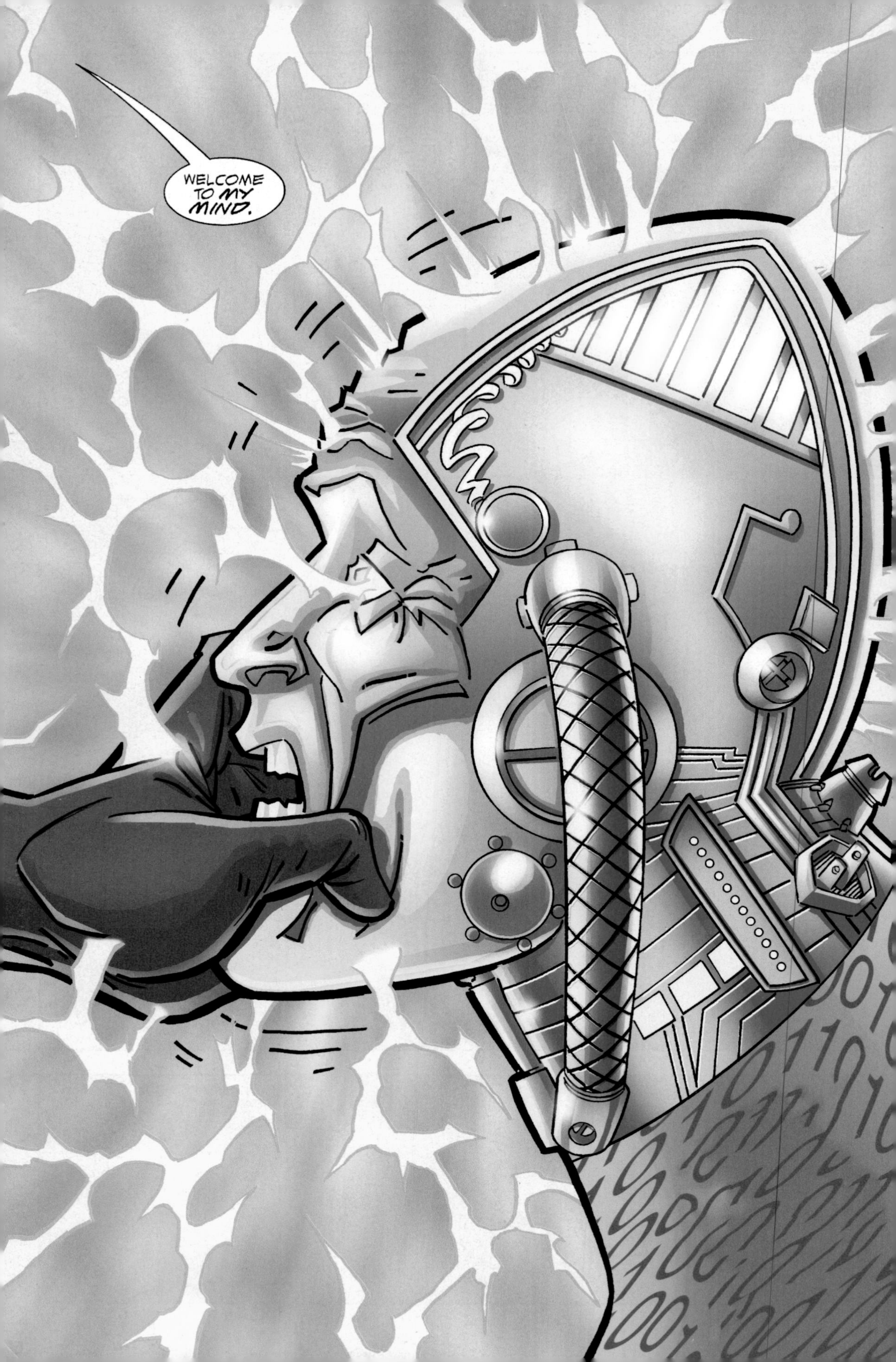
WELCOME TO MY MIND.

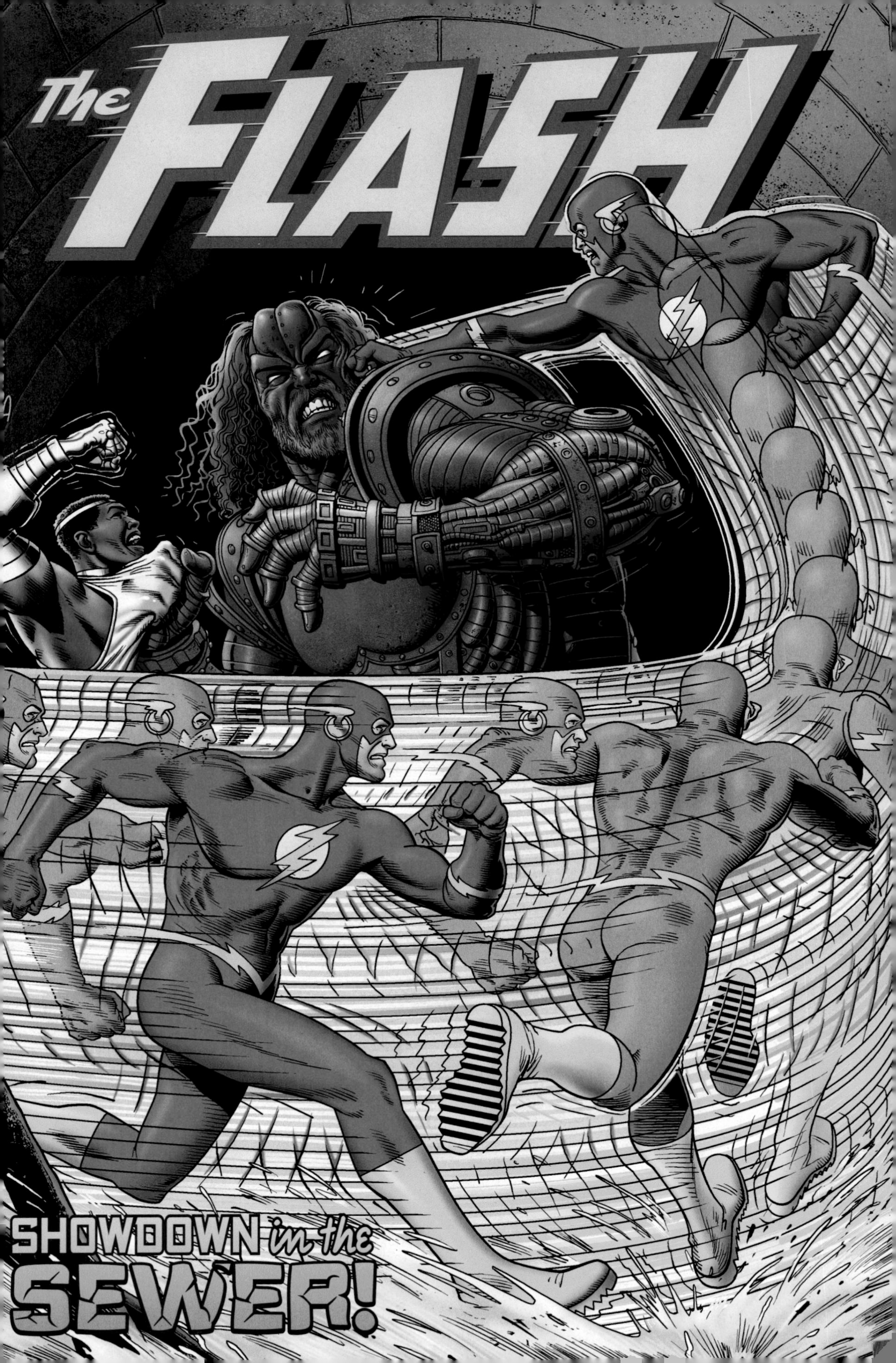
The FLASH
SHOWDOWN in the SEWER!

COVER ART BY **BRIAN BOLLAND**

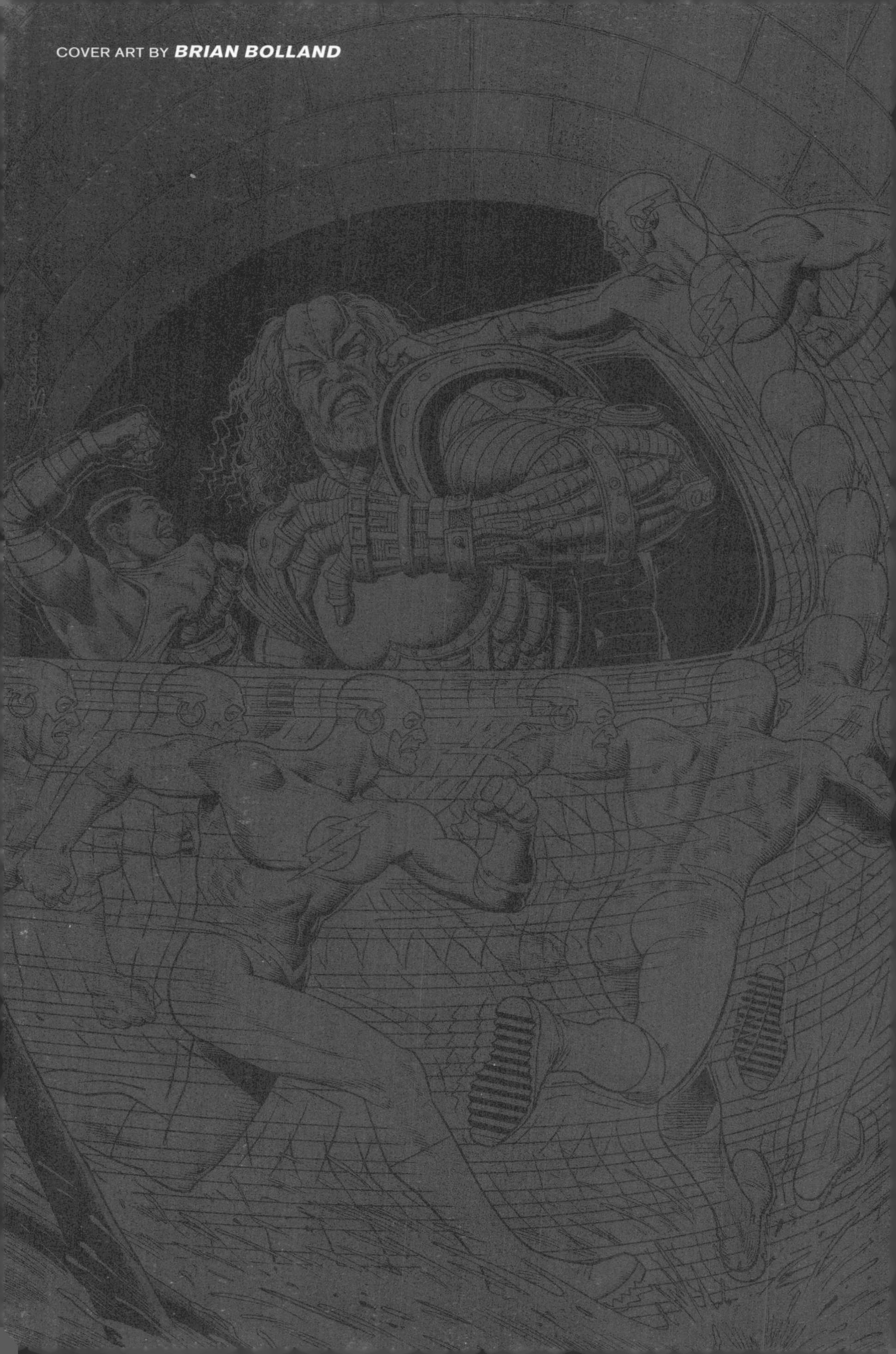

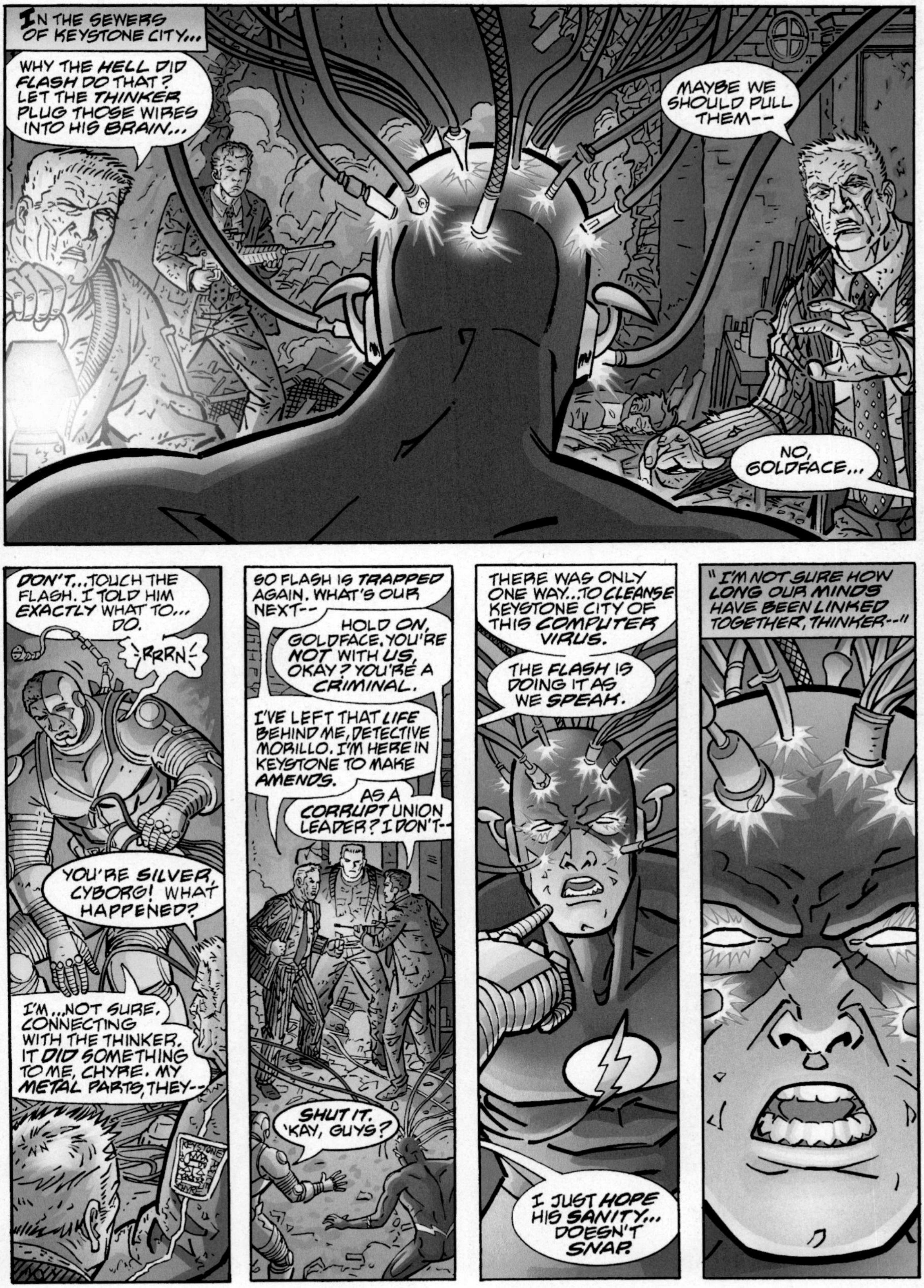
IN THE SEWERS OF KEYSTONE CITY...
WHY THE HELL DID FLASH DO THAT? LET THE THINKER PLUG THOSE WIRES INTO HIS BRAIN...
MAYBE WE SHOULD PULL THEM--
NO, GOLDFACE...
DON'T...TOUCH THE FLASH. I TOLD HIM EXACTLY WHAT TO... DO.
RRRN!
YOU'RE SILVER, CYBORG! WHAT HAPPENED?
I'M...NOT SURE. CONNECTING WITH THE THINKER. IT DID SOMETHING TO ME, CHYRE. MY METAL PARTS, THEY--
SO FLASH IS TRAPPED AGAIN. WHAT'S OUR NEXT--
HOLD ON, GOLDFACE. YOU'RE NOT WITH US, OKAY? YOU'RE A CRIMINAL.
I'VE LEFT THAT LIFE BEHIND ME, DETECTIVE MORILLO. I'M HERE IN KEYSTONE TO MAKE AMENDS.
AS A CORRUPT UNION LEADER? I DON'T--
SHUT IT. 'KAY, GUYS?
THERE WAS ONLY ONE WAY...TO CLEANSE KEYSTONE CITY OF THIS COMPUTER VIRUS.
THE FLASH IS DOING IT AS WE SPEAK.
I JUST HOPE HIS SANITY... DOESN'T SNAP.
"I'M NOT SURE HOW LONG OUR MINDS HAVE BEEN LINKED TOGETHER, THINKER--"

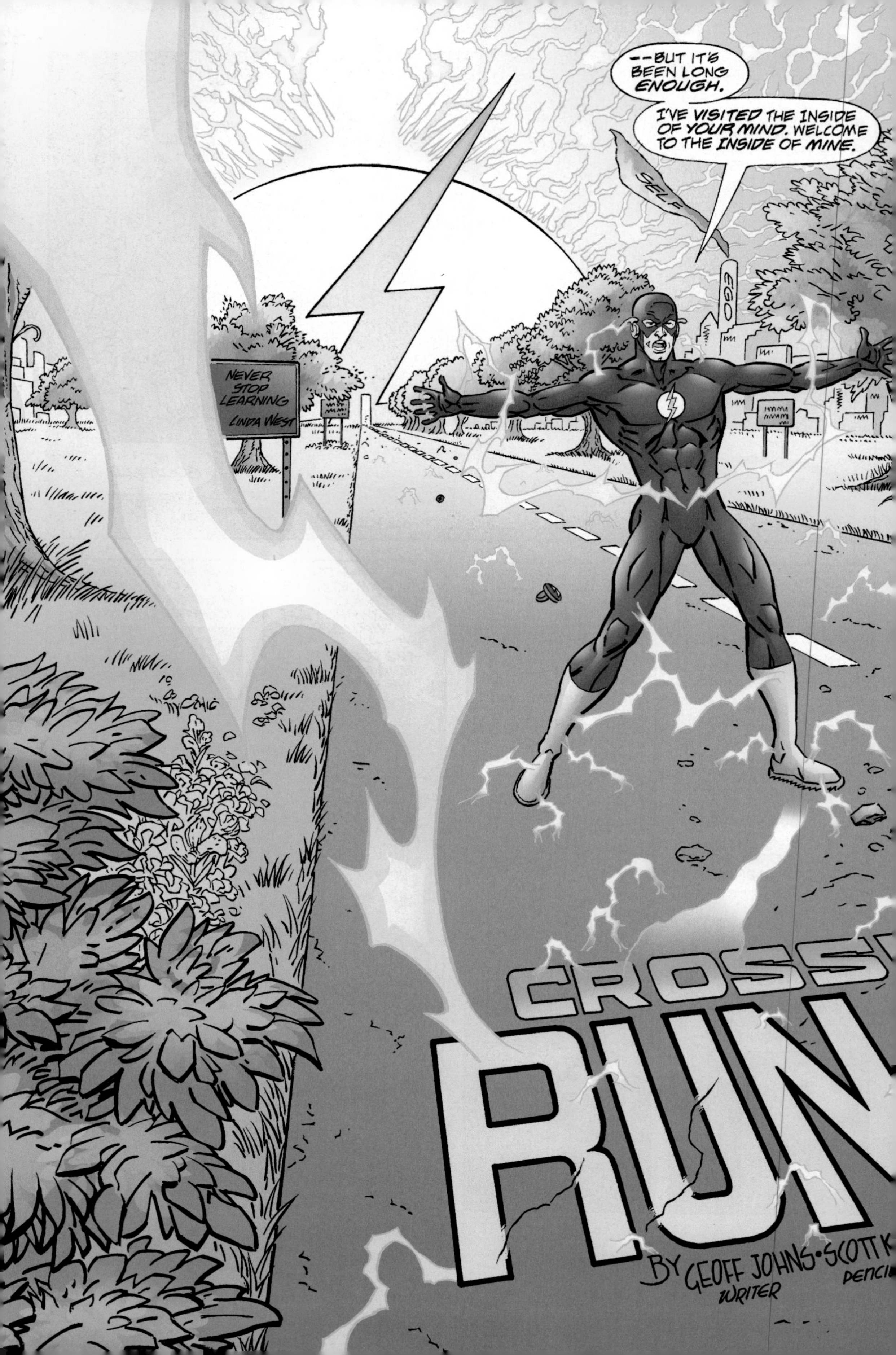
--BUT IT'S BEEN LONG ENOUGH.
I'VE VISITED THE INSIDE OF YOUR MIND. WELCOME TO THE INSIDE OF MINE.
SELF
EGO
NEVER STOP LEARNING Linda West
CROSS
RUN
BY GEOFF JOHNS WRITER • SCOTT K

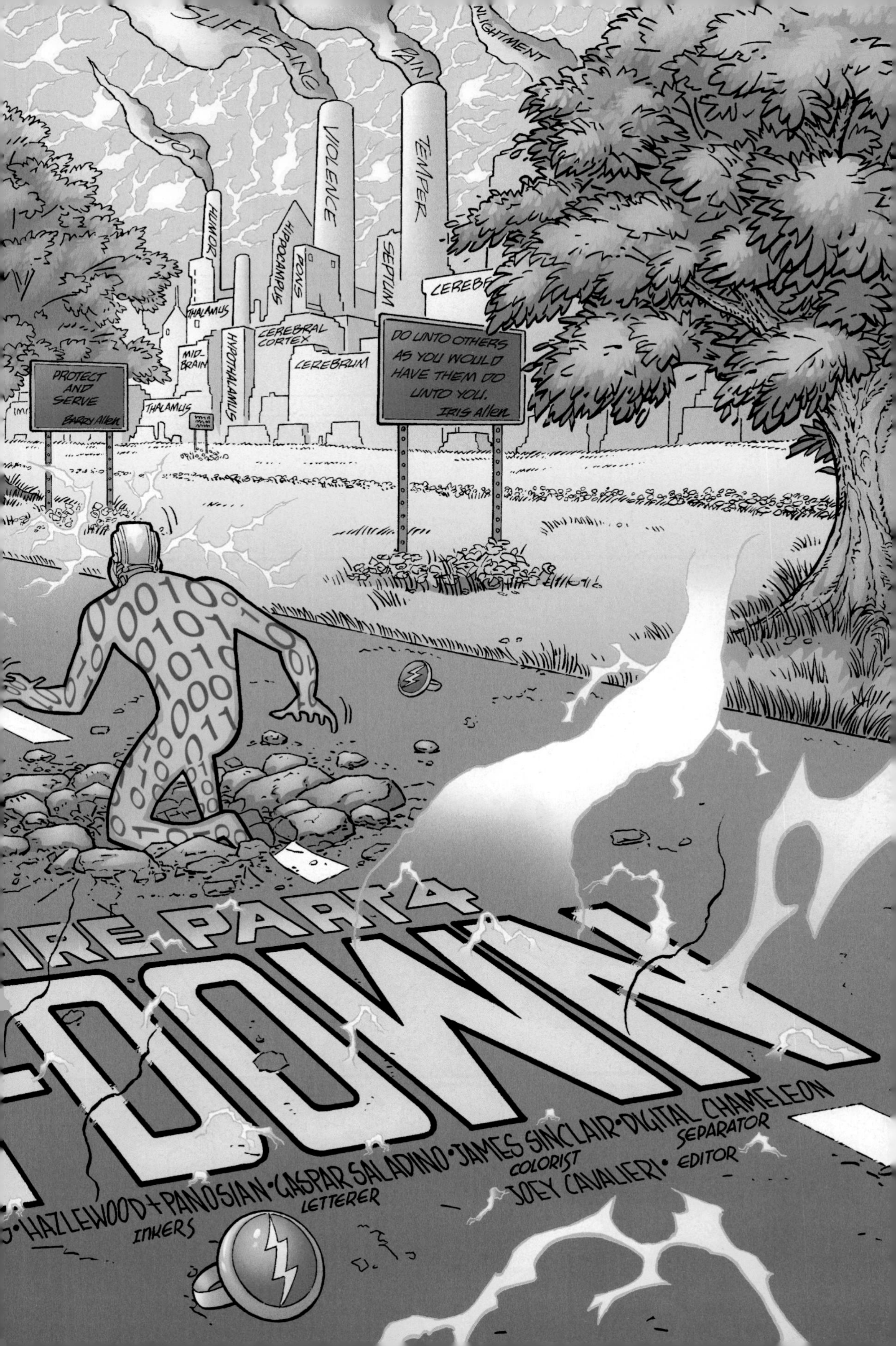

SUFFERING
PAIN
NLIGHTMENT
JOY
HUMOR
VIOLENCE
TEMPER
HIPPOCAMPUS
PONS
SEPTUM
CEREBR
THALAMUS
CEREBRAL CORTEX
MID-BRAIN
HYPOTHALAMUS
CEREBRUM
THALAMUS
PROTECT AND SERVE
Barry Allen
DO UNTO OTHERS AS YOU WOULD HAVE THEM DO UNTO YOU.
Iris Allen
IRE PART 4
DOWN
J • HAZLEWOOD + PANOSIAN • GASPAR SALADINO • JAMES SINCLAIR • DIGITAL CHAMELEON
INKERS
LETTERER
COLORIST
SEPARATOR
JOEY CAVALIERI • EDITOR

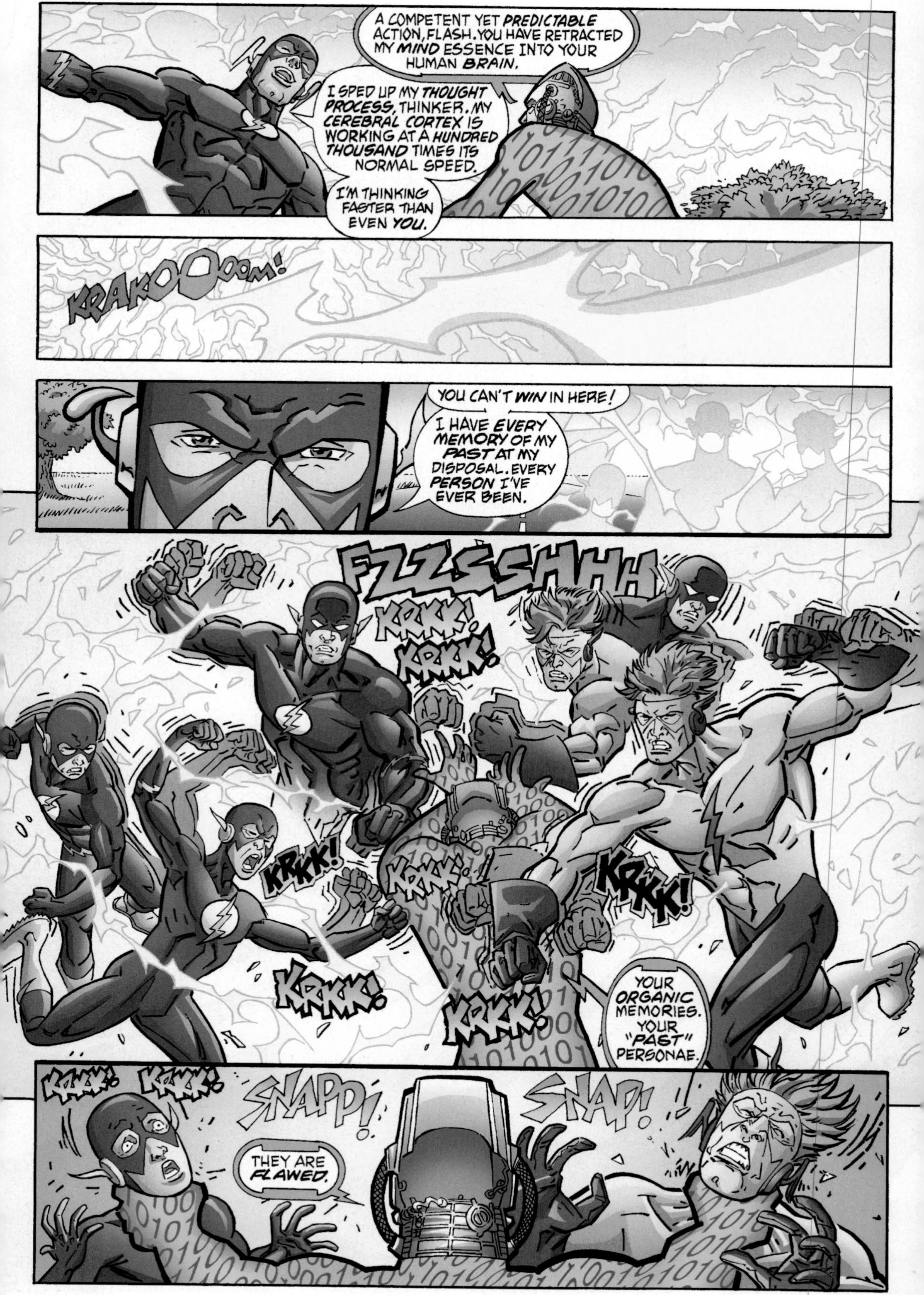
A COMPETENT YET PREDICTABLE ACTION, FLASH. YOU HAVE RETRACTED MY MIND ESSENCE INTO YOUR HUMAN BRAIN.
I SPED UP MY THOUGHT PROCESS, THINKER. MY CEREBRAL CORTEX IS WORKING AT A HUNDRED THOUSAND TIMES ITS NORMAL SPEED.
I'M THINKING FASTER THAN EVEN YOU.
KRAKOOOoom!
YOU CAN'T WIN IN HERE!
I HAVE EVERY MEMORY OF MY PAST AT MY DISPOSAL. EVERY PERSON I'VE EVER BEEN.
FZZSSHHH
KRKK! KRKK!
KRKK!
KRKK!
KRKK!
KRKK!
KRKK!
YOUR ORGANIC MEMORIES. YOUR "PAST" PERSONAE.
KRKK! KRKK!
SNAPP!
SNAP!
THEY ARE FLAWED.

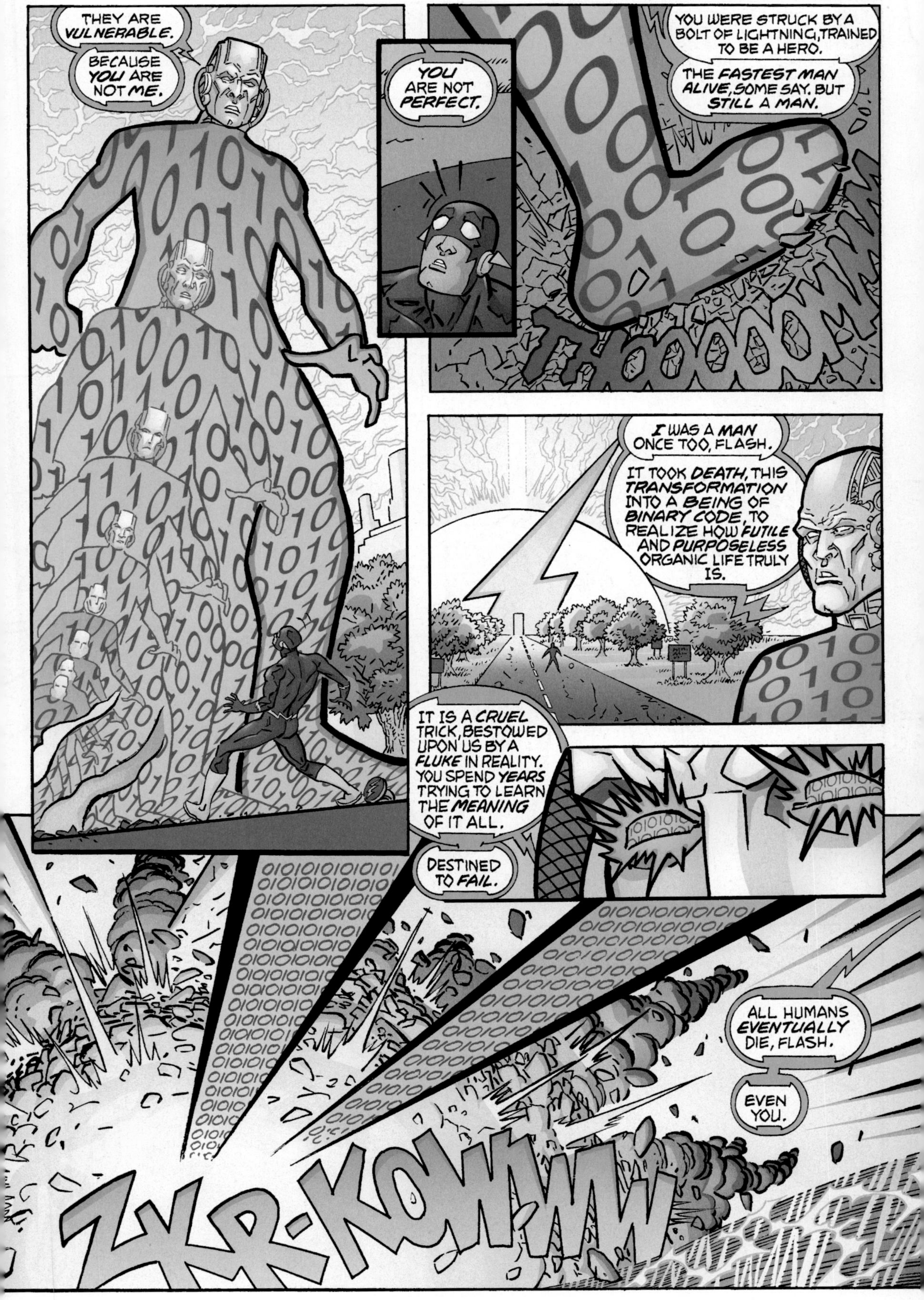
THEY ARE VULNERABLE.
BECAUSE YOU ARE NOT ME.
YOU ARE NOT PERFECT.
YOU WERE STRUCK BY A BOLT OF LIGHTNING, TRAINED TO BE A HERO.
THE FASTEST MAN ALIVE, SOME SAY. BUT STILL A MAN.
THOOOOOM
I WAS A MAN ONCE TOO, FLASH.
IT TOOK DEATH, THIS TRANSFORMATION INTO A BEING OF BINARY CODE, TO REALIZE HOW FUTILE AND PURPOSELESS ORGANIC LIFE TRULY IS.
IT IS A CRUEL TRICK, BESTOWED UPON US BY A FLUKE IN REALITY. YOU SPEND YEARS TRYING TO LEARN THE MEANING OF IT ALL.
DESTINED TO FAIL.
ALL HUMANS EVENTUALLY DIE, FLASH.
EVEN YOU.
ZKR-KOWWW

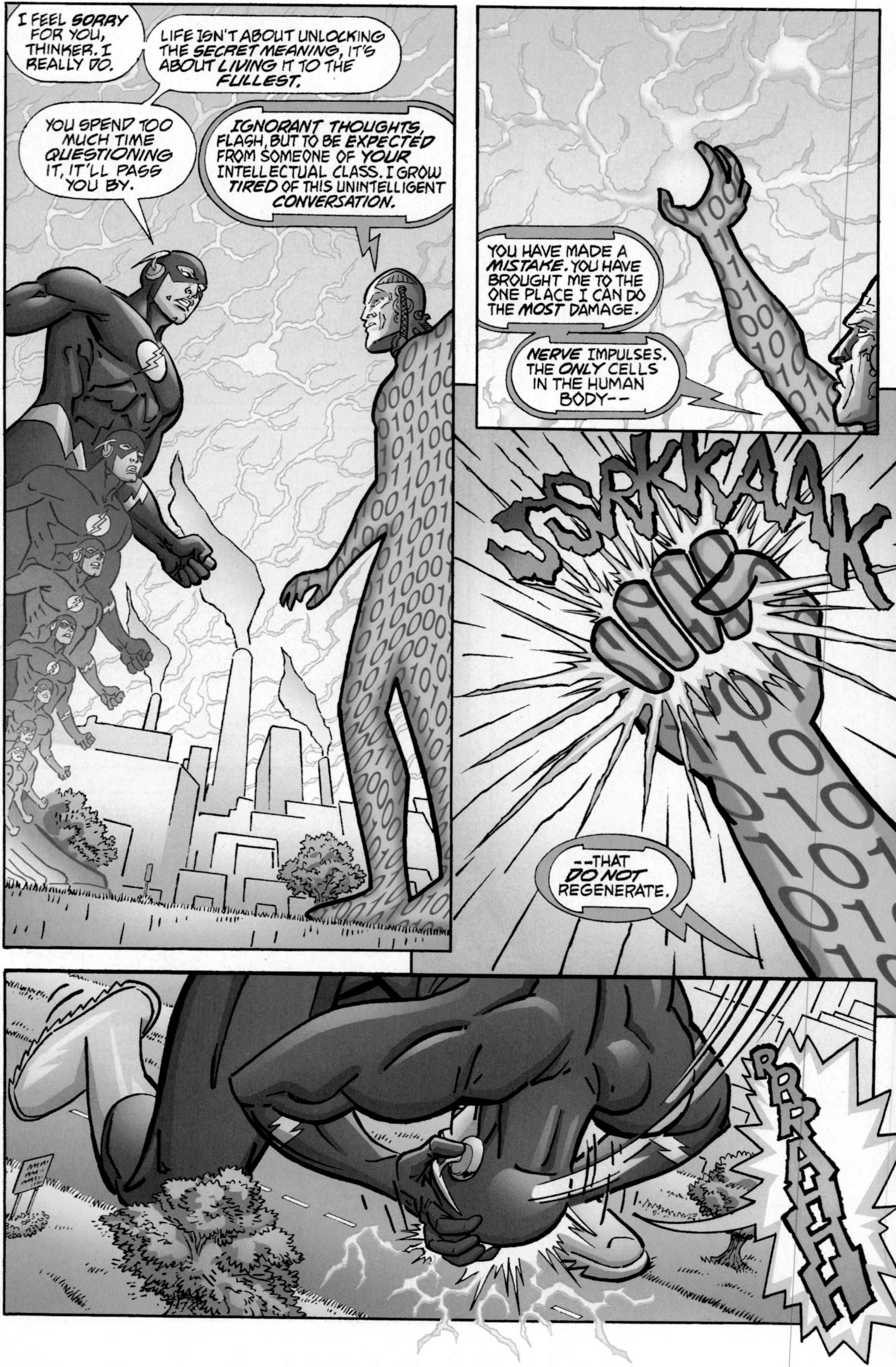

I FEEL SORRY FOR YOU, THINKER. I REALLY DO.
LIFE ISN'T ABOUT UNLOCKING THE SECRET MEANING, IT'S ABOUT LIVING IT TO THE FULLEST.
YOU SPEND TOO MUCH TIME QUESTIONING IT, IT'LL PASS YOU BY.
IGNORANT THOUGHTS, FLASH, BUT TO BE EXPECTED FROM SOMEONE OF YOUR INTELLECTUAL CLASS. I GROW TIRED OF THIS UNINTELLIGENT CONVERSATION.
YOU HAVE MADE A MISTAKE. YOU HAVE BROUGHT ME TO THE ONE PLACE I CAN DO THE MOST DAMAGE.
NERVE IMPULSES. THE ONLY CELLS IN THE HUMAN BODY--
SSRKKAAAK
--THAT DO NOT REGENERATE.
RRRAASSHH

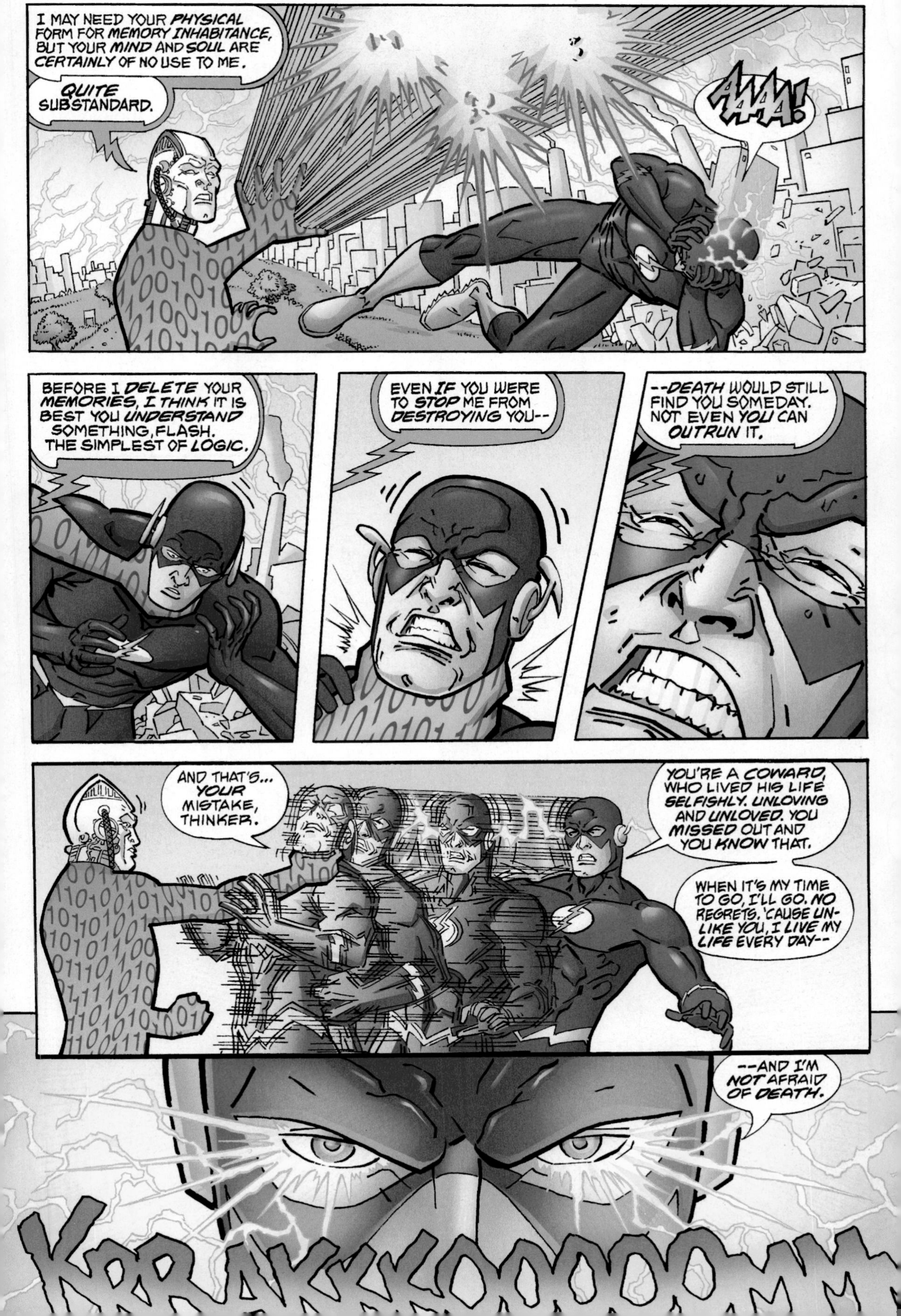
I MAY NEED YOUR PHYSICAL FORM FOR MEMORY INHABITANCE, BUT YOUR MIND AND SOUL ARE CERTAINLY OF NO USE TO ME.
QUITE SUBSTANDARD.
AAAA!
BEFORE I DELETE YOUR MEMORIES, I THINK IT IS BEST YOU UNDERSTAND SOMETHING, FLASH. THE SIMPLEST OF LOGIC.
EVEN IF YOU WERE TO STOP ME FROM DESTROYING YOU--
--DEATH WOULD STILL FIND YOU SOMEDAY. NOT EVEN YOU CAN OUTRUN IT.
AND THAT'S... YOUR MISTAKE, THINKER.
YOU'RE A COWARD, WHO LIVED HIS LIFE SELFISHLY. UNLOVING AND UNLOVED. YOU MISSED OUT AND YOU KNOW THAT.
WHEN IT'S MY TIME TO GO, I'LL GO. NO REGRETS. 'CAUSE UN-LIKE YOU, I LIVE MY LIFE EVERY DAY--
--AND I'M NOT AFRAID OF DEATH.
KRRAKKOOOOOMM

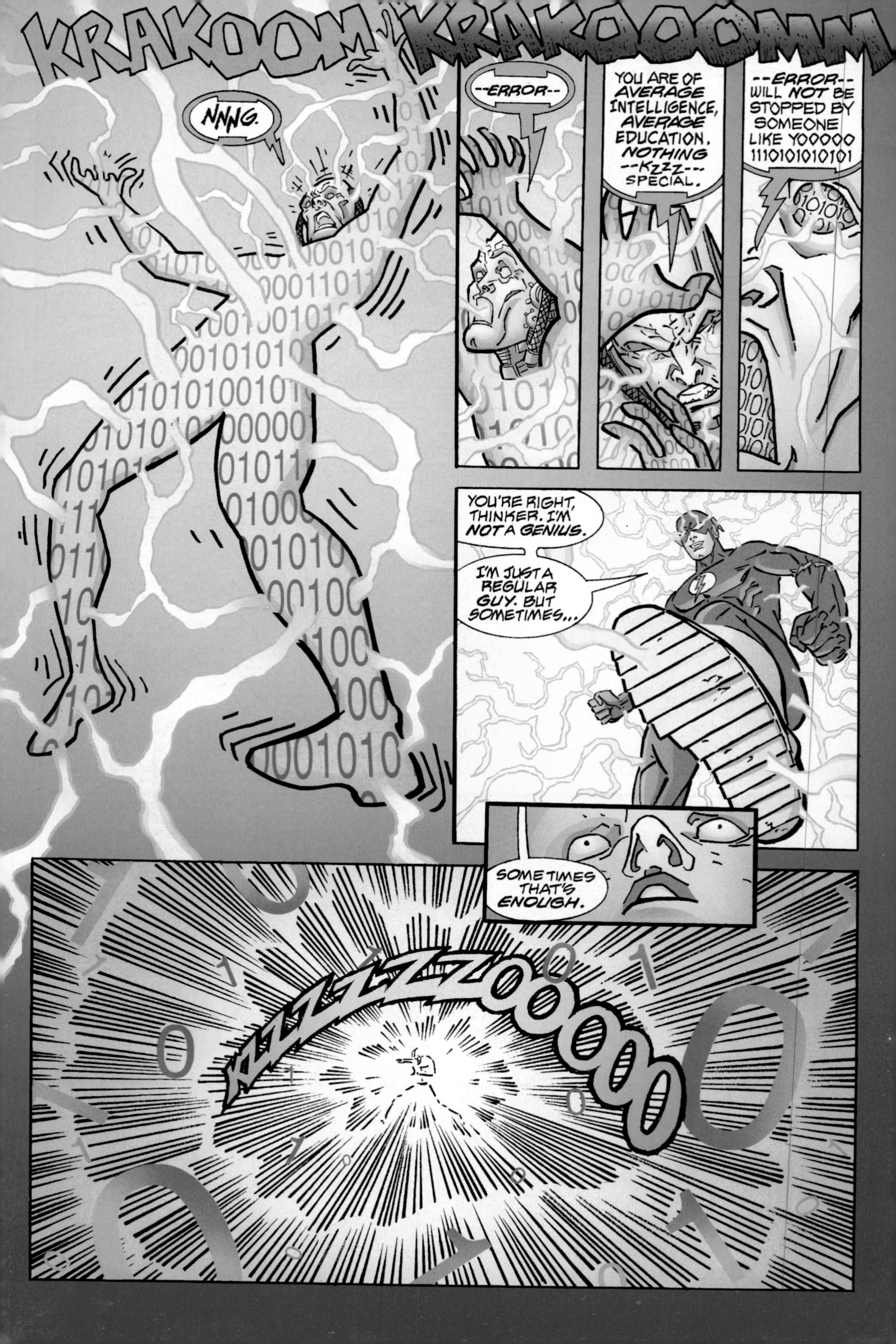
KRAKOOM
KRAKOOOMM
NNNG.
--ERROR--
YOU ARE OF AVERAGE INTELLIGENCE, AVERAGE EDUCATION. NOTHING --KZZZ--- SPECIAL.
--ERROR-- WILL NOT BE STOPPED BY SOMEONE LIKE YOOOOO 1110101010101
YOU'RE RIGHT, THINKER. I'M NOT A GENIUS.
I'M JUST A REGULAR GUY. BUT SOMETIMES...
SOMETIMES THAT'S ENOUGH.
KZZZZZOOOOOO

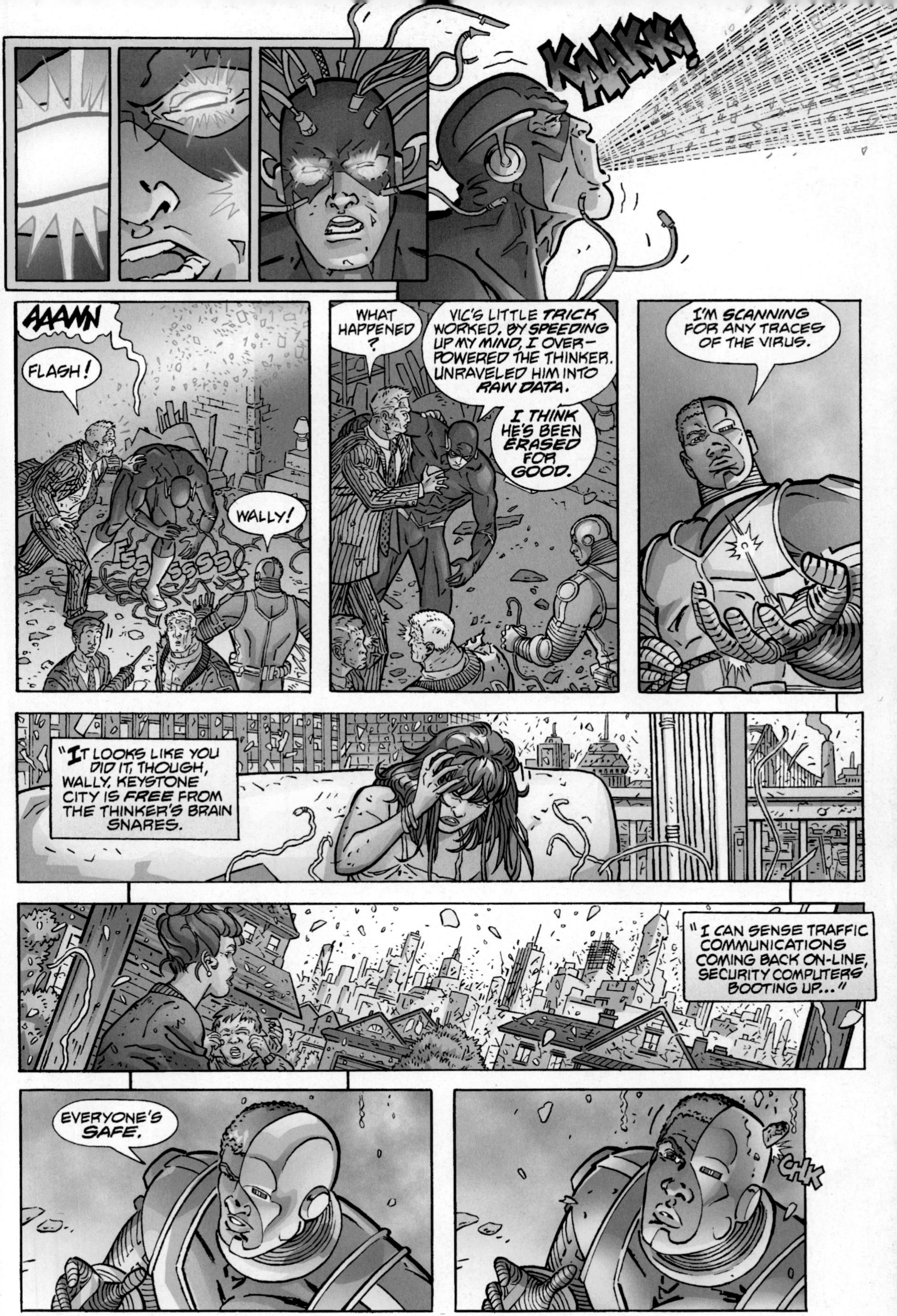
KAAKK!
AAAWN
FLASH!
WALLY!
FSSSSSSS
WHAT HAPPENED?
VIC'S LITTLE TRICK WORKED. BY SPEEDING UP MY MIND, I OVER-POWERED THE THINKER. UNRAVELED HIM INTO RAW DATA.
I THINK HE'S BEEN ERASED FOR GOOD.
I'M SCANNING FOR ANY TRACES OF THE VIRUS.
"IT LOOKS LIKE YOU DID IT, THOUGH, WALLY. KEYSTONE CITY IS FREE FROM THE THINKER'S BRAIN SNARES.
"I CAN SENSE TRAFFIC COMMUNICATIONS COMING BACK ON-LINE, SECURITY COMPUTERS BOOTING UP..."
EVERYONE'S SAFE.
CHK

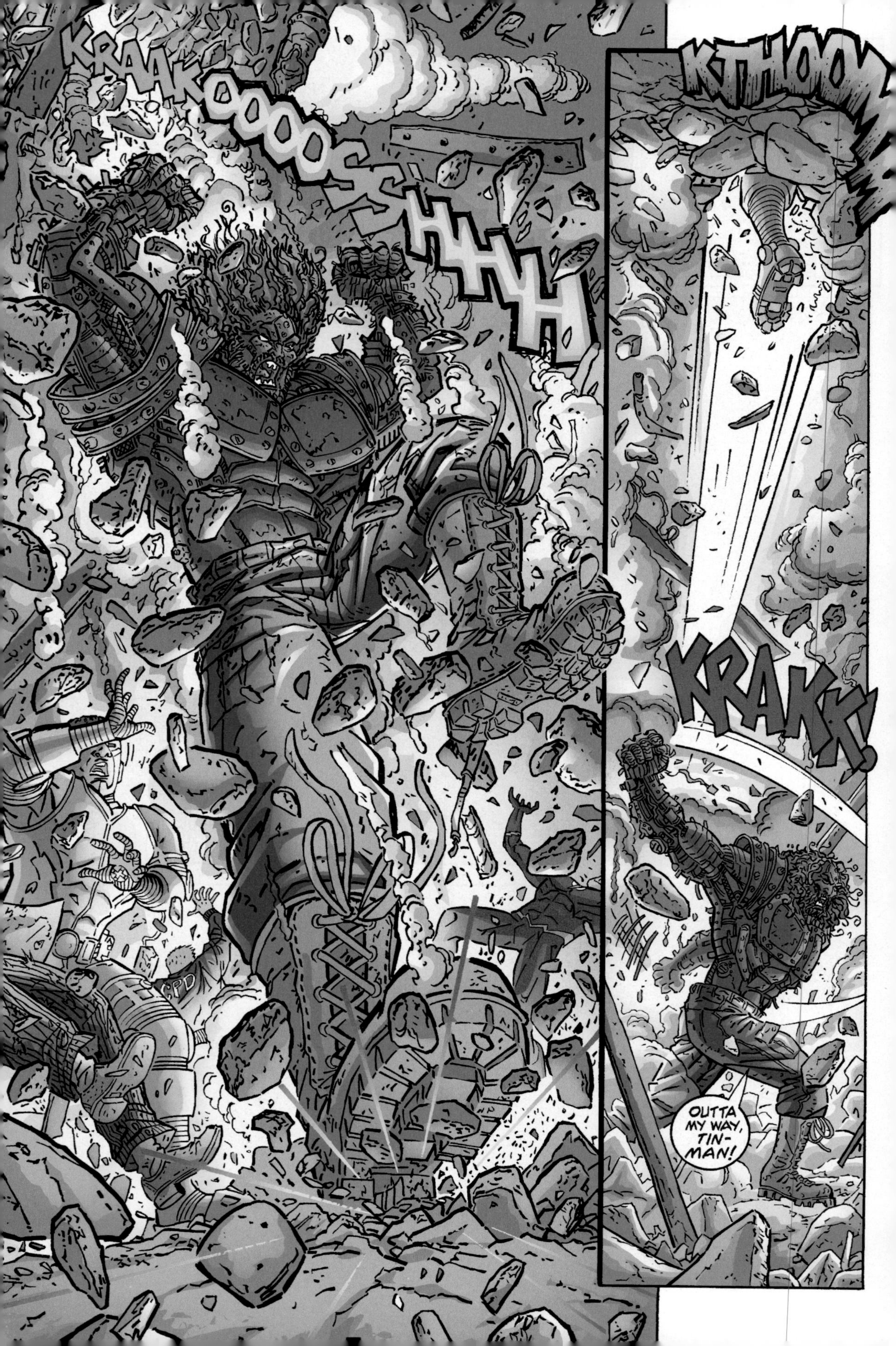
KRAAKOOOOSHHHH
KTHOOM
KRAKK!
OUTTA MY WAY, TIN-MAN!
CPD

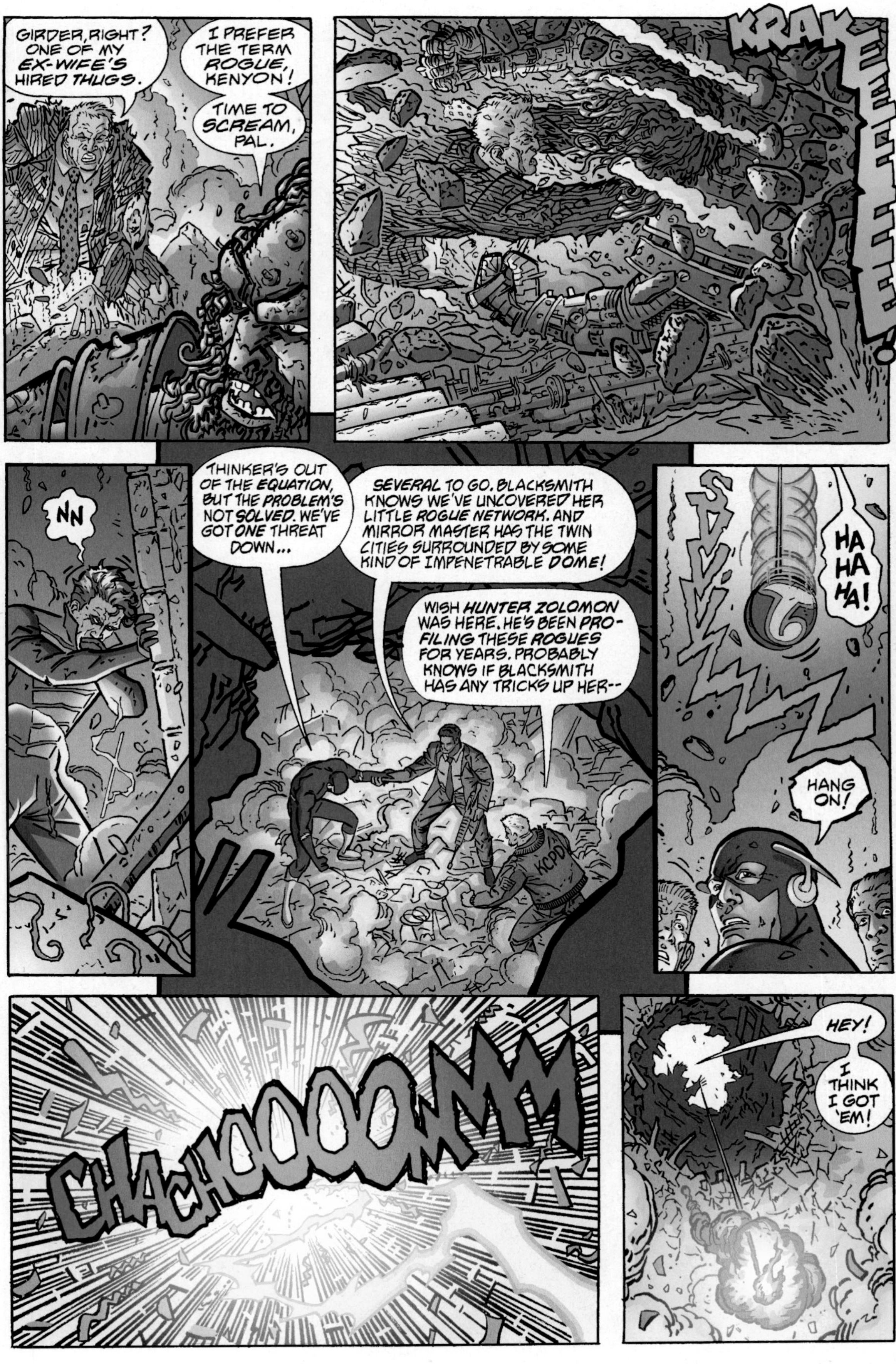
GIRDER, RIGHT? ONE OF MY EX-WIFE'S HIRED THUGS.
I PREFER THE TERM ROGUE, KENYON!
TIME TO SCREAM, PAL.
KRAKEEEEEEE!
NN
THINKER'S OUT OF THE EQUATION, BUT THE PROBLEM'S NOT SOLVED. WE'VE GOT ONE THREAT DOWN...
SEVERAL TO GO. BLACKSMITH KNOWS WE'VE UNCOVERED HER LITTLE ROGUE NETWORK. AND MIRROR MASTER HAS THE TWIN CITIES SURROUNDED BY SOME KIND OF IMPENETRABLE DOME!
WISH HUNTER ZOLOMON WAS HERE. HE'S BEEN PROFILING THESE ROGUES FOR YEARS. PROBABLY KNOWS IF BLACKSMITH HAS ANY TRICKS UP HER--
KCPD
SAVVZZZZ
HA HA HA!
HANG ON!
CHACHOOOOMMM
HEY!
I THINK I GOT 'EM!

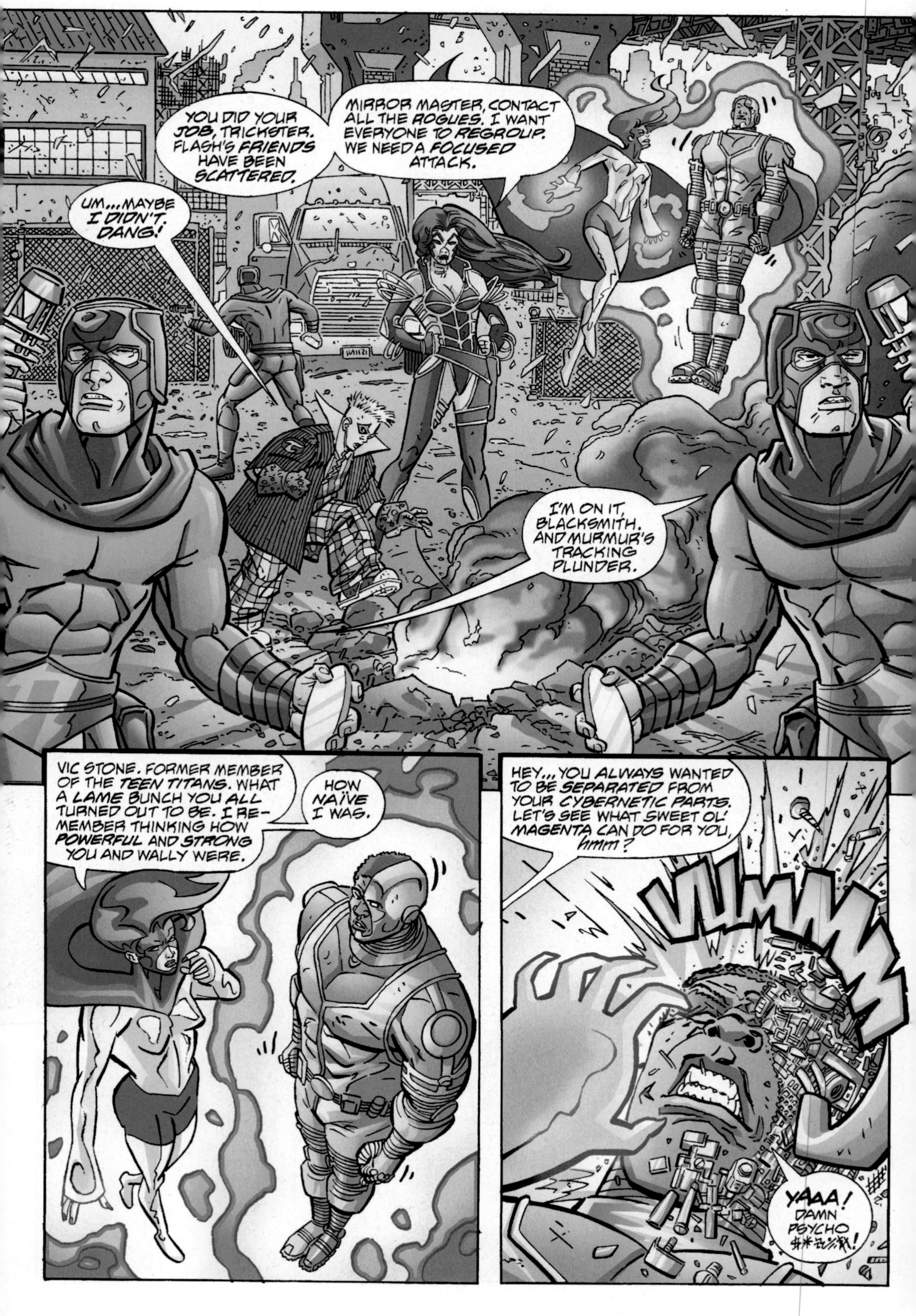
YOU DID YOUR JOB, TRICKSTER. FLASH'S FRIENDS HAVE BEEN SCATTERED.
MIRROR MASTER, CONTACT ALL THE ROGUES. I WANT EVERYONE TO REGROUP. WE NEED A FOCUSED ATTACK.
UM... MAYBE I DIDN'T. DANG!
I'M ON IT, BLACKSMITH. AND MURMUR'S TRACKING PLUNDER.
VIC STONE. FORMER MEMBER OF THE TEEN TITANS. WHAT A LAME BUNCH YOU ALL TURNED OUT TO BE. I RE-MEMBER THINKING HOW POWERFUL AND STRONG YOU AND WALLY WERE.
HOW NAÏVE I WAS.
HEY... YOU ALWAYS WANTED TO BE SEPARATED FROM YOUR CYBERNETIC PARTS. LET'S SEE WHAT SWEET OL' MAGENTA CAN DO FOR YOU, hmm?
VUMMM
YAAA! DAMN PSYCHO

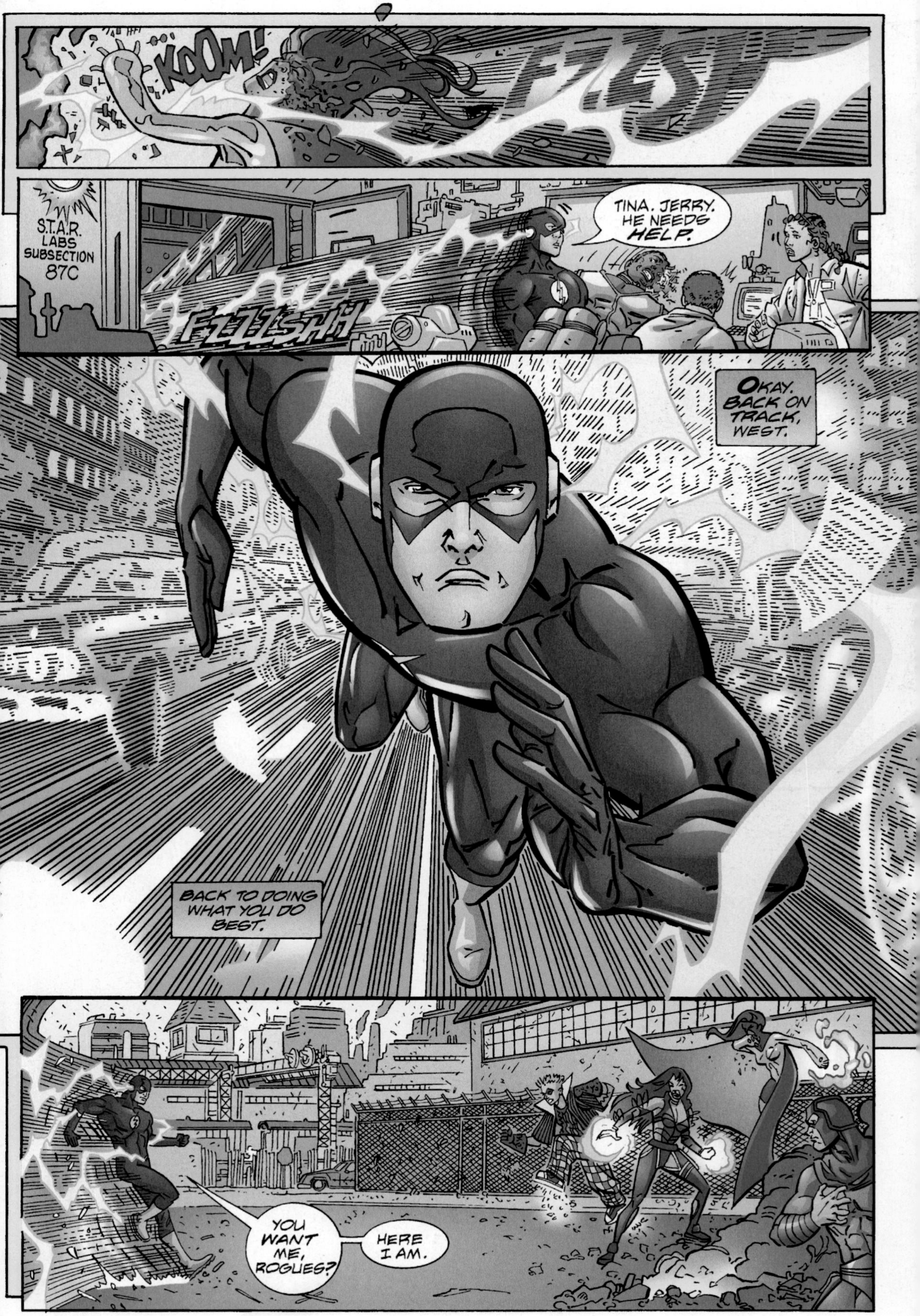
KOOM!
FZST
S.T.A.R. LABS SUBSECTION 87C
TINA. JERRY. HE NEEDS HELP.
FZZSHH
OKAY. BACK ON TRACK, WEST.
BACK TO DOING WHAT YOU DO BEST.
YOU WANT ME, ROGUES?
HERE I AM.

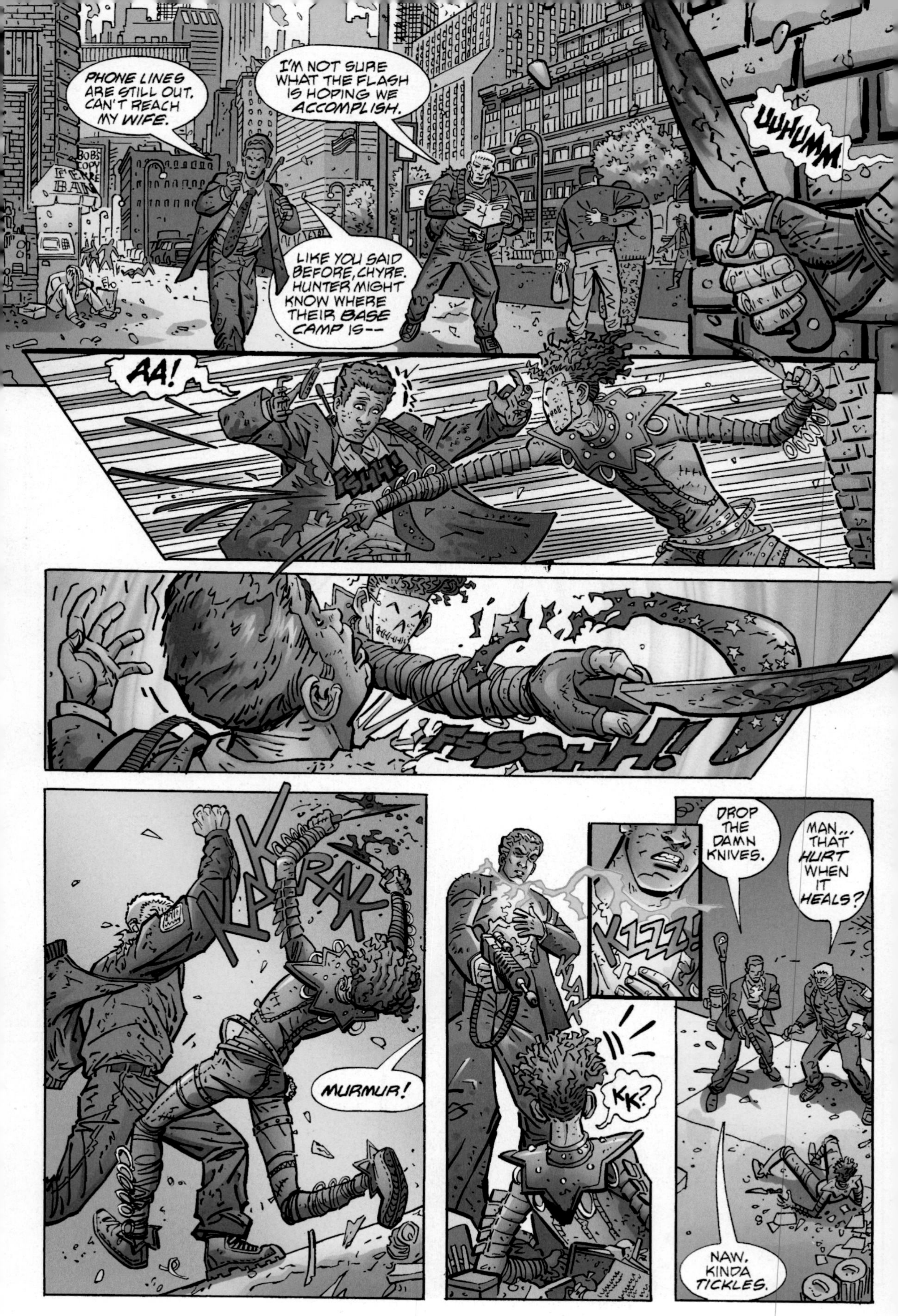
PHONE LINES ARE STILL OUT. CAN'T REACH MY WIFE.
I'M NOT SURE WHAT THE FLASH IS HOPING WE ACCOMPLISH.
LIKE YOU SAID BEFORE, CHYRE. HUNTER MIGHT KNOW WHERE THEIR BASE CAMP IS--
UUHUMM.
AA!
FSHH!
FSSSHH!
KLAKRAK
MURMUR!
KK?
KZZZ!
DROP THE DAMN KNIVES.
MAN... THAT HURT WHEN IT HEALS?
NAW. KINDA TICKLES.

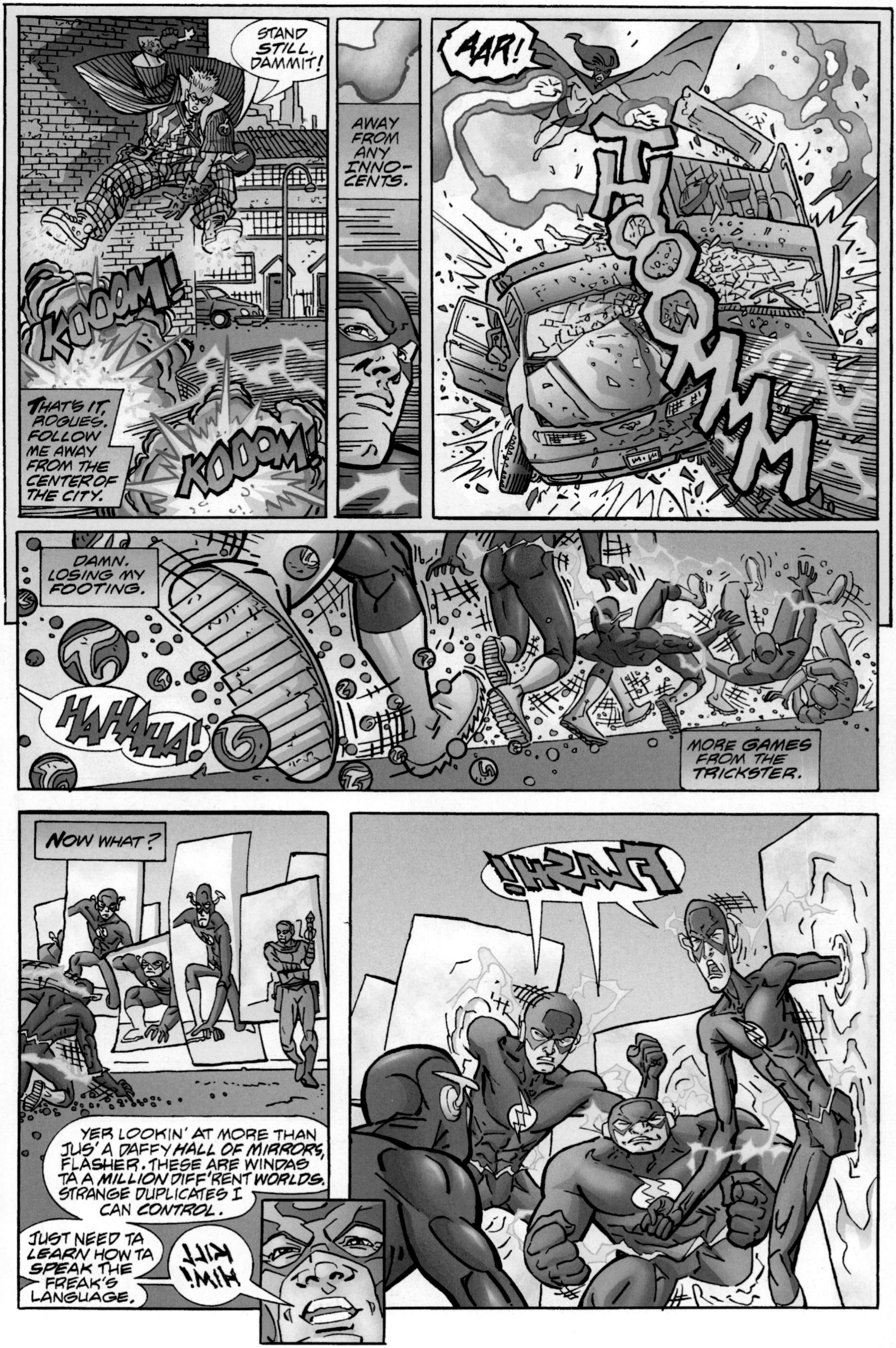
STAND STILL, DAMMIT!
KOOOM!
KOOOM!
THAT'S IT, ROGUES. FOLLOW ME AWAY FROM THE CENTER OF THE CITY.
AWAY FROM ANY INNO-CENTS.
AAR!
THOOMMM
DAMN. LOSING MY FOOTING.
HAHAHA!
MORE GAMES FROM THE TRICKSTER.
NOW WHAT?
YER LOOKIN' AT MORE THAN JUS' A DAFFY HALL OF MIRRORS, FLASHER. THESE ARE WINDAS TA A MILLION DIFF'RENT WORLDS. STRANGE DUPLICATES I CAN CONTROL.
JUST NEED TA LEARN HOW TA SPEAK THE FREAK'S LANGUAGE.
KILL HIM!
FLASH!

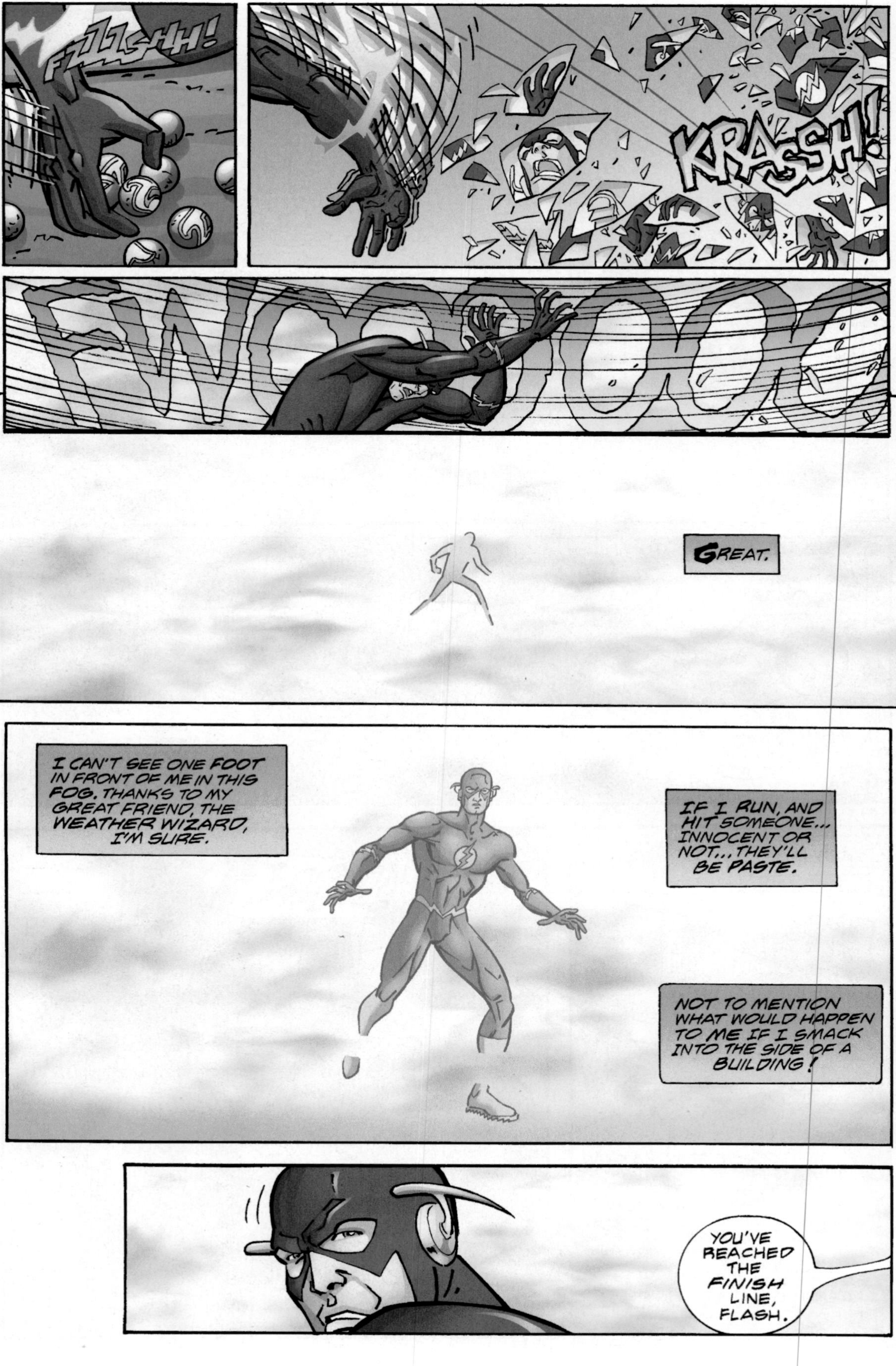
FZZZSHH!
KRASH!
FWOOOOOOOOO
GREAT.
I CAN'T SEE ONE FOOT IN FRONT OF ME IN THIS FOG. THANKS TO MY GREAT FRIEND, THE WEATHER WIZARD, I'M SURE.
IF I RUN, AND HIT SOMEONE... INNOCENT OR NOT... THEY'LL BE PASTE.
NOT TO MENTION WHAT WOULD HAPPEN TO ME IF I SMACK INTO THE SIDE OF A BUILDING!
YOU'VE REACHED THE FINISH LINE, FLASH.

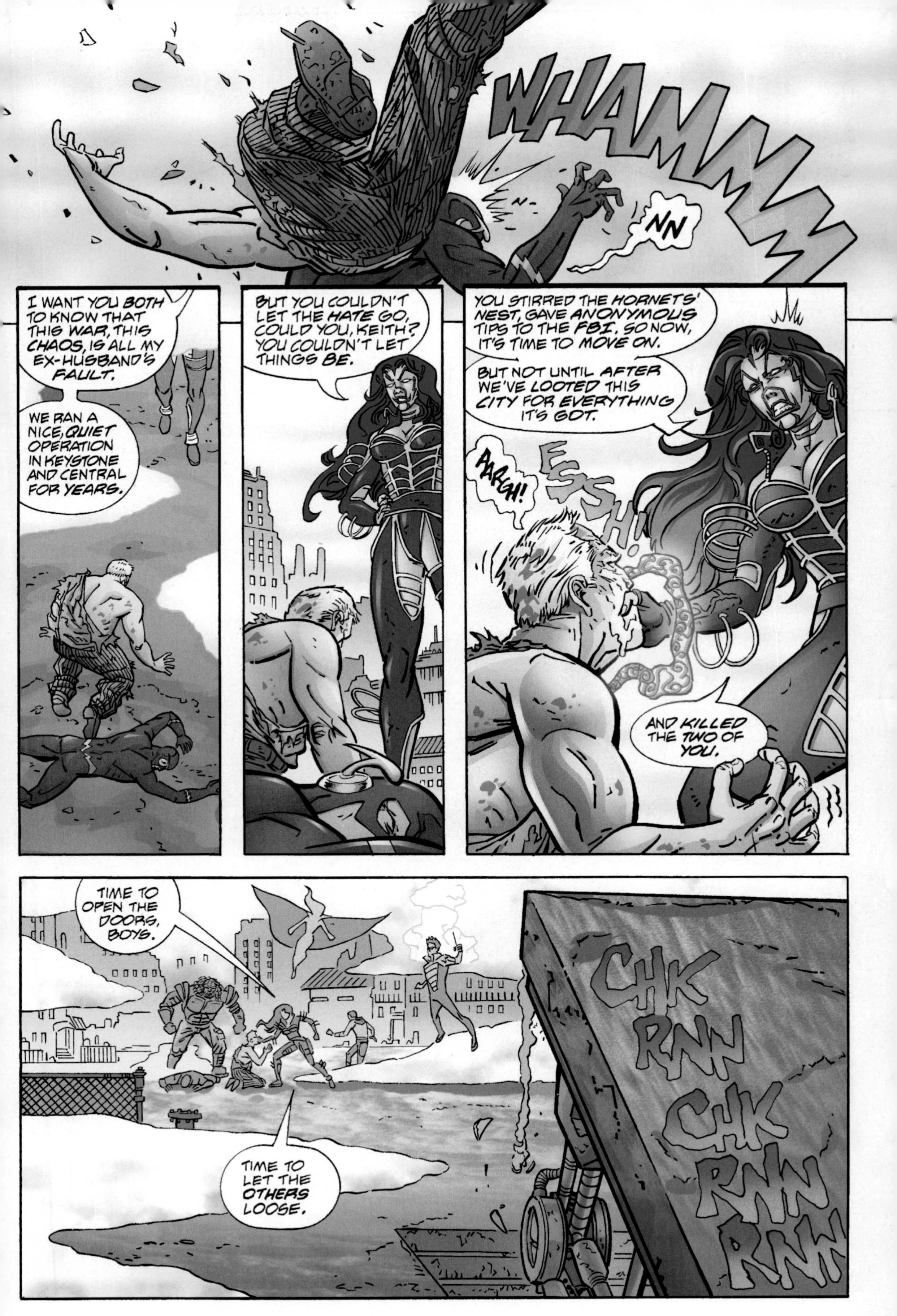
WHAMMM
NN
I WANT YOU BOTH TO KNOW THAT THIS WAR, THIS CHAOS, IS ALL MY EX-HUSBAND'S FAULT.
WE RAN A NICE, QUIET OPERATION IN KEYSTONE AND CENTRAL FOR YEARS.
BUT YOU COULDN'T LET THE HATE GO, COULD YOU, KEITH? YOU COULDN'T LET THINGS BE.
YOU STIRRED THE HORNETS' NEST, GAVE ANONYMOUS TIPS TO THE FBI, SO NOW, IT'S TIME TO MOVE ON.
BUT NOT UNTIL AFTER WE'VE LOOTED THIS CITY FOR EVERYTHING IT'S GOT.
AARGH!
ESSSH!
AND KILLED THE TWO OF YOU.
TIME TO OPEN THE DOORS, BOYS.
TIME TO LET THE OTHERS LOOSE.
CHK RNN CHK RNN RNN

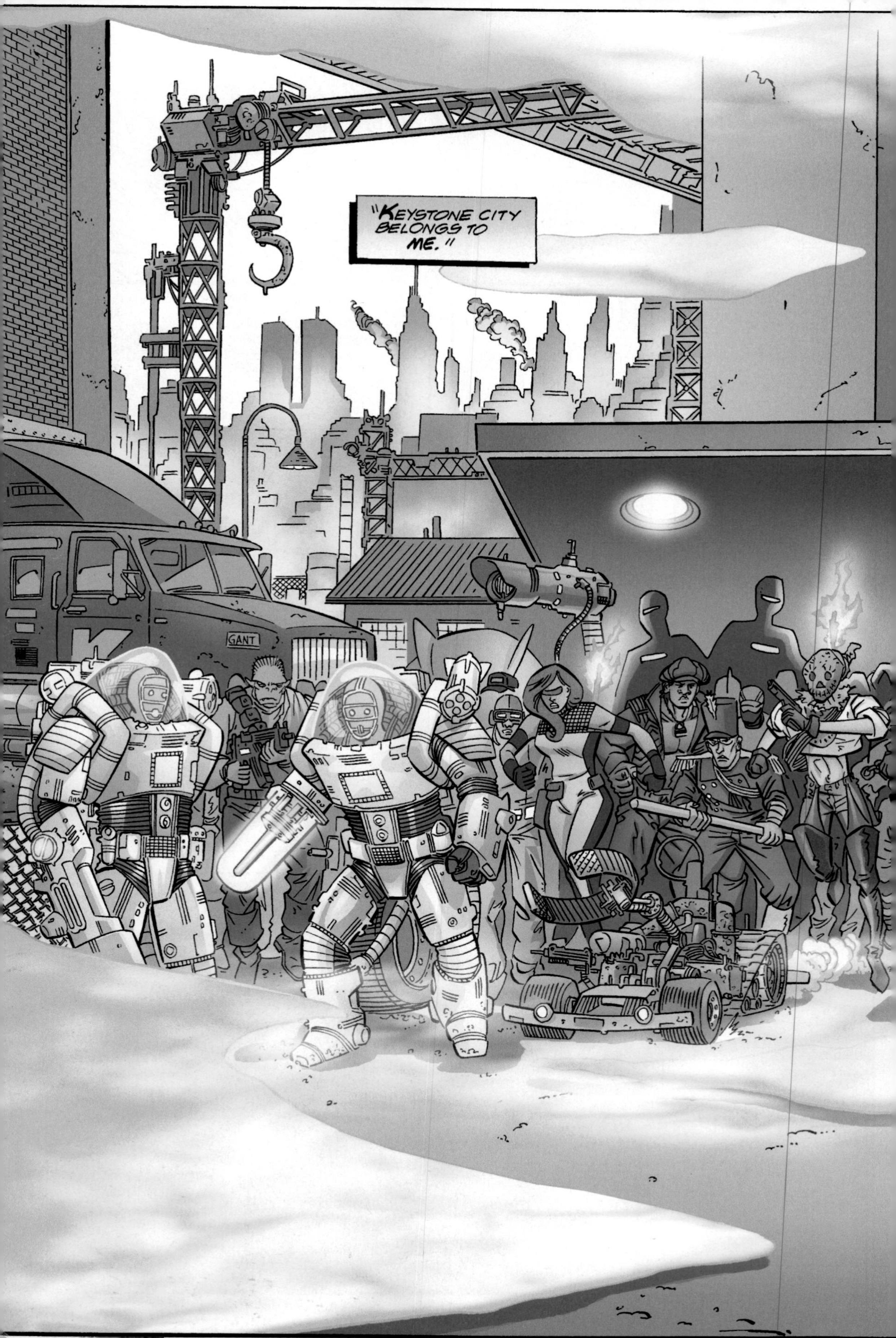
"KEYSTONE CITY BELONGS TO ME."
GANT

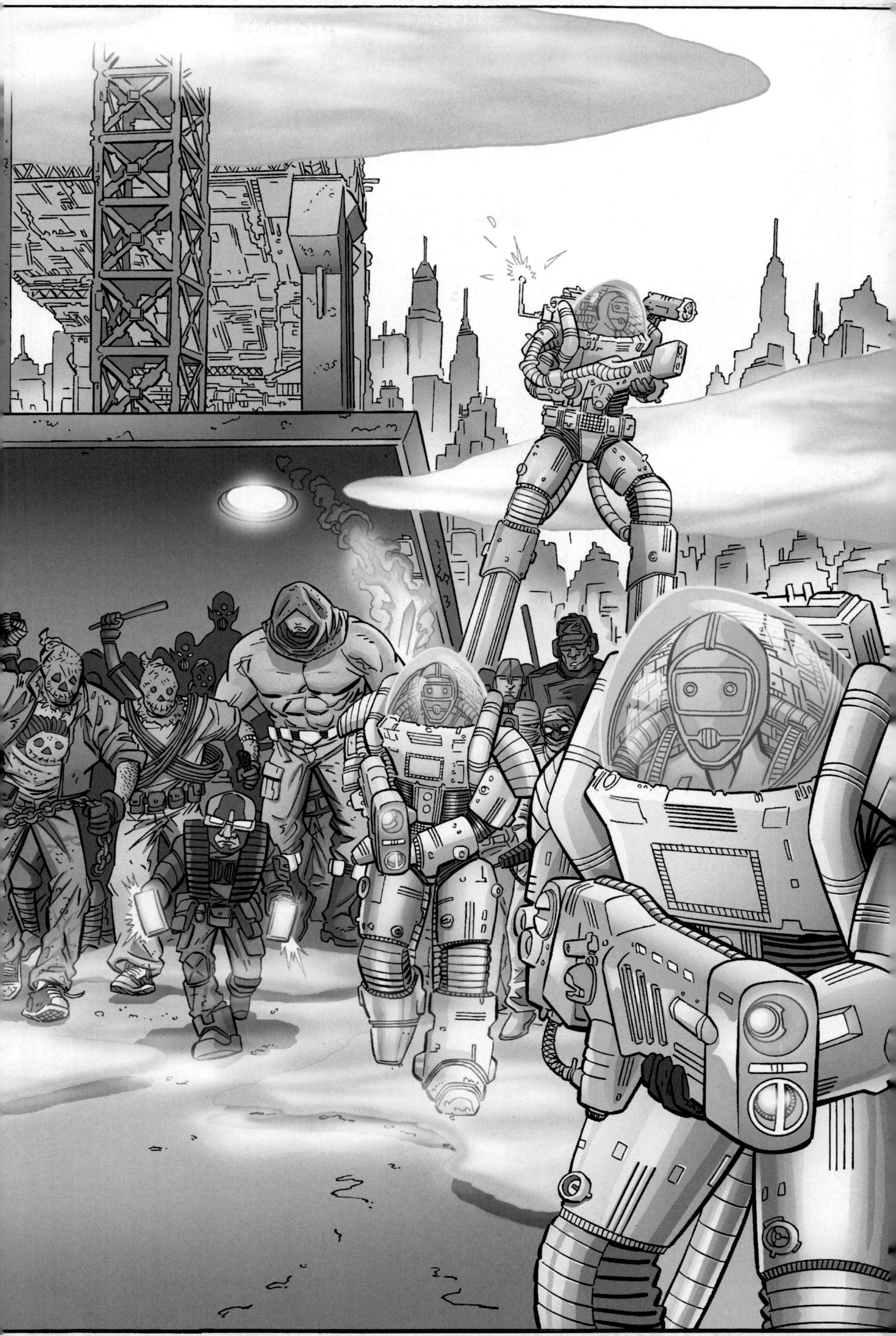

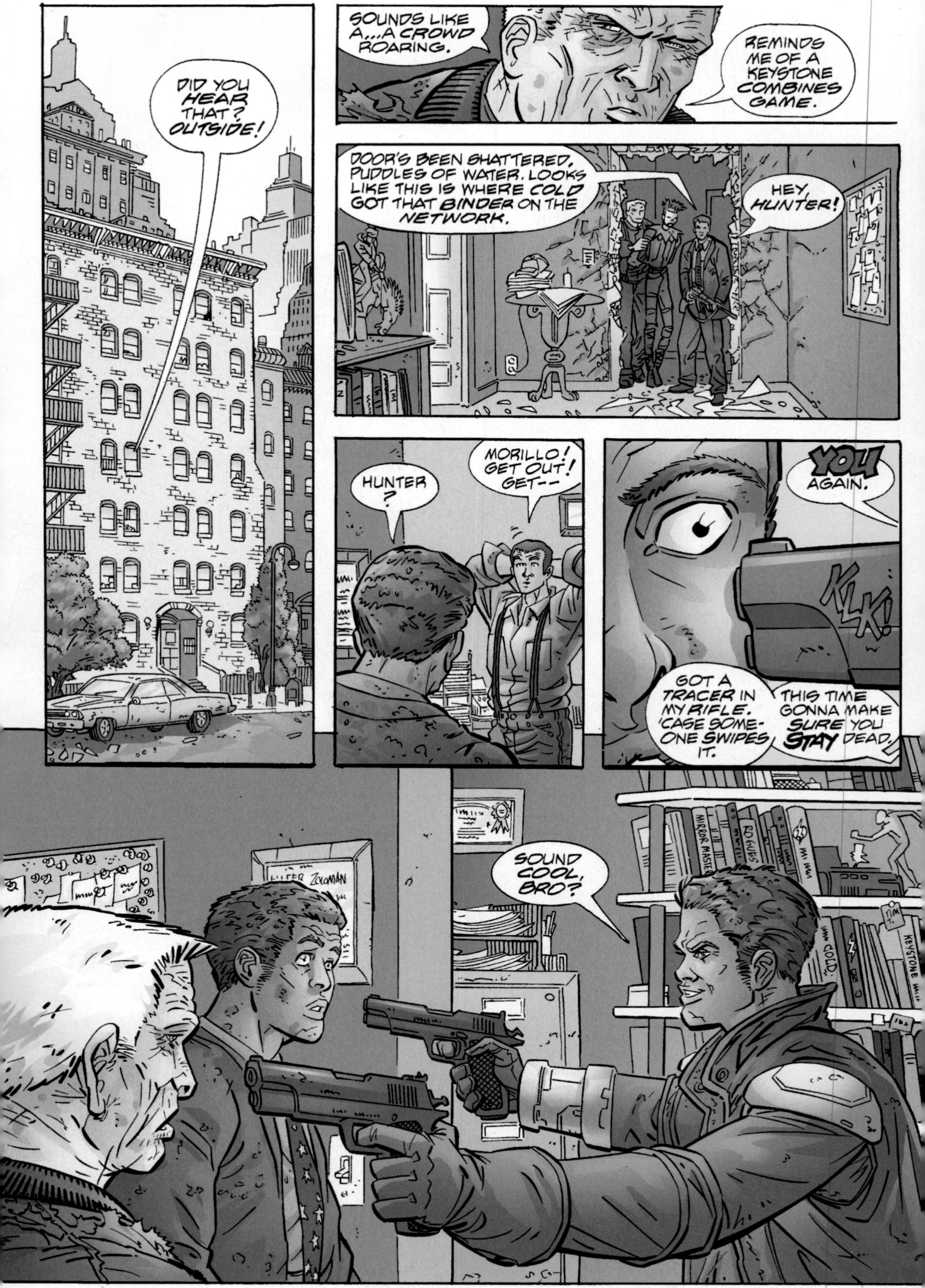
DID YOU HEAR THAT? OUTSIDE!
SOUNDS LIKE A...A CROWD ROARING.
REMINDS ME OF A KEYSTONE COMBINES GAME.
DOOR'S BEEN SHATTERED. PUDDLES OF WATER. LOOKS LIKE THIS IS WHERE COLD GOT THAT BINDER ON THE NETWORK.
HEY, HUNTER!
HUNTER?
MORILLO! GET OUT! GET--
YOU AGAIN.
KLIK!
GOT A TRACER IN MY RIFLE. 'CASE SOME-ONE SWIPES IT.
THIS TIME GONNA MAKE SURE YOU STAY DEAD.
SOUND COOL, BRO?
MIRROR MASTER
RO GUES
KEYSTONE
GOLD

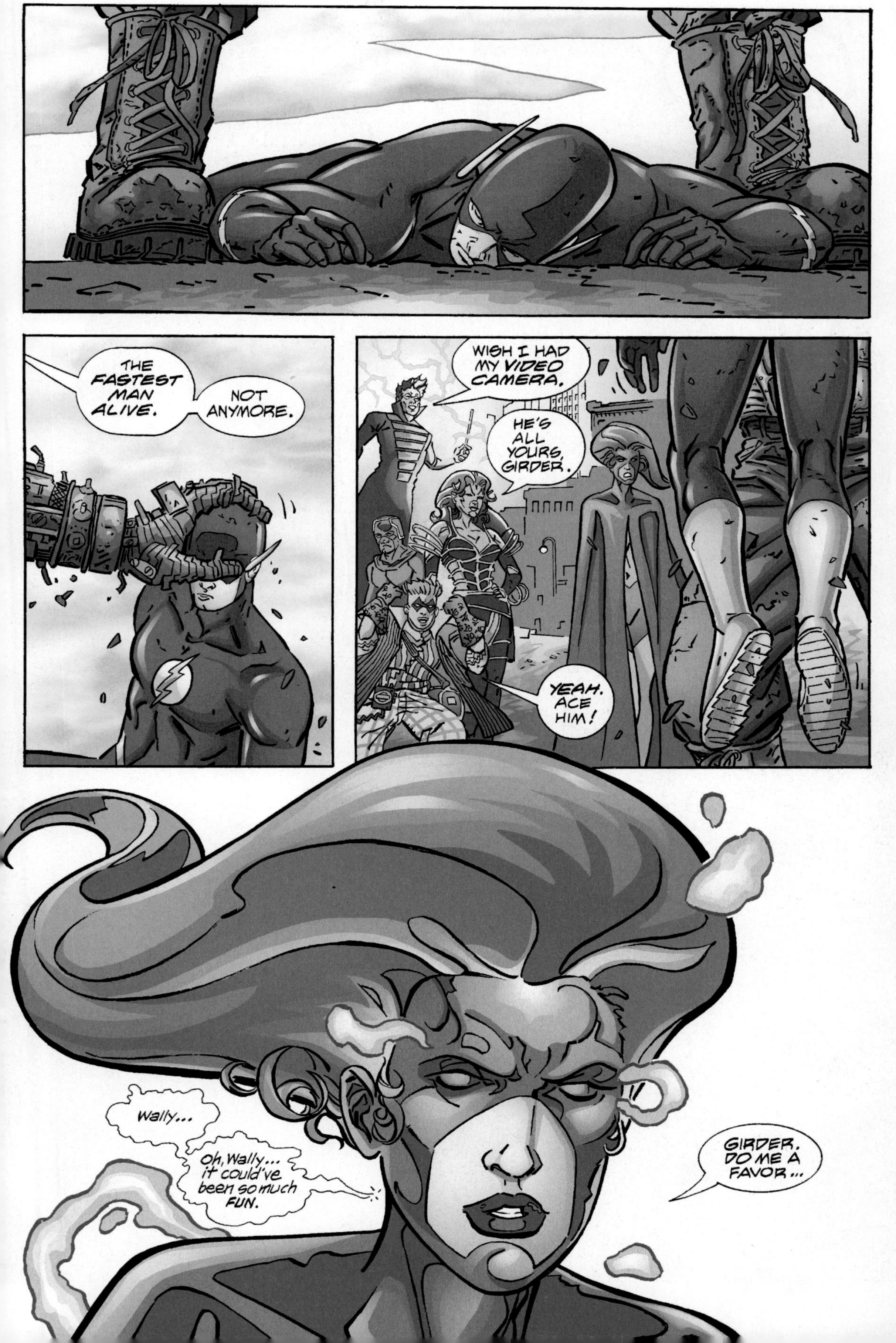
THE FASTEST MAN ALIVE.
NOT ANYMORE.
WISH I HAD MY VIDEO CAMERA.
HE'S ALL YOURS, GIRDER.
YEAH. ACE HIM!
Wally...
Oh, Wally... it could've been so much FUN.
GIRDER. DO ME A FAVOR...

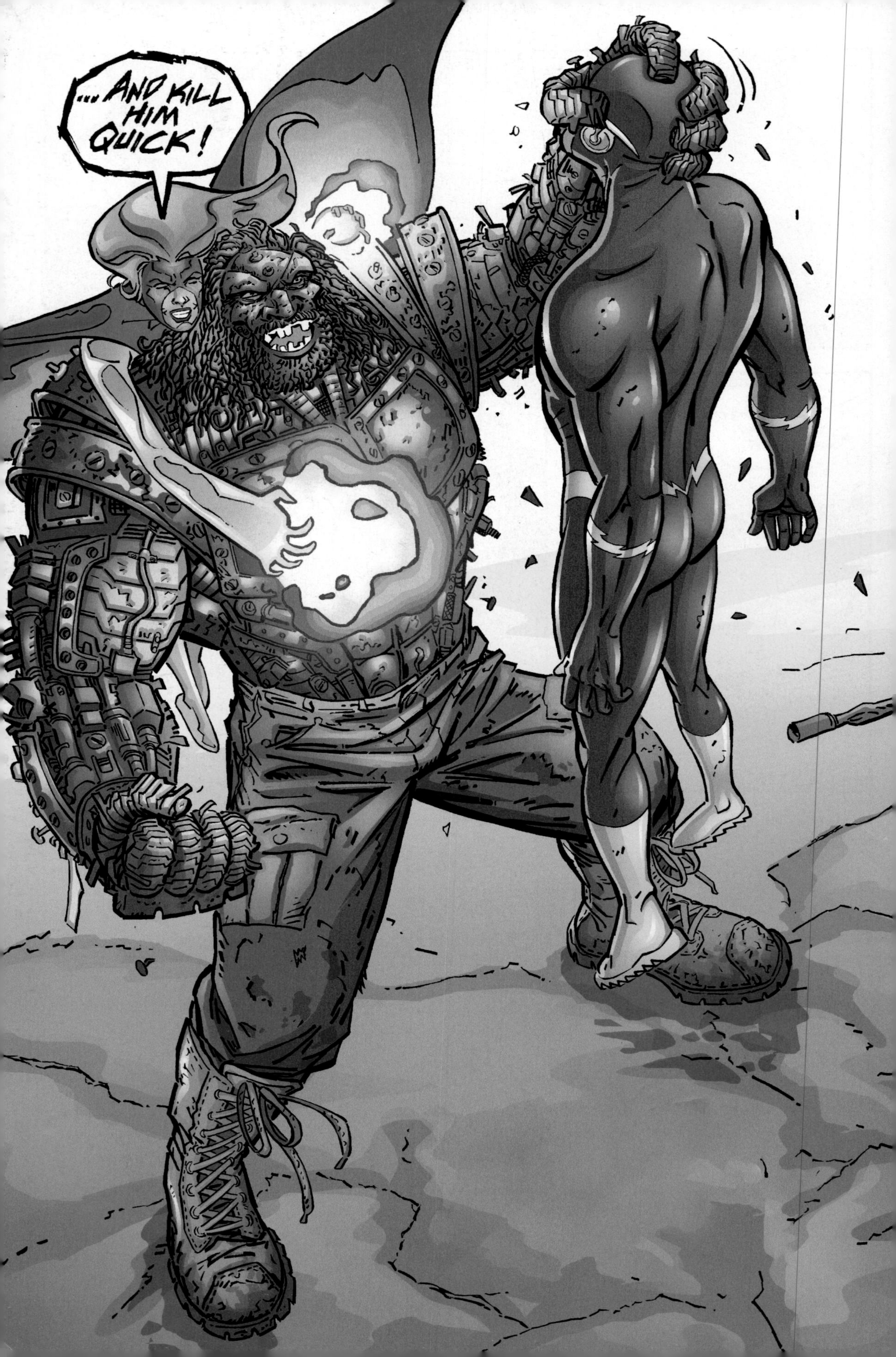
...AND KILL HIM QUICK!

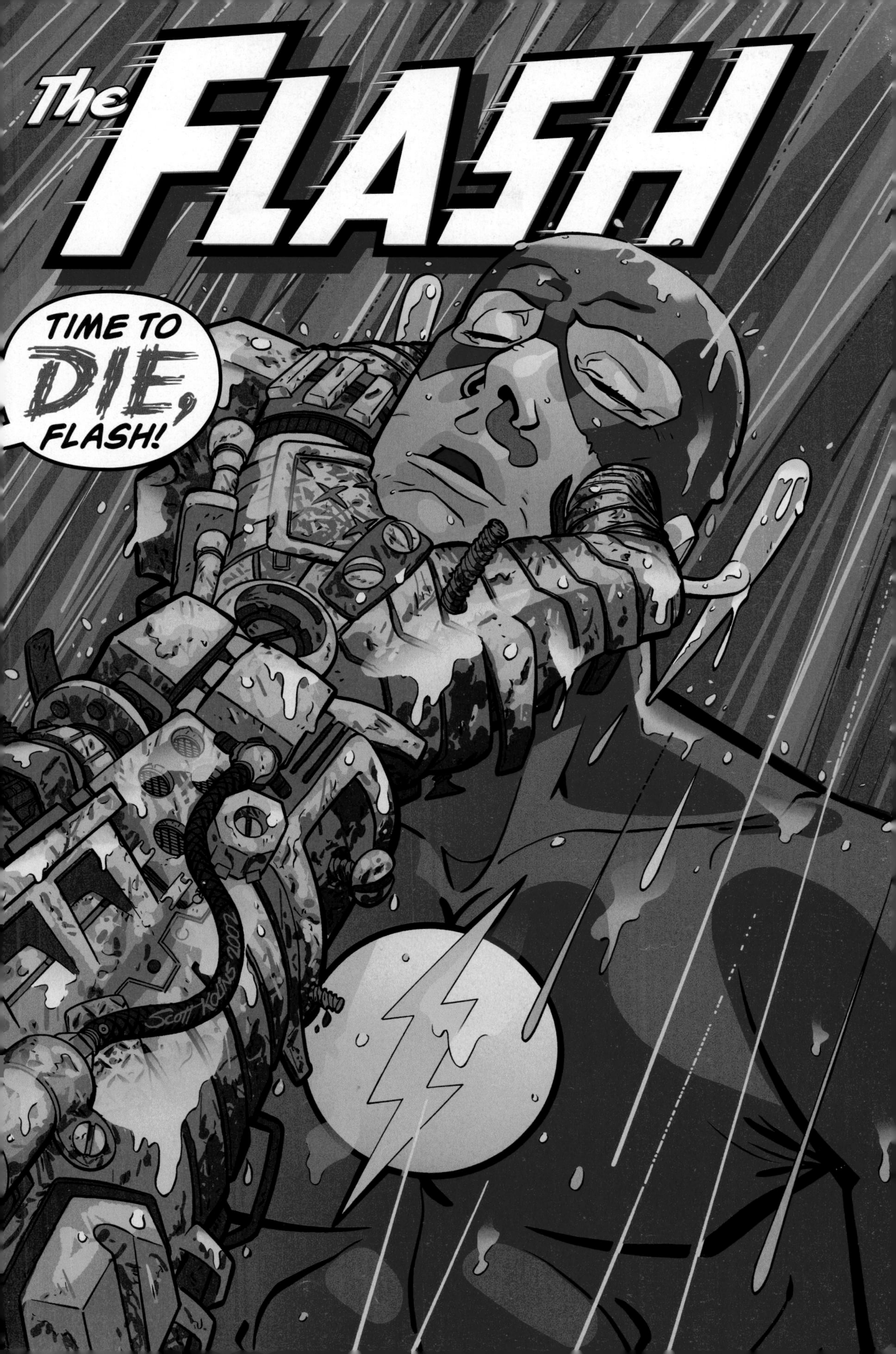
The FLASH
TIME TO DIE, FLASH!
SCOTT KOLINS 2002

COVER ART BY **SCOTT KOLINS**

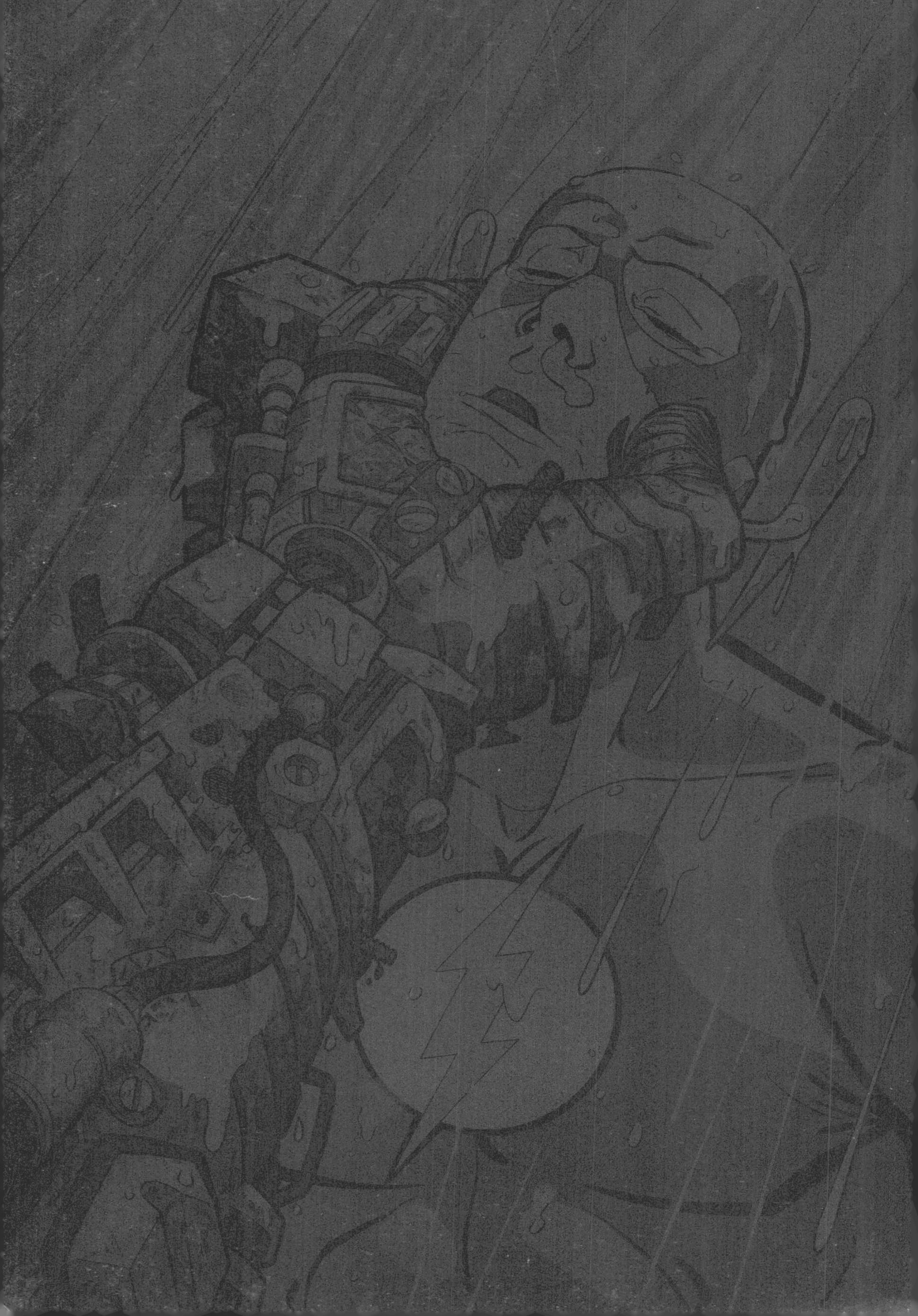

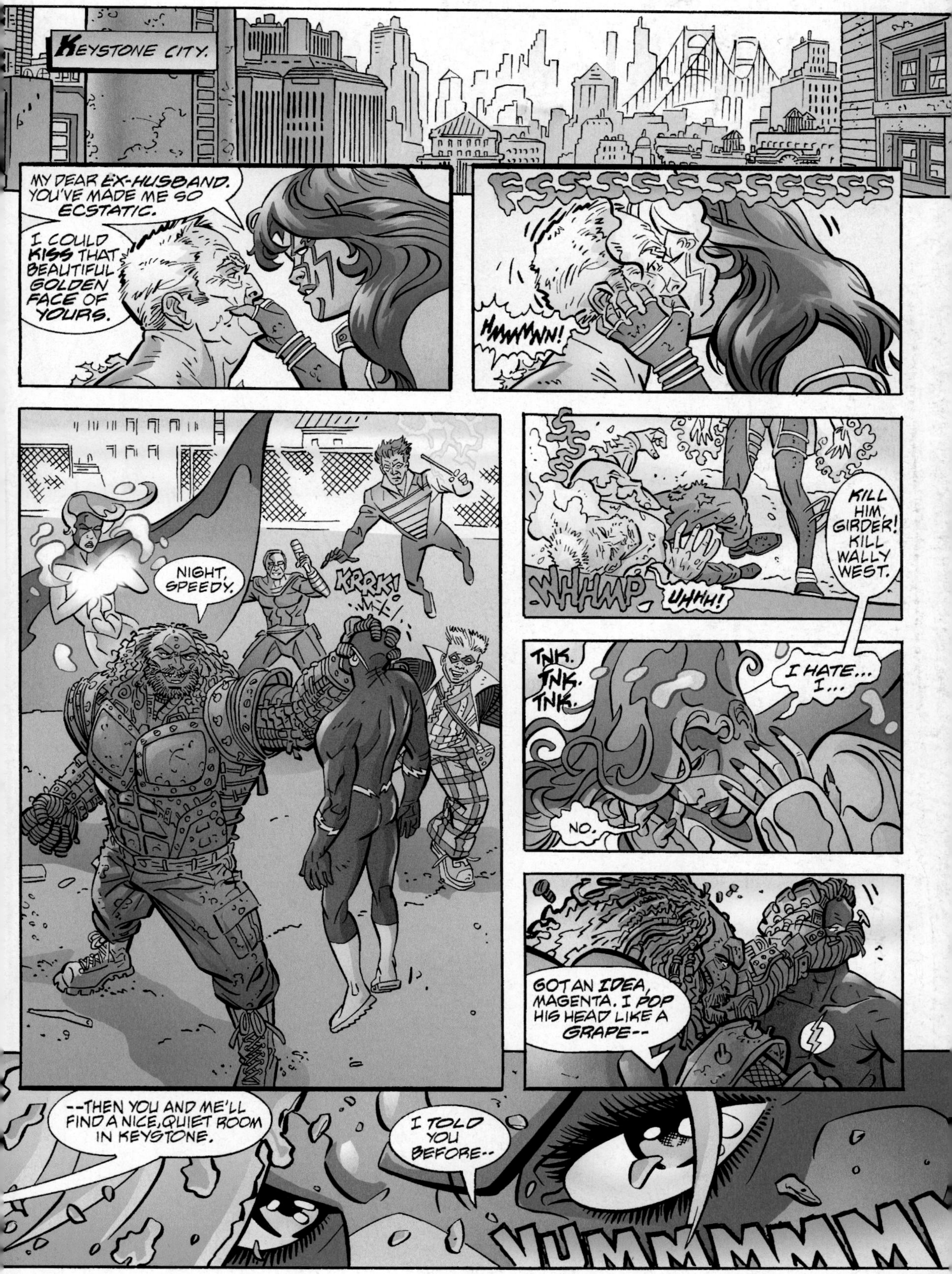
KEYSTONE CITY.
MY DEAR EX-HUSBAND. YOU'VE MADE ME SO ECSTATIC.
I COULD KISS THAT BEAUTIFUL GOLDEN FACE OF YOURS.
FSSSSSSSSSSSS
HMMMNN!
NIGHT, SPEEDY.
KRRK!
WHHMP
UHHH!
KILL HIM, GIRDER! KILL WALLY WEST.
TNK. TNK. TNK.
I HATE... I...
NO.
GOT AN IDEA, MAGENTA. I POP HIS HEAD LIKE A GRAPE--
--THEN YOU AND ME'LL FIND A NICE, QUIET ROOM IN KEYSTONE.
I TOLD YOU BEFORE--
VUMMMMM

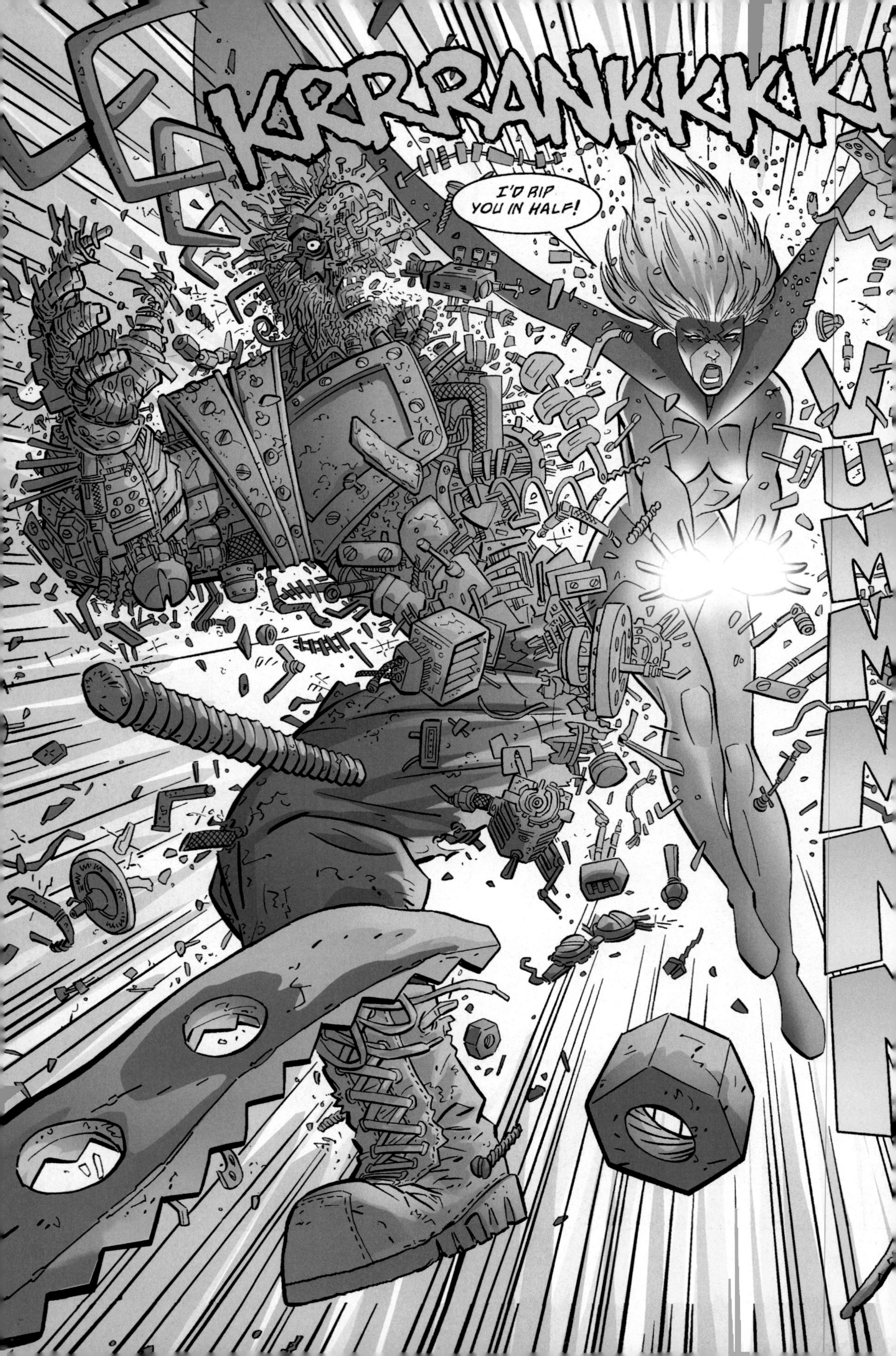
KRRRANKKKKK
I'D RIP YOU IN HALF!

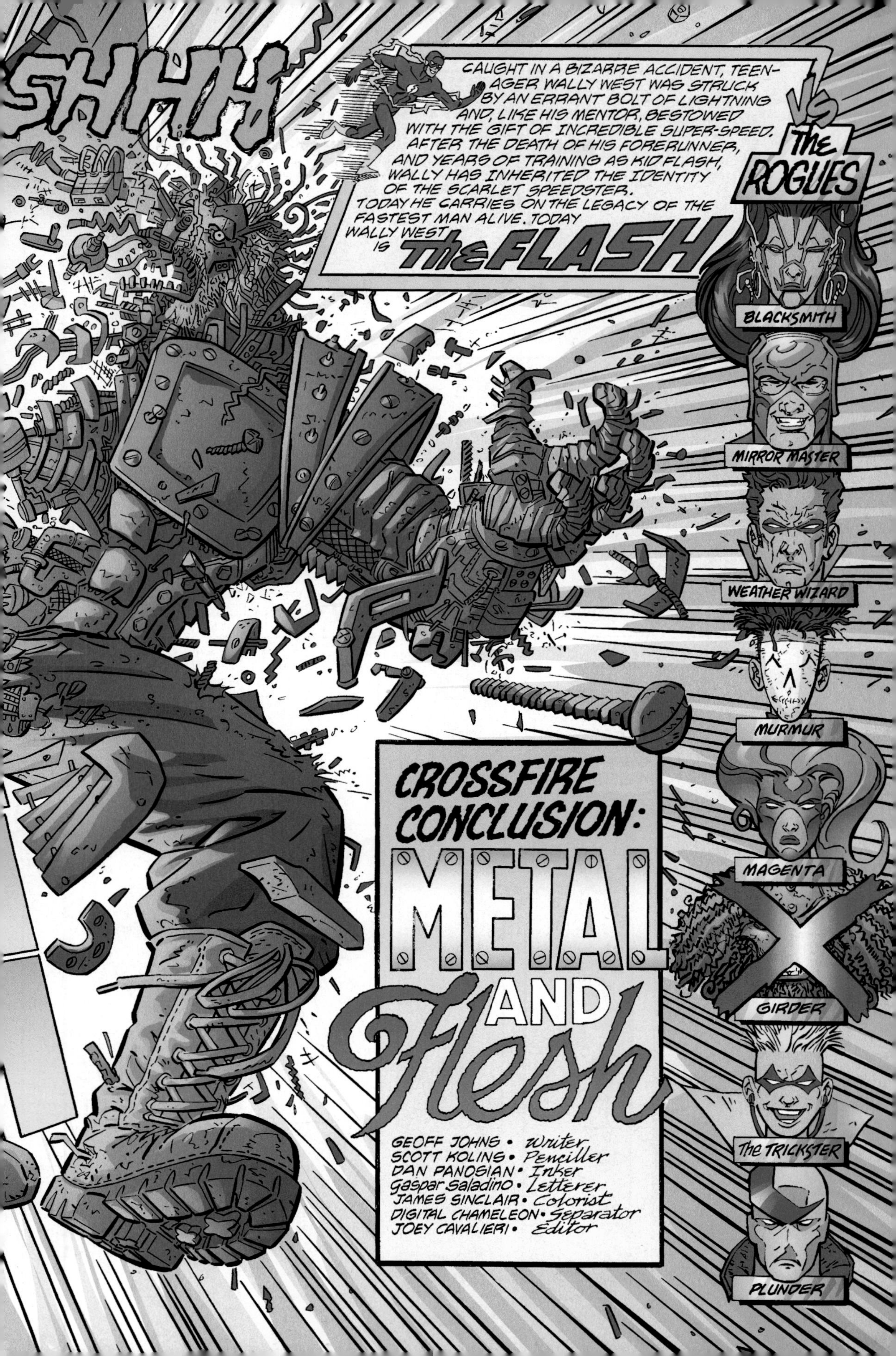
SHHH
CAUGHT IN A BIZARRE ACCIDENT, TEEN-AGER WALLY WEST WAS STRUCK BY AN ERRANT BOLT OF LIGHTNING AND, LIKE HIS MENTOR, BESTOWED WITH THE GIFT OF INCREDIBLE SUPER-SPEED. AFTER THE DEATH OF HIS FORERUNNER, AND YEARS OF TRAINING AS KID FLASH, WALLY HAS INHERITED THE IDENTITY OF THE SCARLET SPEEDSTER. TODAY HE CARRIES ON THE LEGACY OF THE FASTEST MAN ALIVE. TODAY WALLY WEST IS THE FLASH
VS THE ROGUES
BLACKSMITH
MIRROR MASTER
WEATHER WIZARD
MURMUR
MAGENTA
GIRDER
The TRICKSTER
PLUNDER
CROSSFIRE CONCLUSION:
METAL AND Flesh
GEOFF JOHNS • Writer
SCOTT KOLINS • Penciller
DAN PANOSIAN • Inker
Gaspar Saladino • Letterer
JAMES SINCLAIR • Colorist
DIGITAL CHAMELEON • Separator
JOEY CAVALIERI • Editor

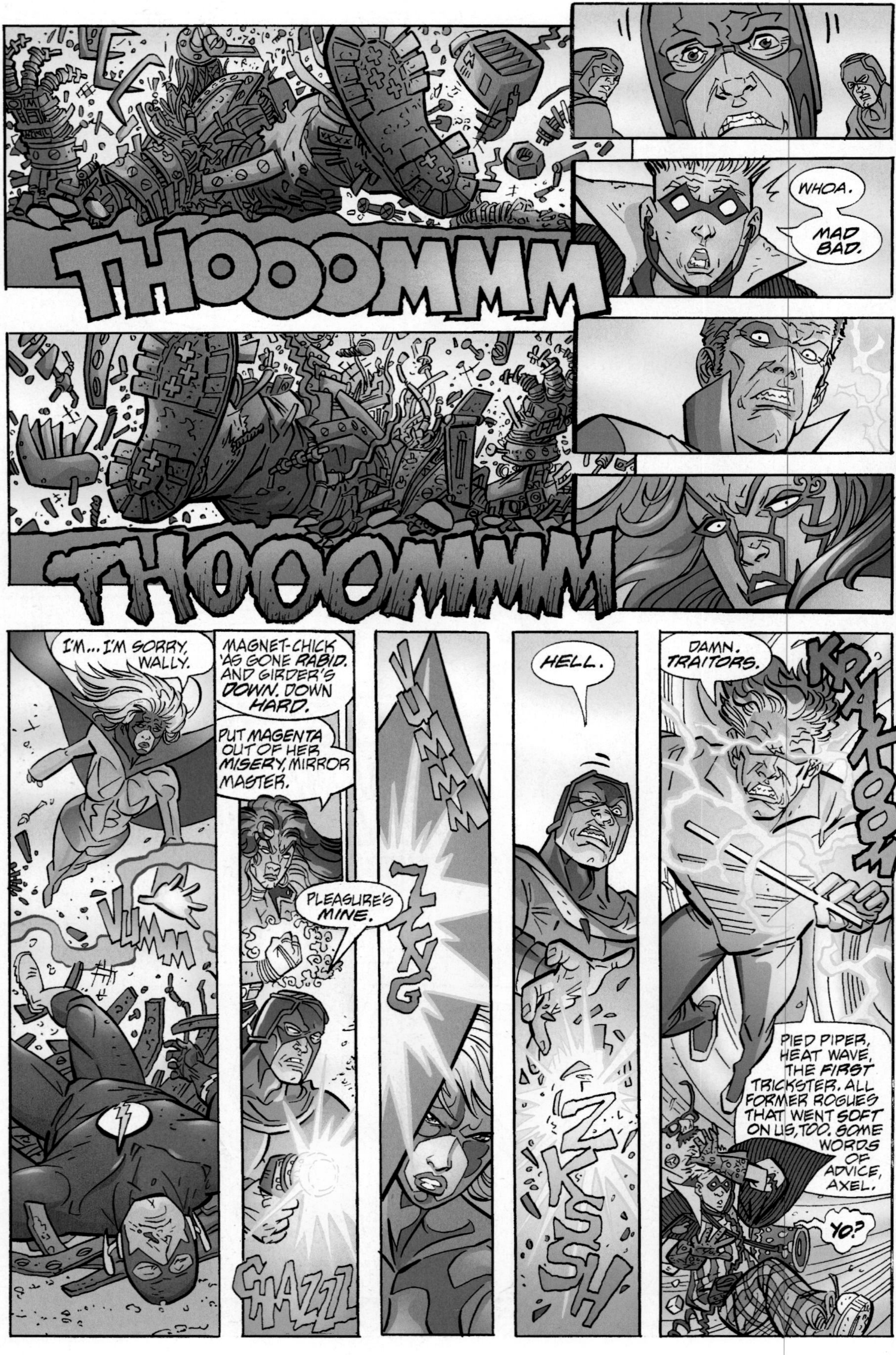
THOOMMM
WHOA.
MAD BAD.
THOOOMMM
I'M... I'M SORRY, WALLY.
VUMMM
MAGNET-CHICK 'AS GONE RABID. AND GIRDER'S DOWN. DOWN HARD.
PUT MAGENTA OUT OF HER MISERY, MIRROR MASTER.
PLEASURE'S MINE.
CHAZZZ
VUMMM
ZANG
HELL.
ZZKSH
DAMN. TRAITORS.
KRAKOOM
PIED PIPER, HEAT WAVE, THE FIRST TRICKSTER. ALL FORMER ROGUES THAT WENT SOFT ON US, TOO. SOME WORDS OF ADVICE, AXEL.
YO?

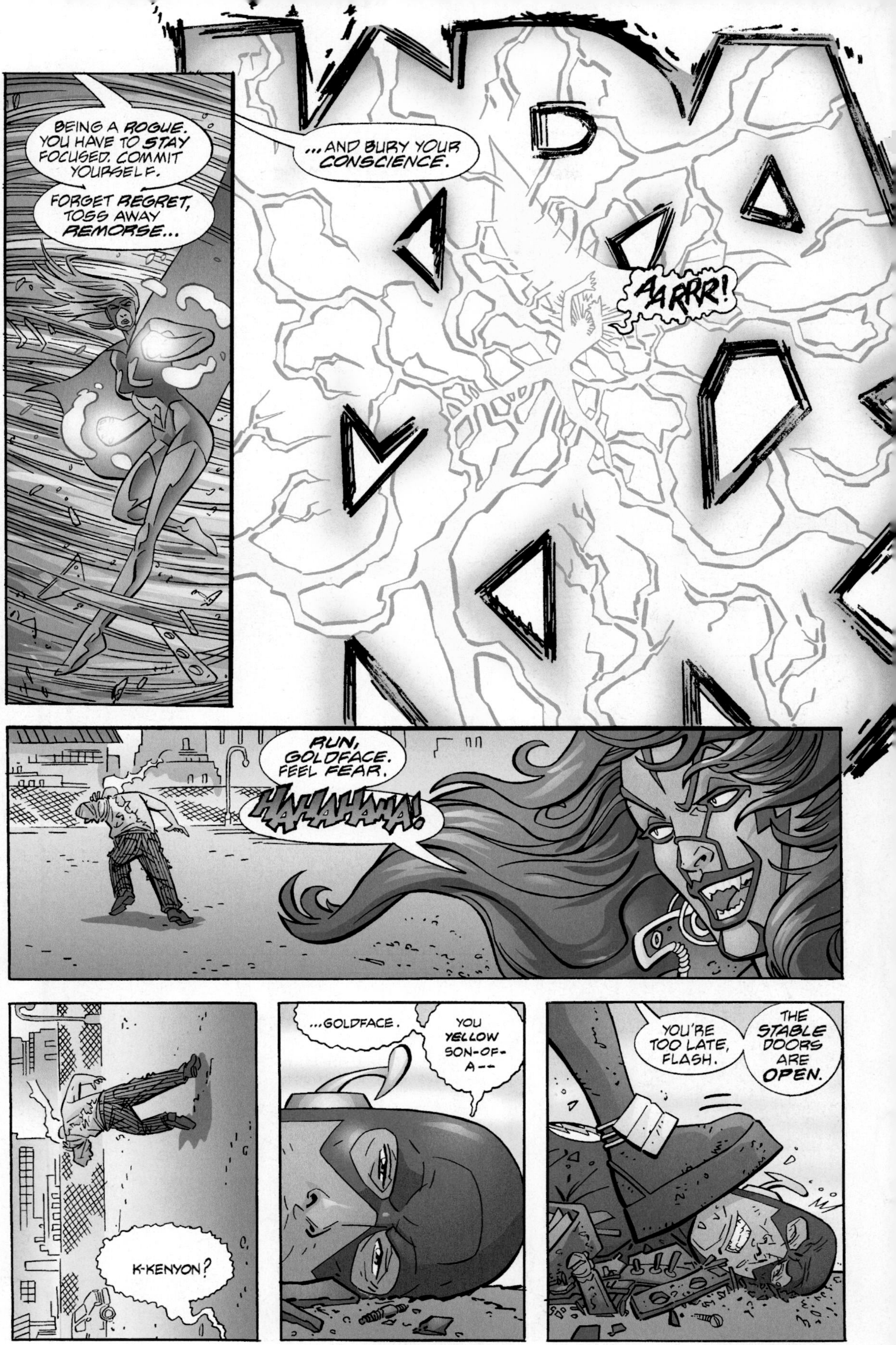
BEING A ROGUE. YOU HAVE TO STAY FOCUSED. COMMIT YOURSELF.
FORGET REGRET, TOSS AWAY REMORSE...
...AND BURY YOUR CONSCIENCE.
AARRR!
RUN, GOLDFACE. FEEL FEAR.
HAHAHAHA!
K-KENYON?
...GOLDFACE.
YOU YELLOW SON-OF-A--
YOU'RE TOO LATE, FLASH.
THE STABLE DOORS ARE OPEN.

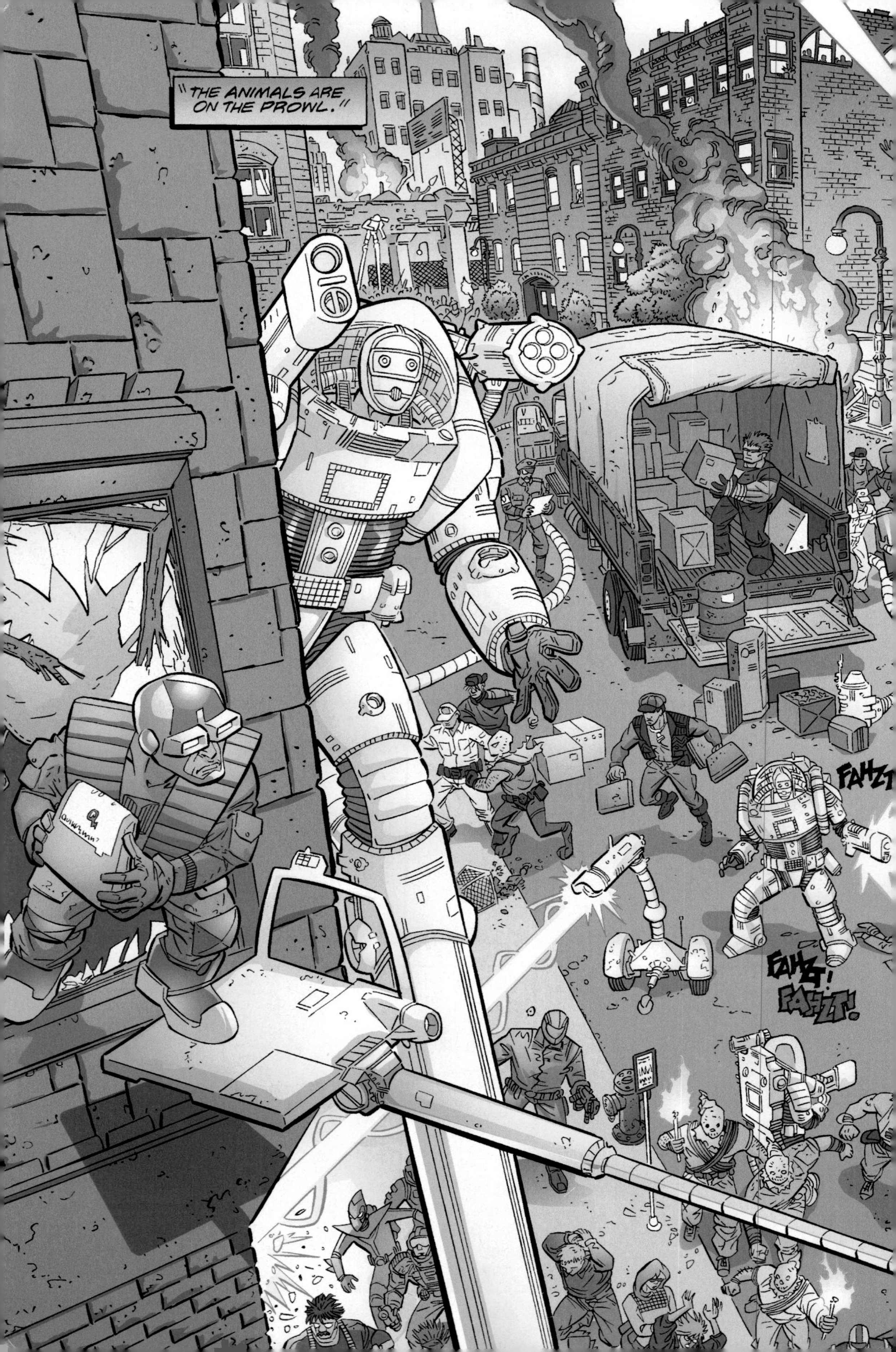
"THE ANIMALS ARE ON THE PROWL."
FAHZT
FAHZT!
FAHZT!

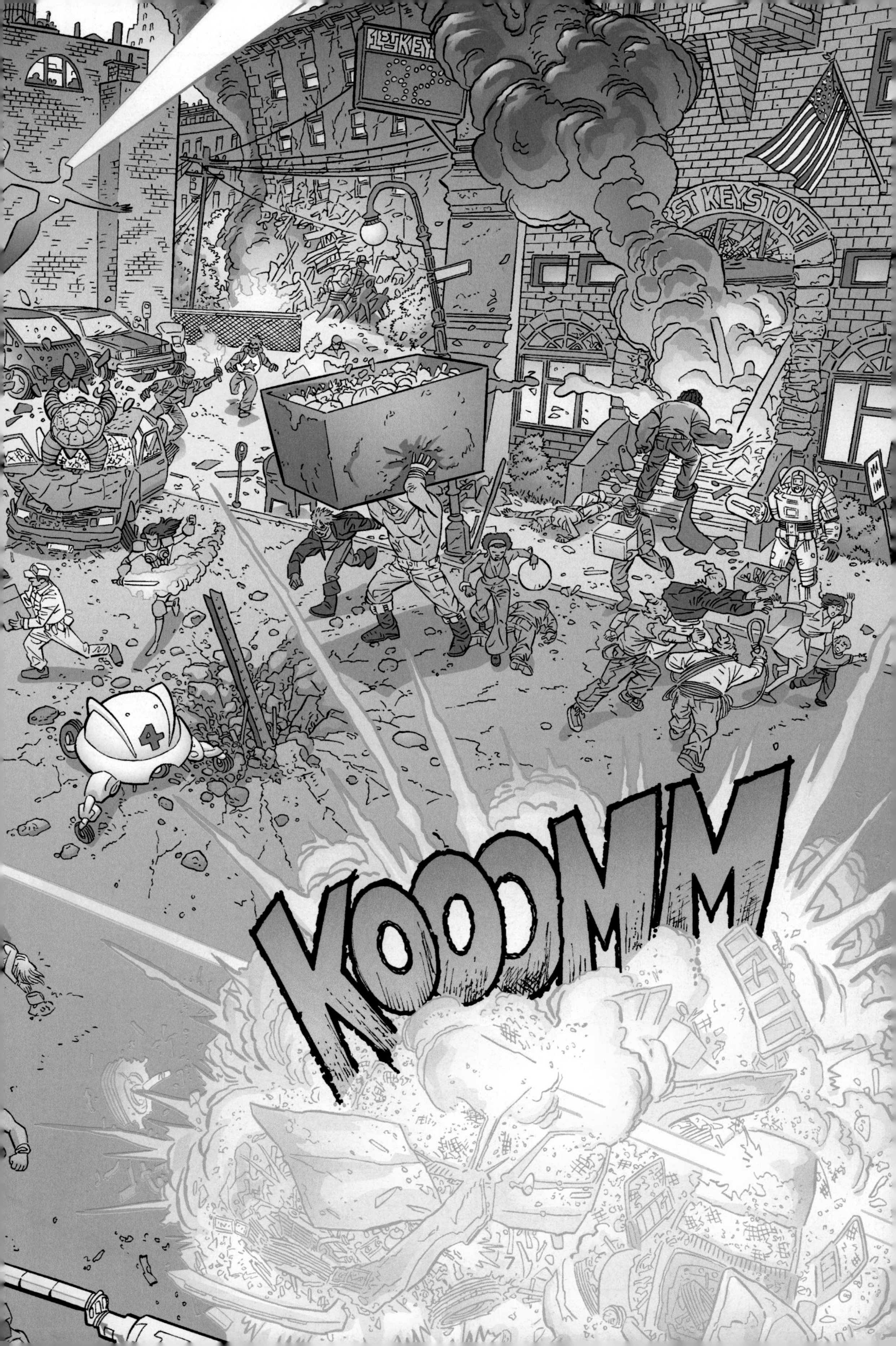
1ST KEYSTONE
KOOOMM

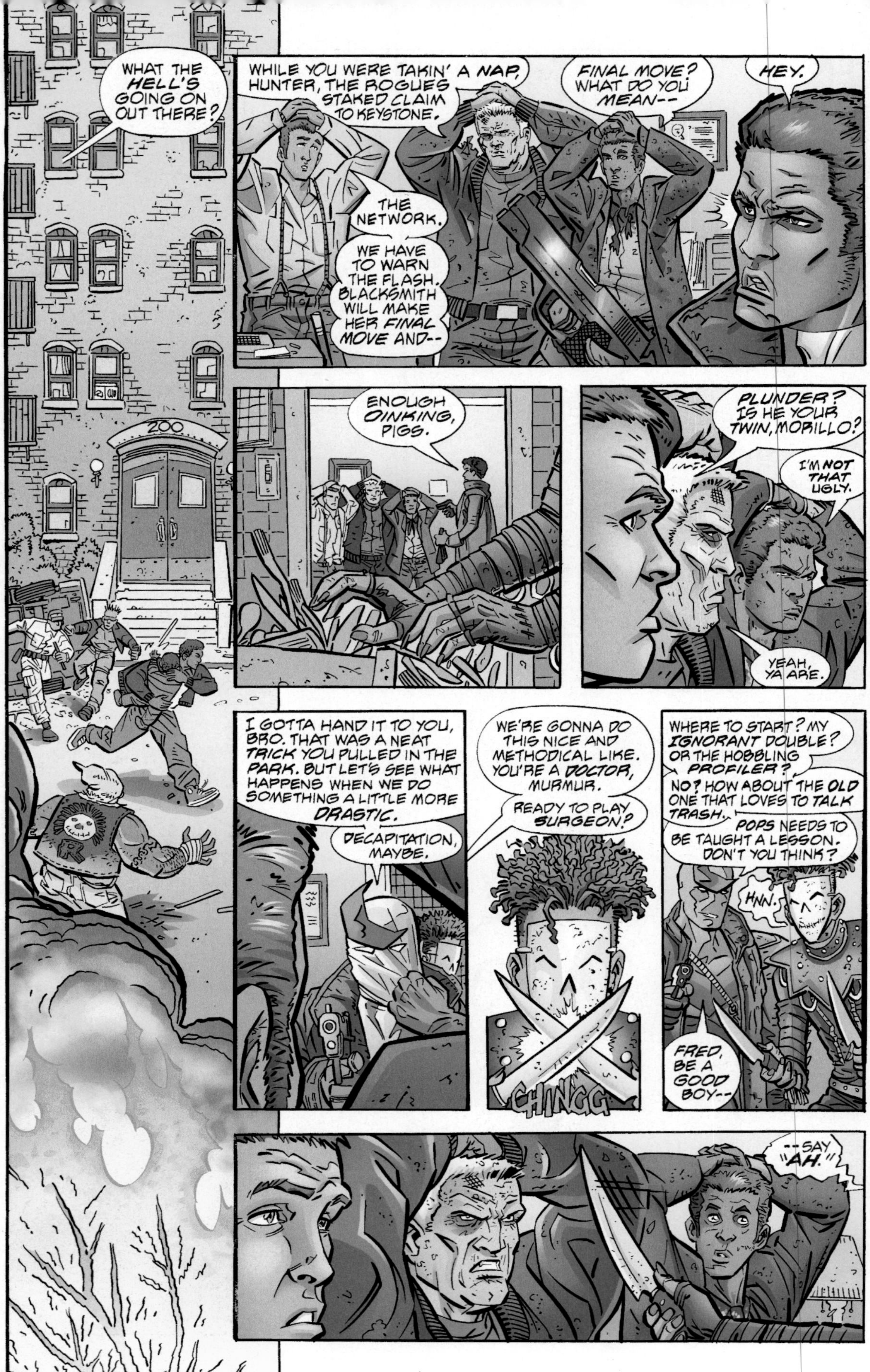
WHAT THE HELL'S GOING ON OUT THERE?
WHILE YOU WERE TAKIN' A NAP, HUNTER, THE ROGUES STAKED CLAIM TO KEYSTONE.
THE NETWORK.
WE HAVE TO WARN THE FLASH. BLACKSMITH WILL MAKE HER FINAL MOVE AND--
FINAL MOVE? WHAT DO YOU MEAN--
HEY.
200
ENOUGH OINKING, PIGS.
PLUNDER? IS HE YOUR TWIN, MORILLO?
I'M NOT THAT UGLY.
YEAH, YA ARE.
I GOTTA HAND IT TO YOU, BRO. THAT WAS A NEAT TRICK YOU PULLED IN THE PARK. BUT LET'S SEE WHAT HAPPENS WHEN WE DO SOMETHING A LITTLE MORE DRASTIC.
DECAPITATION, MAYBE.
WE'RE GONNA DO THIS NICE AND METHODICAL LIKE. YOU'RE A DOCTOR, MURMUR.
READY TO PLAY SURGEON?
CHINGG
WHERE TO START? MY IGNORANT DOUBLE? OR THE HOBBLING PROFILER?
NO? HOW ABOUT THE OLD ONE THAT LOVES TO TALK TRASH.
POPS NEEDS TO BE TAUGHT A LESSON. DON'T YOU THINK?
HNN.
FRED, BE A GOOD BOY--
--SAY "AH."

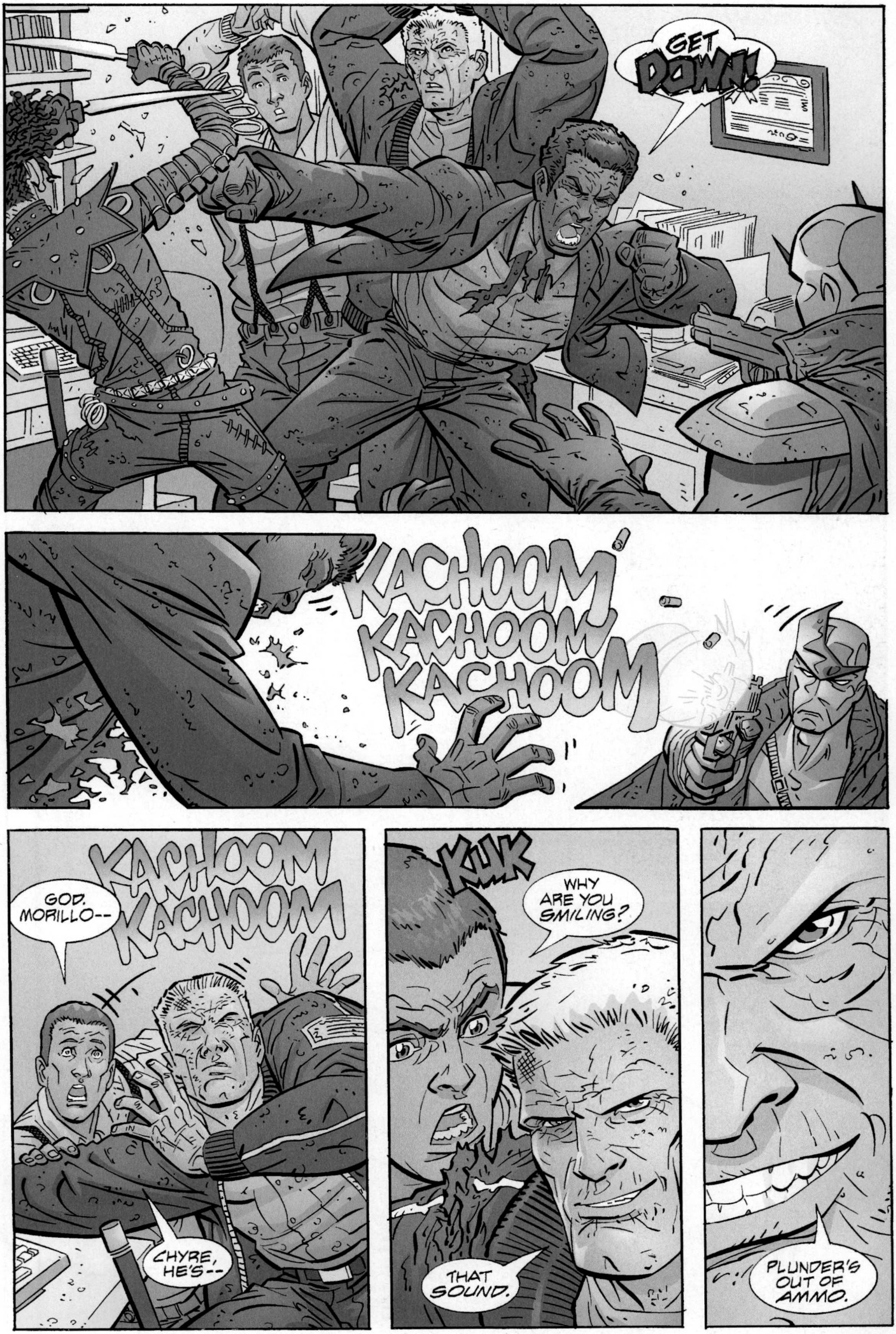
GET DOWN!
KACHOOM
KACHOOM
KACHOOM
KACHOOM
KACHOOM
GOD. MORILLO--
CHYRE, HE'S--
KLIK
WHY ARE YOU SMILING?
THAT SOUND.
PLUNDER'S OUT OF AMMO.

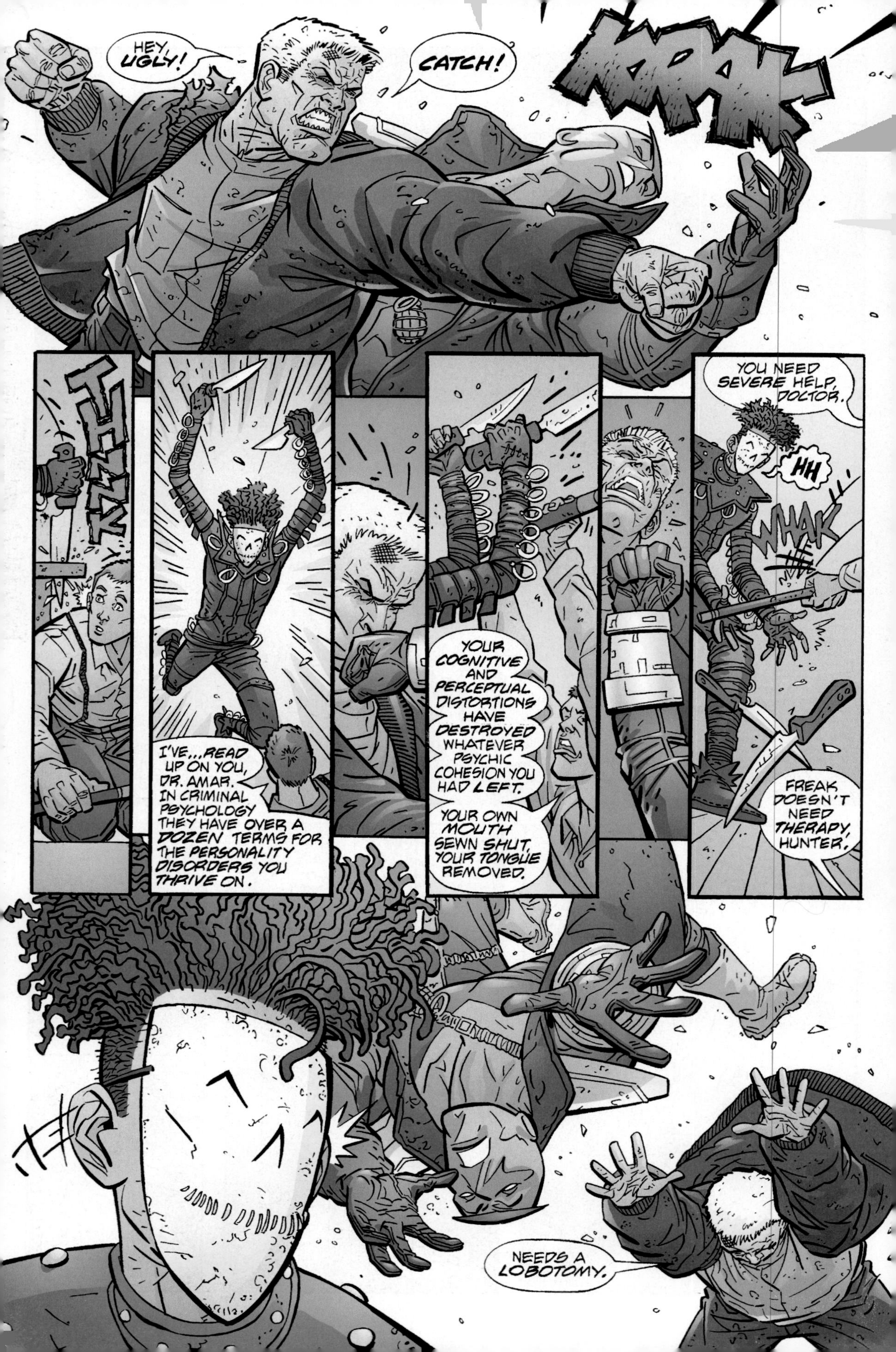
HEY, UGLY!
CATCH!
KRAK
THUNK
YOU NEED SEVERE HELP, DOCTOR.
I'VE... READ UP ON YOU, DR. AMAR. IN CRIMINAL PSYCHOLOGY THEY HAVE OVER A DOZEN TERMS FOR THE PERSONALITY DISORDERS YOU THRIVE ON.
YOUR COGNITIVE AND PERCEPTUAL DISTORTIONS HAVE DESTROYED WHATEVER PSYCHIC COHESION YOU HAD LEFT.
YOUR OWN MOUTH SEWN SHUT, YOUR TONGUE REMOVED.
HH
WHAK
FREAK DOESN'T NEED THERAPY, HUNTER.
NEEDS A LOBOTOMY.

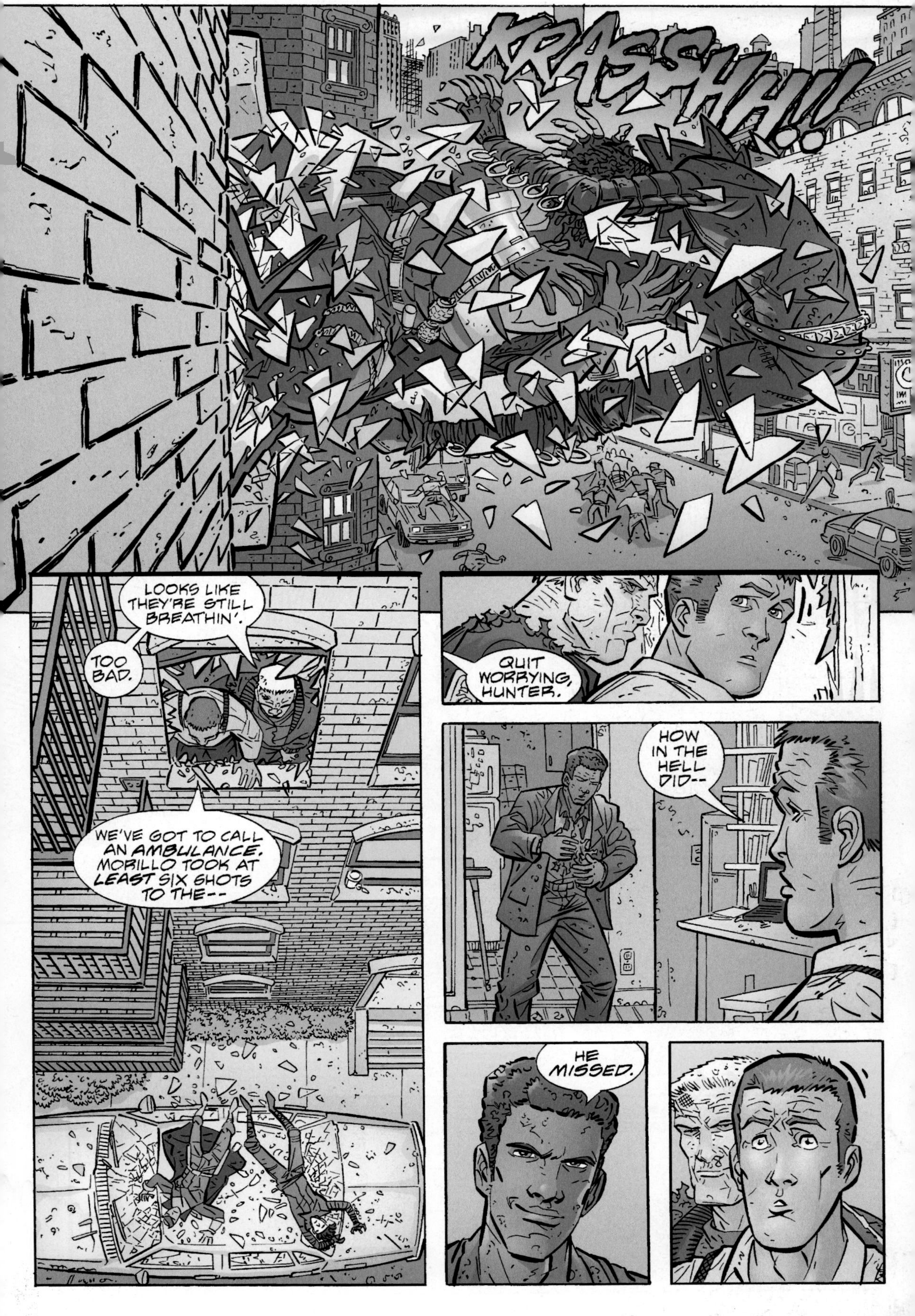
KRASSHH!!
LOOKS LIKE THEY'RE STILL BREATHIN'.
TOO BAD.
WE'VE GOT TO CALL AN AMBULANCE. MORILLO TOOK AT LEAST SIX SHOTS TO THE--
QUIT WORRYING, HUNTER.
HOW IN THE HELL DID--
HE MISSED.

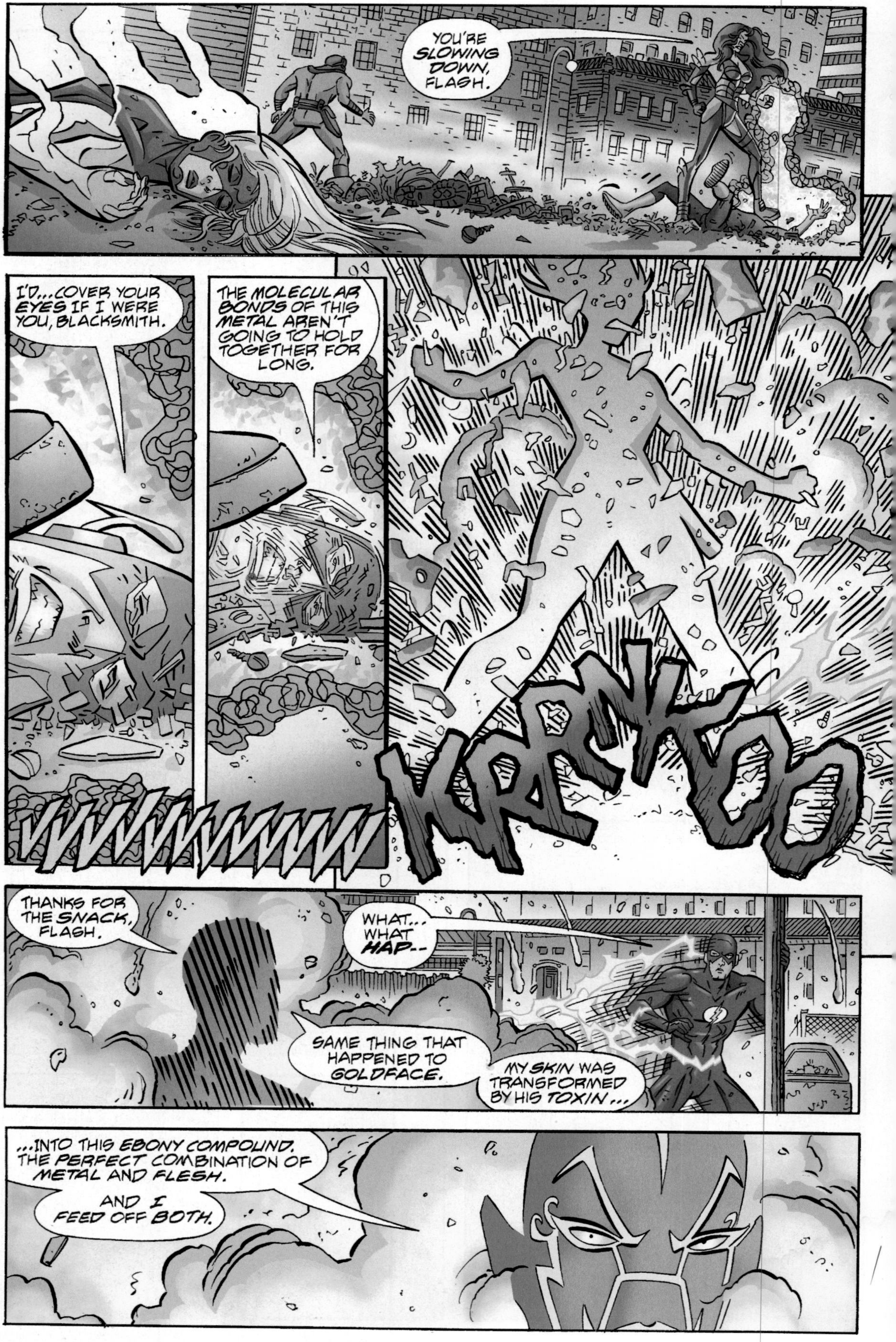

YOU'RE SLOWING DOWN, FLASH.
I'D...COVER YOUR EYES IF I WERE YOU, BLACKSMITH.
THE MOLECULAR BONDS OF THIS METAL AREN'T GOING TO HOLD TOGETHER FOR LONG.
VVVVVVVVVVVV
KRAKKOOO
THANKS FOR THE SNACK, FLASH.
WHAT... WHAT HAP--
SAME THING THAT HAPPENED TO GOLDFACE.
MY SKIN WAS TRANSFORMED BY HIS TOXIN...
...INTO THIS EBONY COMPOUND. THE PERFECT COMBINATION OF METAL AND FLESH.
AND I FEED OFF BOTH.

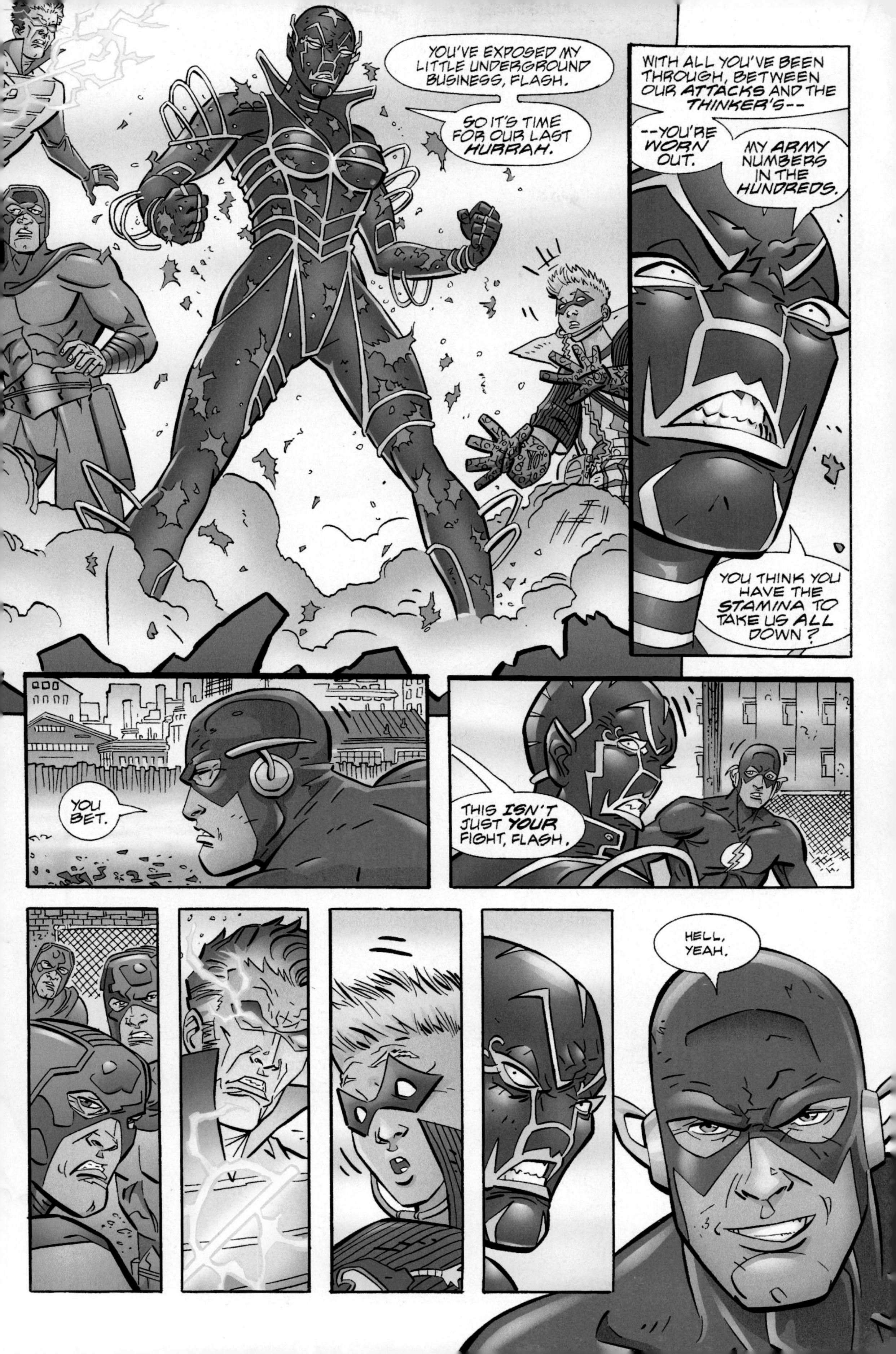
YOU'VE EXPOSED MY LITTLE UNDERGROUND BUSINESS, FLASH.
SO IT'S TIME FOR OUR LAST HURRAH.
WITH ALL YOU'VE BEEN THROUGH, BETWEEN OUR ATTACKS AND THE THINKER'S--
--YOU'RE WORN OUT.
MY ARMY NUMBERS IN THE HUNDREDS.
YOU THINK YOU HAVE THE STAMINA TO TAKE US ALL DOWN?
YOU BET.
THIS ISN'T JUST YOUR FIGHT, FLASH.
HELL, YEAH.

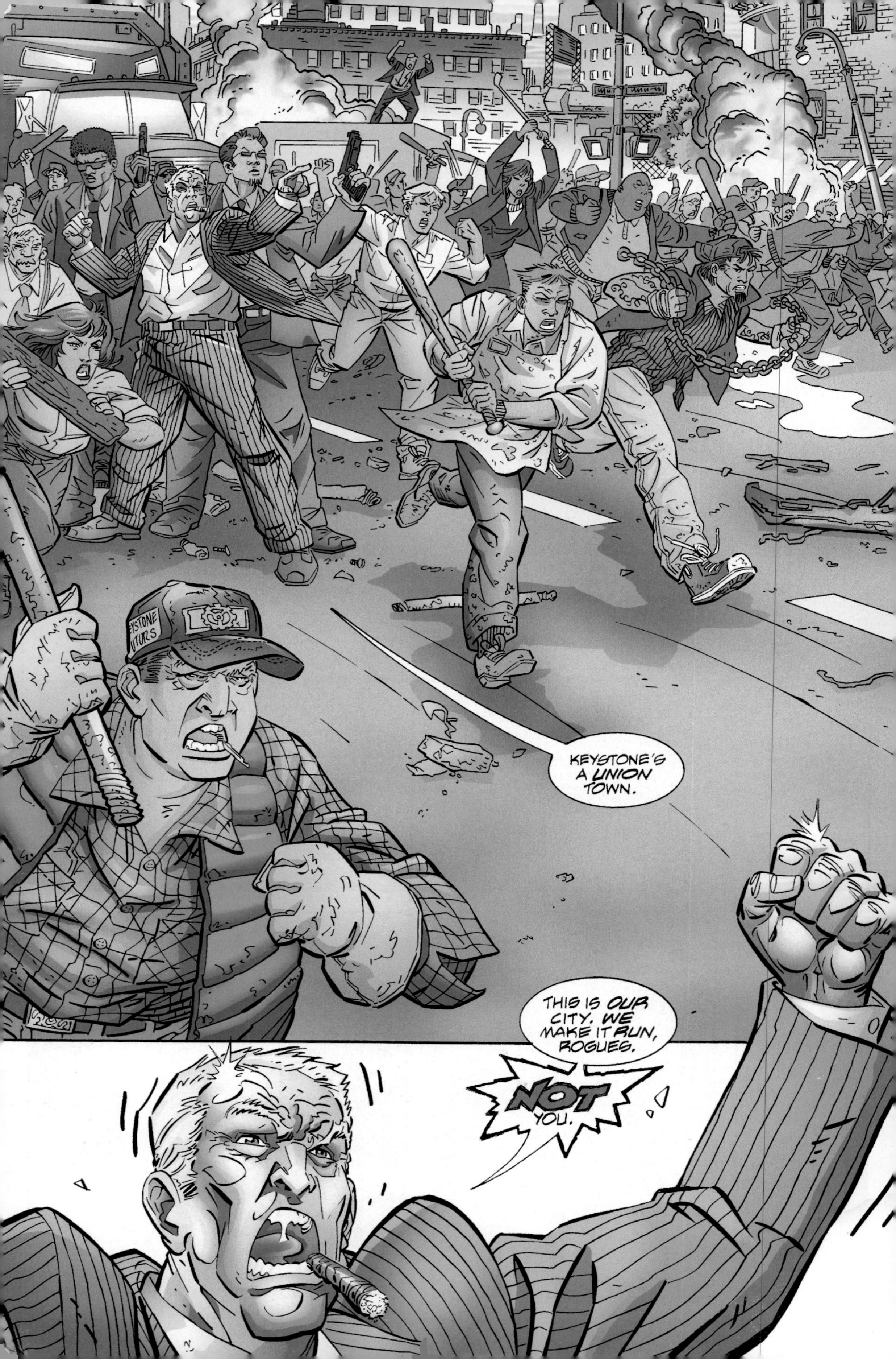
KEYSTONE'S A UNION TOWN.
THIS IS OUR CITY. WE MAKE IT RUN, ROGUES.
NOT YOU.

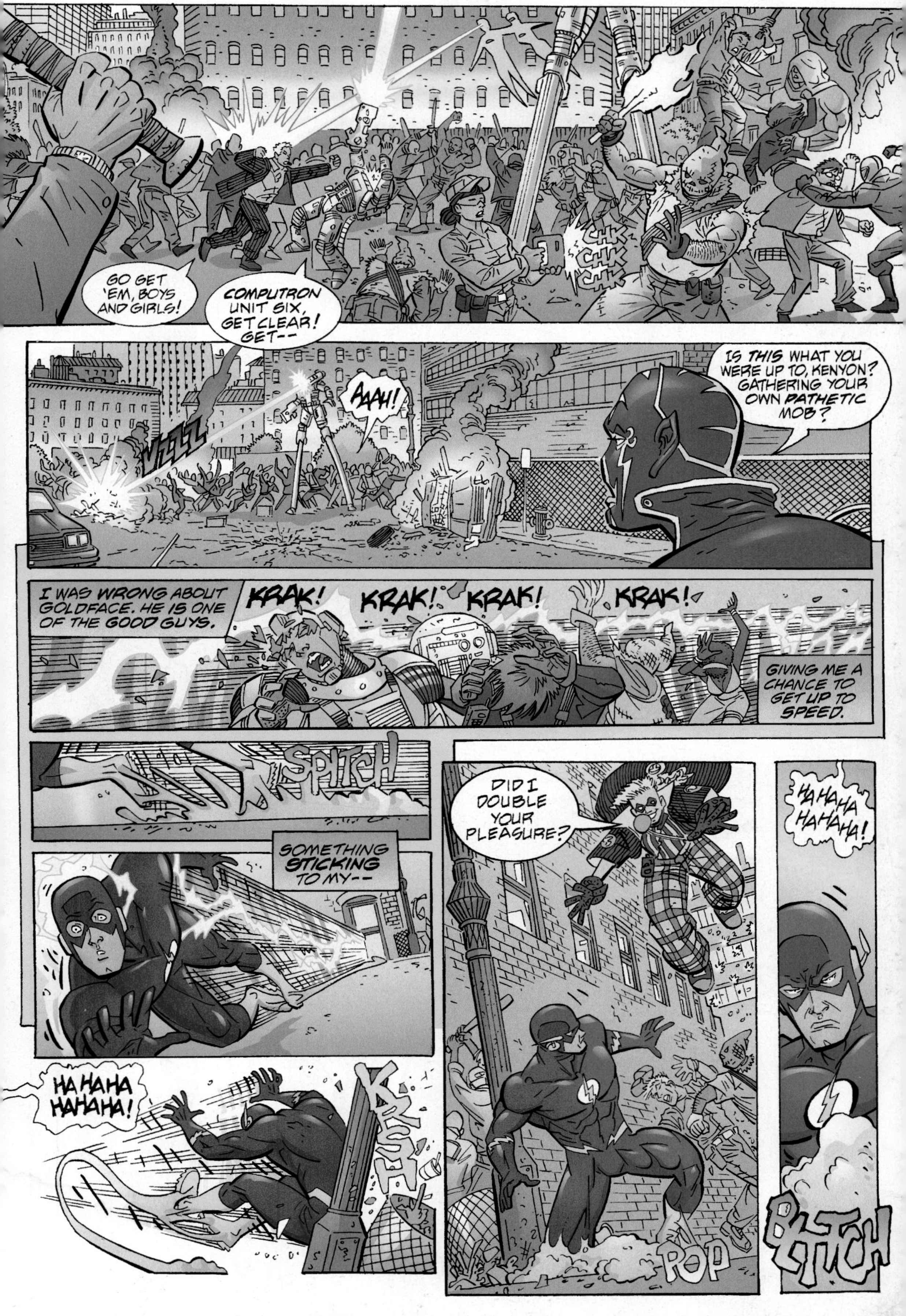

GO GET 'EM, BOYS AND GIRLS!
COMPUTRON UNIT SIX, GET CLEAR! GET--
CHK CHK CHK
AAAH!
VZZZ
IS THIS WHAT YOU WERE UP TO, KENYON? GATHERING YOUR OWN PATHETIC MOB?
I WAS WRONG ABOUT GOLDFACE. HE IS ONE OF THE GOOD GUYS.
KRAK! KRAK! KRAK! KRAK!
GIVING ME A CHANCE TO GET UP TO SPEED.
SPITCH
SOMETHING STICKING TO MY--
HAHAHA HAHAHA!
KRASH
DID I DOUBLE YOUR PLEASURE?
POP
HAHAHA HAHAHA!
BLTCH

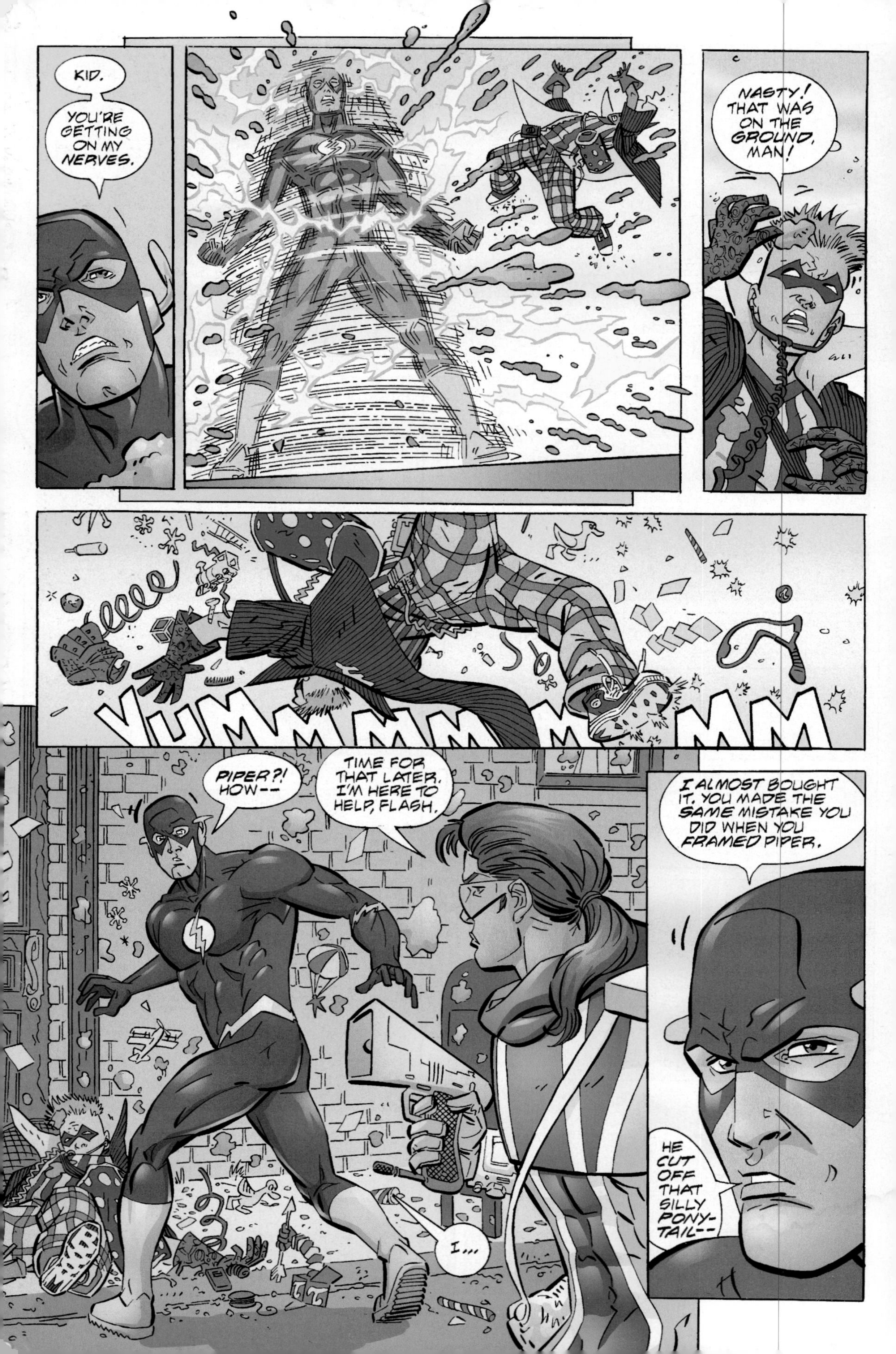
KID.
YOU'RE GETTING ON MY NERVES.
NASTY! THAT WAS ON THE GROUND, MAN!
YUMMMMMMMMM
PIPER?! HOW--
TIME FOR THAT LATER. I'M HERE TO HELP, FLASH.
I...
I ALMOST BOUGHT IT. YOU MADE THE SAME MISTAKE YOU DID WHEN YOU FRAMED PIPER.
HE CUT OFF THAT SILLY PONY-TAIL--

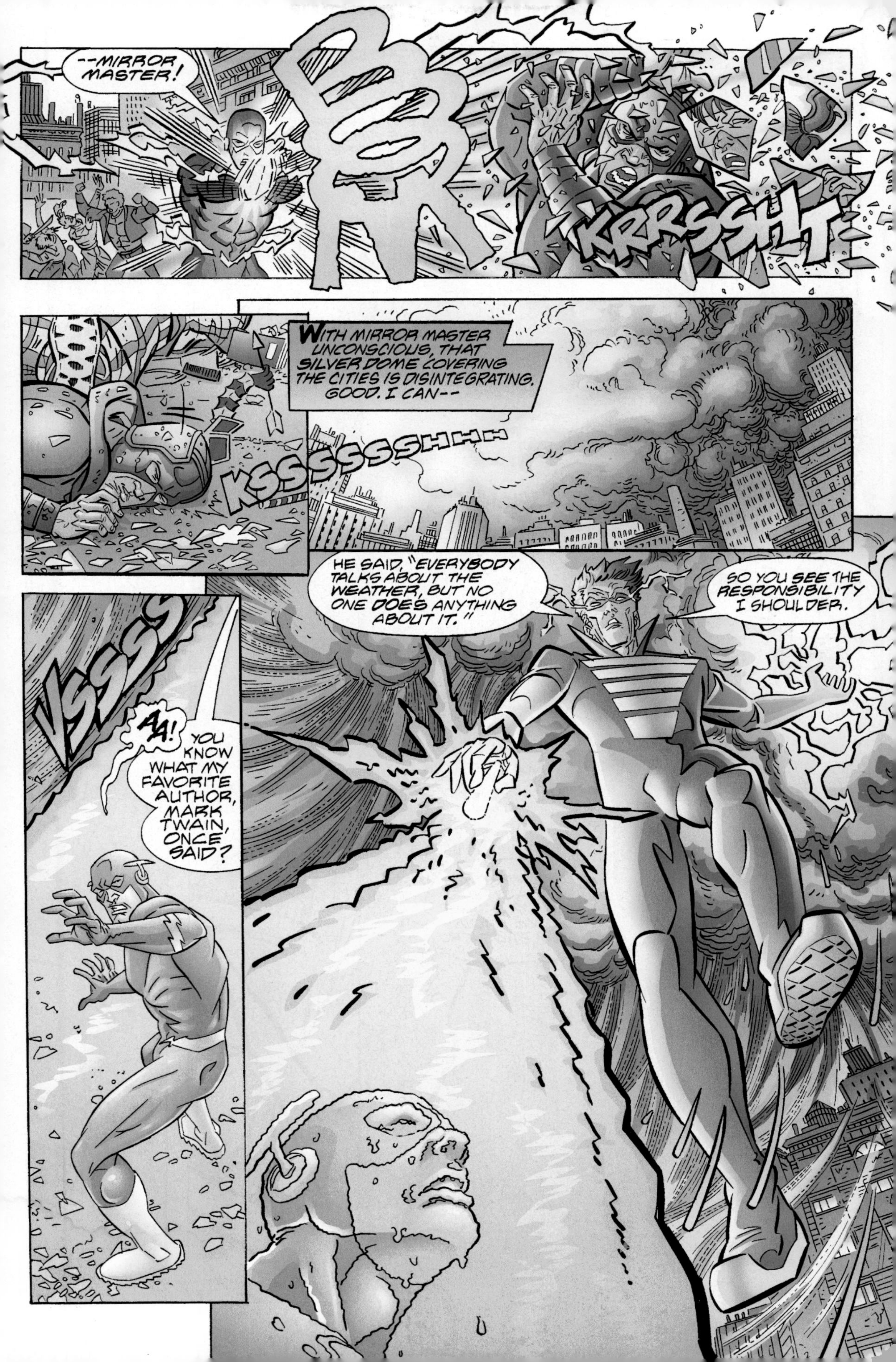
--MIRROR MASTER!
KRRSSHT
WITH MIRROR MASTER UNCONSCIOUS, THAT SILVER DOME COVERING THE CITIES IS DISINTEGRATING. GOOD. I CAN--
KSSSSSSSHHHH
VSSSSS
AA! YOU KNOW WHAT MY FAVORITE AUTHOR, MARK TWAIN, ONCE SAID?
HE SAID, "EVERYBODY TALKS ABOUT THE WEATHER, BUT NO ONE DOES ANYTHING ABOUT IT."
SO YOU SEE THE RESPONSIBILITY I SHOULDER.

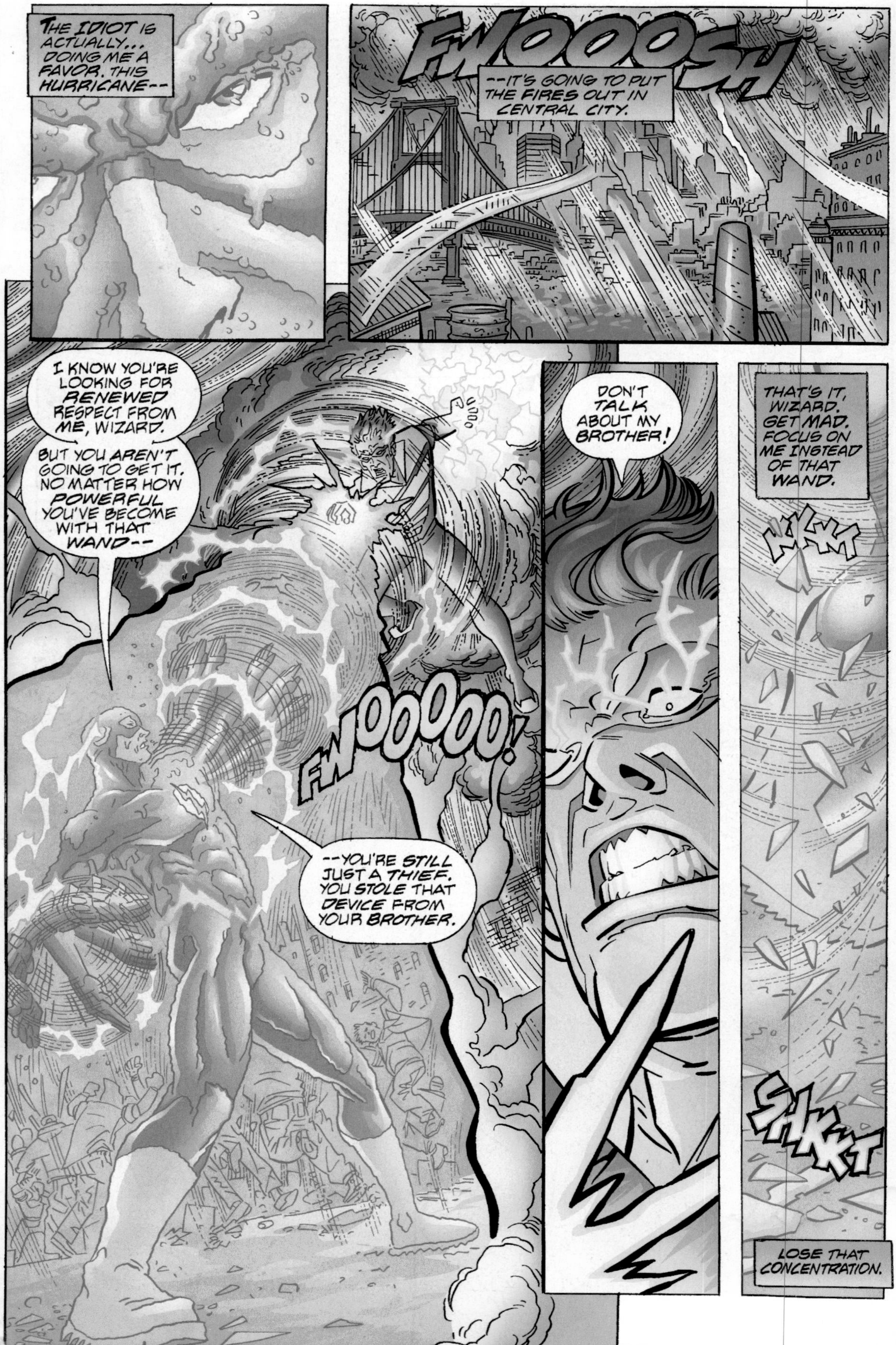
THE IDIOT IS ACTUALLY... DOING ME A FAVOR. THIS HURRICANE--
FWOOOOSH
--IT'S GOING TO PUT THE FIRES OUT IN CENTRAL CITY.
I KNOW YOU'RE LOOKING FOR RENEWED RESPECT FROM ME, WIZARD.
BUT YOU AREN'T GOING TO GET IT. NO MATTER HOW POWERFUL YOU'VE BECOME WITH THAT WAND--
FWOOOOOO!
--YOU'RE STILL JUST A THIEF. YOU STOLE THAT DEVICE FROM YOUR BROTHER.
DON'T TALK ABOUT MY BROTHER!
THAT'S IT, WIZARD. GET MAD. FOCUS ON ME INSTEAD OF THAT WAND.
SHKKT
LOSE THAT CONCENTRATION.

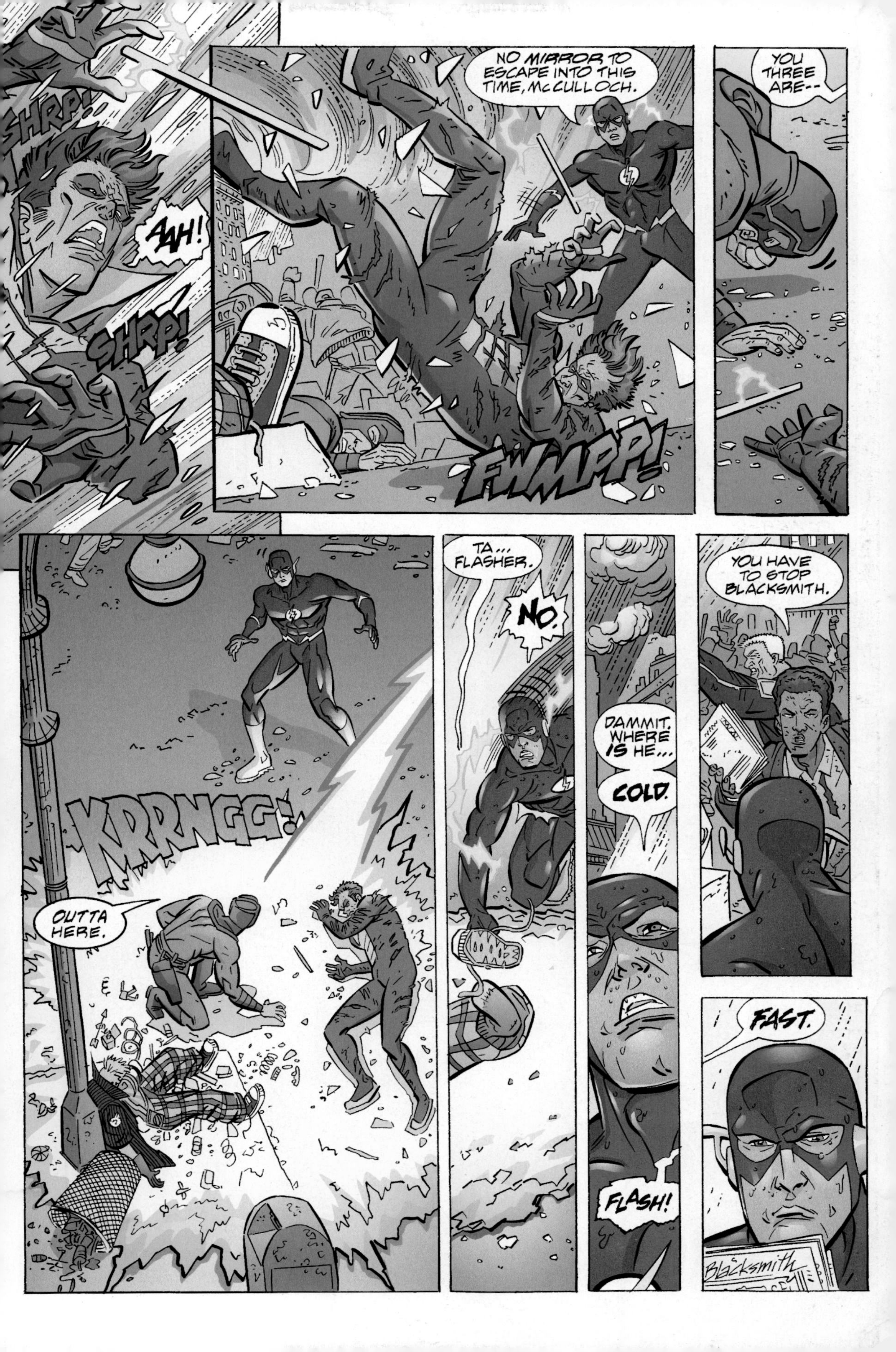
SHRP!
AAH!
SHRP!
NO MIRROR TO ESCAPE INTO THIS TIME, McCULLOCH.
FWMPP!
YOU THREE ARE--
KRRNGG!
OUTTA HERE.
TA... FLASHER.
NO.
DAMMIT. WHERE IS HE...
COLD.
FLASH!
YOU HAVE TO STOP BLACKSMITH.
FAST.
Blacksmith

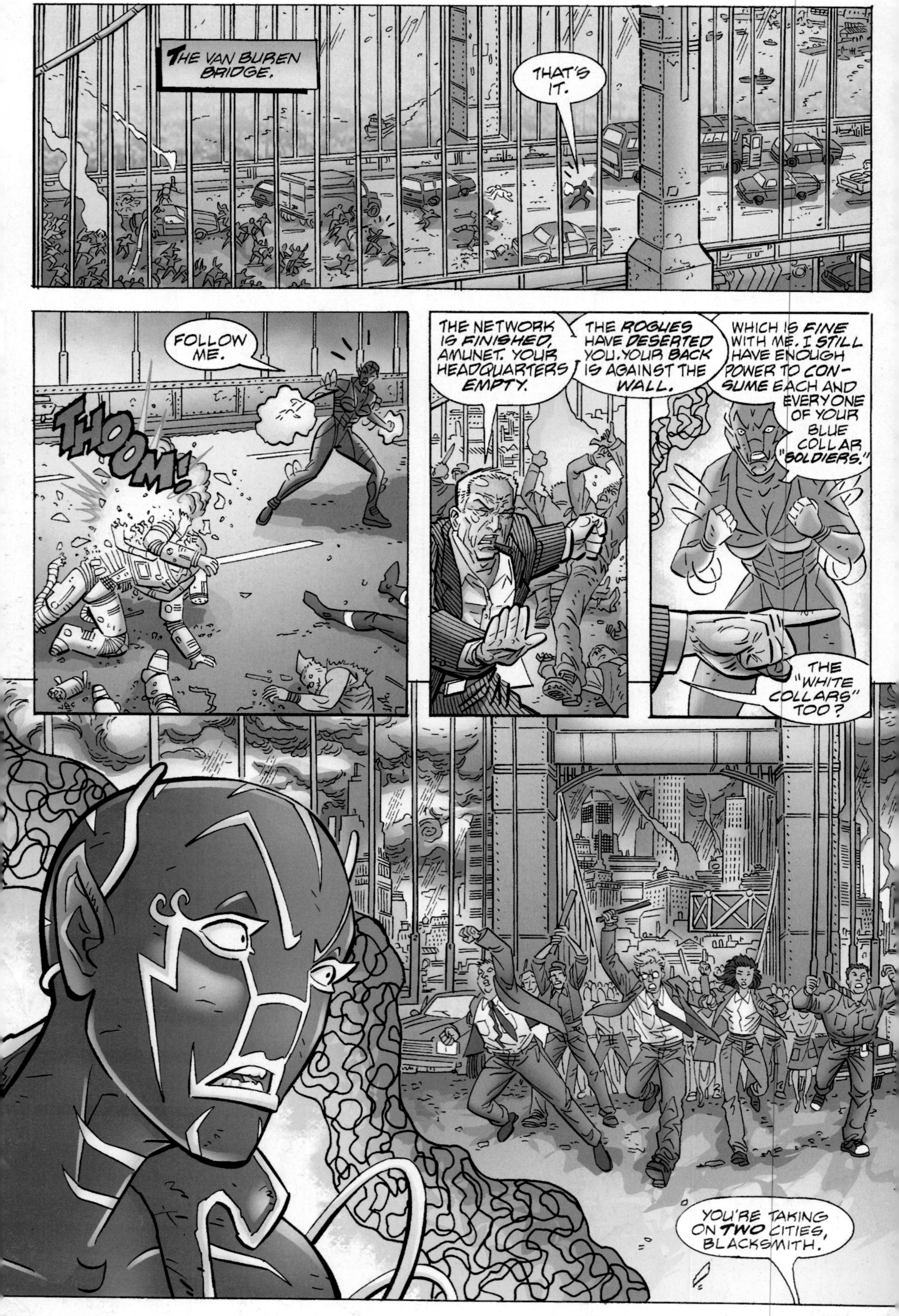
THE VAN BUREN BRIDGE.
THAT'S IT.
FOLLOW ME.
THOOM!
THE NETWORK IS FINISHED, AMUNET. YOUR HEADQUARTERS EMPTY.
THE ROGUES HAVE DESERTED YOU. YOUR BACK IS AGAINST THE WALL.
WHICH IS FINE WITH ME. I STILL HAVE ENOUGH POWER TO CONSUME EACH AND EVERYONE OF YOUR BLUE COLLAR "SOLDIERS."
THE "WHITE COLLARS" TOO?
YOU'RE TAKING ON TWO CITIES, BLACKSMITH!

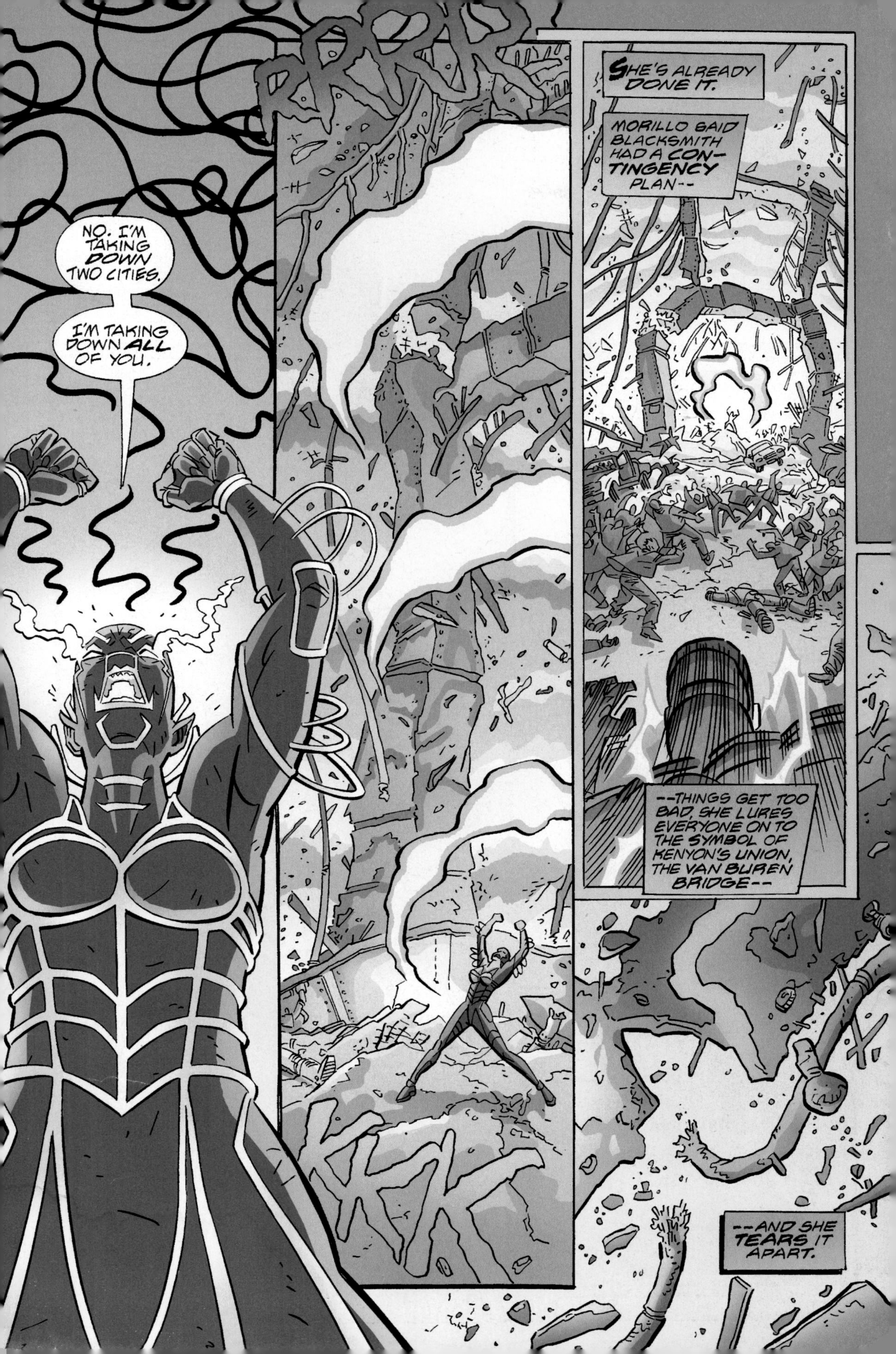
RRRRR
NO. I'M TAKING DOWN TWO CITIES.
I'M TAKING DOWN ALL OF YOU.
KKKK
SHE'S ALREADY DONE IT.
MORILLO SAID BLACKSMITH HAD A CONTINGENCY PLAN--
--THINGS GET TOO BAD, SHE LURES EVERYONE ON TO THE SYMBOL OF KENYON'S UNION, THE VAN BUREN BRIDGE--
--AND SHE TEARS IT APART.

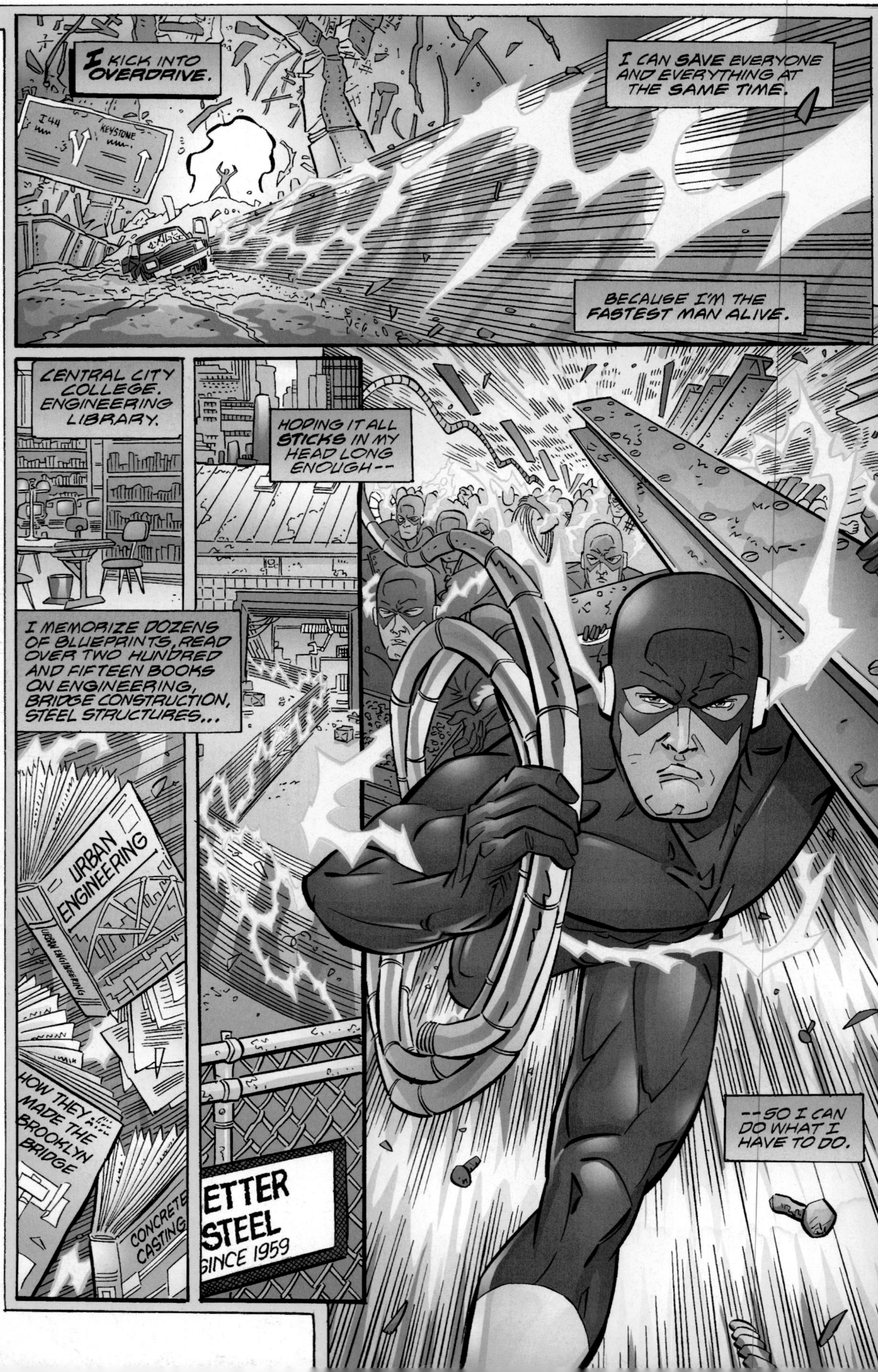
I KICK INTO OVERDRIVE.
I-44
KEYSTONE
I CAN SAVE EVERYONE AND EVERYTHING AT THE SAME TIME.
BECAUSE I'M THE FASTEST MAN ALIVE.
CENTRAL CITY COLLEGE. ENGINEERING LIBRARY.
HOPING IT ALL STICKS IN MY HEAD LONG ENOUGH--
I MEMORIZE DOZENS OF BLUEPRINTS, READ OVER TWO HUNDRED AND FIFTEEN BOOKS ON ENGINEERING, BRIDGE CONSTRUCTION, STEEL STRUCTURES...
URBAN ENGINEERING
HOW THEY MADE THE BROOKLYN BRIDGE
CONCRETE CASTING
ETTER STEEL SINCE 1959
--SO I CAN DO WHAT I HAVE TO DO.

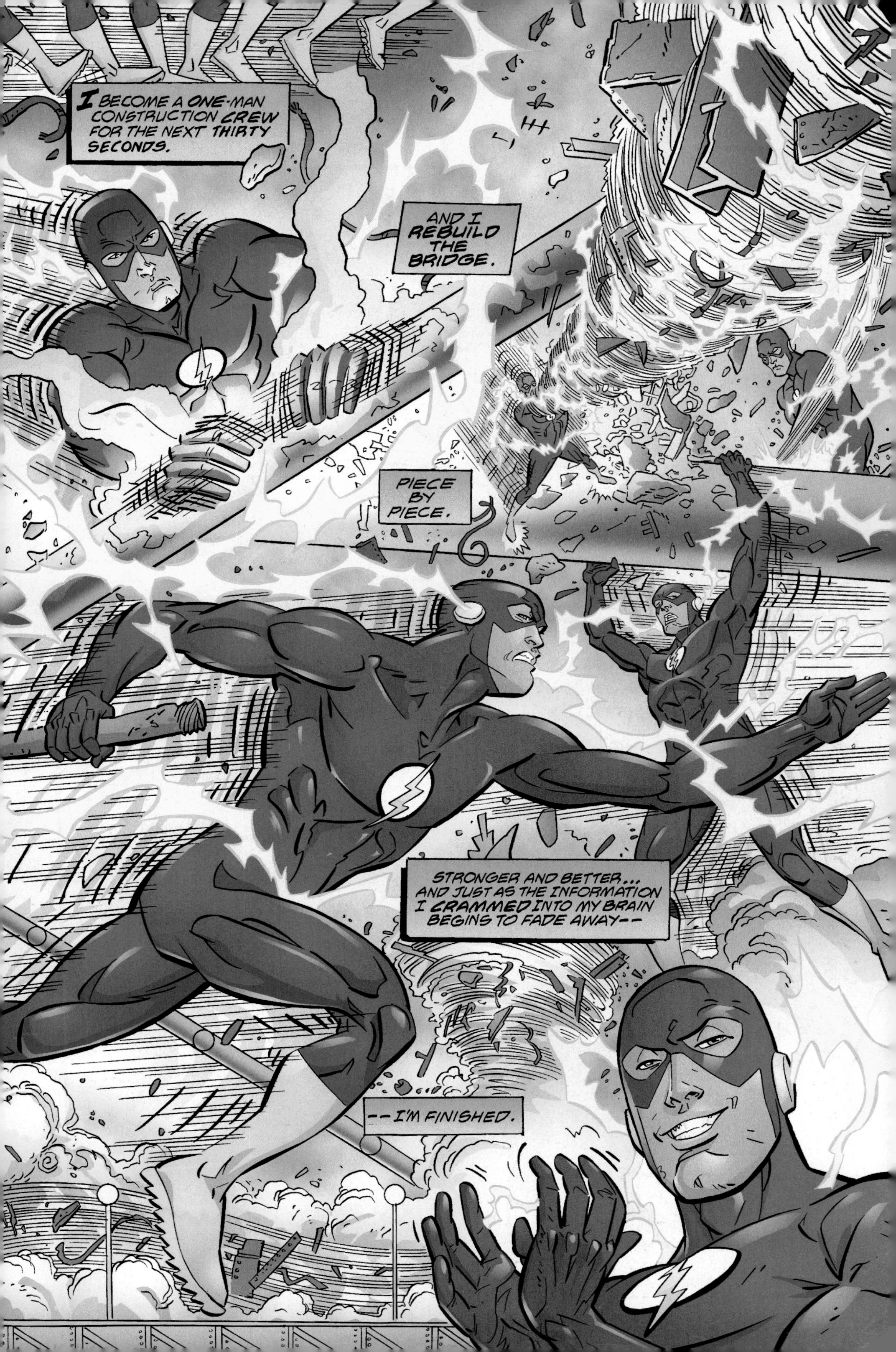
I BECOME A ONE-MAN CONSTRUCTION CREW FOR THE NEXT THIRTY SECONDS.
AND I REBUILD THE BRIDGE.
PIECE BY PIECE.
STRONGER AND BETTER... AND JUST AS THE INFORMATION I CRAMMED INTO MY BRAIN BEGINS TO FADE AWAY--
--I'M FINISHED.

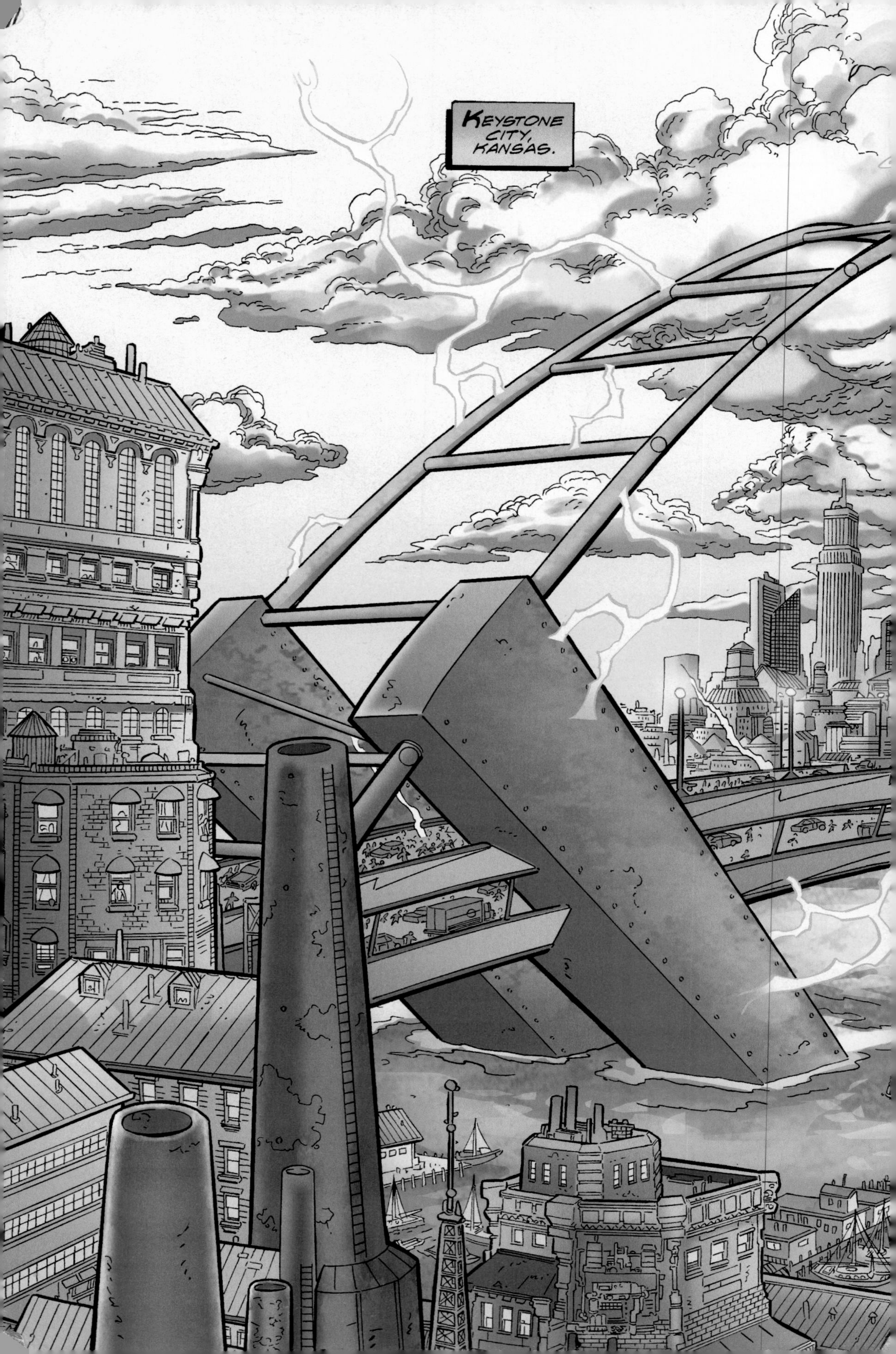
KEYSTONE CITY, KANSAS.

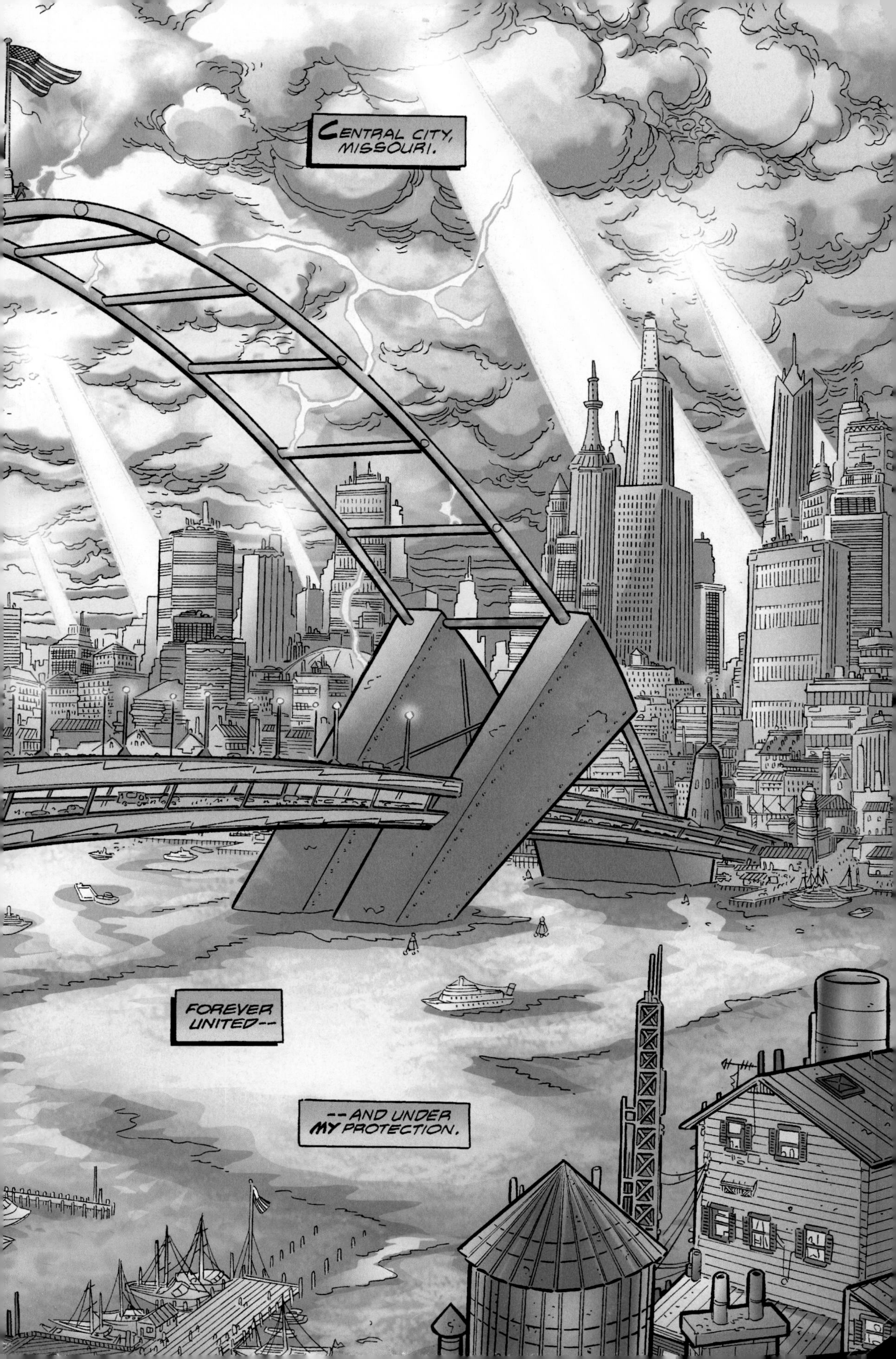
CENTRAL CITY, MISSOURI.
FOREVER UNITED--
--AND UNDER MY PROTECTION.

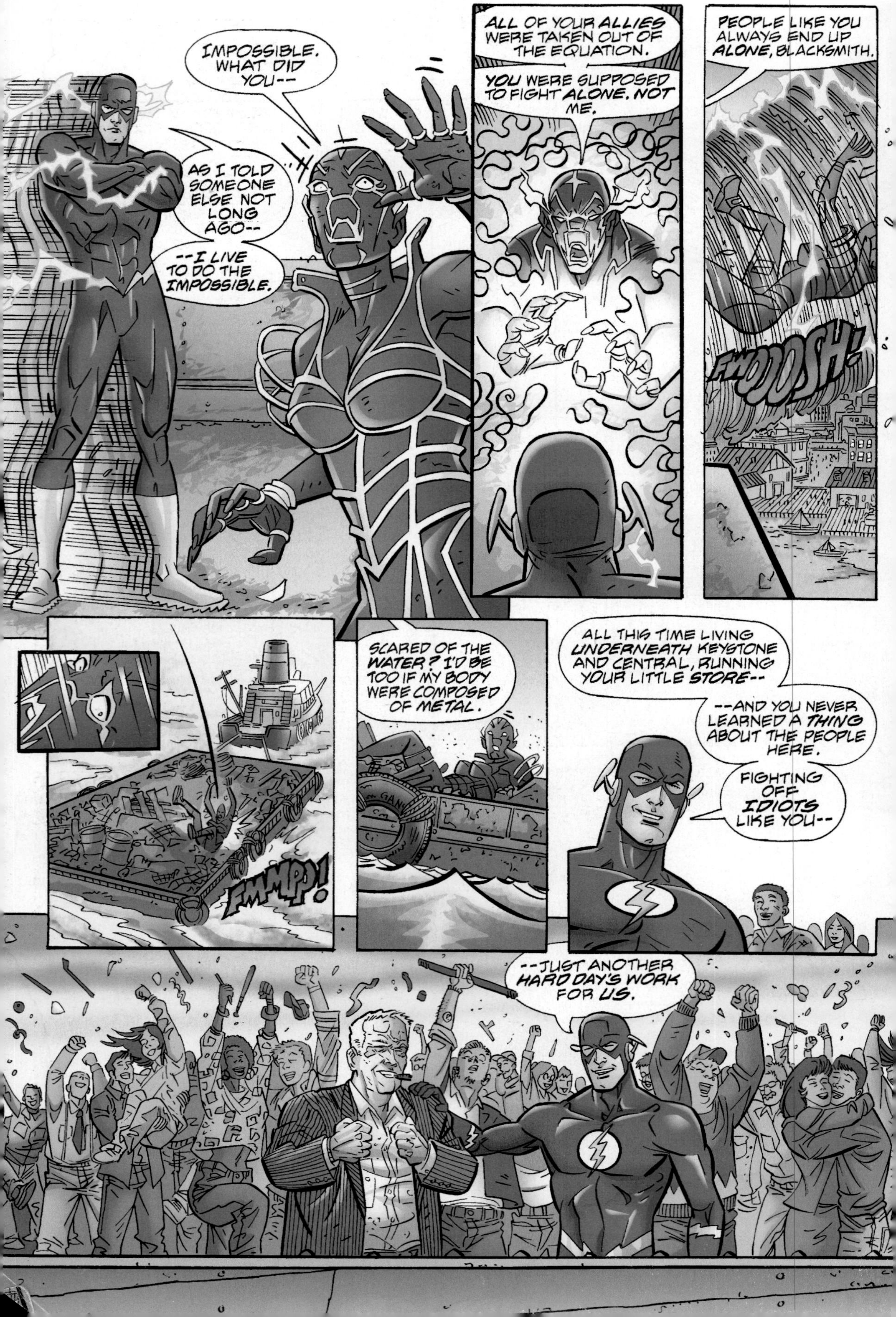
IMPOSSIBLE. WHAT DID YOU--
AS I TOLD SOMEONE ELSE NOT LONG AGO--
--I LIVE TO DO THE IMPOSSIBLE.
ALL OF YOUR ALLIES WERE TAKEN OUT OF THE EQUATION.
YOU WERE SUPPOSED TO FIGHT ALONE. NOT ME.
PEOPLE LIKE YOU ALWAYS END UP ALONE, BLACKSMITH.
FWOOOSH!
FMMPP!
SCARED OF THE WATER? I'D BE TOO IF MY BODY WERE COMPOSED OF METAL.
ALL THIS TIME LIVING UNDERNEATH KEYSTONE AND CENTRAL, RUNNING YOUR LITTLE STORE--
--AND YOU NEVER LEARNED A THING ABOUT THE PEOPLE HERE.
FIGHTING OFF IDIOTS LIKE YOU--
--JUST ANOTHER HARD DAY'S WORK FOR US.

EPILOGUE ONE

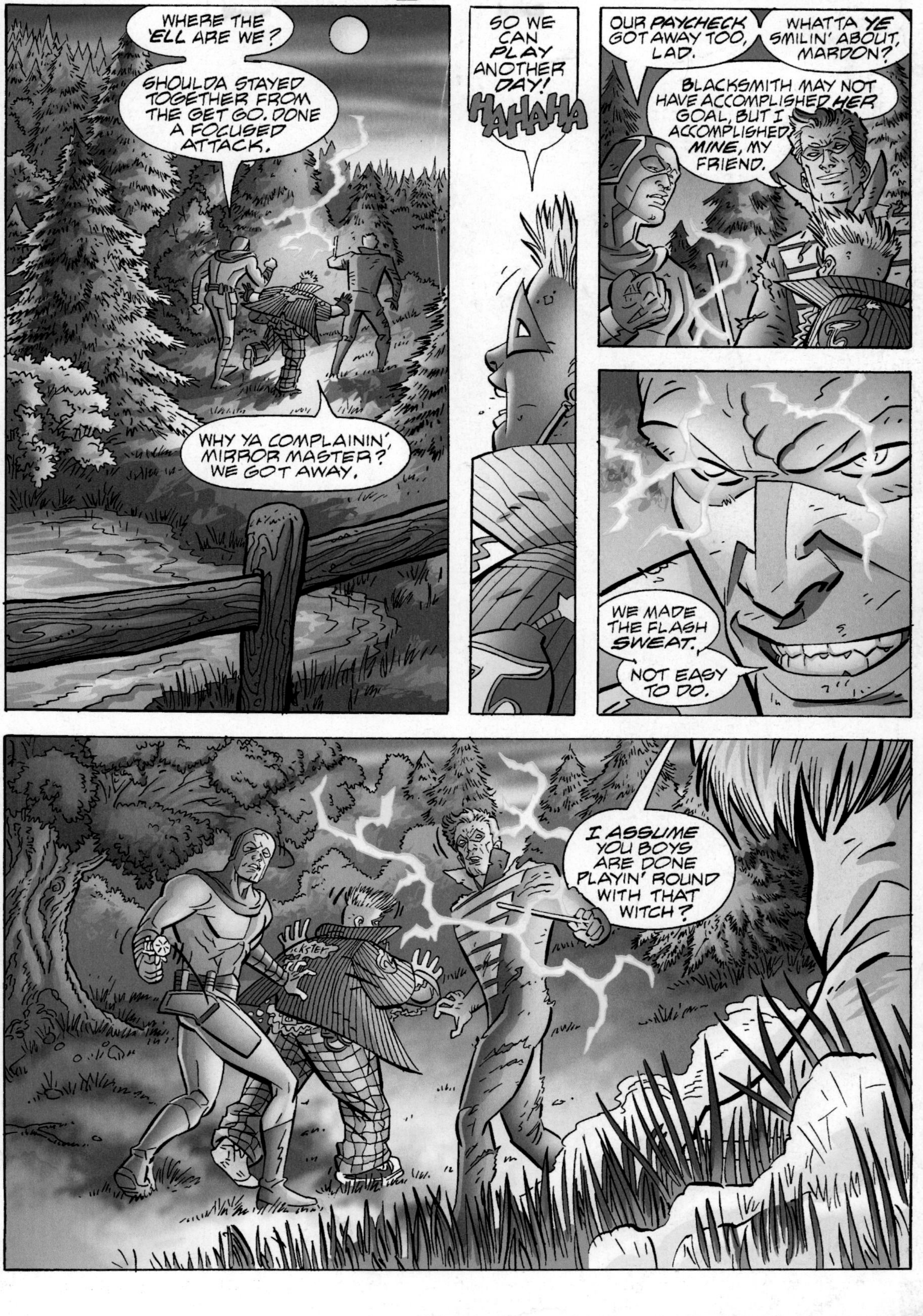

WHERE THE 'ELL ARE WE?
SHOULDA STAYED TOGETHER FROM THE GET GO. DONE A FOCUSED ATTACK.
WHY YA COMPLAININ', MIRROR MASTER? WE GOT AWAY.
SO WE CAN PLAY ANOTHER DAY!
HAHAHA
OUR PAYCHECK GOT AWAY TOO, LAD.
WHATTA YE SMILIN' ABOUT, MARDON?
BLACKSMITH MAY NOT HAVE ACCOMPLISHED HER GOAL, BUT I ACCOMPLISHED MINE, MY FRIEND.
WE MADE THE FLASH SWEAT.
NOT EASY TO DO.
I ASSUME YOU BOYS ARE DONE PLAYIN' ROUND WITH THAT WITCH?

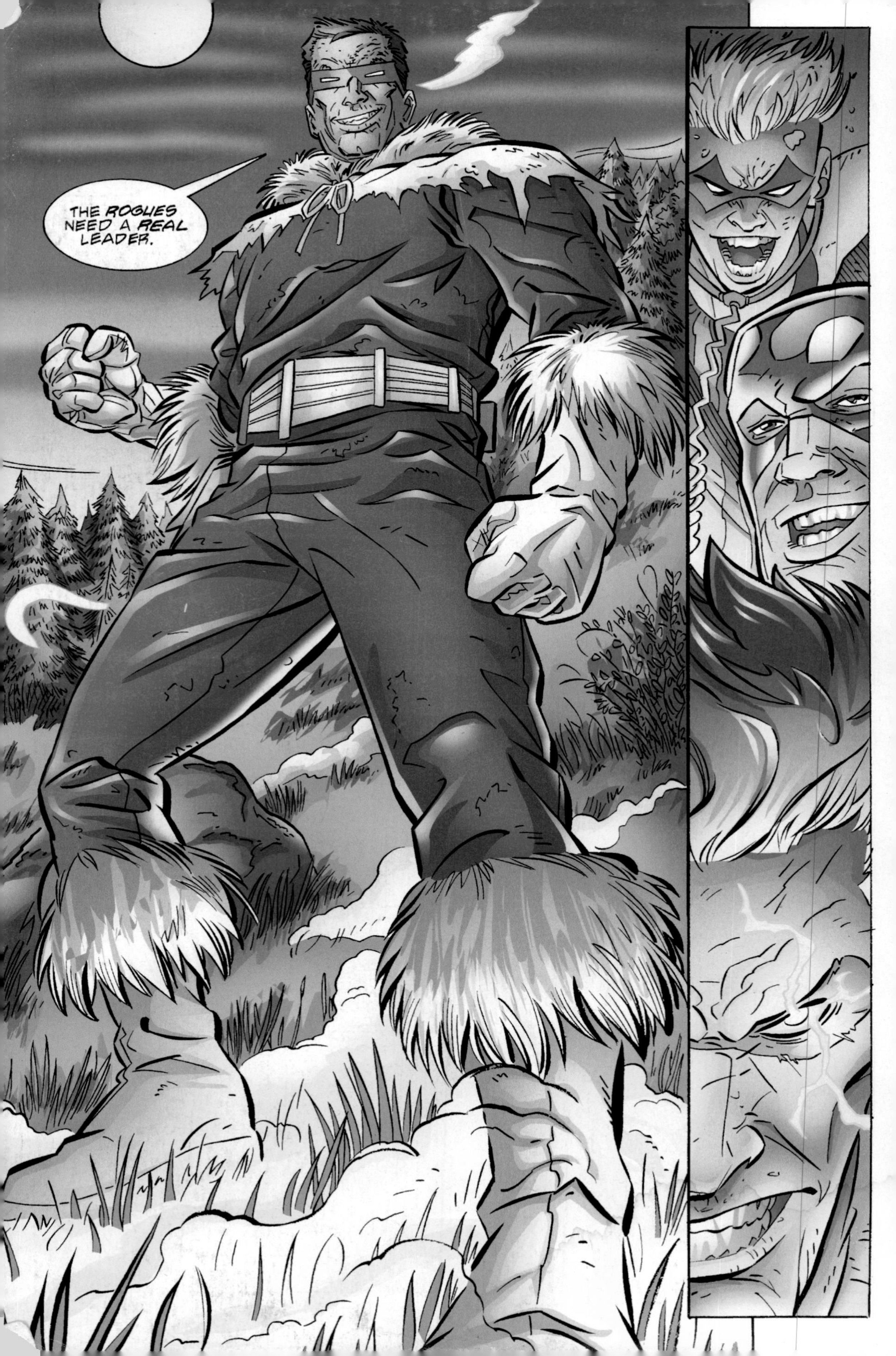
THE ROGUES NEED A REAL LEADER.

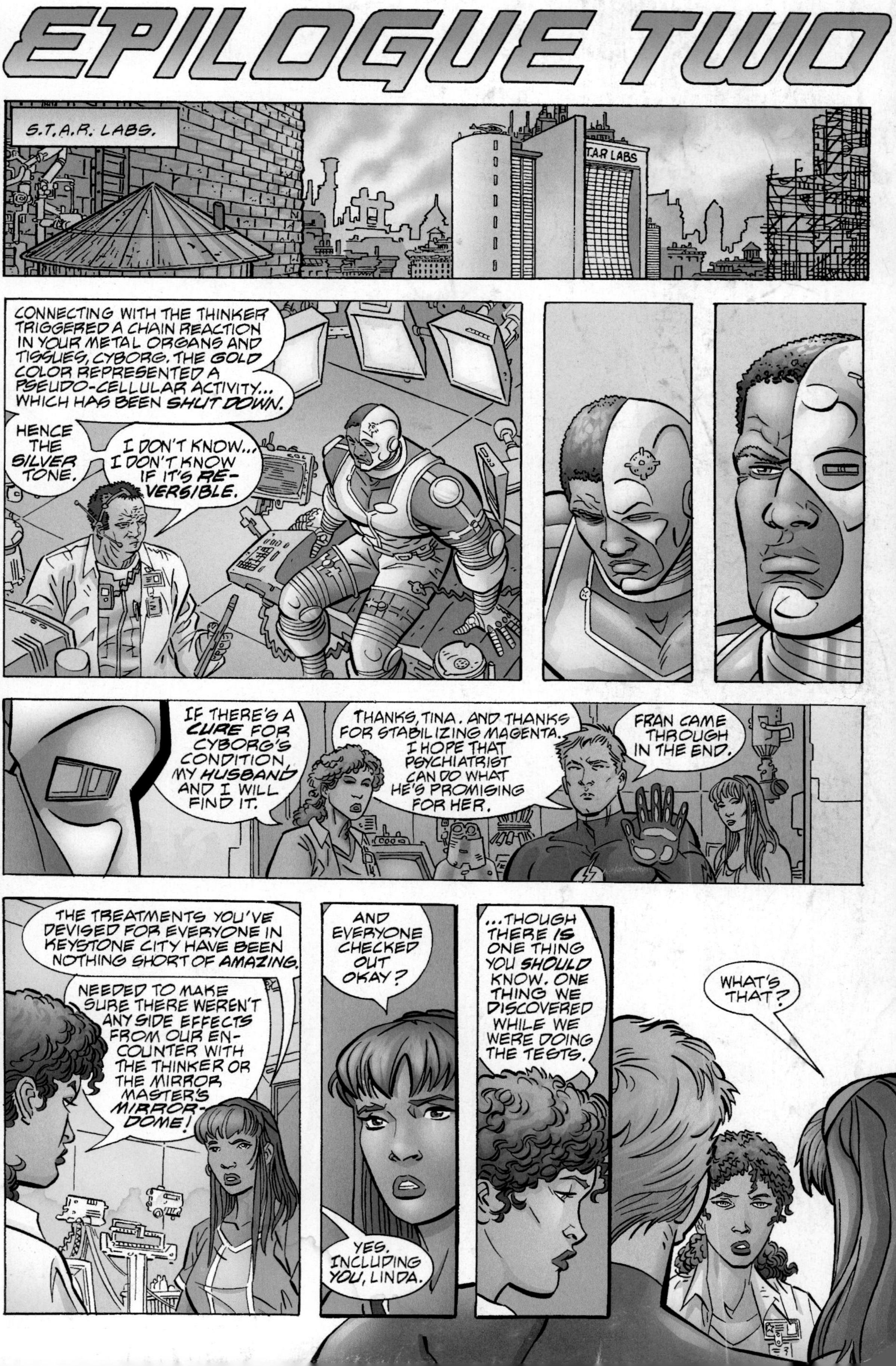
EPILOGUE TWO
S.T.A.R. LABS.
S.T.A.R LABS
CONNECTING WITH THE THINKER TRIGGERED A CHAIN REACTION IN YOUR METAL ORGANS AND TISSUES, CYBORG. THE GOLD COLOR REPRESENTED A PSEUDO-CELLULAR ACTIVITY... WHICH HAS BEEN SHUT DOWN.
HENCE THE SILVER TONE.
I DON'T KNOW... I DON'T KNOW IF IT'S REVERSIBLE.
IF THERE'S A CURE FOR CYBORG'S CONDITION, MY HUSBAND AND I WILL FIND IT.
THANKS, TINA. AND THANKS FOR STABILIZING MAGENTA. I HOPE THAT PSYCHIATRIST CAN DO WHAT HE'S PROMISING FOR HER.
FRAN CAME THROUGH IN THE END.
THE TREATMENTS YOU'VE DEVISED FOR EVERYONE IN KEYSTONE CITY HAVE BEEN NOTHING SHORT OF AMAZING.
NEEDED TO MAKE SURE THERE WEREN'T ANY SIDE EFFECTS FROM OUR ENCOUNTER WITH THE THINKER OR THE MIRROR MASTER'S MIRROR-DOME!
AND EVERYONE CHECKED OUT OKAY?
YES. INCLUDING YOU, LINDA.
...THOUGH THERE IS ONE THING YOU SHOULD KNOW. ONE THING WE DISCOVERED WHILE WE WERE DOING THE TESTS.
WHAT'S THAT?

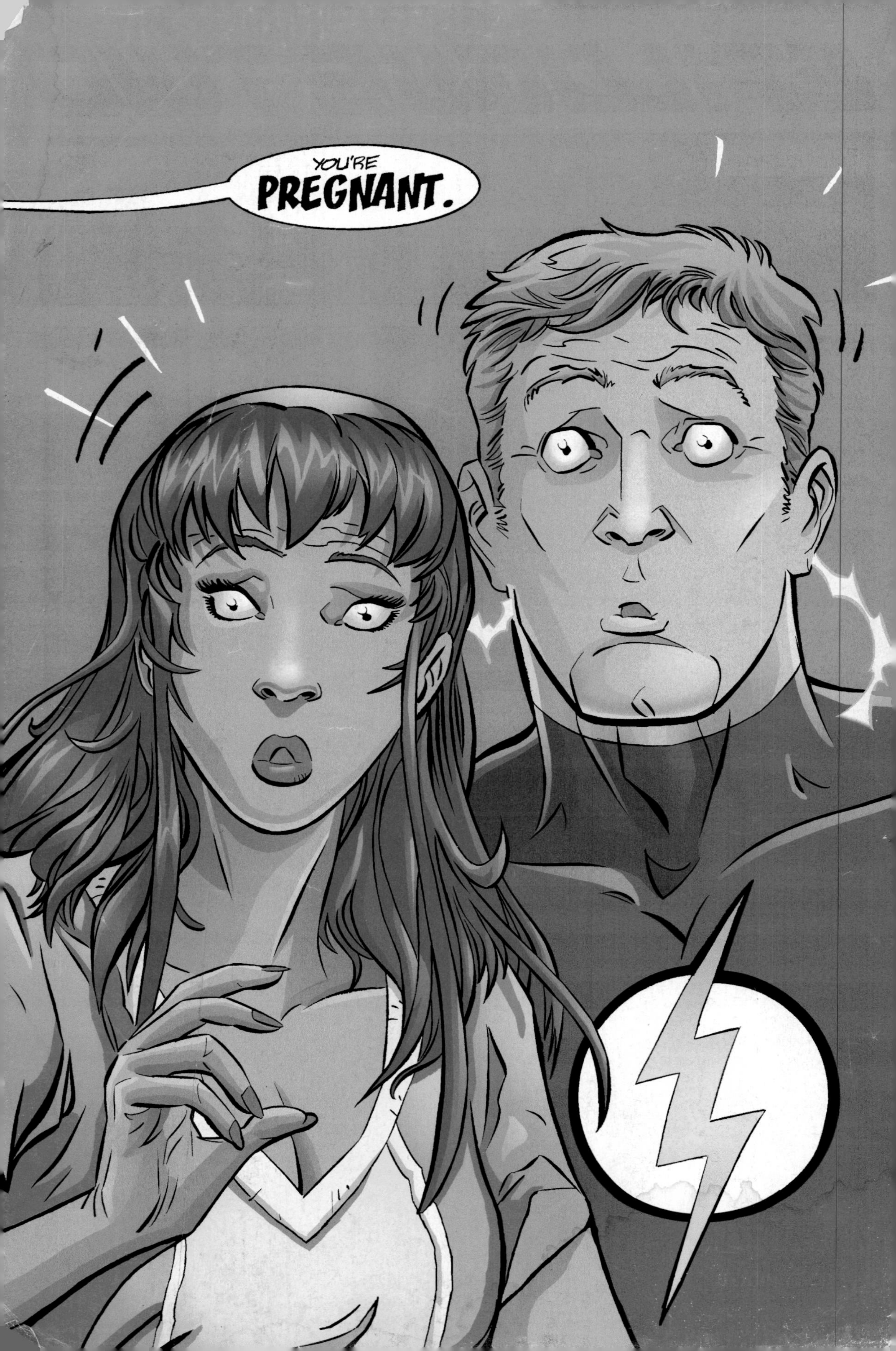
YOU'RE PREGNANT.

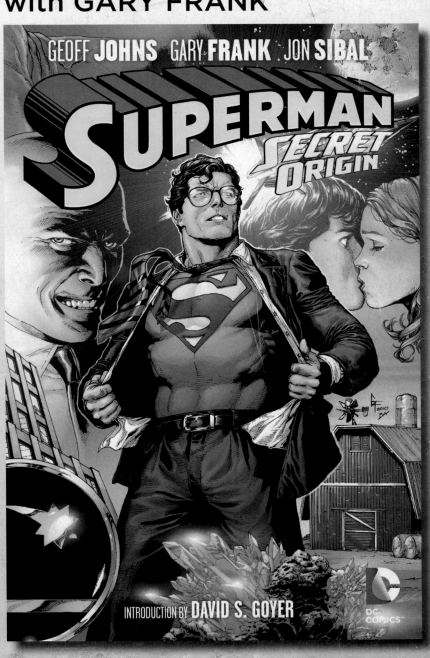

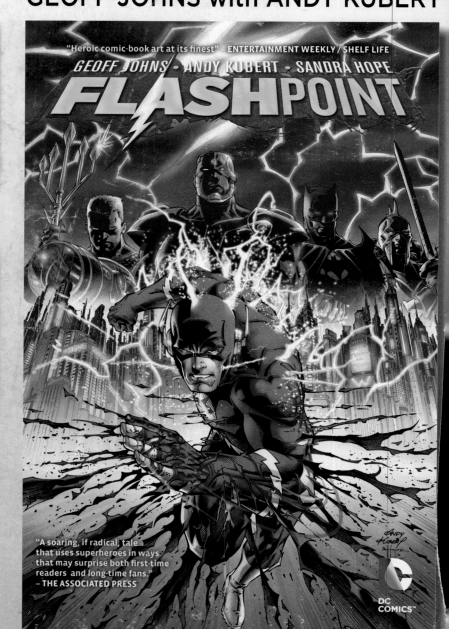